STRANGER
TO HISTORY

Aatish Taseer was born in 1980 and has worked as
a reporter for *Time* magazine. He lives between London
and Dehli. This is his first book.

STRANGER TO HISTORY

A Son's Journey through
Islamic Lands

AATISH TASEER

CANONGATE
Edinburgh · London · New York · Melbourne

This paperback edition published in 2010
by Canongate Books

First published in Great Britain in 2009 by
Canongate Books Ltd, 14 High Street,
Edinburgh EH1 1TE

1

British Library Cataloguing-in-Publication Data
A catalogue record for this book is available on
request from the British Library

ISBN 978 1 84767 131 8

Typeset by Palimpsest Book Production Ltd, Grangemouth,
Stirlingshire

Printed and bound in Great Britain by
Clays Ltd, St Ives plc

www.meetatthegate.com

For Ma

Contents

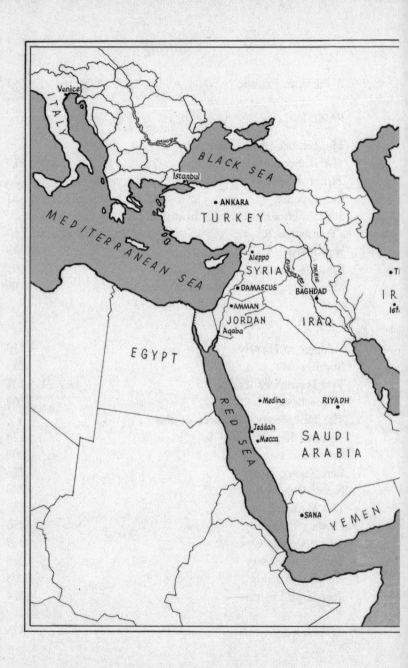

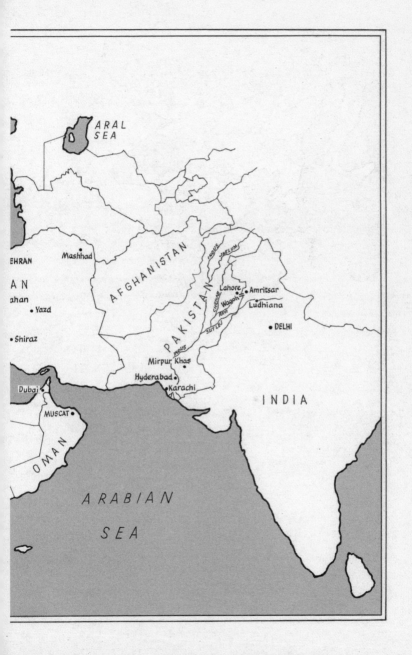

A Pilgrim's Prelude

Once the car had driven away, and we were half-naked specks on the marble plaza, Hani said, 'I'll read and you repeat after me.' His dark, strong face concentrated on the page and the Arabic words flowed out.

Kareem, pale with light eyes, and handsome, also muttered the words. We stood close to each other in our pilgrims' clothes – two white towels, one round the waist, the other across the torso, leaving the right shoulder bare.

'I seek refuge in Allah the Great, in His Honourable Face and His Ancient Authority from the accursed Satan. Allah, open for me the doors of Your Mercy.'

It was a clear, mild night and we were standing outside the Grand Mosque in Mecca. The plaza was vast, open and powerfully floodlit. The pilgrims were piebald dots, gliding across its marble surface. The congested city, the Mecca of hotels and dormitories, lay behind us.

The mosque's slim-pillared entrance, with frilled arches and two great minarets, lay ahead. It was made of an ashen stone with streaks of white; its balustrades, its minarets and its lights were white. A layer of white light hung over the entire complex. Towers, some unfinished with overhanging cranes, vanished into an inky night sky.

We paused, taking in the plaza's scale.

*

I was mid-point in a much longer journey. I had set out six months earlier in the hope of understanding my deep estrangement from my father: what had seemed personal at first had since shown itself to contain deeper religious and historical currents. And it was to discover their meaning that I travelled from Istanbul, on one edge of the Islamic world, through Syria, to Mecca at the centre and the Grand Mosque itself. The remaining half of my journey was to take me through Iran and, finally, into Pakistan, my father's country.

We walked on like tiny figures in an architect's drawing towards the mosque. The plaza's white dazzle and my awe at its scale had made me lose the prayer's thread. Hani now repeated it for me slowly, and I returned the unfamiliar words one by one. My two Saudi companions, experienced in the rituals we were to perform, took seriously their role as guides. They seemed to become solemn and protective as we neared the mosque's entrance. Hani took charge, briefing me on the rites and leading the way. Kareem would sometimes further clarify the meaning of an Arabic word, sometimes slip in a joke. 'Now, no flat-screen TVs and electronics,' he warned, of the prayer we would say inside the sanctum.

We were channelled into a steady stream near the entrance. The pilgrims, who had been sparse on the plaza, gathered close together as we entered. The women were not in the seamless clothes required of the men, but fully covered in white and black robes. Inside, the mosque felt like a stadium. There were metal detectors, signs in foreign languages, others with letters and numbers on them. Large, low lanterns hung from the ceilings, casting a bright, artificial light over the passage. On our left and right, there were row after row of colonnades, a warren of wraparound prayer galleries. The mosque was not filled to even a fraction of its capacity, and its scale and emptiness made it feel deserted. Then, Hani whispered to me the prayer that was to be said around the Kaba. The Kaba! I had forgotten about it. It hovered now, black and cuboid, at the end of the passage. And once again, confronted with an arresting vision, Hani's whispered prayer was lost on me.

The Kaba's black stone was concave, set in what looked like a silver casque, and embedded in one corner of the building. It had been given by the angel Gabriel to Ishmael, the progenitor of the Arab race, when he was building the Kaba with his father, Abraham. Many queued to touch it and kiss its smooth dark surface. We saluted it and began the first of seven circumambulations. Hani read as we walked and I repeated after him. After every cycle, we saluted the stone, and said, 'God is Great.'

The pilgrims immediately in front of us were three young men in a mild ecstasy. They had their arms round each other and skipped through their circuits. The language they spoke gave them away as south Indians. They overlapped us many times and their joy at being in Mecca was infectious. Behind us, a man who seemed Pakistani moved at a much slower pace, pushing his old mother in a wheelchair round the Kaba. She was frail and listless, her eyes vacant: she had saved their fading light for the sacred house in Mecca. Then another overlapper hurried past in an effeminate manner, flashed us a bitter smile, and hastened on.

The vast array of humanity at the mosque, their long journeys encoded in the languages they spoke and the races they represented, brought a domiciliary aspect to the mosque's courtyard. People napped, sat in groups with their families, prayed and read the Book. The hour was late, but no one seemed to notice; this, after all, was the destination of destinations.

When we had circled the Kaba seven times, we moved out of the path of orbiting pilgrims and prayed together. Behind the double-storey colonnades and their many domes, there were brightly lit minarets and skyscrapers. I felt as if I was in a park in the middle of a heaving modern city.

We had rushed things. We sat next to each other, a little sweaty now, at one end of the courtyard. Kareem, prolonging the prayer, sat on his shins. His handsome face, normally bright with an ironic smile, was quiet and closed. Hani's eyes were closed too, his dark lips moving silently. A moment later we rose for the last rite: Hagar's search for water.

There are many versions of the story, but the key facts are that Hagar, Abraham's wife, is stranded with the infant Ishmael in the vicinity of Mecca. She runs seven times between Mounts Safa and Marwa until an angel appears to her. He stamps on the ground and water springs up – where the ZamZam well is – to quench the thirst of mother and child. It was Hagar's steps, her fear and deliverance, a sign of God watching over Muslims, that we were to retrace.

Hani led us out of the courtyard and into a separate part of the mosque. On the way, we stopped at Abraham's feet, gold-plated and in a case. We gazed at them; Hani murmured the prayer that is said at the station of Abraham. We continued towards a long, enclosed walkway. Rectangular pillars at even intervals seemed to make an infinite reflection, like two mirrors facing each other, down the corridor's length. A metal railing ran down the centre, separating those who were going from Mt. Marwa to Mt. Safa, re-created in brown paint and concrete at either end of the walkway, from those who were returning. There was a stretch in the middle, marked out by two green lights, where Hagar's distress had been at its highest. We were obliged to cover this distance at a run. It made the pilgrims sweaty and the air was heavy. On one side of the corridor, there were grilles that let in the cooler night air and on the other it was possible to see the vastness of the mosque, its many floors, with escalators running between them, and black men in blue clothes cleaning the building.

At one point on the run, which was long and exhausting, I caught sight of the Kaba in its courtyard. It possessed the place. Thousands stood in tight circles around it, but they seemed hardly to fill the giant courtyard. I tried to gauge the building's size, but it defied assessment. And this was part of its mystery, like the near invisible, black-on-black calligraphy, woven into the silk covering its solid masonry.

The Kaba could not disappoint because it was nothing. Its utter poverty expressed cosmic contempt for the things of the world. It was solid, mute, no triumph of architecture and virtually impenetrable, more like a rent in the sky than a monument. So silent and unrevealing a sanctum was this, that it implied faith, rewarding the believer with nothing, as if faith itself was the reward, and mosaic ceilings and tiled domes, mere trifles.

This thought of faith seemed to lead into what happened next. A fellow pilgrim approached us at the end of our run. He was dark, with a pointed face and a curt manner. He addressed me in Arabic. I didn't understand so he turned to Hani and Kareem. They nodded and walked on without a word.

'What did he say?'

'He said, "This is the House of God. You will receive divine merit if you make him take those off,"' Hani explained, pointing to the religious strings round my neck and wrists.

I couldn't even remember where the strings were from. Some were from temples, others from Muslim shrines. 'Tell him they're from a Sufi shrine,' I said defensively.

'Don't say that.' Hani smiled. 'That's even worse. The Wahhabis hate Sufis.'

Faith was the reward at the sacred house, and faith would have answered the objection the pilgrim had raised, but I had come faithless to Mecca. And justly, I was found out.

PART I

The Licence-plate Game

My earliest sense of being Muslim was bound to my earliest perception of my father's absence; it could almost be said that it was a twin birth in which one superseded the other.

It was midsummer at my aunt's house, a Lutyens Delhi bungalow, on a wide road lined with *neem* trees. Their fruit, fat green berries, fell everywhere. They lay on the large lawn in front of the house and on the long shallow steps leading up to the pillared veranda; they even made their way into the house on the backs of huge black colonial ants.

I was five, maybe six. My mother was a journalist and used to go away on assignments. When she did, I was sent to spend afternoons and sometimes nights at my cousins' house. My aunt had married the heir of a rich Sikh family and the house was always full of his nephews and nieces, who also lived in big houses on similar wide roads with *neem* berries and fat ants. I lived with my mother, another aunt and my grandparents in a small house past several roundabouts and a flyover that separated the Delhi of white bungalows and *neem* trees from the post-independence Delhi of colonies.

My mother thought that as I had no brothers and sisters it was better for me to be with other children rather than inactive grandparents. But I dreaded the house and if the decision had been left to me, I would not have gone at all. To come from my small uneventful house to the bigger house full of children was to come with nothing to share. Unlike my cousins, I rarely had any opportunity to devise games, especially not for the numbers that came. So on the occasions I was sent, I seemed always to arrive late, or mid-game, with no hope of catching up.

One morning I arrived to find that the cousins, and the cousins' cousins, had all been given notebooks and pens by their fathers and put to the task of recording the licence-plate numbers of passing cars. A special prize awaited whoever at the end of the day had jotted down the most. The game was already underway when I arrived. Main roads surrounded the five-acre property and the cousins were scattered to perches on its periphery from where they could see passing cars. I couldn't find anyone to ask for a notebook, but was quite happy not to play and relieved that my absence would not be felt. I was settling into a planter chair under the portico of the house when my aunt, who had just finished doing the household accounts, found me.

She was furious to discover her only nephew, son of the sister she loved, excluded from the game. I tried to explain that it wasn't anyone's fault, that I had arrived late, but here, she thought she recognised her own family's good manners and it angered her further. She called two servants and sent them to round up all the cousins from the different corners of the property. I withered at hearing these orders and pleaded again to be allowed to join the game on my own terms, but the servants had gone and my aunt, too, in search of a notebook for me.

In a short time, nearly a dozen coloured turbans had assembled at the front veranda, looking at me for an explanation. I muttered something and tried, turbanless, to blend into the crowd by engaging my immediate cousins, but they were irritated by the mid-morning interruption and could speak only of the game.

Minutes later my aunt returned with a notebook, which she handed to me. She explained that she hadn't been able to find one like my cousins had been given, but that this would do just as well. It was much longer and narrower than theirs, and when I opened it, I saw it was the accounts book from which she had torn out the used pages.

She called aside her children, my first cousins, and within earshot of everyone, yelled at them for leaving me out. Then she came up to the other cousins and said that since I had arrived late I couldn't be expected to catch up. In the interests of bridging the gap, I would be given a handicap: they were all to give me twenty licence-plate numbers from their lists before they resumed the game. Muffled groans and cries of 'Unfair!' rose, as they submitted to the slow, arduous process of selecting twenty unique licence-plate numbers to give me. Like an unwilling tax collector, I sat on the shallow steps as my cousins, all older, taller and turbaned, came up to me. My mortification must have appeared as ingratitude, which further annoyed them. When nearly three of my book's long, narrow pages were filled, my cousins vanished. Careful not to be caught alone by my aunt again, I ran after them to find a spot from which to watch the road.

And it was like this that I, who from an early age possessed a horror of competitive games, passed the longest day of my life. Fiats and Ambassadors ambled down the wide boulevards, and wobbly heat strands rising off the tar, nearly concealed their black-and-white number plates. From the roof of the house, it was possible to see the palms around the Imperial Hotel's swimming-pool. The hint of moisture accentuated the dryness of the land. Fumes, dust and temperature came together to form a parched feeling of nausea. The day grew into an impossible fever, rich with boredom and hallucination. If any of my cousins registered the game's monotony, they didn't let on. They ran from perch to perch, sometimes shrieking with excitement at spotting a blue-and-white diplomatic plate, which, like the newly introduced Suzukis, were higher in points.

The game broke for lunch, but its inferences dominated the conversation. Diplomatic cars were easier to spot than Suzukis, but harder than white VIP number plates. Of course an ambassador's car was the hardest to spot and so should be awarded higher points. One cousin claimed to have spotted 15 CD 1, the British High Commissioner's car, but was suspected of lying. Overhearing the conversation, I could tell that the handicap had been unfairly given. I was well ahead, despite being the slowest at spotting cars. The others seemed to register this and left me out of the conversation.

When they returned to their posts, I was determined to spot even fewer cars. I knew the day's humiliations would only increase if I were to end up winning the prize. As the afternoon wore on, I added barely a single entry. The cousins, despite the scorching white heat, remained fanatical. In the worst hours, I had none of the excitement of the competition, just fear of victory. It wasn't till evening when traffic filled the streets, like rising water behind a lock that I could tell I was no longer ahead. With the falling temperature, the sky regained its colour, and birds and insects, also paralysed by the heat, returned to their movements. The vast white torment of the day sank to a compact stratum just above the earth, drawing pinks and blues out of the areas that it surrendered.

At close to six, nearly the time when my mother was meant to pick me up, the nannies came running to call everyone in for milk. Drinking milk was viewed in my aunt's house as the secret to growing tall. Committed to this goal, my cousins drank great quantities of it at competitive speeds. Everyone's nanny brought their child's special milk mug to the house as if it were a piece of professional sporting equipment.

I didn't mind drinking milk, but I wasn't used to the amount drunk at my aunt's house. I hadn't brought a mug, and hoped that if I delayed the process I might be able to slip away with my mother before the points from the licence-plate game were counted. So, as the others ran back to the house, I clambered over a small mound and went to the boundary wall. I unzipped my trousers and started to pee. I was concentrating on the small frothy puddle forming before me when I looked up and saw my first cousin similarly relieving himself. He saw me too, and after staring intently in my direction, his face turned to horror. I looked round to see what had alarmed him and began to say something, but he turned his head away, muttering to himself. Then, squeezing out a few last drops, he pulled up his zip and fled. He ran up the mound and down into the garden, screaming, 'Aatish ka susu nanga hai!'

He had chosen his words well. I felt their embarrassment even before I understood their meaning. '*Nanga*' meant naked; it was a nanny's word used to instil in children the shame of running around with no clothes on. It was used in little ditties to make the point clearer and its resonance was deep. *Susu* was a little boy's penis. And though I knew each word my cousin had spoken, I couldn't piece together the meaning of the sentence. Why had he said that my penis was naked?

I zipped up my trousers and ran down the hill after him in the hope of figuring out what he meant before the others did. I reached the lawn as the news was being broken to the rest of the cousins, who collapsed, coughing and spluttering, when they heard. They were not quite sure what it meant, but the nannies screeched with laughter.

The commotion was so great that the adults were drawn out on to the veranda. Again, my cousin yelled, 'Aatish ka susu nanga hai!' This time, seeing all the adults, including my aunt, laughing, I laughed too, louder than anyone else. The cousins, who earlier had been perturbed rather than amused, were now also laughing. The time for explanations had passed and I decided to ask my mother in private about what the nannies had dubbed my hatless willie. Fortunately, amid the disruption the licence-plate game had also been forgotten and when my mother turned up, she found me agitating to leave before the others remembered.

In the car, as my mother drove from roundabout to round-about, like in a game of joining the dots, I agonised over the day's discovery. I could now tell the difference between my *susu* and my cousin's, but its implication was impossible to guess.

The truth turned out to be more implausible than anything I could have invented. If there was a link between the missing foreskin and my missing father, it was too difficult to grasp. My mother had always explained my father's absence by saying that he was in jail for fighting General Zia's military dictatorship in Pakistan, but she had never mentioned the missing foreskin until now. My idea of my father was too small and the trauma of the day too great to take in the information that he came from a country where everyone had skin missing from their penises.

It was a loose, but not disturbing, addition to my life. I felt oddly in on the joke and laughed again. The sun slipping behind Safdarjung's tomb, the little car climbing up the dividing flyover with my mother at the wheel; it was too familiar a view of the world to change over a *susu* without a hat.

*

I grew up with a sense of being Muslim, but it was a very small sense: no more than an early awareness that I had a

Muslim-sounding name, of not being Hindu or Sikh and of the circumcision. In Delhi, my mother had many Muslim friends; we saw them often, and especially for the important Muslim festivals. On these occasions – in them teaching me the Muslim customs and greetings for instance – I felt somehow that they saw me as one of their own. But in Delhi, steeped in Muslim culture, it was hard to pry apart this sense, here related to food, there to poetry, from the shared sensibilities of so many in the city, Muslim and non-Muslim alike.

On the sub-continent religion is patrilineal so it was inevitable that my awareness of religious identity and my father's absence would arise together. At times, over the years, when the twin birth of that day surfaced again, it was always as a Siamese tangle rather than as distinct questions. My mother didn't raise me with religion, but my grandmother, though Sikh herself, told me stories from the different faiths that had taken root in India. As a child I made my way through all the sub-continent's major religions. When I was five or six, I was a devout Hindu, lighting incense, chanting prayers and offering marigolds to the gods; Shiva remained the focus of my devotion until I discovered He-Man. Then, aged seven or eight, I threatened to grow my hair and become a Sikh, but was dissuaded by my mother and my cousins, who had fought their parents for the right to cut their hair. Through all this, I retained my small sense, gained on that hot day, of being Muslim.

When I was ten a Kuwaiti family, escaping the Gulf War, moved into our building and their three sons became my best friends. One night, sitting on their father's bed, the subject of religion came up. Either from some buried conviction or just the wish to be included, I told them I was Muslim. Their father seemed surprised and asked whether I had been circumcised, making a whistling sound and a snip of his fingers that reduced us to cackles. And just as it began, the question of the circumcision, and the patrilineal connection to Islam that it stood for, was obscured in confusion and laughter.

It was only few years later, when Hindu–Muslim riots erupted across India and Hindu nationalist groups drove through Delhi pulling down men's trousers to see if they were circumcised, that my early memory of the link between my circumcision and my father's religion acquired an adult aspect. But by then, my desire to know whose son I was had consumed any interest I might have had in knowing which religion I belonged to. I was also on my way to a Christian boarding-school in south India, adding the final coat of paint to a happy confusion that was as much India's as my own. And it wasn't until I was in my mid-twenties, far away from my childhood world in India, that religion surfaced again.

The Beeston Mail

The colourful train that took me north on a low, grey morning in 2005 was heading for Leeds. I was twenty-four and had been living in London for a year. A few days before, a group of British Pakistanis had bombed London buses and trains; most had been from Beeston, a small Leeds suburb.

Beeston that morning, with its rows of dark brick, semi-detached houses, could hardly cope with the attention that had come to it. The world's press filled its quiet residential streets with TV cameras and outside-broadcast vans. The police were also there in large numbers and the residents, caught between camera flashes, yellow tape and controlled explosions, either hid in their houses or developed a taste for talking to the press. The majority were Punjabis, Muslims and Sikhs, Pakistanis and Indians, re-creating pre-Partition mixtures – especially evocative for me – of an undivided India that no longer existed.

Walking around Beeston, interviewing its residents, I became aware of a generational divide among its Muslims that I hadn't noticed in previous trips round England. The older generation could have come straight from a bazaar in Lahore. They wore the long-tailed *kameez* and baggy *salwar* of Punjab, their best language was Punjabi, and although they were opposed to

Britain's involvement in the Iraq war and hated America, they were too balanced to be extremists, too aware of their hard-earned economic migration from Pakistan.

Their children were unrecognisable to them and to me. Some were dressed in long Arab robes with beards cut to Islamic specifications. They lacked their parents' instinctive humour and openness; their hatred of the West was immense and amorphous. One appeared next to his father, carrying a crate into their corner shop. He had small, hard eyes, a full black beard, and wore a grey robe with a little white cap. He seemed almost to be in a kind of fancy dress. I asked him why he was dressed that way.

'It is my traditional dress,' he answered coldly, in English.

'Isn't your father in traditional dress?' I asked.

'Yes, but this is Islamic dress.'

His father looked embarrassed.

An older man standing next to me chuckled. 'I was complaining to my neighbour that my son never did any work and the neighbour said, "You think that's bad, mine's grown a beard and become a *maulvi* [priest]."' The joke was intended for me especially because the *maulvi* on the sub-continent is a figure of fun and some contempt.

Walking around Beeston, it was possible to feel, as I had for most of that year, meeting second-generation British Pakistanis in England, that an entire generation of *maulvi*s had grown up in northern Britain. The short exchange with the men at the corner shop was a view in miniature of the differences between the two generations. Though neither felt British in any real sense, the older generation had preserved their regional identity and an idea of economic purpose and achievement. The younger generation was adrift: neither British nor Pakistani, removed from their parents' economic motives and charged with an extra-national Islamic identity, which came with a sense of grievance.

A large, solemn man, the owner of a convenience store, who

knew the bombers, said, 'They were born and raised here. We did the work and these kids grew up and they haven't had a day's worry. They're bored. They don't do any work. They have no sense of honour or belonging.'

Later that week, on the train home, I considered their story. It began in rootlessness, not unlike my own, and led to the discovery of radical Islam, which was largely unknown to me. I had encountered it for the first time the year before when I had met Hassan Butt, a young British Pakistani who had been a spokesman for the extremist group Al-Muhajiroun and active in recruiting people to fight in Afghanistan. (Butt later recanted these views, although in 2008 he was arrested while boarding a flight to Lahore.) We had sat in an Indian restaurant on Manchester's Curry Mile. Butt was short and muscular, with a warm but intense manner. He was exactly my age, and took me into his confidence at least in part because he saw me, on account of my having a Muslim father, as Muslim.

His ambition for the faith was limitless. 'Fourteen hundred years ago,' he told me, 'you had a small city state in Medina and within ten years of the Prophet it had spread to Egypt and all the way into Persia. I don't see why the rest of the world, the White House, Ten Downing Street, shouldn't come under the banner of Islam.' It was Butt's nearness to me in some ways – in age, in the split worlds he had known, in the warmth he showed me – that drew me to him, and the faith he had found that created distance between us. At last, I said, 'So what now? You're as old as I am, where do you go from here?'

'First things first,' he replied. 'Fight to the utmost to get my passport back [the British authorities had impounded it]. The quicker I get it, the faster I get my plan of action together that I have with a group of guys who ... Since leaving Muhajiroun I'm focusing on them. There are about nine of us now and we're not willing to accept anybody else because we have the same ideas, same thoughts. Each one of us will maybe play a different role from the other, but all collectively to gain a wider picture. Once I get my passport back, I definitely see myself, *inshallah*, not out of pride, not out of arrogance, not out of ambition, but rather because I believe I have the ability – I pray to Allah to give me more ability – to become a face for Islam in the future, something Muslims have been lacking for a very long time.'

His answer put still greater distance between us. My small sense of being Muslim, gained so haphazardly over the years, was not enough to enter into the faith that Butt had found.

Now, travelling back from Leeds to London, I realised how short I was on Islam. I knew that the young men I had met in Beeston, and Butt, felt neither British nor Pakistani, that they had rejected the migration of their parents, that as Muslims they felt free of these things. But for me, with my small cultural idea of what it meant to be Muslim and no notion of the Book and the Traditions, the completeness of Islam, it was impossible to understand the extra-national identity that Beeston's youth and Butt had adopted. I wouldn't have been able to see how it might take the place of nationality. My personal relationship with the faith was a great negative space. And despite this, I was also somehow still Muslim.

So, with only an intimation of their aggression; their detachment and disturbance; and some sense that Islam had filled the vacuum that other failed identities had left, I came back to London and wrote my article. It was an accumulation of my experience with radical Islam in Britain. I wrote that the British second-generation Pakistani, because of his particular estrangement, the failure of identity on so many fronts, had become the genus of Islamic extremism in Britain. The article appeared on the cover of a British political magazine alongside my interview with Hassan Butt and, proud to have written my first cover story, I sent it to my father.

I received a letter in response, the first he'd ever written to me. But as I read it, my excitement turned quickly to hurt and defensiveness. He accused me of prejudice, of lacking even 'superficial knowledge of the Pakistani ethos', and blackening his name:

Islamic extremism is poisonous, as is that of the IRA and the RSS [a Hindu nationalist party]. The reason why it is on the rise is because of Palestine and Iraq. If Hindus were bombed, occupied and humiliated you may find the same reaction . . . By projecting yourself as an 'Indian Pakistani' you are giving this insulting propaganda credibility as if it is from one who knows it all.

Cricket, that old dress rehearsal for war on the sub-continent, came up: 'Look at the way the Lahore crowd behaved after losing a Test match and compare that to the "Lala crowds" in Delhi. It seems the Hindu inferiority complex is visceral.' A *lala* was a merchant, and here my father articulated prejudices of his own, textbook prejudices in Pakistan, of Hindus as sly shopowners, smaller, weaker, darker and more cowardly than Muslims. 'Oh, I'm so glad you weren't a little black Hindu,' my half-sister would laugh, or 'I hate fucking Hindus, man,' my half-brother once said. Pakistanis, for the most part converts from Hinduism to Islam, lived with a historical fiction that they were descendants of people from Persia, Afghanistan and elsewhere, who once ruled Hindu India.

I wasn't sure which side my father placed me on when he wrote his letter, whether he thought of me as one of them or, worse, as a traitor he had spawned. He did say, 'Do you really think you're doing the Taseer name a service by spreading this kind of invidious anti-Muslim propaganda?' To me, that was the most interesting aspect of the letter: my father, who drank Scotch every evening, never fasted or prayed, even ate pork, and once said, 'It was only when I was in jail and all they gave me to read was the Koran – and I read it back to front several times – that I realised there was nothing in it for me,' was offended as a Muslim by what I had written. The hold of the religion, deeper than its commandments, of religion as nationality, was something that I, with my small sense of being Muslim, had never known.

When I came to the end of my father's letter, I felt he was right: I couldn't have even 'a superficial knowledge' of the Pakistani, but more importantly Islamic, ethos. I had misunderstood what he had meant when he described himself as a cultural Muslim. I took it to mean no more than a version of what I grew up with in Delhi – some feeling for customs, dress, food, festivals and language – but it had shown a reach deeper than I knew. And the question I kept asking myself was how my father, a professed disbeliever in Islam's founding tenets, was even a Muslim. What made him Muslim despite his lack of faith?

For some weeks, during a still, dry summer in London, the letter percolated. It prompted a defence on my part in which my back was up. My father responded with silence that turned colder as the weeks went by. His wife and daughter tried to intervene, but I wasn't willing to apologise for something I'd written. And although I minded the personal attack, I didn't mind the letter: it aroused my curiosity. Caught between feeling provoked and needing to act, I thought of making an Islamic journey.

My aim was to tie together the two threads of experience from that summer: the new, energised Islamic identity working on young Muslims and my own late discovery of my father's religion. My father's letter presented me with the double challenge to gain a better understanding of Islam and Pakistan.

But I wanted a canvas wider than Pakistan. Something deeper

than national identity acted on my father, something related to Islam, and to understand this, I felt travelling in Pakistan alone would not be enough. Pakistan, carved out of India in 1947, was a country founded for the faith. But it was also a lot like India, and I felt that unless I travelled in other Muslim countries I would not be able to separate what might be common Islamic experience from what might feel like an unexplained variation of India. I also wanted to take advantage of the fact that the whole Islamic world stretched between my father and the place where I read his letter. A strange arc of countries lay on my route: fiercely secular Turkey, where Islam had been banished from the public sphere since the 1920s; Arab-nationalist Syria, which had recently become the most important destination for those seeking radical Islam; and Iran, which in 1979 had experienced Islamic revolution.

In a classical sense, except for Turkey, the lands that lay between my father and me were also part of the original Arab expansion when the religion spread in the seventh and eighth centuries from Spain to India. I decided on a trip from one edge of the Islamic world, in Istanbul, to a classical centre, Mecca, and on through Iran to Pakistan. The first part of the trip would be an old Islamic journey, almost a pilgrimage, from its once greatest city to its holiest. The trip away, through Iran and Pakistan, was a journey home, to my father's country, where my link to Islam began, and, finally, to his doorstep.

'Homo Islamicos'

It was November. The sky was damp and heavy. I waited for Eyup outside a Starbucks on Istiklal. It was an old-fashioned European shopping street, with a tram, in central Istanbul. The road was being resurfaced and rain from the night before spread a muddy layer of water over the newly paved white stone. The youth that filled the street, sidestepping wide, wet patches of sludge and splashing brown sprinklings on the ends of jeans, were of remarkable beauty.

Here, it seemed, was a confluence of racial attributes that produced tall men with high central-Asian cheekbones, light European eyes and the olive colouring of the Mediterranean. They were narrow-waisted and muscular, in close-fitting jeans, small T-shirts and dark jackets. The haircuts were short with cleanly shaved edges and sloping, bristly backs. They walked with a strut, looking ahead, seeming a little vain. The women's painted faces and peroxided hair took away from their looks. Still, the abundance of idle, well-dressed youth gave the street a heady, sexual character.

Istiklal, like its youth, was a hybrid: European archways, fashionable shops and stone apartment buildings, with little balconies and pilasters, ran down its length, while its side-streets led into Eastern bazaars, selling fish and vegetables. It had seen better days, then worse days, and now again its fortunes were turning. There were pick-up bars, cafés, bookshops, an Adidas store, nightclubs, gay saunas, health clubs, embassies and offices. Varied music poured into the street from all sides, not just popular music but Sanskrit chanting with hidden techno undertones.

*

I had arrived a few days before by train, dropping south from Budapest to Sofia and then to Istanbul, a slow movement through the ghostlands of the old Ottoman Empire. Very little remained of its once deep European reach: in Budapest, a reconstructed, tiled shrine, Europe's northernmost Muslim monument, dedicated to a Turkish dervish; and in Sofia, the last of its sixty-nine mosques: small and slightly run-down, it sat at an angle to a busy main road with one stone pillar stepping gingerly into the pavement.

In Istanbul, I was staying in a squat, modern hotel on a central square with a view of the Bosphorus. On the morning after I arrived, I witnessed an amazing scene on the strait's leaden waters. I had come down to the shore, and next to me a few soldiers and old men sipped coffee at a kiosk doing steady business. Then everyone stopped what they were doing and looked at the water. The man at the kiosk turned off his stove and looked too. The soldiers jittered.

The first horn that sounded over the now quiet Bosphorus was like the moan of a great mammal, an elephant or a whale, in lament of a fallen leader. The soldiers stood to attention and their arms snapped into salute. Then other horns, with the eagerness of the young in a tribe, responded. The traffic behind me stopped. Some pedestrians, new on the scene, froze in mid-step. The city ground to a silence. The minute stretched and the city waited. White gulls circled overhead as if fastened by cords to the ships. The horns faded gradually, and after a few stray sounds lost over the water, the Bosphorus came to life again and, with it, the roar of the traffic behind me.

It was 9.06 a.m. on 10 November and the man being honoured in the minute-long silence was Mustafa Kemal Atatürk, the founder of the modern republic of Turkey and the man who had given the state its fiercely secular identity. When Atatürk had founded the modern state in the 1920s, fighting off foreign incursions on all sides, he had shut down the traditional Sufistic centres, thrown out fez and veil, cleansed the language of its Persian and Arabic borrowings, changed the script to roman and abolished the office of caliph. He brought to an end the idea of a sanctifying political authority that had existed in Islam since its founding. It was as if he wanted to break the new state's cultural links to the larger Islamic world, rendering unto Turkey what was Turkey's and throwing out the rest.

My father had mentioned the caliphate in his letter: 'European countries occupied by Muslims for hundred of years, like Greece and Spain, did not enforce conversion. In fact, throughout history the Jews were protected by the Muslim caliphates and Christians were allowed to flourish.' The caliphate was part of my father's idea of a collective Muslim history, which he could possess without faith. It was one of the things – the idea of the great Islamic past – that my small sense of being Muslim didn't cover. And yet my father also admired Atatürk for his strength and modernising mission despite Atatürk's break with the collective Islamic past and his creation of a state that was, in its approach to religion, the exact opposite of Pakistan. So, at the very beginning of my journey, with six weeks set aside for Turkey, and with the words of men like Butt on one side and my father on the other – both, in their way, speaking of

the great Islamic past – I wished to see how the faith had fared
in the state that had broken with Islam.

*

The man I waited for outside Starbucks on Istiklal was a young
Marxist student who, when he heard of my interest, offered to
show me a fuller Istanbul. He appeared a few minutes later
with his hands in his pockets. He was short and wide, with
dark, greasy hair, intense blue eyes and an erratic, jarring laugh.
With Eyup, there were no pleasantries. A quick smile, a hello
and immediately down to business. 'Should we go to this very
religious neighbourhood?' he said, as if it were one of many
possible plans. He hailed a taxi on Taksim Square, close to
where I was staying, and asked the driver to take us to Fatih
Carsamba.

'They are very religious there, and they want to be like Arab
countries and Iran,' he explained. 'It's a kind of sub-culture.'
Istanbul was protean. It became another city on the way to
Fatih Carsamba. Within an intersection, peroxide Turkish
blondes, with lithe bodies, vanished, and stout women, in long,
dark coats and beige headscarves, moved down a busy street,
selling domestic wares and cheap, synthetic fashions. It was
difficult to connect the gaudy advertising, the cars and household goods with the city we had left behind near Istiklal. The
buildings were different, newer, but plainer, more rundown.
There seemed even to be racial differences; the features here
were coarser, less mixed, more Arab somehow. But this area
was not a preparation for the religious neighbourhood: it was
not a sub-culture.

We paid the taxi driver and started to walk. And now Eyup
and I, in jeans and winter jackets, looked out of place. Fatih
Carsamba had made Eyup uncomfortable when he visited it as

a teenager, and I soon began to see why. It came on with sinister suddenness. After a gentle bend in an inclining road, we seemed to come under a new law by which all women wore black and, but for a triangular opening for their noses and eyes, were covered completely. The men were in long robes with shaven upper lips and fistfuls of beard. There were bookshops with names like Dua, or Prayer, more bookshops than anywhere else so far, but they all carried the same green and red leatherbound religious books, Korans of all shapes and sizes and defensive pamphlets – *Jesus and Islam*, *Modern Science and Islam*, *Status of Women and Islam* – forestalling the questions people ask. Other shops delivered a steady drone of Koranic readings. Their racks of religious CDs were on display in polished glass windows, just like on Istiklal. Dull-coloured robes with machine embroidery, black on black, navy blue on navy blue, hung on wire coat-hangers in the doors of clothes shops. All varieties of Arab clothing from slinky latex under-veil garments to white skullcaps were available. It was an Islamic facsimile of a modern high street.

'Sub-culture', I thought, was a good word. It implied an aberration not just from urban Istanbul culture, but also from the traditional Islam of Turkey; it brought out the radical aspect of the new faith. For me, the word suggested punks and hippies, even neo-Nazis. It was a word I would have liked to have been able to use, when I first saw young radicalised British Pakistanis in northern England. There again, people were not simply religious in a traditional way; they were religious in a new way. The religion they embraced constituted an abrupt break from what had come before.

We were attracting hostile attention and Eyup was trying already to edge me out of the area. I suggested we turn into a teashop and reassess the situation.

Eyup seemed nervous. 'Something might happen,' he said ominously, as we entered.

A young man with a light brown Islamic beard and a matching robe worked behind the counter. His eyes fixed on us as we came in. He seemed weary and irritated when Eyup ordered tea, as if he had been denied the opportunity to tell us we were in the wrong place. His gaze remained on us as we drank our tea and he went about his chores, wiping the counter and working the till. The hot sugary liquid and the smells from the stove were just beginning to act against the odourless cold of the street, when my question to the man gave him his chance. I asked him about his dress. Eyup looked nervous, but then translated.

The man stopped what he was doing and his face darkened. When he had finished speaking to Eyup, I could see that the exchange had not gone well.

'He suggests,' Eyup began, looking for solace in the change of language, 'that we don't try to ask any questions around here as there may be a violent reaction.'

The words landed cold and hard on me, more menacing for issuing from Eyup's disinterested lips. The man spoke again and Eyup translated: 'He says, "Our way of life is personal so it's not right for others to ask about it. The Prophet Muhammad wore these clothes and that is why we wear them."'

There was more conversation between Eyup and the man, but when it was over, Eyup did not translate. I heard Pakistan mentioned.

'We should go,' he said. 'Something might happen.' Eyup's natural calm was disturbed. He was not easily excitable and I was keen to follow his judgement. We said goodbye and the man walked us to the door of his shop.

'What else did he say?' I asked Eyup.

'I'll tell you later,' he said. 'We should go.'

It was early in the day and the street was still waking up. Shops were opening and the women who hovered down the street in their long robes turned their triangular faces to us in puzzlement. I asked Eyup if I could find a place like this in small towns or in the countryside.

'No,' he said, 'this is not how they dress.'

The hidden world of Fatih Carsamba fell away as the road sloped downhill. The rest of the city returned and the sub-culture vanished as suddenly as it had appeared. It was only a hilltop of radicalism, but before it was gone, we were met with a haunting scene. In this environment of segregation and austerity, on a cemented quadrangle surrounded by a high chain-link fence, a school was breaking between classes. The screams and laughter from dozens of uniformed young boys and girls disturbed the morning pall.

After the muffled threats from the man in the teashop, the sight of children playing was an unexpected comfort. They were occupied in some variation of catch and mixed teams of boys and girls swept from side to side of the playground. The girls were in skirts and the boys in trousers; they seemed entirely at ease with each other, entirely without inhibition.

Outside their chain-link world, the last shrouded figure vanished over the crest of the hill. I was struck by the thought that these were the children of this neighbourhood. The shrouded figure might have been one of their mothers or elder sisters. Would she have gone to the school too? And, if so, what a strange passage it must have been from this freedom to the violent purity of her dress and the segregation it stood for.

Then, as we turned the corner, we saw a self-standing struc-ture whose presence here was at once fierce and absurd. About three feet from the ground, placed dead centre on the extremity of the playground, and lost in children's games was the unlikely, the implausible, the almost chimeric object: a head-and-shoul-ders bust of Atatürk in smooth black stone, watching over the cemented playground.

In the taxi, Eyup recounted the rest of what the man in the teashop had said to him. Speaking of Fatih Carsamba, he had said, 'This is the only place we can live like Muslims so we have to protect that. If someone comes from outside, like a journalist or writer, he can cause problems for us. The police could come and break up the neighbourhood.' Of his dress, he added, 'I am dressed like this because the Prophet Muhammad dressed this way. None of our other leaders dressed like that, not Atatürk, not anyone else.'

At the time, I didn't appreciate how daring a remark this was. The cult of Atatürk was sacrosanct in Turkey and his forceful brand of secularism, backed by the army, could silence the boldest Islamists. For the man in the teashop to discuss him in disparaging tones, and to a fellow Turk, was a jailable gesture of defiance. It was an introduction to how important physical appearance would become over the course of my journey, especially in regard to Islam's relationship with the modern world; it was part of the completeness of the challenge the faith presented. It had been a battleground for Atatürk and it was a battleground for the man in the teashop.

The man had asked Eyup if I was Muslim. Eyup knew only the facts of my parentage and, though he was not a believer himself, he made a leap of reason that others around me would make for the next eight months: if your father's Muslim, you're Muslim. He might only have been trying to cool the situation, but he knew that the man in the teashop was forced to accept this information. This level of being Muslim was more important than anything that came afterwards, such as the actual components of your faith. It was primary, built into one's birth and recognised by all Muslims, religious or not. 'He is from Pakistan and is a Muslim,' Eyup had said. The man, obligated by his religion to accept this, replied, 'If you're a Muslim, you know that this is how real Muslims dress.'

Muslims living in a Muslim country with a sense of persecution. The link to the great Islamic past, and the cultural threads to the larger Muslim world, proscribed and broken. The modern republic of Turkey aspired to be part of the European Union. Turkey had been among the most open Muslim countries, but its secularism was dogmatic, almost like a separate religion. The state didn't stay out of religion, it co-opted religion: it wrote Friday sermons, appointed priests and hounded people it thought to be religious out of the establishment. Why did it have to be so extreme? What threat to his modern, secular republic had Atatürk perceived in the Islamic identity?

It was the army, along with Istanbul's educated élite, who had enforced his aggressive secularism since the founding of the republic in the 1920s. At first people had obeyed, but in recent years, as migration from more religiously conservative Anatolia to Istanbul increased, people became emboldened, more sure of who and what they were. The radical hilltop, with its high street refashioned along Islamic lines, was the response of a few, but many more wanted to know why they couldn't wear their headscarves. They set up centres of business and capital, 'green capital', to counter the power of Istanbul's secular rich. The prime minister, Recep Tayyip Erdoğan, was of their ilk. The city was full of women wrapped in Versace headscarves driving SUVs. Islam was coming in through the back door. The army and the bourgeois Kemalists eyed them with deep suspicion.

But what was really meant by this reassertion of Islamic identity? What cultural wholeness had been lost and what would it take for the world to be whole again?

*

I don't know what my time in Turkey would have been like had I not met Abdullah. Months later, when I recalled his agony, so difficult to match with his plump face and soft manner – I never forgot that before he gave himself to the faith, before he was penalised for being from a religious school, he was almost a business student. And though he studied Arabic and religion, unlike Beeston's Islamists and religious students in other Muslim countries, he studied them as part of a larger, secular curriculum, and in the way someone in Britain might study divinity. He had not come off a radical hilltop, and though he might always have been a believer, his degree of self-realisation was new. He was like a symbol of the enforced absence of religion in Turkey and of what a conspicuous absence it was.

I had been a few times to the Islamic Cultural Centre on the Asian side of the Bosphorus. Eyup had taken me once to hear a visiting Saudi diplomat speak and then, in his irreligious way and with his Turkish disdain for Arabs, laughed out loud when the man appeared in traditional Arab dress. After the lecture, I had begun a conversation with a student of religion, and it was him who first told us about Abdullah. We tried on many occasions to arrange a meeting with him, but it was only days before I was due to leave Istanbul, when the December rain and wind were at their fiercest and traffic clogged Istanbul's major arteries, that we managed to arrange a time. We took a small, shared bus along the Bosphorus' steely waters and a taxi over a giant, slab-like bridge, entering Asia with an ease that never ceased to delight me.

At the Islamic Cultural Centre, the rain drove us out of the open courtyards into covered walkways that led to the cafeteria. It was a bare white room, with one corner churning out cups of tea. We sat round a Formica table which was too low for me to write on. Eyup went to get us tea and I started to test the language abilities of the two students who had just walked in. Abdullah was heavy-set, with a round face, thick lips and an auburn Islamic beard. He had a friendly, docile manner and spoke English slowly but precisely. Oskan was clean-shaven with an angular face and close-set eyes. He spoke little English and next to Abdullah's smiles and gentle voice, there seemed something hard about his manner. Eyup returned with a round of plain tea, the sugar cubes crumbling at the bottom of the glasses.

'This is something very hard to explain,' Abdullah began, in response to my question about why he had entered the theology faculty. I thought he meant that language would pose a problem, but this was not the case; he was thinking of the actual complication of his decision. 'The simple and basic reason for it is that I want to learn about my religion. I'm studying Arabic language actually, not theology, but as a general education I have studied the Islamic sciences such as *hadi*s [the sayings of the Prophet], and *fiqh* [jurisprudence].' I was still under the impression that Eyup would have to translate from here on when Abdullah surprised me with his fluency.

'You have to be a well-qualified and educated person,' he said, picking his words carefully, 'to represent your religion, culture and point of view in the world.'

'Do you feel you have to do it some service?' I asked, surprised at the new firmness of his tone.

'Yes, of course.'

'What do you have in mind?'

'There is a conflict between the world and our ideas, our beliefs, our culture . . .' Suddenly he was embarrassed at his exclusive conversation with me in English and asked if Oskan could participate. I was happy for him to do so, but wanted Abdullah to continue in English. Oskan seemed to understand better than he could speak, and Eyup agreed to translate where necessary. Abdullah returned to the question: 'We have to understand the conditions we are living in today. This world is a very different world from that of our religion, our history and our background. The first thing we have to do is grasp that, to take the point of what is going on in the world and to understand the political, philosophical and historical root of this system. Of course, we also have to study and practise our own beliefs and culture. It is not easy to take in the culture as a whole because it is a huge culture of more than a thousand years.'

I was forced to stop him; he was losing me in his separations. 'Do you mean Turkish culture or Islamic culture?'

'Islamic,' he replied, 'because we are part of that big culture. For example, Arabic language, there are lots of people who have studied it, Arabs, Turks, Persians. It is a big tradition, hard to grasp as a whole, but we have to do what we can. Then we need to create a response, an answer to this world, and try to solve the problem between the reality around us and our own beliefs and ideals.' It was at this point that I realised that when Abdullah spoke of the 'world', he didn't mean the rest of the world or his world, but something alien, which he later described as a 'world system', shorthand for the modern world.

'What is this conflict?'

Oskan, who had been listening watchfully until now, said, 'The conflict starts with information. All knowledge orders and determines things. It makes the systems of the world. For example, Western civilisation, which is at the centre of the system, is trying to control others. It is getting the knowledge in its hand and trying to control others with it. Once it has, we find that in our practice we no longer think as the early Muslims thought.'

I sensed that I would have to be vigilant about abstraction and the traps of philosophy and theology. 'Do you find that this is something that Western civilisation is trying to do or has successfully done? Do you consider yourself out of the "world system"?'

'I don't mean we are out of the system,' Abdullah answered. 'We are living in it. We are just thinking about what is going on, trying to understand what is being done to us. We are becoming more and more a part of this system, but if you ask me, "Is that OK?" of course the answer is no. For example, Islam says you should live in a particular way, but in today's world system, if you try to follow the orders of your religion, it is really hard to stand up in a capitalist economy.'

'How do you mean?'

'Interest, for example, is such a big problem. This is one of the ingredients of conflict.' I must have looked a little baffled at how the Islamic injunction against usury could make so much difference to Abdullah's life because he added, 'Another example is of some American people I know. One of them said to me last month that he has a son. He is trying to make him fulfil his religious obligations, but is finding it really hard.'

'They're American Muslims?'

'Yes, and his father is trying to make him do his obligations, but the system is working against him. It is stealing your child from you.'

His description of the system as something encircling him, and yet alien, puzzled me. I was part of the system he described, but couldn't think of myself in any other way, couldn't peel away the system. I was curious as to how the other system, the Islamic system, could even remain active within him as something distinct. 'I can see why you describe the system as founded on Western values. I also see why you feel the need for your own system, but why do you think Islam, founded so long ago, would have answers for today?'

'To be a person,' Abdullah answered, 'to be a human being, is one thing, but I have a mode of being. It is to be a Muslim.

It is a unique mode of being because it does not change in any time or in any place. Islam is not something man-made. It was given to us. That means it is above history, above man and above culture, but we are only now beginning to get relevant to it, trying to practise it.'

Abdullah's tone had changed and become tighter. I was worried that the curtain of faith had come down early on our conversation. The certainties of faith had obstructed other discussions I had had, but I was sure that I could find common vocabulary with Abdullah. After all, it was him who brought up this term, the 'world system', which, even though he had never left Turkey, was common to us both. It could mean anything from mobile phones, to air travel, to modern education, but perhaps its most significant component was the exposure to the culture and values of Europe and America that ran like a live wire through Istiklal.

'What is it about the modern experience that is problematic?'

'It is that today's system is putting man at the centre. It is anthrocentric. Our system is theocentric. Western civilisation says we are able to do what we want, that we don't need a God to make a cultural or religious system. That is the difference and it is a big one. This modern system is different from all other traditional systems, not just Islamic but Christian and Judaic systems too.' Man instead of God, progress instead of the afterlife, reason instead of faith: these were the transfers Abdullah felt he was being forced to make, and yet my own feeling was that his regret came not from the prospect of having to make them but from already having done so.

'The modern system has a great power,' Oskan started, 'which is not just against Islam but against Chinese culture too, and other traditional cultures. It's just that any response from another culture may be used by the modern system and made into an empty box, a consumer product. It can't do that to Islam because

Islam is a religion that is interested in this world and the other world.'

'What is the difference in the way Islam treats the physical world?'

'Islam has many rules about this world,' Abdullah said. 'We believe that for a person who is a Muslim the religion will have something to say to him in every second of his life. This is what we try to do in *fiqh*. We try to place value on what a man does. We have a scale and whatever you do must be within that scale. You cannot go out of it. It begins with *farz*, obligation, and ends with *haram*, what is forbidden. There are many levels between these two parameters, but there is no way out of the scale. Other religions don't have these kinds of orders and permissions, but Islam has this unity. It is a whole system for this world and the other world.' Islam offered an enclosed world of prescriptive and forbidden action, which was more detailed than most other religions, but in the end could only cover those things that were common to the world of today and the Prophet's world in Arabia. Within decades of the thousand-year history that Abdullah had spoken of earlier, the Prophet's example was abandoned for the ways of the new worlds of Persia, Syria and Egypt that the early Muslims had gained. But now, in Turkey, that great Islamic past, which had absorbed so much, could not be seen to continue and, with Abdullah, I felt both the nearness and sadness of its end; just the other day, it seemed.

'You think the West is trying to impose its way of life on the rest of the world,' I said. 'Have you ever thought that in the seventh century when Islam was a conquering religion, the Arabs imposed their way of life on the people they conquered?'

Both Oskan and Abdullah choked with laughter and, I thought, some degree of amazement. 'No one has ever asked me that before,' Abdullah said good-humouredly. 'Good question, good question.'

And, although it was as blasphemous a thing as I could have said – that history was a golden history; those Arabs were the bringers of the faith – Oskan fielded it: 'Islam is an organising religion, but these others are destroying . . .'

Abdullah, recovering from his shock, said, 'For example, the Europeans went to America. They found many people living there, but today we don't find many of its original inhabitants living there. But the Ottoman state controlled the Balkans for many hundreds of years, and if you go there, you still find churches.'

The conversation was heading in a dangerous direction: churches destroyed or not in lands Muslims conquered versus mosques destroyed or not in retaliation. I wanted to avoid it, hoping to reach beyond the sanctity with which Muslims viewed their past, a historical perfection held up in contrast to the errors of others.

'If what you're saying,' I said, 'is that there is something in Islam that orders and preserves while there is something in the West that destroys, I want to know what that ordering is.'

Abdullah returned to mosque, temple and church destruction. 'I may say,' he began, 'that if a Muslim has destroyed temples in India, acting as a Muslim, then we can say that that is not OK.'

'Not OK?'

'Yes, definitely without any doubt.'

'Even if he was destroying idols?'

Abdullah smiled. A discussion began between him and Oskan. Arabic verses were traded back forth. At last Abdullah, as if reading the jury's verdict said, 'Our Prophet destroyed idols by his own hand so of course worshipping idols is not OK.' Still smiling, he made a smooth transition to People of the Book. 'But we call all Christians and Jews People of the Book and respect them. If someone who is a Person of the Book cuts an animal, a Muslim may eat it.'

'Tell me one thing: is it possible for someone who is a Person of the Book to follow his own religion, not accepting Islam and Muhammad, and still go to heaven?'

They began to laugh again and traded more verses. 'There are different points of view on that,' Abdullah said, 'but the major and central opinion is that, no, it's impossible.'

My thoughts were on neither theology nor the afterlife. What interested me was Abdullah's mention of an almost biological sense of being Muslim. Perhaps that was why Muslims always wanted to establish – and it had started as soon as I arrived in Turkey – whether or not I was Muslim, and it didn't seem to matter what kind of Muslim I was.

'You have a pan-Islamic idea of the world, yet the Muslim world has been so divided.'

'Sunni and Shia?'

'Yes, but also within countries. Turkey has its eyes one way, Iran another. What gives you hope that Muslims will overcome their differences?'

'Maybe political views will not come together,' Abdullah said, 'but the people . . . You may say there are two levels. The ones at the top care about the political system, but there is something under that. And so if you look at those people in Muslim countries, they are not very different from each other. There might be differences in political structures – and even these are related to the West – but not in people's lives.'

Abdullah had never been to a Muslim country other than Turkey, but he was sure of his brotherhood with Muslims beyond any national or political difference. This was also an aspect of the faith: looking upon governments and political classes as corrupt, in foreign hands, and the average Muslim as inherently good and of one mind. My father later spoke to me of this brotherhood, and what I wondered again and again was what his admission into this brotherhood was based on.

And why was I so definitely shut out of it where he was concerned?

'When you go to a country and you see two groups of people,' Abdullah said, 'you can easily tell who is a Muslim and who is not because to be a Muslim requires many things. For example when the time for prayer is called, he goes to prayer. Another example, a Muslim doesn't lie—'

'Oh, come on, that's nonsense. You might be talking about good Muslims, but good Christians don't lie either. Half the Islamic world is filled with bad Muslims.'

Abdullah laughed. I had heard this talk a lot already. Muslims couldn't kill other Muslims. So what was happening in Iraq? Israelis. Muslims would never have dropped the atomic bomb, and so on.

'You mentioned the conflict between Islamic countries,' Abdullah said, his face growing serious, 'but I'm trying to say that to be a Muslim is a very different experience from any other, no matter where you are. To be a Muslim is to be above history. It is a mode of being, an ideal, but the closer you get to that ideal, the better a Muslim you are.'

To be a Muslim is to be above history. That formulation, like an echo of Gletkin in Arthur Koestler's *Darkness at Noon*, saying 'Truth is what is useful to humanity,' explained so much about the faith's intolerance of history that didn't serve its needs.

Familiar with Islamic logic, Abdullah explained, 'Therefore Islamic countries have an advantage, and that advantage will not go. You say there are differences between them, we accept there are, but these are temporary differences. We can overlook them because we have something that never changes.'

'What do you think the West wants from the Muslim world?'

'That's a big question,' Abdullah said, leaning back a little.

It was nearly dark outside and more glasses of tea arrived.

'I think they realise,' Abdullah said, 'that Islam has an ideal system with the power to make their political and cultural system as a whole go back. Islam has that advantage. It is the unique system with that power. Other systems, Buddhism or Taoism, they don't have that power because the world system can easily turn them into empty boxes. But Islam still has that power because you cannot change it. For example, if you want moderate Islam, you just make yourself far from Islam, but Islam is still there. You cannot do anything to it. If you obey its orders, you're a good Muslim. If you leave it, it's your choice, but you cannot change it.'

For a moment I wondered if the unchanging aspect of Islam that Abdullah seemed so proud of was also the source of his frustrations. After all, it meant living in another still more complete system, the 'world system', that reached into so many aspects of his life and with which he could never be at ease as long as he believed in Islam the way he did. I was grateful for his formulation, 'the world system'. It was like shared experience between us; Islam was his response.

'Fine,' I said. 'This "world system" that you and I are part of, many things come from it, your phone, for instance . . .'

I was looking round the room for other things to mention when he stopped me. 'Everything,' he said, with fresh pain in his voice. 'Everything.'

'Right. Everything,' I repeated, my eyes fixed on him. I felt I had to tread gently now. 'Has anything of value come out of it?'

They talked among themselves. I sensed they understood the question well, but were now picking their way through the rubble of our conversation.

'Marlboro cigarettes,' Oskan laughed, 'and technology are OK.'

Abdullah had thought harder about it. 'No, actually,' he said, 'this is a big issue among Muslim intellectuals. There are many discussions on the subject and, no, it is not so easy to say that technology is OK. For example, let's talk about cinema. The Persians have made many good films. Now, maybe that's OK. By doing that we may stand up against the system by representing our ideals.'

I was about to interrupt him, to say that most of the Iranian films he had spoken about actually stood *against* the Islamic regime, when he introduced a more interesting idea.

'But some other people say we have to discuss the camera itself, not the films. Before making good films, we have to discuss the camera itself. Good or bad? We are not interested in the product, we are interested in the camera.'

'What's the problem with the camera?'

'It's something Western civilisation made. We have to discuss that camera. What does it represent?'

His words chilled me. I thought I heard in them a desire to take the world apart, to have it sanctified in some way by the faith. At the same time, I admired his consistency, the way in which he felt it was wrong to profit from the 'world system' while guarding yourself against its values. Few thought so hard about the issue or cared so much about falling into hypocrisy as Abdullah did, but I couldn't imagine any closed completeness pure enough for him. The world couldn't be put through an Islamic filter: that kind of recasting, like with Fatih Carsamba, could only ever be cosmetic.

He must have seen my discomfort because he tried immediately to console me, supplanting the hate that had risen in him moments ago with reason. 'There was a time in Turkey,' he said, 'when people could not wear turbans and fezes. They had to wear hats. At that time, we discussed whether it was OK to wear turbans or not. It's a very important discussion. There are things that are a symbol of a culture, and if you partake in them, you give a picture of your cultural side.'

'Why is this ownership so important? The West has borrowed from the East, things have gone back and forth. Why must you reinvent everything yourself?'

The irony in what he had said was that for centuries Islam absorbed a great deal that was outside the faith, from Greek medicine and philosophy to Persian architecture, but only at the end of our conversation did Abdullah explain why the faith today was saturated, its cultural circle closed, almost as if American culture, having taken in yoga and Italian food, was to say, 'No more.'

'Of course,' he said. 'Yes, definitely. I don't know what to do. OK? I don't mean that we're going to leave everything that comes from the West. That would be ridiculous. I don't mean that. I'm saying that we have to think and discuss everything that we believe and have today because . . .' The words failed him, '. . . because we didn't do that till today,' he finished a moment later, in a voice that almost broke.

A long, silent moment passed between us. Then, recovering himself, he spoke again: 'We need to discuss everything and maybe we're going to create a new structure. I don't know if we will, but what we need to do is to discuss everything from the beginning, from start to finish. We need to do that.'

Histories swept away, hidden under laminates like Turkey's dogmatic secularism, produced men like Abdullah, who were not content to be told to conceal their religion and wear European clothes. He was studying the past, 'the big Islamic culture' that Atatürk rejected, learning the languages that Atatürk sought to cleanse modern Turkish of, wearing the clothes Atatürk banned; and he had had to pay a price.

'Growing up, what did you and the people around you think of Atatürk?' I asked.

I received the standard embarrassed smile that this question produced in religious people. I pressed Abdullah for an honest answer and assured him that it was not for a newspaper article. 'Of course it wasn't so good,' he said at last. 'We weren't talking so much about the man . . . In my family, you mean?'

'Yes. Just growing up, in school, at home.'

'I would go to school, and Atatürk was in school, just in school. Outside there was no Atatürk. It's difficult to describe. There are some things you don't say but you understand.' Abdullah grew up in a conservative neighbourhood and, briefly, I imagined him in a playground like the one I had seen, a cemented patch of secular life surrounded by men and women of faith.

He complained about secularism: 'It is being used to create a new population, to push Muslims out of the system, and I think they have succeeded on a certain level. For example, if today a religious man, the prime minister, for instance, reaches a high position, it is something we must focus on, something bad. Muslims in Turkey are still out of the system and trying to get in. All the changes in Turkey are coming from the top. They don't ask people if they want these changes.'

Abdullah had suffered at the hands of the system. He came, like Erdoğan, the prime minister, from the religious Imam Hatip schools. He was penalised for this in his college entrance exams; his marks had been docked. It hadn't occurred to me until now to ask him whether he had even wanted to study religion and Arabic.

'There is an ironic story about that,' he said, 'We were meant to write fifteen choices of faculties we wanted to join. Theology was thirteenth on my list. The first was commerce. I was nineteen at the time, not an age when you evaluate things properly, but after entering the theology faculty, I realised that it was the best faculty for me.'

Commerce! I balked. Abdullah, so full of rage against the system, might have been climbing its rungs, drawn in by its rewards. Cast out from that system, he now wanted to be a researcher in the Islamic studies department.

It was late and I rose to leave, but was detained by one last question. It had arisen because I felt at odds with someone I liked. 'You say Muslims have to develop their own system,' I asked, 'separate from the "world system". Why is it not possible for there to be a "world system" that Muslims could be part of?'

'Let me tell you a story,' Abdullah said in reply. 'If a Muslim girl marries someone who is not Muslim, we say that's not OK. She cannot do this. But if a Muslim man marries a girl who is a Person of the Book, that's OK. Jewish people criticise us for allowing our men to marry Jewish and Christian girls, but not allowing our women to marry Jewish and Christian men. You know what the reason for this is? We accept all their prophets, all their books, we don't say anything bad about Christ, but they don't accept our Prophet. They don't accept our Book, they don't accept our religion, they don't accept *our* system. That's the difference. I think that Muslims have to be at the top, at the centre of the system. We have to determine all the things in the world, otherwise we won't be free ourselves. That doesn't mean we will destroy other cultures. No. We want to be at the top so that we can realise what has been ordered by Allah, to make it real in this world by our own hand. We believe that that is the right thing to be done in the world.'

He stopped, and I thought he felt bad that the goodwill between us had evaporated again, but he went on anyway: 'For instance, a Christian may live here with us but not like a Muslim. He may live here, but we have to be dominant.'

I left Abdullah and Oskan on that cold, wet afternoon, in

the cafeteria on the Asian side of the Bosphorus. I was taking the train to Damascus the next morning and had to pick up my tickets.

Abdullah was also planning a trip to Syria the following summer. I wanted him to go; he had asked about Pakistan and the level of freedom its people enjoyed; I wanted him to go there too. Turkey and Pakistan had had similar histories: strong, politically involved armies, a coup every decade and the execution of a sitting prime minister, but Turkey had gone one way and Pakistan another. I felt that travelling in the Muslim world might produce new respect in Abdullah for what his country, outside its Islamic commonality, had achieved.

Pakistan shared an important link with Turkey. When it gained its independence in 1947, carved out of a diverse, pluralistic society, it became, as Turkey had, what it had never been before: an almost pure Muslim state with fixed borders. But while Pakistan, intended as a secular homeland for Indian Muslims, re-asserted its connection to the great Islamic past – even importing Urdu as a suitably Islamic national language – Turkey, founded as a secular state for Turks, broke its links to that past.

I had started out wanting to see how men of faith had fared in the state that had broken with Islam. What I hadn't expected to find was the extent to which Abdullah's faith, in its sense of politics and history, spoke directly to the alien and hostile 'world system' that sought to turn Islam into an 'empty box'. For this aspect of his faith, faith didn't even seem necessary: the same feeling of affront could have come to a people occupied by a foreign power.

The Islamic world also meant something distinct to him: not just a world, but a world order, 'a big culture', to which Arabs, Persians and Turks had contributed. He had never been to any other Muslim country, but he was certain its people would be of the same mind as him, almost in the way that someone in America who'd never left his country might feel about Europe. I didn't ask him about Muslim India, but I'm sure he would have included it as part of what a man in Karachi was later to describe to me as the 'Civilisation of Faith'. To listen to him was almost to feel that a world as complete, as connected, as difficult to contain as the modern world, or the 'world system' that we knew today, had existed, with its origins in faith, in the Muslim world.

The date Abdullah put to its demise, though he would have agreed that its decline was many hundreds of years in the making, was 1924, when Atatürk abolished the office of the caliph in Istanbul. The date chosen was important because it suggested a notion of sanctifying political authority, rule in the name of Islam, that accompanied the millennia-long history that had ended. Its end meant that Islam, at least in the world post-Islamic history, was not as effortlessly complete as Abdullah made out: its completeness had to be asserted. There were constant incursions – technological, moral and political – from the 'world system'. And to realise the Islamic completeness, as Abdullah had spoken of it, the world would have to be recast, passed through an Islamic filter, and the 'world system' kept out. For this reason it was both possible to see why Atatürk had wanted the modern, Turkish state to break its connection with the 'Civilisation of Faith' and how the Turkish approach had been perhaps too extreme, needlessly alienating men like Abdullah.

*

On my last night in Istanbul, a gay couple I had been staying with took me to a club called Love. We entered a dark room where a show was about to begin. I couldn't make out the people around me, but the room smelt of a mixture of sweat and cologne. A dim purple light came on over the stage. My eyes adjusted to the darkness and I saw rowdy transvestites covered with jewellery, a few plain, dumpy girls and, interspersed among the crowd, tall, fine-looking men in their twenties wearing dark trousers and collared shirts. One was telling me about biotechnology when the show began.

In the purple shade, I could make out four men in white underwear. Their bodies were smooth and taut. It made the mind reach for its gym Latin: quadriceps, erector spinae, pectoral major and anterior all toned to the point of plasticity. Their faces showed the best of the region's warm colouring, dark features and high cheekbones. Their hair was shiny and short, and they smirked and joked among themselves as if bound by soldierly comradeship. It was unclear what they intended to do with the green and orange paint in their hands, which glowed luridly in the purple gloom.

Then the music started and the men stopped chatting. Their faces poised and pouting, they broke off in pairs and started to dance. The light dimmed and only their white underwear and the glowing paint were visible. They danced closer together, quadriceps brushed against quadriceps; the crowd let out a scream. Then a diagonal gash of phosphorescent green, from gluteus maximus to shoulder-blade, made it clear what the paint was for, and sent the crowd to frenzy. The two pairs of white underwear moved closer together, the paint changed hands, partners were exchanged and the music picked up. The men rubbed the glowing paint on to each other's bodies in time to the music and as part of a dance. At last so much green and orange paint had been spilt that the figures of the men reappeared like a scene from *The*

Invisible Man. The crowd was cheering in rhythm and the men were laughing, half in embarrassment, it seemed, and half in vanity.

This was the Turkey the visitor could never discount, the Turkey of freedoms such as these, of the Istanbul biennale, of the first Picasso exhibition in the Muslim world, the country a professor living in Istanbul described to me as 'the only livable place from here to Singapore – no offence'. It was this same country that was anathema to men like Abdullah, where freedom meant licence, where secularism was a tool of oppression and foreign values prevailed in place of the rule of God. In secular Turkey, it was impossible to see what his vision of the world was. The Islamic completeness he had spoken of, though touched with a sense of loss and attack, was hard to visualise. It was only in Syria, and later, to a greater extent, in Iran and Pakistan, that Abdullah's words gained physical reality.

The show ended and the activity at Love resumed. My Turkish friend had caught my eye from time to time. And now turning to me, he said, in a sibilant whisper, 'This is why we'll never be Iran.'

Recompense

'**A** human being,' my grandfather always asserted, when people asked whether I was being brought up as a Sikh or a Muslim. 'He's being brought up to be a human being.'

Perhaps all children feel that their grandparents were born for the job. In the case of my grandparents, it was as if their years as very young army parents, distant and old-fashioned, had been a preparation for their true calling as devoted, dependable grandparents. And, as a child, I depended on them a great deal. I lived with them, travelled with them; they were my guardians when my mother was on assignment in Punjab and Kashmir; I was in their care when mobs roamed the streets in 1984, very nearly attacking our house, killing Sikhs in revenge for Mrs Gandhi's assassination at the hands of her Sikh bodyguard.

The religious violence that followed Mrs Gandhi's assassination was a painful reminder of the main historical drama of my grandparents' lives. They had become engaged a few months before the 1947 partition of India. They were married at the end of that year when my grandfather, made homeless by the partition, arrived as a refugee bridegroom in Delhi. And as much as my grandmother rejoiced in the plurality of religion in India, my grandfather kept his distance. Because, if not for religion, he would also have been Pakistani. It could be said, growing up with them in Delhi, that my grandparents were a living historical record of the event whose shadow fell on me four decades later.

In 1947, as landowning people in what was to become Pakistani Punjab, when the time came to divide India, my grandfather's family opted for Pakistan. It was not just a question of land: my grandfather's regiment, Probyn's Horse, just back from fighting the Japanese in Burma and temporarily stationed in southern India, was going to Pakistan. 'We thought,' my great-grandmother once said, 'that first it had been the rule of the Muslims, then it was the rule of the English, and now again if it was to be the rule of the Muslims, what difference would it make?'

She discovered the difference in a painful and abrupt way at Lahore railway station in August 1947. In the weeks before, she had been part of an August insouciance that had prevailed on both sides of the border, a feeling that the partition was nominal and that there would be no transfer of populations. So, when India was being divided, my Sikh great-grandmother, a young widow, spent the summer with her younger son in the hill station of Mussoorie on what was to be the Indian side. When doctors suggested that my great-uncle, suffering from tuberculosis, go up to Kashmir for a change of air, she thought she would stop at their house on the plains before heading north again.

By then the carnage in Punjab, which was to take a million lives, had begun. A Muslim police superintendent recognised their party at Lahore station; my great-grandmother recalled fires swelling on all sides. The policeman told them, with sorrow and disbelief, that there was now no place for them there.

'Where will we go?' my great-grandmother asked.

The policeman put them on a train to Amritsar, the first town on the new Indian side, but the train didn't leave. They waited all day in the monsoon heat and humidity. At last, the policeman took them off the train and put them on another that left soon after, and in this way saved their lives. The train they had been on was a death train, attacked soon after it left the platform. They heard in Amritsar that it had pulled into the station with everyone aboard dead.

My great-grandmother never recovered from Partition. After Amritsar, she and my great-uncle moved to Karnal, a rural town near Delhi, where she lived in a gloomy house till her death in 1989. She never discussed Partition, until four decades afterwards, when my mother interviewed her on the fortieth anniversary. Then she spoke about what had been lost. She mentioned land and silver, but her mind fastened on one genteel image that appalled her especially. 'I can't believe the tenants' wives are wearing my shawls,' she said. 'I used to have the most beautiful shawls.' When I was born and my mother took me to her, she said bitterly, 'Yes, he is lovely, but Muslim nonetheless.'

The resentment my great-grandmother felt for Muslims became, in my grandfather – younger and spared Partition scenes – a general suspicion of religious politics and an unlikely love for Muslims, feeling they were also the victims of the futile wrong committed in the partition of Punjab. What my great-grandmother dealt with by forgetting, my grandfather dealt with by remembering, and remembering well. With age, even as his present perceptions became dull, his memory of the Punjab where he had grown up became sharper. He recalled certain shops, gentlemen's clubs, society beauties, and missed old friends. He thirsted for his Punjab. Cobwebs dropping over his eyes, heavy on the Scotch and prone to tears, his longing for the country he would never see again was touched with the special irony of finding that, after all these years, he had a half-Pakistani grandson.

His face came alive as he'd tell me the story of how he had called my father from London to inform him of my birth. When the operator on the Pakistani side spoke, and my grandfather heard the music in his accent, he gasped, 'He spoke my Punjabi!' It might have been the first time since 1947 that he had heard a voice from the Punjab he had left behind. It was his nostalgia for undivided India, as well as the knowledge that I was twice connected to the land that was Pakistan, that my grandfather transmitted to me as I grew up with him in Delhi.

This feeling for the land and its common culture, deeper than the present boundaries that divided it, might have been a way for him to put to rest some of the absurdities he faced in his lifetime, such as the 1965 war against Pakistan when he fought against the men in his old regiment. Partition was then still a recent event; the men knew each other, and at the end of the day when the fighting stopped, they would call to one other. He was proud of the Pakistani prisoner-of-war from his old regiment who refused to surrender to the infantry, and immediately dispatched an artillery unit to give him the honourable surrender he demanded. It was perhaps the most serious war my grandfather had fought and the heavy casualties on both sides brought home a terrible feeling of futility. He recalled his commanding officer being forced to cremate a large pyre of Muslims – a horror for Muslims – and Hindus together, and when their families came for the bodies, they were given a small urn of ash and told that these were the only remains of their brave Indian dead.

The governments of the two countries parted ways more decisively than the people. My grandfather's best and oldest school friend lives in the Swat valley in Pakistan; in recent years it has become a battleground between Islamic militants and the Pakistani Army. They kept up a correspondence over six decades, even in the days of heavy surveillance, when letters were difficult between the two countries and phone calls virtually impossible.

I came across a recent letter in which, after all the violence, wonder at the passing of time was subject enough:

Dear Amarjit, Many thanks for your letter. I just came down from Swat, where my nephew was killed in a bomb blast. All very sad, a young man of 41 gone for nothing. Things will only change with change in government.

I am not doing too badly for my 80 years. Except that I fell 3 years ago, and developed neuropathy. This has made my limbs very weak and my ears rather deaf. If you had an email, we could correspond more frequently. I am sure one of the children has it. I started using a computer only last year, when my grandchildren began to laugh at me.

If I am 80, you must be 81. Do you realise you're my oldest living friend? So let's communicate more often. Happy New Year. Regards and best wishes, Aurangzeb

'Typical Aurangzeb,' my grandfather said, with glee. 'He's writing from Pakistan to an Indian brigadier and he says, "Things will only change with change in government." Typical Aurangzeb!'

Irony was the great mood of the 1947 Partition of India. The faint, bitter smiles that still cross the faces of that older generation seem like the only fitting response to the friends left behind, the houses and land lost for ever, the wars fought against each other and the two countries made from one shared culture. And though it could be suggested that the same charlatan god who had put up what seemed like absurd divisions between my grandfather and his country was also responsible for landing him after all the violence with a half-Pakistani grandson, he would not have seen it that way. He didn't let the absurdities defeat him. Through his untainted view of the other side, and the hopefulness my mixed birth brought up in him, he cocked a snook at the gods that carved up India. In his hands, the peculiar circumstances of my birth were not strange, unworkable facts but a kind of recompense for all that had been lost, a breach in the historical wall that had put him in one country and his regiment, his house and his 'oldest living friend' in another.

Syria International:
Notes from the Translation Room

I left Istanbul the morning after the Love club. My wish to see the city in snow was unfulfilled, but compensated in part by seeing Anatolia in deep winter. I was on the Taurus Express to Damascus, travelling on what had been the old Hejaz railway. It was built by the Ottomans in their last years, with the intention to connect Istanbul to Mecca, and was famous for being blown up routinely by T. E. Lawrence.

The sleeper was blue and white, the only carriage with Arabic letters on it, sharp-edged sickles and dots, which spelt out the equivalent of 'CFS, Chemins de fer Syriens'. It was to fall away from the rest of the train when we reached the south-east. We drifted past a few coastal towns with red-tiled roofs before I fell asleep, making up for the late night. When I awoke it was just after one o'clock and the winter sun was almost hot. Outside, a brown stream was bubbling past rocks in a shallow chasm. The low branches that hung over it would have brought shade in another season, but were now bare and cast a long, thorny shadow over the water. A single white heron gazed indefinitely over at the muddied winter scene. All around, large, round rocks were heaped on top of one another as if in preparation for a child's game, with snow and shrubs competing for the spaces between them. Gradually, the land became flatter and the winter scene more complete. By late afternoon, the train was racing past snow-covered towns, and only the occasional glimpse of a wall or collapsed house of honey-coloured stone spoke of a warm country. A pale, orb-like sun hung overhead and minarets poked out of the thick snow, forging new associations in my mind, unused to linking Islam with winter.

The next morning, after a night in the train, I was in southern Anatolia and the snow was gone. It was replaced by a land-scape of grey boulders and gentle hills, with a sparse cover of thin, emerald grass. The rocks stayed, but the earth became red and the grass more lush as we continued south. There were few trees and the land's mild, grassy contours met the sky further than the eye could see. Mid-afternoon. We were unhitched and waited for many hours for a new engine. After a small collision, movement one way and then the other, we set off again.

I stepped out of my cabin to ask our large Syrian attendant, with kohled eyes, for some tea when I caught a powerful whiff of marijuana smoke coming from the direction of the engine. I put my head out of the window and it was stronger. I followed the smell, walking the length of the sleeper, until I came to a door with two sealed windows. On the other side, two fine-featured Turkish soldiers with watery red eyes and berets were standing outside their carriage, choking and laughing over a blunt-sized joint.

When they saw me, they bent double with laughter and, arm outstretched, offered it to me. I made a gesture of helpless-ness: the sleeper doors were locked with a nut and a bolt and seemed not to have been opened in years. More out of courtesy to them than from any conviction that it would open, I tried unscrewing the nut. It slid straight off and the bolt fell into my hands. I pulled at the doors; they divided, but no more than six inches, just enough for the soldiers, now in hysterics, to pass me the joint.

In Turkey, military service is compulsory and they were completing theirs in the nearby town of Iskenderun. They spoke little English so we smoked and laughed, and I, more than them, kept looking behind me in fear of the Syrian attendant catching me. He didn't come so we smoked the fat joint to its filter. At one point, we went through a tunnel and the soldiers took great pleasure in passing the burning end in the darkness. Soon after, the train slowed down and the soldiers shuffled off to duty. A few minutes later I saw them disembark. They waved, then pointed ahead, grinning and glassy-eyed. I put my head out and saw two sentry posts, with small Turkish flags, standing alone on a gently sloping grassy stretch. There was no sign of a town, just the changing gradient of the land. We were at the Syrian border.

The Turkish exit stamp came quickly and the train, passing a barbed-wire fence, rolled in the direction of a complex consisting of a grey building with a green roof, an ochre minaret and a water-tank. The sky was a mixture of rain and evening, and beams of religious light broke through the cloudy kaleido-scope on to the lower country ahead. More trains with Arab script appeared, then a portrait of the Syrian leader, Bashar al-Assad, a boyish, fleshy face and chinless; nothing like the tight-mouthed stare of his late father, Hafez.

They kept us at the border for hours. First, a Swiss consultant was questioned for many minutes about his profession. He appealed to me, but the words that might have worked in Turkish didn't in Arabic. The immigration officer was young and cas-ually dressed. He asked whether I spoke Arabic, if I was Muslim, then offered me a cigarette, and moved on to Leon, a Chinese-American software engineer. He was taken away for several minutes and returned shaken. 'I'll tell you about the little bit of theatre that occurred once we get moving,' he said, with a weak smile. He never did.

The rain that began in Aleppo continued through the day and into the evening, following me to Damascus. An Egyptian film played on the Kadmus bus I had boarded. It was a black comedy of sorts in which the main character, a young man, was afflicted with a skin disease that only he could see; its portrayal was vile. I could barely bring myself to look at the green-black slime that spread over his otherwise pleasant face. The film's garish colours and noise were hard to get away from. A soldier sitting next to me with a crew-cut and severe laced-up boots laughed uproariously at the blighted man's fate.

The countryside beyond Aleppo turned to desert, not soft, sandy desert but flat, hard, gravelly desert. The yellowish-brown hills in the distance were bare and gritty. Every now and then we would pass a large mural of Assad *père* or *fils*. The older man's murals were in 1970s socialist style: the grim-faced leader managing a smile as agriculture and industry, combine harvesters and mills, worked in the background. The colours were faded, and in some the paint had flaked off, leaving powdery white patches. The younger Assad had launched a campaign of his own, consisting of a young Syrian man and woman staring patriotically into the distance, with the red, black and white of the Syrian tricolour behind them. This, I was sure, was a response to the wave of international pressure Syria, after so many years in Arab nationalist sleep, was suddenly facing. As it became dark, the bus passed through the towns of Hama and Homs, both ancient, with rich classical histories. In the early 1980s, Hama had been the scene of a crackdown in which the dictator had levelled a good part of the old city and overnight solved the country's Muslim Brotherhood problem, the Islamist movement that thrived in neighbouring Egypt. People spoke of the crackdown with awe; rumours circulated that the government had chased the Brotherhood into Hama's sewers and electrocuted them.

The Kadmus bus dropped us off at a depot some way out of town. It was a bleak spot, open, unprotected and badly lit. There was little of the comfort or wonder of arriving in a new place, just rain, cement block houses and naked bulbs. The city's skyline was low and indiscernible, green tube-lit minarets and white city lights dotting the gloom. The presence of the minarets in this small, makeshift way, at once shabby and ubiquitous, gave the darkness an unexpected, neon edge. It was Christmas Eve.

*

I had first heard of the primacy of Syria as a destination for international Islam from Hassan Butt.

'I do believe I've got a bigger role to play,' Butt said, in the curry house in Manchester, 'and when that time comes, I will make my preparations to play that role.'

He'd been hinting at it so I asked, 'It's martyrdom, isn't it?'

'Absolutely,' he replied. 'It's something that makes me really depressed, being stuck in this country, because I know I'm so far away from it. I know that if I was to pass away in my sleep, I would not have the mercy of Allah upon me because I have been such a bad person. And I don't see myself getting into heaven that easily, except through martyrdom.'

'Where would you go if you got your passport back?' I asked.

'Probably Yemen and Syria initially, because at the moment I'm wanted in Pakistan for supposed involvement in an assassination plot against Musharraf.'

'And after Yemen and Syria, the enemy you would finally confront is the US, right?'

'Yes, but maybe America will be destroyed in my time, maybe

I'll have something completely different to do.' Then his face expressed new urgency. 'But I need to learn Arabic! As an English and Urdu-speaking person, I can see the beauty of Islam from the outside, but I really can't access it without Arabic. It's like having a beautiful house and only being able to see through the windows how beautiful it is inside. That is how I view Arabic. I believe the Arabic language will give me the key to the things I don't have access to at the moment. Once I learn Arabic, *inshallah*, I will get myself militarily trained. It's like the Jews in Israel: conscription is incumbent upon every male and female.'

The presence of international politics and of the traditional enemies of international *jihad* were visible in Syria within hours of my arrival. On Christmas Day in Damascus, as I explored the city's bazaars and baths, I saw a series of red banners, hung in a giant sweep across the breadth of the souk. Their yellow, orange and white painted letters read:

> From Syria the country of peace and loving to the Aggressive Israel and its allied America . . . We are in Syria the country of self-esteem and homebred we refuse your democracy after what we had seen happen in Iraq and Palestine and how your democracy build on people's bodies which you bombed on civilians innocents and when the matter reached the council of security in the United Nations and how you used the rejection right (the Vito) to save Israel for only a suspicious matter, and how America pursued the council of security to issue a decision against Syria followed by new decision even Syria executed first one, but the Syrian people not afraid and whatever the difficulties could be and they are resistant by leadership of dearest the President B. Al Assad.

On Valentine's Day the year before, a bomb killed the Lebanese prime minister, Rafik Hariri, in downtown Beirut. Hariri had played an important role in rebuilding Beirut after its destruction during the Lebanese civil war and was known for his opposition to the Syrian military presence in his country. The Syrians were rumoured to have been behind the bomb, and after an outcry in Lebanon, they withdrew their army from the country. A UN inquiry into Syria's role in the assassination of Hariri had implicated the Syrian high command, and the Americans, perhaps pursuing ends of their own, were putting pressure on Syria for its meddling in Lebanon and for supporting terrorism in Iraq. The air in Syria that winter was filled with rumour.

The country had been closed for decades. The regime, for most of its existence, had been socialist, intolerant of religious politics, and the people had only received propaganda. With their role in the world suddenly internationalised, the city was plastered with these cryptic, high-pitched messages. It was the government's response to trouble in the world beyond. President Bashar al-Assad and the Syrian people were not kneeling before anyone but God. And so, in the absence of a free press, an intellectual life and a political culture, and under the watch of a fierce secret police, the mosque became the only place for people to congregate and discuss politics.

What struck me on that first day, as I read the banner, was how unusual and desperate a message it was, unfurled over the souk, the most public of public places, in the guise of a private citizen's initiative. In Syria, where an email with sensitive content could get you pulled up by the secret service, the banners could only have dominated the great bazaar with the blessing of the regime. In another society, where it might really have been possible for an independent party to rent space and make a political statement, it would be difficult to imagine a message of its kind: a public shriek directed at international enemies, hanging over the equivalent of Times Square or Oxford Street. In India, I couldn't imagine an international issue with enough following to warrant hysteria of this kind.

The shoppers in their polyesters, eating stringy ice-cream and walking down the covered souk, more reminiscent of a Paris passage than a traditional Arab souk, seemed oblivious to the banners. They were mostly young men with light beards, wide trousers and baggy jackets. They wandered about in twos and threes, often arm in arm, here stopping for something to eat, there for a soft drink, seemingly aimless, smoking at will. The main commerce occurred between women, in dark, heavy coats and headscarves, some fully veiled, and moustached shopkeepers with hard, round stomachs. Only foreigners, the odd group of Italian tourists, still visiting Syria despite darkening clouds, on their way to the magnificent Umayyad Mosque at the end of the covered market, stopped to read it. Indeed, the message, translated badly into both French and English, must have been intended, in some measure, for them too.

Syria that winter, despite the threat of war, was full of foreigners. There were English, French, Danes, Norwegians, Indians, Pakistanis and even Americans. And their presence added to a general air of international intrigue. Syria was the first police state I had travelled in; a wrong step could see me escorted to the border. And so, wishing to stay away from the closely watched hotels and to learn the ropes at my own pace, I decided to rent a flat for two months.

In my early days, I met a particular kind of foreigner, namely the international students at Damascus University, wanting to learn Arabic in the post-9/11 era. Though many were toying with an interest in Islam, it was the language that had brought them to Syria, not the faith. I had difficulty in imagining a man like Butt, who wanted Arabic but also a kind of immersion in the culture of the faith, spending his time among this crowd of foreign students. With him and Abdullah in mind, I wanted to find out what men like these, from freer, more open, more prosperous countries, came to Syria in search of. In Britain, and in Turkey, it was difficult to see them as more than individual voices. But because Syria was where they came to develop their ideas, I hoped to see them in the context of a community and to gain a more real sense of what they asked of the world.

It was in the interest of discovering Butt's milieu that I first asked Even, a handsome blond Norwegian, studying Arabic and considering conversion, where he thought a man like Butt would have gone in Damascus. Having listened closely to all I had to say about Butt, Even compressed his lips and emitted a sound that was at once a sigh of understanding and impatience; it must have been annoying for him to listen to my speculations about where Butt would enrol, knowing all the time about Abu Nour. And as he began to tell me, his elfin face brimming with excitement, of a great Islamic university and mosque, drawing students from Mali to Indonesia, words failed him. He knew what I was looking for and his response now became a faint, secretive smile.

A few days went by before we could arrange a time to go to Abu Nour. Even had Arabic classes in the morning at Damascus University and it was late afternoon when we set out from my flat. We walked up an inclined street in the direction of the biblical Mount Qassioun, a pale, treeless peak with a city of cement shacks climbing its base. We passed the famous Jisr Abyad Mosque, with its rose dome, and the French Embassy where we would find ourselves under very different circumstances in the weeks to come.

Just before the foot of the mountain, we went right. The

walk so far had taken less than ten minutes, but within a few hundred metres the city was transformed. Its wide main roads, apartment buildings and embassies fell away, and a tight, congested neighbourhood took its place. The narrow, crowded streets in this part of town had an authenticity that even the old city lacked. There were no tourists or antiques shops here, and the retail did not seem as much of a performance as it sometimes did in the old city. It was a fully functioning traditional souk, alive with oddities. At a butcher's shop, a whole camel's head and shoulders hung from an iron hook. In one covered section, a man spent the whole day drying trotters with a blowtorch. Near him, scorched goats' heads with gummy grins and little teeth were arranged on a wooden table, decorated with fresh parsley. A small blue lorry ploughed through the crowd, with a man sitting in the back on a heap of pomegranates. Dates, olives, cheese and blood oranges were crammed in next to electrical-repair shops, and perfume sellers promising to replicate any Western scent. Old women rested their heads against the cool stone entrances of the Mamluk mosques with hexagonal minarets and stalactites.

Dressed in a dark Arab robe, his long, blond hair held down by a woollen skullcap and a camera kept discreetly at his side, Even was of a piece with the souk. It didn't matter that he was foreign; the souk was a place of curiosity. He prayed regularly in the souk's mosques and, as a white man, his interest in the faith was met with awe and admiration. He also spoke *fusha*, the classical, literary Arabic, rather than the dialects of the Syrian street, and this, too, must have created an impression.

We continued; the souk narrowed and suddenly, well before the university itself, the characters in the orbit of Abu Nour appeared. A couple of South Asians, in white with small faces and thick, black beards, conspicuous and beady-eyed, scurried towards us. They were like a sort of herald before the full diversity of Abu Nour came into view. Then we saw short Indonesians, with conical hats and wispy beards, vast West African women in colourful veils and European Muslims with red facial hair. There were Ethiopian Africans, with high cheekbones and small mouths, more South Asians, this time with English accents, and South East Asian girls, with diaphanous, rectangular veils. Nationality and race were my markers, but for the people coming to Abu Nour, these differences were trumped by a greater sense of allegiance.

The whole scene culminated in a little square, with an internet café, an Islamic bookstore, a gym and a store called Shukr, which specialised in stylish Islamic clothes for Western markets. Even had bought his robe there. The ingredients were the same as they had been in Manchester's Curry Mile where I met Butt, and on the radical hilltop in Istanbul: the ideological bookshop; the gym, as a social centre, when girls and bars are off bounds; and the internet café, to communicate with Muslims worldwide and to browse Islamic websites. From the little square, the white marble minarets of Abu Nour were clearly visible.

Abu Nour had started as a small mosque seventy years ago, but in the last three decades, under the late Grand Mufti, Sheikh Ahmad Kuftaro, it grew to dominate the small, traditional souk. Three Islamic colleges were added, two Shariah schools and nine floors. Courses were offered in Arabic and religion, and more than twelve thousand students from fifty-five countries attended the university. Abu Nour was the pet project of the highest religious leader in the land; its remarkable growth spoke of the growing role of religion in the old Ba'athist dictatorship, and the importance of Syria as a destination for international Islam. The late Grand Mufti was known for his tolerance and for reaching out to other religious groups; Abu Nour prided itself on teaching the 'correct face of Islam'. On Fridays, its vast chambers, and specialised annexes for foreigners and women, were full. Syrians and foreigners alike came to the mosque, but in the non-Arab Muslim's journey in search of the faith and its language, Abu Nour held a special place.

We were looking for Tariq, a fix-it man known to all new arrivals at the university. Even was asking for him in one of the shops when he appeared on a corner of the square, a big, meaty figure with a friendly manner. Though his face had a dark stubble, it was shaved clean just under the chin, an Islamic fashion. He greeted Even warmly. Then, taking one look at me, said, with his Arab deafness to the letter *p*, 'Are you Indian or Bakistani, brother?'

'Pakistani,' I said, hedging my bets.

'We welcome *beebal* from every country, brother, because everyone was very nice to me when I was in Europe. I can help you here, brother, and unlike a lot of guides I don't want any money.' This turned out to be true and made me even more nervous. In a country where 10 per cent of the population were intelligence informants, including taxi-drivers and waiters, I was worried that Tariq was making his money elsewhere.

I asked him about enrolling at Abu Nour, and he said, 'Yes, yes, brother, I can help you. What do you want? Arabic? Islamic classes? A lot of *beebal* come here from all over the world, Norway, England, Africa, Bakistan, to learn about Islam.' He warned us that we couldn't trust others and told us a story from the Traditions about the second caliph, Omar. 'He was with someone who saw another man braying,' Tariq said, 'and the man said, "He is a good man." "How do you know he is a good man?" Omar asked. "Have you done business with him? Have you travelled with him? Until you do these things, you don't know if he is a good man."'

Tariq was a talker and I felt that if we didn't extricate ourselves we would be listening to him for a long time. He promised to help me the next day at twelve thirty 'before Friday brayers'. His mention of the prayers produced panic in me. What if he asked me to pray with him and he saw I didn't know how?

'Tariq, I need to learn how to pray,' I blurted.

'Don't worry, brother,' he said, in his unhesitating way. 'We will teach you how to bray.'

The next day, I waited for Tariq in the internet café on the little Islamic square. He was late and I was worried that, for all his talk, he wouldn't show up. Next to me, a pale European with patches of a curly brown beard surfed a Chechen Liberation website while speaking through headphones and a mic to someone on Skype. I went in and out of the café a few times and was beginning to worry about the time when I caught sight of Tariq. The call to prayer had sounded and Tariq now looked at me in the way that an Olympic coach might look at a substitute just seconds after his star player has been injured. He took my arm and, moving fast for a man of his size, marched me in the direction of Abu Nour. I reminded him that I didn't know how to pray.

'No broblem, brother,' he said, as we approached the doors of the multi-storeyed marble edifice. 'We will teach you everything.' Hundreds of people of all races were filing into the building and depositing their shoes in little cubbyholes near the entrance.

Inside, I saw that Abu Nour was a multi-dimensional maze of doors, corridors and stairways. I stayed close to Tariq and followed him up two flights of stairs as he wove his way through the closely packed crowd. At the top, we took off our shoes and came into a carpeted gallery. Through a glass partition, I could see hundreds of people arranged in neat rows below.

They sat in an enormous white room around which there were two floors of galleries behind glass. Chandeliers and ceiling fans, attached respectively to long chains and thin white poles, reached down from the high ceiling, to a pointillist sea of white skullcaps.

At the end of the gallery, there was a corner room with wall-to-wall carpeting, a window at one end and a view of the action below. Young men of various ages and ethnicities sat around with black headphones, some in armchairs, others on the floor, watching a filmed sermon on a television screen. This was the translation room, Tariq informed me. He seemed to know everyone and, having scanned the room, touched one man in cream robes on the shoulder. He looked up and Tariq said, 'Muhammad, will you blease take care of this brother from Bakistan and teach him to bray.'

Muhammad, small and dark, looked to me like a south Indian. He nodded slowly and said something softly. Tariq thanked him, and flashing a supportive look, he disappeared.

Muhammad offered me a pair of headphones and I sat down next to him. The translation booth asked me if I wanted English (apparently they could do eight other languages). I said, 'Yes,' and a slow voice, with evangelical vocal range, translated the words of the wizened, white-bearded preacher on the screen. He was emphasising the importance of giving alms to the poor, beyond the 2 per cent required of the believer, as a way to show your love for God and His prophet. I didn't know it then, but the preacher was dead; he was Sheikh Ahmad Kuftaro, the late Grand Mufti of Syria and the founder of Abu Nour.

'Should we wash?' Muhammad said, in his soft voice and imperceptible accent, after we had listened for a while.

'OK.'

He rose slowly and I followed him out of the translation

room. Round the corner, there was a bathroom with cold marble floors and a washing area with several metal taps arranged in a row. Muhammad instructed me that I had to wash my face first, then my hands and arms up to my elbows, a portion of my scalp and my feet up to my ankles. 'Make sure the water touches every place,' he said. He began to wash and I, watching him, followed. He washed carefully, prising apart his toes so that the water touched the lighter skin between them. He seemed to notice that I had washed my face only once because he said quietly, 'The Prophet used to wash three times.' I washed some more. 'The reason we wash these parts of the body,' he added, 'is because they are the parts that are exposed, and washing them also keeps the entire body cool.' My body was cooler than cool; it was cold. The marble floors and sharp edges of the washing area made me pick my way out carefully.

I came back into the translation room with wet hands, feet and hair. The video of the late Grand Mufti had finished and there was a break of a few minutes. I took the opportunity to ask Muhammad about himself. He was in Syria, studying Islamic law, he said. He had grown up in Australia. His parents and grandparents had moved there from India to spread Islam.

'Do you like it there?'

'It's very nice,' he said, 'the best country I know.' His dark features were almost African or Aboriginal, and the stillness of his manner allowed them little expression. He asked me why I was in Syria. I said it was out of curiosity for my father's religion, which I hadn't known growing up. 'Islam is needed in societies all over the world in need of peace,' he said, his expression unchanged. 'All religions preach peace, but Islam offers the widest kind of peace.' Before I could ask why, our conversation was interrupted by the arrival of a few figures in the main room below. Their appearance brought many more people into the translation room.

'It's the Grand Mufti of Bosnia,' Muhammad whispered, with excitement.

Because I was new to Abu Nour, I didn't realise what a lucky first visit this was. The university often invited important Islamic leaders to speak from its pulpit but this was, even by its own standards, an august gathering. The men below, three in robes and turbans, were the Grand Muftis of Syria and Bosnia and Salah Kuftaro, the director of the university and the son of the late Grand Mufti. The unbearded man standing next to them in a brown suit was the minister of culture. These attractions were part of the draw of Abu Nour and the little translation room could hardly contain its excitement.

Kuftaro, a corpulent man with a neat salt-and-pepper beard and a prominent nose, spoke first. After Islamic salutations and bearing witness that there was no God but God, and Muhammad, His Prophet, Kuftaro asserted that Islam was a religion of love and tolerance. He mentioned that Abu Nour had never produced a terrorist. But it was outside enemies that Kuftaro had in mind when he introduced the Grand Mufti of Bosnia. He spoke of the terrible and 'arrogant' injustices and atrocities suffered by the Bosnian people. The Prophet had said that Islam would spread from east to west, and so it had, but in Bosnia they had tried to wipe it out. The Bosnian people, though, had remained steadfast: they had kept the faith. Syria, he said, was now facing a similar threat from a foreign enemy and, under the leadership of Bashar al-Assad, she, too, was steadfast.

This was the first time I had heard a *khutba* or Friday sermon and I was surprised by how openly political it was. My few weeks in Syria had been marked by silence when it came to politics. My Syrian friends only ever discussed it in the privacy of their cars, and even mentioning the leader's name publicly was seen as a transgression. And yet here, it seemed, the faith was being used not only to discuss politics but to conflate the enemies of the Syrian government with the enemies of Islam.

The next speaker was the Grand Mufti of Syria, a young, ferocious man with thick lips, a powerful face and build. His short, black beard, along with the gleam in his eyes, made him seem like an old-fashioned grease wrestler coming into the ring. He went over the same formula: foreign enemies of Islam; the great Islamic past; the sense of grievance; praise of the Assads.

Then the Grand Mufti of Bosnia took the stage. He began with a story of an Andalucían princess in the last years of Islamic rule in Spain. During the battle, she was taken captive and was sold as a slave to a Christian family. Her father, in the meantime, fled to Morocco. As the girl grew up, the son of her owners fell in love with her and wanted to marry her even though she was a slave. She had held her tongue until then, but was now forced to speak: 'I am not a slave. I am a princess. I have a father and mother in Morocco. I cannot marry you without their permission.'

'What has the story of the Andalucían princess got to do with Bosnia?' the Grand Mufti asked the congregation. After a pause, he said, 'That princess is Bosnia. One hundred years ago, in Berlin, she was sold as a slave. But when the time came and someone tried to take her for free, she said, "I am not a slave. I have a father in Istanbul, I have a mother in Damascus, I cannot be taken for free."'

I felt unsettled as I heard the Grand Mufti speak. This man of faith, with a measure of dignity and wisdom about him, distorted the history he spoke of. He knew its aims beforehand; the history was merely slotted in. The event in Berlin to which he referred was the 1878 Treaty of Berlin, when the Ottoman Empire had lost a good part of the Balkans. He connected it falsely to the loss of Andalucía several hundred years before. And in the same vein, he went on to join that history to the Bosnian massacres of the twentieth century. The details hardly mattered: it was a long story of aggression and attack from the Christian West, beginning as early as the loss of Andalucía and continuing till the present, in which the sides, as far as he was concerned, were always the same.

It was encased history; I was reminded of Abdullah, in Istanbul, saying that to be a Muslim is to be above history. Nothing in this fixed narrative could be moved or rearranged or made to say something different. Its goal was to forward the idea of the great Islamic past, solidify the difference between Muslim and non-Muslim, and mourn the loss of a great time when Muslims had ruled the world. In the Grand Mufti's account now, the people committing the Bosnian massacres were hardly different from the Americans who allowed them to happen, the Europeans who sold Bosnia as 'a slave' in 1878 and the Spaniards who had pushed out the Moors four hundred years before.

That morning President Ahmadinejad of Iran was in Damascus. The Syrians and the Iranians, both facing pressure abroad, shared a new closeness. The minister of culture had been with him at the Umayyad Mosque before coming to Abu Nour. 'He was on his first state visit,' the minister said, 'and I told him that from this pulpit Islam had spread from China to Andalucía.'

'And so it will again,' Ahmadinejad had assured him.

Kuftaro wrapped up: 'It is easy to get depressed in these times, to see the forces against Islam. The Islamic world, too, is fragmented and divided. It is divided because of the West and the influence of its ideas. First, they rob us economically, then they rob our land, and once they have achieved these objectives, they rob us culturally. They spread their ideas in our society to keep it divided and fragmented.

'But we have our Book,' he added, the message at last uplifting in its own way: it was a long narrative of former greatness and defeat, reversible not through education, new ideas or progress but through closer attention to the letter of the Book.

Then it was time to pray. Quickly, Muhammad described to me what was to be done. We rose. I followed the others, the first part moving quickly, almost like a military formation, putting my hands behind my ears, then across my chest, then on my haunches. And now, the movement seemed to slow, a heightened feeling of privacy crept in and, with it, my own sense of fraudulence. I struggled to keep in time and feared I would fall out of synch. I was up again, then on my haunches, said, '*Amin*,' when the others did, and at last we went down on our knees and submitted. The bowing and touching my forehead to the floor was my favourite part; I enjoyed the privacy it allowed. But there was also a powerful humility in the gesture, which was easily apprehended. After the submission, I sat up with my legs under me, a difficult position that those who prayed regularly took pleasure in prolonging. Through the whole experience, I watched a small boy, sitting at my feet in a white skullcap. He fiddled, then fell occasionally into the prayer position, then got up and looked around. He had beautiful light-coloured eyes. Seeing him near his father, in the all-male environment, it was possible to see how visiting the mosque could become a special rite between father and son.

When the prayers were over, many stayed in the translation room to talk for a while. As if some unspoken connection had formed between us, Muhammad now treated me as a friend and took me round the room, introducing me to the others. I met Fuad, a British Pakistani in his mid-twenties from Birmingham with a serene expression and a thick black beard.

'That's a confusing identity,' he said, his soft mouth and eyes lighting up in a smile when I told him I was half-Indian, half-Pakistani. 'Like us too. When we were growing up we suffered racial abuse. People told us we weren't English. We grew up when racism was still fashionable. I remember Bernard Manning [the comedian], who was very popular when I was growing up, saying about Pakistanis claiming to be British because they were born in Britain: "If a dog's born in a stable that doesn't make him a horse." The choice of dog was not accidental.' Fuad stopped, and as if it had just occurred to him, added, 'He was saying we were dogs.

'Now the home secretary says we're not British enough. We have to be more British.' Fuad worked hard to realise his parents' dream that he enter the corporate world, but he hated it. 'It was so grey,' he said, 'the drive to work every morning, operating on mechanised time, arriving to find you have two hundred emails to answer, no grand narrative. To succeed in that world, you have to serve the corporation. And for what? For money? I decided I wanted to submit to something that was true, something with meaning.'

I asked him where he felt he belonged now: to Britain or to Pakistan?

'I'm both,' he said. 'The ones I pity are my kids. They have a Puerto Rican mother!' He smiled as he said this, an odd, painful smile.

Muhammad was speaking to someone else so Fuad took me up to meet Rafik, a black 'brother' from Connecticut. He was older, perhaps in his early forties, large and jovial. He had moved to Syria with his wife and children after converting to Islam in Florida. He was working as a teacher, married too young and gave me a few tips on how to learn Arabic quickly. I told him about my trip. 'You have to follow the ringing inside you that is Islam,' he said, 'the ringing of what is right and what is wrong. In the West, we learn to question everything. In Islam, we question too, but not just to say, "Ha, ha, you're wrong." You can't prove Allah wrong.'

I took my leave of Rafik and found Muhammad again. He said he would walk out with me. In the gallery outside the translation room, a Koran class had started up and we went through rows of young boys learning the verses. I said goodbye to Muhammad, the man who had taught me to pray. He took my number and said he'd give me a call later. He and a few friends were going over to KFC; maybe I'd like to join them.

I had come to Syria searching for the world of men like Butt and Abdullah and I had found it, but I had also found something else: confirmation of what about them had interested me in the first place: only thinly hidden behind the curtain of faith were the problems of the real world. The issues raised at Abu Nour were modern, directly related to what Abdullah described as the 'world system'. Kuftaro spoke of feeling robbed culturally and coming under the influence of foreign ideas; the Grand Mufti, of modern genocide seen on television sets; Fuad, of racism, of the clutter of modernity – being bombarded by emails and adhering to drab routines – of children from mixed marriages, and of loss of identity, resulting from the large-scale migrations of the last fifty years, in his case from Pakistan to Britain. They were scenarios the entire world faced, that I faced; they defined the modern experience; there was nothing about them that was particular to Islam, and they made the Book seem like an unrelated solution.

Walking back through the souk, I felt a flatness that was like frustration. It arose from a stifled desire to express myself, from the mosque raising important issues and smothering them with prayer. I'm sure there were spheres of faith in which people find refuge from the troubles of the material world, but Abu Nour was not that. Abu Nour was political. It fanned a sense of grievance and, as it could only ever do, offered retreat as the answer. But, unlike other religions, the retreat on offer was not that of the hermitage or the ashram; it was of the physical completeness of the faith, an alternative world on earth, equipped with sanctified history, politics and culture: 'the widest kind of peace.'

It sought to restore believers to a pure historical and political world-order, free of incursions from the modern world. Syria was seen as a good place to begin because it was closed and depressed, with an autocratic ruler who allowed neither a free economic nor a free political life; it was much easier to shut out the world here than it was in Britain or Turkey. But many of the international Muslims I knew in Syria didn't find it pure enough and drifted south to the lawless wilderness of Yemen in search of greater purities and an Islam closer to that of the Prophet's.

In the meantime, the mosque, in its effort to engage the real world, to re-create the time when temporal and religious power were one, dirtied its hands in dealing with bad regimes and cosying up to dictators. Because the faith was such a negative force, because it didn't matter what kind of Muslim you were, just that you were Muslim, because there was never any plan to offer real solutions, only to harness grievance, and because its sense of outrage had much more to do with the loss of political power than divine injunction, it could even find room, as certain decayed ideologies can, for men like my father, who were ready to participate in its grievances but who were also professed disbelievers. It was in the mosque's use of grievance, the way it could make Assad's problems seem like Islam's, but more importantly, the way it could use modern problems to reignite the faith that its great violence was to be found.

And at the end of that cold, tense winter, filled with international fears, what could be easier than to inflame a country in need of release?

Nail Polish

I t was a misunderstanding of giant proportions.
    I first heard of cartoons depicting the Prophet Muhammad
over lunch with my Norwegian friend, Even. They had
been published in Denmark, and then republished in Norway.
We hadn't seen them, but they were said to be generating great
anger across the Muslim world. Syria and Saudi Arabia had
recalled their ambassadors to Denmark. Religious leaders called
for a boycott of Danish products. Within days a painful cycle
had begun in which every republication of the cartoons elicited
more anger, which in turn made the story bigger and forced
republication, if for no other reason than to explain what the
fuss was about. Rights and, more importantly, the separation
of press from government, unknown or hazy to most of the
Muslim world, made the offence seem as if it came from the
entire country rather than from a single newspaper, an individual cartoonist or editor.

Damascus that Friday morning was like a city under curfew.

There were hardly any cars in the street, the shops were
closed and the busy road that ran parallel to mine was so empty
it could be crossed at an absent-minded stroll. The rain, which
began the day before, had stopped but dark, wandering clouds
drifted over the city. Their deep colour and low, predatory

movement over Mount Qassioun made the mountain seem bigger and paler than I had seen it before. The hoary, Biblical mountain, with its petticoat of shanties, seemed that morning to have regained some of the grit and thunder of old days.

Even had mentioned he wanted to come with me to Abu Nour so I stopped at his flat on the way. We walked there through a souk that was much emptier than normal. We arrived at the translation room to find it full, and as I had come regularly over the past few weeks, I now recognised many faces. We had come quite late and the sermon had begun. Kuftaro stood alone at the pulpit.

'Believers, we are living in total darkness,' I heard, as I put on my headphones. 'The enemies of Islam have been conspiring against the Islamic nation. They are trying to suppress the values of our nation. With the beginning of this century, the enemies of Islam have occupied Iraq . . . and now we have the blasphemous drawings. It is war against all Muslim people! They want to destroy our nation and our faith with all the weapons they have.' Even and I glanced nervously at each other. 'Under the pretext of democracy and freedom, they are spreading such blasphemous drawings! Our Lord demands that we be strong, and our strength comes from our love for our faith and for Prophet Muhammad. We call for good speech, but when our sanctity is oppressed, we are all sacrificing our spirits for your sake, O Prophet. We will sacrifice our souls, spirits and bodies for you, O Prophet!'

When he had finished speaking, it almost seemed strange to pray, like trying to sleep after a heated argument. The mood in the translation room was charged. Kuftaro had made a call to arms. It was hard to believe that, after so fiery and shaming a sermon, the vast congregation of young men in the chamber below would do no more than go home and refuse to eat Danish cheese. Kuftaro would not have risked disturbing the peace without the express permission of the regime, and if he was making a sermon like this, other mosques were too. It was the mosque performing its role of infusing temporal power with divine sanction, and we sensed that some bigger response was brewing.

I went up to Brother Rafik when I saw him come in. I asked him if he ever minded the anti-Western and anti-American stance of the sermon. 'No, because as a Muslim,' he said, as if recalling a principle, 'I am first a Muslim, then an American. Even before I came here I had stopped thinking of myself as American.' Brother Rafik had not met Even before and I introduced them. When he learnt that Even was Norwegian, he became solemn and asked how everything was in Norway, in the way people do if there's been a natural disaster.

'It's fine, but there's not much understanding,' Even said. 'People haven't quite figured out why everyone is so upset.'

'You have to remember,' Rafik said, becoming lively, 'that this is offensive not just to Muslims but also to Christians and Jews who, if they went back to their books, would see that they are forbidden to make graven images.' He seemed to enjoy those last words and spoke them with the power they held for him. 'They are so removed from their books that they don't know they are forbidden it. If you make or replicate creation, you are producing an idol and, inevitably, someone to knock it down. So it's not just offensive to Muslims, it's offensive to everyone.'

But it wasn't offensive to everyone. Rafik meant that it ought to have been, and that it wasn't, was a failing on the part of Christians and Jews. That week, Rafik, born and bred in America, along with others who had grown up in the West, was in a unique position in Syria. He could explain to many of the people around him, including some of the senior leaders of Abu Nour who were in the translation room at the time, something they genuinely didn't grasp: that the offending cartoons did not come from the Danish government or from Danish companies and that they were powerless to stop their publication.

'Do you feel the response is appropriate?' I asked.

'Well, they got their response, didn't they?' he said. 'If it's a response they wanted, they have it. There are men sitting outside their embassies with AK-47s. That's the response. I'm not saying it's a good one, but it is a response.'

'Do you think it's outside the parameters from which the offence came?'

Rafik understood my question to an extent most Syrians would have found hard. But he felt it was more important to educate Even and me about the sin of making graven images. 'You see, for most people in this region,' he said in a quieter voice, 'the newspapers are the government so they can't understand how the paper can print the cartoons without the government's permission.'

I asked why he didn't offer this analysis to the people around him.

'We know that the West has technology and democracy, or whatever else turns your crank,' he answered, 'but they don't have a lot of wisdom. There was no wisdom in publishing those offensive pictures just because you have the right. Well, who gave you that right except God Himself? In the West there is constant movement. You're moving without even knowing why. There is no time for reflection.'

Black rainclouds slipped over the souk like a lid. Its narrow streets were packed with worshippers leaving the old Mamluk mosques. When, at last, rain and thunder broke over the souk, trenches of water formed in the tented entrances of shops. The filthy souk cats were drenched and the mud floor ran like weak dye through sloping streets to the city below. The commotion the rain caused was followed by marvel as fragments of exploding hail beat down. Even and I stopped trying to make our way back and gathered under a rain-filled awning.

The stall behind us served corn soup in white Styrofoam cups, which came with such speed that they were hardly optional. The men who gathered round us were mostly in their twenties. There was a smell of worn winter clothes and cigarettes about them. They were well-built, with prominent eyes and noses, and attentive to fashion. Their facial hair was carefully shaved, their jeans and sweatshirts close-fitting with haphazard masculine touches – a motorcycle, an eagle, bits of fake fur on the collars.

When the hail stopped, we made our way out of the souk. Even picked up some vegetables, saying he was cooking at home, and invited me to join him.

At his small, airy flat, the doors and windows were open and a moist breeze came through. He was on the top floor, and from his terrace it was possible to see cemented rooftops and fields of satellite dishes, like sunflowers, with poised, vacant expressions. Their presence, illegal, but tolerated by the regime, perhaps unavoidable, along with the numerous internet cafés in the city, always full of young people, stood out as the most obvious sign of dissent in a system that had depended on controlling information.

The lunch turned out to be a small feast of eggs, an aubergine and tomato stew, and beef with fennel and salad. We ate sitting on the floor.

We had finished, and a kettle was on the stove, when the response of which Rafik had warned rose up from the street. The cheer of lunch had made me forget the tension in the mosque, and as I had never seen the slightest disturbance in Damascus's streets, the sudden loud chanting came as a surprise.

It took the form of the Muslim declaration of faith: 'There is no God but God, and Muhammad is His Prophet. La ilaha illAllah, Muhammad-ur-rasulAllah.' That sentence, with its short, deafening music, audible to believer and non-believer alike, and amplified by the many voices from which it came, reached us like an echo. It came alone, again and again. The first time we heard it, our conversation stopped. The second time we listened from where we sat. The third time we ran on to Even's balcony. From where we stood, it was possible to see the entire sweep of the inclined road.

At the bottom, a small but angry crowd was making its way towards us. Far behind them, the remains of the storm settled in a punctured heap of black clouds, bringing out the green and white colours of the biggest banner. They were a mixed group – fifty to a hundred people – of veiled women, children and young men, like those we'd been with moments before at the soup stall. Turbaned sheikhs, just out from Friday prayers at the city's mosques, led the protest. They carried satiny Islamic and Syrian flags. We watched them pass Even's building and stop no more than fifty metres ahead outside the French Embassy. Days before, *France Soir* had republished the cartoons and its editor had been sacked.

The crowd's shouting grew louder, and Even and I ran down to the street. The demonstrators collected outside the steep, curved walls of the embassy. A few red police cars surrounded them and the officers, who stood at a distance, watched calmly.

Now that they had reached their destination, they seemed unsure of what to do next. Even and I stood still at the edge of the demonstration. There was a little scuffling at the front with the embassy guards, but the protestors lacked the momentum to storm the embassy. For a while, they yelled, 'Get out, get out,' in English, and someone threw a sweet wrapper and a milkshake at the embassy wall. Pink liquid dripped down from the point where the milkshake had hit the wall. There were no speeches, no signed declarations, nothing but anger and frustration. And the message was so simple that a young child in a pink sweatshirt led the slogan in a shrill voice: 'La-il-la, il-allah, Muhammad-e-Rasul Allah' and 'Allah hu Akbar' again and again. There was no response from the embassy, just stony indifference to the angry mob. The street was still wet from the morning shower and a light breeze coming off the mountain threatened to blow away their fury.

Just then, a familiar face appeared from the crowd. It was Basil, a Syrian friend of Even, who had followed the demonstration from the Danish Embassy. He pushed his way through to us. He was in a merry, joking mood and was excited by the afternoon's events. He gave Even a big hug and teased him about being Norwegian. He offered to take us deeper into the crowd. We followed him along the edge of the protest, closer to the front, but at that moment, the protestors pushed harder at the barricades outside the embassy. I felt the squeeze and stopped, but Even and Basil pressed ahead. Within a moment, I had lost them.

The commotion at the front had made me uneasy, but now separation from Even brought on a wave of panic. The mob was searching for a focus at which to direct its anger. I was scanning the crowd for Even when suddenly I heard Basil address the demonstrators in Arabic: 'This is my friend,' he said. 'He is Norwegian and a good man.' Then he raised Even on to his shoulders and said to him, 'Speak for your country.' Not a sound came from the crowd and the new silence chilled me. Now they have an object for their rage, I thought, feeling all my worst fears answered. Even, if he was scared, showed no sign of it. He took in the crowd, his natural repose undisturbed, and then addressed them in Arabic. 'This is just an embassy,' he began, his face still and serious, his hand raised slightly so that the index finger met the thumb in a gesture suggesting precision. 'It is not actually the country. I think that this conflict is caused by lack of understanding. In Norway we don't know much about Islam, and there are not many Muslims there. Norwegians need to learn about Islam, and through knowledge of Islam, we can learn to . . .' He stopped and bent to ask Basil for the right word. The crowd listened in stunned silence. '. . . respect Islam, and live together peacefully. *Inshallah, inshallah, in-sha-llah!*'

At the time I didn't understand what he was saying, but I tried later to imagine the impact of his words: the surprise of them from a foreigner, their clarity and volume, the classical Arabic in which they were spoken, and the simple, helpful message, the only one, so far, that had been more than a cry of hysteria. The words that came so easily to him, words of sympathy and diffidence, keen not to blame but comprehend, clichés in the West, resounded with freshness on the Arab street.

A roar of approval came from the crowd. Someone yelled, 'He accepts Islam!' A small, withheld smile formed on Even's lips. Hands reached up from all sides to shake his; others took his picture with mobile phones; a TV crew squeezed to the front to interview him. His speech brought the demonstration to an end. I knew a great sense of relief; it could have gone so wrong. I thought that Basil had seriously endangered him, but Even didn't see it that way: he felt it had been an act of trust on Basil's part.

Back at the flat, Basil, in his white cap and over-excited manner, was saying that the Israelis were to blame. They had planted the cartoons to poison the close relationship between the Arabs and the Danes. He heard in the mosque that morning that Muslims themselves were to blame because they had failed to tell people in the West how great a man Muhammad was. He took me aside to tell me of the greatness of the Prophet, his flight to Medina, and how Islam was a religion for all people.

'How do you feel?' I asked Even.

'I wish I could have said more,' he replied, the adrenaline still strong in his voice, 'but I didn't have the words. What I really wanted to say was "We know you're angry, but we still don't know why."'

*

On Saturday, we knew less. The cartoons had filtered through outraged governments and clerics to the people. And now the street was on the boil. For the first time since I'd arrived in Damascus, nearly a month ago, I felt unsafe. There was something especially unnerving in watching so controlling a state loosen the reins.

I had just had lunch with an American writer friend, Bartle Bull, and was recounting the events of the day before when cries from a new demonstration rang out. We were walking through a small park in a quiet residential neighbourhood when we heard them. Bartle, as if picking up a scent led us in their direction, out of the park, down a main road and finally on to a wide avenue with palms in the centre. Traffic was diverted because thousands and thousands of demonstrators were marching down the avenue. The crowd here was of a type: angry, available young men, unshaven, sullen, with shiny faces and greased-back hair. This was a different, more orchestrated demonstration than the one the day before: young girls and older men marched too, but at its heart was a large group of the dissatisfied young men that all police states have at their disposal.

Unlike the day before, it was a clear, beautiful afternoon. Following the demonstration down the avenue was no more of a strain than taking an after-lunch stroll. The slogan from the day before, 'There is no God but God, and Muhammad is His Prophet', was shouted now and then, but, for its size, the demonstration was comparatively quiet, focused and on the move. We weren't sure where it was headed, which European nation had published the cartoons now or, since a demonstration of this size clearly had the blessing of the regime, whether all this anger would be channelled in the direction of 'the big Satan', America. It was only when the leaders turned right into a smaller street that we found ourselves standing in front of the Danish Embassy. At first, it was not very crowded, but barricades had gone up on one side of the street and it was impossible to leave, except by the way we had come. That option was blocked by the waves of demonstrators arriving from the avenue. With every minute that passed, the small area in front of the embassy became more compact and the energy of the crowd, like riotous molecules over a Bunsen flame, surged. I became uneasy at the closeness of the mob, and the sudden ripples of mounting energy that travelled through it, drove Bartle and me to a quieter area.

From there we watched the mob turn their anger on the Danish Embassy's dull beige façade. A few stray rocks began to fly. In places where the rocks hit their mark, a cement wound opened on the beige façade and a cry of satisfaction went up from the crowd. More rocks began to come. One hit the embassy's red and gold crest and the crowd screamed with pleasure. A thin line of policemen in helmets, mostly young boys, stood perfectly still and expressionless with their backs to the embassy.

This was not yesterday's demonstration: preparations had been made, and rocks from some mysterious source were now hitting the embassy in a steady barrage. The crowd danced with excitement and a Danish flag was unfurled, burnt, then stamped on many times. Homemade posters were held high: 'We are those who are faster than fate. Vikings beware' and 'We sacrifice ourself, our mother, father and children for you, O Prophet!' A new chant rang through the crowd, and to me, an Urdu speaker, many of the words were familiar: 'Bi ruh, bi dem, rafiki-ya-rasul, With our souls, with our blood, for you O Prophet, O friend!' It was another of those strange moments in which the crowd's rage submerged the meaning of their slogan, in the same way that it was possible to say that Islam was a religion of peace and compassion, then raise a crowd to fury in its name.

A man ran up to Bartle and me. He would have picked us out of the crowd as foreigners or journalists, and this made me nervous. 'Tell your people in Europe that the freedom of journalists is the freedom of madness. Here, here, write down my name, Muhammad Ghazali, forty-nine.' He was a rotund, cheerful man, sick with exhilaration. 'Look and see these ordinary people, not educated people!' he panted. 'And I am ready to die,' he yelled, over the slogans and the cries of the crowd, 'against those who are saying these bad things against our Prophet.' He ran back towards the crowd and was swallowed up in seconds. He was of a piece with the rest: rage and violence on the surface; euphoria and release below.

It was a little after four and the embassy had been stoned for nearly twenty-five minutes without intervention from the authorities. The thin line of boy riot police stood exactly where they had been. I was observing their expressionless faces when a roar from the crowd made me look up. A young man in jeans had got into the embassy and now stood on one of its balconies. He gloried in the crowd's approval for a moment, then reached over the railing and pulled the oval crest off the wall. It came away easily. He held it up like a trophy and threw it into the crowd. Then he took out a green flag with white writing that read, 'There is no God but God, and Muhammad is His Prophet,' and hung it from one of the embassy's slanted flagpoles.

'They're gonna burn this place,' Bartle said. 'This is huge.'

It hadn't occurred to me that they might; the demonstration

had grown so quickly from a few stray rocks to a full-blown attack. The boy policemen continued to do nothing, and watching them, it became clear that the regime had forsaken the small, besieged embassy. More people broke into its compound and a murmur of anticipation went through the crowd.

The black smoke and fire that started appeared at first to come from the compound, not from the actual embassy. But slowly, the embassy building, rather than being consumed by the flames, seemed itself to breathe fire from its ground-floor windows and doors.

Bartle was on the phone to Sunday editors in London. I called Nedal, a Syrian friend who was helping me in Damascus; he said he'd be there in a few minutes. A pinkish dusk hour set in and the flames and smoke, now reaching out of the embassy, mixed with the fading light in a puzzling and primeval close of day. The crowd danced in jubilation. As if re-enacting some ancient rite, they passed round the Danish crest like a holy relic.

The silhouette of a fire engine appeared past the barricades at one end of the street. The other silhouette, its cross and tower framed against the haze of smoke and evening, was that of a next-door church, now threatened by the fire.

A few minutes later Nedal, short, smartly dressed, with a neatly trimmed beard and bright eyes, appeared from among the crowd and we began to make our way out of the crush. I asked him to help me talk to a few people, who were now also moving in the direction of the avenue.

One man shouted, 'They started it. It will not just burn, but be blown to pieces.'

A young girl in a headscarf, called Heba, said, 'This is nothing for us. They have insulted our Prophet. What is an embassy?'

A twenty-six-year-old, bespectacled student, called Muhammad, heard us talking and interrupted her, 'This is wrong. We can protest, we can demonstrate, but we can't do this. Our Prophet would not like it. It is our fault because we are not good Muslims. If we were good Muslims, no one would dare insult our Prophet and our faith. When we were good Muslims, the language of the world was Arabic, not English.'

When he had finished, Heba was silent and nodded. The pain the student expressed was not uncommon: many felt that the insult of the cartoons could only have been inflicted on a defeated people.

The street emptied quickly. The façade of the embassy was charred and soaked where the firemen had doused the flames. On the avenue, a woman with streaked hair and an elegant blue jacket walked past the embassy with her shopping. 'Oh, good, good,' she squealed in English. 'They've burnt it.'

A forty-year-old man, calling himself Jihad, stopped me: 'If you are aware of the Jewish conspiracy, you will see the stamp of Mossad all over this. This is a trick of the Jewish people because they know the Prophet is a symbol of all Muslims in the world.'

'If you know it's a trick, why did you fall for it?'

He wouldn't answer, but wanted to list the wrongs Israel had done. Nedal was visibly upset. He was worried about how this would damage Syria's place in the world and its relationship with the Scandinavian countries that, until now, had been allies and supportive of the Arab cause. He kept asking me how it was possible to have a right to insult the Prophet.

On the way home, I noticed that the violence was spreading from the embassies to the neighbourhood round my flat. Mobs of young men ran from street to street, kicking over dustbins and attacking anything they could find. Now real riot police, with faceless helmets, black uniforms and batons, roamed the streets; a water cannon was brought out. News came in that the Norwegian Embassy had also been burnt and it was at this point, with riots spreading through our part of the city, that I became worried about Even. In Damascus, most people knew their neighbours and could easily point out where the Norwegian who had addressed the demonstration the day before lived. Even didn't have a mobile phone, but I finally got hold of him on Basil's phone. He sounded frantic. He had been at the Danish Embassy and after that at his own. He said he was coming over to my flat.

He arrived twenty minutes later with Basil. Soon after, the police chased a small mob down the street at the end of ours. We saw them like a screeching flicker in the corner window. After a tense few seconds, an expression of relief passed over our faces. Even could hardly think beyond his nerves and excitement. He told me of his afternoon in broken sentences. Outside the Norwegian Embassy, a man had grabbed him and screamed, 'Where are you from? Where are you from?' He had answered, 'Sweden,' and some of the others there had pulled the man away. The demonstration was tear-gassed and Even went with the demonstrators to wash their eyes in a mosque, but the detail that impressed itself on him was that the call to prayer had sounded as the demonstration approached the embassy. The demonstrators had stopped, prayed in the street, then risen and charged the embassy. 'I can't believe they prayed first!' he gasped.

That night the Norwegians in Damascus were meant to have had dinner in the old city, but as rioting continued into the night, it was cancelled. News of the burnings had already made its way from the street to the world beyond and Norway announced it was evacuating its citizens. By four a.m. the first planes were leaving.

*

On Sunday morning, drinking Nescafé on my slim balcony, I looked out on a city in bright sunshine. The neighbourhood was not just calm, it had been cleaned. No trace of the riots remained. There was traffic on the intersection, the shops were open and the baker, just past the traffic-lights, was churning out hot mincemeat pizzas. So much had happened in the last few days, a whole cycle of religious ecstasy, and the final hours of violence had felt almost ritualistic. The mood that morning in Damascus was like the day after a festival in India.

The passions spent, it felt strange to think of their cause: cartoons.

The offensive cartoons could not have been understood Islamically. The democratic rights and interlocking institutions that protected them were outside the faith's compass. Nedal was right: I couldn't explain to him how one could have the right to insult the Prophet unless I was to step outside the circle in which it was written that it was wrong to make graven images. Indeed, to explain to Nedal how one had the right to insult the Prophet, I would have to ask him to suspend his faith for a moment and believe in sanctities greater than that of his Prophet and his Book. But the reverse was not true. Europe had lived through an ugly history of religion intruding on the public sphere. It knew about religious injunctions, and also their dangers. It could be said that the systems that protected the cartoons now had been set up in part to protect public life from the excesses of religion. The cartoons came from places that considered it an achievement for religion to be able to take a joke. It had not always been that way.

In coming to Syria, I had hoped to see the rhetoric of Butt and Abdullah put into practice. I got more than I bargained for. Abdullah's notion of Islamic completeness, a negative concept, possible only as opposition, was already being expressed at Abu Nour before the cartoons had came along. As it was, they provided the ideal grievance: here was an offence from the hostile, alien world, and the faith, for once, knew how to react. But if there hadn't been cartoons, they would have had to invent them: all that preparation and frustration needed release.

What happened in Damascus can be explained in miniature by a story a Syrian friend told me. Its small domesticity hides the hysteria in the background. It is a story of a man who goes to his priest to ask if his wife is permitted to wear nail polish. Expecting the answer to be no, he is surprised when the priest says that of course she can: why shouldn't she look beautiful? However, it is written that when she washes for prayer, the water must touch every part of her body, including her nails. 'The company that invented the polish,' the priest smiles, 'also invented a nail-polish remover.' So, yes, she can wear nail polish as long as she removes it every time she is at prayer: five times a day! And so, the faith deals with the nail polish in its own way but never confronts the real offence: the triumph of the other society, the 'world system', of which the appeal of its nail polish is so soft yet potent a symbol.

Bhutto's Footprint

My parents met in March 1980, in Delhi. My father was in India promoting a biography he had written of his political mentor, the Pakistani leader Zulfikar Ali Bhutto. My mother, a young journalist on a Delhi newspaper, was sent to interview him.

'Which one of you is Salmaan Taseer?' she said, as she entered the room my father and his publisher were staying in at the Oberoi Hotel in Delhi.

Their affair began that evening. My father took my mother's number, they had dinner at a Chinese restaurant called the House of Ming, and for a little over a week, my father disappeared with my mother.

My parents met at a point in their lives when they became politically involved in countries that were experiencing political cataclysm. The state of emergency that Mrs Gandhi declared in 1975 – a month after my mother joined the *Statesman* newspaper – jailing the opposition and silencing the press, had come and gone. Mrs Gandhi had returned to power, and the terrorism in Punjab that would take her life was about to erupt.

In Pakistan the year before, the same year as the Iranian revolution and the Soviet invasion of Afghanistan, Zulfikar Ali Bhutto, to many the great hope of Pakistani democracy, had been hanged. And now General Zia, the military dictator, was settling into the blackest decade Pakistan would know.

My father, who loved Bhutto, could not turn away from these events. He had heard Bhutto speak for the first time as a student in London in the sixties and was moved to his depths. Afterwards, he followed him to the Dorchester and approached him as he sat with a group of friends at the bar. Bhutto invited him to join them for a beer. It was a gesture that meant a great deal to my father. He had lost his own father when he was six – around the same age that I became aware of the absence of mine – and grew up in Lahore with very little money. He was in London studying chartered accountancy, and on most days had little more to eat than a bar of chocolate. Bhutto's generosity and openness at that time in my father's life left more than a strong impression: it was the beginning of a lifelong love for the leader and his family, and excited in him the desire to be involved in Pakistani politics.

For my father, the events of 1979 brought in a time of both uncertainty and possibility. Bhutto's daughter, Benazir, had entered politics and Zia had to be fought. For a man of thirty-six, touched by unusual idealism, the trouble in my father's country had also come with a ripening of purpose. His biography of Bhutto, begun before Bhutto's death, was in many ways a political entry-point.

My parents' affair lasted little more than a week, when my father left Delhi for Lahore, where he already had a wife and three small children. A month later, my mother discovered she was pregnant. The scandal of it was too great to assess. My mother was from an old Sikh family, still carrying the pain of Partition. For her then, to become pregnant out of marriage by a visiting Pakistani was at the time, and still today, incalculable scandal. In a week when she was considering an abortion, my father called unexpectedly from the Club Marbella in Dubai. She told him what had happened.

'What are you going to do?' he asked.

'What do you think I'm going to do?' she replied.

My father asked her what could be done to change her mind. She replied that they would have to at least pretend to be married, and over the course of their conversation, they came to a tenuous agreement to continue their relationship for as long as they could.

The months that followed were defined by secrecy. My parents met again in April, in Pakistan; they went to Dubai; they spent a summer in London, full of bright evenings and the bustle of people in pubs and open-air restaurants; and, all the time, their relationship and my mother's pregnancy were kept from her parents and from my father's family in Pakistan. It was this pact of secrecy that made their relationship possible, and it was from this period that one of the two objects I linked with my father as I grew up came into my mother's possession: a copy of his biography of Bhutto. The inscription, dated '17/5/80', read: 'With love and love, Salmaan Taseer.' The other was a browning silver frame with two pictures of him. In one he's holding me as a baby and in the other he's at a Mughal monument, dressed in white, wearing large seventies sunglasses.

News of my mother's pregnancy was kept from my maternal grandparents until weeks before I was born, in November that year, when my mother's sister presented it to them as a *fait accompli*. They were conservative and old-fashioned and the news would have come as a terrible jolt. But they showed immeasurable bigness of heart when they were told. And with my grandfather, of course, there was the nostalgia for his Punjab. Though it was unsaid, there would have been some secret pleasure in his murmuring, 'I always thought one of you would go back to that side.' Despite the scandal, despite the shock it caused, despite the fact that there was something malicious and teasing in the way the news was kept from them, their first instinct was to get on a plane to London to help with the baby.

It was their first time in Europe and they never went again. They used the trip as an excuse to travel in Europe and always presented it to me, with their many photographs, as something they were grateful to me for giving them the opportunity to do. In Spain my grandfather, with his pointed moustache and turban, was mistaken everywhere for Salvador Dalí.

They returned with me to India in the spring, and that April, they held a reception for my parents in Delhi, publicly acknowledging and legitimising their relationship in front of their friends and family. A few weeks later, events in the Bhutto family intervened. A Pakistan International Airlines flight had been hijacked and forced to land in Kabul. Bhutto's son, Murtaza, was involved in the hijacking. The BBC interviewed my father, who was by then aligned with Benazir Bhutto – herself under arrest – in the fight against Zia. My father was in Pakistan and told the interviewer that, while Murtaza had only hijacked a plane, Zia had hijacked all of Pakistan. Within hours, my father's house in Lahore was surrounded and a warrant had been issued for his arrest. It was no longer safe for him to be in Pakistan. He managed to escape the country and get to Dubai, where my mother joined him, leaving me with my grandparents.

The hijacking brought my father into the long fight against General Zia, and soon after, our small, makeshift family felt the first tremors.

Mecca Reprise: 'Muslims Only'

I left Syria in the aftermath of the cartoon riots and took a car and driver south to Saudi Arabia. The Kingdom's border was a vast complex of warehouses, a mosque with a white minaret and a high shelter with square pillars, also white, which cast strips of welcome shade on the blinding tarmac. The flat, arid land was dotted with barbed-wire fences and tall, stooped steel lights. The glare seemed to suck the colour out of the landscape, and the painted yellow and black paving stones that ran round the square pillars stood out as the only shred of colour. A mid-morning quiet prevailed. Since Syria, the land had turned to desert. Almost everyone was now in full Arab dress, the women heavily veiled, and the Levant's racial mixtures had faded. It was more than a border: it was the ancient boundary between the classical world and Arabia. Visible beyond a narrow stretch of brilliant sea was Egypt.

But for a few men in white robes and pickup trucks – familiar with the routine, arms outstretched with papers – there was hardly anyone at the border. Our SUV drove up to the immigration window as if it were a tolbooth. A man, with a boyish face and a light beard, looked hard at my passport, then glanced at me. Saudi Arabia was a closed kingdom and I was lucky to have the visa. The immigration official seemed impressed and called a colleague to take a look.

'Riyadh?' The colleague smiled.

'No, Jeddah,' I said, smiling back.

He stamped an inky black oval with a little car and the Kingdom's sword-and-palms crest into my passport and waved us through.

'Saudiya,' the driver whispered, as the SUV rolled out of the shade of the border.

My first view of the Kingdom was a hard, arid mountain on whose gritty surface the words 'La-il-la, il-allah' – there is no God but God – were written in huge white chalky letters. Soon after a sign read 'Makkah 1171 km'.

*

Jeddah was the historical gateway city to Mecca. I waited for Hani in a square in its old city. I hardly knew him, but a mutual friend had put us in touch, and when he heard of my plans to go to Mecca, he offered to take me. He also arranged a guide for old Jeddah. 'You don't have to touch the stone,' the old guide advised, after I told him of my purpose that evening. 'People push and shove, but it is enough to salute the rock.'

Around us the maroon and black rugs of the Grand Mosque in Mecca hung outside shops. Jeddah's old city lacked the bustle of markets in other places. The afternoon pall that I now associated with the Kingdom in general prevailed here too. There was also the conspicuous absence of Saudis and women. The men carrying boxes or wheeling carts were Pakistanis in grubby *salwar kameez*. The only woman I saw was a large African, covered, but for her face, entirely in black. She sat in the shade of a *neem* in the middle of the square. Her head was in her hand, and her elbow rested on her knee. She was dusty and her stricken expression spoke of destitution. The complete, virtually enforced absence of women made her, with no male escort and exposed to the gaze of all the men who walked past, seem still more wretched and alone.

A breeze from the sea made its way through the square. Among the tall old buildings and the semblance of trade, it was possible for the first time to think of old Arabia in the Kingdom, and of Jeddah as it had been before the discovery of oil, a major Arabian port and the gateway to the holy city.

The guide said I would enter the mosque from the south-east gate. But first I had to announce my intention to complete the *umrah*, an off-season pilgrimage to Mecca, and to wear the pilgrim's clothes. For this, I was meeting Hani within the hour.

Like many young Saudis, he appeared in his national dress, an off-white robe without the scarf. He was well-built and handsome, with a prominent jaw and cheekbones. His slightly gapped teeth gave him a fierceness unsuited to his warm, friendly nature. He had just finished work at a bank and said that we had to make a few stops before we prepared for Mecca.

The first was at his family house, which, like many, was in a compound where different members of the family also had their houses – low bungalows, spread out over a big lawn. Hani's grandfather's bungalow was a dim, spacious place with a sparsely furnished drawing room, and large windows, overlooking the garden. It had the decorum that elderly people's houses some-times do, of old upholstery, furniture and framed photographs. No one was at home and the reason we stopped there was so that Hani could pray. I wouldn't have thought this about him, this strict adherence to the hours of prayer. Earlier, he had produced two neatly rolled joints from his pocket.

The prayer stop made me a little unsure. We were going to Mecca, but we hadn't discussed my religious credentials, and it would have felt strange for me to join him as if I, too, kept the hours of prayer. Besides, I was still unsure of my co-ordination, especially without the security of other worshippers. So I wandered into Hani's grandfather's study, a comfortable, well-lit room of dark wood and leather, its walls covered with books, many on politics, energy and religion. Through a crack in the door, I caught sight of Hani, his large frame and classically Arab features, kneeling and submitting, muttering the prayers. His ease as he prayed, his comfort with the faith's liturgical language, set against my own unfamiliarity and the impending pilgrimage, gave me a pang of exclusion.

The pilgrim's clothes, a stack of white towels, were already in the car. When Hani had finished praying, we drove to his friend Kareem's house to put them on. It was turning out to be a cool February night.

Kareem was unusually good-looking, in a pale, wolfish way, with light eyes and hair. He had a cynical manner and a mocking smile. The house's high walls were painted a reddish-orange colour. It was modelled on a Spanish *hacienda* with stone arches and a swimming-pool. Kareem's little brother was at home and sauntered past in shorts and a sports jersey. The house had all the comforts of life in the Kingdom – flat, wide-screen televisions, large refrigerators, low, comfortable sofas. We made our way through a den of sorts into Kareem's room, which seemed unchanged from his childhood.

'Should we have a last cigarette?' Kareem asked.

The state we would be assuming was called *ihram*, which literally meant 'prohibiting'. Once we were in it, it was unlawful to do a whole list of things, of which I thought, mistakenly, that smoking was one. As I finished one of Kareem's Marlboro Lights, I had a strange feeling of adolescence. I don't know if it was Kareem's pre-college room or the pleasure of a stolen cigarette or, in a deeper sense, the fraternal connection the faith inspired. There was some current of macho comradeship and familiarity that I'm sure I didn't exude, but felt obliged to slip into when I was with Muslims. That fraternal feeling, whatever it was, was amplified now by the generosity of the two men I hardly knew, who had opened their houses to me and were taking me to Mecca.

This feeling of adolescence was reflected in my awkwardness. I felt a fraud: for not being versed in the meaning of the prayer and rites we were about to perform, but also for being curious, rather than believing. I had a fear of being exposed, which turned out to be well-founded. A few moments later, after we had washed ritually – faces, part of the scalp, hands to the elbows and feet to the ankles – in Kareem's bathroom, we dressed in the pilgrim's clothes, two seamless white garments to be worn with nothing else. One was tied round the waist, the other thrown loosely over the left shoulder. It was important that the right shoulder was exposed as this followed the Prophet's own example. The problem was that, from another far more adolescent experience in Goa, I had a tattoo of Shiva, the Hindu god of destruction, on my right arm. Kareem and Hani looked at it in shock, and then with some amusement. Tattooing was not only forbidden in Islam – 'Muhammad forbade the custom of the idolaters of Arabia to prick the hands of their women and to rub the punctures over with wood, indigo, and other colours', Mishkat, Book 12, Chapter 1, Part 1 – but to have a tattoo of a Hindu god would spoil more than a few pilgrimages and possibly land me in trouble with the religious establishment. It was decided that I would make the pilgrimage with the second white garment wrapped round both shoulders, closer to the example of an old woman in a shawl than the Prophet.

When we were dressed, we prayed together, announcing our intention to make the visit to Mecca. I fell into an easy rhythm in which I paid no attention to my movements in relation to the others'. I took as long as I wanted for the submission, which I liked, and though I had no prayers to say, I enjoyed the privacy so soon after the anxiety the tattoo had caused. By the time I sat back on my legs and felt the ligaments at the top of my feet stretch painfully, my breathing changed and I was aware of a new undeclared ease that had formed between the three of us.

We left Jeddah in Hani's Lexus on an elevated highway. The city's poorer areas were visible below, an expanse of single white lights punctured by dozens of green, tube-lit minarets. Once the road cleared Jeddah, it levelled into a wide, multi-lane highway. The Kingdom's unlikely fusion of grim desert mountains and American chain restaurants gathered close to the road. When their coloured signs grew fewer, we were left with the darkened shapes of hills dotted with floodlights. There was hardly any traffic and the desolation the desert brought on emphasised the security of the fast-moving, air-conditioned car. It was strange, in this prudish country where one could be pulled up for wearing shorts, to be out and about wearing little more than a towel.

On the way, Kareem asked for the story of the tattoo. I told it to him and Hani, complete with details of beer consumed, the little Goan hut besieged by monsoon and the drug-addict tattoo artist who was now dead. Then the solemnity of our present purpose intervened, and I felt uneasy. Hani and Kareem seemed near to me in many ways, but there were aspects of the religion that were written into their cultural framework, such as the visit to Mecca. And, as my exclusion grew, I felt like I implicated them in my discomfort.

My unease must have been apparent because Kareem soon asked the question that had hung over our undertaking since it began. 'So, do you think of yourself as Muslim?' he said, the question's seriousness masked by the lightness of his tone and an artful smile.

'Well, I'm not sure if this is the best time to get into it.'

'No? Why not?'

'Well, sort of,' I answered weakly. 'Culturally.'

A cultural Muslim: a term my father gave me when I asked him the same question. I used it now, not fully knowing what it meant, more as an out than as an honest answer to Kareem's question. I had learnt from my experience with my father that the term meant more than just a lax approach to religion: it contained political and historical allegiance to other Muslims. In the Kingdom, I could see how cultural Islam on the sub-continent would once have been something quite apart from the Islam of Arabia, but I was also aware of a changing balance. In a world that was less local, less particular, Islam, to the detriment of cultural Islam, also became more global, more homogeneous; men in Beeston and men in Istanbul, less far apart.

The journey to Mecca took less than an hour, and before the city, the highway split into two: one was for 'Non-Moslems', known as the Christian bypass, and the other was the one we took, for 'Makkah-Moslems only': an exit for the faithful.

'Where does the other go?' I asked.

'Off a cliff,' Kareem laughed.

The car passed under two vast intersecting concrete slabs that formed a cross.

'What was that?'

'Oh, that's just for tourists,' Kareem said.

It was only when we drove a few hundred metres past the overturned concrete cross that I could make out its shape: it was a colossal Koran stand.

Soon after, Mecca's hills and skyscrapers came into sight. A curved road brought us into the city with unexpected speed. The skyline I saw was nothing like what I imagined. Even though I was prepared not to see an old city, I had imagined a lower city, more scattered. But the city we entered was like the financial district of a metropolis. There were cylindrical, tin-can skyscrapers, with little balconies; white apartment buildings, many storeys high; hotels, with reflective-glass windows; and twin-tower office buildings. I imagined businessmen in hotel suites surfing the web while looking down on the Grand Mosque, or Meccan executives swivelling in chairs as they planned development deals and handled pilgrim tours: their food, their lodging, buses to the different holy points, an apple and a soft drink as a morning snack. We passed one mountainside covered with low, expansive dormitory housing, a sprawling shanty rising from the base of the mountain and reaching close to its summit.

'Many of those houses will be demolished by companies such as Jabal Omar,' Kareem pointed out. 'The whole mountainside has been bought over. Development in Mecca is proving problematic.'

As we got nearer to the centre, Mecca's commerce – dozens of little restaurants, religious bookshops, clothes stores, shopkeepers sitting idly outside them, airline offices, a sign for Pakistan International Airlines – cluttered the bases of the towers. Some of the buildings had Islamic touches, a colonnade of little pointed arches at the base or geometric designs on the façade while others were Marriott-style fronts of blue glass and beige stone. Much of the architecture was from the seventies and eighties: heavy, four-square buildings that gave off a whiff of damp carpets, dim lighting and plywood furniture. At this evening hour, even though it was low-season, there was bustle and bright lights. Men ambled across the road freely and robed figures queued at a fast-food restaurant with a bright yellow and red sign. Descriptions of the old Mecca suggest a similar clutter of tall buildings, but of stone and more along the lines of Jeddah's old houses, narrow with little windows. I felt some sadness at not seeing that old city gathered tightly round our destination, the city's nucleus and main public place.

The other surprise was how African Mecca felt. Everywhere I looked I saw African figures in white, sometimes with skull-caps and sparse, kinky beards. Their sudden presence in Mecca expanded my notion of the Arab world, reminding me of countries like Chad and Mauritania, and Sudan, only a narrow strip of sea away. I felt I entered the deepest sphere of Arabia, where the peninsula faced Africa rather than Asia. It was this proximity that allowed members of the Prophet's family and early Muslims, persecuted by the pagan Meccans, to seek refuge in Abyssinia. There were so many Africans that at last I asked Kareem about it.

'It's a big problem,' he replied. 'They're west Africans who come for *hajj* and stay. Half the domestic help are *hajji*s.'

We drove into a plaza of humbling proportions, composed of white light and marble. Behind us, cranes hung over the skeletons of partially completed towers, their unfinished silhouettes vanishing into the night sky.

'Bin Ladin.' Kareem grinned, referring to the construction empire the al-Qaeda leader's father founded. Relishing the surprise that name brought to the face of a foreigner, he added, 'See? You need to be very close to the royal family to be given a job like that.'

Once the car had driven away, and we were half-naked specks on the marble plaza, Hani said, 'I'll read and you repeat after me.'

*

The Prophet of Islam was born and lived his entire life in what is today Saudi Arabia. There was so little that was old in what I'd seen of the Kingdom that I had to remind myself of that fact. Neither Islam nor the Prophet ventured much further than Arabia during his lifetime. In fact, the entire orbit of

Islam in those early days was concentrated within a radius of a few hundred miles from where I stood. The details of the Prophet's life, unlike Jesus's and the Buddha's, are rich and well documented. He was born in Mecca. He worked in the caravan trade with his uncle, Abu Talib. When he was twenty-five, he went to work for Khadija, a rich, forty-year-old widow, married twice before with children, whom he soon married. The young man without means and the rich, middle-aged woman spent the early years of their marriage trying to have children; the boys died in infancy. During this time, Abu Talib's son, Ali, came to live with the Prophet and Khadija. Ali, the Shia hero who later married the Prophet's daughter by Khadija, was also his cousin and the Prophet himself had lived with Abu Talib when he was a boy.

When the Prophet was forty he had his first revelation. Five years later, he received divine instructions to become a full-time Prophet. The twelve years that followed the first revelation were spent in Mecca and the verses revealed in this period are very different in content from those that come afterwards in Medina, a town a few hundred miles away. The later verses are more specific and grounded in the particular concerns of seventh-century Arabia while the earlier ones concern the universal questions that men face. The years in which these verses were revealed were not easy for the Prophet. The pagan Meccans persecuted his small band of followers and they were beset by financial troubles. In 619, the Prophet lost his wife and his uncle-surrogate father, Abu Talib. Over the next couple of years, his life was threatened and he was driven from his hometown and took refuge in the oasis city of Medina. Ten years later, after another set of revelations, a triumphant return to Mecca and the consolidation of an Arabian empire, he was dead. The glorious years of victories against the world's great empires came later. In the time of the Prophet, the champions of the faith were a small, rag-tag group on the run. The world of Islam was confined to oasis communities, desert valleys and battles between warring tribes.

All this for me was a revelation. Many of the hard facts from the Prophet's personal life make their way into the Book and Traditions. 'Islam has many rules about this world,' Abdullah had said to me in Turkey. 'We say that for a person who is a Muslim, the religion will have something to say to him at every second of his life.' This was one aspect of the faith's 'complete-ness', its detailed control of the believer's life from his personal habits to his food choices.

In Arabia, it was possible to see these commandments as organic, suited to the place, the way Hindu ritual can seem in India. And it was their old tribal past that the Prophet had in mind when he gave the Arabs their religion, a well-balanced reform of the existing way of life and of which the pilgrimage to Mecca, a pre-Islamic custom common to all the warring tribes of Arabia, was an abiding symbol.

Even though the Prophet's family had been custodians of the Kaba, it was not his first choice as the new religion's direc-tion for prayer. Thomas Patrick Hughes wrote, in the nine-teenth century,

At the commencement of Muhammad's mission, it is remarkable that there is scarcely an allusion to the Ka'bah, and this fact, taken with the circumstance that the earliest Qiblah, or direction for prayer, was Jerusalem, and not the Ka'bah, seems to imply that Muhammad's strong icono-clastic tendencies did not incline his sympathies to this ancient idol temple with its superstitious ceremonies. Had the Jews favourably received the new prophet as one who taught the religion of Abraham, to the abrogation of that of Moses and Jesus, Jerusalem and not Makkah would have been the sacred city, and the ancient Rock and not the Ka'bah would have been the object of superstitious reverence.

But the Jews did not welcome the Arabian prophet. Mecca itself only came in the last years of his life. In 629, the idols were still there and the Prophet, according to a treaty with the Meccans, was permitted a visit of three days. At noon, on one of the days, his companion, the slave convert Bilal, climbed on to the Kaba and sounded the first Muslim call to prayer. The next year, the Prophet and his armies occupied Mecca and destroyed the idols in the Kaba. It was then – two years before the Prophet's death – that the ancient pagan pilgrimage common to all the tribes of Arabia was recast in an Islamic mould. Hughes continued, quoting Professor Palmer's Introduction to the Koran:

> Here, then, Muhammad found a shrine, to which, as well as *at* which, devotion had been paid from time immemorial; it was one thing which the scattered Arabian nation had in common – the one thing which gave them even the shadow of a national feeling; and to have dreamed of abolishing it, or even diminishing the honours paid to it, would have been madness and ruin to his enterprise. He therefore did the next best thing, he cleared it of idols and dedicated it to the service of God.

This was another revelation about the pilgrimage to Mecca: it had very little to do with Islam and everything to do with Arabia. It was a pre-Islamic Arabian custom refashioned by the Prophet to unite the Arab tribes and celebrate the fathers of their race, Abraham and Ishmael.

And, just as it was possible to imagine Islam as organic in

Arabia, it was possible to imagine it as alien in places where the faith went. Hybrids would have formed between Arabian Islam and the cultures of the places to which the faith spread. Cultural Islam was the result of these mixtures and it was this, rather than the letter of the Book, that was followed. This Islam, with its mysticism, its tolerance, its song and poetry, its veneration of local saints, often common to Muslim and Hindu in India, was the religion that gave me the string I wore round my wrist. But in modern Saudi Arabia, this type of worship felt like a religion apart from the literalism that was followed. The dark, fleshy pilgrim had approached Hani and Kareem expressly to state his objection. Hani had replied to my weak defence: 'Don't say that. That's even worse. The Wahhabis hate Sufis.'

But even in Arabia it wasn't always like that. The historical events that had made our short exchange possible were also behind the growth of a more global, literal Islam.

In the first years of the nineteenth century, the Wahhabis invaded Mecca. Most of the Hejaz region at the time was part of the Ottoman Empire and the Sultan was perturbed by their success in the region and by the doctrine they propagated. Its founder was Muhammad ibn Abd al-Wahhab, who had made a religious and political pact with Muhammad ibn Saud, a local chieftain and ancestor of the present Saud family, half a century before. The objections of the Wahhabis were to the excesses they felt had come into Islam, indeed to cultural Islam, and taken it away from the pure simplicity of the Prophet's example. In the years they controlled Mecca, they attacked sacred shrines, superstitions, idolatry and luxuries, such as silks, satins and Persian pipes. They attacked shrines like the one from which my string had come, places of music, dance, amulets and comparatively tolerant, flexible doctrines. At the time these attacks were taking place, a large part of the Muslim world would have known faith of this kind.

The Wahhabis' stern rules led to a sharp drop in the number of pilgrims to Mecca. Soon after, they seized Medina, the second of the holy cities, and their reforms were so complete that even the Prophet's tomb, with its ornate dome, was destroyed. The Ottomans at last sent a strong army to retake the holy cities, and in 1818 Saud's descendant Abdullah, who had become the Wahhabi leader, was executed in a public square in Istanbul. After that, the Saud dynasty and the Wahhabi doctrine seemed to vanish for nearly a century, and when the Englishman Wilfred Blunt wrote the *Future of Islam* towards the end of the nineteenth century, he described the Wahhabis as characters from the past:

I believe it is hardly now recognised by Mohammedans how near Abd el Wahhab was to complete success. Before the close of the eighteenth century, the chiefs of the Ibn Saouds, champions of Unitarian Islam, had established their authority over all Northern Arabia as far as the Euphrates, and in 1808 [*sic*] they took Mecca and Medina. In the meanwhile, the Wahhabite doctrines were gaining ground further afield. India was at one time very near conversion, and in Egypt, and North Africa, and even in Turkey, many secretly subscribed to the new doctrines. Two things, however, marred the plan of general reform and prevented its full accomplishment. In the first place, the reform was too completely reactive. It took no account whatever of the progress of modern thought, and directly it attempted to leave Arabia it found itself face to face with difficulties that only political as well as religious success could overcome. It was impossible, except by force of arms, to Arabianise the world again, and nothing less than this was in contemplation. Its second mistake, and that was one that a little of the Prophet's prudence, which always went hand in hand with his zeal, might have avoided, was a too rigid insistence upon trifles.

It was strange now to be in Arabia, more than a century later, and to see that the Sauds and Wahhabis had triumphed. Once again the doctrine had wide international reach, once again it sought to Arabianise if not the world, then the Muslim world, not by force, but by the tremendous wealth at its disposal. And here, once again, I was being pulled up for trifles.

Blunt, writing then, was more forgiving. He saw in Wahhabism similarities to the reforms brought to the Christian Church. He felt that an 'unquiet attitude of expectation' had been an 'unintended result' and 'that Islam was no longer asleep'. A 'wiser' Wahhab, he thought, might 'play the part of Loyola or Borromeo with success'.

An 'unquiet attitude of expectation', Islam 'no longer asleep' but the Wahhabis stronger than ever: these were the mixed, but still potent, still pregnant ingredients that, more than a hundred years later, made the passion, zeal and inevitable frustration in the Muslim world seem as though it was on the verge of some undisclosed outcome. The Muslims themselves, more religious than the rest of the world, closer to the idea of a precipice, gave the impression that something had to give. But what Blunt saw as a failing then was a failing now too: literalism instead of reform.

On the train back from Beeston, I had felt short on Islam, that the small sense of being a Muslim with which I had grown up was not enough. Now, mid-way into my journey, after Turkey and Syria, after much time spent with men of faith, I no longer felt that my idea of the religion was a great negative space. I now had a detailed sense of how the faith's injunctions on dress, food, worship and individual behaviour, as well as in the context of family and society, could form a complete way of life. But learning more about the faith had also extinguished my interest in it. I didn't believe any more that knowledge of the religion, especially its Book, could explain its modern revival. Men like Butt and Abdullah and the people I met at Abu Nour had re-found the faith, but even they thought more about the 'world system' than the Book. And men like my father, who couldn't have been further away from the Book, stood up in surprising ways to defend the faith. So I felt that if I were to understand these emanations of modernity, I would have to look outside the closed circle of faith. And for this I would need a wider view of the societies I travelled in.

It was also for this reason that I felt Mecca had been a wrong turn: Mecca was about faith, faith and tribal Arabia. For the second part of my journey, the journey away from Arabia, through Iran and Pakistan, I didn't feel I needed to be among people of faith. It was more interesting to see how Islam worked on men and societies in ways deeper than the faith, to see how it worked on men like my father, and on countries like Iran where Islamic revolution had redrawn the landscape.

*

After we finished the re-enactment of Hagar's search for water, Hani's Lexus met us directly outside. The Meccan barbers were sitting there and cut a symbolic strand of my hair, bringing the visit to an end. A mood of fatigue and inadequacy hung over our small group. Though full of clues for the journey ahead, it had been a sad, ill-advised undertaking, a wilful misstep on my part, embarrassing for us all. Hani apologised for it not having been a very orthodox *umrah*. I thought of my father who had also performed an *umrah* but hadn't worn the towels;

he had done it in a suit. I apologised for not being a very orthodox candidate. Kareem asked if I would do the *hajj* with him the following year. I thought he was joking, then saw he was quite serious. I wasn't sure if I would, but I was happy to be asked.

It was hard not to be affected by the fraternal attitude of other Muslims towards me. Having grown up without the faith, I was perhaps more aware of this. In a sense, being seen and treated as a Muslim because my father was Muslim constituted the biggest part of whatever Muslim identity I had. My father was also Pakistani, but that didn't automatically make me Pakistani, even in the eyes of Pakistanis. But being Muslim was a different matter.

We took the curved, descending road out of the city. Mecca was quieter now, its lights dimmer. A corresponding gloom grew in the car too, interrupted by flashes of street-light. Then, just before the city limits, I saw two golden arches with no Islamic influence.

'A McDonald's?'

'Yeah,' Kareem said. 'A Muslims-only McDonald's.'

PART II

Stranger to History

'That's Tehran,' Mr Sadeghi said, 'if you can see it through the pollution.' I couldn't. The sun was at a tilt and seemed to make solid the brown skin that hung over the city. The vague shapes of sunlit buildings lost their outlines to the wobbly vapours of heat and haze. There were snow-capped mountains in the distance, above the film that covered the city, and their soiled edges, like dirty bed sheets, produced a special squalor. We came in from the south and the girdle the mountains formed in the north made Tehran seem like a city built in a crater.

'Tomorrow will be clean. It's the birthday of Muhammad,' he sniggered, 'the Prophet of Islam.'

We passed a great golden dome with minarets, bronze now in the murky light.

'What's that?'

'It's Khomeini's . . . Khomeini's whatever,' Sadeghi said, his tired, drooping eyes lighting up. 'Khomeini's palace,' he added, with a chuckle, pronouncing it with a French accent.

With his education, Sadeghi should not have been driving a taxi. And at his age he should not have had to drive more than four hundred kilometres to Isfahan that morning to pick me up, and then the same distance back. But when he told me he had been an economics student in India when the revolution happened, I realised I had misread his age. The lines in his face, the droop of his cheeks and his pulpy, lidded eyes made me add fifteen years to his fifty-something. His master's in economics was interrupted by the revolution. Like many Iranians he came back to take care of his parents. He started a garments business with a friend, but it failed within a few years. 'I had problems with my partner,' he said in a barely audible voice, 'but, besides, those were difficult times for business. It was the time of the war.'

A varied scene opened up before us: apartment buildings with murals of martyrs in poppy fields from the Iran-Iraq War in the 1980s; a detailed digital gauge showing red levels of pollution; a green plastic cactus and a neon-orange coconut palm; a network of highways choked with traffic; and a mismatch of four- and five-storey buildings. Some had reflective silvery squares between blue borders; others were colourless and rectangular with dusty aluminium windows. One rust-coloured giant grew outwards from a circular base and had no windows except a thin, hidden strip at every level. As the city went north, the buildings grew taller. There was more reflective glass, mostly ice blue, sometimes black, and many clusters of white towers. Nothing seemed old, nothing especially modern, nothing particularly Iranian, nothing so Western; it was a bleak, unplanned vista without landmarks, a city on the edge of history, free of the stamp of any one culture, free of design, guided only by human multiplication. Urban snobbery was written into its geography. It was built on an incline: the rich lived at the top and the poor at the bottom where the pollution seeped deepest.

The traffic was hypnotic. The overspill from the main arteries, tar gashes with lush traffic islands, reached the avenues, and from the avenues, the smaller streets, so that the city seemed always either paralysed or spasmodic. At the traffic-lights where we waited for many minutes, I rolled down the window and let in the warm, smoky air. A girl walked by, wearing huge oval shades with a yellow and black polka-dot headscarf. The only other flashes of colour came from yellow taxis and pink buses.

I had been delayed by my travelling in Arabia, then by the two-week-long Iranian New Year and lastly by my journey north to Tehran from the southern city of Shiraz. It was April, and I had a month-long tourist visa.

My relatively trouble-free experience in the Arab police states – Syria and Saudi Arabia – made me feel that my work could be done more easily than I had thought. I had managed to fly under the radar in these countries, and so long as I didn't ask about politics or approach people connected with the state, a renewable tourist visa had been the best way to operate.

An Iranian journalist friend lent me his flat, leaving his keys and mobile phone with Sadeghi. It was off Shiraz Avenue, a road devoted to bathroom fittings. Down its entire length, and even on the streets leading off it, all the shops sold gold-plated taps, four-spray shower heads, shallow basins, toilet seats, cisterns and bowls. It seemed impossible, even in this city of fifteen million, for demand to match supply.

The flat was in a large building complex, overlooking the city on both sides: mountains, some greenery and taller buildings in the north; low, boundless sprawl and smog to the south. Around me, there were cemented rooftops with a busy organisation of air-conditioner exhausts, blue coolers on stands, television antennae and discreetly positioned satellite dishes. Besides the congestion, the roar and the greyness of Tehran, something else, like a drone, an alloy of noise, fumes and concrete, tapped against your equilibrium. It was a city you longed to turn off or escape. The only visual respite, indeed the only reason for building a city in this spot at all, was the mountains. Below, but for three feet of wretched green water in the deep end, the building's swimming pool was empty. Graffiti in red, on the boundary wall, read, 'Life = A Sexually Transmitted Disease'.

*

For me, even in those first few days, Tehran was addictive: a modern crisis city, full of energy, anonymity and menace. It was also a city full of talk. Summer was on its way and there were rumours of girls rounded up for not being correctly dressed, cars stopped for playing Western music, raids, confiscations, a general tightening of the belt. At the same time, the news carried reports of women being allowed to enter stadiums for the first time, despite the religious men in Qom creating an uproar about it. The regime was keeping people busy interpreting these mixed messages.

My guard was down in Tehran for no other reason than that the Iranians I met spoke openly and freely, and were so trusting that I stopped feeling as if there was anything to be worried about. In Syria, even people I knew for weeks remained guarded and never spoke in public places or on telephones. But in Iran, people not only seemed to speak without fear, they seemed to take special pleasure in the volume of their dissenting voices. On the way north, a student I met at the university in Yazd relished telling me, 'Our revolution has expired.'

This mood suited my ambitions. I was at a turning-point in my journey. Rather than meeting specific people of faith, I wanted to gain a sense of what kind of society the Islamic Revolution had created. I wanted to know what the desires of men such as Butt and Abdullah looked like when they were realised in a larger, more macro sense, when they became more than just voices in Manchester and Istanbul. I also felt that this would be a preparation, or rather a coalescence, for the second part of the challenge my father's letter had presented me: to know Pakistan better. But first, I wanted to meet a man who had made good under the Islamic Republic.

*

Muhammad Rahimi was twice as old as the Iranian Revolution. The first half of his life was spent under the Shah, the second under the Islamic Republic. Like my driver Sadeghi, he had been a student in India. He attended the Indian Institute of Technology in Delhi, a highly competitive university, in the late 1970s – interesting years in India, cataclysmic years in Iran. His level of involvement in the events of 1979 was unique. He was politically active, had been anti-Shah, and when the revolution came, he was part of a small group of Iranian students in India who took over the Iranian Embassy in Delhi and proclaimed the new Islamic Republic. Nearly a quarter of a century later, he was a private-sector businessman who had thrived in the post-revolution years. On paper, he was a sort of golden child of the Islamic Revolution.

I knew very little about his student years when I met him on one of my first days in Tehran. The building he owned, in a stylish section of town, and the dark, wood-panelled board-room where I waited for him, showed signs of his prosperity. At even intervals, there were framed photographs of ricefields in Bali, desert sunsets in Arizona and other natural vistas. Muhammad came in wearing a tan linen jacket over a blue shirt. He was large and pale, with a goatee and a warm, jovial manner. His easy self-confidence and personal style, the finely made gold glasses he wore and his diving Breitling spoke of his success. I had known him as a child in India, and his warmth and laughter were what I remembered about him.

I had barely reintroduced myself when the conversation turned to politics, and the summer crackdown on women's dress. He screwed up his face and became serious: 'We were more moderate before, under the Shah, but it is still a moderate country and will be again when this regime is gone.' To hear him speak in this way, knowing he had supported the revolution, brought an unsettling personal note to the remark, like listening to someone you hardly know speak of a family feud.

'I hear this a lot,' I said, 'talk of when the regime is gone. Do you think it will happen soon?'

'It is the younger generation who will change it,' Muhammad said, 'and they could do it very soon, even in, say, one or two years. But the foreign powers mustn't intervene. If they don't, it will happen very soon. If they get involved, these guys will stay because they will be able to unite the people. They mustn't do here what they did in Iraq.'

There was a strong air of the self-made man about Muhammad and perhaps this, along with his political past, reminded me of my father. He spoke in a lecturing way, a little pleased with himself, certain of all that he said. The conversation created a premature intimacy between us. Then he seemed embarrassed to have begun on so serious a note. He suggested we walk to a restaurant for lunch and ushered me out of the boardroom. The quiet side-street where he had his office led on to the city's main avenue, Vali Asr – where I would find myself again for less appetising reasons, in the days to come. For now it was painted in the spring sunlight that came in patches through the *chenar*s, the Oriental plane, a magnificent tree, redolent of the Kashmir Valley, with a broad canopy and leaves like the hands of a child. At one end of Vali Asr were the mountains, so close that morning that they seemed part of a film set. The avenue was lined with coffee shops, women's clothing stores, small businesses, hotels and embassies. It also housed the Discplinary (*sic*) Force of the Islamic Republic of Iran. On certain nights cars would collect in a line along the avenue and car-flirting would begin. It was a Tehrani activity in which carfuls of boys rolled past carfuls of girls, looks were exchanged, smiles, paper chits, and if the bearded men showed up, the scene scattered.

The restaurant was called Bistango. It was down a short flight of stairs, a smart, well-lit place, with crisp white tablecloths, heavy glasses and peach-coloured wallpaper. The manager knew Muhammad and, greeting him warmly, seated us at a table in the centre of the room. Muhammad scanned the other tables quickly, as people do when they're having lunch at a place where they're used to running into people they know. The other diners were mostly older men in dark suits and I could almost have felt I was in a corporate lunch place in mid-town Manhattan. It seemed natural to reach for a wine list.

I hadn't seen Muhammad since I was a small boy in India, but when he said he had returned to Iran in 1980, between revolution and war, I realised I must have known him as a visitor to India, and not when he was living there. In 1980, the entire Muslim world was in spate: events from the year before – the Soviet invasion of Afghanistan, the attack on the Grand Mosque in Mecca and the execution of Zulfikar Ali Bhutto – would bring a decade of political Islam sponsored by the Saudis, Pakistani intelligence and the CIA.

'So, right in the middle of things?'

'Yes.' He smiled, as if surprised himself by what an eventful year it was. 'Seven days after I came back the war started.'

The war with Iraq became the instrument by which Khomeini was to enforce the Islamic Republic, eliminate all opposition and extend the war into the carnage it became. Half a million Iranians died. It was started by Saddam Hussein and prolonged by Khomeini. The Iraqis, backed by the Americans, lost half a million people too. Those numbers, and so recently, had to be remembered; it was the event that touched people's lives even more than the revolution.

But 1980 was still a year of possibility in Iran: the Shah and Savak, his vindictive secret service, had gone the year before; a wide political spectrum was still in play; the religious regime had not begun in force and some even believed that Khomeini might step down now that the revolution had come.

'If I had entered politics at that time,' Muhammad smiled again, as if withholding a secret, 'I could be at the level of a minister now, you know. The guy who's the foreign minister today was also Indian-educated, but I realised from an early age that politics was a very dirty business and I never wanted to enter it.'

Muhammad returned to Iran with an Indian wife and a small child. The foreground of his young life mapped perfectly on to the drama of Iran's revolution and war. But despite his own success, financial and personal, against the toughest odds, he became disenchanted with the revolution he had proclaimed in India. Looking at me from deep within his finely made glasses, he said, 'You know why we had the revolution?'

'Why?' I asked, after some silence, in which his mood seemed to change from combative to maudlin.

'Because the people had nothing else to do,' he said. 'There was so much money from oil that even a teacher could take his family on a tour of Europe. The people had everything. Every one of us students had scholarships to go abroad for university. We didn't understand the meaning of any of it! The Shah was introducing democracy. We thought democracy meant standing outside his palace yelling, "Down with the Shah!" We were moving too fast. The Shah considered himself a modern man and he was moving the country too fast with President Carter behind him, yelling at him to go faster.' Muhammad had been one of the people outside the palace, yelling, 'Down with the Shah!'

'You know I spent forty-five days in prison here under the Shah?' He grinned, relishing the surprise it caused. 'Yes – because we stormed the Iranian Embassy in India and took the ambassador hostage. There was a student demonstrator who had come from Iran to India. The Iranian government wanted him and had asked the Indian government to extradite him to Iran. So we broke into the embassy and took the ambassador hostage in his office.

'The ambassador swore to us,' Muhammad went on, after a dramatic pause, 'in this fatherly voice, on his dignity and honour, that it was not him who had issued the extradition order. He said it in such a nice and fatherly voice that we believed him. We let him go. There was nothing we could have done anyway. We didn't have any guns or knives or anything. Only after we had let him go did we get hold of the records of who had issued the order.' He paused again. 'It was him!

'Some time later, I was at a celebration in Tehran and I saw him. He saw me too and sent for me. When I went up to him, I reminded him that it had been me in the embassy that day. He said, "I know."

'"Why did you swear on your integrity and lie?" I asked him. And, do you know what he told me?'

'What?'

'He said, "Politics does not understand integrity. Take my word for it, you have a bright future ahead of you. Stay out of politics." Before I left, he said to me, "If you're ever in the same situation as me, please remember my words."

'I was so angry!' Muhammad cried, reliving the feeling from that time. 'I went around saying, "Our leaders are terrible."

'It was only later,' he said, a touch of sadness entering his voice, 'when the revolution happened and we stormed the

Iranian Embassy . . . It was me who suggested we do it, by the way, and declare the revolution. You know we held the embassy the entire night until the Indian government recognised the Iranian revolution. That night I was around people who were drinking and partying; the next day they stood at a formal cere-mony in front of the embassy reading the Koran! It was then that I remembered what the ambassador had said to me.'

He stopped to gauge my reaction and, perhaps feeling I had misunderstood him, glowered at me. 'I have nothing against drinking – but then to stand there and read the Koran! I didn't stay. I told them that my university was very hard and that I had to go back. It was then that I decided to stay away from politics.'

Muhammad was shocked that the religious revolution had been a cover for something else. I was less surprised. Before the revolution, Iran was bombarded with a wide distillation of foreign influences, the onslaught of the world beyond. Very quickly that world came to be linked with Tehran nightclubs, half-dressed women on television and the excesses of the Shah and the wealthy Westernised circle around him. It was oil money that brought the sudden wealth to Iran, and yet Iran was not Saudi Arabia; it had a significant educated and professional middle class; its collapse was not easily explained. Neither, once the old system was dismantled, were the religious ecstasies and retreat that followed.

But hearing the innocence of Muhammad's story, it was possible to believe his description of the almost childish wilful-ness with which the world was taken apart. I was not nearly as appalled as Muhammad by his fellow revolutionaries drinking at night and reading the Koran the next day. But for Muhammad, who might truly have believed in the faith as providing the guidelines for a new world, this was the first wrong step. It was as if what had been rejected would always have been more powerful than what was meant to supplant it. But could any Islamic Utopia have been pure enough? His idealism, his religious idealism increased my eagerness to see the country the revolution had created.

In Muhammad, that idealism had been replaced with a kind of Islamic doubt, a world of cobwebs, oil companies and the foreign hand; a suspicion about the work of men. The Iranian Revolution happened in part as a response to this meddling foreign hand, but even now, after the country's closing off, he felt it had not been complete enough; he still felt his country was being played with.

'You know,' he said, 'we had everything, but I sometimes wish we hadn't had oil because that brought all the attention from outside. Even now with this atomic-energy business, the Chinese and Russians support the government because they want oil. The Americans have put up with this Ahmadinejad because he makes it possible for them to play a role in the region.'

'You think he's their guy?' I asked, with some wonder how Muhammad could believe that the Iranian president, Mahmoud Ahmadinejad, the man who with every passing day came to seem like America's nemesis, was an American stooge?

'One hundred per cent,' Muhammad replied. 'You have to look at his political career. Where did this guy come from? Nowhere. Nobody supports what he says. Wipe Israel off the map? Who are we to wipe Israel off the map when even the Palestinians haven't been able to do it?'

Seeing the scepticism form in my face, Muhammad said, 'It's like when I was sixteen and in love with a Christian girl. I wanted to get to know her so I arranged with my friend that he would push her. The plan was that when I saw this I would slap him, and like that I'd be able to get close to her. So, when the moment came I really slapped him hard and the girl and I became friends.'

The friend in the story stood for Ahmadinejad, Muhammad for America and the girl for Iran.

'This is how it is with America,' Muhammad went on. 'They need a problem in the country so that they can get involved.'

'But isn't the president in Iran just a puppet of the mullahs?' I said, playing along.

'Yes, but they're in with the Americans too,' Muhammad returned.

'You think Khomeini was?'

'Absolutely. Otherwise, how did he fly into the country on a private plane from Paris? We have such a great country,' he spat, 'but it's just this bloody politics.' It was remarks like these that could make conversations in the Islamic world seem to contain an element of fantasy.

Then, with no warning, Muhammad asked me if I knew who Cyrus, the classical Persian king, was. It was a shift in conversation that reflected the extent to which the new regime was a reminder of old, historical wounds.

'The Achaemenian king? Yes.' Cyrus the Great in the sixth century BC founded what became a vast global empire, the first of its kind, and whose further expansion led to the legendary wars with Greece.

'Cyrus two thousand five hundred years ago had laws that today are displayed in the United Nations!' Muhammad exploded. 'He set out human rights and said that no human being has the right to enslave other beings. This was two thousand five hundred years ago! And these mullahs try and tell us that if the Arabs hadn't come and saved us we'd be eating ants now.'

Muhammad was talking about much more than politics now. I was amazed by the freshness of this fifteen-hundred-year-old history, resurrected by the Islamic Revolution in Iran. The awareness Iranian Muslims had of the time before Islam, and their conversion, didn't exist among the sub-continent's Muslims, most of whom believed they came with the Muslim invader.

Muhammad spoke with such passion about distant history that it seemed his words contained some other, hidden meaning. In Bistango's air-conditioned seclusion his tone, and not his actual words, seemed to speak of a more real and closer threat.

'And you know what's worst?' Mohammad cried. 'They burnt our libraries and books. They tried to kill Farsi!' he ranted. 'Avicenna was a Persian writing in Arabic!'

Returning finally to the regime, he said that in textbooks they were shortening the country's pre-Islamic history. 'And this is what I always say,' he continued, his voice dropping. 'The youth of today are strangers to their history. I met one of the people from the regime the other day – they had invited me to represent the private sector – and I told him that you can't make the youth strangers to their history. You can't build a country like that.'

In the end, he came full circle back to despair. But his earlier urgency and the hint of hysteria in his voice lingered. They took hold of this last idea of his, haunting as it was, of being estranged from history. And from this big, jovial man I had not expected so abstract, and shrill, a cry of loss.

Rupture

A pact of secrecy had made my parents' relationship possible, but soon after they went to Dubai, leaving me with my grandparents in Delhi, this pact began to unravel. News of my birth was travelling.

In Dubai, there was a false alarm. My father was cooking dinner when his sister's husband walked up to him and said, 'How's Aatish?' My father dropped the pan he was holding and recovered himself only when he realised that his brother-in-law didn't in fact know of my existence, but was using my name – not normally used to mean 'fire' in a banal sense – to check the stove's fire.

But soon after, real transfers of information began. Uncles of my mother who had been at the reception in Delhi went to Lahore for a rare school reunion at Aitchison College where they made enquiries about the Pakistani she was said to have married. My father's eldest daughter, a teenager by then, heard about me from an aunt and confronted him. Until that point, my father might have believed he could lead two lives. He had said to my mother – in that time before mobile phones and email – that there had been no contact between the two countries for so long, why should there be any now? But as news spread, my father, more determined than ever to be in politics in Pakistan and knowing it would be impossible with an Indian wife and half-Indian son, began to lose his nerve; and, as secrecy unravelled, so did my parents' relationship.

After they had spent a short time apart, my mother rejoined my father in London, bringing me with her. She found him changed. He was colder, more aloof, and as she walked about their flat off Baker Street, she saw from the long, black hairs strewn around the place that he had had an affair. It was a public affair with a well-known Indian actress, and my mother felt sure that he had wanted her to find out about it so that she would end their relationship. Many years later, my father's sister told me he had written to the papers himself to publicise the affair. He wanted his relationship with my mother to seem like part of the excesses of a Pakistani playboy, rather than a serious involvement with an Indian woman. He calculated correctly: his affair with the Indian actress ended their relationship.

My father left, and my mother and I stayed on for a few months at the Baker Street flat. They saw each other only a few times after that, once formally to decide what would be done with me. My father's approach was 'Either you take him or I do, but it must be a clean separation.' My mother was clear that she would have me, but she hadn't anticipated how ugly things would become over money. My father had given her a thousand pounds, but when she wrote to him asking for more, he accused her of being a 'bottomless pit'.

By 1982 my mother, still in London, was borrowing from friends. She sold the diamond earrings her grandmother had given her – one of the few family heirlooms to survive that sudden departure in 1947 – at a shop off Bond Street. In the spring of that year, my father let her know through a mutual friend that she had to leave the Baker Street flat. 'Where should I go?' she asked.

'I don't know,' the friend replied, 'but you have to go.'

My father had told her that the flat had been bought for me, and at first she resisted leaving, even changing the locks, but when he threatened to inform British Immigration of irregularities in her visa, she gave in.

By the summer, she had moved back to Delhi and my father to Pakistan. Soon after, he was married again, and the following year he had the first of three more children. What I heard of my father over the next two decades came from my mother. She supported us with her career as a political reporter in India, covering secessionist movements and terrorism, first in Punjab and later in Kashmir. Because she was a political journalist we followed my father's progress across the border closely, through multiple imprisonments in the 1980s, to the restoration of democracy and Benazir Bhutto's landslide victory in 1988, to the failed governments of the 1990s and his eventual exit from politics. His fears of being politically harmed by his connection to me were perhaps real, and despite our separation, his opponents would distribute copies of my birth certificate to undermine his bid for election.

It was during the years that I was growing up in Delhi that I had my first questions about my father, but like so much else about that early absence, they were lost in confusion and laughter. One day, my second-year teacher telephoned my mother, concerned that I was suffering from some kind of emotional disturbance. When my mother asked her why she felt this, she said I showed a tendency to tell wild, obviously untrue stories. My mother pressed her and she said she had asked the class what their fathers did for a living and I replied, 'My father is in jail.'

'It's absolutely true,' my mother said, and left it at that.

Then, aged seven, I met a friend of my mother's, and discovering his name was Salman, asked him, to my mother's great embarrassment, whether he was Salmaan, my father.

We lived at first on our own in a small terrace flat, for which my grandmother paid the rent, and later with my grandparents in the small house, past the flyover, from which I would go to the Lutyens bungalow on the *neem*-lined avenue.

When I was very young, my mother explained her separation from my father in terms of a fight with a friend, not unlike those I had routinely with my friends. When my questions became more sophisticated, she told me about his political career and how it would have been impossible if we had been in his life. And though I didn't have a good impression of my father, I don't think I had a bad one either. My mother was always very clear about who he was. She supported my interest in meeting him, and made sure that I saw the Pakistani friends they had in common whenever any came to India. She seemed also for many years, and I don't know how I know this, still to be in love with him, or at least thought of their relationship, as the big love affair of her life. She often said, 'Sometimes people come together for a reason, to create something or someone, and then they go their own ways.' This made me think, at least when I was child, of my father's departure as something unavoidable for which no one was to blame. My grandfather, of course, made it seem like just one more chapter in the Partition saga he had lived through.

When I was eight or nine, I wrote my father a letter, expressing my desire to see him, which I sent with my mother to Pakistan where she was covering the election. 'If I see him, I'll give it to him,' she said, 'but be prepared that he may not reply. What will you do if he doesn't?'

'I'll leave it and never get in touch with him again.'

As it happened, with my mother covering the election and my father contesting it, they did run into each other. My mother gave him my letter. He took it and told her he would reply, but never did. And for years I made no effort to contact him again.

The Tyranny of Trifles

At the start of my third week in Iran, I sat with Muhammad's son, Payam, in the food court of a mall. The regime had taken away a friend of his.

'Disappeared?'

'Yes, for one year.'

The mall had been shut down by the government for promoting 'mingling', but had recently reopened. Its top floor had brightly painted walls and brushed-steel chairs and overlooked a park. It seemed to commit no more offence than offering bad world cuisine, but I soon saw that it attracted undesirables in the Islamic Republic. As we came in, an effeminate boy in low jeans and a black tank top, with spiky hair, dozens of earrings and glittering blue mascara kissed three times a more discreetly dressed figure with greasy coils. They giggled at the entrance for some minutes, then vanished into an alcove. The Islamic Republic had put homosexuals to death and it was in little glimpses like this – from a yellow and black polka-dot scarf to my driver, Hussein, insisting I play 'Like A Prayer' from my iPod at top volume as he rolled down his windows – that I saw gestures of dissent every day in Tehran.

'Yes, there was a student demonstration,' Payam continued, 'and he just happened to be in the area. He wasn't taking part, just buying something nearby. They started rounding up students and they took him along because he was there. His family, his friends, no one knew where he was.' Payam was an industrial-engineering student in his early twenties. Unlike his father, he was quiet and soft-spoken. He had large, sorrowful eyes and dark skin, inherited from his Indian mother. He seemed protected and young.

'And then, a year later, they just released him on a road somewhere. He's so scaredy now, he doesn't go out after seven. He's scaredy of everything. He told us what they did with him.'

'What?'

'They would make him and the other guys stand in a half-filled pool of water up to their waists. Then they would put on a cooler, an air-conditioner, over them and if they moved out from under it, they would hit them . . .' His English wasn't good and he reached for the word. 'With cables,' he said unsurely.

'Where is he now?'

'He's in Tabriz. He's so scaredy of everything. He came back really thin. He used to have perfect eyesight. Now, he wears glass that are this thick.'

Payam left half an inch between his thumb and index finger. I asked if I could meet his friend and he said he would speak to him, but he thought there was little chance; he had become paranoid. Listening to Payam, I was struck by how unlikely a character he was to be near a story like this. In another country, it would be possible to describe him as a nerd or even a mama's boy, but in the Islamic Republic, no one's innocence was spared. Everyone had stories like this.

In Syria, I felt that when the faith was made to explain aspects of the world beyond its circle of completeness, such as how rights and judiciaries worked in a modern society, it could force the faith into trifles. I also felt that it could force the faith into hypocrisy. But I was really saying the same thing: that when the faith was made to understand a world that was beyond its grasp, a world that could feel like an affront, for reasons other than faith, it could end up, as it imposed its simplicities, in doing the little right at the cost of committing a greater wrong.

But while Abdullah in Turkey was just one man, and Abu Nour in Syria just one mosque, the Islamic Republic was an entire country that had been passed through an Islamic filter. The emphasis on trifles, and the hypocrisies that came with it, had been institutionalised, turned into a form of control over the people who posed the greatest threat to the republic: its young.

In my optimism, I had missed something important. When I saw that Iranians were no longer looking to religion to solve their problems, I concluded that they were on a healthier path than other Muslim countries I had visited. But though the mosques were empty in Tehran, though I hardly ever heard the call to prayer, never saw a woman fully veiled or a man with a beard, unless he was a government man, the revolution had not been kind; it had brutalised its children. And where religious feeling had departed, new psychoses had crept in. People had been twisted. There were small signs of this as I made my way up from the south, but it was only after seeing Tehran and the shrill panic it could awaken, that it was possible to know how bad the revolution had been.

*

Amir only ever wore black. He wore loose black trousers with a collarless black shirt. His hair was long, as was his beard, and he wandered about barefoot. We shared a taxi one day and the driver asked why he was wearing black.

'For me, every day is Ashura,' he replied, referring to the tenth and most bloody day of the Shia mourning.

Amir was a film director and lived with his beautiful actress wife, Anahita, in a small house in a residential colony in northern

Tehran. The couple were part of the country's loudest collective dissenting voice: its film industry. Over the past two decades, it had produced some of the strongest films anywhere in the world. But the industry, which grew in the brief spring it had been allowed under President Khatami, was now being suppressed. Ahmadinejad's government had given permission for no more than two or three films in the last year and Anahita's most recent film had been shot without permission, secretly, in Kurdistan. 'I feel as if I'm starting to censor myself,' she said, her almond-shaped eyes widening. 'My thinking is changing. I don't think of things outside the censorship because I know it won't be possible. It's terrible because I know that this is what they want.' We sat in their small, cluttered kitchen. Its colourful cabinets, little stove, solitary table and weak light from bulbs and candles gave it a protected atmosphere. A big spring night came in through an open door that led onto a paved veranda. Anahita, her thick black hair in a plait, talked between preparing yoghurt, kebabs, salad and Iranian smoked rice.

Amir poured us red wine and a newly invented cocktail called Whisky Albaloo. Alcohol was banned in the Islamic Republic, but could be bought fairly easily through bootleggers and in grocery shops once they knew you. 'The people suffer from a kind of schizophrenia,' Amir said, 'because in the day even a little girl has her head covered in school and has to learn about religion, but when she comes back there's no religion and she takes her headscarf off.' I realised I had heard the same words in reverse from Abdullah in Istanbul. 'For example,' he had said, 'I would go to school, and Atatürk was in school, just in school. Outside there was no Atatürk.'

'Have you seen the mosques?' Amir said. 'They're empty except for a few people and Basiji. People use them as bathrooms!' The Basiji were a militia of young Iranian men whom the regime allowed to enforce religious morality. 'They're like a different species of people,' Amir said. 'If you look in their eyes, they seem like a different species. We call them *Homo Islamicos.*'

Anahita's father was a theatre director whose plays the regime suppressed. On one occasion the censors showed up three hours before his play was to go on and made him perform the play, itself three hours long. When it was over, they proposed cuts and revisions. He said he couldn't possibly introduce them at this late stage. They said he would have to or they would stop the performance. The actors did the best they could, but the regime's inspectors were not pleased and during the interval, the theatre owner appeared to say that there had been a power cut. The director turned to his audience and asked if they would mind the actors performing the rest of the play in the dark, using light from candles and torches. There was a roar of approval. But the owner declined, stating a security risk. He turned them out on to the street where they saw that the entire neighbourhood, but for the little theatre, had lights.

Amir told the story not to show artistic repression in the Islamic Republic but to point out the sophistication of the regime's methods. 'You say Syria is a police state,' he said. 'In Iran, they've planted the police state in our heads.'

A candlelit sadness lingered in the kitchen as Amir and Anahita spoke. My heart went out to the young Iranians I met. Anahita described Iran as a place where she felt she kept hitting her head as she tried to grow: 'There is no appreciation for what I do here, no appreciation, and that's why I'll have to leave one day.'

I didn't think she would. Her resistance was like a kind of addiction. It would be difficult to feel as worthwhile elsewhere. And, besides, there must have been some appreciation because everyone knew her name. For people with no outlet, it was a different matter.

*

In Tehran, I reconnected with Reza, a young vet I had met on my journey north. He was a light, jovial character with floppy black hair and teeth that clambered over one another, but when he spoke of the Islamic regime, his lightness vanished. 'It'll be the death of this religion at least in Iran. Seriously, if they continue like this, religion in this country is finished. Do you know how many spiritual groups are cropping up now? There are Hare Krishnas, a man who teaches the *Mahabharata*, three hundred followers of the Sai Baba. People understand they need spirituality, but they are sick of this religion.'

Hare Krishnas in Tehran! I couldn't believe it. In the Islamic Republic, and in Islam, to convert out of the religion was apostasy, for which the sentence is death. I couldn't believe people would take risks like that. What interested me was not the rejection of faith – I had met many Muslims without faith – but the potential rejection of its political and historical character.

Reza roared with laughter when I said I wanted to meet the Hare Krishnas, making me think I had fallen for an elaborate joke. But then he assured me that the Hare Krishnas did exist and said he would speak to his friend, Nargis. He warned me that he thought her teacher, Gulbadi, was a fraud. 'He teaches celibacy!' Reza cried. 'The whole country is exploding with sexual frustration and he teaches celibacy!' A few minutes later he rang again with Nargis's number, saying she was expecting my call.

The voice on the telephone seemed much older. It was slow, languid, and though the words came, there were no extra words, no colloquialisms, to iron out the discomfort of a first conversation. Nargis wanted to know what my project was, and though I was happy to tell her, I was nervous for her sake and mine about speaking on the telephone. We arranged finally to meet at her flat early the next morning. She said she would speak to the taxi-driver and explain where to come.

For the rest of that day a sly, superstitious uneasiness crept up on me, as if I had been right to be nervous about talking to Nargis on the telephone. It began at a lunch appointment with Violet, a half-German, half-Iranian ex-journalist who came to me through the Rahimis. I had found no equivalent in Iran of Eyup and Nedal, the students who helped me in Turkey and Syria, and I was beginning to need help, especially as I planned to travel to the religious cities of Qom and Mashhad in the next few weeks. Violet had been a reporter in Iran for a major Western news agency for many years and I thought she might be able to suggest someone safe and reliable.

I met her at her house in a dim room with heavy carpets. She was a pale, watchful girl, who had spent the last few years surrounded by sickness and death. She and her German mother had nursed her Iranian father who, after many months of illness, had just died. Violet was still finding her feet, still seeming to take solace from the endless duties that arise when someone dies. She had quit her job in the hope of writing a book, but found herself too tired and 'burnt out' to begin. The story she wanted to tell was semi-autobiographical and linked to other Iranian women's stories, but the material was sensitive and she didn't have the strength for it. The other reason she had left her job was because after 9/11 her employers pressured her to come up with certain angles and stories that amplified the dangers of radical Islam. It had been too much of a strain. I felt more than her fatigue in her: in that low, dark room, still heavy with the late presence of death, I felt her disturbance.

In the taxi on the way to lunch she asked me not to talk because it made her feel sick. She rolled down her window and looked out. We passed Vanak Square, at this hour crowded with buses, taxis and pedestrians. Even in bright sunshine, Tehran had a vertical, gassy quality; the light didn't burn away the city's black edges, or its fever. Violet stared at a green patch in the middle of the square, then turned to me and said she could recall when public floggings happened there; they had stopped under Khatami. It was hard to graft that image onto the square: it was so ordinary and congested, like a bus terminal. There was special menace in thinking of that desert cruelty transposed to the drab, municipal atmosphere of Vanak Square, with its crowds and traffic.

We went to an air-conditioned windowless restaurant decorated with mirrors and Persian scenes of banquets and the hunt. Once we sat down, Violet became more relaxed. She said she knew a few people she could call about my work in Tehran. She suggested Jasib, a young Iranian who had worked with her at the press agency. She said that when he arrived he had been very religious and conservative, but had opened up at work and improved his English. He was now working night shifts at another news agency and she thought he would be an ideal guide for me.

As she described her work as a journalist in Iran, I began to feel that Violet, with a foot in and a foot out of the Islamic Republic, was even more damaged than the people whose stories she recorded. She was over-exposed. I could see why she was having trouble with her writing. She was like an artist who had begun a creative work that took more and more out of her until she was too implicated in it to continue. She covered the 1999 student protests, which had led to a severe crackdown from the regime. Earlier that morning I had driven past the dormitories where it had taken place. I had wanted to stop but it was forbidden. The regime's men had forced students to jump from their windows and the site had become an unmarked memorial to those who died. 'They had thought a revolution would happen,' Violet said, 'and basically it didn't. They counted on Khatami coming out in support of them, but there was just a neutral statement from his office. It was very disappointing.' Violet added that though many felt Khatami hadn't gone far enough, a great deal was accomplished in those years, especially in the area of press and individual freedom.

Jasib called while we were still at lunch. Violet suggested a few coffee shops and restaurants where we could meet but he insisted on a public park. We paid and left the restaurant. A taxi took us down an avenue, then on to a long, quiet street running next to the park. We stopped in front of a small kiosk that sold internet cards, chocolates, soft drinks and magazines. The park at this mid-afternoon hour was quiet, except for a few lone figures strolling down its paved paths. The foliage, still new and bright green, seemed almost to glow against the blackness of the branches.

I wandered up to the kiosk and was looking at an Iranian magazine with an Indian film star on the cover – the always amazing reach of Bollywood – when Violet gestured to me to come over. A man on a bike had dropped off Jasib, then driven off without a word. Jasib was a large, friendly man, heavyset and broad-chinned, but nervous. He smiled and looked behind him, smiled and scanned the street, the park and the kiosk. He managed to say hello to Violet in Farsi, but could hardly focus enough to greet me. I put out my hand for him to shake, but he offered me his wrist. He flicked his thumb up for a second; it was covered with blood. The sight of blood, breaking the afternoon stillness, made me recoil. Jasib kept shrugging his shoulders and smiling. I focused on his thumb. I had assumed at first that he had cut it on the bike, but now, as I looked closer, I could see that the thin stream of watery blood was not coming from a clean gash but from a cuticle; it was the worst I had ever seen. A whole piece, about a millimetre thick and wide, was bitten fresh from a torn cuticle.

His nervous, unfocused manner, interrupted by unprovoked bouts of laughter, made me uneasy. Also, his English was not good enough to interpret. He could barely understand me and was trying to hide it by answering me with a quick phrase, a nod, a laugh, then a full sentence in Farsi to Violet.

Violet looked sternly at him. She had insisted I keep up formalities and call him Mr Jasib. 'Mr Jasib,' she now said herself, 'you haven't been practising your English. It used to be much better.'

'No!' he said, with emphasis to imply fluency, and smirked awkwardly. Then, picking his words carefully, he said, 'It – wasn't – better.' His large, ungainly figure shook with laughter.

'Yes, it was!' Violet scolded. 'That was why I suggested you for this work.' She seemed to be speaking more to me than to him.

'I didn't promise my English was perfect!' he burst out.

'No, the fault is mine. I thought it was much better. You haven't been practising, Mr Jasib,' she said again, in a tone of matronly reproach.

Turning to me, she said that it was a shame about his English because his contacts, especially in Qom, were very good. I made a last attempt to explain my interest in Qom, the Islamic Republic's clerical capital. I could see he wasn't following so I stopped.

'I'm sorry,' Jasib murmured, like an overgrown child about to start writing lines. 'I am very sorry I haven't been practising my English.'

In the car on the way back, I said, more out of politeness than sincerity, that I wished it could have worked because he had seemed ideal otherwise.

Violet's pale face became serious. 'You know,' she said, 'I'm beginning to think he wouldn't have been. In fact, I think it's a good thing it didn't work out.'

'Why?'

'You have to watch these guys very carefully to see if they change when they join these agencies. Once the government knows they're working for foreign publications, they come to them for information. Did you notice how agitated he became when you were putting your number into his phone?' I did remember. He wrote down the wrong number so I corrected it and entered my name. He had jumped at me. 'What are you doing?' he exploded. It was one of his few fluent sentences. 'And his insistence,' Violet said, 'that we meet at a park. It's very strange. You see, they can't obviously go to the foreign journalists so they go to these guys.' I couldn't understand why Violet, if she had known all this, hadn't warned me of this in advance or met Jasib on her own first.

It was almost evening now. I was seeing some people for dinner and wanted to do some exercise at the gym I had just joined. I got out of the taxi and caught another one to Shiraz Avenue. Violet gave the driver clear instructions on how to get there. He nodded as she spoke, then, looking over his shoulder, stared with aimless intensity at the roaring street behind him. He was a lean man in his twenties. He wore a loose shirt through which his hard, wiry frame was visible. His collarbones were exposed and jutted out, seeming to hold up the rest of his bent torso. His eyes were small and sunken with a vacant polish, like billiard balls, and his stubble, though almost a shadow, was black against his unhealthy skin. He looked at me for a moment, thin-lipped and smiling, as if he knew me from before.

Once we were moving, he said in English, 'I don't know where Shiraz Avenue is,' and laughed. 'These women are driving me crazy.' For some reason I thought he meant a private domestic situation, but I soon discovered he meant the women of Tehran. On the heavily trafficked avenue, his eyes fixed on a pretty, made-up face under a light pink and blue scarf in a nearby car. She was worn out by the traffic delays. Her head rested against the car door and her delicate wrist hung out of the window. As soon as the traffic moved, the driver inched his car up to hers and slammed noisily on the brakes, making her look up.

He asked her where Shiraz Avenue was, but as she collected her thoughts to explain to him, he leered at her. He was unin-terested in what she said, and when the traffic moved, he made a sucking sound and a kissy face and drove on. He drove fast, in an unsettling, predatory manner so that he seemed almost disappointed when his risk-taking did not cause an accident. After the first woman, there were one or two more. All the time, despite his speed, he didn't seem to know where he was going. I began to question him. He dismissed me with a nod. Then absent-minded, his eyes scanning the traffic, he found himself channelled on to an exit for a multi-lane highway.

Sloping, grassy traffic islands came into sight, the familiar tall buildings of the avenue fell away and the road veered up ahead. Now I knew we were going in the wrong direction and raised my voice. He nodded and braked, causing the cars behind us to erupt into angry honking. Then already fifty metres or so up the exit ramp, he rested his arm on the seat, turned to face me and began reversing into the oncoming traffic. I started screaming at him, but his face was expressionless. He ploughed through the traffic, the other cars now as hysterical as I was, honking and swerving to avoid him. People rolled down their windows and hurled abuse at him as he went past, but he seemed untouched by their anger. His face, after the leering and the frustration, was serene, as if he had found the release he was looking for. When he reached the point where the road had forked, he swung the car back on to the avenue.

I called an Iranian friend, explained what had happened and passed the driver the phone. He spoke to my friend and now seemed to know where he was going. He made a few swerves, a jolting progress down an avenue, and soon a familiar blue-glass tower came in sight, the row of mountains swung to the right and before long we were going past bathroom-fittings shops on Shiraz Avenue. When we reached the multi-storey concrete blocks where my friend's flat was, the driver asked for no more money than we had discussed. He just looked on as I paid him, one arm on the wheel, distracted again, frustrated, of a piece with the traffic.

I had barely arrived at my friend's flat and was checking

emails when the phone rang. It was a friend of Jasib. He spoke fluent English with an American accent, rattled off his CV and said he was the official stringer for ABC News in Iran. 'I had a seminary training myself,' he said, unprompted, 'so I've been good for a lot of sensitive stories. I think because you're writing on religion Mr Jasib suggested me.' His constructions seemed to be from Farsi, but the language came easily to him.

'Where did you learn English? Did you live abroad?' I asked.

'No.' He laughed a cheesy American soap-opera laugh. 'I've not had the opportunity to go abroad. I learnt my English right here in Tehran.' He pronounced it Teh-*ran*.

'How old are you?'

'Thirty-six.'

I thought Violet should speak to him first. He said he'd call her and get back to me. I went to the gym, and by the time I returned to the flat, its windows showed a dark sky with bright city lights beyond.

I was in the shower when the phone rang again. The cordless lay on the bed and I came out to answer it. It was the translator. He said he'd spoken to Violet, and began to give me the names of some people he'd worked with. He mentioned Jeremy someone from a news agency, then Daniel Pearl.

'Daniel Pearl?' I said, feeling a sudden chill.

'Yeah,' the translator breathed, in his American fraternity accent, 'and then he went off to Pakistan and got himself killed, which wasn't so cool.'

Daniel Pearl, of the *Wall Street Journal*, had been beheaded in Pakistan while chasing a lead. His story was among the most grisly in recent memory. To hear it referred to in this casual, artificial voice, here in Tehran, scared me profoundly. It was fear of my own inexperience, of coming into a milieu of foreign journalists and stringers with dark cameos that I knew nothing about. I wanted to get off the phone. I had no taste for the journalist's thrills, not even a good writing style for it. I thanked him and put down the phone. For the first time since I arrived in Tehran, I was aware of being alone in the flat and of its quiet, broken by the cyclical groan of a lift.

I called Violet back. 'You know, I don't think he should be working for anyone,' she said. Apparently he had also worked for an old news-agency chief who was forced to flee the country with his wife, who later wrote a book scattered with suspicious Tehran characters. He was banned now from working with anyone other than ABC, and Violet assured me that he was watched.

She could tell she had unsettled me and asked if I would like to come over for some take-away food. I cancelled my other plans and went because I thought I might feel more at ease if I could go over the day with her, the day with its ambiguous sense of danger and unexplained premonitions.

That night in Violet's drawing room, lampshades casting low-voltage parabolas across the walls, she began to tell me a story from when she was a child in Tehran.

Her parents had gone out to dinner, leaving Violet and her sister alone at home. The girls had a white West Highland terrier called Emily, and after their parents left, they took Emily for a walk. The streets around the house were quiet and residential. They would have been familiar to Violet, and walking the dog was a nightly ritual, which held perhaps, the possibility of bumping into neighbours. But that night the moral police were patrolling the streets and came down Violet's.

When they saw Emily, their car stopped and a few men got out. Dogs, according to a Tradition, are unclean animals, but while the Tradition only discusses how many times a vessel should be cleaned if a dog drinks from it, the Islamic Republic incorporated the Tradition as another aspect of its tyranny of trifles. The men, despite appeals from the sobbing girl, arrested Emily.

Violet would not let the car go. One of the men said, 'It's

either you or the dog.' If they took Emily, they said, they would kill her. Just as the girls surrendered the little West Highland, an uncle or a friend appeared. He knew how to speak to the men and succeeded in arranging a bribe for the dog's life. The weeping girls went back into the house with Emily. That night, Violet said, perhaps thinking only of the bribe and not of herself, 'I wrote in my diary, "Tonight was my introduction to corruption."'

People made corrupt, people stunted, twisted, criminalised by the tyranny of trifles. That was what the faith had become available for in Iran. The faith that Abdullah described as having something to say to the believer in every second of his life had been turned against the people of Iran; the regime used it to deal obsessively, almost voyeuristically, with the private details of people's lives. Though Iranians had not known the great machines of socialist and Fascist repression, they knew a subtle, daily harangue. That it was conducted in the name of Islam was a great pain: the people's deepest allegiances were used to subdue them, their religion turned to nonsense. It left a terrible vacuum. The young, who suffered most, didn't remember a time when Islam was not in the hands of the Islamic Republic. The Book was not clear on the varied meanings drawn out of it. As in the case of dogs, some obscure Tradition, locked in the context of the Arabian oasis, was used to control everything from satellites to hairstyles, music, dress, socks and even elbows – in the worst days, men had been pulled over for wearing T-shirts because their elbows were considered attractive to women. At a time when people might have needed religion most, a hybrid of the world's two most pernicious varieties, the bureaucrat and the cleric, was in charge of it.

*

It was pouring the next morning when I went to see Nargis, spring rain washing clean the city's smoky air, its sooty buildings, making the fumes vanish in swirls of cold mist. The traffic was worse than normal and I spent many minutes behind a green van with 'yah Mahdi!' written on the back. We were on an avenue festooned with political slogans.

'Imam Khomeini's supporters are always supporting Palestinians and fighting their enemies' was painted in white letters on a black background next to an American flag and a blue Star of David. Then we passed a powder-blue mural on the side of a grey building with blue-glass squares on the front. Half a dozen young faces with short beards, some smiling, others wistful, one with spectacles, gazed over the street. A huge billboard several feet high showed the famous Palestinian mother suicide-bomber against an astral background that made her look more like an astronaut than someone entering the afterlife. The words below said: 'My children I do love, but martyrdom I love more.' The Islamic Republic enjoyed provocations.

Nargis lived in a small flat in an angular white building, five or six storeys high. It was on a narrow street, with hardly any traffic, and large over-hanging canopies. She waited for me on her landing as I came up. In her twenties and strikingly beautiful, she had tight coils of thick black hair, bronze skin, round, slightly bulging eyes and a slim body, with heavy breasts. She wore a white net sweater with a purple skirt, and bits of turquoise dangled from her ears.

It was very early in the morning and I felt a little confused to enter a flat painted mauve, powder blue and beige with streams of incense smoke rising rapidly into the air. The room was full of things from India: little colourful stuffed birds and dolls, chimes, Krishna cushion covers, a standing rack of clothes with glass and stitch work. Hindi phrasebooks and India Lonely Planet guides lay about; a Krishna temple had been constructed near the kitchenette. Electronic music played in a monotonous cycle in the background. Nargis wandered into the kitchenette and put the kettle on for tea.

It was easy to see the effort that had gone into making the flat a cheerful place. Nargis was someone with an idea of how she wanted to live. She had realised this as fully as it was possible to do in the little space, down to its colours, the fittings, the choice of stone for the kitchen counters. There was a touching attention to order, detail and the *objets* from India that made the place distinctively hers. My feeling for it must have come in part from hearing that it had been ransacked not so long ago. It was only when I thought of the little flat's plants ripped up, its temple broken, the clothes thrown everywhere, its careful, new-age serenity overturned, that I was moved by the optimism with which it had been restored.

'They didn't like us having a satellite dish and receiver so they broke into the building,' she said, eyes wide, reliving her surprise at their arrival. Tehran was full of satellite dishes and the crackdowns were more a moneymaking enterprise than a concerted effort at stopping their spread. 'They came in and broke everything,' she continued, looking about the place as though making an inventory of what 'everything' meant to her. 'When they began to search the flat, I said, "If it's the satellite dish you want, then take it, here." But they said, "Maybe you have guns or something." Then they took my husband and made him spend the night in jail. We had to buy his lashes. Forty lashes. The government has a little package.'

'Buy his lashes': the phrase brought back the feeling from Vanak Square, the anachronism of Islamic punishment, so clearly outlined in the Book, and its savagery amplified by the modern bureaucracy that dealt it out. Her husband managed without faith, but Nargis, naturally inclined to spiritual quests, rejected it for a philosophy derived from Hinduism. Nargis grew up in a religious family. Her mother was a believer and her aunt a servant in one of the most sacred mosques in the country, the Shrine of the Imam Reza in Mashhad. It wasn't easy for Nargis to reject Islam. 'She cries for me,' Nargis laughed, speaking of her mother. 'She doesn't understand why I would worship what she thinks of as pieces of wood. She tells me she prays that I won't go to hell.'

'What drew you to Hinduism?' I asked, watching her put teabags into mugs of hot water.

'Before we were Zoroastrians,' she said, 'and that is so close to Krishnaism and so far from Islam. Both use nature. Krishnaism is more natural in its eating, its culture. It uses the sun and the moon, and for me that is so much more comfortable than the government's version of Islam where they just do whatever they want and say it is Islam.'

Nargis was too open, too spiritual in a real sense, to damn any faith, but she couldn't have gone on with the republic's religion. The tea made, she stared at it vacantly, and shrugging her shoulders, said, 'Real Islam is not like what we have in Iran. We have Shiite Islam here, which people made after the Prophet, and it's totally different from the real Islam. During Muharram [the Shia month of mourning] we have half the Muslims celebrating and the other half beating themselves and crying. It confuses me. Just because some people did something fifteen hundred years ago we don't have to go on doing it. Shias don't like to be happy, they prefer to be angry.' My amazement made her smile. One really needed to come to the Islamic Republic of Iran to hear a Shia Muslim speak in this way. The ability to look hard at your own faith, to reject it, to consider another: I sometimes thought I must have travelled through a good part of the Muslim world in search of this intellectual openness and not found it until now. It made it possible for Nargis to think of herself as once Zoroastrian and to care as much about Tibet's freedom as Palestine's; it made it possible for her to overcome the agony at the deaths of Ali and Hussein; it freed her judgements from the motives of faith.

Gulbadi, her teacher, had reached her through vegetarianism. He gave cooking classes in extreme vegetarianism in which eggs, onions and garlic were prohibited as well as meat. Nargis didn't seem to know it, but the diet was classically Jain, a derivative religion of Hinduism that practises extreme non-violence. For fear of the regime Gulbadi devised an ingenious way of reaching people – ingenious because the emphasis on eating meat, especially red meat, was part of the culture of the faith, part of its seemingly limitless compass. And yet, vegetarianism was not prohibited; it was just unusual for Muslims. Gulbadi, knowingly or not, walked the finest line between the commandments of the faith and its culture. He drew people to his classes who, if considering extreme vegetarianism, would in all likelihood have also had doubts about Islam.

'What is the punishment for apostasy?' I asked Nargis, who was watering the plants now. I was trying to broach the subject of the risk she took in embracing 'Krishnaism'.

Her eyes showed white. She looked at me in disbelief as if *I* were considering this path. 'In Iran,' she whispered, looking up from a money plant, 'they kill you for it. If Muslims change their religion, they are killed. They believe here,' she added, by way of gentle explanation, 'that Islam is the last religion, so if you are a Muslim, you have the best religion. That is their mentality.'

Nargis slipped on a white muslin 'manteau', a long coat with buttons down the front, and threw a purple scarf over her springy black hair. She was ready to take me to meet the other Hare Krishnas. We went down to the ground floor in a very small lift, then raced across a cemented driveway in the rain. Nargis drove a jeep, which was parked in the street. The sight of her wet, white manteau clinging to her, the coils of black hair pushing up the purple scarf and the dark, delicate Nargis behind the wheel made me wonder if we weren't committing some kind of offence; cars had been pulled over for much less.

The rain made the traffic worse and I stopped paying attention to where we were going. On a busy main road, Nargis veered left and parked at the side. A gushing open drain, clean as ever, divided the main road from a narrow service lane. Nargis moved stealthily across the lane. I followed her as she slipped behind a black gate on to the paved drive of a low, double-storey bungalow with tinted sliding doors. The rain fell lightly around us and there wasn't a sound. It was still very early and it felt as though everyone was asleep in the house. We made our way round an empty swimming-pool in the garden towards the sliding doors. Outside them, on a veranda, were the first signs that the house was not asleep: dozens of shoes and sandals were strewn about.

As Nargis approached, the doors opened and we were ushered into a dark anteroom by a tall, smiling man with a short grey beard. The little house was crowded, and after the silence outside, I suddenly found myself in a warren of rooms alive with murmurs, chanting and clashing cymbals. My eyes had not adjusted when I lost Nargis. The man who showed us in took my wrist and led me into a blue room with a dim green chandelier. Inside, forty or fifty people sat, rotating rhythmically, in front of a painting of the blue god, his head cocked to one side, a peacock feather in his crown. At one end of the room, two women in white, one with a drum round her neck, were singing and gently rocking forward and back on the balls of their feet. 'Hare Krishna, hare rama' went through the room again and again. Some faces watched the women, feeding off their ecstasies, others looked ahead at Gulbadi, a little bespectacled man with a greying crew-cut and a youthful face, chanting behind a low desk with a book on it. Outside, through the tinted glass doors, the garden was quiet and wet, revealing nothing of the warmth and throng within.

From Nargis, I had gained the impression that the Hare Krishnas would be like her, young, rebellious, slightly new age.

But the faces I saw in the blue room were nothing like what I expected. Though there were several young people, there were also older women, mothers and wives, some fully covered. On the other side of the room, I saw balding, middle-aged men, who looked like bankers and shopkeepers, in beige trousers and checked shirts, with gold rings on their fingers. The average age of the men was well over forty. Somehow the middle-aged, middle-class aspect of the crowd, the men's slightly embarrassed faces, brought vulnerability to the group – the vulnerability of people making a great change late in life. As though submitting to some hidden desire, balancing something that felt right yet seemed wrong, they let their voices catch the increasingly rapid pace of the chanting. One or two eyed me with suspicion. The energy between Gulbadi's chanting and the two musicians was building.

The room was covered with stylised pictures and icons in vivid colours, of Swami Prabhupada, the twentieth-century founder of the Hare Krishnas; of Krishna as a child playing with butter; Krishna, in a Bollywood-style love scene with his girlfriend, Radha; Krishna with his flute; Krishna in grand format; Krishna in a small, makeshift temple with fake yellow flowers placed outside; and, most significantly, a picture of Narasimha, the god Vishnu's half-lion, half-man incarnation tearing to pieces a king who won't allow his son freedom of worship. It was not an image I had seen often, even in India, and I couldn't help but think that its presence in Tehran was Gulbadi's own private stab at the Islamic Republic.

Gulbadi, caught up in a chanting fever, was now hardly able to separate consonant from vowel. The 'Hare' had gone and the blue god's name was now just a breathy whisper: 'Krish-na, Krish-na, Krish-na, rama, rama, rama.' Just at the point when it seemed the momentum had to break, it got faster and louder. I was watching Gulbadi when someone walked into the room behind me. It was the expression on his face, of fear and resignation, that made me turn. I saw a tall man with a stoop, and a short, salt and pepper beard, come in and sit down. His entry coincided with Gulbadi upping the ante: 'Krishna, Krishna, Krishna, rama, rama, rama, Ali, Ali, Ali, Allah, Allah, Allah.'

What?

I didn't know it then but the man who'd just walked in was the regime's spy. Gulbadi had been closed down, put in jail, faced court trials, but he hadn't given up. The Islamic Republic, at last, acting always with the subtlety of which Amir had spoken, decided to use him rather than silence him.

Soon after his arrival, the chanting died down and Gulbadi began a sermon in Farsi. I got up and went to find Nargis. A number of people were sitting round a dining-table next to a refrigerator, listening to the sermon; it was just an ordinary house when it wasn't a temple. Nargis was listening from just outside the room. When it was over, Gulbadi fielded questions. He made a comparison between Kalki, the final incarnation of Vishnu, who comes on a white horse to bring in a better age and the Shia Mahdi, who also comes on a white horse at the end of the world. A schoolteacher was asking if, perhaps, they might come sooner. 'No,' Gulbadi said, and Nargis translated, 'He must take his time.' With this, the meeting was dismissed and tea and sweets were served on the dining-table. Nargis took the opportunity to introduce me to Gulbadi.

He was nervous. He gave me a long, involved speech on how he hadn't rejected Islam. 'People in India ask me if I converted,' he said, 'but Prabhupada's instruction is about the love of God and he has many names. I am a Muslim, I love God and Muhammad. I didn't reject one for the other, I accepted them all.' Then he came out with what was really on his mind. 'He is a judge of the courts,' he whispered, looking at the man who had come in late, 'and a very Islamic person. He became interested in our classes. I had a case in the courts, but by his mercy he talked to the other officers and saved us.'

This was not quite true. The man was a government monitor.

On the way to Gulbadi's vegetarian restaurant, Nargis told me that the judge often disrupted Gulbadi's sermons by saying that Islam was superior to Krishnaism and suggested books that showed how the Koran was more powerful than the Bhagavad Gita. That morning his presence led Gulbadi to make an energetic sermon cast in Hindu terms against democracy, America and the material world. 'How can they bring democracy when they don't even have it in their own countries?' he had asked. 'They are in passion, and passion makes anger, which makes war. That's why America makes these wars against Afghanistan and Iraq.'

Gulbadi's vegetarian restaurant was on the veranda of an attractive red-brick building, near the embassies. This was an older part of town, with wide boulevards and low, heavy bureaucratic buildings. The old American embassy was just next door, its walls now covered with vivid, anti-American murals and slogans, the faint outline of its defaced crest still visible at the gate. Houshmand, a friend of Nargis, had joined us. He was a slight, fine-featured student with dark, intelligent eyes.

'In this country, the government can do what they like,' Nargis explained, referring to the earlier episode of the government spy.

'Did Gulbadi switch to saying "Ali" because he came in?'

'You can make this connection,' she laughed.

Houshmand looked at me intently. Minutes ago he had also been laughing, telling me how they had picked up his brother and given him a full eighty lashes because they had found a picture of him at a party from the year before in his car glovebox. 'We have a thousand experiences like this. Maybe I do a business with the government and make them whips for lashing.' Now, becoming serious, he said, 'You must understand the difference between the real Islam and what you see here, which is not Islam, and the real Muslims and these Muslims you see here. All religions try to give you inner peace, but only a few intelligent people understand the real religion. Even with Hindus, you have the bad ones, who tell me to go out of the temple, but with our Muslim religion, we have more of a problem.'

'Why?'

They talked between themselves for a few seconds, Houshmand arranging the words he wanted to give me. Then he looked up and said, 'I think Muslims are more strict because, I don't know when this happened, they started to feel danger from other religions, maybe three or four hundred years ago. And the father started telling his son that you must fight the other religion and the son tells his son the same thing. And now, today, we have this.' Arm outstretched, he pointed at the city around us, still drying after the morning shower.

The 'other religion' was the growth of the West and the dates were roughly right: between two and three hundred years ago European powers, charged with new learning, grew stronger and Muslim empires everywhere began to fail. The faith's response was to retreat behind the purity of its Book and Traditions and to assert its simplicities more forcefully. Wilfred Blunt, writing in the interim between what seemed like the end of the Wahhabis and their resurgence in the twentieth century, had seen in their literalism a spirit of reform, but felt that their two mistakes, which were really the same mistake, were an over-insistence on trifles, the letter of the Book, and the attempt to Arabianise the world. But to be in Iran, and Saudi Arabia, more than a century after Blunt was writing, it seemed as though the trifles, rather than holding back the literalist imposition of Islam, had become the instrument by which regimes that sought to execute these programmes could control their population. But an entity like the Islamic Republic, perhaps many hundreds of years in the making, had, in imposing the modern tyranny of trifles, opened itself up to the charge of not representing the 'real faith' and, more importantly, of being mired in the corruption that lay behind the insistence on trifles.

*

Nargis wanted me to meet another friend, called Desiré. We drove over to her flat later that evening. Desiré was always in trouble with the regime, and within minutes I could see why: she was eccentric and outspoken. I could barely make out her features because her flat was in darkness. The whole place was lit with dim ultraviolet light. The walls were painted white and mauve, and the seating consisted of several fat saffron-coloured cushions. All the colours glowed. On the wall there was a huge painting from the Hindu epics of Krishna driving Arjun's chariot into war. Incense sticks burnt in the fireplace, a wide-screen Panasonic TV sat darkly on one side of the room, and under a reading lamp, the only real light, a DJ's mixing equipment was laid out.

Desiré was dressed in a red, sleeveless vest and tight beige tracksuit bottoms that followed her legs closely to the knee, then flared. Her hair was short, but with bleached dreadlocks tied into it. In another country, she might have gone to music festivals and raves, or hung about on beaches in Goa, been at Burning Man, or known full-moon parties in Bali, but in Iran the tyranny of trifles had made something of her. She was far too essential to their programme to be ignored and she, as if addicted to the attention, violent as it was, couldn't get away. They picked her up all the time, sometimes just for laughing in a public place. But the most recent episode had been the most serious.

Desiré spoke in a torrent of chaotic accented English, stray laughter and impassioned exclamation marks. 'So many times! So many times, I'm telling you!' she cried, when I asked her if she'd been picked up before. 'But the thing is that every time I knew how to get away. I look like a foreigner, I don't look that much like an Iranian, and so many times I would start pretending that I am French, that I am Indian maybe, too. I knew how to bribe them and talk to them, but this time it wasn't talkable.'

'Why did they come?'

'Because my friend and I, we wanted to go and party in Shemshak.' The place she spoke of was a ski resort north of Tehran. 'And my friend, she wanted some drugs, you know, and there was this guy who used to always come and give it to her. But this time he arrived at her house with the police because they had taken him.'

'This is the dealer?'

'Yes, they took the dealer and came to my friend's house, and they were there waiting when I arrived, waiting, talking, speaking to my friend. My friend had called before to say, "Come pick me up and we'll go party in Shemshak for my birthday." So I went to pick her up and suddenly I come in and see this guy with a gun to my head.'

'Was your friend also in the room?'

'Yes, they were searching her house when I rang the bell.'

'She didn't call to say don't come?'

'She couldn't! She can't! They don't let you do anything. So, anyway, they're standing there all rough and tough. You see, most of these people, they grow up in these houses without their mother and father . . .'

'Orphanages?'

'Yes. Or even if they have parents, in their . . .' she paused in search of the right word '. . . culture, beating a woman is very easy. From the time a boy is a little boy, the father says,

"Beat your mother," so he starts beating his mother, his sister, anybody. So, beating us is nothing for them.'

'Did they beat you?'

'Of course!' she said, with near-jubilation. 'Once we were in Shemshak. Nargis was there.' Nargis, sitting on a saffron cushion, looked over. 'We were walking,' Desiré continued, 'it was night time, and we were going from my house to Nargis's house. I had a car, but I just felt like walking. And a car, not even a Komiteh car or a police car, just a white Pride, came near us. We saw them, but thought they were these guys who say things to girls. OK? Suddenly we see four big guys come out of their car and come to take us. They take one of my friends and they want to put her in the car. She was like, "*Aein, aein* . . ." She emitted a girly nasal noise to indicate that she had put up no resistance. 'But I wasn't . . . I said, "Leave me alone! Don't touch me! Don't touch me!" I wanted somebody to help us because I didn't know these were police.'

'Were they Basiji?'

'No, no! They were so clean, in their white shirts, nothing. Normal people. I tell you, after that night I was scared of everybody because those men were so normal. You might even party in front of them.' Desiré said 'party' with special emphasis, drawing out the word, as if the world was divided into people who partied and people who didn't. 'We didn't know where they were from! I was scared that these were people who wanted to steal us and rape us, you never know! I was screaming, "Show me your paper, show me something," and they were like, with their big batons, beating us! Nargis was funny,' she chuckled. 'She's big, you know, so when they wanted to put her in the car, I was screaming, "Nargis, don't get in, don't get in!" So she put her hands up and they were pushing and pushing, but they couldn't get her into the car.' Desiré laughed out loud, and for the first time I could make out her features, her strong, square jaw, her red lipstick, her light, tanned skin. She was right: she could have been from anywhere. 'And they were beating me and beating me like hell!' She said it with so much energy and lightness that it didn't feel real.

'With a baton?'

'Yeah, with baton. I swear if I didn't do this,' she said, raising her arms over her head, 'I would be dead because my arms were black. Suddenly I saw Nargis was getting away and the baton guy was going to hit her on the head. I jumped in front of him because I thought maybe it would hit me somewhere but not on the head. So I jumped in front of him. I screamed, "Don't touch her, don't beat her," and I went in front of the Komiteh. Nargis was smart, she used that, and she started running. Running and running! The Komiteh was yelling, "Stop, stop," and she was running. I was yelling, "Run, Nargis, run, Nargis," and – and, oh, stupid Nargis! After running, she comes back! Running back! I said, "What the fuck is she doing? She's coming back!"' Desiré was reliving every second, laughing now, sipping vodka and cranberry juice with ice, standing in front of her refriger-ator. 'She came running back to me, screaming, "Listen, listen, your car is there, I saw your car." I said, "Fuck the car, just run, man, run." And she was worried about my car!'

It was disturbing to hear Desiré speak this way. There was something hard and desensitised about her. She seemed to boast, her voice full of bluster; her eyes were frazzled and glassy.

'What did they want?' I asked, hoping to ground her story a little.

'It was a football thing,' she answered. 'Everyone was cele-brating in the streets. There were so many people in the street and, oh, I think it was the time the Americans came into Iraq and TV programmes started to say something.' She meant the American-based Iranian TV channels that broadcast anti-regime propaganda to the Islamic Republic. 'And they [the regime] said,

"Fine. Wherever we go, we're going to do this." And that was one night in Shemshak that they did this.

'They knew that Shemshak was an easy pick-up for them. Anyway, Nargis ran away, I don't know, but she ran away. Me, I was getting beaten because I made her run away. They beat the shit out of me. I was numb. I said to myself, "Just cover your face and head." Their boss was down there and they were taking all the young people and they were beating them. They beat so many people that night, it was like, I can't tell you, it was like a disaster! They would scream, "Whore, you mother-fucker whore," and I was saying, "Oh, I get it, it's because your mother was a whore that you think I'm a whore. Don't fucking beat the shit out of me." And he would beat the shit out of me.' She laughed uproariously.

'I said to one of them who was beating me so hard, "Do you have a mother? Do you have a sister? Do you know that beating a woman like this hurts so much? Don't, please, have mercy on me!" And he wouldn't have mercy. I was bloody and down on the floor.'

'They must have given some reason? What do you think was their reason?'

'Nothing. They didn't have any excuse. They never have any excuse.'

'If you had to say . . .'

'They just wanted to show, "What's going on here? It's like Europe here? What is it? What is this? Girls and boys walking in the street, very cool, it's not possible here. You're not allowed to have fun. You have to always cry, beat the shit out of your-self and be in misery so they would love you." You're not even allowed to look nice. I had a nice picture of myself, I gave it for my passport. They gave it back! They said, "This picture looks nice, we don't take it." And they took such an ugly picture and they put it in!' Desiré laughed.

The regime was the biggest figure in Desiré's life; it seemed to consume her.

'I tell you,' she said, 'when they beat me, they pulled me on the floor because I couldn't walk any more. They dragged me by the hand and put me in the car. It was a bus full of young people crying.'

They had put up roadblocks and were stopping cars, making people get out. They went from door to door, raiding chalets. Nargis and Desiré said the police took thirty busloads of people to Tehran that night. Influence in Shemshak got Desiré off the bus, and one other thing, the horror of which must have registered on my face, because she said, with some anger, 'I am not a young person. Why? What did you think?'

I tried in the half-light to see her face more clearly. I had put her age somewhere in the late twenties, perhaps early thirites. But now as I looked closer, I could see that her skin was slacker than I first thought, and lined. She was forty with a son of twenty. It was not that she looked young; it was that her growth was stunted. She was an absurdity. She dressed and behaved like a teenager. Her whole life had been given to fighting for the right to party.

Coming back to her original story, I asked her what happened after the gun was removed from her head. 'Did they take you to prison?'

'No,' she answered. 'They told me to give names of people. And they had this electric thing, this shocking thing. They would put it to me and ask me to give names. I would say I don't know any names. They would say, "No?" and shock me. "If you want us to free you, you have to give somebody's name."' Desiré claimed she gave no names so they took her to her house and searched it.

'Did they find anything?'

'Of course, of course,' she smiled, more sedate now, 'grass, drink, satellite. Whatever's good in life is not good here in Iran, man. My house was not good! When I was in court, the guy was saying to the judge, "Judge, you have to see her house. I have to go and film her house and show you. If you see her house, you will give her six months in Evin."'

She was referring to Evin Prison, renowned for its cruelty both under the Shah and during the Islamic Republic. A trial of sorts followed, in which Desiré was allowed neither lawyers nor family. When her father came looking for her, he was told falsely that the trial was over and that his daughter had been given six months in Evin.

In the courtroom, Desiré was accused of making pornography and of living as a kept woman. Her accusers' vendetta was so obvious that the judge became suspicious. 'What do you want?' the judge finally said. 'Do you want me to stone her? Do you hate her so much?'

Five minutes later, Desiré's father walked through the door, furious at having been lied to. By this point Desiré had already spent four days in jail.

'They didn't try to get you out earlier?'

'You can't,' she said. 'Four days is nothing. That's the pre-prison. The real prison is Evin.'

'What were the four days like?'

'Oh, fine,' she said. 'It was dirty, there were druggy people, heroin people, vomiting everywhere. We were all in a small room, we slept together. The sheets were smelly and dirty, everyone was smelly and dirty. I was able to take a *hijab*, which was like a kimono, and I would crawl into that at night so that nothing would touch me.'

When she came out of prison none of her old friends would see her. They hung up the phone when she called.

'Why?'

'They were scared.'

'Of what?'

'That I would give their names. And because my best friend told everybody that I had given her name. She wanted to run away from Iran and needed an excuse. Afterwards I said to her, "What were you thinking? How could you do this to me?" She said, "I thought your ass was on it so a little bit more wouldn't matter."

'"What?" I shouted. "Do you know that little bit more was the worst part? You have to take pain away from me, not give me more!"

'So I stayed home. I started not to call people. I started not going anywhere because I would go places and people would be uncomfortable. They would think I was working for the government. Because most of the time when they take you, if your punishment is a lot, they make you work for them instead. In this way you never know if your friend is an informer or not. Everybody becomes an informer. You have to be scared of everybody.'

I believed Desiré when she described this as the worst part, and yet I couldn't help but feel sympathy for her friends too. Not everyone was capable of Desiré's heroism, and one of the most treasured aspects of a state that didn't brutalise and spy on its own people was that it allowed people without a hero's courage to live with dignity, without the guilt of having betrayed friends from fear. Heroes, then, were saved for when they were needed, for truly heroic acts, and Desiré's heroism, if it was real, would not have been squandered on the freedom to 'party'.

'Why do you stay?'

'My land,' Desiré muttered. 'I don't know. It attracts me wherever I go. I speak French, I speak English. I am an English resident. I had a husband, my son is in England, some of my family is there. Everyone asks me, "Why are you here?" I go there, I spend time there.' Then, as if telling me a great secret, she whispered, 'But then I want to come back. Krishna always says, "Wherever you were born is your root, and wherever else you might go, you always come back." She stopped, and those frazzled eyes glistened with a few stray tears. 'I don't know why. Shit, I hate it. But I'm comfortable here.' Then, choking with fresh laughter, she added, 'And it's not comfortable.'

*

Desiré mentioned the word 'Islam' only once to me. At her trial she had asked, 'You don't know anything about me so how can you judge me? Is Islam something that has to judge people like this?' Houshmand also differentiated between the 'real Islam' and the Islam of the Islamic Republic. It was true that, as I encountered the Islamic Republic in the lives of its people, I made no separation between the republic's Islam and the 'real faith'. Did it really matter whether the Islam of the Islamic Republic was the 'real Islam' or not? Did it matter whether the socialism of Stalin or Mao was the real socialism?

The rush of sudden oil wealth, 'the country moving too fast', unstable, undemocratic governments interfered with by foreign powers: these were the components of the Islamic Revolution. This was what had mattered before the society was put through the Islamic filter. It was a distortion of the faith's rule now, always happier dealing with trifles, to shut out those questions and to choose instead to harass Desiré.

Even as I heard these stories, my own luck was running out. It was as if tales of this unseen regime made certain our meeting.

Phone Booth

I didn't try to contact my father again until I was seventeen. I was in my last year of boarding-school in the hills of south India and about to go to college in America.

The school had been started by American missionaries in the early part of the last century and grew into a 'Christian international school', drawing a bizarre mixture of Midwestern missionaries and hippies who wanted to spend time in India. The school therapist was an old American hippie who had set up a peer-counselling programme that I joined. She trained us in one-to-one meetings in her sunny office near the chapel. Together, we would invent hypothetical problems and work through them, employing the methods of parroting, paraphrasing and open-ended questions to arrive at a made-up solution. She was a large, blonde woman, with protruding blue eyes and thick spectacles. She listened carefully to everything I said, her lips adjusting themselves over the braces she had recently started wearing to take in an overbite. 'I'm sorry, they still cut my mouth a bit,' she would say, if she saw that I was distracted by the movement.

On one of these afternoons, playing shrink and patient, I found myself recounting the real facts of my life to the therapist. I suddenly felt awkward, but found it comforting to talk to someone so removed from my life. I also liked showing off my surprising indifference to my father.

'But wasn't it difficult for your mother to marry a Pakistani?' the therapist asked.

'Oh, yes, it really was. She was a total outcast,' I exaggerated.

'That must have been hard for you to handle those social pressures at such a young age.'

'Well, yes, but I had a lot of support. You know, the Indian family system, so strong, so inclusive.'

'And what was it like to grow up in Indian society without a father?'

'Well, as my mother always says, it was the biggest favour he could have done me.'

'Who? Your father? Why does she say that?'

'She's only joking.'

'Oh, I see. Do you have any memory of him?'

'No, none at all. He jumped ship when I was two.'

'When you were two? And you never heard from him, no letters, no phone calls?'

'I think he wanted it to be a very clean separation.'

'And how does that work for you?'

'It's fine. See, the thing is that while a lot of children get messed up because of fathers that are there and then not there, for me the idea of a father never took root at all. And since these things are all social constructs, it's possible to do without them just as long as you get love and attention from somewhere else.'

'Uh-huh. And who were those people in your life?'

'Oh, lots.'

'Grandparents?'

'Yes. Grandparents, aunts, uncles, cousins. You're never alone.'

'Uh-huh. And now?'

'Now what?'

'How do you feel about your father today?'

'Nothing. I mean, the man is obviously a shit. He abandoned my mother with a baby to bring up on her own in India. Everyone gets shitty people in their lives. Some have shitty mothers or grandmothers, some even have shitty children. You take advantage of the good ones and let the bad ones find each other.'

'You seem to be very decided about it. How did you come to feel this way?'

The therapist had an awful way of depriving any experience of its uniqueness. I felt threatened by the equalising character of her questions. I realised then that the particularity of my story had been a refuge and that much of what I told her was related to the peace my mother had found, derived in part from the thrill of the cross-border romance, the love-child, the challenge and excitement of an unconventional life. These things could get her through, but they would never have been enough for me because they were not of my making. Rather than comfort me, they made me feel the absence in my life more acutely, as though someone else had lived and I hadn't.

The therapist's technique prevailed; the seclusion of her office was too great; for once I shrugged off my stock answers.

'And why,' she continued, 'leaving your mother's problem with him aside, have you not tried to contact him?'

'I honestly don't think my mother would like that.'

'Yes, but, Aatish—' She stopped.

'What?'

'No, I shouldn't. It's not for me to disturb whatever equilibrium you have come to. It's really moving to hear you talk with this resolve about what must have been such a painful side of your life, but I feel you must also consider yourself when you make this decision about your father. It is your right to know him. It is your right not to have to live with his ghost.'

The therapist chewed her braces for a moment. 'You are not betraying your mother by seeking out your father.'

'Oh, please, stop it. This isn't America. What am I going to do after all these years? Just call him and say, "Hello, Abba, this is Aatish"?'

'No, deciding the best approach is another matter. First, you have to be willing to address the subject.'

That day as I left her office I knew I would do it. Her words had binding force; it was harder not to act.

I took advantage of the free period after my meeting with her to go back to my dormitory. Everything felt vivid and new: the wooded road leading up to the dormitory, the occasional views of blue eucalyptus hills, the old colonial club where retired army officers gathered in the evening to play bingo. Why should this hill station in deepest south India, full of hippies and Christians, be the setting for one of the most important decisions of my life?

I slipped into the dormitory building without my housemistress noticing and went into my room. Leafing through my address book, I already felt a tinge of guilt. I was looking for the number of an old friend of my mother, an ex-friend, really, because he had remained friends with my father after the split. He was the friend who had asked my mother to leave the Baker Street flat. I chose him because my mother wouldn't find out. I found the number and scribbled it on to a phone pass. Then, to avoid coming back for another, I changed the 'number of calls' from one to two, and in place of my father's telephone number, I put the country code for Pakistan. It was all I knew of his whereabouts. I approached my housemistress who spent several minutes searching for her spectacles, then examined the pass closely.

'First call, England. And second to which country, please?' she asked.

'Ma'am, to my mother's mobile phone.'

'Mobile phone?'

'Yes, ma'am.'

'Mobile phones require international standard dialling?'

'Yes, ma'am,' I lied.

'Oh, God, please save us from this new technology,' she said, and signed the slip.

I made my way along the uphill road, past the chapel and the therapist's office to the telephone operator in the main administrative section of the school. There was a ten o'clock assembly and a degree of commotion in the normally quiet corridors. There were two phone booths: a cramped wooden one with graffitied walls and a naked yellow lightbulb, and a newer one with a window and stool.

I handed the signed phone pass to the operator and asked for the wooden booth. I was reading the graffiti when the phone started ringing. I answered it and the operator's voice bellowed, 'Trunk call from India. Mr Nath? Mr Nath?'

A sleepy voice answered, 'Yes.' I realised that in my excitement I hadn't taken into account the time difference.

The man, though surprised to hear from me, was friendly and gave me my father's number so quickly and with so few questions that it felt as though he had been expecting my call for years. I wrote down the numbers and apologised for waking him up.

The assembly was still going on when I left the phone booth. I walked in its direction hoping to find the therapist. I caught sight of her in a far corner, leaning against a pillar. When the assembly was over, I rushed up to her and asked if I could see her in the next class period. I would have to miss Hindi, but was sure I could get away with it. We agreed to meet back in her office in ten minutes.

Sitting again on the sofa in her office, I asked, with new purpose, the same question: 'So what am I going to do? Just call him and say, "Hello, Abba, this is Aatish"?'

'Well, first,' she began, 'it's important to establish that he's in a position where he can speak to you. He has a new wife and more children, right?'

'Yes.'

'Do they know about you?' she asked.

The question stung, but I could see that she hadn't intended it to. 'I don't know. Maybe.'

'Well, then, you're going to want to make sure it's a good time. You don't want to phone him just after he's had a big fight with his wife and suddenly say, "Hello, it's me, your long-lost son."'

I heard her out, then left her office. My only thought was that I would telephone my father later that day, and that I had to convince the operator to connect the call with my dormitory. I hoped my father, like my mother, was better disposed to dealing with important matters in the evening.

The operator said his colleague would be taking the evening shift, but that he would pass on the request for the nine-fifteen call.

'Operator, one other thing,' I said. 'When you connect the call, could you not say where it's from? It's a surprise of sorts.'

The operator didn't object so I left the slip with him and headed off to my classes.

It was a difficult day to get through, with a double-science period in the afternoon, during which my thoughts were fixed on the evening call. Practical considerations troubled me most. How would I make sure that my housemistress or friends wouldn't interrupt me? Would I take the call in the corridor or in the housemistress's apartment? If a servant should answer, who would I say was calling? How would I greet my father? Surely not 'Abba', but by his first name then? I'd never addressed any Indian adult in that way.

I decided to return to the dormitory early and make some headway with my homework as I was sure it would become harder to do as nine fifteen approached. I met my housemistress on the way and told her I was expecting a trunk call that evening so that I could wish my mother a happy birthday.

'Your mother's happy birthday today?' She grinned.

'Yes, ma'am.'

'Good, good. Please also convey my very best wishes to her. Please feel free to speak in my apartment.'

'Thank you, ma'am,' I said, sidling off to my room.

The study hour began, and my two roommates came in. I wished I could tell them of the error I was making. I felt in unsafe hands with the therapist, yet in a day she had reduced the greatest gulf in my life to a tantalising two-hour wait. For all that I didn't trust her, I was excited and willing to believe. My caution was just fear of disappointment.

By nine, the study hour was over and I escaped the clamour of the corridors for the quiet of my housemistress' apartment. In the fifteen minutes I spent by the phone, I took in every minute detail of the apartment, from my housemistress' shrine to the late Princess Diana to the needlework pastoral scenes, with religious messages.

At ten past nine, I focused on the task ahead, as if I were doing last-minute revision for an exam. I prayed the call wouldn't go through. But the operator was following a simple instruction, and the line was connecting as it had before, and the phone rang.

I answered it, expecting to be flung straight into conversation with my father, but the operator's voice spoke instead. 'Call to Lahore, Pakistan. Should I connect?'

'Yes, please,' I managed, shuddering at the mention of Pakistan.

Then, as if performing a magic trick, the operator's voice was gone and a gruff voice at the other end of the line, said, 'Hello.'

'*Salam Olaikum*,' I said, recalling a Muslim friend of my mother teaching me the greeting. 'Is this Salmaan Taseer's house?'

'*Olaikum*,' the gruff voice replied, with some puzzlement. 'Yes, who's speaking?'

'May I speak to him, please?' I asserted.

'Speaking,' the voice said in English.

'This is Aatish Taseer,' I said, blushing at my own heroism.

The voice did not respond. I imagined the comfort of an evening at home ruined.

Then the therapist's suggestion came to mind, and I said, aware that I had not banished the flutter from my voice, 'Is this a good time to talk?'

'No,' the voice said. Then, as if explaining a hard concept to a child, 'This isn't actually a very good time.'

'Will tomorrow morning be better?' I offered.

'Yes, it will be better.'

'Should I try the office number?'

'Yes, do that. Where are you?' the voice asked, with sudden concern.

'In India, at my boarding-school in southern India. It's in Tamil Nadu.'

'OK,' the voice said, losing interest.

I said goodbye and hung up.

The next morning I rushed into the therapist's office, furious at the disappointment. She was engaged in another one-to-one peer-counselling session, but she asked the person to leave. She listened to every last detail about the sound of his voice, his choice of words, the way he had said goodbye. Then she asked, like a mantra, 'How has it made you feel?'

'Extremely disappointed.'

'Have you thought yet of why?'

'Yes, I've been thinking about this man all my life and I got the courage to call him only to be told that it wasn't a good time.'

'Maybe it wasn't,' she said stubbornly.

'What? Do you mean you think he was telling the truth?'

'Perhaps not, but we have to take people at their word.'

'You think I should call him back?'

'What harm is there? If nothing else, you'll hear his voice again, which will only affirm that he is a creature of flesh and blood, and not some over-built-up myth.'

She was an infuriating woman to share a secret with, but she had one unique quality: she was never dissatisfied with an outcome, no matter how far it was from what she expected. It made me want to call my father, if only to throw it in her face.

Later that day, I returned to the original wooden booth and waited to be put through to my father's office. My mood was not unlike that of someone calling a customer service or IT help desk for the tenth time. When the number finally rang, I could tell the operator was still on the line. He said, in a heavy south-Indian accent, 'Hello? Hello? Stand by for trunk call.'

The voice at the other end was quiet. I said, 'Hello, can I speak to Salmaan Taseer?'

'Who's calling?' the voice said. I recognised its gruffness as my father's.

'His son,' I said firmly.

Then the voice changed. The gruffness was gone and the tone was meek, like a servant's. 'He is not in at the moment,' the voice said, now in Urdu.

I hadn't planned for this. 'What?' I said, certain that the voice sounded like my father's, but unsure how to proceed.

'He is out,' the voice, still servile, repeated.

The cowardice enraged me and I felt a strange sense of power over the voice. I wavered between pressing on and giving up. Then, a sense of fatigue took over. I made the owner of the voice write down my number and hung up.

I never found out if it was really my father.

The Disciplinary (*sic*) Force of the Islamic Republic

> In the Name of God. As Long as a Tourist is in an Islamic country, the Islamic government is responsible to guarantee his safety and comfort. If a Tourist in an Islamic country loses his properties, the government should support and provide him with the lost property.
>
> *Imam Ali, from a sign in a travel agent's office*

The Disciplinary (*sic*) Force of the Islamic Republic of Iran and Department of Aliens' Affairs in Tehran had a bad reputation for inefficiency and unpleasantness. I was thinking of going out of town to renew my visa, but as it was about to expire I had little choice. I still had a lot more to do in Iran. I wanted to go to Kurdistan and to the holy cities of Qom and Mashhad. Reza, my vet-friend, and I organised our train tickets to Mashhad at a travel agency on Tehran's congested south side. Then, to renew my visa, we took a taxi north into cleaner air and *chenar*-lined avenues, with glass-fronted boutiques and coffee shops.

In that hour before lunch, the office was empty. I followed Reza in past a guard; we signed our names in a visitors' book and dropped off the forms. I was requesting a month's extension but was willing to settle for a fortnight. The man who took them said I could pick up my passport on Saturday, the night before we were meant to leave for Mashhad. It seemed straightforward enough.

Saturday came and, as instructed, I returned to the Disciplinary Force of the Islamic Republic on the long, tree-lined avenue. This time, the office was airless and crowded. The main room was full of Africans, South Asians and Asians standing around for varied consular services, such as visa extension, pick-up and delivery. Many had dazed, puzzled expressions, showing the effects of indefinite waiting. The usual religious decorations and instructions hung on the walls: 'Honourable aliens, Islamic *hijab* is necessary,' 'Yah Fatima' in gold letters and a romanticised portrait of Ali's son.

In a far corner of the room behind a glass partition, I saw a sign that said 'Visa Pickup and Interview Box'. A couple of Europeans were standing near it and I made my way over. The man working behind the partition with two stars on his epaulettes was bald, with a moustache and a cold, stern mouth. His eyes darted from person to dossier to person, giving the impression that the two were interchangeable. After a short wait, I handed him my pickup slip. He fingered a few dossiers, then went away, came back and searched again for mine. I saw it before he did and gave him some indication of where it was. He picked it up and scanned its contents quickly. Then his eyes rested on something in it.

'I can give you two days,' he said blandly.

'Two days?' I blurted.

'Two days,' he replied, paying no attention to the emphasis in my voice.

'But I asked for a month.'

'I'm sorry, I can't help you.'

'But why? Why have I just been given two days?'

'I'm sorry, I can't help you.'

'But I haven't even made transport arrangements to leave in two days.'

'I'm sorry I *can't* help you,' he said, then turned to the next person.

I had prepared myself for a variety of surprising outcomes, but two days was less than my lowest estimate. It would not give me time to travel by land to Pakistan, which was my plan, let alone to the religious cities of Qom and Mashhad. It was hardly any more time than my visa already allowed so I didn't bother to ask for the two days he offered.

Panic rose from my stomach. There was so much I still needed to do in Iran! The bald man's answer didn't just alter my plans but altered me, bringing me into line with the level of distress in the room. I pushed my way out of the window-less office and on to the street.

I walked up and down the block, past a pastry shop, and crossed the black metal rails that bridged the clean waterway, bright from light driven in spokes through the *chenar*s above. In the other direction, the incline took the eye past the broad stretch of avenue, culminating in the snow-capped mountains that, despite the dark layers of pollution, gave Tehran an aspect of spring. This strange city could turn like a hologram: at one instant it was spring, greenery and white mountains; at the next, traffic, pollution, black outlines and hazard.

I was still under the impression that my two-day extension was the result of a bureaucratic accident and could be amended with the help of someone who knew the country and the language. I couldn't decide who to call. Most of the people I knew in Iran were young and would have no influence. The only older people I could think of were Muhammad Rahimi and his Indian wife, Sita. She had been away since my arrival in Tehran, but had returned in the past few days and I was meant to be meeting her anyway.

'I'm sorry to call you with this, Sita,' I said, 'but I have a bit of a problem. They've given me forty-eight hours to leave the country. I have a lot of work still to do. Is there any way you can help?'

'Well,' she answered, perhaps a little put off by the urgency in my voice, 'Muhammad's office is always getting visa extensions for people who work for the company. You should have let us know you were doing this. Let me call him and then I'll call you back.'

Sita called back within minutes and sounded reassuring. She asked where I was, then said she would have their son, Payam, who I already knew, pick me up and take me to Muhammad's office, which was off Vali Asr.

Payam's arrival was a comfort after the large and inscrutable government apparatus, but the doubt I had sensed in Sita must have been playing on his mind too: had I only been offered a two-day visa because of a bureaucratic error or because I had run into trouble with the regime? In the first case, it made sense to contest the decision; in the second, it would be reckless to do so.

Muhammad, sitting in his elegant, wood-panelled office, squinting through his gold-rimmed glasses, traced my story back to the flat I was staying in. He was certain that my friend's links with the press had brought me under scrutiny from the Islamic Republic. 'Is your friend Iranian?' he asked.

'Yes.'

'Then be sure he's an informer,' he said, with the special confidence he reserved for expounding conspiracy theories.

'He's hardly ever lived here,' I protested. 'I know him from England. He's only just started to work here. Besides, he's not even in the country.'

'Be sure he is an informer,' Muhammad said, shaking his head from side to side.

We waited for Mr Valaie to show up. He handled Muhammad's business visas for his foreign employees. He was someone who, Muhammad said, 'knows how to speak to those people'. I liked the description: it was exactly the kind of knowledge I felt I lacked. I was still more comforted when Valaie arrived. He was a tall, burly man, with a quiet but substantial presence, and wore the short, stubbly beard of the Basiji. He had the appearance of an insider. We recounted to him the morning's events and he suggested we go directly back to the office and speak to them.

Soon we were back in the car, finding openings in the giant traffic formation heading down Vali Asr.

Using back-streets, and side-streets, and outmanoeuvring other cars, we arrived at the Disciplinary Force of the Islamic Republic of Iran. Again we went straight past the bearded sentries into the main room, which had cleared since I'd last seen it. The bald man, with the hard mouth, was immediately visible and I pointed him out to Valaie. Valaie told me to stand back and moved his large, impressive form in a swift, self-assured step toward the man, who was now standing up but looking down. When Valaie approached, he glanced up for a second to take him in, as if he had been expecting him all along.

Valaie explained himself, then asked, 'May I take some of your time?'

'I have no time,' the man replied, and returned to his work.

'Could you just say what the problem is?'

'No, I cannot, and you must not ask me.'

As soon as he had said this, he moved away from the desk. Valaie appealed to him again as he withdrew. He did not answer, but when the appeal came again, he snapped, in a louder voice so that his other colleagues heard, 'Two days and don't ask for an explanation.'

A woman came up to the desk, like an apologetic wife, and explained politely that a Mr Rashidi had denied the visa; we had to speak directly to him. When Valaie asked where Mr Rashidi was, they said he had left for the day.

Valaie looked as if he was unused to being spoken to in this way. It was as if a kinsman or relation had insulted him. He advised that we take the two days and try again for more days tomorrow when we came to collect the passport. Since the extension fees were paid and the two days would give me at least one day more than my visa allowed, I agreed. Valaie took the slip back to the counter. This time someone else dealt with him.

My relief at having escaped the government office, and its bitter disappointments, was so great that it was some minutes before the realisation of what had occurred sank in. I had a two o'clock appointment with Hosseini, who had recently returned from America and was a senior administrator at Tehran University. He was to help me in the religious cities of Mashhad and Qom. Now I was not sure if there was any point in seeing him. I still wanted to complete the trip by land and had already begun to calculate how long it would take me to reach the Pakistani border. Iran's border with Pakistan, in the southern region of Balochistan, is a heavy smuggling route and rumoured to be dangerous. It was the riskiest part of the entire trip, and while I could muster the courage to do it in normal circumstances, I wasn't sure I wanted to cross it if I was already in trouble with the Islamic Republic. I called Hosseini to tell him what had happened. 'I think I can help you,' he said. 'Let's meet as planned, at the hotel.'

The Homa had once been the Sheraton. Like many Iranian hotels, it was trapped in the past, a past that was once not a bad present but today showed its backwardness. The lobby was dark, musty, and seemed to reflect the state's enthusiasm for foreign visitors. Old cutlery and plates from the Sheraton days remained, but the coffee shop was run like a college canteen.

The place was teeming with staff, but the service was hope-less. As I entered, the sofas in front of the reception desk were filled with people waiting. None could have been Hosseini so I veered off to the left to inspect the bookshop. It sold soft, old paperbacks, outdated guides for Iran, airport thrillers, James Baldwin's *Another Country*, with the *Spectator* calling him 'the greatest Negro writer'. If I hadn't grown up in the frozen socialist days of India in the 1980s, I don't know if I could have placed the exact year when the clock stopped in Iran. As it happened, it was familiar and stirred a degree of nostalgia.

When I went back to the lobby, I saw a small, elderly man sitting in a corner with one leg outstretched. We caught each other's eye and he rose with difficulty, then walked with a limp in my direction. He was clean-shaven and distinguished, and didn't look like a government man, but his being in a senior position at Tehran University, which had only just received a mullah as its president, made me wonder. But even as these judgements became harder to make in the rest of the Islamic world – people you never expected to be religious, surprising you with their piety – in Iran, the positions became always clearer. As I would come to learn within the next twenty-four hours, Islam in Iran was not religion; it was politics. And my having confused this landed me in trouble.

I spent a few hours with Hosseini. He told me he had been appointed to a position that dealt specifically with international relations for Tehran University and he would let the people at the government office know I was a former student of his, working on academic research in Iran. 'But I don't have a visa for that,' I said. 'I have a tourist visa.'

'That's OK, but don't say anything about religion. Say you're working on a thesis about the cultures of people in the East.'

It sounded vague to me, but I guessed that was the idea. It was evening and Tehran's main arteries were clogging when

Hosseini dropped me off at Shiraz Avenue. On the way I asked him why he had left Iran. 'I didn't like this government,' he said. 'Also, I wanted my children to grow up in a free country. One goes to Harvard, the other to Stanford, and my son goes to Northeastern for engineering. They wouldn't have had those opportunities here. I value very much freedom of expression, freedom of thinking. I value these things very much.'

Hosseini's family had owned a construction company, which they lost in the 1979 revolution. He spent many years in America and had only recently come back after being offered a senior position at the university. Like so many other Iranians, a sense of loss and love of his country brought him back. His main reason for leaving, as he said, was his children and how growing up in the Islamic Republic would limit them.

'You know what happened in Iran?' he said, after the traffic slowed again, 'People were very connected to religion even though the government was not religious. But now that the government is religious, most of the people want to get away from religion. They see it as killing people, putting journalists in jail. That is the true religion. It is very hard for me to say I am a Muslim. Most of the terrorists today are religious. I prefer to say I have no religion.' Then, as if in an afterthought, he said, 'We are a talented, enthusiastic people, but with a bad government.'

'It's funny that everyone always says "government",' I said, 'when they mean "regime" or "state".'

'Yes, because every year we say this is the last year, but they're still here.'

We agreed to meet the next morning at nine fifteen outside the office of the Disciplinary Force of the Islamic Republic of Iran.

That evening I had an urge to go out. Nightlife in Tehran happened at private houses, and as my absent host once said to me, 'It's filthy.' Most of the time I was too busy or un-prepared for its excesses, but that night, like many young people in Tehran, I felt in need of release.

I called Amir. When I told him what had happened, he became quiet. I still expected Hosseini to perform a miracle, but Amir smelt trouble. 'This can also happen,' he said, after a long silence. 'Don't push too hard.' We talked of other things and I said I'd like to see him in case I was leaving tomorrow.

'Yes,' Amir said. 'In fact I'm taking you to a party. It's the birthday of an actor friend and I think it'll be fun.' I readily agreed and he said he'd pick me up in a few hours. I was standing on the balcony when I spoke to Amir and caught a glimpse of the lights coming on in the city. My eyes had fixed on this view so many times over the previous month and, despite its ugliness, it was a captivating and dark urban vision.

Amir and Anahita arrived in high spirits. They drove an elegant, cream 1970s Paykan – Iran's Volkswagen – and Anahita was holding a large tambourine. The party was in another high-rise building, which, like mine, was constructed in the time of the Shah.

At the party, beautiful made-up girls threw off manteaux and scarves to reveal *décolleté* tops and long, flowing hair. The room was dark, the music loud; a famous Iranian hit song played; a light came from the kitchen where several kinds of spirits and beer lay around the sink.

Most of the crowd were in the film business, and when I told them I was Indian, they tittered about Bollywood. A girl in a red and white satin blouse danced close to me, a man smoked a joint on the balcony and Anahita beat on a drum while others, including the host, who was bearded, with clear blue eyes, danced round her. Fun of this kind in Tehran always seemed to be had with the accompanying awareness that it could land you in trouble. Almost everyone present had had a brush with the law; almost everyone had been at a party that was busted; many of the girls had been picked up for stretching decency laws. An entire urban youth had been criminalised. Most of the people there were almost exactly the same age as, or slightly older than, the revolution. They had lived through times when T-shirts, Western music, certain haircuts, the mingling of the sexes, dancing and, of course, intoxication could have you hauled in. And yet they took their chances – in fact, too many; they were hooked on dissent.

Leaving the party, two girls reeled ahead of us, carrying a giant ten-foot sandwich from the party on their shoulders. They rocked from side to side and their headscarves slipped off. One climbed drunkenly into our car. Anahita, who had been drinking through the evening, drove and sang. She tore down highway after highway, veering the car towards traffic islands, then pulling away with a laugh at the last minute. Amir looked serene. It was behaviour that would have got us arrested in London, let alone Tehran. I leant over to him and said, as if consoling him, 'Fuck the Islamic Republic of Iran.' He laughed, and Anahita and he stuck up their elbows and rotated them, a jeer at the regime from the time when elbows were sexy.

We ended up at some house, sitting about the floor, drinking cheap vodka in plastic cups. A painter friend of Amir, a dark man with a shaved head, began a story. Addressing me, he said, 'I was the most religious guy. I believed in Muhammad and Ali for years. But I have seen all the propaganda in schools and now I don't believe in religion. One day I started thinking and I stopped believing.'

'How?'

'I was driving with my friend and I had a Koran kept in that . . . How do you say it, the sun thing in the car?'

'Visor?'

'Yes, visor. And the road was very bumpy and the Koran fell down. So I picked it up and kissed it. And my friend, he saw me, and he said, "Oh, your Koran fell down. Let me kiss it too." So I give it to him and he takes it, kisses it and throws it out of the window.'

The room erupted in laughter, but the painter withheld his smile, eager to continue. 'And . . . and my friend says, "This is nothing." And I start to think, How can he and how can't I? How can he and how can't I? All night I lay in my bed, thinking, How can he and how can't I? All night. And then it came to me: Islam was nothing but history written by victors. So before, when I was religious, I was a big fighter. Now I give a prize to anyone who can make me fight.'

No one laughed now. They smiled knowingly at the painter, nodding and sipping their drinks. He described Islam as 'history written by victors'. He made a haphazard connection between being a 'big fighter' and religion. His description of himself reminded me of Muhammad Rahimi's student days. Religion overcome, the painter knew a kind of peace; he saw empowerment in his transformation from believer to thinker. His tracing his former rage to the religion's view of history was the most significant thing I heard on my journey. It was at the heart of my problem with my father, with whom, but for religion, it could be said I shared a single history.

The next morning, I felt the effects of the night before. Payam was downstairs at eight fifteen, alert in a crisp white shirt. The highways had burst their banks and even the exits were filled with slow-moving traffic. Our maddeningly slow pace, leagued with my dehydration, brought on nausea and sweatiness. When we reached Muhammad's office, Valaie was already there but was caught up with work and took many minutes to come down. I was anxious not to keep Hosseini waiting, but when I called him, he was already outside the government office. We were fifteen minutes late for him.

This time Hosseini, dignified despite his limp, led us into the office. It was as crowded as it had been the day before. I caught sight of the man whom I had dealt with previously. I pointed him out to Hosseini and he signalled to me to stand back. Watching from afar, I could see that the man had spotted the large figure of Valaie slouching towards him behind Hosseini. He looked irritated, but when Hosseini approached and introduced himself, his manner became courteous and helpful. It was the first encouraging sign so far.

The man retrieved my file and began to leaf through it as Hosseini, occasionally throwing a glance in my direction, stood in front of him. After the man looked over the file carefully, Hosseini and he had a short exchange. Then Hosseini nodded and limped slowly back to me.

'There's nothing wrong with your application,' he said. 'He says he'd give you the extension right now, but since Mr Rashidi has denied it, he says we must speak to him to find out why. He's from a different agency.'

'Where is Rashidi?'

'He's not in yet, but should be here soon.'

A moment later Valaie came up to us. He had enquired about Rashidi and been told that he would be in at eleven. It was ten o'clock and we decided to take a break for an hour and meet back at eleven. I hadn't had breakfast so Payam took me to the former Miami Hotel. We went to a breakfast room on the top floor and I fell upon a plate of fried eggs, cheese and cold meat. Two cups of coffee later, I felt much better.

When we met up again with Hosseini at eleven, Rashidi had still not arrived. We decided to wait for him outside. A couple of Pakistani women in *chador* were slumped on a bench with their chins in their hands as if in grief. A heavyset man in Pakistani *salwar kameez* stood in front of them, staring in bewilderment at a set of pink forms. Hosseini and Valaie were deep in conversation. Hosseini was saying how in the past you could send someone to pick up your US or UK visa for you but now, since the revolution, it was different: if you hadn't been in the Islamic Republic for a long time, it was important not to lose your cool when dealing with bureaucracy.

Then he grew impatient and moved towards the office again. I was going to stay outside, but decided to follow him in so that I could take a mental note of what the office looked like. The crowd had thinned, but the windowless room was still almost full. I had barely an instant to take it in when across the room past dozens of people and behind the glass partition, I saw a man who could only have been Rashidi. The words 'He's from a different agency' shot into my mind and, guessing which agency it was, the blackest fear sprang up in me.

I had seen an intelligence man only once before. It was in Damascus and I remember I was struck then by the certainty with which I recognised him. Rashidi, too, was a breed apart from the other officials in the room. In plain clothes, he wore a dark blue jacket over a dark blue shirt, had a short salt-and-pepper beard and his eyes gleamed from behind a pair of silver spectacles. There was an air of extra-legality about him. He looked like a man who had been sent to override the system, to get the job done quickly and efficiently. He spoke rapidly into a mobile phone, and though I'd never laid eyes on him till that moment, the instant he saw me he knew who I was. His eyes burned and he made a violent gesture with his arm for me to come over. Payam, who had followed me in, saw the gesture, and it was only when I recognised the fear in his face, like a man made aware he's bleeding by another's reaction to it, that my heart sank.

I grasped for Hosseini. He had seen the gesture too, and continued to walk at a steady pace ahead of me. His presence shielded me from the anger that Rashidi was ready to direct at me. When he saw that the small, elderly man was with me he seemed to show the disappointment of a dog restrained by the appearance of his master. We went up to the window together. Hosseini and Rashidi began to speak energetically to each other in Farsi. I could only make out the odd word in common with Urdu: '*saval*', question, '*javab*', answer, 'Afghanistan' and 'Pakistan'. They spoke for many minutes, Rashidi shaking his head vigorously and answering the professor politely, but assertively, and Hosseini stubbornly persisting. At last they came to an impasse and Hosseini turned to me to say, 'He won't give it because apparently you filled in your visa application incorrectly. You have to review it before you apply again.'

At the time, Rashidi's sarcasm was lost in translation, but the extension was the last of my concerns now. I wanted to take my passport and leave immediately. Hosseini said, 'I told him you were my student.'

To which Rashidi had replied, 'Don't get involved with these foreign students.'

It was an easy lie to uncover and it scared me more.

'I'm already involved,' Hosseini said. 'I represent the international relations of Tehran University. He is doing research for a humanities thesis on Eastern peoples.'

Rashidi gave the old professor a long, cold stare, then picked up the telephone and made a call. When he hung up, he gestured to two young military recruits in dark green fatigues to take us somewhere. The bearded men, with sunken eyes, came up to us. Only Hosseini and I were to go. We followed them out of the office and into a small lift. The building was not just that one office, but a complex. The recruits pressed the button for the fifth floor and the small lift made a slow ascent. When the doors opened, we were met with a series of green arrows. Four pointed left, indicating services such as passport renewal and licence-plate registration. A single arrow pointed right. It read

'Offend'. Hosseini looked at me and shrugged. For the second time that morning I felt sick.

We were brought into a lobby of sorts, with rooms leading off it, and were seated next to two European men. We waited in silence again. A few minutes later, three plain-clothes men showed up and *salaam*ed everyone before vanishing into different rooms. One of the Europeans was called in. They began to speak and I heard something about a camera. Photography in the wrong places could get you into serious trouble in the Islamic Republic. Then suddenly, I felt my notebook in my pocket and became nervous. If they went through it, they would find all they needed. I whispered to Hosseini that I should do something with it. He nodded his approval. I looked at the door and saw it was not guarded. I took the opportunity and ran out, down five flights of stairs, past the guards at the main office and into the street. Payam and Valaie were waiting for me outside. I indicated that they should come with me into a side-street.

'What's going on?' Payam asked frantically.

'I don't know. I have to go back up, but keep this.' I gave him my notebook and had to fight the temptation to jump into the car and leave.

On my way back up the five flights of stairs, I passed Rashidi. He darted a suspicious look at me. I nodded and continued upstairs. When I came back into the room Hosseini was still sitting where I had left him. He seemed to have digested the sinister colour of the place and looked nervous now. In a few minutes, two men appeared. One was small and dark with lively eyes and a sparse grey beard, the other was fairer, larger, with a broad face and a grim aspect. These were our interrogators. With a wave, they cleared a room of the two *chador*ed women manning a desk, and asked Hosseini to come in. I couldn't hear what was said, but it was a short conversation, and in a few minutes, Hosseini reappeared. The small, dark man came out after him, flashed me a smile and asked me in.

The large, fair man was the interrogator and he took his position behind a long desk, sprawling comfortably in a chair with wheels. The small, dark man was the translator. The larger man would ask a question in Farsi to his small, mean conduit. While he translated, his beady eyes glued to me, the larger man reclined in his chair, swivelled slightly and watched. The round-about way in which the questions reached me caused so much discomfort that I was inclined to think the larger man spoke perfect English and only introduced the other as part of a strategy to break me down. They told me to sit on a straight-backed chair placed against a pale, yellow wall.

The questions began immediately without any explanation of why I had been brought there in the first place.

'Who are your other two companions?' came the question in Farsi, then the anticipation, and finally the translated echo.

'One is the son of a family friend,' I said. 'The other works in his father's office.'

'What are their names?'

'Payam and Mr Valaie.'

'Their full names?'

'Payam Rahimi.'

'Rah?'

'Rahimi.'

'What is their connection to you?'

'His father is a family friend.'

'What's the father's name?'

'Muhammad Rahimi.'

'Rah?'

'Rahimi, like the son's name.'

'Are you staying at a hotel?'

'No, at a friend's flat.'

'Where?'

'Saman building, off Shiraz Avenue.'

'What number?'

'719C.'

'Whose flat is it?'

'Bahador,' I answered, swearing to myself that I would tell the truth, but try to withhold information where possible.

'Afkhami?' The larger interrogator snapped, relishing the surprise it created in me.

'Yes.'

'Bahador is here?'

'No. He's in London.'

'But you say you're staying in his flat?' the little man asked, his eyes widening.

'Yes, he let me stay there while I'm here.'

'Are you paying him money?'

'No. He's let me use it.'

'How do you know Mr Bahador?'

'From London.'

'Can you describe the exact circumstances of your first meeting?'

'Yes, we had lunch in London.'

'Who did you meet him through?'

'Through a mutual friend.'

'Can you say where you first heard of Mr Bahador?' I didn't know where this was leading, but the questions were coming so quickly I felt I could only rely on telling the truth, even though the truth was turning out to be more complicated than I first imagined.

'In Indonesia,' I answered, mystified by the strangeness of the word in this room.

'Do you know his job in Iran?'

'No. I don't think he has one.' Bahador was not connected

to any network, and as I didn't know much about his work in Iran, I hoped to get away with genuine ignorance.

'No?' the little man said, his voice brimming with sarcasm.

'As far as I know.'

'You have known him four or five years, Mr Aatish, he's letting you stay in his flat and you don't know what he does?'

'It's hard to say,' I mumbled aimlessly. 'I'm not sure he does anything.'

They looked at each other. The little one's beady eyes flashed and the big one leant back in his chair with a shrug, as if to say 'How can we help someone who won't help himself?'

'Then how can he live?' the little one asked, of his own accord.

'Perhaps he's well-off.'

'What?'

'Perhaps his family is well-off.'

They both looked away in disgust.

'You say Mr Bahador is not in the country so how did you get into his flat?'

'He sent me his keys with his driver to Isfahan.'

'Who was this driver?'

'Mr Sadeghi,' I answered, sad to drag his name into this.

'What's his number?'

'I'm sorry, I don't know it by heart. I have it at home.'

'He's based in Isfahan?'

'No, Tehran.'

'You said he picked you up in Isfahan.'

'Yes. He came from Tehran to Isfahan in order to pick me up.'

'Mr Aatish, you have a mobile phone in Iran.' This was not a question.

'Yes, I'm borrowing one.'

'What's the number?'

'I can't be sure, but I think it's . . .' As soon as I said it, I knew I'd made a mistake. I had given them a variation of my passport number, which began in a similar way, but I couldn't bring myself to correct it.

He wrote down the number and examined it closely. 'Where did you get this phone?'

'It's also Bahador's.'

'He gave you his phone?' the little man asked, always with his tone of incredulity.

'Yes.'

'How did he give you his phone?'

'Mr Sadeghi brought it to Isfahan.'

'Mr Sadeghi had his phone?'

'Yes.'

'What is Mr Sadeghi's phone number?'

'I told you, I don't know it by heart. I have it at home.'

'How much did you pay him?'

'I don't know – maybe sixty dollars?' I had spoken in a tone of exasperation and they eyed me as if to say, 'Watch it.'

'Mr Aatish, what is your purpose in Iran?'

'I'm writing a travel book. I've been travelling from Istanbul by land and hope to finish in India.'

'What is the book about?'

'It's a travel book based on my impressions,' I answered, hoping to find a middle route between Hosseini's suggestion and my actual purpose. 'I'm interested in religion and culture.' Religion had been an innocuous way of approaching more sensitive subjects in other countries and I hoped it would be the same in Iran.

'Did you have an interpreter in Iran?'

'No, I didn't,' I answered, thinking of all the interpreters I nearly had.

'You didn't need an interpreter?'

'No, I didn't.'

'Why? Do you speak Farsi?' The little man's face gleamed.

'No, but I'm just travelling through, recording my impressions, talking to people where I can. I haven't been doing interviews.'

'Mr Aatish,' the little man began, with an assertiveness that suggested someone who took pleasure in language and the sound of his own voice, 'we hear that you have been asking about religion, the changes in religion, and politics somehow.' I nearly smiled: it was a glorious, subtle formulation, encapsulating perfectly the closeness of religion and politics in Islam and the Islamic Republic, just in case I was confused.

'I've been asking only about religion, not politics,' I answered, with failing conviction.

'You were seen attending the Friday sermon given by Mr Rafsanjani.' This was not true, but it was nearly true. I had asked Payam's friend to take me to the Friday sermon at Tehran University. If the interrogators knew this, they would have overheard it on the telephone, and if they had been tapping my phone, they knew a great deal more.

At this stage, I made a mental shift from thinking of this as a short interrogation to just the first stage of a much longer detention.

'No, I did not attend the Friday prayers.'

'You were seen there.'

'That's impossible,' I said, with as much conviction as I could muster. 'I wasn't there.'

'Have you been visiting any seminaries in cities like Mashhad and Qom?' Now, a further wave of doubt came over me. Had they spoken to Reza?

'No.'

'But wouldn't you like to?' the little man asked patronisingly. 'They're very interesting for your work.'

'Yes, I would,' I answered, seeing no point in lying. 'I was hoping to go to Mashhad tomorrow night. But I've been to other places too.'

'Where?'

'I've been to Shiraz, Yazd, Isfahan . . .'

'From Tehran?'

'No, I flew to Shiraz and worked my way up.'

The big man got up and walked out of the room for a moment. The little interrogator's tone became suddenly friendly. 'Which city did you like the most?'

'Yazd,' I smiled.

'Why Yazd?' he asked, now sly again.

'I liked the desert nearby, the colour of the buildings, the Friday mosque.'

The other man walked back into the room. He spoke to the little one, who nodded. 'Mr Aatish, don't you need someone to arrange your travel for you, buy your tickets?'

Now I was sure they knew something about Reza. 'No, I do it myself.'

'All of it?'

'Yes – why not? For instance, I bought my ticket in Dubai for Shiraz. The hotel in Shiraz organised the car to Yazd.'

'How much did you pay him?' he asked, always relying on the relentlessness of his questions to wear down his subject.

'Oh, I don't know! Same as the other one – forty or fifty dollars?'

They looked between themselves, mean and dissatisfied.

'Mr Aatish,' the little man said, with his special sarcastic voice, making me feel as though I was in a Dickensian orphanage, 'you do know that you must always tell us the truth?'

'I am telling the truth,' I cried.

'I hope so,' said the little man, putting down his pen and rifling through some papers. Then, looking up, he added, 'For your sake.'

I became subdued and a new cycle of questioning began.

'Mr Aatish, how long have you been travelling for?'

'Since November, so six, seven months.'

'How did you have the money to travel?'

'It was my own money.'

'Yes, but who gave it you? A newspaper, an organisation or are you also "well-off"?'

'Yes, my family gave it to me,' I lied.

'Your father?'

'My mother, actually.'

'Where are your parents from?'

'My mother's Indian and my father's Pakistani.'

'What does he do?'

'He's a businessman.'

'What kind of business?'

'Telecommunications.'

'And your mother?'

'She's a writer.'

'In India?'

'Yes.'

A kind of fatigue set in. The interrogators looked thoroughly unhappy.

'Mr Aatish, why are you doing this trip in Iran?'

'I'm exploring the lands of my father's religion,' I said, surprising myself with how pompous I sounded.

'You are Muslim?'

'Yes!' I answered hopefully.

'Sunni or Shia?'

'Sunni,' I replied, realising too late that this wouldn't help me in the least.

'Mr Aatish, you know you have a tourist visa. You're not meant to be writing a book and asking questions. When you're a tourist, you just see the sights and then go home. Do you know what you've been doing in Iran is illegal?'

'No, I didn't. I was just talking to the people I met on the way.'

They looked at me sadly. I had no idea how much more they had up their sleeve. They told me to go out for a while and Hosseini was called back.

Hosseini was in for a few minutes, then came out, shaken. Poor man, I thought, he was too old to go through this. He made out that nothing was wrong. 'They're letting me go,' he said quietly. 'They want to ask you a few more questions. It's nothing. Should I wait downstairs?'

'Yes, please,' I said, hoping that it really would be 'nothing'.

They called me back into the room with the frosted-glass windows. Sitting behind the desk, from which the women in black had shuffled off like birds, now nearly two hours ago, they watched me as I sat down on the straight-backed chair against the wall.

'Mr Aatish,' the little man sighed, 'we hope you have thought about your answers and are now willing to tell us the truth. Do you have something new for us?'

'No,' I said, with fresh conviction. 'I'm doing a travel book. I've been travelling from Istanbul to India and I spoke to people on the way. That's all.'

'Mr Aatish, do you know Ms Violet?'

Of course! That was what this was about. Violet, the agency journalist who had introduced me to Jasib.

'Yes,' I said, slightly broken.

'How do you know her?'

'She was introduced to me by the Rahimis.'

'By whom?'

'My Iranian family friends.'

'They introduced you to her?'

'Yes.'

'What is your relationship with her?'

'I've only met her a few times.'

'When?'

'For dinner and for lunch.'

'When was the last time you saw her?'

'A few days ago.'

'When?'

'Two or three days ago.'

'What was the exact time?'

'I'm not sure, about noon.'

'It was only a few days ago. Try to remember.'

'Noon on Friday?'

'And what was the occasion?'

'We met some friends of hers.'

'Who?'

'Humeyra and her husband.'

'Their full names?'

'I don't know.'

'What do they do?'

'They're artists.'

It had been a very strange lunch full of expat Iranians who had recently moved back to Iran. Everyone spoke French and English and the lunch had become very drunken. Madonna played. A homosexual in a printed shirt danced close to a small, voluptuous woman. There was something childishly defiant about Madonna in Tehran, especially late in the afternoon. The gay man said, 'I hate this fucking revolution. Why us? It's not fair. Why not Turkey? We just picked the wrong number.' He enjoyed provoking me. 'We're waiting for the Americans,' he hissed, 'waiting for bombs!'

'And the time before that?' the interrogator asked.

'I met her for lunch.'

'Did you meet anyone with her?'

Now I could see what all this had built up to.

'Yes. We met a friend of hers who she thought could be a guide for me in Tehran.'

'Jasib!' the big man exclaimed, as he had done with Bahador at the start of the interrogation.

'Yes,' I replied.

He emitted a satisfied grunt. 'Mr Aatish, you've had no problem in the other cities, why did you need a guide here?'

'No, I've had no problem,' I answered, pretending to misunderstand him.

'Yes, so why did you need a guide here?'

'The other places were small cities, more manageable. Tehran is vast. I thought I'd need some help.'

They seemed content with this explanation.

'So he was your guide?'

'No, his English wasn't good enough. I met him once and that was that.'

'Mr Aatish, when did you arrive in Tehran?'

'On the fifteenth.'

'So, two weeks ago?'

'Yes, about.'

'Two weeks in Tehran! What did you do for so long?'

'I met my family friend, saw the city, saw how people lived here.'

'For two weeks! What did you see?'

'I saw your palaces, the Gulestan, Sadabad,' I said, reaching in my mind for other tourist destinations. 'Your crown jewels, the national museum, the museum of contemporary arts.'

'And what else?'

'The museum of ceramics?' I managed. 'Which used to be the Egyptian embassy.'

I could see from their bored expressions that they already had what they were looking for.

'Can we see your mobile phone?'

I handed it to them. It was the worst moment in the interrogation because I knew, now that they were through with me, they wanted to go after all the people who had helped me in Iran. I recalled Desiré not giving names under duress. 'I don't know all the numbers in it,' I said, trying to make up for the cowardice of handing them the phone. 'It had some from before.' Fortunately, none of the names had surnames and I could pretend I didn't know them.

'You have a number in here that says Bahador's flat,' the interrogator asked, 'but it's a mobile-phone number.'

I asked to look at it and saw that it was the number of my mobile phone. 'This is the number of my mobile phone.'

The bigger man examined his sheet and shook his head.

The little interrogator said, 'But this is different from the number you gave us.' He read the number back to me.

'No, that was a mistake,' I stammered. 'I told you I might make one. This is the number of the phone. You can try it if you like.' For a moment, everything seemed to hang in the balance. Then they returned to the phone list, writing down all the names and numbers.

When they came to the end, they looked up at me and a neutral silence fell over the room.

'You would like an extension?' the man said at last.

'Yes, I would have liked an extension. I would have liked to travel more.'

'Why is your visa issued in Damascus?'

'I was there when I needed it. I've been getting them as I go along.'

'Did you get your Pakistani visa here?'

'I had that from before. My father's Pakistani.'

'What will you say about Iran?'

'Very positive things. I liked it very much.' I wanted to add, 'Until now!' 'I hope you'll let me come back.'

'Did you take notes?' he asked, ignoring the question
'Yes.'

'On paper or the computer?'

'On the computer,' I answered, with relief at having got rid of my notebook.

'How many pages on Iran?'

'I'm not sure, eight to ten.'

'What will you write about Iran?'

'Very good things, I've really enjoyed my time here and wish I could stay on.'

'And you have Mr Sadeghi's number at home?' they asked again, making me think they would come for both that and the notes.

'Yes.'

'And where do you go next?'

'Pakistan.'

'When?'

'Well, in the next day or so, I only have two days.'

'And then you finish travelling in India?'

'Yes.'

They handed me back the phone and said, 'Have a good trip.'

'I'll try.' I smiled, walking out of the room, half expecting to be cut down before I reached the door.

*

That night as I drove to the airport I felt a childish excitement at leaving Iran. My last hours in the Islamic Republic, and the nature of my departure, gave me a sense of escape. It made me feel the country's impoverishments more acutely. I would never have believed I could look forward so much to the freedom of the Dubai Duty Free.

Earlier I had gone to the flat for the last time. It was quiet, as always, and the windows showed another spring storm building over the hills. I packed all my things and went to Payam's house. The storm broke later that afternoon. Reza called and I agreed to meet him for coffee. The sky was black when I crossed the busy main road in front of Payam's house and the wind made the new leaves on the trees cling to their branches.

The coffee shop was in an open-air arcade. Reza arrived, looking sombre. He said he would have our tickets refunded and was sad I was leaving. He asked me what flight I was on. I didn't tell him I was booked on the Emirates night flight to Dubai. I didn't want to trust anyone: I was still worried they would come after my notes.

The three-hour interrogation covered every aspect of my shortened trip to Iran. When I looked back on the transcript of my interrogation, drawn from memory as soon as I left the country, I was amazed by its thoroughness. The questions that seemed incessant, and cut with fear in the interrogation room, were now a helpful way to retain everything about my time in Iran. Every car I hired, every kilometre I covered, every person I encountered made its way on to the interrogators' notepad. They took my phone, wrote down every name and number in it, making me fear for those who had helped me and now could end up in more trouble than me for the generosity they had shown to a visitor. I had vowed to tell the truth, but seven months of travel from Turkey to Iran can sound incredible. In the closed-off world of Iran, these strange, doubtful threads seemed to excite the interrogators' worst suspicions. At times, even as the interrogation was going on, I was grateful for it, grateful that I did not leave Iran disarmed, unaware of the regime's constant presence in the lives of the people I liked so much.

Then came that formulation I could hardly believe: 'Mr Aatish, we hear that you have been asking about religion, the changes in religion, and politics somehow.' Politics somehow! All the faith's inability to deliver in the modern sense was contained in that 'somehow'. What I had discovered in Iran, and had sensed in Syria, was how violent and self-wounding the faith could become when it was converted from being a negative idea, a political and historical grievance against the modern world, into a positive one.

I had wanted to see what Butt and Abdullah's vision of Islamic completeness looked like when it was implemented in a modern society. In Iran it had been, and its small, irrelevant rules were turned on the people to serve the faith's political vision. For the faith to remain in power in a complex society, it had to beat down the bright and rebellious members of that society with its simplicities. In the end the big unpurified world won anyway, but terrible hypocrisies took shape: short marriages were condoned to allow prostitution; lashes were bought from the municipality as if they were no more than gas bills; and little girls were sexually taunted because Islam forbade West Highland terriers.

We drove through a velvety, smoke-filled night and passed a great white arch that looked as if its base was caught in a wind, causing it to fan out on all sides like a frock. The driver said it was the Azadi Monument. '*Azadi*' – 'freedom'; one of the many words that Farsi had in common with Urdu.

Imam Khomeini airport at that hour was deserted. The imam would have liked it the way I saw it: its sparseness, white lights and purple seats, its porters in red waistcoats gliding across the sparkling floors, or dozing against a trolley, gave it a heavenly aspect. To me, it was menacing. It stood for all that I had learnt about the Islamic Republic in the last twelve hours: brutality wrapped in godliness.

The airport was not real; it was a showpiece. The real airport was down the road and handled most of the air traffic in and out of Tehran. It was there that the noise, grime, long queues and commotion of other airports collected. None of that was permitted in the tube-lit serenity of the imam's airport. It was a symbol, more shrine than airport. It was big and modern, ablaze with fluorescent light; every surface spoke of newness. It didn't matter that the world had to be kept out for it to look as it did. The ideal was achieved – the simplicity, the quiet, the decorum – and that was all. It didn't matter that the ideal served, the Islamic perfection, had played no part in its construction. It was like the Islamic Republic in miniature: a violent imposition of religious perfection on the modern world, driven to illogic.

I bristled when I presented my passport and visa to Immigration, with its rude notation in red, stating that I had two days to leave the country. But the young woman inspecting it was unfazed and put a red-domed exit stamp over the blue one that had allowed me entry into Shiraz twenty-five days before. As the announcement for the Emirates flight came, and a small group of passengers walked on to the jet-way, I noticed some young female Tehran–Dubai regulars. The scarves were already slipping.

Continuities

It was July in Delhi, 2002, when I made up my mind to visit Pakistan for the first time. The rains had broken, and for a short spell the air was hot and gassy; earthworms were flooded out of their holes and the fruit from *neem* trees, the same fat berries of my childhood, lay mashed in the wet earth. I was twenty-one.

All summer Indian and Pakistani troops had brooded on the border in huge numbers, and though foreign diplomats had been evacuated, and news bulletins flashed with talk of nuclear conflict, the joy and lethargy of the rainy season felt too deep that year to be interrupted by the sound of war. I'd wanted to go many times since the abortive phone conversation with my father, but was prevented by being at college in America and by worsening relations between India and Pakistan. This time, seeing a lull in hostilities, I decided I'd catch the cycle at its trough in case the next one was deeper still.

Getting to Pakistan from India in those months posed so many practical problems that meeting my father for the first time became more of a logistical challenge than an emotional one. There were no flights, trains or buses between the two countries, and it looked as though I would have to fly to Dubai, and from there to Lahore. This seemed complicated and expensive so I went to see the acting Pakistani high commissioner in Delhi to ask his advice. The High Commission, a blue-domed mausoleum of a building, enveloped in afternoon gloom, was deserted, like some embassy of a former ally after a revolution. I found the acting high commissioner surprisingly receptive to my problem. 'Why don't you drive?' he suggested.

'Isn't the border closed?'

'Only to Indian and Pakistani nationals. You have a British passport. I can give you a visa and you can cross by land at Wagah.'

By land! I thought. That moody frontier! It seemed impossible. I grew up thinking of the physical border as a land fault, a crevasse in the earth spitting fire. I would cross that border in a car?

'No, not in a car,' the acting high commissioner said. 'On foot.' Apparently, I could drive up to the border, but then would have to walk across it and someone else would have to meet me on the other side. With that, the high commissioner had a little blue and purple rectangle stuck in my passport that read: 'Islamic Republic of Pakistan, 28 days, Multiple Entry'.

'Do say hello to your abbu for me. I know him,' he said slyly, handing back my passport. 'They have a very nice farm near Lahore.'

My mother was not in Delhi at the time, but offered her full support for the trip. She called a friend of hers in Pakistan, also a friend of my father, to ask if I could stay with her. The friend said she would be happy to have me and would send her son to the border to pick me up.

I thought my mother must have suffered at my going, both out of concern for my well-being and for her own makeshift peace with that time. 'Just remember, my darling,' she said, 'you'll find him charming, interesting, very funny, but he'll always let you down.'

That morning, my flat in Delhi was dark and quiet, except for the dull hum of the air-conditioner. The marks of the morning were apparent. A crack of light came from the kitchen where Sati, the servant, moved around before anyone else; a Thermos of coffee had been left for me on the dining-table; newspapers lay unopened on the floor.

Sati came out of the kitchen when he heard my footsteps. I had been at university for many months and he still beamed at seeing me after so long. He handed me a blue polythene bag with my breakfast in it.

'Is Keval up?' I asked.

'Yes, he's in the car.'

Downstairs, it was a beautiful, clear dawn. The rain had come and gone, and though the night faded from one pale patch in the sky, no direct light had crept in yet. The brightening of the day could not be separated from the adjusting of the eyes.

Keval sat in the car, smoking a cigarette. When he saw me come out, he brought the car up, with no more fuss than if he were taking me to school.

'*Chalo* Pakistan,' I said, as if we were refugees in 1947.

'*Chalo* Pakistan!' he chortled.

We drove through the Delhi of roundabouts, long avenues and white colonial bungalows. Long stretches of dark, empty road, with off-duty traffic-lights, gave way to a headlight parade of trucks. Keval would accelerate until he was just inches behind one, and its bright, painted colours were visible, then he'd sidle over to the right to see if it was safe to overtake. Sometimes he'd overtake with oncoming headlights close in the distance, slipping between yellow lights and coloured trucks. We passed factories and warehouses, agriculture marooned in every corner of free space, until we were only among fields. I remember falling asleep just after we drove through the city's red stone gates.

When I woke up, a heavy pink sun was blanching fast. Salmon, gold and saffron light seeped into the hot haze, lifting from green, waterlogged fields. The town we drove into was Ludhiana. It was a town of cloth mills, and the evidence of this was everywhere. The industry invaded the inner streets. Rough mountains of fabric were heaped precariously outside every shop so that only wholesale purchases seemed possible. Trucks, with sack-cloth posteriors, bursting with cotton, clogged the town's narrow arteries. The bypass was under repair so highway traffic, impatient from recently moving at a steady pace, now inched behind the cotton trucks. Bicycles, two- and three-wheeler scooters completed the chaos, driving one little wheel into any opening. But for the porous fortification of open drains, the only indication of municipality, the street caved in on itself. Ludhiana itself was a town inside out, in which factories and highways sprung up in its centre and the people lived outside.

It was the first large Punjabi town we passed through. In my own complicated situation, Punjab was a way through the confusions of nationality and religion. My father was from Punjab across the border, but so was my mother's Sikh family. There was Punjab in India and Punjab in Pakistan. It was like a network of cultural familiarity that stretched over the two enemy countries. It was made up of language, song, poetry, clan affiliation, and a funereal obsession with certain tragic romances. Decades after Partition, it clung on, like the rods in a crumbling building, bent, mangled, but somehow, still fierce. More than India, it was Punjab that was divided to make Pakistan, and the pain of it was felt acutely on both sides.

There was a time when my entire journey from the moment we left Delhi would have been through Punjab. But what was left of the state in India after Partition was further divided into three smaller states. So, of the state that once stretched from Delhi to Kabul, only a patch remained in India, carrying the name Punjab. And when my father first saw Indian Punjab, all those years ago, he said, with characteristic delicacy to my mother, 'We got Punjab, you got the foreskin.'

There had been a substantial monsoon, and in this river country, every little stream and canal ran unsteadily, like an over-full glass, to drop-off points in the fields. The villages we drove past were single-storey brick constructions containing a surprising number of auto mechanics and chemists. The rains did the job of the municipality, producing a large patch of wet black mud, which served as a town square. Vegetable sellers, tea stalls and outdoor eating places fought for space. The idle-ness of cows and buffaloes seemed to rub off on the people, who lazed on rope beds.

Stout yellow and white milestones now read 'Jalandhar'. A functioning bypass swept away the town, and a cement bridge took us across a wide, muddy river. The Beas. One of the five rivers of Punjab, two of which remained in India, and from which the state derived its purely Persian name: *punj*, five, and *ab*, water; five waters.

Then, abruptly, in this landscape of fields, tractors, canals and red-brick houses, a road sign read: 'Lahore 43km.'

'Forty-three kilometres!' Keval cried. 'I could drive there in less than an hour!' Until now there had been no indication of the closeness of the border, and I hadn't expected to see any before Amritsar.

Keval was still shaking his head, his crooked protruding teeth frozen in a grimace, when the road took on a new aspect. It was no longer the busy run-down highway leading to Amritsar, but a leafy dual-carriageway with little traffic. Its construction and maintenance bore the unmistakable mark of military effi-ciency. The first signs of an army presence were soon visible: cadets and young recruits peered inquisitively out of the back of their camouflaged trucks; the Border Security Force's bases appeared, and some of the army vehicles turned into them. Their high walls, with bright bougainvillaea hanging over them, suggested army schools and peacetime routines. The occasional armoured car appeared, but there was nothing threatening in its heavy tread. The entire place possessed an old-fashioned cantonment atmosphere of good food and officers' evenings.

The only unnatural element was the fields: the massive, unending expanse of agriculture, which threatened to engulf the neat academies and bases that had been set up so incongruously on its stretch. These fields, heavy with rice and water, so removed from everything, seemed strange things to defend. Keval and I pushed on along this unexpected road, eaten up by fertile land, until we came at last to the moody frontier.

It appeared like a roadblock, at best a scenic stop, to interrupt the land's flat expanse. Hawkers and agents fell upon the car, selling soft drinks and postcards of the border-closing ceremony. It was a difficult moment for Keval and me. I felt bad at having to leave him behind. I also felt a degree of fear because I couldn't see into Pakistan and wasn't sure if my mother's friend's son would have come to pick me up. Keval registered my nervousness and said, 'No reason to worry. I'll wait for you for an hour until I know you've crossed.'

Shooing off hawkers, he led the way past the car park and refreshment stalls and through a small black gate. Here, an attendant asked for our passports. Keval gave me a tight hug and sent me off.

Through the gate, I could see the lavish excesses of the governments' imagination. A pink amphitheatre had been constructed where spectators at the daily border-closing ceremony could sit. It consisted of an exchange of huffs and salutes performed in symmetry by the Indian and Pakistani sides. Then two gates, painted to look like iron flags, were slammed shut before a hooting crowd. It was a choreographed piece of officialdom, a military extravaganza for the bureaucrat. Two concrete arches stood at equidistance from the open gates. In their shade, two men from the respective sides sat with ledgers in their laps. Someone had gone to a lot of trouble to finesse these symmetries in concrete.

I was ushered into a cool, dark office on the Indian side where a man inspected my passport. Then a coolie in a blue shirt and white pyjamas pushed my bag through an X-ray that wasn't switched on. I picked it up at the other end and was directed out of the office on to a bleak stretch of road leading up to the arches. The great trees of the sub-continent lined the road: dark green mango, frangipani, pale eucalyptus, dour, drooping *ashok* and the patriarchal and sacred *peepal*. Among them, appearing intermittently, were rusty billboards advertising Pepsi. Following the coolie, I saw the fields again. A great black two-faced fence, with a stooped back and tense barbed wire, ran for miles through them. On the other side, past the barbed wire, the fields continued. The morose screech of a koel broke the quiet.

When we reached the Indian arch, I saw in the ledger that the last person to cross had been a Nigerian some weeks before.

The coolie walked a few yards further, past the short shadow cast by the arch, to where another coolie in identical white pyjamas, but with a green shirt, took my bag from him. The exchange was made with so little ceremony that its meaning was nearly lost on me. The coolies' faces, tired and lined in the same way, next to the detail of their ragged shirts in different colours, seemed to mock the place. After the pomp before, that was all: I was in Pakistan.

The gate on the other side was of rust-coloured brick, with cream crenellations and turrets. In gold Urdu letters a sign read: 'Gate of Freedom.' Above it, the green – the darkest of all greens, a black forest green – and white of the Pakistani flag raced in the wind.

In the old-fashioned colonial offices on the other side, the reception was warm. They read the name in my passport and asked, unprompted, 'This is the People's Party Salmaan Taseer?'

'Yes,' I answered.

'You're not carrying alcohol, I hope?'

'No.'

I knew that my father was well-known in Pakistan for his political role, and later his businesses, but not the extent of it. Sitting in those shaded offices, heat and heavy trees outside, I knew that I had set in motion one of the biggest decisions of my life.

Then an unsettling exchange occurred. One of the men, effusive and warm at first, asked in Urdu, 'So, what brings you back this time?'

Urdu and Hindi were hardly different so I replied easily, 'Not much, boss. Just my friend's birthday.'

The hospitality evaporated and they stared at me in silence.

One of the men repeated the word I used for 'birthday', and suggested another. Then, he said, 'Oh, you've come from *India*?' The differences between the two languages were very slight and, growing up in Delhi, my language was heavily influenced by Urdu, but I had used the one word that only someone who grew up in India could have used.

And so it was that I took my first steps into Pakistan aware of my unique patrimony, knowing at once familiarity and unfamiliarity.

Renaissance Now

Karachi, Pakistan, four years later. My arrival in Pakistan was sudden and unplanned. Two weeks ahead of schedule, I was on an Emirates flight, covering the short distance from Dubai to Karachi. We flew like a small plane, close to the land, sometimes over bright blue water, sometimes over desert, before dropping toward the Indus's saline mouth and the hard yellow land of Sind.

I chose Karachi, rather than Lahore, because I wasn't ready yet to see my father. I was also thinking of his letter and wanted to travel in his country before making my way north to him.

It was my first time in Karachi. The highway that brought me into town didn't bring me far enough for me to have a feel of the city. I expected a noisier, more congested city, more like Bombay or Tehran, but the city we entered was spread out, with empty residential streets. Long, unshaded main roads connected little markets and offices to colonies of golden-brown, California-style bungalows, with green, reflective-glass windows. There was in the hot breeze, the listless neighbourhoods, the bungalows, with large balconies, and the bleak, grid-like streets, here and there with the cowering shadow of a palm on them, seeming to rise to a distant point, and then dropping, a hint of the sea. There was also, in the high walls of houses, armed guards standing outside, white cars with tinted windows, through which it was possible to make out the silhouettes of body-guards, a hint of crime.

There was some talk of my staying at my father's guesthouse in Karachi, but my elder half-brother, whom I hardly knew, insisted I stay with him. He lived in one of Karachi's newer bungalows. It was a small, well-proportioned house, sparse and functional, with a large balcony. Most of the day it was quiet, except for the hum of an air-conditioner. Large Indian blinds kept the sun's blaze out and gave the little house a permanent feeling of afternoon. My brother ran it like a bachelor's home, with a single servant who brought up beers, lime water and meals on TV trays. I had a basic room, with a narrow bed, next to my brother's, which, after all these years of being an only child, gave me a taste of living with siblings.

I felt unexplained tenderness for my brother. My father and he had always had a complicated relationship, often related to my father's disapproval of the women he dated. I sensed damage in my brother, the kind that can sometimes occur in children whose parents have been too powerful or too successful. After years of being my father's heir, of being told who to marry and who not to marry, groomed at the best schools and universities in Europe, he was about to find himself, at the age of thirty-five, beginning life alone in a country where connections and influence were everything. He had known about me for many years before that first trip to Pakistan, and perhaps because of our troubled relationships with our father, we shared a special connection.

After Iran, and my sudden arrival in Pakistan, I was happy to rest for a few days. I felt the delayed strain of my night flight from Iran, of connections made and hours lost. I wanted to put off travelling, calling my father, and even thinking too much about Pakistan. But on that first evening, I had a fore-taste, among educated Pakistanis, of a great double-edged tension. As India came up again and again, in big and small ways, sometimes through caste references, sometimes through Bollywood, I was reminded, as I had been unexpectedly four years before at the border, that I was a stranger in Pakistan.

The evening I arrived, my brother was holding a business meeting. It was for his own pet project, a half-hour comedy show that dealt with the week's news called *The Cutting Edge*. Those present were the two hosts, an attractive single mother in her thirties and a paunchy, older man who was the star of the show. There was also a young, pretty girl, with an American accent, whom everyone called 'Princess', and a dark, effeminate man, who was just sitting in. The targets for the satire beyond what was in the news were Bush and Islamic fundamentalism; the General was liked and spared.

That day there had been a news item about a study by an American think tank that placed Pakistan at nine in the top ten failed nations of the world. The study was based on a number of indexes ranging from 'chronic and sustained human flight', to 'criminalisation and delegitimisation of the state', to 'progressive deterioration of public services' and 'rise of factionalised élite'. The year before, according to the same report, Pakistan had been at number thirty-four. The group now worked out how to tear apart the report on the show.

'We want to be number one,' the dark, effeminate man cooed. 'I hate competition.'

Another asked where India was in the list.

The effeminate man rolled his eyes and his gapped teeth closed over his lower lip. 'Why can't we just accept that they are a better, greater country?' Everyone looked at me and laughed.

'Is it my imagination,' my brother said, 'or are there just many more ugly people in India?'

'Yes!' the effeminate man hissed. A short discussion began about how ugly Indians were, especially in the south. I listened for a while, then mentioned that some of India's best-looking models and actors come from the south.

'Well turned-out,' the effeminate man said archly. 'Not beautiful.' Then suddenly, he thought I'd taken offence, and said how much he loved India and that he was there recently. 'But I really gave it to them for running after the Americans,' he added, lifting his limp wrists to his chest and making the sound of a dog panting. He was referring to the nuclear deal that America and India were working out.

The next news item was about a threat from fundamentalist groups, saying they planned to host parties for young, liberal people in order to bomb them.

'They're hitting us where it hurts,' the attractive presenter said.

'We've been to these parties,' my brother nodded. 'This is serious.'

They decided it was so serious they wouldn't satirise it. At most they would say, 'Islamabad, you needn't worry, but Karachi and Lahore, beware.'

The next news item said that ten Americans had been killed in Afghanistan. 'I know this is politically incorrect,' my brother said, 'but *yesssss*!'

There was some stray laughter, then the group set to work on how to satirise the American 'occupations' of Iraq and Afghanistan. The middle-aged presenter said they had to keep up a sustained campaign against George Bush. A song was devised. It was a spoof of 'This Land'. 'This land is my land, this land is *not* your land . . . from Iraq to Guantánamo Bay,' or somesuch variation.

My brother said that the programme was creating a sensation. He was very pleased that many of the jokes were too sophisticated for the censors to catch, jokes such as the attractive host yelling, 'It's coming, it's coming, it's coming, I'm coming!' and faking an orgasm on television.

'But you really have to do it properly,' someone said. 'Can you go through with it?'

The female presenter smiled uneasily and nodded, like a great actress agreeing to do all that was necessary for a part.

Many of the show's jokes were too sophisticated for me to catch, some mismatch of what the show's creators had picked up at university in Britain and America. My brother hoped the programme would be shown in other places. Apparently, networks in India had expressed interest. He asked me what I thought. I told him it wouldn't work. It would be difficult to air a show that so many people wouldn't understand.

'Yes, but what about your small niche audience?' my brother asked.

'It's not as influential as it is here.'

When everyone had gone, the servant brought up a few beers and I sat for a while with my brother. In Karachi, there had recently been bombs. There were often bombs in Karachi, but this was more serious. A suicide-bomber had come into a prayer meeting of a Sunni political group on the Prophet's birthday and, along with himself, blew up the group's leadership and nearly sixty other people. The tensions the bombing brought to the surface revealed divisions and sub-divisions of denomination, language and sect that were hard even for Pakistanis to follow. There was not just the Sunni–Shia divide, but identities within identities, and corresponding political parties. And then, of course, there was the perpetual tension between the old inhabitants of Sind and the *Muhajjir*, the Muslim immigrants from India, who came in 1947 to realise the dream of a homeland for Indian Muslims.

'It's a different religion,' my brother said of Shiism, 'make no mistake. It's linked to a state, like Israel, and Iran can draw the loyalty of Shias worldwide, over and above the loyalty to the country their passport says they're from. They say they have seventy thousand Shias in Pakistan, armed and ready to strike US interests, which include Pakistan. If they don't have seventy thousand, they at least have a thousand! And that will cause chaos in Pakistan.'

The post-9/11 climate affected him more than I thought. It came out as excitement at Pakistan having become an international story, and instead of encouraging reflection into the reasons for the country's new fame, it brought out a kind of exhibitionism.

'There's a feeling of total civilisational defeat,' he said.

'What civilisation do you have in mind?'

'European, non-European, Christian, non-Christian, Caucasian, non-Caucasian,' my brother answered.

'It's interesting that you don't think of your civilisation as Indian,' I said, now feeling directly, as I had with my father, that the 'Civilisation of Faith' stood between me and someone I felt culturally close to.

'Yes, that is very interesting. There has been a complete rejection of the sub-continent.'

'But do you consider it your own, a part of your history?'

'No, we don't own it,' he answered. 'I'll tell you. No matter how much education a Pakistani gets, his mindset is fixed at the age of ten or eleven. If you write in your exams that the devious – you have to write devious,' he said, noticing my surprise at his use of the word, '– that the devious Hindu did this and did that, then you pass.' Not religious himself, but perhaps questioning his own convictions, my brother continued, 'At a certain time in Europe, learning and education were in the hands of the religious orders. Perhaps here, too, some kind of renaissance could begin with education in the hands of the religious orders.'

A renaissance! The revival of the great Islamic past in Pakistan. It was the country's present darkness, what my brother said earlier, 'the feeling of total civilisational defeat', the contents of the American think tank's report, that made him dream of renaissance. In his excitement, he forgot what constituted the kind of renaissance he was thinking of. He forgot the industry of those European monks all those centuries ago, translating books from Arabic into the European languages. I'd been to enough *madrassa*s in my life, in enough places, to know that the majority not only ignored books outside the Islamic past, they ignored the Islamic thinkers too; they taught only one Book. Pakistan, the country founded for the faith, never part of the tradition of high Islam, always, culturally, an adjunct of Persia and Arabia, the country that today supplied the oil-rich sections of that world with its menial labour, was alone left to believe in a great Islamic future. And with that belief came always the unsaid horror of India.

*

Karachi was a British city and hardly older than a hundred and fifty years. Until the 1960s, it was one of the cleanest, pleasantest cities in the sub-continent to live in, a city whose older inhabitants remembered the streets being washed in the mornings. But immigration, and the transfer of the capital from Karachi to Islamabad, initiated its decline, leaving it today riddled with armed crime, sectarian strife and its old British streets in ruins. In the most crowded sections, cluttered with mean, bright little billboards, chemists, 'footwear' shops, electrical appliances and mangled nests of wires, there were the remains of the city's finest buildings.

Behind one pale yellow façade, exquisite with sleeping columns, little raking cornices, blackened dentil ornaments and balustrades, the actual building had fallen away. Through the mask-like façade's semi-circular windows, it was possible today to see the white open Karachi sky. In the street of elegant buildings, domes and clock towers were barely hanging on, and in many the second storey was sealed with splintering sheets of plywood. Scattered across the old British city were Karachi's squat administrative buildings and hotels, many with 1970s patterned concrete screens in front of them so that they looked as if they had no distinct levels or windows.

The Sind Club was in this part of the city, and women were not allowed into its billiards room and bar, not for Islamic reasons but for old-fashioned colonial ones. Uniformed bearers glided through the high-ceilinged room, bright where light escaped from low shades over green felt tables. They brought members the Scotch and soda that the club kept for them under lock and key. There were hunting trophies on the walls, a smell of kebabs in the air, and from the lights in the garden, I could see waterfalls of red bougainvillaea. I'd gone there with my brother a few evenings after I arrived. We sat outside with some businessmen at a round table under a portico of sturdy arches.

'I saw you the other day at the airport,' one stout man in a silky shirt said to another sitting next to him.

'I wasn't there,' the other, taller, more sober, replied.

'You were boarding a first-class flight to Dubai.'

'No.'

'You were complaining about your air miles and saying you had nine hundred million in your account.' The man who had initiated the conversation, seeing the confusion on the other's face, guffawed, 'It's a joke, man!' Then he became confidential and they began to discuss a deal. I heard him say, 'You approached me about it when I was drunk, but if you're serious you can have it for thirteen million.'

On certain nights of the week, the club went a little further and organised a dance called Casablanca. In a darkened room, a disco light threw red, green and pink patterns on the walls. Waiters in white, with red fezes, moved quickly through the room, serving girls in little black dresses and paunchy men in fussy shirts. Through a glass partition close to the ceiling, it was possible to see a library of sorts, not a great library, but like something you'd find in a school, deepening my sense of being at a middle-school dance. A Bollywood hit song played several times over, filling the dance-floor each time.

A cousin I had recently met yelled over the music, 'She assaulted him three times. One time she tore his shirt and twisted his Bulgari cufflinks. Her family are *choodas*!' She was talking about her brother and his wife, but what interested me was her use of '*chooda*', which was used like the word 'nigger', to mean low-caste. But in Islam there was no caste. My cousin, who used the world freely, as did my brothers, grew up with it. It had resonance all over Pakistan, but many people used it without knowing where it came from or that it denoted caste. It was part of an unacknowledged carryover from India. It was like the song that brought everyone to the dance-floor.

But these commonalities, these memories of plural India, were not always easy for Pakistanis to take on. They were a hazy reminder of what had been lost. Pakistan's assertion of Islamic identity was not the theocracy of Iran. It was through purifying its population of non-Muslims, conducting the transfers of people, of which my maternal great-grandmother had been a part, that the new state realised its aims. But India, on the other side, was still as it had been, still plural, not symmetrically Hindu and with as many, if not more, Muslims than Pakistan. And there was no escaping the strangeness of that.

The Bombay film industry was a powerful reminder of composite India. It was full of Muslim stars and the Hindustani language it kept alive was replete with Urdu words. Though the films were officially banned in Pakistan, 'unofficially', my brother's dark, effeminate friend explained, 'Hindi films are released on

Fridays in India and the same night – the same night! – via piracy, they release in Karachi!' It meant that Pakistanis had a view of India every day in their homes. The reverse was not true. Pakistan's once significant film industry had sunk. The cause of its demise was like a roll call of the country's tragedies: the loss of half its audience when East Pakistan broke away to become Bangladesh, Bhutto's economic nationalisation in the 1970s and Zia's Islamic censorship in the 1980s.

'We used to have fifteen hundred cinemas,' my brother's friend moaned, 'and now we have some two hundred.'

He was worried about the tighter hold of religion in Pakistan. 'In Punjab and Sind,' he said, 'our Sufi culture will save us, but I worry about the North West Frontier Province and Balochistan. They could flood us. Otherwise, we are deeply immersed in our Sufi culture. And also our diversity will save us.'

'Are you religious?'

'It depends by whose definition.'

'By your own?'

'Well, I say my prayers and pray to Allah that I win the lottery. People say that that's gambling, but I say, 'Hey, thank Allah.' Then as if remembering what he had said earlier, he added, 'I think it's because they're LMC and there's a lot of guilt.' 'LMC' meant lower-middle class and it was a term rich Pakistanis used often to mean a rising section of the country that was also more religious. The remark was at once flippant, an aspect of his bitter wit, and significant. 'Guilt,' he went on, 'is the reason people are turning to religion. Many rich people made their money by illegal means and now they feel guilty.'

Corruption in Pakistan was something one always heard about, but I had never thought of it before as something for the religious imagination to seize on. Later, I would meet many admirable young people who made these kinds of connections.

'Your mother is a Sikh,' the effeminate man continued, 'but do you know that sixty per cent of the *Guru Granth Sahib* was written by Baba Farid?'

Farid was a twelfth-century Sufi teacher and his writings are included in the Sikh holy book, but the figure was an exaggeration. 'The tolerance!' the effeminate man hissed. 'The tolerance! That period should have had a renaissance, and it's all because of the white man, all because of him.'

The white man doesn't mean well for us. Nearly six decades after the 'white man' left, this weak refrain was all that could be found by way of self-examination. But it was not enough to blame the white man. It didn't explain why the white man's world should have posed such an affront to Muslim India and not to non-Muslim India. With my special feeling for undivided India, I would have liked nothing more than for the period he described to have a 'renaissance' – how strange it was to hear the word twice in such a short time from different people – but how could it when even men like my brother dreamed of Islamic renaissances in *madrassa*s?

The party came to an end. Men in blue and brown safari suits, seeming like chaperones, appeared and oversaw the winding up. The girls in black dresses and their short, paunchy men, the country's 'factionalised élite', staggered out. The waiters in white became scarcer, then appeared with dishcloths, and were bald under the fezes they now carried in their hands. A small sadness, as at the end of a children's birthday party, prevailed. And finally, just before everyone was gone, bent, old women, in white cotton *salwar kameez*, their faces tired at this late hour, came out with plastic dustpans and little brooms to sweep up the broken glasses and cigarette butts, the remains of Casablanca.

*

Soon after arriving in Karachi, I called my stepmother. She was warm and welcoming, as always, and said that, despite the heat, Sind's interior was very romantic. It was where I was intending to travel before I made my way up to Lahore. After we talked of the small regional towns and the important shrines I would visit, she said, 'Call Abba.'

'I will.' Then I squirmed.

'No, call him,' she stressed.

I thought up a few conversation points that would see us through the first few minutes of stilted conversation and called him. He was quiet but not unfriendly. I told him about Iran and my planned travels in Pakistan.

When I received my father's letter the year before, I knew nothing of Pakistan and even less about Islam. I wanted now, through travelling in Pakistan, to answer the second challenge his letter had posed, even though the two seemed in important ways to coalesce: of understanding 'the Pakistani ethos'. In the month in which I would travel, moving from south to north, I wanted to understand my unfamiliarity in Pakistan. I felt that this would help me understand the differences that had come up between my father and myself. My upbringing in India, together with seven months of travel in the Islamic world, formed a kind of Venn diagram, a problem in set theory, in which Pakistan, carved out of India in 1947 for the faith, was a common set between India and Islam.

My father listened to my travel plans, but there were no questions or comments. Before he hung up, he said, 'Call if you need anything.' And that was all.

Four years after our first meeting – and one, since the letter, spent in silence – I felt the thinness of our relationship.

Nerve Blindness

That summer of 2002, I crossed the border and my mother's friend's son met me on the other side. I could make him out, standing by his car, in tight jeans and a close-fitting shirt. He had gelled hair and reflective sunglasses.

We drove away from the border in his air-conditioned car. The country that opened up, of mud chimneys, canals full of bathing children and small, congested neighbourhoods, with bright-coloured Urdu writing on the walls, might have been a Muslim neighbourhood in India. It seemed so familiar that one expected the diversity of the Indian scene to reveal itself. And when it didn't, it was unsettling. It really was an India for Muslims only.

The other feature of the landscape that troubled the eye was the absence of women. On the other side of the border, women had been riding bicycles – some in Punjab, with long plaits, had been on scooters and mopeds – but here, in crowded places, I could see thousands of men, many dressed like the officials at the border in *salwar kameez*, the same macho ease about them, but few women. When women did appear, they were either with other women, moving purposefully, as if with little time to spare, or with their men on an outing. There were no women waiting at bus stops, on their way to work, or canoodling with men in parks, or leisurely enjoying the weather. Their presence, slight as it was, seemed to be a matter of permission.

As the car entered the sections of Lahore built since Partition, I saw a strong resemblance to Delhi: dusty greenery, lazy flyovers passing from one quiet residential neighbourhood to another, the diffused sense of the city.

I was to stay with Nuscie, a friend of both my mother and my father. She lived in a large, whitewashed house off a main road. It was run the way houses in regional towns in India ran, with many servants, food at all times, long afternoons and family coming and going. Nuscie turned out to be a warm, hospitable woman with a keen sense of intrigue. She had fair skin, bright green eyes, and the lines on her face seemed to come as much from laughter and mischief as age. And like her greying hair, they emphasised her once considerable beauty. She had met my mother through my father and they remained friends despite my parents' separation. She had always wanted me to meet him, and took me in knowing that he would be furious with her for helping me to do exactly that.

'Would you like me to call him first?' Nuscie asked, sipping tea, her eyes dancing with excitement.

'No, no, no, Nuscie, you mustn't. It's very important that an element of surprise works in my favour or he'll have time to back out.'

'Yes, of course, that's what I was thinking.'

I had cast aside earlier notions of just turning up at my father's house and introducing myself. It was totally impractical: there would be too many servants, guests and family to achieve the result I had fantasised about. In all likelihood, even if I was let into a room in which my father was, it would be full of people where my only line of introduction would be a stammered 'I'm Aatish Taseer.' I also found fault with my plan to meet my father on my own terms, anonymously, at a dinner party. I imagined we would spend many minutes talking, before he discovered I was his son. Absurd though they seemed, now that I was really in Lahore, these were some of the bizarre, cinematic ways that, as a child, I imagined our first meeting to be like.

Finally, against my imagination and with the dread of failure still in me, I realised I would have to telephone my father again. The thought of it aroused the worst feelings of disappointment in me. I had a superstitious fear that the bad luck from the time before would work against me. But I could see no way round it. No sooner had I decided on this course of action than, again, the foreignness of the place descended on me. Here I was, having travelled for fourteen hours to arrive at a near-stranger's house to make one telephone call that could end in anti-climax.

Once I resolved to do it, instinct told me to get on with it, as quickly, and with as little interference, as possible.

I excused myself and asked permission to go to my room.

'Yes, of course. You must be tired. Have a rest. Tonight we can go to the old city for dinner. There's a lovely little place there.'

I was not in the least bit tired; I was terrified. With meat patties and tea as the only weight holding down my body, I left the room. No sooner had I let the door close behind me than my eyes raced in search of a telephone, as if it were the antidote to my desperation. I went over the lines I had prepared, not caring any longer for their meaning but only that I was able to say them without my voice wavering. 'I can understand . . . why you may not . . .' I mouthed, as I saw the bright red instrument. I had written the number on a small chit, and held it now, tightly pressed between two fingers. I found the phone in a quiet corner between the drawing room and the kitchen. I was too restless to sit so I stood, leaning against the doorway, yawning with nerves. I dialled the number, and again, as I had years ago in my housemistress' apartment, hoped that there would be no answer.

The number this time, procured from Nuscie, was for a mobile phone. I took advantage of the personal access the technology afforded and began to talk mechanically as soon as I heard a voice.

'Hello, Salmaan. This is Aatish Taseer. I am in Lahore now and would like to see you.'

There was a brief silence and my father, as if his response had been years in the making, said, 'What would be the objective?'

I was grateful for the sting it caused. It gave me the indignation I needed. As long as I didn't give in to rudeness and insensitivity, I would retain the higher ground. It didn't feel like a tender reunion with my long-lost father but a contest, a Saturn and Jupiter fight to the finish.

'I can understand,' I started slowly, 'why you may not,' no waver, 'want to see me, but it is important to me that I see you, if only for a short time.'

He said nothing.

'Will this be possible?' I asked, in a still steadier voice.

'I'll have to think about it,' my father said. 'There are many things to consider.' He hung up.

I had failed to secure a meeting with my father. The anti-climax I was warned of had come and it felt worse than I imagined. I thought of my mother's words, 'Just remember, he'll always let you down,' and felt a kind of dread at having to face the other people in the house.

But that night my half-sister intervened. I bumped into her at a 'GT' – short in Lahore for a get-together – to which Nuscie's son had taken me. We spotted each other among a handful of attractive young people, dancing close together in a small, dimly lit, drawing room. I had met her once before in London. It was in 2000 after she sent me an email, having discovered that I was at college with a friend of hers. We met a few months later and liked each other very much. But my father was enraged when he found out. And as my sister was moving back to Pakistan to work for him, she couldn't afford to be on his bad side. We hadn't spoken since.

But seeing me now, unexpectedly in Lahore, she was full of warmth and affection. She said we would see each other over the next few days, even if we had to meet secretly. I told her of my conversation with our father; she said she would help, but couldn't tell how he would react.

Then, two days after my arrival, my sister called to say that my father had agreed to meet me. She would pick me up the next morning and take me to him.

*

I met my father, for the first time in my memory, at his low, red-brick house in the cantonment area of Lahore. It had a large lawn, and a Land Cruiser brooded outside the front door. My sister led the way in, but disappeared almost immediately, with a smile and a supportive wave. I stopped at a large pencil portrait of my father as a young man. It gave me my first real sense of being in his house. It seemed to have hung there for years and it emphasised my absence from his life. To see the old yellowing portrait, which had been made at roughly the same time as my pictures of him had been taken, was to know that he had lived and that I had been elsewhere.

A moment later a servant showed me into his library. It was a room with floor-to-ceiling books and windows overlooking a swimming-pool. On a slim, marble table there were family pictures in polished silver frames. The physical resemblance of the people in them to me was another reminder of my absence. It was as if a kink in time and space had air-brushed me out. I didn't feel emotional or even nervous; I was overwhelmed by the unreality of the moment. Tea and sandwiches laid out on a tray seemed to mock me.

My father walked in a few minutes later with his young wife. Her hair was blow-dried and she had diamonds in her ears. He was in blue, wearing soft boots with tan insides. I noticed them because my mother would tell me he had weak ankles and bought expensive boots. Though I couldn't have known it at the time, I must have sought to bridge the time when she and I had known him with the time now. It was why I asked his wife if she would leave us alone. It was perhaps also why the pictures and the portrait had unsettled me.

My father's physical appearance riveted me. The man who walked in was a fatter, balder version of the man from my browning silver frame. I had seen him last when I was not even eighteen months old and had no image of him except from those old pictures. I noticed the light, greenish-amber eyes that my mother had described to me, the lines around the mouth that were like mine, and the way he dropped into his chair, uncaring of where his hands and legs fell. I would have liked to know what he smelt of.

I must have been in some state of shock because I can hardly remember a word that was said. I know that I wanted very quickly to provide him with good reasons for why he hadn't been in my life and offered his political career, which he took up readily. I also made a point of saying that now that he was no longer in politics, perhaps it would be easier for us to meet, even if we couldn't have a conventional father–son relationship. This, too, he accepted. And then we spoke of generalities: my journey, the differences between India and Pakistan, how similar the two countries were. I felt the conversation was stilted, but I didn't realise how much more open it would seem when compared with our later conversations. My father asked after my mother and said he had no hard feelings towards her. It was almost the only time in our relationship that he acknowledged I had known him in the past. It helped me to ground myself in the present situation.

Then, as we got up, he asked if I had any questions for him. I had many, but felt that since the meeting had gone well and he seemed open to seeing me again, there would be time later. But when his life in Lahore, the life I had not been part of, closed around him again, he was less willing.

The Mango King

'I feel I've made a mistake in my attitude to Pakistan,' I said to the publisher. 'I arrived treating it as just another country. I was still thinking of Turkey, Syria and Iran when I got here. But I feel now that I'm more invested in Pakistan than I thought. I need to see more of it.'

He frowned and his eyebrows collected tightly above his eyes. He was a heavy man in a white *salwar kameez*, with short greying hair and moustache. His face was large and pinkish and his eyes intense. He published a major Pakistani newspaper. My mother had put us in touch, and though he wasn't sure what I was writing about, he seemed to understand my urgency. He did for me what I would have liked my father to have done: he insisted on my connection to Pakistan, the land, deeper than the border that divided India and Pakistan. He made no outward attempt to do this, but by arousing my interest in the cultural bonds that still existed between the two countries, in speaking to me of my paternal grandfather, an Urdu poet, in the pre-Partition years, and, most importantly, by communicating his own feeling for my situation, the publisher gave me the other side of the romance of an undivided India on which my maternal grandfather and my mother had raised me. Here was Pakistan, a whole country of unexplored connections. But where to begin?

Karachi, though it was the closest thing to a representative Pakistani city, was not like Istanbul was to Turkey or Tehran to Iran, not a city where a fifth or a sixth of the population lived. No one knew the exact figure, but a rough estimate put it at 16 million in a country of about 160 million. Pakistan, unlike any other country I had been in so far, was largely rural. People had said to me, 'You don't know the soul of Pakistan till you know feudal Pakistan.' And charged by the desire to see this feudal life, I asked the publisher if he could help.

We sat in his grand old Karachi house. He lay on a very high bed, smoking, dictating itineraries and making phone calls to people who might help me. The most famous twentieth-century Indian and Pakistani artists covered the high walls of his room; boxes and precarious stacks of books lay on the floor. The house had long dark corridors and whole wings seemed to be closed off. After a few hours of messages left, phone calls returned, lists made, lectures on safety and extreme heat, the publisher looked up at me, scribbling as he spoke. 'Can you leave tonight?'

'Tonight?'

His fierce, pinkish face, the face of a man used to getting things done, fixed on mine; something twitched. He seemed to show disappointment and anger that I had wasted his time and betrayed his romantic vision of travelling in the country of the Indus, of Mohenjodaro, of Sufi shrines and the oldest Indian civilisation.

'Yes,' I stammered. 'I can leave tonight.'

'Good.'

It was early evening when I went back to my brother's to pack my bags. I was to leave late that night with the Mango King for his lands in interior Sind.

*

I had dozed off on my brother's beanbag when the Mango King called to say he was outside. I looked at my watch and saw it was well past midnight. I picked up my bag and went downstairs. A warm breeze was blowing and the street, lit with flickering tube light, was quiet. A white car, with heavily tinted windows, stood outside. As I approached, one of its back doors opened, but no one stepped out. Instead, cold, air-conditioned air infused with a faint smell of cigarettes drifted out. I put my head into the car and saw a young man in the back seat, with a black moustache, fair skin and a handsome, slightly puffy, face. He peered at me through a dense haze of smoke and gestured to me to get in.

The chauffeur drove off as soon as I shut the door. I turned now to the Mango King, who lit another cigarette. The air was so smoky, so cold and unbreathable, and the black windows wound up so deliberately, that my first exchanges with him were a series of polite half-smiles, confused looks, gentle prodding, anything to steer the conversation in the direction of why we were driving in these conditions. The Mango King, if he registered my objections, showed no sign of it. He smoked continuously, slowly and deeply, looking out at the deserted streets. I could tell from his eyes and the thickness in his voice that he had been drinking.

'In the city I am a different person,' he said abruptly, 'and, you'll see, in the village I am a different person. One has to adjust. It gets pretty nasty,' he added suddenly. 'People steal water. Typical *vadhera*.' A *vadhera*, or landlord, was what the Mango King had become after his father died; his family were among the largest producers of mangoes in the country. 'But things won't change.'

'Why?'

'Not for another fifty years. There will still be feudalism.' I nodded and saw that he was drinking from a hip flask.

'Do you know why Sindi society is a failure?' the Mango King asked, in his abrupt way.

'No.'

'There's no middle class. There's us and there's them. We had a middle class, but they took off when what happened?' I thought it was a rhetorical question and didn't answer, but the Mango King's gaze held me, expecting a reply.

'Partition,' I answered obediently.

'Exactly. But, you know, life goes on, one day to the next. My father trained me to be a farmer.' The Mango King spoke in broken sentences, disconnected in thought and language. After a long silence, he said, 'Do you know why religion was invented?'

'Why?' I asked, wondering if some vague précis of my purpose had been passed on to him.

'A man can deal with everything but death.'

The Mango King lit up again, but this time my eyes focused on a new discomfort: an AK-47 was placed between him and me, and the ribs of its magazine, its short barrel, and bulbous sight shone in the yellow streetlight. The Mango King was silent now, still drinking and smoking. The car's cold, fetid air made me feel ill. The gun's silhouette came in and out of shadow as we left Karachi. I kept catching it in the corner of my eye, and as there was a lull in the conversation, I thought I'd ask why the AK-47, particularly, was so popular.

'Three things you have to be able to trust,' the Mango King answered. 'Your lads, your woman and your weapon. It'll never jam on you. Anyone can fire it and it'll never jam.'

I don't know when I fell asleep, but I woke up once to see the Mango King still smoking. The next time, he was asleep, his head bobbing from side to side, the gun still visible at his feet, matt black with occasional yellow lustre.

I fell into a deeper sleep and woke next when I felt a touch on my hand. It was dawn, and we drove down a deserted country road, amid acres and acres of flat, empty fields.

'The estate begins here,' he said. The car swung left. 'This, on both sides, is my estate.' I looked around and saw that there were only shrubs and small trees on the land, thirsty even in the half-light. 'This is the land I don't grow.'

'Why?'

'No water.'

'How big is it?'

'Six thousand acres.' By the sub-continent's standards, this was a large holding.

Then after some silence, he straightened his posture and, with pregnant solemnity, said, 'This is my territory.'

We passed several acres of dense, low crop, then just before the house, like some last battalion of a great regiment or a vanishing tribe of horses, seeming almost to smile at their own dignity in the desolate fields around them, were the mango trees. The Mango King stared in dull-eyed wonder at the dark green, almost black canopies, heavy with fruit and dropping low in a curtsy against an immense saffron sky.

As we came closer, the trees that seemed to have a single, pointed canopy, concealing their short trunks, were in fact distinct clusters of long, curled leaves, as though warped by the heat. Their contours contained a bewitching interplay of pigment and shadow. The fruit was small and mostly unripe, but the end of each was yellow as though some tropical poison gathered its reserves before overwhelming the whole.

When we got out of the car, I saw that the Mango King was tall and well-built. His cream *salwar kameez* partially concealed a new paunch, and like the puffiness of his face, it was unattractive on a man of his looks.

A few men were stooped in greeting. The Mango King waved at them, then stumbled through a doorway. We entered a walled garden of palms, droopy *ashoka* trees and buoyant rubber plants. A cement walkway, like a Pac-man trail, led to the house. The

Mango King's fluttering cream figure reeled, tottered, straightened, and lurched down the narrow path, as his servants and I followed. The walkway finished in front of a low white bungalow. Darkness and a musty stench from thick, beige carpeting hit us as we entered. I couldn't make out much of the house in the dim morning light. At the far end, there was a square arrangement of low sofas.

The Mango King collapsed into one, and stared vacantly at me, as if only now seeing me. I wondered what he thought I wanted with him. Among pictures of the family, and one of the Mango King in a yellow tie, there were many books: a pictorial biography of Hitler, *National Geographic*s, Frederick Forsyth, *Jane's Aircraft Almanacs*, *Animals in Camera* and dozens on travel. I felt from the books, and from the framed posters of impressionist paintings, a longing for other places; it was like a longing for clemency, in colour, temperature and degree.

'Did your father read a lot?' I asked, scanning the shelves.

'Yes,' the Mango King replied. 'He was the sort of man you could talk to about anything and he would always have the right answer.' The description suggested a nightmare person, but the Mango King hadn't intended it to sound that way. 'I used to read,' he added, 'but I don't get the chance any more.' He showed me a book he'd recently bought. It was a guide to being a gentleman. 'It says that a gentleman never adjusts his crotch in public.' The Mango King chuckled and then we fell into silence. He sat there, looking neither at me nor at his men, but ahead, into the gloom, like a man who had just lost all his money. A servant brought him some water and a new AK-47, this time with a drum magazine. He leant it against the leg of his chair and, turning to me, said that this one was Chinese; more than a hundred countries produced them now. He asked me if I'd like to fire one.

'Yes,' I said, surprising myself.

'She wreaks havoc when she opens her mouth,' he smiled mirthlessly. He was prone to theatrical utterances and to clichés like 'Different strokes for different folks' or 'You can take the boy out of the country, but you can't take the country out of the boy,' which he said as if they'd never been said before. The idea of firing the gun was forgotten for now.

My own fatigue deepened just as the Mango King had a second wind. He ordered wine and asked if I'd like some dinner. The wine was unusual in the sub-continent, whisky and soda would have been more standard, but this, like the cigars and brandy that came afterwards, and the guide to being a gentleman, seemed like a recent feudal affectation.

I laughed at the suggestion of dinner, as it was already dawn; he stared at me.

'No, thank you,' I replied, more soberly.

'Yum-yum,' he said, looking at the feast that was now being laid out before us. There were several kinds of meat, rice, lentils, bread and more wine.

The Mango King rolled up his sleeves to eat and I saw that there were cigarette burns branded into his arm. The cutlery was Christofle, scattered stylishly among the ovenproof crockery and dinner trays.

Two minutes later he asked again. I declined once more and said that I'd like to go to bed. He gestured to a man to show me to my room, and just as I was leaving, he enquired one last time if I wouldn't have any dinner.

*

When I awoke a few hours later, I was lying under a wooden fan, with an inbuilt light, and a small chandelier. Next to my bed there was a copy of *Time* magazine and a guide to nightlife in Thailand. The little room, despite the air-conditioning, was suffocating. From the edges of tightly drawn curtains, a white blaze broke through. It was about ten o'clock and the house was quiet. I stepped into the drawing room and felt a wave of compressed heat. The room could not have been more badly designed for the fierce temperature beyond its darkened, sliding doors. It was low, like a garage, heavy with carpeting and velvety sofas, and without ventilation. I stepped out on to a white tiled courtyard and soon retreated. It was dangerous heat, the worst I'd ever experienced, sharp, unshaded, asphyxiating. It could make you sick if you went unprotected into it. Yet to be back in the room, in the bad, stale air, was hardly better. Outside, buffaloes lay in the shade of trees; little villages of straw, with brambly fences, dotted the Mango King's lands; and slim, black women, in bright colours, with white bangles all the way up their arms, walked along the edges of mud paths.

After tea, breakfast and a shower, I came into the main room of the house to find that the Mango King was up and inspecting weapons. 'You can't get this on licence,' he said cheerfully, as the man brought out an Uzi. The Mango King was freshly bathed, his eyes alert, his manner sprightly in a way I wouldn't have thought possible the night before. The deadened glaze had gone from his eyes and his mind made connections easily. He seemed to read my face and sense that I might be a little surprised at the gun parade before lunch. 'A lot of people in Karachi don't like farmers,' he said. 'They say they're feudal, but my feeling is that there are good and bad people in every field.' Still fixing magazines, looking through sights, handing back guns, he said, 'Can you imagine? Even I was kidnapped.'

I thought he was being deliberately provocative now and, concealing my surprise, I asked casually, 'How old were you?'

'I was twelve and when I came back I was thirteen. It was from 1984 to 1985, for six months. I was chained for the last two. My father wouldn't pay the ransom. When they called he started abusing them so they only called once. After that, they dealt with my uncle.' The kidnappers had picked him up outside his school in Hyderabad.

The Mango King did not alter his short, offhand style. His point was not to emphasise the violence in his life but to make clear that he had paid his dues.

It was difficult to take anything away from the story. The Mango King drank heavily; he had suspicious cigarette burns on his arms; he played with guns; his father, who knew the right answer to everything, sounded as if he had been difficult; and yet what might have seemed like cause for alarm was presented instead as emblematic of the feudal life. The violence he had experienced, and perhaps inflicted, became like a rite of passage.

'Was it traumatic?'

'Yes,' the Mango King replied, 'but you get used to anything.'

His reply reminded me of a story my father once told me of being in prison in Pakistan. His jailers had put him in a metal cage in heat similar to the kind outside. Then they threw a leather blanket over the top and sprinkled it with water so that the humidity made the air even less breathable. They wanted my father to sign an admission of guilt, which they didn't bring him until several hours into the process of breaking him down. When finally they did bring it, he wouldn't sign. His explanation was that they tortured him for too long: if they'd brought it sooner, he might have signed, but once he realised he could bear the unbearable, new resolve hardened in him.

Like the Mango King's, it was difficult to draw a message of courage from my father's story. At most, and this in part was why my father told it, it could give an idea of what was needed to enter politics in Pakistan. But that kind of mettle could not be asked of everyone. It couldn't be made a requirement of office, like promising to tell the truth. Most people would bend and enter a state of corruption, which wasn't really corruption given the duress. In the end, the story could only be seen in its context, a vignette in Pakistan's Hobbesian political life. The extreme shows of defiance – not signing the admission or not paying the ransom – could also come to seem like bravado rather than courage when the people who endured them saw them as training rather than injustice.

That evening the Mango King suggested I go with him to Mirpur Khas, a nearby town, to meet a lawyer who was working on a case he was fighting. The sun at last was loosening its grip on the day and the land, stunned and silent for many hours, came to life with the screeching of birds and the movement of animals. The evening brought with it colour that, after the white blaze, made it seem as if the sun was sinking behind a mountain of prisms.

Driving out of the Mango King's gate, I noticed something I hadn't seen earlier: under the name of the estate, it said, 'Veni Vidi Vici'.

'We used to send mangoes to the Queen of England,' the Mango King said proudly.

'You should start again.'

'No,' he smiled, 'but we send them to Musharraf.'

In the car, the Mango King and his tall, thin lieutenant discussed feudal revenge. The lieutenant was a *muhajjir* or immigrant from India. His family came to Pakistan after Partition from Jodhpur in Rajasthan. The feudal life needed men like the lieutenant. He was dark and bald, with the aspect of a grand vizier, and after the Mango King's father died, he served the son as a loyal adviser. They talked about how another feudal had killed the Mango King's friend in an argument over 350 acres. The Mango King said that the other landlords still teased the dead man's son for having been unable to exact revenge. 'What can he do?' The Mango King laughed. 'His father's killer is hardly in the country, and when he is, he's guarded heavily. There's a Sindi saying: "Love and revenge never get old."'

'Don't the police ever get involved?'

'Not in these things. The people come to me with their problems and family matters. If you're the landlord, you're politician and policeman too. The landowner's word is law.' Then, thinking about it for a moment, he said, 'In the end, it's not even about land. It's about who gets to be head honcho.' I thought he put it well: land at last was stabilising; this was about arbitrary power and the Mango King was also vulnerable.

The Mango King's lieutenant had been back to Jodhpur just once, in 1990, and from the moment he heard I was Indian, he could speak of nothing else. He craned his long neck forward and asked if I saw much difference between India and Pakistan.

'Not much,' I said, meaning to be polite. 'There's more feudalism here.'

'But between human beings, on a human level?'

'No, not really.'

'But there is!' He smiled.

'What?'

'In Pakistan, the clothes people wear are much better. There's far less poverty. India makes its own things, its own cars, but then you don't get Land Cruisers. In India, you get Indian needles. In Pakistan, we get Japanese needles!'

In India you now got Japanese needles too. The lieutenant had visited before economic liberalisation, but that was not the point. What struck me was how this man, who would never come close to owning a Land Cruiser, could talk of such things as core human differences. The poverty around him was as bad as anything I had ever seen, yet he spoke of expensive cars. It was as if the mere fact of difference was what he needed. It hardly mattered what the differences meant: that was taken care of by the inbuilt rejection of India. In the confusion about what Pakistan was meant to be, whether it was a secular state for Indian Muslims, a religious state, a military dictatorship, a fiefdom, that rejection of India could become more powerful an idea than the assertion of Pakistan.

'What other differences did you see?' he asked.

'It's hard to say as there's so much change within India. There are more differences between the north and the south than there are between north India and Pakistan.'

The lieutenant was not to be put down. He wanted to get something off his chest. 'The other difference,' he began, 'was that while men here wear flat colours, the men there are fond of floral prints, ladies' clothes.' Hindus weaker, more feminine, and Muslims stronger, manlier: this was the dull little heart of what the lieutenant wanted to say and a great satisfaction came over his face as he spoke. This was the way he reconnected with the glories of the Islamic past, of the time when the 'Civilisation of Faith' remained and the martial Muslims ruled the 'devious Hindu'.

The heat that seemed inescapable earlier had lifted magically and the din of insects made its way into the car. The land around us was completely dark, but for the occasional tube-light over a small structure somewhere in the fields.

'Were you scared when they kidnapped you?' I asked the Mango King, hoping to hear the rest of the story.

'The first fifteen minutes were scary, but then it was all right.'

After many minutes of silence, the Mango King began again, with a new softness in his voice, 'They said, "Now, OK, say your last prayers," but fortunately,' he chuckled, 'they did not kill me.' After four months he had tried to steal a kidnapper's gun and use it on two of them, but just as he picked it up, the third returned and wrested it from his hands. That was when they chained him as punishment. It was painful to think of the Mango King, so hard now, in so vulnerable a position.

I thought he wanted to say more, but his lieutenant interrupted: 'Tell me,' he said, 'why do you wear a *kara*?' He was referring to the steel bangle on my wrist.

'Because my grandmother is a Sikh and wanted me to wear it.'

'Your mother's Sikh and you're Muslim.'

'No,' I said, wishing to annoy him, 'my mother's Sikh and my father's Muslim.'

'Yes, yes, so you're Muslim.'

'I'm nothing.'

The lieutenant seemed to ask the question in the most basic sense. He could tell I wasn't a practising Muslim, but he wanted to know if I was Muslim somehow, in the way that my father was Muslim. My experience with my father had shown that this vague sense contained passions I didn't share so I thought it better to dissent early rather than have to explain myself later.

'Come on, you're Muslim. If your father's Pakistani, you're Muslim.'

'If you say so, but don't you have to believe certain things to be a Muslim? If I don't believe, can I still be Muslim?'

He looked at me with fatigue. It was almost as if he wanted to say yes. It was as though, once acquired, this identity based on a testament of faith could not be peeled away, like caste in India. And really, I felt that if I could know the sanctity of his feeling of difference in relation to non-Muslim India, and the symbolic history that went with it, I would be as Muslim as he was.

'It's his decision,' the Mango King laughed.

The lieutenant fell into a moody silence. 'It's hotter in India than it is in Pakistan, isn't it?' he started again.

The Mango King groaned with irritation.

'No, it's the same!' I said. 'You see too many differences.'

Perhaps sensing that he had created bad feeling with a guest, he said, 'Sikhs have a very sweet way of speaking.'

'Their way of speaking is the same as ours!' the Mango King snapped, and the lieutenant retreated with a sad, stung expression.

Pakistan's economic advantage, the manliness of Muslim men, Land Cruisers and Japanese needles, even an imagined better climate: these were the small, daily manifestations that nourished a greater rejection of India, making the idea of Pakistan robust and the lieutenant's migration worthwhile. The Mango King didn't need the lieutenant's sense of the other. He was where his family had always been, sure of himself and, if anything, he felt the lack of the Hindu middle class that once completed his society. It reminded me of a story of a Pakistani aunt of mine: as a child, she had seen the waves of Muslim migration from India and said, 'Oh, look, the Pakistanis are coming!' The Mango King, unlike his lieutenant, hadn't migrated in search of a great Muslim homeland and found himself, still after six decades, an immigrant.

On the way into town, the Mango King explained the legal dispute. It was a complicated scenario in which the laws of the country, British law, with Islamic accents, came into conflict with the feudal agreements in his family. The Mango King's aunts inherited a small parcel of the land, which they wanted the Mango King to inherit, but as his cousins – with whom he'd had gun battles – would contest this, a spurious sale of sorts was organised, by which the land would come indirectly to the Mango King. The cousins were contesting the sale and the Mango King was looking for a way out.

The section of town we entered in moonlight had old-fashioned whitewashed buildings and tube-lit streets. Outside the lawyer's office there was an open drain from which a vast *peepal* tree grew at an angle, its prehensile roots threatening the foundation of both street and building. In the soft, pale light, the *peepal*'s long-stalked flat leaves with their pointed apexes were like little bits of silver foil, flittering noisily in the slightest wind. Under the tree, a man sold hot food from a cauldron of boiling oil and behind him colourful posters advertised a wrestling match. A bright red fire truck, with white Urdu writing on it, blocked the entrance to the lawyer's office.

The man inside the pistachio green room was like a caricature of a small-town lawyer. He was a squat, smiling man, with dimples, clefts and greasy hennaed hair. His eyes vanished when he smiled and light brown moles dotted his face and neck. His office contained a black briefcase, a glass-topped desk, green metal filing-cabinets and shelves stacked with volumes of *Pakistani Legal Decisions*.

He had been briefed about the case and, after offering us tea and soft drinks, he began immediately: 'You have two options, either of speaking the truth or . . . I've heard, sir,' he said, a smarmy smile lighting his face, 'that it is hard for you to tell a lie.'

The Mango King looked sternly at him. 'No, there's no such problem.'

'Another situation is that we tell the truth,' the lawyer said, shaking his head mournfully, as though drawing some pleasure from the foreplay of an illegal act.

'Please leave truth and lies aside,' the Mango King said. 'Let's just do what favours us.'

The lawyer, bowing from the waist, grinned. 'Are both women educated?'

'Yes, a little.'

'English-speaking?'

'Yes.'

The lawyer nodded sadly, feigning gloom.

'What difference does it make?' the Mango King barked.

'Because we could say the transaction was a fake,' the lawyer sputtered rapidly. 'The ladies did not understand what they were doing. We could make the plea that they didn't know what was in the documents when they signed them.'

'But then, wouldn't I, myself, end up looking like a fraud?'

'No, no,' the lawyer assured him, regaining his composure, 'you weren't present. We can say the ladies never sold the land. They received no monies.'

'But then you're making me a liar.'

'Just wait,' the lawyer replied, a tantalising smile coming to his lips. 'This is our ladies' plea. The court will accept it. We'll make this plea, but we'll have to tell lies.'

'Leave lies aside,' the Mango King snapped. 'Let's do what will help us.'

'See? The ladies will support us in this. We'll say the ladies knew nothing of this, that they were misguided,' he added, with relish. 'We'll have to interview the ladies beforehand and prepare them. I think this is better. There's more truth in it.'

'Leave truth—'

'No, no. One lie leads to another. Even smart people get caught out.'

'But they'll lie too.'

'Yes, but they have only one lie to tell.'

The Mango King looked as lost as I was. 'Does the judge accept bribes?' he asked. 'Can't we just bribe him?'

'He does in some cases and not in others,' the lawyer replied, as if delivering an official statement. 'But the other party can bribe him, too, so it doesn't matter.'

'Yes, but it shouldn't be that they just bribe him and close the whole matter. Anyway, so you think this is better?'

'Yes, because the women can speak the truth.'

'Leave the truth!' the Mango King roared. 'I want to do what will help us win.'

The lawyer, still smiling, winced. But I could see now that he was only interested in the truth because it made a simpler story for the old ladies to retell. 'Yes, yes,' he said. 'This will be easier to prove.'

'All right.' The Mango King nodded.

The lieutenant, who watched the rapid exchanges with keen interest, now said, 'Leave it. The case will keep going. You'll become old.'

'Can't we give them a little *danda* too?' the Mango King said, using the word for 'stick' to mean a beating.

The lawyer smiled serenely.

'The case will go to appeals,' the lieutenant said, 'It'll take ten years just there.'

'And if in twenty,' the Mango King asked, 'the court rules in their favour, how will they take possession of the land?'

'The police will come on order of the court,' the lawyer replied, defending the system of which he was a part.

'And if I resist?' the Mango King asked, seeming to threaten the lawyer.

'There will be cases against you, criminal cases.'

'Can the property be put in my mother's name?' the Mango King asked, then mentioned she was a German national, which created other problems.

'Why don't you get married?' the lawyer suggested.

'I have to find the right girl,' the Mango King laughed. 'Then I'll get married.'

We stood up to leave and the lawyer rose too, bowing and smiling.

Outside, the Mango King lit a cigarette. Turning to me, he said bitterly, 'Bloody feudal family disputes.' He seemed a little depressed and lonely.

In the car on the way back his lieutenant tried to convince him to get married. He said it would increase his strength.

251

'If we lose in the court, how soon can they take control of the land?' the Mango King asked, thinking aloud.

'We'll take it to a higher court,' the lieutenant comforted him.

'And if we lose there?'

'They can take control of the land, but then we'll bring it back to the lowest court on some excuse. Whole lifetimes go by and these things remain unresolved. You know you've done nothing illegitimate. And as long as you have done nothing illegitimate, Allah will protect you.'

What he could mean by 'legitimate' in this legal desert eluded me, but he seemed to summon up some higher notion of legitimacy and justice. The temporal example he gave a moment later was as ambiguous as the circumstances he'd begun with. 'Look,' he said, 'I'll give you an example. Nawaz Sharif tried to get rid of Musharraf in Pakistan and now Nawaz Sharif is in the black water.' But even as the lieutenant spoke, the general seemed to be heading towards 'black water' of his own, just one set of illegitimate circumstances replacing another.

'They've done a lot to subdue me,' the Mango King said.

'You just get married quickly,' the lieutenant said, trying to arrest the gloom that grew in the Mango King, 'and then you'll have a wife and an heir and at least they won't be able to say "he's all on his own." Your strength will improve greatly.' Strength was the right word: it was all that could make sense of the landscape around the Mango King. In the absence of a credible state, crude power, loose and available, was all there was to seize on to. 'Find a good relationship and get married. Aren't I right?' the lieutenant asked me.

'Yes,' I said.

'People are scared of my house,' the Mango King replied. 'Girls run away from it.'

'Why?'

'You know my pool in Karachi, right?'

'Yes,' I said, half expecting him to say it was having its water changed.

'Well, I had a party,' he said, 'and a guy drowned in it. And my cousins said that I paid money to the police and to the guy's family. Can you imagine? You have a party and a guy dies in your pool. It's terrible. And they say it's because I'm feudal. I think the guy was on drugs or something.'

*

That night I sat with the Mango King on his veranda drinking whisky-sodas and talking. Though occasionally I felt his pain, I didn't understand his world; I didn't think it was a world that could be made understandable to someone who wasn't obliged to work by its arbitrary laws; its brutalities were its own. The Mango King said that things wouldn't change and that feudalism would go on. He also spoke of the importance of the Hindu middle class who left in 1947 and in doing so identified the key component in the change that came to feudal India but not to Pakistan: the middle class.

It was India's middle class, its growth and energy, more than anything else that set the two countries apart. The power of the middle class in India dismantled the old feudal structures. In Sind, the cost of realising the purity of the Indian Muslim state was the necessary departure of Sind's Hindu middle class. The *muhajir* population that arrived in its place had not been able to replace its social function; the bonds that had held together the diverse society of Muslims and Hindus had not arisen among the co-religionists. And, without its middle class, Sind was not merely unchanged from 1947, not merely feudal: it was lawless, divided acrimoniously within itself; town and country were divorced from each other; 'the factionalised élite' that the think tank's report described had been created; and even men like the Mango King knew insecurity. The society had been dismembered.

The lieutenant, who had been sitting quietly on the edge of the veranda, now whispered slyly to me that he was a Rajput. This was another reference to the Hindu caste system, in this case high-caste, going deeper than Islam in Pakistan. But the lieutenant didn't know he spoke of caste. When I suggested to him that Islam, with its strong ideas of equality, forbade notions of caste, he became defensive and said that this was a matter of good and bad families. The Mango King thought it was tribe, but it was really caste.

'If you can have Rajputs, then you can have *choodas*,' I said, using the derogatory word for 'low caste' that my cousin had used on the night of Casablanca.

'Of course you can have *choodas*,' the lieutenant replied.

'Would you let your daughter marry one?'

'Never.'

'Even if he was Muslim?'

'Even if he was Muslim.'

On the one hand, there was the rejection of India that made Pakistan possible, and on the other, India was overwhelmingly at play in the deepest affiliations of Pakistanis, sometimes without their knowing it. It made Pakistan a country in which everything just existed because it did, eroded haphazardly by inevitable change. The country's roots, like some fearsome plumbing network, could never be examined to explain why something was the way it was, why the lieutenant, perhaps centuries after conversion, could still think of himself as a Rajput. And though I, with deep connections on both sides, could see the commonalities, they were not something to be celebrated: we spoke instead of difference. It was a country where you could imagine that, one day, no one would know where anything had come from.

Before I went to bed, the Mango King came to the end of the story of his kidnapping.

'Were you afraid they would harm you?' I asked him.

'Twice,' he said. 'Once when I tried to escape and the second time after my father had abused them and I heard them saying, "Should we bury his body or throw it in the river?" "I'm still alive," I was saying to myself, and that was pretty scary.'

Finally, after six months, the kidnappers gave him a bus ticket and released him in the Sindi town of Sukkur from where he made his way back to his father's house in Hyderabad. His hair had grown longer and when he got home, the watchman didn't recognise him. The Mango King said no ransom was ever paid.

When he was released they danced in the village. He went to get a passport photo taken, and the man in the shop had baked a cake for him. These were the details that remained with him after two decades. The whisky worked on the Mango King, at once deadening his eyes and bringing up unprocessed emotion. He'd gone to get a passport picture because he was going to Germany to see his mother for the first time in fourteen years. His separation from her was another secret in the life of the Mango King, but I had a feeling it was related to the father who always had the right answer for everything.

The next morning I left the Mango King's lands for Hyderabad. He was still asleep when I walked out, and even at that early hour, the small, musty house was filling with heat.

Contact Paper

The answers to the questions I had wanted to ask my father at our first meeting were a way for me to string the world together. I wanted, with whatever shred of common memory I could find, to close the gap between the world that ended in 1982, when my father left my mother, and the world as it was now that my father and I had met. I was ready to shuttle between two families in two countries, but it helped to know that they had begun as one life, just as it helped to know that the two countries were once the same country. Like slipping a sheet of clear contact paper over another, both with partial images on them, to make a complete one, I sought to stabilise the new world I had gained with the one I had always known.

Even as our relationship grew, my father seemed resistant to my efforts to bridge the two worlds. Between my first and second visits, a few weeks apart, when he invited me to stay in his house, the initial openness between us had narrowed. I asked him a question about a time when he had known my mother and he reminded me bluntly, 'I asked you when we first met whether you had any questions for me.'

On one occasion he mentioned the plane Murtaza Bhutto hijacked and the comment he made to the BBC. I had heard about the event from my mother. To hear of it now from my father filled me with a kind of child's wonder. It was like hearing about what your parents had been doing just before you were born. In an effort to bring together the two versions of the same story, I asked him where my mother and I were when it happened. My father's face soured. 'I don't know what anyone else was doing at the time. I can tell you what I was doing. I was getting away from the police, who wanted to put me in jail.'

Despite the gaps and silences, our relationship grew over the next four years, during which I became a regular visitor to Lahore. The more I went, the less I saw of the country or even the city. My father's house became my world in Pakistan. On my first visit I had met three siblings: my elder sister from my father's first marriage and a younger brother and sister from his present marriage; over the next few months, I met three more. They, and my father's young, beautiful wife, were full of goodwill and affection for me. Having grown up as an only child, I was so overwhelmed by suddenly having brothers and sisters that getting to know them took up much of my time in Lahore. I managed to sneak into some of the small, exquisite mosques in the old city, saw the important monuments, the museum and that fine stretch of red-brick British buildings, which were like a lesson in civic planning, but that was all. I went with my sister to many more GTs. I met fashion designers, Lahore beauties, and spent more than a few orange dawns eating hot meat in the old city. In summer, we'd end up in my father's mango-shaped swimming-pool as the muezzin's cry broke over the dark trees in his lawn. In those twice-yearly visits to Lahore, I felt at home and yet not, as if I was in a place I had been before but couldn't recall.

After university in America, I worked as a reporter for *Time* magazine, first in New York and then in London. During that time, my father and his family paid me a surprise visit in New York, and later I saw them regularly in London. Benazir Bhutto's self-imposed exile during the Musharraf years and my father's own electoral failures had distanced him from political life. Though politics was still his passion, he was now a far more successful businessman than he had ever been a politician. Still, some of the old embarrassment at having an Indian son lingered, and he was much more at ease with seeing me abroad than he was in Pakistan.

His embarrassment in Pakistan surfaced in small, telling ways. He prevented my siblings throwing a party they had planned for me; he rarely spoke to me at social occasions and never introduced me to anyone. I interpreted this as a hint that he didn't want to see me any more, but his family assured me that it was just his way and he enjoyed my visits. Sitting on worn sofas in his TV room, children and servants coming in and out, a drinks trolley in one corner, with an ice bucket on it, I felt that a kind of closeness had arisen between us. My father would often engage me in some long conversation about the great Punjabi Urdu poets of Lahore. His father was part of this milieu but died when my father was a child. Though it was never expressed, there was irony in our shared experience of absent fathers. He also let it be known that I was his only child who was like him – interested in books, politics and history – and though this also contained irony, it gave me great joy to have a kind of male approval I had never known. One last irony was that during a family holiday in Italy in 2005, a few weeks before the London bombings, before my article and my father's letter, and before the pain of the new silence between us, we were closer than ever before.

Sind 360: The Open Wound

It was a great relief to be on the road and independent of the Mango King's uncertain hours. It was from him that I gained an idea of Sind's composite society, complete with Hindus and Muslims. That completeness ended with the 1947 transfers of population. I looked now for what had taken its place. My father had spoken of the 'Pakistani ethos' in his letter, and with this in mind, I set out for the desert city of Hyderabad. My travelling was to be different from anything I had done so far. I wanted to avoid focusing on any one group but to see an array of life, a panorama, in a typical Sindi town. And for this I was meeting Laxman, one of the publisher's most trusted managers, on the outskirts of Hyderabad. My brother had arranged a driver, a dark, moustached man with kohled eyes.

The road to Hyderabad through the bleached, shrub-covered country was full of unexpected bursts of colour and activity. There were black flags with gold borders, their masts covered with coloured bulbs, commemorating the Shia mourning; tiny pink and orange figures of women working in sugar-cane fields; and green pools of water with children bathing in them. The shade of mango trees attracted old people in white and animals escaping the heat, including a hennaed donkey, with an impossible burden. The road was crowded with camels pulling carts, cattle crossing from one side to the other, and small, painted mosques, with grey loudspeakers, huddled close to the road.

We covered the distance at an irregular pace, stopping or slowing for varied traffic. At one point, we hit a little goat that the driver calculated would make way for him. I thought we'd killed it, but it picked itself up and, indignantly, with hardly any change in its pace, made its way across the road to join the herd. We passed a gold-domed and yellow-tiled Shia mosque, whose opulence among the surrounding thatched houses suggested Iranian contributions.

Laxman was waiting for us near a canal on the outskirts of Hyderabad. He was a stocky man, with thick, greasy hair and shiny black skin. He had a bristly moustache over a set of pearly, capped teeth. He greeted me in a furtive, hurried manner, and within minutes was organising me, making phone calls and giving the driver orders. He suggested we go first to a shrine just outside Hyderabad, where Sind's Muslims and few remaining Hindus prayed together. Sind's countryside was covered with the Sufi shrines of saints who were often honoured by Muslims and Hindus alike. They were part of a local form of Islam that served a once diverse society. It was this kind of worship that gave me the protective string on my wrist that the men in Mecca had minded so much.

An armed guard, who provided security to the newspaper's people when they travelled in the countryside, accompanied us. Laxman said the road was often struck at night by dacoits. Their ploy was to throw a stone or a bale of straw into the middle of the road, and to surround the car as soon as it slowed down. He said a man from the newspaper had been robbed recently. The dacoits had thrown a briefcase in front of the car. I didn't think that this was a particularly obstructive object so I asked him about it.

'He got greedy.' Laxman chuckled. 'He thought there was money inside it so he stopped.'

In the open land outside Hyderabad, a still, hot afternoon came to an end, solitude and isolation giving way to a more social hour. Children came out to play, truckers stopped for tea, and a wrestling match began in a clearing at the side of the road. Dozens of people gathered round a sandy ring, children watched from the branches of trees, and loudspeakers energised the crowd. The wrestlers, bare-chested and in tied-up *salwar*s, prowled around the edges of the ring, awaiting their fights. They were of varied ages and physiques, some young with slim, hard bodies, and others with heavy shoulders and barrel stomachs. It was clear from the dark brown welts on some of the younger men's backs that they were Shia and had flagellated themselves during the period of mourning.

The wrestlers had thick ropes tied round their waists. When their match was called, they approached each other as if about to give one another a low embrace. Then they grabbed their opponent's rope and began to pull. Sometimes one wrestler would do a kind of dance round the other, hoping to tire him out before leaping on him with all his weight and pushing him to the ground. At others, the heavier wrestler would engage the lighter one as soon as possible, entwining his more powerful legs round his opponent, causing him to lose his balance.

We drove past men on rope beds drinking tea, and boys playing in the hollow of a haystack, until the white shrine appeared among flat fields, dotted with large trees.

'It's proof of the Sufi time in Sind when Muslims and Hindus prayed together,' the driver said, as we approached. 'I think there's even a mention of it in the Indian movies.'

The story of the white shrine, with its turrets and little crenellations, was typical of what made the religious commingling of

Sufi India possible. An oppressive, fanatical king ill-treated his people, Hindu and Muslim alike, until the saint Oderolal, a white-bearded miracle man, arrived out of the water, preaching love and oneness, and used his powers to end the cruel king's abuse. He came to be loved by both Muslims and Hindus and, honouring his memory and message of unity, they prayed next to each other, though not actually together. 'Here the *azan* is about to be called,' a white-bearded man, in sunglasses and a red cap, explained, 'and there you can see Hindus are praying. That is the miracle.'

'Is it still like that today?'

'Like brothers. There is a lot of love.' He pointed me in the direction of a tree, which the saint had put down in the dry earth. 'That's the miracle,' the man said gaily. 'It needs no water. Look!' The leaves at the top are green.' The tree was in bad shape and I wasn't too surprised that it grew from a little patch of dry earth. Most of Sind was dry and only a few days before I'd seen a much bigger tree growing out of a building and a drain. The bearded fakir yanked down my head and said, 'Aatish, may you become cool,' then demanded money.

Laxman let out an evangelical cry and said, 'Ask! This is the time. Ask, if you ever meant to ask! Open your heart and ask!' The call to prayer sounded and a few Muslims on the other side of the white courtyard congregated. 'This was once the world!' Laxman said dramatically.

It was easy to see how the true relevance of a shrine like this would have grown from the society's former diversity. Unlike the idea on which the state was founded, here, the commonality of culture, language and local faith trumped doctrinal differences. One could imagine how it would have made the heart leap to put aside religious differences, Hindu caste notions or the Muslim horror of idols and images, in favour of a larger cultural unity.

In the white courtyard, under the shade of a *neem* tree, a

group of farmers and their families discussed something in low, serious tones. Laxman and I went up to them and sat down to listen. They spoke in Sindi and Laxman translated. They seemed upset. One man was saying, 'Conditions are so bad these days, we don't know how we can continue.' Having just been with a landlord, I was keen to hear what else they would say, but Laxman was in a hurry: it was evening and he was worried about dacoits. After some persuasion, I managed to get the farmer's problem out of him. Three young men from the community, sitting solemnly together on one side, had struck a deal with the landlord in the hope of improving their lot. They had his land from him at a fixed price, with an eye to cultivating it and keeping whatever profit they made from the crop. But that year everyone's crops had failed. The three enterprising farmers found that not only had they made no profit, they hadn't even made enough to pay the landlord his rent. They approached him and begged him to excuse part of their debt. The landlord agreed and said he would excuse them 40,000 rupees (some £490), leaving them still to pay 50,000 (£600). They managed to collect this amount, pooling together all that they had and borrowing the rest. But when they appeared at the landlord's with the money, he denied any recollection of their first meeting and demanded the entire sum.

Sitting in the shrine's courtyard, as they might always have done, the community elders, with leathery faces and white stubble, considered the dilemma. Children climbed over colourfully dressed mothers and the three young farmers listened in gloomy silence. They had just reached some kind of solution when Laxman insisted we leave immediately, promising to explain the meeting's conclusion to me later.

In the car, he murmured something in his alarmist fashion about dacoits. It was hard to sense the danger in the sociable, rural scene, but Laxman was convinced that just after we had left the shrine a group of men had taken a picture of the car on a camera phone, with the intention of marking us for robbery. I hadn't seen them, but the driver said he had and accelerated down the country road. We passed police posts on the way, which I pointed out to Laxman, but he said it made no difference: the police were in collaboration with the dacoits. The driver agreed and said we were running just as much from the police as from the dacoits. Then, looking at our bodyguard, he added tenderly, 'Don't worry, we don't think you're police.'

'It's always an inside job,' Laxman explained. 'First, the dacoits gave the police ten per cent, then the police started demanding more, twenty, thirty, forty. Finally it was *phipty-phipty*. Then the police said, "Why let them do it when we can do it ourselves?" So now the off-duty policemen are the dacoits.'

When we were safely on the main road to Hyderabad, Laxman relaxed and I was able to extract from him the meeting's conclusion. I understood now why I had missed it the first few times: its innocence was like a failing of logic. The elders had decided, since the landlord could not remember excusing the debt, to approach two of the landlord's friends who were present at the time the debt was excused. Surely they would remind the man of his promise. If not, the community would pay off the young men's debt. In any event, it was clear that they were ruined.

Did they really not know that the landlord lied when he said he didn't remember excusing their debt? Had it not occurred to them that the landlord's friends would lie too? Or that they would be beaten for trying to get round the landlord in this way? I tried to put the scenes of disappointment or, worse, open flailing out of mind. It was an affecting final image of feudal life before the city.

*

Hyderabad was older than Karachi. Stray images from lithographs of a great fort and the Indus ran through my mind as we entered it. The Indus still unseen! Almost a lost river for Indians as only a shred of it remained in India. There was something especially evocative for me in thinking of my longer journey as ending near the Indus.

The traffic into Hyderabad showed signs of a city whose organisation had broken. Hundreds of small industries gathered close to the road. Trucks, carrying anything from cattle to black electrical meters, clogged the main road.

'Why electrical meters?' I asked Laxman.

'They've been confiscated because they've been tampered with,' Laxman replied. Lost in his own thoughts, he suddenly said, 'Because of the problem in Karachi, I don't know if it'll be all right for me to take you into a Sunni shrine or *madrassa*. Even though they say,' he added nervously, 'that the MQM did it.'

The 'problem in Karachi' was the bombing that had occurred a few weeks before my arrival. Hyderabad was once a Muslim town, with a highly successful Hindu merchant community. It was a perfect example of the society, complete with its Hindu middle class, whose loss the Mango King had mourned. After 1947, much of that middle class left and made good in places as far away as West Africa. *Muhajjirs* took their place, and a great urban tension existed between Sindi and *muhajjir*. The MQM Laxman spoke of was the *muhajjir* party.

I tried to unpack the varied currents in Laxman's comment. 'Why would it be a problem for me to go to Sunni *madrassa*?' I asked.

Laxman, with an evasiveness that I was beginning to recognise in him, said, 'Well, don't tell them you come from Iran.'

'I don't. I was just travelling through Iran.'

'Oh, that's fine,' he said quickly, seeming to adjust his judgement of me.

The communal landscape was hard to make sense of. Difference of denomination, region and political affiliation were on everyone's mind.

Laxman had booked a room for me at the Indus Hotel. It was a modern place, on a bleak stretch of road, full of fake flowers and scenic pictures of places cooler than Hyderabad. He told me he would give me some time to 'get fresh', but almost as soon as we arrived, he was keen to get going. He wanted me to meet his bureau chief at the newspaper's offices. He even followed me upstairs, extolling the man's merits and usefulness to me. My room was reached by a transparent lift that was out of order, and overlooked the driveway and main road. The hotel's designers must not have envisaged it breaking down because the only staircase provided was a grubby service entrance.

The room had a large white plywood bed, with a satiny bedcover and thin, dirt-encrusted carpeting. As we entered, Laxman asked, unprompted, if I'd like some beer.

'No, thanks,' I said, finding the question strange, given the hour and that alcohol was illegal in Pakistan.

But he seemed to be trying to tell me something else. A moment later, he came out with it. 'There's no problem for me,' he said. 'I am a minority. I am allowed a permit.'

'What minority?' I asked, then felt like an idiot. Of course I knew that Laxman was Hindu, but outwardly the similarity between India and Pakistan was so great that my awareness of being in Pakistan had faded momentarily. I had stopped thinking of him as a Hindu in a state for Indian Muslims; I had forgotten about the transfers of population. But he, a member of a tiny minority, a remainder of the city's once great diversity, never forgot he was that rarest of rare things: a Pakistani Hindu. It made him want to know where everyone else stood and I saw now that the offer of beer, had, perhaps been a way to find out whether I was Muslim and, if so, how Muslim.

'What's happening underground will definitely burst,' he said mysteriously, as he loitered in the doorway.

'What's underground?' I asked, unpacking my bags, and truly confused by all this intrigue.

'Hatred,' he replied.

'Between whom?'

He looked at me, a suspicious eye-darting look, at once worried about who was listening and whether I was playing with him. 'Sindi and *muhajjir*.'

The road on which the Indus Hotel stood was called Cool Street. It formed, I discovered from Laxman as he bundled me out of my room, an enemy line between the Urdu-speaking *muhajjir* section of town and the Sindi-speaking Sindi section. On the way to the newspaper's offices, it was possible to see from the systematic organisation of the streets, and the occasional fine row of whitewashed buildings, with Hindu names and motifs, that Hyderabad was once an attractive town. And the black wires, starved animals, paper and polythene that grew over the scene only made its past harmony more apparent.

The newspaper's offices were in an old building, up a darkened flight of stone steps. Its wood and glass partitions, old furniture, typewriters and yellowing files seemed to have been unchanged for decades. The bureau chief was at his desk, a tall, elderly man, with thick glasses, deep lines on his face and neatly combed grey hair.

He was full of gloom. Minutes after we met, he launched into talk of religious and regional divisions, corruption, water shortages, feudalism and crime. 'The MQM is trying to start a problem between Sunni and Shia to have in-fighting while they keep their vote bank.' The religious parties, which came up under General Zia, have come of age, and are instilling in the minds of youth that death is imminent, and that they must fight the enemies of Islam. Crime is rampant: you can't go ten kilometres outside Hyderabad without someone throwing a stone in front of your car and taking your money at gunpoint. The Indus, which used to roar like a lion through Sind, is running dry.

'The Indus dry?' I said, hoping to stop the torrent.

'Yes,' he replied. 'There's dust flowing in it now.'

He was in a panic because some nights ago he had had to hold back the paper's printing to include the speech of the MQM leader. 'The district news must be finished up by ten,' he cried, 'because the page is laid out. But the story of the leader's speech was filed at a quarter to one in the morning and a paper like ours had to wait for it. We don't even wait for the president, but we had to wait for this story because they have Kalashnikovs in their hands so we are helpless. Just imagine one thing. Their leader had only a 50cc Honda and a small house, but he's living in London now. You know how costly that is, and with secretaries? Where is the money coming from? That is the question nobody in Pakistan dares to ask.'

I didn't know the answer. 'This is the worst time I've seen!' he cried. 'We've lived through difficult times, but this is the worst.'

'Why?' I asked, thinking of the Zia years.

'Because there's no faith in anyone. Someone becomes your friend and the next minute they stab you in the back. There are suicides because people are so short of money. The frustration is terrible.'

I spoke to him for nearly an hour, told him something of

my travels so far, and he offered to help me meet some people over the next few days. I didn't have a fixed plan. I was happy to be in other hands; happy to be shown what people thought I should see. We arranged to meet the following morning at the newspaper offices.

When Laxman and I walked down the dark flight of stairs, a sandstorm had begun on the once beautiful street. It cleared the crowds and traffic of a few hours before, and brown swirls of smoke and dust now pounced on little scraps of paper, and raced down the empty street. A purplish-brown haze made it seem later than it was. We drove over a truss bridge. Below there was a vast bed of white sand, reeds and a ribbon of green water. Laxman, looking down at it, shook his head. 'There were times when they would warn the residents on the shore to leave their houses because a flood was coming,' he said. 'And now, look, in the same river children are playing.'

His words didn't sink in immediately. Then, with the special horror reserved for something close to death, I turned again to look through the lattice of iron beams at the remains of one of the world's great rivers. 'That's the Indus?'

Laxman nodded. I told the driver to pull over. The car took a left and stopped near a large *peepal* tree, under which a man sold balloons and green-bottled soft drinks lay about on plastic tables. Steep black steps led down to the Indus. From just the height and gradient of the bank I could imagine what the river had once been. Halfway down the stairs, the strip of greenish water was lost in the white dunes and reeds. I walked for some minutes across the riverbed, over sinking sand, before I came upon it again. It was possible at this dusk hour to see the clear outline of the moon and this, along with the darkened sky and the wind blowing the green water in the opposite direction from the one in which it flowed so frailly, gave the scene a final, twilight aspect. A line of roaring traffic went by on the bridge many metres above. A small blue boat bobbed in the narrow strip of water, spanning half its breadth, and the river seemed, at once and ever, like a scene of beginnings and of endings.

Laxman crept up behind me. 'It's an amazing thing. We are standing in the Indus, not in a boat or anything, but in the Indus. People pray to this river. The Sindhu river! But where is the water? It's just sand.'

Laxman, the Hindu, thought of the river with the special, religious regard much of the sub-continent gave its rivers. In Sind, the story was that Punjab was stealing the water. Some wanted Punjab to be divided again, not because that would make a large state easier to govern, but so that it would not dominate the other states. There was an irony to these regional differences coming up on account of the Indus because it was the closest thing Pakistan had to a national river. It was almost like a symbol of national unity, a coronary artery flowing through the middle of the country, for which the scattered rivers of Punjab came together to feed its once great expanse. Sindi nationalist parties had taken up the issue and the splintering, faction within faction, difference within difference, that I had seen since I arrived in Pakistan, and was hardly able to follow, was spreading through the political arena.

And here there was a deeper irony. It was thought that the faith, as the basis of Pakistan, would trump all other identities. It didn't matter what kind of Muslim you were, what language you spoke or even if you lived at the other end of India. As long as you were Muslim, Islam would bridge the differences. It reminded me of the faith Abdullah, in Istanbul, placed in all the Muslims of the world he hadn't met. 'You mentioned the conflict between Islamic countries,' he had said, 'but I'm trying to say that to be a Muslim is a very different experience from any other, no matter where you are. To be Muslim is to be above history.' But history did matter, not just the faith's encased and symbolic history, but history as realised in language and culture. It was a distortion of faith that all this didn't matter, and in Pakistan people seemed to fall back on regional, linguistic and denominational differences.

Laxman, now determined to exercise his minority privileges, insisted I join him for a beer. On the way to his house, we drove through a gated urban colony, with run-down buildings, open drains and walls covered with slogans. '"Sunnis, when will you awake?"' Laxman read, in a fearful whisper, as if the words leapt off the walls at him. It was a reference to the bombing in Karachi and, Laxman thought, a call to arms. As we left the quiet, concrete colony, domestic scenes overhead and hatred on the walls, Laxman hissed, 'See? See? It's boiling. If something doesn't happen, it'll rip.'

*

That night at Laxman's house, the bureau chief called, wanting to know my father's name. That made me nervous. My father was well-known in Pakistan and I would have preferred to travel with a degree of anonymity; I had done well so far. Laxman gave it to him, then put down the phone and gave me his hunted-minority look. His room was filled with fake flowers, dusty stuffed toys, calendars and pink curtains. His bed was of a black and gold laminate, and a fake vine of maple leaves in autumnal colours drooped over one corner. A drinks trolley, still in its plastic covering of years, came in.

'What is it, Laxman? Why did he want to know?'

'Nothing, Aatish. God is great.' I noticed as we fled the men who'd marked our car that he had said, 'God is great.' It seemed he always did when trouble lay ahead.

'Laxman?'

'No, it's just that this is the time that the ISI [Pakistani Intelligence] come round to his office. He's their man. He does their drafting and translation.'

'What? Why didn't you tell me?'

'It was only when he called that it came into my mind. But, don't worry, Aatish, God is great.'

'Please, let's leave God out of this for a minute. I really don't want to be stuck in an interrogation room again.' I told him about Iran.

'Is it possible they have informed him?' he asked, taking pleasure, I thought, in the world turning out to be just as shadowy as he imagined it.

'I don't know. Listen, I hate this sort of thing. I needn't have met him. Why didn't you warn me?'

Two doubts circulated in my head: the first was that perhaps Laxman wasn't trustworthy, the second was how the bureau chief could have informed Pakistan's intelligence services about me when I was a guest of his boss, the publisher. I felt I was being brought in line with the level of suspicion that people in Hyderabad felt for one another.

'I'll tell you what, then,' Laxman said. 'Don't stay in the hotel tonight. We won't meet him tomorrow. We'll leave for Sehwan Sharif [a shrine] and come back in a day or so when things have calmed down.'

'No, Laxman. That's not how I want to work. Either it's safe for me or it's not.'

'It's safe. God is great.'

I said I was calling the publisher, half expecting Laxman to admit he was being alarmist, but he said, 'Good idea.' I tried a few numbers, then finally had the man on the phone. He listened to what I had to say and then, with a protective growl, said, 'Give me Laxman.'

I handed over the receiver. They spoke for a few minutes and hung up. Laxman tittered with excitement at the scene unfolding.

A few minutes later the publisher called back. 'Remember that you're a British national, that you have done nothing wrong and have nothing to worry about. I have spoken to him [the bureau chief] and have told him in a chilling, but indirect, way that you are my friend and he'd better take care of you.'

'I can't face another interrogation.'

'It's a minor inconvenience!' the publisher bellowed.

'Should I see him tomorrow?'

'Yes, yes. It's fine.'

Laxman was in a state of high excitement. 'See?' he said. 'See how disloyal these people are who only want money despite how well *saab* keeps them? Us minorities are much more loyal.'

I liked the bureau chief and could only think that in his way he had warned me. I thought he spoke from the heart when he said, 'The frustration is terrible.' And it was the most basic frustration of how to survive and earn an honest living, free of coercion and fear. In calling the publisher I'd put a counterweight to the fear the intelligence men would have exerted on the bureau chief, the fear of losing his job, and the smaller man had come into line. It was so easy to slip into the interplay of corruption and power that made the society work and I, who felt quite righteous when I arrived, was less full of high sentence when I left.

*

The next morning in the Indus Hotel's breakfast room, a boy on television sang in a shrill voice about the rule of God and never uttering a lie. He was in his early teens and wore a red tunic and a black turban. He smiled as he sang, his hands opening and closing to the beat of his own moral tunes. There was something grotesquely compelling about him. I drank a cup of unusually good coffee and waited for Laxman.

We were such an unlikely pairing, Laxman and I: a Pakistani Hindu showing an Indian, with Pakistani origins, Pakistan. It was as if the publisher, with his feeling for undivided India, was having a joke. But it was not an insignificant joke. I think that because Laxman was my guide, I felt closer to Sind's multi-religious past and, also, to its decay. I found it interesting that Laxman's distrust of others was not along religious lines but cultural ones. He was suspicious, as were Sindi Muslims, of the non-Sindi; he had close relationships with Sindi Muslims. (And I think even his problem with the bureau chief boiled down to him being Punjabi.) In his like-mindedness to his Muslim counterparts, Laxman was like a living relic of what had been Sind's composite culture.

He appeared a few minutes later in high spirits; he was taking me to a wedding. I tried to resist, citing the meeting with the bureau chief, but Laxman was insistent and said we'd meet him after the wedding.

I'm not sure how I was able to tell any longer – and maybe it was only because I'd left an air-conditioned room – but when I stepped out on to Cool Street that morning, I was sure it was the hottest day so far. It was barely nine and white vapour sucked the colour out of the day.

The heat in this treeless desert city was made worse by the kind of work people did, work which involved vats of boiling oil and colourfully painted blowtorches. Men came out of their industrial cubby-holes to water the searing streets. No sooner had the water touched the grey-white surface, robbed for a moment of wobbling mirages, than it vanished and the hypnotic heat returned. The earth at the roadside was so dry that the water skittered over the surface like mercury, and it was a few moments before the tension around the dust-covered drops broke. Skeletons of buses lay bent and mangled in unclaimed plots of destroyed earth and the backs of old trucks, propped up on stocky, wooden beams, were used for storage.

The drive to the wedding took us past the full destruction that had come to Hyderabad. In front of a pink sandstone colonial mansion, once the lord mayor's residence, there was a blue and green sign that read 'Govt. Khadija Girls H/S School'. The building's stained-glass windows were broken, their old shutters fell from their frames like dead skin, and many were boarded up. The balcony railings were rusted over, the sunken pillars cracked, and even the decorative urn on the left side of the building had fallen over and smashed in two.

In another area, the buildings once belonged to Hindu merchants. One had an especially fine façade, on which the Hindu name of Hassaram Vishindas 1924 still remained. It stood on a hairpin bend and had what was once a semi-circular balcony. A wall of unplastered bricks now rose from the balcony's balustrade and the space was divided into little rooms.

'Is anyone living there?'

'No. Now they're just *muhajjirs*,' Laxman said.

'Maybe, but are they living there?'

'Yes, and they have their shops below.'

Further on, whole streets of pale town-houses were deserted, entire neighbourhoods abandoned. It was amazing to see how, even after six decades, the city's once effortless harmony had not been regained. As if mourning the wholeness of its society, the breaking up of its diverse, interlocking components, the city retreated into ghettos. The *muhajjir*s, who had left behind diversities of their own, felt the worth they knew in other societies – a usefulness formed over centuries – extinguished in the one they came to. The disappointment would have been immense: to have begun with the idea of the religious homeland and to have ended with the divisions between the old and new Muslims deepening into walls, political parties and militias. My mother's family were the equivalent of *muhajjir*s in India – they had come as refugees from the Pakistani side, just as the people here had come from the Indian side – but in India there was no equivalent grouping: the concept didn't exist.

The *muhajjir*s in Hyderabad were holed up, as if in a communal sulk, in the fort I remembered from the lithographs. They lived in a warren of tight, winding streets among the ramparts where Laxman was too scared to go. The fort's red-brick walls were falling away, its crenellations crumbling, and the windows of people's homes had been broken into its walls. Outside, in the heat, a market had sprung up next to an open cesspool, with a giant slab of concrete lying in it. A polio victim sat in a wooden cart under a blue tarpaulin. Gearboxes, grey car seats, lubricants and the greasy coils of suspension springs baked in the sun near him.

Next to a particularly beautiful yellow house, with gables and a balcony of high pointed arches, the wedding preparations were under way. A rectangular section of the street, crowded with donkey carts, sacks of cement and yellow phone booths, had been tented off. No one had arrived yet, but a woman of the house welcomed us in a state of high excitement. 'The big function is tonight,' she said. 'There'll be dancing and singing, you watch. Yes, yes, the whole society will come! We won't sleep, it'll go on all night! We don't even have to tell people, they will come on their own.'

With this, she rushed off. I was introduced to a bearded old man in blue, with a skullcap and a prayer mark so high on his head that I wondered how he was able to touch it to the floor. It turned out that he was the father of the groom. He knew Laxman as the man from the newspaper and must have thought I was a journalist because he began to grumble to me about the government: 'Ask me why they have forbidden us to serve food at our weddings.'

'Have they?'

'Yes.'

'Why?'

'Just like that.'

'No reason?'

'No reason.'

'They must have said something.'

'No, and they've also banned the loudspeaker at the mosque, even when there's a visitor from out of town.'

'They've banned singing and dancing too,' Laxman said.

'No,' the man interrupted, 'that's allowed, but we can only serve one dish at the wedding.'

'They want to discourage all this extra spending,' Laxman said.

Though Pakistanis denied it, in places like Iran where laws of this kind existed, the practical justification was only a cover for a deeper Islamic desire to rid the marriage ceremony of all things that were cultural and not strictly Islamic. I couldn't see why else, in this lawless region where the state could not be relied on to bring basic governance, it would bother to make sure that ordinary people followed hospitality guidelines for weddings.

Laxman went off looking for food, and the old man turned to me with a gleam in his eyes. 'I shouldn't say this,' he said, with a crooked smile, 'but my son works at the paper. His position there is not permanent. Do you think you could help him become permanent? He's been there seven or eight years and his position is still temporary.'

'I'll try,' I said, not wanting to disappoint the man on his son's wedding day.

We were still talking when the son arrived. He was dark and heavy, with a thick, black beard and a prayer mark that was just a dot. I saw these marks with a feeling of dread now, as if everywhere one looked people were catching a terrible new disease. All the trainers in my brother's gym had them. In seven months in the Muslim world, I had seen the prayer callous, with its rough, thick texture only once, in Syria, and now in Pakistan every other man had one. He was speaking on his mobile phone and continued to do so as he told us that we were to make our way to a mosque across the street for the wedding.

A small gathering of men left the tented area and walked to the white marble mosque. It was crowded, with a pungent smell and fluorescent and tinted glass lights. There were other worshippers too, some with red, hennaed beards. Laxman tried to make me wear a plastic skullcap for those who didn't have their own, but when I saw him in his red shirt and white plastic cap, looking so foolish, I couldn't bring myself to do it. I sat down next to the old man, and as we watched the bustle at the front of the mosque, he said, 'There was a time when the priest came to the house. Our weddings used to last seven days, but today many of the traditions are dying out. There's only one day for the wedding and we have to come to the mosque for the ceremony. When I was little, weddings took place with great festivity. They're forgetting how to get married!'

The old man put it well. This was the loss of history that was not just in books, but real and felt. The weddings he described were like weddings I knew in India; often the only difference between religions was the ceremony, which was the shortest part of the occasion. It was easy to imagine, as with the Sufi shrine, how weddings would have been an event for people of all faiths. There would have been a special feeling of goodwill at attending the wedding of someone from another faith, yet of the same culture. There was no cultural familiarity for me now: it was only a Muslim wedding. The dumbing-down of the wedding to its bare Islamic essentials was part of the rejection of India as a cultural entity, part of the rejection of the composite culture, which left only the bare bones of religion. The old man was religious, but he missed his culture. That culture, like the Sufi religion of Sind and the city of Hyderabad, had relied on its diversity. The sudden fact of homogeneity in a composite culture was a shock, like imagining London or New York stripped of their diversity. It affected values, and the assumption of homogeneity in my father's house – the jibes against Hindus, Jews, gays, blacks and Americans, the language untempered by just the awareness of others – was more alien to me than anything else.

In my confusion, I kept expecting a bejewelled bride in red to appear so I was little surprised when the father indicated that his son, after signing a few documents, had become married while sitting next to another man who was also getting married.

We walked back to the rectangular tent and the women beat kitchen utensils and sang songs about their brother's happiness. When they saw that the groom was lagging behind on his mobile phone they stopped, and started again a few minutes later. Many more people arrived and men who looked like blacksmiths, in greasy vests and beards, brought in great metal pots of steaming food.

The attorney general drove up in an air-conditioned car, opened his window and shook the groom's hand. Laxman ran up to him to introduce me as a journalist from London. He smiled, gave me his card and then the tinted windows went up. We had to go too; we were meant to meet the bureau chief. I looked into the tent before leaving. Large, listless men, with hot faces, were standing by a row of blue tables, putting away great mouthfuls of rice and chicken.

When we arrived at the newspaper offices, the bureau chief wanted me to meet someone who had just stepped out of the office to prayer. I felt some tension from the night before pass between us, then he said, 'I don't know if I should be telling you this, but only twice in the twenty years that I've been working here has *saab* called me. But he called yesterday and he said, "What you do for him, you'll be doing for me." So, you have asked for the moon and I will move heaven and earth.'

I was embarrassed to see the dignified old man put in this position, but Laxman's face gleamed with satisfaction. The awkwardness in the room ended with the appearance of a tall, fair man, with a thick, black moustache and a prayer mark.

The man was a member of Sind's legislative assembly. He had made his way up in Pakistani politics through channels that were now closed. He began his career in the student unions in 1971, the year East Pakistan was lost. 'That time was good.' He smiled. 'Student life was very good. We were getting a lot of talent, but then Zia banned the student unions and their leaders. All the good politicians you see now, who aren't scared of the army, came up during that time.' The student unions, like the film industry, never recovered. They were one of those fragile organisations that take decades to build but only months to smother. And in 1979, the year Bhutto was executed, the year before my parents met, the young politician who in all likelihood would have joined a large, secular party, like the People's Party, joined a religious one instead. Though his aspiration for Pakistan was the most basic, non-religious desire for good government, he felt that only Islam could bring true democracy.

'The army won't let it come,' he said. 'They listen to what America says. When they wanted to fight the Russians, the army brought the Taleban and General Zia and it was all *namaz* and *Allah Allah*. Then they wanted the Taleban out and they brought Musharraf who knows nothing about these things. The Islamic movement is strong, and if there were free and fair elections, we would sweep into power. But there are bogus elections and ballot stuffing. In 1947, *madrassa*s were only a few hundred and now there are twenty-five thousand. Isn't religion growing? Do you see the attendance at religious events?' In the past, religious parties had never swept the ballot boxes, but the politician was sure that the mood had changed.

'People are becoming more Islamic-minded. When Muslims are being killed in Waziristan, won't religion increase? Musharraf says, "Take Islamic culture out of textbooks," and people say, "Fine, we'll teach it at home." Religion is growing because they're trying to suppress it. They did away with the Taleban, which controlled the people very well, curbed crime, stopped opium, ended injustice, and it just made people turn more towards religion.'

'How do you want religion in Pakistan to be?'

'In everything.'

'Shariah?'

'Yes.'

'Saudi?'

'No, that's a kingdom.'

'Iran?'

'No, that's something else.'

'Then what?'

'Like in the time of the Prophet. An Islamic republic.'

'But there was no republic then.'

'Yes, but what is a republic, after all?'

'A European concept coming out of ancient Greece.'

'No. A republic,' he said, 'came from Islam.'

What he had in mind was not really a political entity but a vision of a just society. He quoted a story I had heard many times now about the caliph Omar. In the story, the caliph is questioned publicly over why he uses more cloth in his dress than his fellow Muslims. Despite his high office, he is not offended by the query and explains that he has more cloth because his son has given him his share. Muslims liked the story for its message of equality and political accountability. But beyond these simplicities, when the young politician's demands were boiled down to details, they bore a resemblance to a modern, Western-style republic, not a Taleban-style state.

'We want to improve education. We want full education – maths, chemistry, economics. We want to improve hospital facilities, services, utilities. We are not allowed to present these things in the Assembly. We present them and they block us.' But how could it happen in a deeper sense until men like the young politician stopped standing for the faith and stood instead for what they wanted? Wouldn't the Islamic lens always distort the real priorities? Wouldn't it be better to think of models in places where republics of this kind had been achieved, rather than the Prophet's example? The reason it couldn't work, this finding something in one place and recasting it in a palatable Islamic mould, was that the faith's distortions were too many. Even now, in the country founded for the faith, the young politician was ready to blame foreign powers for the inefficiencies of the local legislature.

'The Sind Assembly hasn't passed a single law in three years!' he cried. 'It's huge, with money and ministries, but the people have no relief. But ask us to find Osama bin Laden in Waziristan and we're doing it. That's why I think my government is in foreign hands. Because it is not a republic, it is not in our hands. One man, controlled by international powers, is controlling everything, a controlled and engineered democracy.

'I have a constituency,' he continued, 'I want to get it medicine, but I can't. There's a board, but they don't give us a vote on it. There's no elected representative on it! People are corrupt, and in this country they make corruption files only to blackmail people, not to bring them to justice. The rate of commission for any government development project is thirty per cent. I was given five million for development in my constituency, but out of that the government contractor wants thirty per cent. That's just the rate. My guy wants even more. He says, "Let's speak in terms of fifty."'

In the end, the young politician came back to religion. He quoted the great slogan of the religious parties, the final logic of the secular state for Indian Muslims: 'Pakistan ka matlab kya, la illa il allah. What is the meaning of Pakistan? There is no God but God.'

The politician struck me as sincere and I felt that the corruption he saw around him drove him to the purities of faith. He offered to take me to the Assembly and we exchanged details. When I told him my name, he smiled and said, 'Taseer. I'll remember it. It was the name of a great Pakistani leader.'

This mention of my father, like the one at the border when I first came to Pakistan, surprised me. I wouldn't have thought the young politician would know of him. The respect people in Pakistan had for my father complicated my assessment of him. I felt a certain pride when ordinary people spoke of his courage in the Zia years, and when young executives looked up to him for the business empire he created at the age of fifty in a country where it wasn't easy to rise on your own. But I didn't know how I could let their opinions influence my own difficult relationship with him. I think it's impossible to see your parents in any role other than the intense, personal one you need with them. My peace with my father couldn't include knowledge of his success in public life. What good was he to me as a charismatic politician and businessman if he wasn't willing to be my father?

In his letter, my father had mentioned the 'Pakistani ethos'. I had had it in mind all the time in Hyderabad, but how strange it was to think of that phrase now, in this desert city, where in the name of a Pakistani ethos the city's harmony, still engraved in its buildings, had been carved into ghettoes of faction. Pakistanis offered their natural differences, differences in culture and language, as an explanation for the battle lines that had come up, but this was hardly an explanation when next door in India deeper differences had been bridged. Not only that, but in Sind too, where once great variety had been absorbed, bitter division was to be found in what was now relative homogeneity. And Sind, for centuries so diverse, its culture and worship formed from that diversity, was for the first time in its history no longer a place of confluence.

As we walked down the stairs, Laxman scuttled up to me. 'Now, he's set.' He meant the bureau chief, whom we were dropping off at the Press Club. The bureau chief had mentioned earlier that one of the political parties had called for a strike and the streets now were emptier than usual. It was early afternoon and the heat that had been building since the morning surpassed all expectations. The stillness of the trees, the knife-like edges of Urdu slogans on the walls, the near-solidity of shadows brought a phantasmagoric aspect to the day. The greenery of trees seemed sometimes to be red, and the whole scene was stained like a photographic negative. The heat pressed against my head and it took all my strength to get out of the car and thank the bureau chief for his help.

I was leaving Hyderabad later that afternoon for a rally in another town. I had just said goodbye to the bureau chief and was turning away to get back into the car when, barely a few feet from me, there was a man wearing nothing but a fragment of cloth. It was his nakedness that made me look again, and when I did, I saw that sections of flesh had been torn from his legs, his arms and his chest. A blue polythene bag hung from his wrist. His frail, dark body trembled and shook and tears streamed down his small, bearded face. He wasn't with anyone, he didn't approach anyone, he just stood alone outside the Press Club, almost naked, covered with open wounds, looking up at the white sky with his glassy eyes, and weeping, not like a child but like a fully grown man, a deep broken groan from the depths of his wretched body.

It was as complete an impasse as I had ever found myself in. I had turned away from all kinds of horror in my life, but this man, the extent of his injuries, the climate he stood in and the cry coming from his mouth made it impossible to look away. Laxman and I ran up to him and yelled to the bureau chief, who turned and came back. The man could hardly speak, but he managed to tell the bureau chief that he had been burnt, and it was possible now to see that the wounds were broad swathes of burns. As the man tried to speak, a young man in a powder blue *salwar kameez* appeared. He said that a fire had broken out and the man had been burnt in it. He was taken to the civil hospital burns ward, but because he told the press he was not being treated properly, they had left him without treatment as punishment. 'For twenty days,' the young man said, 'he has been lying without treatment.'

'These stories happen every day, Aatish *saab*,' the bureau chief said. 'Best to leave it alone.'

'How was he burnt? In a factory or house?'

'In a garbage dump,' the man said.

'What was he doing there?'

'He's an addict.'

'In Hyderabad,' the bureau chief clarified, 'garbage is disposed of by burning.'

'Yes, but what was he doing in it?'

'He's an addict. He doesn't feel anything,' the chief said. 'He was lying in the garbage when they burnt it. Don't worry too much about these cases. They are a daily occurrence.'

Pakistan had among the highest number of heroin addicts in the world and this, too, like so much else in Pakistan, had happened since 1979.

'What's he going to do?'

'I'm treating him,' the man in blue said.

'Who are you?'

'Saeed.'

'Who's he?' I asked the bureau chief.

'A quack,' the bureau chief replied, 'In Pakistan, if you cannot afford a doctor, you go to a quack.'

The man had run away from the hospital when it refused to treat him and Saeed found him. He seemed now to be using the burnt man to some end of his own. He had brought him to the Press Club in the hope of calling attention to the story. He seemed half amused, a little exhilarated. He asked me my full name and then, trying to form some religious judgement about me, asked why I wore the Sikh bangle on my wrist. I ignored him.

It was a story full of ambiguity. Everyone seemed to have some incalculable motive; no one's account was clear; the press, the hospital, the authorities, the quack were all implicated, but then there was the bare, inadmissible fact, the fact big enough to stop anyone in their path, of a man, half burnt to death, standing in the street sobbing in fifty-degree heat. I could hardly believe – after a cycle in feudal Sind, after the violence of the Mango King's world, after Dickensian lawyers, informant journalists and bloodthirsty slogans – that this was my last vision, the most voiceless creature in this degraded chain. When this reality was seen against the exalted expectations for the religious homeland, it was possible to imagine that this was the darkness, the almost religious darkness, so potent a myth in the Muslim imagination, of a time when no man was left uncorrupt, and from whose depths, surely, a messiah was at hand.

The Idea Country

My father had written about India and Pakistan in his letter and now the publisher wanted me to write about continuities between the two. I felt I couldn't. He said I was in a unique position to see them. And perhaps I was. But after my panorama in Sind, I felt that what remained common were remains; the countries had gone their own ways. He became irritated. Educated Pakistanis didn't like to hear of the inroads the faith had made over the past fifty years. They pointed to the Sufi religion of Punjab and Sind, how so many people were as they had always been, hardworking, no veils, no beards. And they were right. But that Sufi faith, with its shrines and poetry and wide appeal, was not the religion that was gaining ground in Pakistan, but a more literal, streamlined faith. In many who didn't have veils and beards, it had made its trespasses. The secular state for Indian Muslims had been muddied over the decades; democracy with dictatorship; Bhutto's populism died with him; and after everything else had been allowed to fall away, the men who believed that Pakistan was created for faith would always have the force of logic on their side.

The 'Pakistani ethos' was hard to pin down, but I could tell that the rejection of India was an important part of it. So it was not because continuities did not exist that I didn't wish to write about them, but because their reassertion was not part of the Pakistani story. To write about them was to write about obscurity.

If Iran found Islamic expression in a modern context through the Islamic Republic, so did Pakistan, but the nature of the republic, and even the impulses behind it, were very different. At first, it hadn't been an Islamic republic at all, the 'Islamic' was added a decade later; it was a secular state for Indian Muslims. And, in the beginning, that was all: no Shariah, no clerics, no ban on alcohol; people remembered women on bicycles. It was as if a trust like Abdullah's – that the Muslims he had never met possessed a certain basic identity – had been the impulse behind gathering the sub-continent's various and disparate Muslims into a single state. That was Pakistan's first religious battle: the cleansing of the population.

Pakistan's founders were not clerics and fanatics, but poets and secularists. It was from the most sophisticated Muslims of that time that the case for the country was made. The poet Iqbal, the country's intellectual founder, was a contemporary of my grandfather. He actually wrote and performed my grandparents' marriage ceremony. And yet among these genteel people an idea was expressed whose full ugliness, and violence, only became clear in the cruder, more basic articulations that followed. For me, until I saw the faith's unspoken hold on my father's notions of history and politics, and the chauvinism it could produce, the idea would almost have been too strange to understand. Though it was disguised as an economic argument, a fear of being swamped by money-minded Hindus, it was really just a refinement of what Abdullah had said to me half a century later in Istanbul, also now free of its diversity: 'I think that Muslims have to be at the top, at the centre of the system. We have to determine all the things in the world, otherwise we won't be free ourselves . . . A Christian may live with us here, but not like a Muslim. He may live here, but we have to be dominant.'

Translated into political terms, he was saying that Muslims needed their own state. This had also been the demand for Pakistan. But despite its apparent political objective, the demand was less concrete than it seemed. Its impracticality, but also the frustration that arose from its failure, became clear when, in my last few days in Karachi, I met an Islamic ideologue.

'When you see him,' Salim, the reporter, said, 'you would never expect him to be such an Islamist, but he's a real hard-liner.' Salim was stocky and bearded, with tired eyes. He was a star reporter at the publisher's paper and obsessed with the war on terror. The ideologue, he said, supplied some of the country's fiercest religious groups with their philosophy. His description of an outwardly irreligious man, with political ideas that had all the force of religion, made me want to meet the ideologue.

We arranged lunch at the Usmaniye restaurant in the outer reaches of Karachi, deep within the city of cement and corrugated-iron. Once we left the broken streets on the outskirts of Karachi, the road signs and pavements continued for some distance, then fell away in parts. At traffic-lights, a couple of black eunuchs dressed in pink, with cloudy eyes and yellow teeth begged for money. It was a big, treeless intersection full of open-backed trucks and scooters. The heat and the smoke made the outlines of the buildings tremble. On a grey cement wall, a colourful scrawl read, 'Crush Israel' and 'Down with Denmark'. A boy salvaged pens and plastic bags from a mountain of hardened garbage at the centre of which there was a half-full dumpster. The flags of local parties appeared in clusters, reds, greens and a worn-out Pakistani People's Party flag. It was Bhutto's party, my father's party, at times the great hope of Pakistani democracy, still popular, especially in Sind, and now awaiting another life.

We passed another mountain of waste and compressed polythene, from which shreds of pink and blue fluttered in the hot breeze. Below it I saw a still body of black water, disturbed now and then by a mysterious sputtering of bead-like bubbles. Where there might have been rocks at the edge, there were hillocks of filth and little clumps of bright grass.

The restaurant was cool and dimly lit, away from the roar of the street. The ideologue wore an olive green shirt. He was dark, clean-shaven and his eyes were sunken. He smoked many cigarettes.

He didn't want to talk about himself. 'Nothing is personal in all of this. I don't believe in personal opinion as far as religion is concerned. Nothing I say has to do with who I am or my own experience.'

He had grown up in Karachi, born just before the first war with India in 1965. In 1971, he told me, 'Pakistan became two pieces. I have very little memory of that time,' he recalled, his thin lips pulling at the cigarette, 'but I was aware that we didn't cook three meals a day in our house. The good thing about our house, though, and many others was that we read a lot, two or three papers a day, literature, we discussed politics. I had read all of Premchand [the short-story writer] by the time I was ten. We might have been misguided, but the political motivation was there. At times it might have been wrong, but it was there, and this was without it being associated with any one political party. But now all that is gone.'

The ideologue spoke some English, and refined Urdu. His intense, studious manner and nicotine-stained fingertips reminded me of an old-fashioned Marxist intellectual. But there was something missing about him – humanity, perhaps. He seemed hard and hollow.

'Why is it gone?'

'The people became disillusioned. We always thought Pakistan was made to be realised. This sense was lost, and with it, we lost many other things.'

'What else?'

'A sense of destiny, collective self-confidence. Our political framework was dismembered. But with Muslims, geography is not very important. If even after 1971 our ruling élite had bounced back, we would have bounced back because we've never been fascinated with geography. We are fascinated with ideas. If even then an idea could have come . . .'

The ideologue grew up talking about the idea of Pakistan. 'Discussing Pakistan,' he said, 'was like discussing Islam. Pakistan was made in the name of Islam. It had to be a role model for the rest of the Islamic world. We identified characters who were responsible for its failure: Mujibur Rahman [the founder of Bangladesh], Bhutto, India, Mrs Gandhi. We thought one day we'd become one again. It was a very simplistic world-view. We were closely associated with the notion of Pakistan. It was more like a being than a country. It was all-living. It wasn't geography or politics. It was more than that. It was a collective conscious-ness. This was the idea of many.'

And now, put this way, I felt the ideologue's description wasn't of a real place but of a religious Utopia. This man who could be so clear and down-to-earth had an almost magical side to him.

'But this is such a country,' he said, with new softness in his voice, 'that has never let it be decided where it was headed. That's why you see the situation of today. Look at the India of 1946. It was fractured, but then one idea came and the whole sub-continent was united and held together by this idea. Even if we had decided to become a secular state or a nation state, we would be in a good position now. But we did not follow a liberal model or an Islamic one. Nor did we achieve material success or build a bond. We have a lot of diversity, rare diversity, of language, of culture, of religion. This could have been a great force, but it was turned into contradiction by our political élite.'

'Why was it so bad here?'

'Our ruling élite was such that it never thought of anything but its own vested interest. It never thought of Pakistan as a nation, only as a private limited company.' It was the first time in months that I had heard a Pakistani blame Pakistanis, not the foreign hand, for the country's failures. Hearing him speak, I felt as I had when I met the young politician in Hyderabad: the faith was getting all the good people.

'And the idea now?'

'It's still alive and kicking,' he said sadly.

'Of a state that embodies Islamic principles?'

'Absolutely.'

'Have you thought more about a model?'

'Islam doesn't depend on form,' he said. 'Form is not important. Essence is the main thing. If the essence is there, you can derive from it any kind of model.'

It was the most untrue thing I had heard. This dependence on sacred essence, and disregard of form, political models and institutions, had been the undoing of Pakistan, and Iran.

'Do you think that if Pakistan had been a successful secular country, you would be writing about political Islam today?'

'There is no such thing as political Islam. There is just Islam, which has a political component. That is a Western phrase designed to distort the totality of Islam.

'The problem with us,' he said, 'is that somewhere along the way we stopped being a country guided by an idea and just became a place where people lived.'

That remark stopped the ideologue's torrent; he seemed to

sense that he'd said a painful but amazing thing. So many places were just places where people lived, but Pakistan, which was made for an idea, and which had broken with history for that idea – which, if not for that idea, was just a handful of Indian Muslim states, with linguistic and cultural differences – depended on it for its survival.

'There are two kinds of history,' he said, of the connection to India, 'dead history and living. Dead history is something on a shelf or in a museum and living history is part of your consciousness, something in your blood that inspires you.'

'But why is the pre-Islamic history of Iran living?'

'There is a reason for this,' he replied. 'If all India became Muslim, we might have been able to identify with the Hindu past. We would have modified something. But since it didn't happen that way, we can't choose something that goes against our taste. You won't wear a T-shirt you don't like.

'It's very unusual,' he continued, 'in the case of Europe, that the Christian world should have abandoned its roots and looked to Hellenistic civilisation. It ran away from the Christian golden period, when Constantine accepted Christianity and it spread through Europe. They abandoned it and ran towards Greece. It shows that they did not have a law, and that for the law, they had to run to Rome. They didn't have *shariat*. We have spirituality and we have a law.' The ideologue knew that those histories had flowed from each other, but couldn't accept an origin other than in faith. It was interesting that he didn't choose Jesus as a starting-point, but Constantine and Christianity's political triumph.

'Who's "we"?'

'The Muslims.'

'You say it as though you were Arab.'

'This doesn't arise in the case of Muslims – Arab, non-Arab. It's a civilisation of faith. We are Muslims.'

A 'Civilisation of Faith'. This was also the civilisation to which my father belonged. It was the thousand-year culture, of which Abdullah had spoken. It was what all Muslims had in common, believing or non-believing, moderate or extremist. For me, there was something miraculous in this transfiguration of one's culture and history, by either a profession of faith, or an inherited profession of faith. There was something miraculous in the idea that if Even, my Norwegian friend, converted to Islam that this would also become his history. The poet Iqbal's family, after all, were only recent converts to Islam. And how had I fallen through the cracks? What would it take to believe in a history like that? A profession of faith? My father had made none, but believed in the history. My mother gave me no religion, so how was it that my father and I had ended up being from two different nations having been once from the same country, and even, the same region? Perhaps it was like retaining certain moralities without believing in God, or religion. Perhaps it was kept in place by everyone around you believing.

It was time for me to make the final part of my journey north to see my father.

Articles of Faith

I made my way to Lahore by train. My father hadn't called me once during my time in Pakistan and I feared an unfriendly reception.

In Karachi railway station, beyond a line of peach-coloured arches, listless railwaymen sat with their feet on desks in dark offices, with open doors and brown mesh windows. One picked at his feet as he spoke to his colleague. An old-fashioned red metal roof came down over the arches, protecting the platform from the late-afternoon blaze. Among the hurried movements of porters in orange, men sat on their haunches next to swollen plastic sacks and women, on the floor in groups, fanned themselves. A great brass bell, a blue phone booth, a Pizza Hut and a black-tiled water fountain were arranged in a line down the platform. Sunken polythene bags and candy wrappers hung in the few inches of grey water that lay between the tracks. The large families and skullcapped men waiting for a train under droning fans seemed like characters in a Partition scene.

Talk of the train began. The crowd on the platform compressed, then broke loose, all moving at once with the arrival of the Tezgam, an elegant pool-table-green train with beige and red stripes. My brother's driver, who waited quietly with me, now said, 'Wherever you look, there's public. People I've spoken to say the condition of India is better than Pakistan.'

I didn't answer, wishing to avoid the conversation of differences. What I did know was that discovering Pakistan, its closeness to India and the trap I felt it had fallen into where religion was concerned, filled me with an affection for the country that I hadn't expected.

'Yes, on our side, things have yet to be established,' the driver said. He spoke in Urdu, but said 'establish' in English.

We found the sleeper by the numbers written in white chalk on the side of the carriage; a crest said 'Islamabad Carriage Factory'. The cabin was air-conditioned with its own bathroom and the most spacious since Istanbul. The dark green seats were wide and springy, the walls were of plywood, and the windows darkened. A smart, painted sign with yellow letters and black outlines, reminiscent of another time, read: 'To seat 3 sleep 2;' I had it to myself. My brother's driver put the white box of Sind Club sandwiches that the publisher sent for me on the table. His large, mascaraed eyes scanned the carriage and he said, 'If there's been any error on my part, please pardon it.' Then he went off and stood on the platform until the train left.

The sign for the Inward Parcel Office, a mountain of packages, men sleeping on plastic sacks, and a policeman lying on a bench, drifted by as the Tezgam left Karachi. We passed heaps of burning garbage, smoke rising against cement walls, with black writing on them. I thought of the bureau chief's words, 'In Hyderabad, garbage is disposed of by burning.' The train climbed past the top of the city, and a final film reel played out through tinted windows: the coloured roofs of buses, the upper storeys of small apartment buildings, corrugated-iron roofs held down by bricks, mango-tree canopies, bougainvillaea from terraces, barbers' shops, the green and white domes of mosques modelled on Medina's, the span of a flyover, water tanks and green satiny flags, with gold trimmings, fluttering in the black smoke from burning garbage. A village of cloth and sticks appeared near the tracks amid the devastation of blue plastic bags. Thorny bushes reached out to touch the train. The cement city, with men sitting on rooftops, families of buffaloes in manure and the watermarked walls of warehouses, passed just before sunset.

At dusk, the eternal Sind scene: flat, dry land throwing up magnificent, double-storey cacti, with fleshy depressions and sparse giant thorns.

The next morning we were in Punjab. At Multan station, the carriage attendant looked into my cabin and smiled. I asked for some tea.

'Yes, yes,' he said. 'Everything is available. I'll send the boy.'

A few minutes later an old man in a green uniform arrived to take my order. 'Just tea?' he said, with surprise.

'What else is there?'

'Eggs, double *roti* and butter.'

'OK. Bring them all.'

He came back with bread, marmalade, teabags, real milk and sugar, and an omelette on a white napkin and a steel plate. One station later, a young man with long, greased-back hair and a silver wire in his ear came into my cabin with a red brush to sweep the place while I sat on my haunches. The station, though smaller than Karachi's, had the same colonial elements: sloping metal roofs with a carved skirting; a whitewashed platform, blackboards and blue and white signs that said 'Battery Room'; 'Unity – Discipline – Faith', the motto that Pakistan's founder gave the country hung on a wall. There was a pink marble mosque and people washing for prayer outside.

Soon afterwards, a boy with a pointed face and crooked teeth knocked on my door. He was looking for a plug point to charge his phone. I said I hadn't seen one, but that he was free to look. He went away, then came back and sat down. His name was Rizwan and he was an electrical-engineering student in Karachi. 'Where are you from?' he asked.

'Karachi.'

'But in reality where are you from?'

'London.'

'I could tell from your accent.'

'Is it apparent?'

'Slightly. Are you Muslim?'

'Yes,' I replied, not wishing to enter into a long explanation.

'Nationality is British?'

'Yes.'

'I can tell.' He smiled. 'If you have any need in Pindi, I'm there. For a hotel, car, whatever.'

'Thank you.'

He said he had two more years left before he got his BSc in electrical engineering.

'Then?'

'Middle East. There's a lot of demand there. Maybe UK too.'

'Aren't visas tough, these days?'

'Yes, very. Don't even ask how tough, but Allah will help and when it happens I won't even know how it happened.'

'Where in the Middle East?'

'Dubai and Saudi. Both have a lot of demand, but Dubai is like ours.'

Just then, the carriage attendant and a man in a white uniform, with shiny silver buttons, knocked on the door, came in and asked to see my ticket.

'Who's he?' he asked, seeing that my ticket was for one person.

'We were just talking.'

299

The man turned to Rizwan and said sternly, 'Please go back to your seat.'

'No, no, we were just—'

'Please go back to your seat! You're lucky it was just me. Another conductor would have fined you.'

Rizwan rose, I made one last plea on his behalf, but the conductor reminded me that I was lucky it was just him.

Outside, a few boys in *salwar kameez* played in a canal. Another defecated near the tracks while a friend kept him company, running to get him water when he needed it. Under a cloth roof held up by four poles, a few women lazed next to a buffalo in a patch of mud. In Punjab, the houses were firmer and the majority in red brick. White domes and rust red minarets rose out of the low townscapes. There were big-leafed papaya trees in the fields and a golden layer of ripening corn. There was also much more water: in the fields, in the tube wells and in the wide network of canals. At the stations, men used old-fashioned hand pumps outside signs that said 'Lamp Room'.

Being in Punjab made me think ahead to my arrival at my father's house. My doubts had faded; the travelling made me optimistic. I felt that it would appeal to my father's sense of adventure that I was showing up on his doorstep after eight months of journeying from Europe to Pakistan. I also thought that if we were to move forward from our recent problems, we might set a new tone in our relationship. Fighting with someone, whatever its other effects, was at least a sign of emotion and openness. I thought that it might help make our relationship more instinctive.

At sunset, not far from Lahore, Adil, a Kashmiri boy, knocked on my door. The train had stopped and he felt like a chat. He had pale skin, light brown hair, amber eyes and prominent, very pink gums. He was a marine-biology student in Karachi and there was something intense and restless about him, even about the way in which he'd barged into my cabin for a friendly chat. He was off to Kashmir for a memorial service to his uncle who died in the October earthquake, which happened a few weeks before my trip began.

Adil had a brother in Abu Dhabi, but he was reluctant to go abroad. 'You can say you're a Muslim abroad,' he said, 'but you can't say you're a Pakistani because immediately people will say, "He's a terrorist." You tell me, how can you go to a foreign country and not even be able to say what your nationality is?'

'Do you think Pakistan's reputation has become that bad?'

'It didn't become bad. It was broken.'

'Who broke it?'

'Indians. They really maligned us abroad.'

I started to become nervous as the conversation grew more sub-continental.

'Are you Muslim?' he asked.

'Yes.'

'Then why do you wear that string?'

'It's from a shrine in Sind,' I lied.

'OK, then why do you wear this bangle?'

'My grandmother gave it to me. She's a Sikh.'

'But you?'

'Muslim. My father's Muslim.'

'And your mother?'

'She was Sikh,' I lied further, 'but she became a Muslim.'

'What does your father do?'

'Business.'

'What kind?'

At last I got him off the topic by asking how Karachi was. He said it was great, and that it was fun to tease the girls there.

'How do you tease them?'

'We go up to them, a few friends and I, and we sing songs to them.'

'Like what?'

He laughed and began to sing: 'Come, come, my little queen, tonight I have the emperor's right on you. Who will free you from my grip? Tonight, you've been caught, caught, caught . . .'

He laughed again and stayed talking until the silver-buttoned conductor appeared to eject him and announce the train's destination.

*

And so, with the ease and inevitability of a train pulling into a station, I found myself, one hot evening in Lahore, almost at the point where I had begun a journey to find my father four years before. But for the short flights in and out of Iran, I had travelled by land and it amazed me now that the journey which had begun in Europe, by train from Venice to Istanbul to Damascus, and by road through Arabia, had yielded the sub-continent, Lahore and, even more miraculously, my father. I had travelled eight months for this meeting, but the confluence of time, distance and expectation made it feel even longer.

I arrived to a house full of people. My younger sister was graduating from Lahore's American School and brothers, sisters, their spouses, uncles and grandparents had all flown down for the ceremony. My stepmother was involved in organising the graduation. There was to be a party at the house, and a few days later, it was my father's birthday. The level of activity was close to that of a wedding. Tents went up in the lawn as I drove in and a steady stream of tailors, caterers and hairdressers passed in and out of the house.

The mistake I made with my father was to be ready for anything other than indifference. That evening, standing on his doorstep after a year of silence, I thought we'd do something we'd never done before: have a meal together, a drink, a conversation about what had happened since we'd last met.

The trip had not left me unchanged. My relationship with Islam was no longer a negative space. I had learnt about the faith in the early part of my journey. Then, from my conversations with men like Abdullah, I discovered it wasn't faith in an obvious way that I needed to understand, but the political and historical demands it made and how it reshaped countries like Iran and Pakistan. This aspect of the religion, which could make my half-brother feel 'civilisational defeat' without being a believer, and which my father could possess without the faith, was not open to me. The way into that kind of faith was closed. It would once have been part of a whole system of belief, complete with ideas of politics, law and behaviour. In Pakistan and Iran, I had been shocked by the violence of reviving the faith in the form of Islamic republics and religious homelands. But all this seemed very far away now that I was at my father's doorstep. At that moment I thought only of our relationship. I couldn't see how these amorphous things, politics and history, could bring up real differences between two people. I had never lost a relationship over such differences and I couldn't believe that they might encumber my relationship with the father I had found after so many years.

And though I was more confident in some ways, arriving into the commotion at that low, red-brick house, I felt my courage fail me at an emotional level. Somehow I was a weaker man than I had been four years before when I walked boldly into his life. It was easier then for me to be the person I wished to be with him, to be able to say frankly that I'd like to talk to him alone. Now, even before I walked into my father's house, I felt myself fall into line with the rules of the place.

I found my father, as I had always known him, lying on his

bed surrounded by family. He didn't get up, but from the nod and smile in my direction, I could tell that there was no bad feeling. He was in high spirits. At one minute he was answering his phone or laughing as he read aloud a funny text message, at the next he was serious, discussing the price of his shares with his brother-in-law. My stepmother sat on the bed, speaking to friends, organisers, dealing with my sister's sartorial panics. My two younger brothers came in from a football match on the lawn. An older sister was arriving later that night with her husband, who worked at one of the American banks. It was a scene I had witnessed many times before and occasionally felt part of. It was a scene in which you could be present yet sink into your own thoughts without anyone noticing.

My stepmother, always very welcoming, managed between many chores to ask me about myself and if I needed anything while I was in Lahore. Over the next few days my father and I came to rely on her to defuse the awkwardness of speaking directly to one another. Our conversation became neutered. In the past, we spoke openly about history and politics, but this time, those topics were off limits. Though I could tell from my father's manner that he meant to make amends, it was as if an unspoken distance, a sense of my having joined another camp, had arisen between us. I found it strange that, over the next few days, he didn't ask me once about my trip through the Muslim world or my travels in Pakistan. It was as if he didn't want to know.

At last I felt I had to raise the subject and I walked into his room, three or four days after I arrived, with that purpose. He seemed pleased to see me, but after a while, when some of the family had dispersed and I told him what I wanted to talk to him about, his face darkened. 'It depends on what you're writing. If it's another filthy anti-Pakistan diatribe, I want no part in it.

I've read some of what you've written and I don't think much of it.'

He said that what angered him about the article I wrote after the London bombings was that I had posed as a Pakistani. He said that he and his father were known as defenders of Pakistan and had been patriots all their lives, that he could play no part in an attack on Pakistan and Islam.

He lay on his bed as he spoke, occasionally turning to me, but mostly text-messaging. He seemed bored yet irritated. He described the faith as a brotherhood, something he'd grown up in. He said that the other day he'd been in Udaipur where some numbers, '786', were written on a wall. He asked his guide what they meant and the man replied that they were a lucky charm. 'No,' my father had said, 'it's bismillah ar rahman ar rahim [in the name of God, the compassionate and the merciful].'

'Oh, you're Muslim,' the guide replied, and shook his hand.

'So, yes, there is a brotherhood,' my father said. 'People are warm to you, they bring you in, show you friendship.'

I asked him what it meant to be a 'cultural Muslim'.

'You see it all around you,' he replied. 'Everyone I know is Muslim. You see *namaz* [prayers], and *roza*s [fasts], all the servants are Muslim, and with Islam, people believe deeply. It happens that I don't privately, but I wouldn't dream of criticising Islam. I am not a practising Muslim, but my wife is and it would hurt her feelings.' He compared it to drinking in front of your friends when you wouldn't dream of doing so in front of your grandmother. 'It's offensive.'

His description of the 'cultural Muslim' seemed hardly different from my earliest idea of it, nothing more than festivals, ritual and language, but my journey had made me feel it contained deeper elements that he was not raising. My first hint of this was my father stressing many times that I was not Pakistani and not Muslim. The way he said it, with relish, he seemed almost to suggest that I wasn't really his son either. He stressed my not being Muslim so strongly that I became curious about the question with which my journey had begun: how could he be Muslim, if he claimed not to believe? How were we at this strange impasse where he, who didn't believe in the faith's most basic law, its Book, was telling me as a Muslim that I wasn't Muslim when by every law of the faith I was, and certainly if he was? He spoke with such passion, attaching some deeper importance to the idea of being Muslim, that I felt he couldn't be speaking only of culture.

During those days I spent in my father's house, I wanted very much for us to do something together that would help us regain the closeness we had known before I had received that letter. But our conversations now, with all that remained unsaid, reminded me of the first few years when I had known my father. There was the same embarrassment, but it was touched now with lack of interest.

And then, amid a minefield of family occasions, the perfect opportunity seemed to arise. I received a call from Yusuf, a cousin of my father, and on his mother's side the grandson of Iqbal, the poet and intellectual founder of Pakistan. It was Yusuf's great-grandmother who had rescued my grandfather all those years ago when the plague killed off his family. My grandfather grew up in Yusuf's *haveli*, or mansion, in the old city and I had been in touch with him since I arrived to find out more about my grandfather. Like the publisher, Yusuf had a special feeling for my connection to Pakistan and arranged meetings for me with his ancient uncles, who drank Chivas Regal in the evenings and had known my grandfather. That night Yusuf was calling to say that the famous Pakistani singer, Farida Khanum, was practising in the *haveli* and would I like to come? I accepted his invitation immediately, then asked my father if he would like to come with me. Even for

people who lived in Pakistan, the chance to hear Farida practise was rare.

His eyes brightened. 'Farida Khanum in the *haveli*?'

'Yes.'

Then, inexplicably, his mood changed and he declined. It
was the way it always with us: we were forever on the verge of
doing something that might deepen our relationship so that it
might be relied on, but it never happened.

So, I went off that night to Yusuf's *haveli* on my own. It
was in the heart of the old city, which, after the still heat of
the day, had come alive. A great doorway and a red-brick
drive rose out of the tightly packed streets, leading up to the
house, full of courtyards, slim balconies, leaning trees and a
collage of old city houses peering down at the scene below.
I found Farida Khanum in a room reached by a narrow staircase. She sat on the floor, in a pistachio green sari, eating
mangoes. She ate them with her hands and off the skin, her
dark red lipstick smudged. She was large and old, with dyed
black hair, her skin drooped, but her every gesture was touched
with femininity and whimsy: the gentle theatrics of an ageing
star. When, finally, she began to sing, all that melted away.
Her voice was insistent, filled with regret and seduction. She
seemed to notice that she'd moved a new, young admirer
nearly to tears and decided to drive the knife deeper. Yusuf
had told her when I came in that I was my grandfather's
grandson and now, helped by him, she put one of my grandfather's poems to music. Awakening his ghost in this house
where he'd lived, she gave me, couplet by couplet, the one
thing of my grandfather's that all poets hope will remain of
them.

As soon as she finished singing, Yusuf slipped away. He returned
a few minutes later and said he wanted to give me something.
He held a beautiful handmade watch with a grey face and a

shabby black strap. He said that my English great-grandfather had presented the watch to the head of Yusuf's family when my grandparents had got married. The watch had come down to Yusuf, and though my father had insisted on having it, Yusuf wanted to give it to me because I'd been Dr Taseer's only grandchild ever to ask about him. He warned me that it would probably cause more problems for me at home, but that I should stand firm. I was thrilled to have the watch. I already felt a connection to my grandfather, in part because he was a poet but also because I had been named after his main work.

The next morning, my stepmother said, 'Please don't tell Abba. He'll be really angry. He really wanted that watch.' Her mother suggested I give it to him for his birthday, but I decided, recalling the affection with which it had been given to me the night before, that I would wait. By now, it was as if everyone in the house sensed the strain between my father and me.

In the breakfast room, newspapers strewn everywhere, I found my father sitting in his blue cotton nightsuit with his legs up on the sofa, sometimes flicking through TV channels, sometimes playing with his phone. He was always up early and I was hoping to catch him alone, but a few minutes later, my elder sister, my stepmother and her father, who was old and in a wheelchair, joined us. A conversation began about a circle of homeopathic doctors in New York to which my sister belonged. They had received a group email about Ahmadinejad's denial of the Holocaust.

'I never respond,' my sister said in a loud voice, 'but this time I said, "There'd better have been a Holocaust because the only people who've paid for it for the last fifty years have been Muslims."'

My father sniggered. 'All the Germans paid was the gas bill.' He felt that the number of people who had died in the Holocaust was wildly exaggerated. Even if the Germans were working day and night through the whole war they couldn't have killed as many people as it was claimed. 'The job was too big. I've seen Belsen by the way,' he sneered. 'I was expecting a big warehouse or something. It was hardly bigger than this room. There's no way they could have fitted in more than three hundred people a day. Then they brought them in a train, which had to go back and forth . . . I'm not denying the Holocaust, the Jews were definitely gassed, but not so many.'

He said that the people who trumped up the Holocaust were like those who said the Pakistanis killed a million people in Bangladesh in 1971. He was about to use the same argument he did for Bangladesh, about to ask where the graves were, when he must have remembered that the Nazis hadn't bothered with graves.

I had said nothing so far because I had the incredible suspicion that he was needling me. I say 'incredible' because if this was needling what possible 'us and them' theory could be behind it? What group was I part of that made it automatic for me to object to a derisive attitude towards a well-documented genocide? But he must have been right because the satisfaction, with which, my sister made her remark, and the pleasure my father seemed to derive from downplaying the Holocaust, disgusted me. It was not just disgust at their hatred for the Jews and Israel, but at the smallness of my father's world, the homogeneity of the place, in which people voiced ugly opinions without challenge: a safe area for casual hatred.

My father, returning to the subject of the Holocaust, made the point more than once that he was not denying the Holocaust, just objecting to the figures. At last I became curious as to what number he could have arrived at that made the Holocaust not such a bad thing after all.

'So, how many?' I asked.

His amber eyes shone with irritation. 'I don't know, but the eight million figure people quote is rubbish.'

'Six?'

'No, and by the way, there were Romanians and Gypsies too.'

So what? I wanted to say.

'Four and a half million Jews?'

He shrugged. 'When I hear people go on about the Holocaust,' he said, 'I just shake my head and keep silent because the whole might of the Judaeo-Christian lobby will come down on you.'

My sister said that she objected to anyone who doubted the Holocaust being labelled anti-Semitic. I had heard that before, but usually it was framed as an objection to anyone criticising the State of Israel, not the Holocaust, being labelled anti-Semitic. Knowingly or unknowingly, my sister distorted this little bit of college speak. But it was a revealing error: it prompted my curiosity about what lay behind this wrangling over numbers.

'What has made you adjust these numbers?'

'What I've seen,' he answered, 'and what I've read.'

I knew the historians who refuted the Holocaust. When I thought of my father, who read vast amounts of history, reading these discredited historians, I thought that he would have had to go against all his better instincts, abandon all the ways in which he formed his other historical opinions, to believe what those books said.

I heard the Muslim denial or downplaying of the Holocaust many times in my journey, especially during the cartoon riots in Syria. It was done because the Holocaust was thought to have played a part in the creation of Israel. Muslims felt Jews had occupied a Muslim country and that their cause was taken up by the West in part out of guilt that the Holocaust had taken place. The politics of faith then, produced a distortion that was both ugly and magical: the Holocaust never happened or was grossly exaggerated; it was a myth concocted by the enemies of Islam. The chain of Islamic logic ended with Muslims denying a well-documented genocide that they hadn't committed.

The deeper reason, I felt, that my father chose the Holocaust was that in the West its memory was sacred. Perhaps he thought he would provoke me, show me how it felt to desecrate something sacred. He made a mistake for two reasons: I wasn't Jewish or from the West, and the Holocaust was committed in the West by the West. For the West then, to hold up the Holocaust with near holy dread, forcing itself never to forget the evil of those years in which it considered itself, not just the Germans, as complicit, was one of the most important treatments of history in modern times. It could not be reduced to the founding of Israel; it hadn't happened with a political end in mind; and it happened as much for the sake of the victimisers as for that of the victims. For me, on the outside, not from the West, to see the beauty of how another part of the world could move forward, could grow from such a terrible history, was a testament to history standing alone. You didn't have to be Jewish or European to accept the truth of it.

It was precisely the opposite of how the faith viewed history. Throughout my journey, this was the obstacle I had encountered: history fused with faith; the robbery of the great Islamic past, the pain and resentment that followed. It was what I, with my small idea of the faith, could not have acquired. It didn't need faith but, like faith, it had to be felt. And it was the reason why I had come to believe that there was more to being a 'cultural Muslim' than was apparent from the description.

'The real horror of the Holocaust,' I said, surprised at the tone in my voice, 'is not whether two, three or four million were killed, but that it was a mechanised, systematic extermination of a people. The state of Israel was many years in the making. It's possible to pry apart the causes for the creation of Israel from the fact of the Holocaust. You don't have to deny a Holocaust you didn't commit just because you hate Israel.'

Suddenly I looked round the room and felt bad. I thought,

I'm making such a nuisance of myself. My sister and step-mother looked worried about the direction the conversation was taking. My stepmother's father, his mouth open, was staring at me, wide-eyed.

My father nodded, then began on Israel and on the massacres in Sabra and Shatila, how women and children were killed, and what made that so different from the Holocaust. I didn't say any more. I had begun my journey asking why my father was Muslim and this was why: I felt sure that none of Islam's once powerful moral imperatives existed within him, but he was Muslim because he doubted the Holocaust, hated America and Israel, thought Hindus were weak and cowardly, and because the glories of the Islamic past excited him.

The faith decayed within him, ceased to be dynamic, ceased to provide moral guidance, became nothing but a deep, unreachable historical and political identity. This was all that still had the force of faith. It was significant because in the end this was the moderate Muslim, and it was too little moderation, and in the wrong areas. It didn't matter how someone prayed, how much they prayed, what dress they wore, whether they chose to drink or not, but it did matter that someone harboured feelings of hatred, for Jews, Americans or Hindus, that were founded in faith and only masked in political arguments.

Later he confessed that though he didn't believe Lahore drawing-room talk that 9/11 was a conspiracy, unanswered questions about the size of the hole in the Pentagon and Muhammad Atta's passport turning up at the crash site, produced doubt in him. 'I just don't know what to say when people bring up these things.' The 9/11 conspiracy theory was being added as the most recent article of faith for believer and non-believer alike.

I rose to leave the room. It was as if a bank had burst. My father and I, for the first time, were beyond embarrassment.

I returned a few moments later to say goodbye to him, but

he had left for the day without a word. The now empty room produced a corresponding vacancy in me that was like despair. I wanted somehow to feel whole again; not reconciliation, that would be asking too much, just not this feeling of waste: my journey to find my father ending in an empty room in Lahore, with the clear light of a bright morning breaking in to land on the criss-crossing arcs of a freshly swabbed floor.

As the crow flies, the distance between my father and me had never been much, but the land had been marked by history for a unique division, of which I had inherited both broken pieces. My journey to seek out my father, and through him, his country, was a way for me to make my peace with that history. And it had not been without its rewards. My deep connection to the land that is Pakistan had been renewed. I felt lucky to have both countries; I felt that I'd been given what Partition had denied many. For me it meant the possibility of a different education, of embracing the three-tier history of India whole, perhaps an intellectual troika of Sanskrit, Urdu and English. These mismatches were the lot of people with garbled histories, but I preferred them to violent purities. The world is richer in its hybrids.

But then there was the futility of the empty room, rupture on rupture, for which I could find no consolation except that my father's existence, so ghostly all my life, had at last acquired a gram of material weight. And, if not for that, who knows what sterile obsessions might still have held me fast?

Postscript: Distrust

A year later, in a Lahore shoe shop full of bulbs and mirrors and the smell of leather, the shopkeeper swivelled round to turn off a small television before he took my money. But I had seen something and so had a few bejewelled ladies standing next to me, so we asked him what had happened. His thick dyed moustache clamped shut over his mouth and his expression grew dark. He muttered, 'Benazir Bhutto has expired.'

He was aware of what happens when a demagogue dies on the sub-continent. 'When a big tree falls, the earth is bound to shake,' Rajiv Gandhi had said, when violence broke out against the Sikhs after his mother, Indira Gandhi, was killed. And violence was my first thought when I stepped out of the shop's bright lights and mirrors on to a cold, smoky Liberty Market, swiftly waking up to the fact that Benazir Bhutto was dead.

That name – Benazir Bhutto – already filled with music, a name that was more like a chant, a carryover from the greatness of the father, a name perhaps bigger than the person to whom it belonged, now linked with death, which brought drama to ordinary names, had alarmed the shopkeeper. Benazir Bhutto is dead. It was too much. We were in a city of slogans and the Lahore shopkeeper, who would have heard that name turned to slogan on so many memorable occasions and so often in relation to long life, knew that he had said something he would only ever say once in a lifetime. It began the last rite in the life of a demagogue, that one moment when the indestructible icon of the people, the person who replaced institutions, who herself was an echo of her name, was human, cut down and sacrificed, before becoming immortal again, her spirit passed to the heir on the back of a sympathy vote.

Benazir Bhutto is dead! Long live Benazir Bhutto!

*

There was to have been an election.

The year had been full of events. In the summer, there was the siege and storming of the Red Mosque in Islamabad where more than a hundred people were killed. In the autumn, the country's major political leaders tried to return from exile to take charge of their parties. Nawaz Sharif, allowed by the Supreme Court to return, was deported on arrival. Benazir Bhutto, as part of a deal with the Americans, returned in October and narrowly escaped a bomb blast at her welcome rally. In November, the General put an end to his year-long battle with the Supreme Court and declared a state of emergency, rescinding press freedom, imprisoning his opposition and sacking over sixty judges. By the end of the month, he had removed his uniform and installed himself as a civilian president in preparation for the election. And all the time the bombs had continued, and parts of the country that were once holiday destinations were in the hands of extremists. The demand for more literal Islam, so long in the background and often absorbed electorally, had turned renegade and become the country's main battle. By the time December came round and the emergency was lifted, it was difficult to trust that anything as positive as a genuine election could occur in this climate of extremism and extra-legality.

Interwoven in these national dramas was a personal surprise for me. Watching Musharraf swear in his caretaker government on television in November, I noticed my father's brother-in-law in the audience. And in the next bulletin I saw, in the foreground, that my father, the lifelong PPP man and the once close ally of Benazir Bhutto, was being sworn in as a minister to the ex-general's new cabinet.

Though I congratulated him, his elevation ensured that when I arrived in Lahore a few weeks later to cover the elections, I wouldn't stay with him. His political aspirations had been the reason for our original distance. I felt that staying with him now that he was in an official position, and especially after the ill feeling that had arisen between us, would cause embarrassment. So I asked my uncle Yusuf, with the rambling house in the old city where my grandfather grew up, if I could stay with him. 'On the condition you don't write anything about your father or Pakistan,' he pleaded. I half agreed.

And when I arrived there was not much to write about. Lahore was full of Christmas and New Year parties and election posters – white bicycles on green backgrounds, promoting the pro-Musharraf alliance, lined the city's canals. But there was a general air of malaise and distrust. People talked of rigging and pre-decided elections. After a few days of watching the atmosphere in the old city, usually the nerve centre of election excitement, my uncle declared, 'Such a cold election I never saw. At least a few gunshots should have gone off.'

We sat on low beds in the courtyard of his house near the Royal Mosque. There was much about the *haveli* that I missed in my earlier visits: frangipani trees and the lamp-lit shadows of their long leaves; semi-circular transoms in green, red and orange glass, particularly beautiful in the evenings;

chocolate-coloured screens of varying size, bringing harmony to the mismatch of whitewashed buildings. I had recently begun to read and understand my grandfather's poetry, and it was a source of wonder to inherit and slowly decipher a book in a new script from a dead, unseen grandfather. Yusuf was keen that I try to make contact with my father, and at his behest I did, but after a few unsuccessful attempts, un-returned calls and messages, I gave up.

Shortly after I arrived, Yusuf left to spend New Year in India. The election was still 'cold' when he left. Looking back at the year of protest, and how it had been subdued – the emergency that was like an act of irritation on the General's part at having to deal with real constitutional constraints – it didn't seem as if the election would ever warm up or become more than an ornament in the General's make-believe democracy.

And yet Benazir Bhutto and Nawaz Sharif, whatever their sins, were not part of this world of cosmetic democracy. The sight of a giant billboard of Benazir at the edge of the old city, pictured in blue against a vast crowd holding red, black and green People's Party flags, was enough to renew my faith in a genuine fight, if not a genuine election. The reason in part was that Benazir's fight, the fight my father had been part of, was the truest fight Pakistan had known against its inner demons, military dictatorship and fundamentalism. And though it had not fulfilled its promise, Benazir still seemed to have so much fight in her.

Benazir, unlike the general, didn't have to say she was liberal; people knew she was liberal. She was also one other thing that no one in the race could stake claim to: she was the only national politician, with support in all four provinces, in a country threatened with dissolution. So I felt that, despite talk of deals with the Americans and with Musharraf himself, if Benazir was in the race she would bring the 'noise and chaos' of democracy that her father had once written kept India in one piece.

But now, like her father, Benazir Bhutto was dead.

My thoughts went to my father. I knew he would be devastated. He'd fought General Zia alongside Benazir througout the eighties, been jailed for their shared cause, seen her triumphant return and electoral victory in 1988, been her party spokesman and travelled with her. And there was also the special pain he would feel of being estranged at death from someone he'd known and loved. But though my heart went out to him, the distrust that had grown between us in the past year made me feel that if I went to see him he would think I had come in bad faith.

I stood now, alone for a moment in the crowded market, naked bulbs coming on and evening traffic clogging the narrow street. I saw my brother's friend waiting for him to bring out the car and told him what I'd heard in the shop. He took in the information greedily, leant into the car as soon as it pulled up and told the others.

Before we had left the market, phone calls were coming in, telling us to get off the streets. We flicked through radio stations, hoping for more information, but the news had either been suppressed or the radio stations hadn't picked it up because they were leading with electoral stories. And what election could there be now? My brother wondered if there would still be a New Year's Eve ball. He wasn't being callous: he had paid a lot of money for the ticket and we were in an enclosed setting, with no perspective from TV or radio, trying to link the world as we'd just known it to the news that seemed to alter it so profoundly.

I called Nuscie, my mother's friend with whom I had stayed when I first came to Pakistan. She was sobbing and saying again and again, 'I just can't believe it. I can't believe they killed her.'

The news rebounding, forming webs, made real what was fantastical in the car's sealed environment. Then the mobile phones jammed, a sure sign of the city, so indifferent moments ago, becoming aware that Benazir Bhutto was dead.

The night was changing fast as we drove to my father's house. The street- and traffic-lights stopped working; there was a power cut of sorts; the traffic became more frantic and police barricades appeared.

When we reached my father's house, no one was sure whether or not I should go in to see him. 'This is the worst time,' my brother kept saying. My sister said she would go and see how he was taking the news before advising whether I should go in or not. In the meantime my mother called, also on the verge of tears. She had covered Pakistan for decades. In November 1988 she was in Lahore for Benazir's arrival. She wrote:

> I arrived in Lahore on the night of Nawaz Sharif's last rally of the campaign. The night before it had been Benazir's turn and everyone was still talking about the unbelievable welcome she had received. The city waited till dawn to hear her speak. It took all night for her to drive in from Gujranwala because of the thousands who lined the route. They lay down in front of her Pajero [a Japanese Land Rover that has become a political status symbol since she started using one], they danced in the streets, and when she finally spoke many wept. 'Lahore,' she said, 'is a city of lights,' quoting Faiz Ahmed Faiz's famous poem. 'Lahore is a city of people whose hearts are alive. Lahore is Benazir Bhutto's city.'

'It's too awful,' my mother wept. 'I first saw her when I was with your father. We were in Islamabad and he said, "That's Benazir Bhutto." She was so young, so pretty. She had no business dying.

Whatever her faults she didn't deserve to die like this.' My mother had witnessed the death of the great Indian demagogues, Indira Gandhi and her son, Rajiv. She understood demagoguery. She knew that in countries like ours, more so in Pakistan, where institutions are weak, where the state is threatened, these seemingly indestructible icons thrown up by the people bring a kind of solidity to the political landscape: they make it impossible to imagine the world without them.

I was still wavering when my father's brother-in-law entered the room. He had just been with my father and seemed to reflect the heaviness of his mood. 'Go in and see your father,' he said.

I began to say I wasn't sure that this was the right time.

'He's your father,' he said firmly. And then an old courage sprang up in me. I thought, I've met him in circumstances far more strained than these. How can I stand in the same house dithering over whether or not I should go in and see him?

I grabbed my little brother and walked into my father's house, past the pencil portrait of him, the courtyard, through the corridors that always smelt of food, and into the television room where we had parted on bad terms a year before. My father sat in his blue cotton nightsuit with his legs up on the sofa. He looked in my direction, a glimmer of surprise passing over his face, but didn't say a word. 'Abba,' I managed quietly. His gaze returned to the television, but he was haggard, his shock and grief written into the droop of his face and the dullness of his eyes. For forty minutes we sat in silence, our eyes following an Urdu/English news cycle of the bomb scene, riots spreading through the country, the PPP spokesman breaking the news, then breaking down. My father watched with two lenses: in one lens he was the lifelong PPP man, shaken to his core at seeing his leader cut down. He knew whose car she travelled in; he recognised all the people around her; as the one-time spokesman of the PPP, he had been in those situations so many times. In the other lens, he was a minister in Musharraf's caretaker government, fearful of what this could mean for it.

In that silence, I wondered why I was there. How despite our distances and unforeseen plans had the small works of Fate brought me to my father on the night Benazir Bhutto was killed? What was I to understand of the man – what was I to offer him? – on that cold and tense night, in a country that was noticeably more desolate, and by degrees, more violent?

When his shock subsided enough for him to speak, he said that the terrorists deliberately sought to rid the political landscape of its heroes. The men who wanted the faith to triumph knew that the country had to be destabilised, the robust society made bleaker. The ideologue in Karachi was right: the faith encouraged essence, and form was unimportant. But it also encouraged a dismantling of existing forms. Intellectual life, student unions, film industries and, eventually, judiciaries and constitutions were swept away; the cricket team began to focus on prayer; and, as the landscape became more desolate, the religious vision grew clearer, the anticipation of it more urgent. With every cycle, the conditions for faith were increased and the world was gradually undone till only the essence, of which the ideologue had spoken, remained.

I didn't need to be Pakistani to understand what my father meant, only perhaps the degree to which he meant it. The death of the demagogue would demoralise the population. But in a country with few national leaders, removing Benazir made the very idea of the federation less viable. 'And now you'll see the disintegration of the PPP,' my father said.

That disintegration was part of the Pakistani story. Just that year, Musharraf had hobbled the judiciary, and that institution, once one of the better ones in Pakistan, would not recover. My father now spoke of the country's biggest political party disintegrating.

But there was something else: no one believed the regime when they said the Taleban and al-Qaeda killed Benazir. The great majority of people believed some combination of the agencies, Musharraf and his allied party killed her. It was witnessing this distrust that made me understand what it meant to live in a state that had been discredited. And at a time when the regime claimed to be fighting the gravest threat to the state's existence!

My father's mind, with its double vision, fastened on a conundrum: on the one hand, elections couldn't be held in the present environment; on the other, the nation was in need of release, in need of legitimacy. Perhaps sensing his own mortality, he said, 'You can't have a caretaker government go on and on.'

Then images of the coffin flashed on the screen. Party workers handled it and beat their heads on it; the camera panned to a glass aperture on it its lid through which a white sheet was visible. My father's face turned to horror; he sucked his teeth and pressed his folded hands against the bridge of his nose. It was the same gesture Benazir had made when she stepped off the plane in Karachi a few months before, unspeakably moving, a gesture of fighting emotion in public.

'Like her brother,' my father said, 'shot in the neck.' He referred to Murtaza Bhutto, who was gunned down outside his house in 1996 when Benazir was prime minister.

'And in the same place as her father,' my brother-in-law added.

'What?' my father said, a flicker of his normal, energetic manner returning to him.

'Bhutto was executed in Rawalpindi,' my brother-in-law clarified. My father nodded and sank into silence.

Zulfikar Ali Bhutto had, in a way, also died from a wound to the neck. That had been the beginning of my father's political fight. The person we watched taken away in a simple coffin, now with no fight left in her, was his leader when that career came to fruition. It could be said that all my father's idealism – his jail time, the small success and the great disappointment, the years when he struggled for democracy in his country – were flanked by this father and daughter who both died of fatal wounds to the neck. And running parallel to these futile threads, with which my father could string his life together, were the generals, one whom he had fought and the other in whose cabinet he was now a minister.

For it to be possible for men to live with such disconnect, for my father to live so many lives, the past had to be swept away each time. The original break with history that Pakistan made to realise the impulses of the faith, and which gave it the rootlessness it knew today, had to be repeated. Like the year of events, which had ended in trauma, all that could be wished for was the distraction of the next event. But in these small interims when the past could be seen as a whole, when my father could cast painful bridges over history, I felt a great sympathy as I watched the man I had judged so harshly, for not facing his past when it came to me, muse on the pain of history in his country. And maybe this was all that the gods had wished me to see, the grimace on my father's face, and for us, both in our own ways strangers to history, to be together on the night that Benazir Bhutto was killed.

Acknowledgements

The journey I made for this book was longer than the text suggests. It began in Venice and ended in Delhi. There were countries like Jordan, Yemen and Oman that I travelled in, but was unable to write about. In eight months of travel, many more people helped than I can remember here. In some cases, I've had to leave out people because of the nature of the regimes they live in. For the same reason, certain names in the text have been changed. There are a few people whose generosity stands out, but I must emphasise it can only be attributed to the best traditions of warmth and hospitality, and is not an endorsement of what I have written, for which I am solely responsible. In Turkey: Eyup Ozer; Ömer Koç; Cigdem Simavi; Ömer Karacan. In Syria: Chad Sherif-Pasha; Even Nord. In Saudi Arabia: Fady Jameel; Salman bin Laden; Hisham Attar; Kareem Idriss. In Iran: Jack Gelardi. In Pakistan: Salmaan and Aamna Taseer; Shaan Taseer; Nuscie Jamil; Hameed Haroon; Yusuf Salahuddin.

I would like also to thank Claire Paterson, Andrew Kidd, Andy Miller, Anya Serota, Chiki Sarkar, Nick Davies.

Ajit Gulabchand, for his belief in me, and his unfaltering support.

And Ella Windsor, whose love and friendship run silently through each of these pages.

A Clinical Guide to Cancer Nursing

JONES AND BARTLETT SERIES
IN ONCOLOGY

A Clinical Guide to Cancer Nursing

A Companion to *Cancer Nursing,* Fourth Edition

Edited by

Susan L. Groenwald, RN, MS

Assistant Professor of Nursing—Complemental, Department of Medical Nursing, Rush University College of Nursing, Rush-Presbyterian-St. Luke's Medical Center, Chicago, Illinois

Margaret Hansen Frogge, RN, MS

Vice President—Strategic Development, Rush-Riverside Cancer Center, Riverside Medical Center, Kankakee, IL, Assistant Professor, Rush University College of Nursing, Chicago, Illinois

Michelle Goodman, RN, MS

Assistant Professor of Nursing, Rush University College of Nursing, Oncology Clinical Nurse Specialist, Section of Medical Oncology, Rush Cancer Institute, Rush-Presbyterian-St. Luke's Medical Center, Chicago, Illinois

Connie Henke Yarbro, RN, BSN

Editor, *Seminars in Oncology Nursing*
Clinical Associate Professor, Division of Hematology/Oncology, Adjunct Clinical Assistant Professor, Sinclair School of Nursing, University of Missouri, Columbia, Columbia, Missouri

JONES AND BARTLETT PUBLISHERS
Sudbury, Massachusetts
Boston   London   Singapore

Editorial, Sales, and Customer Service Offices

Jones and Bartlett Publishers
40 Tall Pine Drive
Sudbury, MA 01776
(978) 443-5000
(800) 832-0034
info@jbpub.com
http://www.jbpub.com

Jones and Bartlett
Publishers International
Barb House, Barb Mews
London W6 7PA
UK

Senior Production Editor: Lianne Ames
Editorial Assistant: Karen McLure
Director of Manufacturing: Jane Bromback
Editorial Production Service: Clarinda Publication Services
Cover Design: Dick Hannus
Cover and text Printing and Binding: Courier Companies

Library of Congress Cataloging-in-Publication Data

A clinical guide to cancer nursing: a companion to cancer nursing.
    fourth edition/edited by Susan L. Groenwald . . . [et al.].
        p. cm. — (Jones and Bartlett series in oncology)
    Companion v. to: Cancer nursing/edited by
        Susan L. Groenwald . . . [et al.]. 4th ed. 1997.
    Includes bibliographical references and index.
    ISBN 0-7637-0540-3 (pbk.)
    1. Cancer—Nursing—Handbooks, manuals, etc.
        I. Groenwald, Susan L. II. Cancer nursing. III. Series
    [DNLM: 1. Neoplasms—nursing—handbooks. 2. Onco-
    logic Nursing—methods—handbooks.   WY 49 6412 1998]
    [RC266.C55   1998
    610.73'698—dc21
    DNLM/DLC
    for Library of Congress   97-46106
                                                                    CIP

Printed in the United States of America.
        02 01 00 99 98   10 9 8 7 6 5 4 3 2 1

CONTENTS

PREFACE

In our continuing commitment to provide resources to all nurses who come in contact with individuals with cancer, we designed *Clinical Guide to Cancer Nursing* as an easy-to-use general nursing reference. Information most pertinent to the care of individuals with cancer has been gleaned from *Cancer Nursing: Principles and Practice, Fourth Edition,* and consolidated in this pocket-size clinical reference.

The content of this clinical guide follows the general outline of *Cancer Nursing: Principles and Practice.* Some chapters were deleted, and other chapters were split into smaller, more specific topics to foster clinical utility. Content has been thoroughly updated throughout and is presented in an abbreviated outline format to enhance the readability and aid in locating desired information quickly.

Part I, the Cancer Problem, covers epidemiologic and pathophysiologic aspects of cancer. Content on the biology of cancer has been completely updated to reflect the latest research. Part II, Diagnosis and Treatment, outlines standard and emerging treatment modalities and diagnostics, including an updated chapter on allogeneic and autologous bone marrow and a new chapter on blood cell transplantation. Part III, Symptom Management, provides step-by-step management of common symptoms in cancer patients. Chapters are alphabetized by subject, as they are in Part IV, The Care of Individuals with Cancer, for easier access by the reader. Part IV details the specific medical and nursing management for patients with 26 system- or location-specific types of cancer.

Part V, Issues in Cancer Survivors, includes a new chapter on spiritual and ethical concerns of cancer. In Part VI, Delivery Systems for Cancer Care, unique concerns related to the ambulatory, home, and hospice settings are covered. And finally, Part VII, Professional Issues for the Cancer Nurse, includes a chapter on ethical issues and a new chapter on cultural diversity.

Suggested readings have been included to direct the reader to more comprehensive information on the subject, including reference to the chapters in *Cancer Nursing: Principles and Practice* from which the content was extrapolated.

We sincerely hope that this book will be an easy-to-use, quick, and helpful reference to nurses—wherever they are caring for people with cancer.

ACKNOWLEDGMENTS

Our special thanks to the nurses who continue to provide us with feedback, suggestions, and encouragement regarding the information and resources they need in caring for patients with cancer. Thanks to Jones and Bartlett Publishers for their assistance and their commitment to providing quality textbooks to oncology nurses. Finally, we acknowledge and thank the following authors whose chapters in *Cancer Nursing: Principles and Practice, Fourth Edition* were used to derive the content contained in this guide:

Andrea M. Barsevick, RN, DNSc
Director of Nursing Research
Fox Chase Cancer Center
Philadelphia, PA

Karen Belford, RN, MS, OCN®, CCRN
Clinical Instructor, Department of Nursing Education
Memorial Sloan-Kettering Cancer Center
New York, NY

Connie Yuska Bildstein, RN, MS, CORLN
Vice President of Operations
Northwestern Memorial Home Health Care/Services, Inc.
Chicago, IL

Carol Blendowski, RN, BS, OCN®
Oncology Clinical Nurse
Rush Cancer Institute
Rush Presbyterian St. Luke's Medical Center
Chicago, IL

Karen Smith Blesch, RN, PhD
Documentation Specialist
Hoffman-LaRoche
Nutley, NJ

Debra L. Brock, RNC, MSN, CS, AOCN, ANP
Nurse Practitioner
Nashville Family Medicine
Nashville, IN

Patricia Corcoran Buchsel, RN, MSN
Senior Research Associate
University of Washington
Transplantation Consultant
Issaquah, WA

Dawn Comp-Sorrell, RN, MSN, AOCN, FNP
Oncology Nurse Practitioner
University of Alabama at Birmingham Hospital
Birmingham, AL

Brenda Cartmel, PhD
CPS/CARET: Yale University
Occupational Health Center
Groton, CT

Dianne D. Chapman, RN, MS, OCN®
Coordinator, Comprehensive Breast Center
Genetic Counselor
Rush Inherited Susceptibility for Cancer (RISC) Program
Rush Cancer Institute
Rush Presbyterian St. Luke's Medical Center
Chicago, IL

Jane Clark, RN, MN, OCN®
Clinical Nurse Specialist
Emory University Hospital
Atlanta, GA

JoAnn Coleman, RN, MS, CRNP, OCN®
Case Manager for Pancreas and Biliary Surgery
Department of Surgical Nursing
Johns Hopkins Hospital
Baltimore, MD

Jan M. Ellerhorst-Ryan, RN, MSN, CS
Oncology/HIV Clinical Nurse Specialist
Vitas Health Care Corporation
Cincinnati, OH

Ellen H. Elpern, RN, MS
Coordinator, Lung Transplant Program
Rush Presbyterian St. Luke's Medical Center
Chicago, IL

Ann T. Foltz, RN, DNS
Breast and Cervical Cancer Program Director
Louisiana Office of Public Health
New Orleans, LA

Susan M. Fox, RN, MS, OCN®
Oncology Research
Nurse
Indiana University
Cancer Pavilion
Indianapolis, IN

Margaret Hansen Frogge, RN, MS
Assistant Professor,
Associate Faculty
Rush University College
of Nursing
Rush Presbyterian St.
Luke's Medical Center
Chicago, IL
Vice President, Strategic
Development and
System Integration
Riverside Medical Center
Kankakee, IL

Barbara Holmes Gobel, RN, MS
Oncology Clinical Nurse
Specialist
Gottlieb Memorial
Hospital
Melrose Park, IL
Instructor,
Complemental
Rush University College
of Nursing
Chicago, IL

Michelle Goodman, RN, MS, OCN®
Assistant Professor
of Nursing
Rush University
College of Nursing
Oncology Clinical
Nurse Specialist
Section of Medical
Oncology
Rush Cancer Institute
Rush Presbyterian St.
Luke's Medical Center
Chicago, IL

Susan L. Groenwald, RN, MS
Assistant Professor of
Nursing, Complemental
Rush University College
of Nursing
Rush Presbyterian St.
Luke's Medical Center
Chicago, IL

Carol Guarnieri, RN, MSN, AOCN
Oncology Clinical
Nurse Specialist
Samitivej Srinakarin
Hospital
Bangkok, Thailand

Lynne Hagan, RN, BSN, CETN
Enterostomal Therapy
USC Kenneth Norris, Jr.
Cancer Hospital
Los Angeles, CA

Jeanne Held-Warmkessel, RN, MSN, CS, AOCN
Instructor, Roxborough
Memorial Hospital
School of Nursing
Philadelphia, PA

Laura J. Hilderley, RN, MS
Clinical Nurse Specialist,
Radiation Oncology
Radiation Oncology
Services of Rhode Island
Warwick, RI

Linda Hoebler, RN, MSN
Oncology Clinical
Nurse Specialist
Allegheny General
Hospital
Pittsburgh, PA

Rebecca J. Ingle, RN, MSN, FNP, AOCN
Oncology Clinical
Specialist
The Dan Rudy
Cancer Center
Saint Thomas Hospital
Adjunct Instructor of
Nursing
Vanderbilt University
School of Nursing
Nashville, TN

Joanne K. Itano, RN, PhD, OCN®
The University of Hawaii
at Manoa
School of Nursing
Honolulu, HI

Patricia F. Jassak, RN, MS, CS, OCS
Rush Cancer Center
Rush Presbyterian St.
Luke's Medical Center
Chicago, IL

Barbara Hansen Kalinowski, RN, MSN, OCN®
Clinical Research Nurse
Joint Center for
Radiation Therapy
Boston, MA

Marsha A. Ketcham, RN, OCN®
Senior Research Nurse
Arizona Cancer Center
Tucson, AZ

Paula Klemm, RN, DNSc, OCN®
Assistant Chair
University of Delaware,
College of Nursing
Newark, DE
Clinical Nurse
Department of GYN/OB
Johns Hopkins Hospital
Baltimore, MD

Jennifer Lang-Kummer, RN, MN, CS, FNP
Oncology Case
Management Services
Pitt County Memorial
Hospital
Adjunct Assistant
Professor of Nursing
East Carolina University
Greenville, NC

Paul J. LeMarbre, MD
Medical Oncology/
Hematology
Waukesha Memorial
Hospital
Waukesha, WI

**Julena Lind, RN, MN,
MA, PhD(c)**
Assistant Professor of
Clinical Nursing
University of Southern
California
Los Angeles, CA

Lois J. Loescher, RN, MS
Senior Research
Specialist, Cancer
Prevention and Control
Arizona Cancer Center
Tucson, AZ

**Jeanne Martinez, RN,
MPH**
Clinical Nurse Manager
Northwestern Hospice
Program
Chicago, IL

**Mary B. Maxwell, RN, C,
PhD**
Clinical Specialist/Nurse
Practitioner in Oncology
Veterans' Affairs Medical
Center
Adjunct Assistant
Professor of Nursing
Oregon Health Sciences
University
Portland, OR

**Mary Ellen McFadden,
RN, MLA, OCN®**
Clinical Support
Specialist Amgen
Baltimore, MD

**Deborah B. McGuire, RN,
PhD, FAAN**
Edith Folsom Honeycutt
Chair in Oncology
Nursing
Associate Professor
Nell Hodgson Woodruff
School of Nursing
Emory University
Atlanta, GA

**Joan C. McNally, RN,
MSN, OCN,® CRNH**
Director, Health Care
Services
Karmanos Cancer
Institute Home Care
and Hospice Programs
Detroit, MI

**Theresa A. Moran, RN,
MS**
AIDS/Oncology Clinical
Nurse Specialist
University of California,
San Francisco/
San Francisco General
Hospital
Assistant Clinical
Professor
Department of
Physiological Nursing
University of California
San Francisco, CA

Judie Much, MSN, CRNP, AOCN
Oncology Clinical Nurse Specialist
Psychosocial Support Nurse
Fox Chase Cancer Center
Philadelphia, PA

Lillian M. Nail, RN, PhD, FAAN
Associate Professor
Associate Dean for Research
University of Utah College of Nursing
Salt Lake City, UT

Cathleen A. O'Conner-Vaccari, RN, MSN, OCN®
Manager/Clinical Nurse Specialist
Memorial Sloan-Kettering Cancer Center
New York, NY

Sharon Saldin O'Mary, RN, MN, OCN®
Director of Hospice Services
Nations Health Care Hospice
San Diego, CA

Diane M. Otte, RN, MS, ET, OCN®
Alegent Health
Administrative Director, Cancer Center
Immanuel Medical Center
Omaha, NE

Patricia A. Piasecki, RN, MS
Clinical Coordinator, Orthopedic Oncology
Rush Presbyterian St. Luke's Medical Center
Chicago, IL

Sandra Purl, RN, MS, AOCN
Oncology Clinical Nurse Specialist
Lutheran General Hospital
Park Ridge, IL

Mary Reid, RN, MSPH
Research Specialist
Department of Family and Community Medicine
University of Arizona
Tucson, AZ

Mary Beth Riley, RN, MS
Oncology Clinical Specialist
Rush Cancer Institute
Rush Presbyterian St. Luke's Medical Center
Chicago, IL

Kimberly Rohan, RN, MS, OCN®
Patient Services Coordinator
Edward Hospital
Naperville, IL

Vivian R. Sheidler, RN, MS
Clinical Nurse Specialist—Neuro-Oncology
Johns Hopkins Oncology Center
Baltimore, MD

Carol A. Sheridan, RN, MSN, AOCN
Clinical Support Specialist
Amgen
New York, NY

Carole Sweeney, RN, MSN, OCN®
Fox Chase Cancer Center
Philadelphia, PA

Karen N. Taoka, RN, MN, AOCN
Clinical Nurse Specialist
The Queens Medical Center
Honolulu, HI

Elizabeth Johnston Taylor, RN, PhD
Assistant Professor
University of Southern California
Department of Nursing
Los Angeles, CA

David C. Thomasma, PhD
The Fr. Michael I. English S.J. Professor of Medical Ethics
Director, Medical Humanities Program
Loyola University of Chicago Medical Center
Maywood, IL

Peter V. Tortorice, PharmD, BCPS
Oncology Clinical Pharmacist
Illinois Masonic Cancer Center
Chicago, IL

Steven Wagner, RN, BSN
Nurse Clinician
Northwestern Hospice Program
Chicago, IL

Janet Ruth Walczak, RN, MSN
Clinical Nurse Specialist
The Johns Hopkins
Oncology Center
Clinical Associate
The Johns Hopkins
University, School of
Nursing
Baltimore, MD

Vera S. Wheeler, RN, MN, OCN®
Consultant, Cancer
Nursing and Biotherapy
Vancouver, WA

Rita Wickham, RN, PhD(c), AOCN
Assistant Professor,
College of Nursing
Rush University
Rush Presbyterian St.
Luke's Medical Center
Chicago, IL

Debra Wujcik, RN, MSN, AOCN
Clinical Director
Affiliate Network Office
Vanderbilt Cancer Center
Clinical Trials Office
Adjunct Instructor
Vanderbilt University
School of Nursing
Nashville, TN

Connie Henke Yarbro, RN, MS, FAAN
Editor, *Seminars in Oncology Nursing*
Clinical Associate
Professor
Division of
Hematology/Oncology
Adjunct Clinical
Assistant Professor
Sinclair School of
Nursing
University of
Missouri–Columbia
Columbia, MO

John W. Yarbro, MD, PhD
Professor Emeritus,
School of Medicine
University of
Missouri–Columbia
Columbia, MO
Editor, *Seminars in Oncology*

PART I

The Cancer Problem

CHAPTER 1

Cancer Epidemiology

Overview

Cancer epidemiology is the study of

1. Frequency of cancer in populations
2. Risk factors
3. Interrelationships between host and environment

Cancer Causation Factors

Environment

1. Tobacco

    * Most important known cause of cancer
    * Causes about 30% of cancer deaths

* Cigarette smoking causes 90% of lung cancers

2. Diet

   * Proposed as contributing factor in 20% to 70% of cancer deaths
   * A modifiable risk factor

3. Alcohol

   * Causally linked with cancers of the oral cavity, pharynx, larynx, esophagus, and liver; may be linked to cancers of the breast and rectum
   * Accounts for 3% of cancer deaths
   * Appears to be synergistic with smoking

4. Physical activity

   * Protective for colon cancer and precancerous colon polyps
   * May be protective for breast cancer

5. Occupational exposure to carcinogens

   * Accounts for 4% to 9% of cancer deaths
   * Related primarily to lung cancer

6. Pollution

   * Accounts for less than 1% to 5% of cancer deaths in U.S.
   * Related primarily to lung and skin cancers

7. Reproductive factors and sexual behavior

   * Endometrial, breast, and ovarian cancers related to unopposed estrogens

* Cervical cancer related to number of sexual partners

8. Viruses and other biologic agents

   * Viruses account for 15% of worldwide cancer incidence
   * Implicated viruses include

     Hepatitis B virus (HBV)

     Human T-lymphotropic virus type 1 (HTLV-1)

     Epstein-Barr virus (EBV)

     Human papillomavirus (HPV)
   * Gastric cancer may be linked to infection with *Helicobacter pylori*
   * *Schistosoma haematobium*, a parasitic flatworm found in Egypt and Africa, may cause bladder cancer

9. Radiation

   * Responsible for 3% of cancer deaths
   * Types of radiation

     Ionizing

     Nonionizing

     Ultraviolet (UV)

10. Drugs

    * Second malignancy is late effect of cell damage resulting from chemotherapeutic agents
    * Phenacetin is associated with cancers of the lower urinary tract

* The immunosuppressive drug azathioprine is associated with increased incidence of non-Hodgkin's lymphoma and squamous cell cancer of the skin

* The immunosuppressive drug cyclosporine is associated with increased risk of lymphoma

* 8-Methoxypsoralen combined with UV radiation, used for treatment of psoriasis and vitiligo, is associated with increased risk of squamous cell cancer of the skin

11. Exogenous hormones

* Diethylstilbestrol associated with vaginal and cervical cancers in daughters of treated women

* Combined oral contraceptives associated with decreased risk of endometrial and ovarian cancer

* Increased risk of liver cancer associated with oral contraceptive use in young women

* Estrogen replacement therapy has been shown to increase the risk of endometrial cancer in postmenopausal women

Host factors

1. Age

* Individuals over age 65 are 10 times more likely to develop cancer because of

    Prolonged lifetime exposure to cancer-inducing agents

Declining efficacy of immune system

2. Sex

   * Incidence of non–gender-specific cancers is lower in females

3. Genetic predisposition

   * Associated with certain types of cancer, such as familial polyposis

   * Aggregates in families due to inherited susceptibility or to common environmental exposure

   * Two genes, *BRCA1* and *BRCA2,* are associated with 5% of breast cancers

4. Ethnicity and race

   * Biologic and cultural factors cause differences in incidence and mortality

5. Socioeconomic status (SES)

   * Low SES associated with some cancers, independent of race

   * Strongly associated with lifestyle

   * Low SES strongly associated with smoking prevalence and higher lung cancer rates

Application to Cancer Nursing Practice

Epidemiologic data are used by nurses to

1. Identify high-risk patient populations
2. Develop and evaluate effectiveness of cancer prevention programs

3. Understand survival rates

   * Calculation of the probability that an
     individual with a specific disease will be
     alive at a particular time after diagnosis
     (usually 5 years)

Suggested Readings

1. Cartmel B, Reid M: Cancer control and
   epidemiology. In Groenwald SL, Frogge MH,
   Goodman M, Yarbro CH (eds): *Cancer Nursing:
   Principles and Practice* (4th ed). Boston: Jones
   and Bartlett, 1997, pp 50-74.
2. Cartmel B, Loescher LJ, Villar-Werstler P:
   Professional and consumer concerns about the
   environment, lifestyle and cancer. *Semin Oncol
   Nurs* 8(1):20-29, 1992.
3. Oleske DM: Epidemiologic principles for
   nursing practice: Assessing the cancer
   problem and planning its control. In Frank-
   Stromborg M, McCorkle R, Grant M, Baird S,
   (eds): *Cancer Nursing: A Comprehensive Textbook*
   (2nd ed). Philadelphia: Saunders, 1995,
   pp. 119-137.

CHAPTER 2

Carcinogenesis

Overview

Body cells are held under rigid growth control

Control of cell division is maintained by oncogenes (growth promoters) and cancer-suppressor genes (growth-inhibitors)

Carcinogenesis is the process by which these genes are damaged to the extent that clones of cells lose their normal control mechanisms of growth and proliferate out of control

Stages of Carcinogenesis

In the past, carcinogenesis was divided into three stages—initiation, promotion, and progression

1. Initiation indicates a primary change in the target, produced by a carcinogen
2. Promotion is the secondary effect of a promoter, which alone might not be able to induce a malignancy
3. Progression designates the process by which tumors go from bad to worse

Distinction among the three stages is blurred, and many more steps are involved

1. More than one type of initiating event is probably common
2. In some cases, initiators may act as their own promoters (a complete carcinogen)
3. An initiator may be a complete carcinogen for one organ and an incomplete carcinogen for another organ

Chemical Carcinogenesis

There are few chemicals for which there is strong evidence of cancer causation in humans

1. Tobacco
2. Benzene
3. 2-Naphthylamine
4. Vinyl chloride
5. Some metals

Only 4% of cancer deaths in U.S. are from occupational exposure

Chemotherapeutic agents are associated with subsequent development of cancer, especially leukemia and myeloproliferative syndromes

Familial Carcinogenesis

15% of human cancers may have a hereditary component

1. Breast cancer estimated to have familial component in about 13% of cases
2. Some genes, when inherited, increase the risk of cancer
3. Genes have been isolated for several classic family syndromes

   * *RB1* in retinoblastoma
   * *WT1* in Wilms' tumor
   * *NF1* and *NF2* in neurofibromatosis types 1 and 2
   * *APC* in familial polyposis associated with colon cancer
   * *RET* in syndromes of multiple endocrine neoplasias
   * *VHL* in von Hipple-Lindau syndrome
   * *FACC* in Fanconi's anemia
   * ATM in ataxia telangiectasia
   * *BLM* in Bloom syndrome

* *P53* in Li-Fraumeni syndrome
* *RAD2* in xeroderma pigmentosum
* *MSH2*, *MLH1*, *PMS1*, and *PMS2* in hereditary nonpolyposis colorectal cancer (HNPCC)
* *CDKN2* in dysplastic nevus syndrome
* *BRCA 1* in breast and ovarian cancer
* *BRCA2* in breast cancer

Physical Carcinogenesis

Agents damage oncogenes and cancer-suppressor genes by physical means

1. UV radiation from the sun induces cancers of the skin
2. Ionizing radiation, mostly from natural sources, is carcinogenic
3. Asbestos causes mesothelioma and bronchogenic cancers

Viral Carcinogenesis

Evidence for viral etiology of cancer is strongest for relationship between

1. Hepatitis B virus (HBV) and hepatocellular carcinoma
2. Human T-cell leukemia virus type 1 (HTLV-1) and T-cell lymphoma
3. Association between Burtkitt's lymphoma and Epstein-Barr virus (EBV) is also strong

4. Evidence for role of viruses in other cancers:

  * EBV and nasopharyngeal carcinoma in Chinese persons
  * Herpes simplex virus type 2 (HSV-2) and human papillomavirus (HPV) in cervical carcinoma

Bacterial Carcinogenesis

Relationship discovered between *Helicobacter pylori* and the mucosa-associated lymphoid tissue (MALT) lymphoma of the gastric mucosa

Suggested Readings

1. Yarbro JW: Carcinogenesis. In Groenwald SL, Frogge MH, Goodman M, Yarbro C (eds): *Cancer Nursing: Principles and Practice* (4th ed). Boston: Jones and Bartlett, 1997, pp 39-49.
2. Mettlin C, Michalek AM: The causes of cancer. In Frank-Stromborg M, McCorkle R, Grant M, Baird S: *Cancer Nursing: A Comprehensive Textbook.* Philadelphia: Saunders, 1995.
3. Shields PG, Harris CC: Principles of carcinogenesis: Chemical. In Devita VT Jr, Hellman S, Rosenberg SA (eds): *Cancer: Principles and Practice of Oncology.* Philadelphia: Lippincott, 1993, pp 200-212.
4. Howley PM: Principles of carinogenesis: Viral. In Devita VT Jr, Hellman S, Rosenberg SA (eds): *Cancer: Principles and Practice of Oncology.* Philadelphia: Lippincott, 1993, pp 182-199.

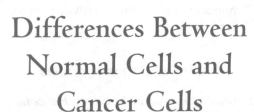

CHAPTER 3

Differences Between Normal Cells and Cancer Cells

Differences in Growth

Primary feature of cancer cell is uncontrolled growth

1. Normal cells are carefully regulated; number of new cells formed in tissues equals number lost by cell death or injury
2. In cancer, cells continue to divide without regard to needs of host

Average human neoplasm doubles in size every 2 months

1. Cell cycle time of cancer cells is not much different from that of normal cells

2. Number of new cells is greater than number of cells lost, resulting in tumor mass

Uncontrolled growth of tumors occurs from

1. Cancer cell immortality

    * Most normal cells divide only approximately 50 to 60 times before they die; cancer cells are immortal

2. Loss of contact inhibition

    * When placed in a petri dish, normal cells in culture divide until they form a single layer of cells on the bottom of the culture dish, when they stop dividing

    * Cancer cells do not stop dividing; they pile on top of each other in an unorganized mass

3. Diminished growth factor requirements

    * Cancer cells appear to

       Divide without or with lower concentrations of normal serum growth factors

       Make their own growth factors

4. Ability to divide without anchorage to a surface

    * Most normal cells will not divide in liquid medium or in suspension surface; they require anchorage to a surface to divide

    * Cancer cells grow in suspension or gel

5. Loss of restriction point in cell cycle

   ∗ "Decision" of cell to enter G0 (resting
     phase) of cell cycle or to continue into G1
     occurs at point in G1 called the restriction
     point
   ∗ G0 controls cell division
   ∗ When cell passes restriction point, it is
     committed to cell division
   ∗ Cancer cells do not have this control, and
     therefore do not enter G0

Differences in Appearance

Normal cells have well-organized and extensive cytoskeleton providing cell structure and shape

Transformed cells have

1. Variable sizes and shapes
2. Darker-staining nuclei (hyperchromatism)
3. Larger nuclei
4. Variety of abnormal mitotic figures

Differences in Differentiation

Differentiation: Process by which cells become specialized for specific functions

1. All cells derive from one cell
2. Occurs by "turning on and off" of certain genes
3. The more differentiated a cell, the more its potential is restricted

4. Fully differentiated cells are often incapable of replicating

Cancer cells may arise at any point in differentiation

Oncogenes active in embryos but suppressed during differentiation can be reactivated by carcinogenic agents

Cancer cells tend to be less differentiated than cells from normal tissue

Anaplasia occurs when cancer cells are so undifferentiated that tissue of origin cannot be identified

During shift from normal to undifferentiated cells, a sequence of tissue alterations occurs

1. Metaplasia
2. Dysplasia
3. Carcinoma in situ
4. Invasive carcinoma

Differences in Cell Surface

Cell membranes of animal cells determine which molecules can enter and leave cell

Numerous changes take place in cancer cell surface

1. Glycoproteins are missing or altered
2. Absence of fibronectin prevents cancer cells from attaching to other surfaces

3. Secretion of proteolytic enzymes promotes metastasis

4. Content and complexity of cell surface glycolipids are reduced

   * Increases responsiveness of cancer cells to growth factors

   * Reduces cell-cell recognition by altering glycolipid surface markers

5. Tumor-associated antigens appear on surface of cancer cells

   * Used as tumor markers in

     Cancer detection

     Monitoring prognosis

     Evaluating treatment measures

6. Permeability and rate of transport of materials across cell membrane are increased

Biochemical Differences

Biochemical substances are altered, missing, abnormally secreted, or secreted in increased amounts by tumor cells

1. Altered biochemical substances include

   * Cyclic adenosine monophosphate

   * Cyclic guanosine monophosphate

   * Nutrients

   * Chalones

   * Growth factors

2. Cell growth and cell-cell interactions are affected

Genetic Differences

Cancer arises from single altered cell that acquires heritable and selective growth advantage over other cells

1. Each daughter cell inherits genetic defect
2. Tumor cells are genetically unstable
3. Tumor progression results from additional mutations in cells within clone
4. Result is sequential appearance within tumor of subpopulations of heterogeneous cells

Tumor heterogeneity identified as most significant cause of cancer treatment failure

Suggested Readings

1. Clark WH: Tumor progression and the nature of cancer. *Br J Cancer* 64:631-644, 1991.
2. LeMarbre PJ, Groenwald SL: Biology of cancer. In Groenwald SL, Frogge MH, Goodman M, Yarbro C (eds): *Cancer Nursing: Principles and Practice* (4th ed.). Boston: Jones and Bartlett, 1997, pp 17-37.
3. Groenwald SL: The behavior of malignancies. In Gross J, Johnson BJ (eds): *Handbook of Oncology Nursing* (2nd ed). Boston: Jones and Bartlett, 1994, pp 3-20.
4. Lind J: Tumor cell growth and cell kinetics. *Semin Oncol Nurs* 8(1):3-9, 1992.

CHAPTER 4

Invasion and Metastasis

Overview

Most cancer deaths are related to uncontrolled progression of metastasis

Microscopic colonies of cancer cells are often present in other areas of the body when symptoms of cancer first appear

Factors Contributing to Metastatic Potential

Tumor Factors

1. Progression of tumors from benign to malignant is associated with structural alterations in genes and changes in genetic expression

2. Genes controlling proliferation appear to be different than those related to invasion and metastatis

3. Heterogeneity

   * Clones of cells isolated from tumors vary in metastatic potential

   * Tumors are comprised of resistant cells that prosper and produce more and more unstable cells

   * Even if 99.9% cell kill is achieved with therapy for a 1-cm lesion, a significant number (105) of resistant cells will remain and continue growing

   * Heterogeneity explains differences in growth and metastasis of similar tumors in different individuals

4. Production of angiogenic factors

   * Assists metastatic clones to establish blood supply

5. Motility factors

   * Necessary for tumor cells to move away from primary tumor site

6. Specific cell-surface receptors

   ∗ Integrins are crucial for binding of
     fibronectin and laminin to basement
     membrane, enabling tumor cells to breach
     tissue barrier

Host Factors

1. Deficient immune response

   ∗ Contributes to development of cancer and
     metastases

2. Intact hemostatic system

   ∗ Platelets play central role in metastatic
     process
   ∗ Antiplatelet drugs inhibit experimentally
     induced cell metastases in mice

Metastatic Sequence

Tumor neovascularization and growth

1. Growing tumor establishes its own blood
   supply through angiogenesis
2. New tumor blood vessels are disorganized,
   with prominent gaps in their walls that allow
   tumor cells to gain entrance and potentially
   travel away from primary site

Tumor cell invasion of surrounding tissue

1. Local invasion of tissue surrounding tumor
   can be by single cells or groups of cells
2. Invasion begins with destruction of basement
   membrane of cells of host tissue

3. Abnormal cell motility and chemoattractants in tumor tissue cause cells to push through tissue to spread to distant sites

Detachment and embolism of tumor cell aggregates

1. Early movement of tumor cell is by pseudopodia protrusion
2. Random tumor cell motility and dispersion from primary site are regulated by cytokines
3. Tumor cells may enter the lymphatic or circulatory system
4. Once in a vessel, tumor cells may localize at entry site or disseminate to other locations
5. Some tumors have tendency to spread locally through lymphatics before metastasizing, while others involve the bloodstream early
6. Eventually, if cells survive, they will enter the circulatory system, where they face threats such as

   * Mechanical forces of blood turbulence

   * Immune defenses

7. Tumor cells form aggregates to other tumor cells or blood cells, such as platelets, for protection against immune cells

Arrest

1. Tumor cells arrest in capillaries and attach to endothelial cells or vascular basement membrane, or both
2. Approximately 50% to 60% of metastatic distribution can be predicted from knowing

anatomic route followed by disseminating tumor cell

3. In approximately 40% to 50% of tumors, distribution of metastases appears

   * To be selective
   * To depend on growth factors and match between tumor and organ chemotaxis

Extravasation

1. Once tumor cell arrests in capillary bed of target organ

   * Degradative enzymes are produced by tumor cells that break down capillary basement membrane
   * Tumor cell penetrates through capillary into organ tissue

Proliferation within organ parenchyma

1. Metastatic tumor grows and proliferates by

   * Establishing a blood supply (angiogenesis)
   * Restarting metastatic cycle

Genetic Control of the Metastatic Continuum

Many genes have been implicated in formation of a metastatic phenotype

Current evidence suggests that invasion and metastasis require activation of a set of effector genes over and above those required for unrestrained growth alone

A metastasis suppressor gene, *NM23,* may be a most important factor in determining metastatic potential

Antimetastasis Therapy

Prevention of metastasis lies in ability to interrupt one or more steps in metastatic process

Many substances that interfere with metastatic process have been studied

1. Inhibitors of proteinase activity interrupt tumor cell invasion
2. Synthetic peptides with sequence Arg-Gly-Asp block tumor cell adhesion
3. Monoclonal antibodies prevent tumor cells from binding to and invading basement membrane
4. Razoxane restores structure and integrity of capillary vessels in tumors
5. TNP-470 and other agents inhibit angiogenesis
6. If it is found that certain genes have a significant impact on metastatic potential of cancer cells, genetic manipulation of tumor cells to restore them to normal may be possible

Clinical Application

Clinical challenges of cancer metastasis include

1. Accurate identification of metastatic potential of primary tumor
2. Diagnosis and localization of clinically silent micrometastases at time of initial diagnosis of cancer
3. Complete eradication of all tumor cells in heterogeneous tumor with primary tumor treatment
4. Selective eradication of metastases during treatment of primary tumor
5. Prevention of invasion and metastasis

Suggested Readings

1. Holzman D: New view of metastasis is spreading. *J Natl Cancer Inst* 88:1336-1338, 1996.
2. Ruoslahti E: How cancer spreads. *Sci Am* 275:72-77, 1996.
3. LeMarbre PJ, Groenwald SL: Biology of cancer. In Groenwald SL, Frogge MH, Goodman M, Yarbro CH (eds): *Cancer Nursing: Principles and Practice* (4th ed). Boston: Jones and Bartlett, 1997, pp 17-39.

PART II

Diagnosis
and Treatment

CHAPTER 5

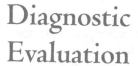

Diagnostic
Evaluation

Overview

Major goals are to determine

1. Tissue type
2. Primary site
3. Extent of disease
4. Potential for recurrence

Approach depends on

1. Patient's presenting symptoms
2. Patient's clinical status
3. Patient's tolerance of invasive tests
4. Anticipated goal of treatment
5. Biologic characteristics of suspected tumor

29

6. Availability of diagnostic equipment
7. Third-party payor approval

Early detection and treatment are key to survival

The seven warning signals of cancer are

1. Change in bowel or bladder habits
2. Unusual bleeding or discharge
3. Sore that does not heal
4. Obvious change in wart or mole
5. Thickening or lump in breast or elsewhere
6. Nagging cough or hoarseness
7. Indigestion or difficulty in swallowing

Nursing Implications in Diagnostic Evaluation

Role of nurse

1. Determine an individual's risk for cancer
2. Facilitate entry into the health care system
3. Provide information on cancer detection and diagnostic procedures
4. Clarify misconceptions
5. Refer patient to appropriate health care providers
6. Provide information to reduce stress of diagnostic procedures
7. Assess for possible complications from procedure
8. Design education programs that target populations at risk and those who are likely to delay seeking medical attention

Diagnostic Methods

Laboratory techniques

1. Biochemical analysis of blood and urine
2. Tumor markers

   * Produced by tumor

   * Produced by other cells in response to tumor

   * Can be used to detect cancer or monitor response to therapy

   * Most commonly used markers are

   Carcinoembryonic antigen (CEA: elevated in colo-rectal, stomach, pancreas, lungs and breast)

   Alpha-fetoprotein (AFP: elevated in testicular cancer)

   Human chorionic gonadotropin b-subunit (B-HCG: elevated in choriocarcinoma, germ cell testicular cancer)

   Prostate-specific antigen (PSA: elevated in prostate cancer)

   Cancer antigen 125 (CA 125: elevated in ovary, pancreas, breast and colon cancer)

   Cancer antigen 19-9 (CA 19-9: elevated in pancreas, colon, gastric cancer)

   Cancer antigen 15-3 (CA 15-3: elevated in breast cancer)

   Cancer antigen 72-4 (CA 72-4: elevated in gastric cancer)

3. Flow cytometry

  ∗ Measures and indentifies DNA characteristics

    Helps determine DNA content (ploidy)

    Helps determine percentage of cells undergoing DNA synthesis

  ∗ (S phase fraction)

    Aneuploidy and high S-phase fraction correlate with a more aggressive disease

Tumor imaging

1. Radiographic techniques
2. Nuclear medicine techniques
3. Positron emission tomography
4. Radio-labeled monoclonal antibodies
5. Ultrasonography
6. Magnetic resonance imaging

Invasive diagnostic techniques

1. Endoscopy

  ∗ Provides direct view by insertion of endoscope into body cavity or opening

  ∗ Permits visual inspection, tissue biopsy, cytologic aspiration, staging of disease, and excision for pathology

2. Biopsy

  ∗ Provides tissue for histologic examination

* Common techniques include

Needle biopsy   *Punch biopsy*

Incisional biopsy   *Bone marrow biopsy*

Excisional biopsy

Suggested Readings

1. O'Mary SS: Diagnostic evaluation, classification, and staging. In Groenwald S, Frogge MH, Goodman M, Yarbro CH (eds): *Cancer Nursing: Principles and Practice* (4th ed). Boston: Jones and Bartlett, 1997, pp 175-197.
2. Frank-Stromborg M, Rohan K: Nursing's involvement in the primary and secondary prevention of cancer. *Cancer Nurs* 15:79-108, 1992.
3. Williams NN, Daly JM: Flow cytometry and prognostic implications in patients with solid tumors. *Surg Gynecol Obstet* 171:257-266, 1990.
4. Lind J: Tumor cell growth and cell kinetics. *Semin Oncol Nurs* 8:3-9, 199-217, 1992.
5. Shellock FG: MRI biologic effects and safety considerations. In Higgins CB, Hricak H, Helms CA (eds.): *Magnetic Resonance Imaging of the Body.* New York: Raven Press, 1992, pp. 233-265.

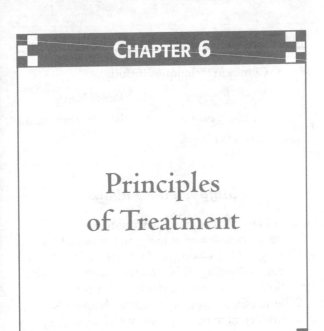

CHAPTER 6

Principles of Treatment

Classification and Staging

Basic terminology

1. *Tumor:* Mass of tissue that may be benign or malignant
2. *Cancer:* Malignant tumor capable of metastasis and invasion
3. *Primary tumor:* Original histologic site of tumorigenesis
4. *Secondary or metastatic tumor:* Resembles primary tumor histologically
5. *Second primary lesion:* New, histologically separate malignant neoplasm in the same patient

6. *Unknown primary:* Biopsy of metastatic site reveals cells that are markedly anaplastic, making it impossible to determine tissue of origin

Pathological classification

1. Tumors usually retain sufficient characteristics of normal cells to allow recognition of type of tissue from which they were derived
2. Tissue of origin is basis of distinguishing tumors in histogenetic classification system (see Appendix 6–1)

Clinical Classification

1. Method of classifying malignancy by extent of its spread
2. Cancers of similar histologic features and site of origin invade locally and metastasize in a predictable manner
3. Objectives of staging for solid tumors are to

   * Aid in treatment planning

   * Give prognostic information

   * Assist in treatment evaluation

   * Facilitate exchange of information

   * Compare statistics among treatment centers

4. Tumor-Node-Metastasis (TNM) staging system

   * Internationally accepted method of staging solid tumors

   * Solid tumors are classified by anatomic extent of disease:

Tumor (T): Extent of primary tumor evaluated on basis of depth of invasion, surface spread, and tumor size

Node (N): Absence or presence and extent of regional lymph node metastasis

Metastasis (M): Absence or presence of distant metastasis

* Tumors are further classified by

  Clinical extent of disease

  Extent of disease after pathologic review

  Extent of disease at retreatment

  Extent of disease at autopsy

* TNM permits staging groups (I, II, III, and IV) and therapeutic planning

5. Other staging systems are

  * Clark level: Melanomas are staged histologically by level of invasion of primary lesion

  * Duke's staging system: Colorectal cancer is classified by depth of invasion and presence of nodal metastasis

  * The International Federation of Gynecology and Obstetrics has an accepted staging system for cervical and endometrial cancers

  * Hodgkin's disease and non–Hodgkin's lymphoma are described by the Ann Arbor classification, which recognizes disease distribution and symptoms

* Leukemias are classified according to their predominant cell types, cell maturation, and acute or chronic nature

Grading

1. Method of classification based on histopathologic characteristics of tissue
2. Reveals degree of malignancy of tumor cells
3. Compares cellular anaplasia, differentiation, and mitotic activity with normal counterparts
4. American Joint Committee on Cancer recommends the following grading classification

   * GX: Grade cannot be assessed
   * G1: Well differentiated
   * G2: Moderately well differentiated
   * G3: Poorly differentiated
   * G4: Undifferentiated

Determining the treatment plan

1. Involves interdisciplinary decision-making based on

   * Aggressiveness of tumor
   * Predictability of spread
   * Morbidity and mortality that can be expected from treatment
   * Cure rate
   * Patient's wishes

2. Involves entering patients into clinical research trial if one is available

3. Factors influencing cancer treatment choices

* Tumor factor

   Size, anatomic location

   Histology, sensitivity to chemotherapy, radiation

   Natural history

   Survival statistics

* Treatment Factors

   Availability of treatment modalities

   Availability of research protocols/clinical trials

   Prior cancer treatment

* Patient factors

   Age, psysiologic factors

   General Health

   Psychological status

* Treatment goals

   Cure

   Control

   Palliation

* Ethical factors

   Patient participation and quality of life issues

   Informed consent

Assessing response to treatment

1. Objective criteria are

   * Complete response (CR): Complete disappearance of signs and symptoms of disease for at least 1 month

* Partial response (PR): 50% or more reduction in sum of products of greater and lesser diameters of all measured lesions for at least 1 month, with no new lesions appearing

* Minimal response (MR): Same as for PR but less than 50% reduction

* Progression: 25% or more increase in sum of all measured lesions, or appearance of new lesions

* Stable disease: Measurable tumor does not meet criteria for CR, PR, MR, or progression

2. Parameters for assessing objective response to treatment

* Tumor size: palpation, X-ray measurement

* Gonadotropin titer: decrease or increase

* Serum/urinary: decrease or increase
  Paraproteins, CEA, CA 153, CA 125, CA 159

* Bone marrow biopsy: decrease, increase, or blasts

* Organ function: improve or worsen

3. Subjective criteria include

* Increased feeling of well-being

* Increased strength

* Decreased fatigue

* Improved appetite

* Weight gain

* Decreased pain

Suggested Readings

1. Fleming ID, Cooper JS, Henson DE, et al: *American Joint Committee on Cancer: Manual for Staging of Cancer* (5th ed). Philadelphia: Lippincott, 1997.
2. Maxwell MB: Principles of treatment planning. In Groenwald S, Frogge MH, Goodman M, Yarbro CH (eds) *Cancer Nursing: Principles and Practice* (4th ed). Boston: Jones and Bartlett, 1997, pp 214-228.
3. Yarbro JW: Future potential of adjuvant and neoadjuvant therapy. *Semin Oncol* 18:63-69, 1992.

Appendix 6-1

Select Benign and Malignant Neoplasms Listed
by Histogenetic Classification

TISSUE OF ORIGIN	BENIGN NEOPLASM	MALIGNANT NEOPLASM
Epithelial (Endodermal)		
Squamous	Squamous cell papilloma	Squamous cell or epidermoid carcinoma
Glandular	Adenoma Papilloma Cystadenoma	Adenocarcinoma Papillary carcinoma Cystadenocarcinoma
Respiratory tract	Bronchogenic	carcinoma
Renal epithelium	Renal tubular adenoma	Renal cell carcinoma (hypernephroma)
Urinary tract	Transitional cell papilloma	Transitional cell carcinoma
Placental epithelium	Hydatidiform mole	Choriocarcinoma
Testicular epithelium		Seminoma
		Embryonal carcinoma

(continued)

Appendix 6-1—*Continued*

TISSUE OF ORIGIN	BENIGN NEOPLASM	MALIGNANT NEOPLASM
Liver	Liver cell adenoma	Hepatocellular carcinoma (hepatoma)
Biliary tree	Cholangioma	Cholangiocarcinoma
Stomach	Gastric polyp	Gastric carcinoma
Colon	Colonic polyp	Adenocarcinoma of the colon

Mesenchymal (Mesodermal)

Connective

Fibrous tissue	Fibroma	Fibrosarcoma
Adipose tissue	Lipoma	Liposarcoma
Cartilage	Chondroma	Chondrosarcoma
Bone	Osteoma	Osteosarcoma

Muscle

Smooth muscle	Leiomyoma	Leiomyosarcoma
Striated muscle	Rhabdomyoma	Rhabdomyosarcoma

Endothelial

Blood vessels	Hemangioma	Hemangiosarcoma

(continued)

Appendix 6-1—*Continued*

TISSUE OF ORIGIN	BENIGN NEOPLASM	MALIGNANT NEOPLASM
Lymphatic vessels	Lymphangioma	Lymphangiosarcoma
Hematopoietic and lymphoreticular		
Hematopoietic cells		Leukemias
Lymphoid tissue		Lymphomas Hodgkin's disease
Plasma cells		Plasmacytoma (multiple myeloma)
Neural (Ectodermal)		
Meninges	Meningioma	Meningeal sarcoma
Glia	Astrocytoma	Glioblastoma multiforme
Nerve cells	Ganglioneuroma	Neuroblastoma
		Medulloblastoma
Melanocytes	Nevus	Malignant melanoma
Mixed Tissues		
Kidney		Wilms' tumor
Salivary gland	Mixed tumor of salivary gland (pleomorphic adenoma)	Malignant mixed tumor of salivary gland

CHAPTER 7

Surgical Therapy

Overview

Approximately 55% of all individuals with cancer are treated with surgical intervention

Using combinations of surgery, chemotherapy, radiotherapy, and biotherapy, disease-free intervals have been significantly lengthened and survival advantages have been realized

Surgery can be used for

1. Cancer prevention
2. Diagnosis

3. Definitive treatment
4. Rehabilitation
5. Palliation

Factors influencing surgical oncology

1. Over 50% of surgical procedures performed in U.S. today occur within an ambulatory setting

   * Educating the patient and family in self-care is a significant challenge to health care workers

   * Educational materials are needed to supplement patient/family teaching

2. Advances in surgical technology have led to greater acceptance by patients, because less invasive surgical procedures result in fewer surgical risks, less pain, and a less extensive recovery period

3. Advances in surgical techniques have resulted in less blood loss, which has reduced operative mortality

4. Economic forces and managed care have precipitated development of aggressive measures to reduce lengthy and costly hospital stays

Factors influencing treatment decisions

1. Tumor cell kinetics

   * Radical surgical procedures used to treat cancer have failed to significantly increase cure rates

   * New knowledge of tumor cell kinetics has helped to identify tumors best treated with surgery

2. Growth rate

   * Slow-growing tumors, consisting of cells with prolonged cell cycles, lend themselves best to surgical treatment because they are more likely to be confined locally

3. Invasiveness

   * A surgical procedure intended to be curative must resect entire tumor mass and normal tissue surrounding tumor to ensure margin of safety for removal of all cancer cells

   * Less radical procedures are indicated where radical surgery has not enhanced results

4. Metastatic potential

   * Initial surgical procedure has better chance for success than subsequent surgery performed for recurrence

   * Knowledge of metastatic patterns of individual tumors is crucial for planning most effective therapy

   * Some tumors metastasize late or not at all and may respond well to aggressive primary surgical resection

   * Some tumors predictably metastasize to local or regional sites; cure may be achieved by removal of primary tumor-bearing organ and adjacent tissues or lymph nodes

   * For tumors known to metastasize early, surgery may not be appropriate, or surgery may be used to remove all visible tumor either in preparation for adjuvant systemic

therapy or after chemotherapy to resect remaining disease

5. Tumor location

    * Location and extent of tumor determine structural and functional changes after surgery

    * Learning about anticipated changes assists patient and family in weighing benefits and risks of treatment

    * Superficial and encapsulated tumors are more easily resected than those embedded in inaccessible or delicate tissues or those that have invaded tissues in multiple directions

6. Physical status

    * Preoperative assessment identifies factors that may increase risk of surgical morbidity and mortality

    * Systems to be evaluated are

        Respiratory

        Cardiovascular

        Nutritional

        Immunologic

        Renal

        Central nervous system

    * Patient's rehabilitation potential is assessed before surgery, and determination is made as to whether individual is capable of handling anticipated physiologic alterations

7. Quality of life

* Goal of surgical therapy varies with stage of disease

* Selection of treatment approach takes into consideration quality of individual's life when treatment is complete

Preventing Cancer Using Surgical Procedures

Surgery may remove nonvital benign tissue that predisposes individual to higher risk of cancer, such as prophylactic removal of breast in women with high risk of breast cancer

Role of surgery in cancer prevention is limited

Diagnosing Cancer Using Surgical Techniques

Surgical techniques used with biopsy cells or tissue specimens for histologic examination

1. Selection of biopsy technique depends on possible treatment methods if cancer is diagnosed
2. Site of biopsy should be removed at surgery, or biopsy should contain tumor in toto
3. Biopsy specimen should contain both normal cells and tumor cells for comparison: specimen should be

* Intact and not crushed or contaminated

* Labeled and preserved properly for complete evaluation

4. If multiple biopsy specimens are taken, instruments that may have contacted tumor should not be used for other sites
5. Only positive biopsy findings are definitive
6. Possible complications of biopsy include

   * Pain

   * Infection

   * Bleeding

   * Dehiscence

   * Hematoma

   * Tumor-cell seeding

7. Tell patients when biopsy results will be available and how physician will give results

Needle biopsy

1. Performed in outpatient setting
2. Local or topical anesthetic used
3. Limitation is the possibility that tumor will be missed because of narrow tract of needle

Surgical biopsy (extracted with needle)

1. Excisional biopsy is performed on small, accessible tumors to remove entire mass and little or no margin of surrounding normal tissues
2. Incisional biopsy is used to diagnose large tumors that require major surgery for complete removal

3. Endoscopy is used for diagnosis of tumors in accessible lumen

Staging Cancer Using Surgical Procedures

Exploratory surgical procedures important in defining extent of tumor involvement

The American Joint Committee for Cancer Staging and End Results Reporting developed the TNM system for staging many cancers by site (see Chapter 6)

Determining stage of disease is important in selection of therapy

Astute nursing care may alleviate profound anxiety patients experience during diagnostic phase

Surgery for Treatment of Cancer

Surgery aimed at cure

1. Surgical approach for cure has changed from "more is better" philosophy to consideration of tissue and functional preservation; relies more on adjuvant therapy
2. Type of surgical procedure selected depends on specific tumor cell characteristics and site of involvement
3. Adjuvant or combination therapy including radiotherapy or chemotherapy may be used to improve cure rates and survival

4. Surgery may be used to resect a metastatic lesion if primary tumor is believed to be eradicated and

   * Metastatic site is solitary

   * Patient can undergo surgery without major morbidity

5. In preoperative period, nurse instructs individual as to what to expect in postoperative recovery and rehabilitation

Surgery aimed at palliation

1. For palliation of debilitating manifestations of cancer, such as pain and obstruction
2. Aimed at controlling cancer and improving quality of life

Surgery for rehabilitation

1. Used for cosmetic reasons or to restore function after surgery, such as breast reconstruction, head and neck reconstruction, and skin grafting
2. Goal is to improve quality of life
3. Rehabilitation potential considered before surgery

Special Considerations for Nursing Care

Since 1990, more surgical procedures have been done on an ambulatory basis than on an inpatient basis

Presents challenges for nurses in regard to minimizing postoperative complications and maximizing inpatient support and education

Challenges in surgical care are rapidly changing as the technology of surgical instrumentation and role of adjuvant therapies advance

Particularly challenging is the patient with concomitant diseases receiving aggressive treatment for cancer

General surgical complications and nursing care considerations include

1. Acute respiratory distress syndrome (ARDS)

   * Maintain patent airway

   * Optimize mechanical ventilation, avoid toxic levels of oxygen, use positive end-expiratory pressure (PEEP) as tolerated

   * Administer corticosteroids and/or anti-inflammatory agents, such as indomethacin, as ordered

   * Use colloid if fluid replacement is necessary—invasive hemodynamic monitoring

   * Optimize nutrition

   * Add mucolytic agents via nebulizer

   * Turn and reposition often

   * Monitor chest with x-ray films

2. Aspiration pneumonia

   * Keep head of bed elevated 30°
   * Maintain NP0 status if gag reflex is not intact—use nasogastric (NG) tube
   * Consult speech therapy for swallowing techniques
   * Avoid excessive sedation in nonintubated patients
   * Soft mechanical diet once taking PO
   * Frequent suctioning when intubated
   * Keep patient in lateral position
   * Monitor chest with x-ray films
   * Monitor daily complete blood cell (CBC) count

3. Infection

   * Assess vital signs often
   * Check insertion sites, IV lines, suture lines, and wounds for signs of infection
   * Isolation as indicated—no fresh flowers or fresh fruit for neutropenic patients
   * Institute skin care precautions
   * Minimize invasive procedures
   * Direct all visitors to use strict handwashing techniques
   * Check daily CBC count (absolute neutrophil and lymphocyte counts)
   * Monitor chest with x-ray films

* Obtain blood culture if temperature higher than 101°F

4. Bleeding

   * Place bleeding precautions sign at bedside
   * Observe for signs of bleeding: purpura, oozing, pallor, hemoptysis, petechiae, hemorrhage, and ecchymosis
   * Test all excreta for blood
   * Turn and reposition often
   * Monitor CBC count, prothrombin time (PT), partial thromboplastin time (PTT)
   * Eliminate aspirin-containing compounds and heparin from IV lines
   * Avoid invasive procedures
   * Secure peripheral arterial lines and observe site for bleeding

5. Poor wound healing

   * Assess wound for drainage and erythema
   * Keep dressing dry and secure with a nonirritating tape
   * Optimize nutrition
   * Consider vitamin E cream

6. Stomatitis

   * Assess oral membranes for ulcerations
   * Administer frequent oral care with cleansing agent, such as chlorhexidine or hydrogen peroxide

* Moisten membranes and lips with water-soluble gel or artificial saliva preparation

* Secure endotracheal tubes with tape, avoiding contact with lips

* Avoid mouth rinses containing alcohol

* Watch for oral candidiasis and administer topical or systemic antifungal agents

Autologous blood donation

1. Patients may donate one or more units of their own blood to bank before surgery (autologous blood donation)
2. Autologous donation may be done from 42 days to 72 hours before surgery

Anxiety and pain control

1. Patient teaching about pain control begins preoperatively and includes

   * Expectations of pain and its relief
   * Dosing of analgesic medicine
   * Use of rating scales to measure pain
   * Nonpharmacologic methods to decrease pain and anxiety

Nutrition

1. Nutritionally debilitated person with cancer is a poor surgical risk
2. Before surgery, protein calorie malnutrition is reversed, and weight loss prevented
3. Patients may receive aggressive preoperative nutritional support to improve nutritional status

Hemostasis

1. Person with cancer is highly susceptible to postoperative thrombophlebitis
2. Early postoperative ambulation is instituted
3. The nurse observes patient closely for signs and symptoms of phlebitis

Wound healing

1. Postoperative complications include

   * Wound dehiscence
   * Infection

2. When surgery is performed on previously irradiated tissue or when chemotherapy is initiated early in the postoperative period, potential complications include

   * Postoperative wound dehiscence
   * Infection
   * Tissue and bone necrosis

Combined modality therapy

1. Combined modality treatment of cancer has introduced a new set of challenges for health care providers
2. Synergistic and augmented effects of combined therapies can produce postoperative reactions and complications that may be difficult to manage

   * Radiotherapy and chemotherapy compromise wound healing

- * Organ toxicities from radiotherapy or chemotherapy increase postoperative complications

3. Intraoperative radiotherapy and intraoperative chemotherapy may decrease recurrence and metastases

Suggested Readings

1. Balch CM, Pellis NR, Morton DL, et al: Oncology. In Swartz SI, Shires GT, Spencer FC (eds): *Principles of Surgery* (6th ed). New York, McGraw-Hill, 1994, pp 305-385.
2. Frogge MH, Kalinowski BH: Surgical therapy. In Groenwald SL, Frogge MH, Goodman M, Yarbro CH (eds): *Cancer Nursing: Principles and Practice* (4th ed). Boston: Jones and Bartlett, 1997, pp 229-246.
3. Steele G, Cady B: The surgical oncologist as the patient manager. In Steele G, Cady B (eds): *General Surgical Oncology*. Philadelphia: Saunders, 1992, pp 18-21.

CHAPTER 8

Radiotherapy

Overview

Radiotherapy may be used

1. As the sole treatment for cancer
2. In combination with surgery or chemotherapy and immunotherapy

The goal may be to

1. Cure (e.g., skin cancer, carcinoma of the cervix, Hodgkin's disease, or seminoma)
2. Control (e.g., breast cancer, soft-tissue sarcomas, or lung cancer)
3. Palliation (e.g., relieving pain, preventing pathologic fractures, returning mobility

in metastatic bone lesions, and relieving
central nervous system [CNS] symptoms
caused by brain metastasis or spinal cord
compression)

Equipment and beams used in radiation are

1. Teletherapy (external radiation)

   ✳ Conventional, or orthovoltage, equipment

   Produces X rays of varying energies

   *The higher the voltage, the greater the depth of
   penetration of the x-ray beam*

   Disadvantages include

   Poor depth of penetration

   Severe skin reactions because of high dose at
   skin level

   Bone necrosis because bone absorbs more than
   soft tissue

   ✳ Megavoltage equipment

   Has distinct advantages over orthovoltage

   Deeper beam penetration

   More homogeneous absorption of radiation
   resulting in less bone necrosis

   Greater skin sparing

   Equipment includes

   Van de Graaf generator

   Cobalt and cesium units

   Betatron and linear accelerators

2. Brachytherapy

  * Use of sealed sources of radioactive
material placed within or near tumor

Often combined with teletherapy

May be used preoperatively and postoperatively

Contained in a variety of forms

    Wires (^{182}Ta)

    Ribbons or tubes (^{192}Ir)

    Needles (^{137}Cs, ^{226}Ra)

    Grains or seeds (^{198}Au, ^{222}Rn)

    Capsules (^{137}Cs, ^{226}Ra)

Source selected by radiotherapist according to

    Site to be treated

    Size of lesion

    Whether implant is temporary or permanent

Used in treatment of

    Head and neck lesions (needles, wire, and
ribbons)

    Intra-abdominal and intrathoracic lesions (gold
or iodine seeds)

    Gynecologic tumors

May be

    Preloaded (radiation present when applicator
placed in tissue)

    Afterloaded (radioactive source added after
applicator is in position)

* Brachytherapy is either

  Low-dose rate

  High-dose rate (produces same radiobiologic effect in short period of time)

Simulation

1. Localizes tumor
2. Defines volume to be treated
3. Determines field of treatment

   * Radiation therapist duplicates markings on patient's skin by tattooing (dropping India ink on patient's skin and introducing ink into skin using needle)

   * Patient is immobilized with headrests, armboards, and handgrips

   * Blocks to protect vital body organs and tissues are secured to plastic tray placed at head of treatment machine between beam and person being treated

   * Careful explanation about purpose of simulation and equipment allays patient's anxiety

Radiobiology

1. Cellular response to radiation

   * Direct radiation hit at cellular level occurs when any key molecule within cell (DNA or RNA) is damaged

     Unrepaired breaks or alterations lead to mutations and altered cell function or cell death

     Most effective and lethal injury

* Indirect hit occurs when ionization takes place in medium (mostly water) surrounding molecular structures in cell

  Results in free radical that may trigger variety of chemical reactions, producing compounds toxic to cell

  More likely to occur than direct hit

* Radiosensitivity maximum just before and during actual cell division

* Sensitivity of cells to irradiation is directly proportional to their reproductive activity (radiation most effective during mitosis) and inversely proportional to their degree of differentiation (the more differentiated, the less sensitive to radiation)

* Cell death from radiation can be immediate or delayed

* Radiation can inhibit cell from reproducing

* Other factors that directly affect biologic response to radiation include

  Oxygen effect: Well-oxygenated tumors have greater response to radiation

  Linear energy transfer (LET): Rate at which energy is lost from different types of radiation while traveling through matter

    Higher LET has greater probability of interacting with matter and producing more direct hits

  Relative biologic effectiveness: Compares dose of test radiation with dose of standard radiation that produces same biologic response

Fractionation: Division of total dose of radiation into a number of equal fractions to accomplish

Repair

Of intracellular damage by normal cells between daily dose fractions

Major advantage of fractioning dosages

Redistribution (within cell cycle)

With subsequent daily doses of radiation, more and more tumor cells are delayed in cell cycle and reach mitosis as the next dose is given, increasing cell kill

Repopulation (new growth of normal tissue)

Takes place some time during fractionated treatment course

Fractionation favors normal tissue but eradicates tumor

Reoxygenation

Oxygenated cells are more radiosensitive

Fractionating dose allows time between treatments for tumors to reoxygenate

Chemical and thermal modifiers of radiation

1. Radiosensitizers

   * Increase radiosensitivity of tumor cells
   * Achieve greater cell kill
   * Prevent repair of cellular radiation damage
   * Side effects include

Neurotoxicity

CNS symptoms of somnolence, confusion, and transient coma

Dose-related nausea and vomiting

* Results are disappointing because of severe toxicity and lack of significant efficacy

2. Radioprotectors

   * Protect aerated (nontumor) cells but have limited effect on hypoxic (tumor) cells

   * Increase therapeutic ratio by promoting repair of irradiated normal tissues

   * Nursing responsibilities include

   Providing patient and family education

   Participating in obtaining informed consent

   Administering investigational agents

   Timing and coordinating drug administration with radiotherapy treatment

   Observing and documenting expected and previously unreported effects and side effects

   Managing side effects, including developing interventions for those newly observed

3. Hyperthermia

   * Heat is cytotoxic to cancer cells

   * Hyperthermia combined with radiotherapy produces greater effect than either modality alone

✱ Parameters that may influence tumor response to combined hyperthermia and radiation therapy include

Tumor size

Histologic findings

Disease site

Total dose of radiation and dose per fraction

Thermal dose

Total and weekly number of hyperthermia sessions

Sequencing of hyperthermia and radiation

✱ Hyperthermia is achieved by

Immersion of local area in heated bath

Ultrasound

Microwaves

Interstitial implants

Perfusion techniques

✱ Side effects include

Local skin reaction

Pain

Fever

Gastrointestinal (GI) effects

Cardiac arrhythmias

Late effects, such as necrosis and ulceration; these are generally not severe enough to discontinue use

* Nursing responsibilities

  Pretreatment evaluation phase

  Assess for

  > Suitability for treatment
  >
  > Ability to tolerate treatment
  >
  > Cardiac and neurologic status
  >
  > Presence of metal objects in treatment field

  Provide thorough patient and family education

  Treatment phase

  Monitor vital signs

  Prepare patient's GI tract

  Administer sedation

  Assist during surgical placement of thermometry probes

  Position patient for comfort and access to applicator probes

  Monitor patient throughout treatment

  Provide physical and emotional support

  Post-treatment phase

  Clean and dress cannula sites

  Observe and document thermal changes at treatment site

  Provide discharge instructions

  Manage subsequent local reaction

Tissue and Organ Response to Radiation

Integumentary system

1. Skin is irradiated when any site within body is treated
2. Skin of exit portal may also be affected
3. Skin reactions may range from erythema to dry, and then moist, desquamation
4. Healing may be slow, but is usually complete, leaving minimal residual damage, except for change in pigmentation
5. Fibrosis, atrophy, ulceration, necrosis, and skin cancer may occur after high doses but are uncommon with modern equipment
6. Skin in warm, moist areas, such as groin, gluteal fold, axilla, and under breast, exhibits greater and often earlier reaction to radiation
7. Radiation of hair follicles and sweat and sebaceous glands results in loss of hair and decreased activity of glands; both generally return to normal after therapy

Hematopoietic system

1. If large areas of red bone marrow are irradiated (i.e., ilia, vertebrae, ribs, metaphyses of long bones, skull, and sternum), the number of circulating mature blood cells decreases because production is suppressed

    * Erythroblasts (red blood cell precursors) are damaged, causing anemia, but recovery is rapid and anemia is transient

* Myeloblasts (white blood cell precursors)
  are suppressed at same rate as erythroblasts,
  but rate of recovery is much slower

* Megakaryocytes (platelet precursors) are
  affected 1 to 2 weeks after exposure and
  take longest time to recover (2 to 6 weeks)

Gastrointestinal system

1. Oral cavity

   * Oral mucous membrane may develop a
     confluent mucositis

     *Occurs especially on soft palate and floor of
     mouth*

     *Occurs during third and fourth weeks of
     therapy at usual dose rate*

   * Salivary function is altered from damage to
     serous and mucous acini

   * Saliva becomes viscous after moderate
     doses

   * Higher doses lead to atrophy of salivary
     glands, with greatly diminished saliva and
     increased acidity

     May be permanent

     May lead to radiation caries and infection

   * Alterations in taste occur early in treatment
     but are rarely permanent, depending on
     dose

2. Esophagus and stomach

* Gastric secretions of mucus, pepsin, and hydrochloric acid are reduced and may be accompanied by nausea, dyspepsia, and pyloric spasm

* Gastritis and esophagitis occur with moderate to high doses and produce dysphagia, anorexia, and sometimes nausea and vomiting

* Late changes may include atrophy, ulcerations, and fibrosis

3. Small intestine

* Most sensitive area of the GI tract

* Radiation reaction characterized by shortening of villi and loss of absorptive surface

* Prolonged and severe reactions may cause major nutritional consequences

* Late changes after high doses of radiation include fibrosis, ulceration, necrosis, and hemorrhage

* Intestinal obstruction may occur

* Most common symptoms are anorexia, nausea, diarrhea, and cramping

4. Colon and rectum

* Effect is similar to that in small intestine

* Tenesmus may occur when anal sphincter is irradiated

5. Liver

* Greatest damage to liver is vascular injury

* Early changes detectable only by liver function test
* Radiation hepatitis is possible consequence of high doses

Respiratory system

1. Hoarseness caused by laryngeal mucous membrane congestion sometimes occurs
2. Radiation pneumonitis may be a transient response to moderate doses
3. Later changes are fibrosis in lung tissue and thickening of pleura

Reproductive system

1. Cervix and uterine body are radioresistant
2. Vaginal mucous membrane responds with mucositis and inflammation
3. Vaginal stenosis may be result of brachytherapy
4. Radiation to ovaries may produce temporary or permanent sterility, depending on age of person being treated and radiation dose
5. Hormonal changes and early menopause may occur after radiation of ovaries
6. Genetic damage may occur after radiation of gonads in both males and females
7. Radiation to male testes damages and prevents maturation of sperm
8. Sterility may be permanent even in low doses

Urinary system

1. Radiation-induced cystitis and urethritis are early and transient effects

2. In high doses, nephritis may occur, which may result in renal failure and death
3. Kidneys are protected when abdomen is irradiated

Cardiovascular system

1. Damage to vasculature of an organ or tissue can be primary reason for its radioresponsiveness
2. Blood vessels may become occluded when excessive cell production takes place during repair and regeneration in response to radiation injury
3. Thrombosis may be induced by the thickening that occurs during regenerative activity, further occluding vessels
4. Late changes are telangiectasia, petechiae, and sclerosis
5. Heart muscle is relatively radioresistant, although pericarditis may occur

Neurologic system

1. Brain, spinal cord, and peripheral nerves are relatively radioresistant; damage relates to vascular insufficiency
2. Higher doses may produce transient symptoms in CNS
3. Lhermitte's sign may occur

   * Follows irradiation to cervical cord

   * Characterized by paresthesia in form of shocklike sensations that radiate down back and extremities when neck is bent forward

4. Myelopathy usually is transient but at higher doses may lead to paralysis or paresis

5. Radiation of large volumes of spinal cord produces transverse myelitis
6. Radiation to neurons in olfactory, gustatory, and retinal receptors alters or destroys function of sense organ
7. Preexistence of diabetes, hypertension, and arteriosclerosis enhances radiation effects on nervous tissue

Skeletal system

1. Mature bone and cartilage are radioresistant
2. Late avascular necrosis

    * Is rare but can occur after high doses

    * Causes pain and possible pathologic fracture

3. Radiation has severe effect on growing bone and cartilage, causing deformities and stunting growth

Systemic Effects of Radiation

Patients may experience systemic effects of radiation including

1. Nausea
2. Anorexia
3. Malaise resulting from release of toxic waste products into bloodstream from tumor destruction

Nursing Care of the Patient Receiving Radiotherapy

General

1. Develop nursing care plan
2. Assist patient in coping with diagnosis
3. Teach patient what to expect
4. Teach patient about expected side effects
5. Assist in arranging transportation for outpatients
6. Prepare patient for

    * What equipment looks like

    * Where radiation department is located

7. Coordinate complex treatment schedules

For fatigue

1. May be pronounced during and after course of radiation treatment
2. Potential causes include

    * Recent surgery

    * Prior or concurrent chemotherapy

    * Pain

    * Malnutrition

    * Medications

    * Frequency of treatment visits

    * Maintaining usual lifestyle

    * Tumor burden

    * Anemia

    * Respiratory compromise

3. Extra rest and reduction in normal activity level may be necessary

For mucositis

1. Tell patient to avoid irritants, such as

   * Alcohol
   * Tobacco
   * Spicy or acidic foods
   * Very hot or very cold foods and drinks
   * Commercial mouthwash products

2. Tell patient to gargle

   * As often as every 3 to 4 hours and especially before bed
   * With solution of 1 ounce of diphenhydramine hydrochloride (Benadryl) elixir diluted in 1 quart of water

3. Outpatients can irrigate mouth with this solution sprayed into the mouth from an air-powered spray apparatus

   * Loosens retained food particles
   * Breaks up mucus and soothes mucosa

4. Inpatients can modify technique by using disposable irrigation bag hung from pole to deliver spray of solution
5. Do not dislodge plaque-like formations of mucositis
6. Agents that coat and soothe oral mucosa, such as Maalox, are sometimes used
7. Lidocaine hydrochloride 2% viscous solution may provide some relief from discomfort, but

anesthetic effect, especially to the tongue, is
objectionable to some

For xerostomia

1. Often accompanied by alterations in taste
2. Little can be done to relieve this symptom
3. Best method is frequent sips of water
4. Frequent mouth care provides relief from thick
   and viscous saliva
5. When inflammation has subsided, some
   individuals benefit from use of saliva
   substitute for periods of 2 to 4 hours

   * May assist individuals who otherwise
     awaken during night because of dry mouth

   * Packaged in small container carried easily
     in pocket or purse

   * Formula is

     Cologel   98.2 ml
     Glycerin   110.0 ml
     Saline   1000.0 ml

   * Solution is mixed well and refrigerated

   * Patient uses 1 to 2 teaspoons every 3 or 4
     hours, swishing in mouth and swallowing

For radiation caries

1. Potential late effect of radiation to mouth and
   oropharynx
2. Can be greatly reduced or avoided by proper
   care before, during, and after course of
   treatment
3. Before therapy, thorough dental examination
   and prophylaxis should be carried out

4. For poor dentition, full mouth extraction is treatment of choice
5. If teeth are in good repair, vigorous preventive program is begun

   * Daily diphenhydramine hydrochloride mouth spray for cleansing effect
   * Follow with 5-minute application of fluoride gel

6. Patient should brush teeth with soft-bristled brush several times daily

For esophagitis and dysphagia

1. Occurs when radiation is directed to mediastinum
2. Transient
3. First signs are difficulty swallowing solids, progressing to esophagitis, with painful swallowing
4. Administer following mixture to provide relief

   Mylanta: 450 ml (three 5-oz bottles)

   Lidocaine hydrochloride 2% viscous solution: 100 ml

   Diphenhydramine hydrochloride elixir: 60 ml

   Shake well and refrigerate. Dosage: 1 to 2 tablespoons 15 minutes before meals and at bedtime

5. In place of regular meals, encourage high-calorie, high-protein, high-carbohydrate liquids and soft, bland foods (e.g., eggnog, milk shakes, "instant" liquid meals,

commercially prepared liquid supplements,
and blenderized foods)

For nausea and vomiting

1. Not common, but occur when treatment is
   directed to whole abdomen or portions of it,
   large pelvic fields, hypochondrium,
   epigastrium, or para-aortic areas
2. Occurs from 1 to 3 hours after treatment
3. Delay intake of full meal until 3 or 4 hours
   after treatment

For diarrhea

1. Not an expected side effect
2. Occurs if areas of abdomen and pelvis are
   treated with high doses of radiation
3. Ranges from increased number of bowel
   movements to loose, watery stools and
   intestinal cramping
4. Occasionally, treatment interrupted to allow
   bowel to recover, especially in elderly or
   debilitated individuals
5. Intravenous fluids for short-term replacement
   may be needed
6. Low-residue diet and loperamide
   hydrochloride are usually sufficient to control
   diarrhea

For tenesmus, cystitis, and urethritis

1. Infrequent
2. Occur in some individuals receiving pelvic
   irradiation

   * Tenesmus

Produces persistent sensation of need to evacuate bowel or bladder

Relief may be obtained from GI and urinary antispasmodics and anticholinergic preparations

May persist until treatment has ended

* Cystitis and urethritis

Result from radiation to bladder

If clean-catch urine specimen shows positive results, antibiotic therapy is instituted

Usually no infection is found

Treatment consists of urinary antiseptics and antispasmodics for symptomatic relief

High fluid intake is encouraged

Sitz baths contraindicated if perineal area is being irradiated

For alopecia

1. Occurs during treatment of whole brain
2. Follows typical pattern

   * First, patient notices excessive amounts of hair in brush or comb, and gradual thinning of hair; this continues about 2 or 3 weeks

   * Suddenly, most of hair comes out—patient awakens to find remainder of hair on pillow

   Prepare patient with wig or attractive scarf or hat

   Occasionally hair loss occurs regionally or in patches

Encourage patient to grow hair longer to cover spot

3. Care of hair and scalp during radiation treatment includes

   * Gentle brushing or combing
   * Infrequent shampooing
   * Permanent waves and hair coloring are contraindicated

4. Top of patient's head should be protected from sunburn with a cap
5. Forehead, ears, and neck may be more sensitive to sun

For skin reactions

1. Response of skin varies from mild erythema to moist desquamation, which leaves raw surface similar to second-degree burn
2. Healing and cosmesis usually are satisfactory
3. Some individuals exhibit permanent tanning effect in treatment area, with no change in texture of skin
4. Others have

   * Fibrosclerotic changes in subcutaneous structures
   * Skin is smooth, taut, and shiny
   * Telangiectasia may be evident

5. Skin reactions in groin, perineum, buttocks, inframammary folds, and axillae are more severe because of warmth and moisture in these areas

6. Skin care measures during treatment and until skin reaction has disappeared include

   * Keep skin dry

   * Avoid powders, lotions, creams, alcohol, and deodorants

   * Wear loose-fitting garments

   * Do not apply tape to treatment site when dressings are applied

   * Shave with electric razor only and avoid preshaves or aftershaves

   * Protect skin from exposure to direct sunlight, chlorinated swimming pools, and temperature extremes

7. Treatment of skin reactions includes

   * Use light dusting of cornstarch for pruritus from erythema and dry desquamation

   * For moist desquamation and denuded areas, use thin layer of a & D ointment plus nonstick dressing

8. Treatment may be required on exit portal as well as marked area

For bone marrow suppression

1. Occurs when large areas of active bone marrow are irradiated (especially pelvis or spine in adult)
2. Blood counts are done on all individuals receiving radiotherapy weekly or two to three times weekly
3. Transfusions of whole blood, platelets, or other components may be necessary for patient with dangerously low blood counts

4. Treatment may have to be adjusted or suspended
5. Nurse observes for signs of bleeding, anemia, and infection
6. Patients and families are taught what to look for and to report whenever symptoms occur

For uncommon side effects

1. Transient myelitis

   * Occurs when lymph nodes in cervical region are radiated

   * Lhermitte's sign (a shocklike sensation radiating down back and over extremities when flexing neck) may occur 2 to 3 weeks after treatment ends

   * Symptoms improve gradually or spontaneously with no residual effect

2. Parotitis

   * Painful swelling and inflammation of parotid glands

   * Occurs in individual receiving radiation to maxillomandibular area

   * Onset is sudden and follows first two or three treatments

   * Symptoms subside quickly and require no treatment

3. Visual and olfactory disturbances

   * Occur during radiation to pituitary area

   * Manifest in person seeing lights or smelling something burning after several treatments

* May relate to irritation of optic nerve and olfactory bulb

* Reassurance and explanation are best means of handling

4. Radiation recall

* Can occur in a previously irradiated site that exhibited mucositis or erythema

* Occurs in response to systemic administration of certain chemotherapeutic agents several months to a year or more after radiation received

* Person develops intraoral mucositis or skin reaction in exact pattern corresponding to previously treated radiation portal

* Treatment is symptomatic

Nursing Care of the Patient with a Radioactive Source

Specific safety precautions must be observed by patients who are receiving brachytherapy

To design an appropriate care regimen and safety precautions, the nurse must know the answers to the following questions

1. What is the source being used?
2. What is the half-life of that source?
3. What is the type of emission (alpha, beta, gamma)?
4. How much radioisotope is being used?
5. What method of administration or application is being used?

6. Is the source metabolized? Absorbed? Neither?

Three major factors are considered in developing safety plans

1. Time: Exposure to radiation is directly proportional to time spent within a specific distance from source
2. Distance: Amount of radiation reaching a given area decreases as distance increases
3. Shield: Sheet of absorbing material placed between radiation source and detector; amount of radiation reaching detector decreases, depending on energy of radiation and nature and thickness of absorbing material
   * Portable radiation shields are available
   * Useful for doing tasks within room but not for direct care

Patient education includes

1. Description of procedure
2. Preparation for potential change in appearance (needle implants in facial area)
3. Knowledge of anticipated pain or discomfort and measures available for relief
4. Knowledge of potential short-term and long-term side effects and complications
5. Restrictions on activity while radioactive sources are in place
6. Visiting restrictions
7. Radiation precautions observed by hospital personnel

8. Preparation for isolation by planning suitable activities, such as reading, doing handiwork, and watching television

Suggested Readings

1. Hassey-Dow K, Hilderley L (eds): *Nursing Care in Radiation Oncology.* Philadelphia: WB Saunders, 1992.
2. Hilderley LJ: Radiotherapy. In Groenwald SL, Frogge MH, Goodman M, Yarbro CH: *Cancer Nursing: Principles and Practice* (4th ed). Boston: Jones and Bartlett, 1997, pp 247-282.
3. Mauch PM, Loeffler JS (eds): *Radiation Oncology, Technology and Biology.* Philadelphia: WB Saunders, 1994.
4. Sitton E: Early and late radiation-induced skin alterations. Part I: Mechanisms of skin changes. *Oncol Nurs Forum* 19:801-807, 1992.
5. Sitton E: Early and late radiation-induced skin alterations. Part II: Nursing care of irradiated skin. *Oncol Nurs Forum* 19:907-912, 1992.

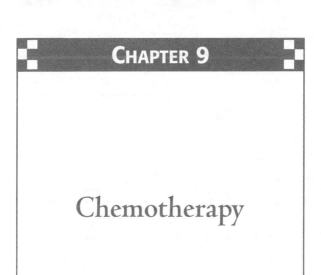

CHAPTER 9

Chemotherapy

Scientific Basis of Chemotherapy

Factors influencing chemotherapy effectiveness

1. Biologic characteristics of tumors

   * *Growth rate:* Actively dividing cells are most sensitive to chemotherapy

   * *Growth fraction:* Number of cells dividing at one time is small

   * *Tumor cell heterogeneity:* Tumor cells vary in their sensitivity to chemotherapy

   * *Tumor burden:* The larger the tumor burden, the more likely it is that resistant cells will emerge

* Genetic instability: Tumor cells can mutate, becoming resistant over time to chemotherapy

2. Host characteristics include the patient's

* Nutritional status
* Level of immune function
* Physical and psychological tolerance to treatment
* Response to supportive therapies

3. Response to a specific drug or drug regimen is related to

* Dose
* Schedule of administration
* Toxicity of drug
* Route of administration
* Drug resistance

4. Tumor cell biology

* The cell cycle includes 5 phases:

    G1- synthesis of RNA and cellular proteins

    S- DNA is replicated

    G2- Cell prepares for division

    M- Mitosis-cell divides

    G0- Following mitosis the cell may either enter cell division again or rest in the G0 phase

* Tumor cells are different from normal cells because:

they do not stop dividing

they lack differentiation

they can invade local tissues

they can establish new growths at distant sites

* Tumor cells accumulate because their proliferation exceeds cell death

* Cytotoxic drug resistance is a major factor in response to chemotherapy.

  Drug resistance arises from spontaneous genetic mutations

  Primary drug resistance is present prior to treatment

  Secondary drug resistance develops after exposure to chemotherapy

Therapeutic Strategies

Combination chemotherapy

1. Use of multiple agents with different actions may

   * Provide maximal cell kill for resistant cells

   * Minimize development of resistant cells

   * Provide maximum cell kill with tolerable toxicity

Scheduling and drug sequencing

1. Measures to prevent acquired drug resistance include

* Administering intermittent high doses of drugs
* Alternating non–cross-resistant chemotherapy regimens
* Minimizing interval between treatments to coincide with recovery of normal cells
* Maintaining optimum duration of therapy without dose reductions or treatment delays

Dose

1. Dose reductions and treatment delays most often account for suboptimal response to chemotherapy
2. Critical aspects of dosing

   * *Dose size* refers to amount of drug delivered to patient when corrected for physiologic variables, such as creatinine clearance and weight

   * *Total dose* is sum of all doses of drug for an individual

   * *Dose rate*, or *dose intensity*, is amount of drug delivered per unit of time $(mg/m^2/week)$

   * *Adjuvant chemotherapy:* Administration of chemotherapy as a strategy to increase cure rates in individuals with presumed, not proven microscopic disease

   * *Modifying agents:* Drugs that are used to enhance efficacy of an antineoplastic agent

Reversing multidrug resistance

1. Multidrug resistance occurs when exposure to a single drug is followed by cross-resistance to other drugs
2. Major strategies to overcome multidrug resistance include

   * Increasing intracellular drug concentration using high doses of drugs
   * Using chemoprotective agents to permit higher doses of chemotherapy

     Amifostine (reduces DNA damage in the kidney in patients receiving cisplatin therapy and may reduce neorpathies as well)

     Dexrazoxane (inhibits free radical formation in patients receiving doxorubicin therapy)

     Leucovorin (rescues normal cells from toxicity associated with methotrexate)

     Mesna (protects the bladder in patients receiving Ifosfamide or cyclophosfamide)

   * Combining high doses of chemotherapy with peripheral blood stem cell transplant
   * Alternating noncross-resistant chemotherapy regimens
   * Using monoclonal antibodies
   * Maintaining intracellular drug concentration by enhancing the membrane permeability and drug efflux pump
   * Administer chemotherapy according to the patient's circadian cytokinetic rhythm to maximize therapeutic effect and minimize toxicity.

* Liposomal encapsulation of doxorubicin and daunorubicin allows a longer half-life and increased uptake by tumor cells with less toxicity.

Clinical Trials

Clinical trial is a scientific study designed to answer important clinical and biologic questions

Conducted according to a written guideline for the study (protocol)

Provides mechanism to test effectiveness of new therapies

Clinical trials are categorized as

1. Phase I studies

   * Testing done on patients who may benefit from the drugs and for whom there is no treatment known to be superior

   * Goals of phase I study are to

     Evaluate acute toxicities

     Establish maximum tolerated dose

     Analyze pharmacologic data

2. Phase II studies

   * Goals of phase II study are to

     Determine tumor activity

     Design administration techniques

Identify precautions and toxicity

Determine dose modifications

Identify need for supportive care

3. Phase III studies

   ✳ Goals of phase III study are to

   Compare drug(s) to standard

   Evaluate response and duration of response

   Evaluate toxicity and quality-of-life issues

4. Phase IV studies

   ✳ Goals of phase IV study are to

   Determine new ways to use drug

   Determine effect of drug in adjuvant therapy

Pharmacology and Classification of Antineoplastic Agents

Principles of pharmacokinetics

1. Pharmacokinetics is the study of the movement of drugs in the body:

   ✳ Absorption–the amount of drug that reaches systematic circulation and the tumor depends on the degree to which the drug is absorbed.

   ✳ Distribution–determined primarily by the drugs ability to penetrate different tissues and bind to various plasma proteins.

* Metabolism–metabolic activation and inactivation or catabolism of drugs is carried out primarily by the liver.

* Elimination–the kidneys are responsible for the majority of the elimination of drugs and drug metabolites

Alkylating agents

1. Cell cycle nonspecific
2. Mechanism of action is cross-linking strands of DNA
3. Examples include

   * Nitrogen mustard

   * Carboplatin

   * Cyclophosphamide

   * Ifosfamide

   * Melphalan

   * Dacarbazine

   * Lomustine

Antitumor antibiotics

1. Cell cycle nonspecific
2. Interfere with DNA function
3. Examples include

   * Bleomycin

   * Doxorubicin

   * Mitomycin C

   * Mitoxantrone

   * Daunorubicin

Plant derivitaves

1. Topoisomerase inhibitors
2. Interfere with mitotic activity
3. Cell cycle specific
4. Examples include

   * Vincristine

   * Teniposide

   * Vinblastine

   * Vindesine

   * Etoposide

   * Vinorelbine

Camptothecin Analogs:

1. Examples include

   * Topotecan

   * Irinotecan

Taxanes

1. Cell cycle specific
2. Promote microtubule assembly
3. Examples include

   * Taxol

   * Taxotere

Antimetabolites

1. Cell cycle specific
2. Interfere with DNA synthesis
3. Examples include

   * Methotrexate

   * Mercaptopurine

* 5-Fluorouracil
* Cytarabine
* Gemcitabine
* Trimetrexate
* Cladrabine

Chemotherapy Administration

Professional qualifications

1. Current licensure as registered nurse
2. Certification in CPR
3. Intravenous therapy skills
4. Educational preparation and demonstration of knowledge in all areas related to antineoplastic drugs
5. Drug administration skills
6. Policies and procedures to govern nursing actions include

    * Chemotherapy drug preparation and handling guidelines that comply with occupational Safety and Health Administration guidelines

    * Chemotherapy administration procedures

        Vesicant management

        Management of allergic reactions

        Safe drug handling and disposal

        Patient and family education

        Management of vascular access devices (VADs)

        Documentation methods

        Outcome standards

Oncology quality improvement process

Handling cytotoxic drugs

1. All chemotherapy drugs are prepared under a class II biologic safety hood
2. Personal protective equipment (PPE) is worn during handling of chemotherapeutic agents
3. Direct exposure to cytotoxic drugs can occur during admixture, administration, or handling; specifically, by inhalation, ingestion, or absorption
4. Drugs are known to be mutagenic, teratogenic, and carcinogenic

Nurse's role in patient and family education about cancer and its treatment

1. Identify specific learning needs related to chemotherapy
2. Prepare teaching aids such as written materials, calendar, video, teaching guides
3. Describe various sensations patient will experience during treatment; e.g., stuffy nose, lightheadedness, dizziness
4. Describe specific side effects and measures to prevent these complications
5. Teach patients self-care measures and give clear instructions on how to report symptoms
6. Ensure that informed consent has been obtained
7. Document teaching in patient's medical record and describe method of follow-up

Administration principles

1. Steps to administer an antineoplastic drug

* Verify patient's identity
* Check and double-check drug order
* Calculate body surface area to confirm dosage
* Ensure informed consent
* Evaluate laboratory results
* Locate extravasation kit or supplies, if giving vesicant
* Wash hands, don gloves, and other PPE
* Select equipment and site for venipuncture
* Use an appropriate sterile technique for venous access
* Tape needle securely, without obstructing site
* Test vein with at least 5 to 8 cc of normal saline
* Administer chemotherapy with even, steady pressure
* Check for blood return every couple of cubic centimeters (milliliters) of drug given
* Flush between each drug to avoid incompatibilities
* When the injection or infusion is complete, dispose of all equipment according to policies and procedures of the institution
* Arrange for follow-up care
* Document procedure in patient's medical record

* Preventing drug errors

  Verbal orders are never given or taken for chemotherapy drugs

  Physician responsible for the care of the patient and most familiar with the drug and dosing schedule should write the chemotherapy orders

  Avoid abbreviations, especially for similar sounding and spelled drugs (E.g. mitomycin and mitoxantrone, vinrelbine and vinblastine, 5-fu and 5-fudr_)

  The drug name, dose in mg/m2 (if appropriate) total daily dose, and cumulative dose should be written

  The drug order should never be transcribed before it reaches the pharmacist

  All orders are checked by the pharmacist against previous orders.

  Variations are verified

  Avoid the use of extraneous ".0"s as this leads to errors where 100 becomes 1000. Better to spell out the amount rather than depend on interpretation

  Drugs need to be dispensed in large trays or large z-lock bags to contain the drug and avoid confusing one patient's drugs with another

  The individual giving the drug should not be the same person preparing the drug unless another individual has double checked the order

  All persons handling chemotherapy should be properly trained

*Policies and procedures for drug preparation
and administration should be updated once a
year*

Vesicant extravasation

1. Vesicant drugs can cause tissue necrosis if they infiltrate soft tissue from blood vessel
2. Vesicant drugs include

   * Dactinomycin
   * Vinblastine
   * Daunomycin
   * Nitrogen mustard
   * Doxorubicin
   * Idarubicin
   * Mitomycin-C
   * Teniposide
   * Vincristine

3. Extravasation of vesicant can result in physical deformity or functional deficit
4. Measures to minimize risk of extravasation

   * Identify patients at risk

     Patients who are unable to communicate clearly

     Elderly, confused, debilitated patients with frail, fragile veins

   * Avoid infusing vesicants over joints, bony prominences, tendons, or antecubital fossa
   * Avoid giving vesicant drugs in areas where venous or lymphatic circulation is poor
   * Give vesicant agent before other agents

* If vesicant is ordered as an infusion, it is given only through central line
* Have on hand extravasation kit and all materials necessary to manage extravasation

5. Symptoms of extravasation include

   * Swelling at injection site
   * Stinging, burning, or pain at injection site
   * Redness
   * Lack of blood return

6. If extravasation is suspected, stop infusion and follow official policy and procedure for extravasation

Irritant drugs

1. Irritant drugs cause localized irritation, even burning, but no tissue necrosis if infiltrated.
2. Examples include

   * Etoposide
   * Carmustine
   * Gematabine
   * Dacarbazine
   * Streptozocin
   * Taxol
   * Taxotere

Routes of drug administration

1. Topical
2. Oral
3. Intramuscular

4. Subcutaneous
5. Intravenous
6. Intrathecal
7. Intraperitoneal
8. Intrapleural
9. Intravesical

Vascular access devices (VAD)

1. Nontunnelled central venous catheters

   * Indicated for short-term use
   * Multilumen catheter permits polydrug therapy
   * Easily removed
   * Sterile technique used during care

2. Tunnelled central venous catheters

   * Indicated for frequent IV access
   * Cuff surrounds catheter, permitting fibrous ingrowth
   * Require sterile site care with dressings until formation of granulation tissue (about 7 days)
   * Require flushing every other day or weekly (Groshong catheter)
   * Flush with 3 to 5 cc of heparinized saline (10 to 100 U/ml)
   * Avoid intraluminal mixing of potentially incompatible drugs by flushing with saline between each drug

3. Implantable ports

   * Completely implanted under skin

* Permit access to venous or arterial system, or peritoneal, pleural, or epidural space

* Accessed by noncoring needle

4. Complication management

* Intraluminal catheter occlusion

    Complication arises from

    Blood clot within catheter

    Crystalization or precipitate

    Improper needle placement in port

    Prevention and management

    Maintain positive pressure during flush

    Avoid excessive manipulation of catheter

    Vigorously flush with 20 cc (ml) saline after blood draw

    Flush between each drug to prevent incompatibility

    Flush every 8 to 12 hours when giving total parenteral nutrition (TPN) or lipids

    Urokinase may be used if blood clot is suspected

* Extraluminal catheter occlusion

    Complication arises from

    Fibrin sheath formation

    Thrombosis

    Catheter position

    Pinch-off syndrome

    Prevention and management

Vigorously flush to prevent fibrin sheath formation

Lyse fibrin sheath with urokinase with dwell time of 24 hours

Low-dose warfarin may prevent or decrease incidence of thrombus formation

Anticoagulants may be necessary to treat venous thrombosis

* Infection

Manifestations

Most common in patients with neutropenia and/or multilumen catheters and in those receiving TPN

Local skin infections are common

Symptoms include redness, warmth, discomfort, exudate and fever

Prevention and management

Provide meticulous catheter care

Obtain culture of area

Increase frequency of catheter care

Administer appropriate antibiotics

Take blood cultures (intraluminal and peripheral)

Management of Chemotherapy Toxicities

Acute and long-term toxicities are often function of effect of drugs on rapidly dividing cells

Incidence and severity of toxicities are related to

1. Drug dosage
2. Administration schedule
3. Specific mechanism of action
4. Concomitant illness
5. Measures employed to prevent or minimize toxicities

Pretreatment evaluation: Vigorous treatment course is not tolerated in

1. Patients in weak physical condition
2. Patients with poor nutritional status
3. Heavily pretreated patients who may lack marrow reserve, placing them at higher risk for infection, bleeding, or anemia
4. Individuals who are unable or unwilling to care for self
5. Patients with pre-existing hepatic or renal dysfunction, which can alter absorption, distribution, metabolism, and elimination of drugs
6. Patients with hypovolemia and dehydration from nausea, vomiting, or diarrhea, which may increase risk of acute renal failure
7. Patients with a concomitant illness that affects individual's ability to metabolize drug or to care for self
8. Patients for whom compliance with treatment program may be influenced by financial and third-party payment concerns

Patient education and follow-up goals

1. Provide support and information
2. Empower patient to care for self

3. Reduce patient's fear, increase his or her self-confidence, improve compliance
4. Help patient adjust to treatment
5. Increase patient's understanding of treatment goals
6. Help patient recognize and control side effects
7. Enhance patient's ability to report side effects early
8. Document and follow-up to reinforce teaching and to evaluate patient's condition

Grading of toxicities

1. Grading is a means of standardization of assessment and documentation of side effects
2. To assess toxicity, knowledge of the following is necessary

   * Which toxicities occurred

   * Toxicity severity

   * Time of onset

   * Duration of effect

   * Interventions used to minimize effect

Systemic toxicities

1. Bone marrow suppression

   * Most common dose-limiting side effect of chemotherapy

   * All hematopoietic cells divide rapidly and are vulnerable to chemotherapy

   * Point of lowest blood count (nadir) occurs about 7 to 14 days after chemotherapy

* Alkylating agents and nitrosoureas are toxic to noncycling and cycling cells

* Antimetabolites, vinca alkaloids, and antitumor antibiotics are less toxic because they are cycle specific

* Risk factors for bone marrow suppression

    Tumor cells in bone marrow

    Prior treatment with chemotherapy or radiation

    Poor nutrition

* Thrombocytopenia

    Lifespan of platelets is 7 to 10 days

    Thrombocytopenia occurs on days 8 to 14

    Manifestations of thrombocytopenia

    Easy bruising

    Bleeding from gums, nose, or other orifices

    Petechiae on extremities and pressure points

    Platelet transfusions are indicated if platelet count drops quickly to dangerous level (20,000/mm³ or less) or if patient is bleeding

* Anemia

    Red blood cells have a lifespan of 120 days

    Manifestations of anemia

    Pallor

    Fatigue

    Hypotension

    Tachycardia

    Headache

    Tachypnea

    Irritability

Transfusions are indicated when

    Hemoglobin goes below 8 g/100 ml

    Patient is symptomatic, e.g., short of breath

    Patient is bleeding

Consider the growth factor erythropoietin

✶ Neutropenia

Lifespan of granulocyte is 6 to 8 hours

Neutropenia usually develops 8 to 12 days after chemotherapy

Chemotherapy is often withheld if white blood cell (WBC) count is below 3000/mm3 or if absolute neutrophil count (ANC) is below 1500/mm3

Profound neutropenia (grade 4) is defined as an ANC of less than 500 cells/mm3

ANC is calculated by multiplying WBC count by neutrophil count

(Segmented neutrophils + bands) × WBC = ANC

Infections from invasion and overgrowth of pathogenic microbes increase in frequency and severity as ANC decreases

Risk of severe infections increases when nadir persists for more than 7 to 10 days

Chemotherapy-induced damage to alimentary

canal and respiratory tract mucosa facilitates entry of infecting organisms; 80% of infections arise from endogenous microbial flora

When neutrophil count is less than 500 cells/mm3, approximately 20% or more of febrile episodes are accompanied by bacteremia caused principally by aerobic gram-negative bacilli and gram-positive cocci

Treatment involves culture and broad-spectrum antibiotics for a minimum of 7 days

Fever persisting for more than 3 days without identification of infected site or organism suggests

Nonbacterial cause (may begin antifungal therapy)

Resistance to antibiotic

Emergence of second bacterial infection

Inadequate antibiotic serum and tissue levels

Drug fever

Infection at avascular site (abscess)

Colony-stimulating factors can shorten duration of neutropenia

2. Fatigue

* Common and distressing side effect of chemotherapy

* Cause in cancer patient is unknown but may relate to

Changes in musculoskeletal protein stores

Metabolite concentration and accumulation

Changes in energy usage or disease pattern

Anemia and psychologic distress

Metabolism of end products of cellular destruction by chemotherapy

* Manifestations of fatigue

  Weariness

  Weakness

  Lack of energy

* Interventions to overcome fatigue

  Energy conservation

  Rest

  Setting priorities for activities

  Delegating tasks

3. Gastrointestinal (GI) toxicities

   * Anorexia

     Characterized by abnormalities of carbohydrate, protein, and fat metabolism

     Alterations in food perception, taste, and smell are commonly caused by chemotherapy

     Anorexia can lead to

     Decreased calorie intake

     Weight loss

     Compromised immune status

     Decreased macrophage mobilization

     Depressed lymphocyte function

Impaired phagocytosis

Management includes

Nutritional and physical assessment

Dietary diary

Consultation with dietitian

Dietary plan

Degree of anorexia and success of any dietary plan depends on

Patient motivation

Nutritional status at time of diagnosis

Site of cancer

Type of treatment

Severity of side effects

* Diarrhea

Results from destruction of actively dividing epithelial cells of GI tract

Degree and duration of diarrhea depend on

Drugs (e.g., 5-fluorouracil, methotrexate)

Dose

Nadir

Frequency of chemotherapy

Abdominal cramps and rectal urgency can evolve into

Nocturnal diarrhea

Fecal incontinence

Lethargy

Weakness

Orthostatic hypotension

Fluid and electrolyte imbalance

Prolonged diarrhea causes

Dehydration

Nutritional malabsorption

Circulatory collapse

Management often includes

Temporarily discontinuing chemotherapy

Low-residue, high-calorie, high-protein diet

Pharmacologic measures

Stool cultures to rule out infectious process

Clostridium difficile infection has been reported in patients receiving chemotherapy who have had prior antibiotic exposure

Antidiarrheal agents are not given to counteract diarrhea resulting from infection, since these agents promote slow passage of stool through intestines, prolonging mucosal exposure to organism's toxins

Pharmacologic intervention for diarrhea includes

Anticholinergic drugs to reduce gastric secretions and decrease intestinal peristalsis

Opiate therapy binds to receptors on smooth muscle of bowel, slowing down intestinal motility and increasing fluid absorption

Octreotide acetate

Synthetic analog of hormone octapeptide

Inhibits release of gut hormones, including serotonin and gastrin, from GI tract

Prolongs intestinal transit time, increasing intestinal water and electrolyte transport and decreasing GI bloodflow

* Constipation

Infrequent, excessively hard and dry bowel movements result from decrease in rectal filling or emptying

Risk factors

Narcotic analgesics

Decrease in physical activity

Low-fiber diet

Decrease in fluid intake

Poor dentition in elderly population

Bed rest

Diminished rectal emptying caused by vincristine or vinblastine therapy; these drugs cause autonomic nerve dysfunction and symptoms may include peripheral nerve dysfunction

Prevention of constipation

Prophylactic stool softener before beginning vincristine or vinblastine therapy

Increase fiber, fluids, and physical activity

Notify physician if more than 3 days has passed without bowel movement, because impaction, ileus, or obstipation can occur

✳ Nausea and vomiting

Vomiting center (VC) contains neurotransmitter receptors sensitive to chemical toxins in blood and cerebrospinal fluid

Major receptors are

Dopamine

Serotonin (5-HT3) in central nervous system (CNS) and GI tract

Muscarinic cholinergic receptor in chemoreceptor trigger zone

Muscarinic receptor in VC vestibular apparatus

Efferent vagal motor nuclei

Histamine in VC and vestibular apparatus

Emesis can be induced by

Stimulation of VC

Obstruction, irritation, inflammation, or delayed gastric emptying

Conditioned anticipatory responses

Nausea

Subjective conscious recognition of urge to vomit

Manifested by unpleasant wavelike sensation in epigastric area, at back of throat, or throughout abdomen

Mediated by autonomic nervous system and accompanied by symptoms such as tachycardia, perspiration, lightheadedness, dizziness, pallor, excess salivation, and weakness

Retching

Rhythmic and spasmodic movement involving diaphragm and abdominal muscles

Controlled by respiratory center in brainstem near VC

Negative intrathoracic pressure and positive abdominal pressure result in unproductive retching

When negative pressure becomes positive, vomiting occurs

Vomiting

Somatic process performed by respiratory muscles causing forceful oral expulsion of gastric, duodenal, or jejunal contents

Classifications of nausea and vomiting

Acute: Nausea and vomiting 1 to 2 hours after treatment

Delayed: Nausea and vomiting persisting or developing 24 hours after chemotherapy

Delayed nausea and vomiting are less common if acute emesis is prevented

Anticipatory: Nausea and vomiting occuring as result of classic operant conditioning from stimuli associated with chemotherapy

Conditioned responses experienced after few sessions of chemotherapy

Occurs most commonly when efforts to control emesis are unsuccessful

Prevention and management

Risk factors include

Emetic potential of drug(s)

Onset and duration of emetic response

Dose of drug

Schedule of drug

Age: Younger are more susceptible

Prior chemotherapy

Anxiety

Gender: Women more than men

Management strategies

Treat prophylactically, before chemotherapeutic treatment

Combination antiemetic therapy: e.g., serotonin antagonist plus Dexamethasone

Employ behavior strategies; e.g., progressive muscle relaxation, hypnosis, and systematic desensitization

Organ toxicities

1. Cardiotoxicity

   ∗ Acute cardiac toxicity

     Characterized by transient changes on electrocardiogram (ECG)

     Occurs in about 10% of patients receiving chemotherapy

   ∗ Chronic cardiac toxicity

     Characterized by onset of symptoms weeks or months after therapy

Cardiomyopathy is irreversible

Congestive heart failure presents as low-voltage QRS complex

Less than 5% of patients develop chronic cardiotoxicity

* Signs and symptoms

Nonproductive cough

Dyspnea

Pedal edema

* Risk factors

Anthracyclines directly damage myocyte of heart

Total cumulative dose of doxorubicin reaches 550 mg/m² and daunorubicin, 600 mg/m²

If mediastinal radiation has been given, dose of doxorubicin is reduced to 450 mg/m²

High doses of cyclophosphamide or 5-fluorouracil increase risk for cardiac damage

* Prevention

Limit total dose of anthracycline

Low-dose continuous infusions minimize cardiac toxicity

Administer chemoprotectants if appropriate

Use less cardiotoxic analogs if possible

* Management

Monitor ECG and radionuclide scan to evaluate heart function

Instruct patient to conserve energy

Manage fluid retention and minimize sodium intake

Digitalis therapy may enhance cardiac output

Diuretics may be useful to decrease cardiac load

Oxygen may be useful to manage dyspnea

2. Neurotoxicity

   * Chemotherapy-induced neurotoxicity may result in direct or indirect damage to CNS, peripheral nervous system, cranial nerves, or any combination of these

   * CNS damage primarily involves cerebellum; this damage produces altered reflexes, unsteady gait, ataxia, and confusion

   * Damage to peripheral nervous system produces paralysis or loss of movement and sensation to those areas affected by the particular nerve

   * Damage to autonomic nervous system causes ileus, impotence, or urinary retention

   * Drugs most commonly associated with neurotoxicity

     Vincristine

     Peripheral neuropathy

     Myalgias, loss of deep tendon reflexes at ankle, progressing to complete areflexia

     Distal symmetric sensory loss, motor weakness, footdrop, and muscle atrophy

Autonomic neuropathy can also occur with vincristine and is characterized by ileus, constipation, impotence, urinary retention, or postural hypotension

Cisplatin

Damages large-diameter fibers of neural tissues, causing sensory changes

Paresthesias of hands and feet are common

Sensory ataxia

High-tone hearing loss

Taxol

Peripheral neuropathy

Myalgias and arthralgias are dose-dependent

Autonomic neuropathy

Symptoms gradually improve after cessation of therapy

Other drugs associated with neurotoxicity

Ifosfamide

High-dose methotrexate

High-dose cytarabine

5-Fluorouracil

Navelbine

Prevention and Management

Neurologic assessment before treatment

Dose modification may be necessary to prevent irreversible damage

Vitamin B6 injections may help to minimize neuropathy

3. Pulmonary toxicity

* Chemotherapy can damage endothelial cells, resulting in pneumonitis

* Long-term exposure to chemotherapy causes extensive alteration of pulmonary parenchyma

* Presenting symptoms

  Dyspnea

  Bilateral basilar rales

  Unproductive cough

  Tachypnea

* Risk factors

  Age: Very young and elderly

  Preexisting lung disease

  History of smoking

  Cumulative dose

  Long-term therapy

  Mediastinal radiation

  High inspired concentration of oxygen

* Drugs commonly associated with pulmonary toxicity

  Bleomycin: Cumulative dose should not exceed 400 to 450 units; it induces interstitial changes with hyperplasia

  Cytarabine directly damages pneumocytes

  Mitomycin C causes diffuse alveolar damage

  Cyclophosphamide causes endothelial swelling

    * Prevention and management

     Symptoms of pulmonary toxicity

       Low-grade fever

       Nonproductive cough

       Dyspnea

       Tachycardia

       Diffuse basilar crackles

       Wheezing

       Pleural rub

       Fatigue

     Management

       Conservation of energy

       Corticosteroids

       Diuretics

4. Hepatotoxicity

    * Chemotherapy can cause damage to parenchymal cells

    * Obstruction to hepatic bloodflow results in fatty changes, hepatocellular necrosis, and veno-occlusive disease

    * Risk factors for veno-occlusive disease

     Increased age

     Hepatitis

     Elevated serum glutamic oxaloacetic transaminase (SGOT) level

    * Clinical signs of veno-occlusive disease

Weight gain

Jaundice

Abdominal pain

Hepatomegaly

Encephalopathy

Elevated bilirubin level and SGOT values

* Chemotherapy drugs commonly associated with liver toxicity

  Methotrexate

  Nitrosoureas

  6-Mercaptopurine

  Etoposide

  Cytarabine

  Taxotere

  Taxol

* Symptoms of hepatotoxicity

  Elevated liver function test results

  Chemical hepatitis

  Jaundice

  Ascites

  Decreased albumin level

  Cirrhosis

5. Hemorrhagic cystitis

   * Results from damage to bladder mucosa caused by acrolein, a metabolite of cyclophosphamide and ifosfamide

* Symptoms of hemorrhagic cystitis

  Microscopic hematuria

  Transient irritative urination

  Dysuria

  Suprapubic pain

  Hemorrhage

* Risk factors

  High doses of ifosfamide or cyclophosphamide

* Prevention and management

  Adequate hydration

  Frequent bladder emptying

  Mesna therapy

  Test urine for occult blood (Hemastik)

6. Nephrotoxicity

   * Damage to kidneys is caused either by direct renal cell damage or obstructive nephropathy; i.e., tumor lysis syndrome or uric acid nephropathy

   * Risk factors

     Elderly patient

     Preexisting renal disease

     Poor nutritional status

     Dehydration

     Large tumor mass

     High cumulative dose of nephrotoxic drug

Concomitant administration of aminoglycoside therapy

✳ Symptoms

Increased blood urea nitrogen and creatinine

Oliguria

Azotemia

Proteinuria

Hyperuricemia

Hypomagnesemia

Hypocalcemia

✳ Drugs commonly associated with nephrotoxicity

Cisplatin: *Damages renal cell*

Methotrexate: *Damage occurs because drug precipitates out in an acid environment to obstruct renal tubules*

Streptozocin: *Directly damages tubules, causing tubular atrophy*

Nitrosoureas: *Cause delayed renal failure: azotemia and proteinuria followed by progressive renal failure*

Mitomycin C: *Renal failure and microangiopathic hemolytic anemia occur in approximately 20% of patients who have received cumulative dose of 100 mg or more*

✳ Prevention of nephrotoxicity

Evaluate renal status before therapy

Adequately hydrate patient

Encourage patient to drink 3 liters of fluid per day

Decrease uric acid production with allopurinol in patients with high tumor load

Ensure that patient receiving methotrexate has pretreatment with sodium bicarbonate to alkalinize urine

Mannitol induces diuresis with cisplatin therapy

Amifostine reduces the cumulative renal toxicity associated with repeated cisplatin therapy

* Acute tumor lysis syndrome

  Occurs most commonly in patients who have a highly proliferative tumor (high grade lymphomas)

  Characterized by hyperuricemia, hyperkalemia, hyperphosphatemia and hypocalcemia with or without acute renal failure

  Uric acid crystallization in the renal tubules causes obstruction, decreased glomerular filtration and possible acute renal failure

  Prevention of acute tumor lysis syndrome includes:

    urinary alkalinization

    diuresis

    maintain fluid balance

7. Gonadal toxicity

  * Chemotherapy effects on the gonads include:

Gonadal failure

Infertility

Premature menopause

★ Risk factors for gonadal toxicity

Age: Women over 30 are less likely to regain ovarian function because they have fewer oocytes than younger women

Cycle nonspecific agents are most toxic and include

Busulfan

Melphalan

Nitrogen mustard

Procarbazine

Chlorambucil

Drug-induced testicular damage results in azospermia, oligospermia, and abnormalities of semen volume and motility

Sperm banking is an option for men to preserve their ability to produce children

8. Secondary and therapy-related cancers

★ Risk factors

Long-term survivors are at highest risk for second primary cancer

Alkylating agents are most often implicated as risk factors for second malignancies

Long-term survivors and their children should be monitored for their lifetimes

Suggested Readings

1. Tortorice PV: Chemotherapy: Principles of Therapy. In Groenwald SL, Frogge MH, Goodman M, Yarbo CH, (eds.): *Cancer Nursing: Principles and Practice* (4th ed.) Boston: Jones and Bartlett, 1997, pp 283-316.

2. Camp-Sorrell D: Chemotherapy: Toxicity management. In Groenwald SL, Frogge MH, Goodman M, Yarbro CH, (eds.): *Cancer Nursing: Principles and Practice* (4th ed.) Boston: Jones and Bartlett, 1997, pp. 385-425.

3. Goodman M and Riley MB: Chemotherapy: Principles of Administration. In Groenwald SL, Frogge MH, Goodman M, Yarbro CH, (eds.): *Cancer Nursing: Principles and Practice* (4th ed.) Boston: Jones and Bartlett, 1997, pp 317-384.

4. High Dose Cancer Therapy, (2nd ed.) Armitage JO and Antman KH, (eds) Baltimore: Williams and Wilkins, 1995.

5. Maxwell MB, Maher KE: Chemotherapy-induced myelosuppression. *Semin Oncol Nurs* 8:113-123, 1992.

6. Hoagland HC: Hematologic complications of cancer chemotherapy. In Perry MC (ed): *The Chemotherapy Source Book*. Baltimore: Williams & Wilkins, 1992, pp 498-507.

7. DeVita, VT: *Principles of Cancer Management: Chemotherapy*. In DeVita VT, Hellman S, Rosenberg SA (eds): *Cancer Principles and Practice of Oncology*, (5th ed.) Philadelphia: Lippincott-Raven, 1997, pp. 333-344.

8. Wickham R, Purl S, Welker D: Long-term central venous catheters: Issues for care. *Semin Oncol Nurs* 8:133-147, 1991.
9. Vose JM, Armitage JO: Clinical applications of hematopoietic growth factors. *J Clin Oncol* 13:1023-1035, 1995.

CHAPTER 10

Biotherapy

Overview

Biotherapy is based on hypothesis that immune system can be manipulated to restore, augment, or modulate its function

Evidence from animal and human trials indicates that, under proper circumstances, malignant tumors are susceptible to immunologic rejection

Biologic response modifiers (BRMs) are soluble substances capable of altering immune system with either stimulatory or suppressive effect

127

Three major categories of BRMs

1. Agents that restore, augment, or modulate host's immunologic mechanisms
2. Agents that have direct antitumor activity
3. Agents that have other biologic effects

   * Agents interfering with tumor cells' ability to survive or metastasize

   * Differentiating agents or agents affecting cell transformation

Types of Immunotherapy and Their Side Effects

Antibody therapy (serotherapy)

1. Promotes specific targeting of cells through antibody-antigen response
2. Monoclonal antibodies (MAbs) may be used alone or in combination with radioisotopes, toxins, or chemotherapeutic drugs (immunoconjugates) to stain, destroy, or identify cells with specific antigens on their cell surfaces
3. Also used in vitro to remove tumor cells from bone marrow before autologous bone marrow transplantation and in conjunction with other BRMs
4. Toxicities most often occur within 2 to 8 hours after antibody administration and include

   * Anaphylaxis (infrequent)

     Signs and symptoms

Predicted by presence of generalized flush or urticaria followed by pallor or cyanosis, or both

Patient may complain of tickle in throat or feeling of impending doom

Complaints of bronchospasm are common

Hypotension and unconsciousness may result

Nursing measures

Stop antibody infusion immediately

Assess patient's vital signs often

Alert physician

Administer 0.3 cc aqueous 1:1000 epinephrine subcutaneously, if patient is conscious and has detectable blood pressure

For patients who cannot be aroused, epinephrine 1:10,000 is administered by intravenous push

Additional therapeutic measures may include

Administration of oxygen

Administration of antihistamines, corticosteroids, and aminophylline

Cardiopulmonary resuscitation

* Fever

* Urticaria

* Chills

* Pruritus

* Diaphoresis

* Dyspnea

* Rigors
* Nausea
* Malaise
* Vomiting
* Pallor
* Diarrhea
* Weakness
* Hypotension
* Generalized erythema

Cytokines

1. Substances released from activated immune system cells that affect behavior of other cells
2. Activate variety of biologic activities that may alter growth and metastasis of cancer cells
3. May be administered directly to patients for control of cancer, or may be used to manipulate immune response in vitro to generate products used to treat individuals with cancer
4. Examples include

    * Interferons (IFN)

        Naturally occurring cytokines that interfere with virus activity in cells

        Have antiproliferative effect

        Three major types

        α-IFN

        β-IFN

        γ-IFN

Each type originates from different cell and has distinct biologic and chemical properties

IFN Tau, or trophoblastin, is similar to α-IFN and may be antiviral and antineoplastic

Routes of administration

Subcutaneous

Intramuscular

Intravenous bolus

Intravenous continuous infusion

Intrathecal

Intralesional

Intracavity

Route significantly alters pharmacokinetics

Toxicities are dose-related and include

Flulike syndrome: Fever, chills, malaise, fatigue

Central nervous system (CNS): Headache, lethargy, somnolence, seizures, confusion, impaired concentration

Renal/hepatic: Elevated transaminase level, proteinuria

Reproductive: Impotence, decreased libido

Gastrointestinal (GI): Nausea, vomiting, diarrhea, anorexia/weight loss

Hematologic: Leukopenia, thrombocytopenia, anemia

Cardiovascular: Hypotension, tachycardia, arrhythmias, myocardial ischemia

Integumentary: Alopecia, irritation at injection site

Treatment is symptomatic

✴ Interleukins (IL)

Regulatory substances produced by lymphocytes and monocytes

Variety of immunoregulative biologic activities that stimulate proliferation and maturation of immune cells

Types include

Interleukin-1

Potential clinical applications

- Prevention or reversal of iatrogenic neutropenia
- Reversal of thrombocytopenia
- Bone marrow transplantation
- Antiproliferative effects
- Infectious disease
- Dysmyelopoietic states
- Combination therapy with other cytokines

Administered subcutaneously to rotating sites on arms, abdomen, and thighs, with ice applied after injection to prevent bleeding

Toxicities include

- Fever
- Asthenia

- Chills
- Anorexia
- Headache
- Hypotension
- Nausea and vomiting
- Myalgia
- Tachycardia
- Diarrhea

Hypotension is dose-limiting toxicity

Interleukin-2

Supports proliferation and augmentation of natural killer (NK) cells

Is critical for generation of lymphokine-activated killer (LAK) cells

Augments various other T-cell functions

Activates cytotoxic effector cells that produce cytokines

Used in conjunction with LAK cells or tumor-infiltrating lymphocytes (TILs), in combination with other biologic agents, and in combination with chemotherapeutic agents

Produces objective tumor responses in 15% to 45% of patients with renal cell carcinoma and malignant melanoma

Toxicities are multisystem and may be life-threatening; however, all are usually reversible within 24 to 96 hours after therapy

- CNS

  Disorientation

    Monitor for overt and subtle changes in mental status

    IL-2 held or discontinued if agitation, restlessness, or increased anxiety are present

    Some patients progress rapidly to somnolence, disorientation, or severe agitation, and require restraints

    Symptoms resolve within 24 to 48 hours after therapy ceases

- Cardiovascular/pulmonary

  Marked cardiovascular and pulmonary toxicities occur when IL-2 is administered at high dose

  Capillary leak syndrome, characterized by marked extravascular fluid shifts, consistently occurs

  Peripheral vasodilation occurs, with significant decrease in systemic vascular resistance and increase in heart rate

  Hypotension begins soon after onset of treatment

  Plasma protein fraction or albumin is administered

  Dopamine HCl or phenylephrine HCl (Neosynephrine) is administered to keep systolic blood pressure greater than 90

  Tachycardia occurs as compensatory response

Cardiac dysrhythmias occur in 10% of patients

Respond to traditional medical management with digoxin or verapamil

Daily ECGs and increased vital sign monitoring are indicated for patients taking vasopressors

Transient cardiac ischemia has been reported; myocardial infarction is rare but has been reported

Pulmonary congestion is common

Patients may require oxygen therapy

Oxygen saturation is monitored by pulse oximetry

Patients with histories of cardiac or pulmonary dysfunction are not eligible for treatment with IL-2

• Renal

Oliguria, anuria, azotemia, and elevations of serum creatinine and blood urea nitrogen levels occur

Progressive respiratory alkalosis and hypophosphatemia, hypocalcemia, and hypomagnesemia may occur

Low-dose dopamine assists with renal perfusion

Normal renal function returns spontaneously after IL-2 therapy is stopped

Patients with prior nephrectomy are at high risk and should be monitored closely

• GI

Nausea and vomiting are controlled with antiemetics

Diarrhea is common and may require administration of bicarbonate

Stomatitis is frequent but not severe

Malaise and anorexia are not treatment-limiting

- Hepatic

Increased levels of serum bilirubin and liver enzymes and progressive hypoalbuminemia occur with IL-2 therapy

Mild to moderate hepatomegaly without abdominal tenderness occurs commonly

- Hematologic

Severe anemia occurs in 77% of patients who receive IL-2

  Warrants transfusion of packed red blood cells

Thrombocytopenia is common, but platelet therapy is rarely indicated

No severe coagulopathies have been reported

- Integumentary

Diffuse erythematous pruritic rash progresses to desquamation in IL-2 therapy

Desquamation can be severe, involving soles of feet, palms of hands, and moist, intertriginous areas

- Flulike syndrome

Patients develop fever, chills, rigors, and malaise

Managed by prophylactic administration of acetaminophen, diphenhydramine, and indomethacin

If fever or chills develop, meperidine, 25 to 50 mg intravenous push, or lorazepam, 1 to 2 mg intravenous push, is effective

- Endocrinologic

20% of patients receiving high doses of IL-2/LAK develop hypothyroidism

Other IL-2 endocrinologic effects include increases in blood levels of adrenocorticotropic hormone, cortisol, prolactin, growth hormone, and acute-phase reactant C-reactive protein

LAK cell reaction

Mild to severe chills followed by transient fever have been reported within 1 hour after first administration; reactions are less severe with subsequent administration

Tumor necrosis factor

Produced by macrophages

Cytotoxic or cytostatic on tumor cells with no effect on normal cells

Therapeutic effects under clinical investigation

Administered

- By intravenous bolus

- By continuous intravenous infusion

- Subcutaneously

- By intramuscular injection

- Optimal route has not been established

Clinical toxicities are similar to those of IL-2

Colony-stimulating factors (CSF)

Regulate hematopoiesis

In culture, stimulate growth of colonies of maturing blood cells from their hematopoietic precursors

Used prophylactically or therapeutically in treatment of disease states in which myelosuppression, anemia, and thrombocytopenia limit therapeutic treatment options

Allow increased or scheduled doses of chemotherapeutic agents to be given with long-term myelosuppression

Effective in other hematologic diseases, such as AIDS, in which abnormalities of blood cell components exist

CSFs include erythropoietin, granulocyte-CSF (G-CSF), granulocyte-macrophage-CSF (GM-CSF), IL-3, and macrophage-CSF (M-CSF)

Examples include

- Erythropoietin

  Treats anemia related to cancer

  Administered subcutaneously

Response seen (increased hematocrit) within 14 to 21 days after initiation of treatment

Minimal side effects

- G-CSF

Used to treat chemotherapy-induced neutropenia

Administered subcutaneously, or as short intravenous infusion

Side effects include flulike syndrome with fever, myalgias and headache, generalized rash, and bone pain

- GM-CSF

Broader spectrum than G-CSF

Stimulates both macrophages and neutropenia

Decreases requirement for platelet and red cell transfusions in addition to its effect on granulocytes

Permits dose intensification and enhances myeloprotection before and after chemotherapy

Approved by Food and Drug Administration for treatment of neutropenia associated with autologous bone marrow transplantation

Administered by subcutaneous or intravenous infusion

Side effects include

Flulike syndrome (fever, chills, rigors, myalgias, headache, fatigue)

Facial flushing

Generalized rash

Inflammation at injection site

Leukocytosis

Eosinophilia

Dyspnea

Bone pain

Fluid retention

Nursing Management

Flu-like Syndrome

1. Premedicate with acetaminophen and indomethacin one hour prior to first dose of biologic therapy.
2. Use warm blankets at the first sign of a chill.
3. For rigors, administer meperidine 25-50mg parenterally as appropriate
4. For arthralgia, myalgia, or headache, continue acetaminophen as appropriate
5. Consider giving biological agent at bedtime rather than in morning.

Fatigue

1. Assessment: determine peak severity, patterns of activity and sleep, impact on self-care activities and nutritional balance
2. Patient education: teach patient and family methods of saving energy and value of activity in spite of fatigue
3. Maintain activity: Prevent prolonged bedrest.

Capillary leak syndrome (CLS)

1. Monitor blood pressure, pulse, respiratory status, urine output, and body weight during therapy
2. Remove all jewelry, particularly rings before treatment
3. For hypotension and oliguria, administer fluid boluses. Low-dose dopamine may be administered intraveneously to increase urine output
4. Instruct patient to report any feelings of dizziness.

Dermatologic changes

1. Apply hypoallergenic emollient lotions and creams on the skin frequently.
2. For pruritis

   * Administer antipruritic medications such as hydroxyzine HCL, or diphenhydramine
   * Use lorazepam with severe itching as needed.
   * Try colloidal oatmeal baths

3. For subcutaneous site inflammation

   * Rotate sites and do not reuse until firmness resolves

Gastrointestinal symptoms

1. Steroids should not be used as an antiemetic because of their effects on immune function
2. Administer antiemetics and anti-diarrheal agents as needed.

Neurological effects

1. Assess baseline neurologic function
2. Instruct family members on the early signs of mental status changes that should be reported to the patient's health team
3. Monitor patient throughout therapy as symptoms, especially mental status changes, can be subtle.

Suggested Readings

1. Wheeler VS, Biotherapy. In Groenwald SL, Frogge MH, Goodman M, Yarbro CH (eds): *Cancer Nursing: Principles and Practice* (4th ed). Boston: Jones and Bartlet, 1997, pp. 426-458.
2. *Biotherapy: A Comprehensive Review*. Reiger, PT (ed) Boston: Jones and Bartlett, 1995.
3. Rosenberg SA: The immunotherapy and gene therapy of cancer. *J Clin Oncol* 10:180-199, 1992.
4. Carter P, Engleking C, Rumsey K, et al: *Biological Response Modifier Guidelines. Recommendations for Nursing Education and Practice*. Pittsburgh: Oncology Nursing Society, 1989.
5. *Biologic Therapy of Cancer*. DeVita VT, Hellman S, Rosenberg SA (eds). Philadelphia: JB Lippincott, 1995.

CHAPTER 11

Allogeneic Bone Marrow Transplantation

Overview

Types of bone marrow transplantation (BMT)

1. Syngeneic

   * Donor is an identical twin (perfect human leukocyte antigen [HLA] match)

2. Allogeneic

   * Depends on availability of HLA-matched donor

   * Graft-versus-host disease (GVHD) is unique complication

143

✳ Diseases treated with allogeneic BMT include

Acute and chronic leukemias

Lymphomas

Myeloma

Aplastic anemia

Immunologic deficiencies

Inborn errors of metabolism

✳ Most appropriate donor chosen by means of tissue typing of HLA

✳ Donor marrow is harvested in operating room

3. Autologous and blood cell (see Chapter 12)

BMT Process

Candidates and donor require comprehensive evaluations

Pretransplant conditioning regimens involve high-dose chemotherapy alone or with total-body irradiation

Marrow is infused through central lumen catheter over several hours

Toxicities and complications are most severe before marrow graft becomes functional

Acute Complications of BMT

Gastrointestinal (GI) toxicity

1. Occurs 0 to 28 days after BMT
2. Clinical manifestations include

   * Mucositis

   * Nausea and vomiting

   * Diarrhea

Acute GVHD

1. Occurs 10 to 70 days after allogeneic BMT
2. Clinical manifestations

   * Maculopapular rash progressing to erythroderma with desquamation

   * Elevated liver enzyme levels, right upper quadrant abdominal pain, hepatomegaly, and jaundice

   * Green, watery diarrhea and abdominal cramping

   * Anorexia, nausea, vomiting

3. Prophylaxis and approaches to care

   * Administer cyclosporine and methotrexate to inhibit T-lymphocytes

   * Administer antithymocyte globulin

   * Assess patient's integumentary system

   * Monitor liver function tests, guaiac stool test, patient's weight, intake and output, and electrolytes

   * Assess patient's nutritional status

Hematologic complications

1. Bleeding can occur from all body orifices

   * Requires irradiated blood products, HLA-matched platelets

   * Follow appropriate nursing interventions for bleeding

2. Hemorrhagic cystitis from high-dose cyclophosphamide

   * Assess patient's fluid intake and force fluids

Renal insufficiency

1. Occurs 1 to 50 days after BMT
2. Early clinical manifestations include

   * Anuria

   * Acid-base imbalances

   * Doubling of baseline creatinine level

Veno-occlusive disease of liver

1. Almost exclusive to BMT
2. Occurs 6 to 15 days after BMT
3. Clinical manifestations

   * Fluid retention

   * Sudden weight gain

   * Abdominal distention

   * Right upper quadrant pain

   * Increased bilirubin and serum glutamic oxaloacetic transaminase (SGOT)

   * Hepatomegaly

* Encephalopathy

4. No known treatment; provide symptom management and supportive care

Infection

1. Most common sites of infections are

   * GI tract
   * Oropharynx
   * Lung
   * Skin
   * Indwelling catheter sites

2. Most common infections from days 0 to 30 are

   * Bacterial: gram-negative and gram-positive
   * Herpes simplex viruses I and II
   * *Candida* and *Aspergillus* species

3. Most common infections from days 30 to 90 are

   * Cytomegalovirus (CMV)

     CMV pneumonia is a common occurrence

   * Gram-positive bacteria
   * *Pneumocystis carinii*

4. Most common infections after engraftment are

   * Encapsulated bacteria
   * Varicella zoster

Clinical Management of BMT Outpatient

Hospital discharge after BMT averages 30 to 35 days

Common discharge criteria are

1. Availability of 24-hour outpatient medical care
2. Evidence of oral intake
3. Nausea, vomiting, and pain controlled without IV medications
4. Diarrhea controlled at <500 ml/day
5. Platelet count supportable at 5000 to 15,000/mm^3
6. Granulocyte count >500/mm^3 for 24 hours
7. Hematocrit >25%
8. Patient tolerating medications by mouth
9. Family support at home

Patients experience at least 3 months of severe immunodeficiency

Immune function generally returns in 6 to 9 months

Immune recovery delayed in allogeneic patients with chronic GVHD

Numerous tests and evaluations are needed for follow-up care

Late Complications of BMT

Chronic GVHD

1. Major cause of morbidity after allogeneic BMT
2. Onset is 100 to 400 days after BMT
3. Clinical manifestations

   * Skin involvement

     Itching, burning rash

     Erythema

     Hypopigmentation and hyperpigmentation

     Fibrosis

   * Liver disorders

     Jaundice

     Abnormal liver function test results

   * Oral involvement

     Pain, burning, dryness

     Loss of sense of taste

     Stomatitis

     Dental decay

     Xerostomia

   * Ocular involvement

     Burning and itching

     Dry eyes

   * GI tract

     Anorexia, weight loss

    Dysphagia

* Vaginal involvement

    Inflammation

    Dryness

    Stricture formation

4. Treatment

   * Long-term administration of cyclosporine with or without prednisone

   * Symptom-related supportive measures

Late complications of high-dose chemotherapy or total-body irradiation are

1. Gonadal dysfunction
2. Thyroid dysfunction
3. Cataracts
4. Dental decay
5. Radiation nephritis
6. Impaired memory and learning disorders
7. Second malignancy

Psychosocial Issues

Stresses encountered with each phase of BMT process

Counseling and education promote realistic expectations

Support should be available for nurses

Moral and ethical issues include

1. Allocation of resources
2. Competitive selection of marrow recipients
3. Life support in irreversible organ failure

Research studies on quality of life after BMT are emerging

Suggested Readings

1. Buchsel PC: Allogeneic bone marrow transplantation. In Groenwald SL, Frogge MH, Goodman M, Yarbro CH (eds): *Cancer Nursing: Principles and Practice* (4th ed). Boston: Jones and Bartlett, 1997, pp 459-506.
2. Buchsel PC: Ambulatory care for the bone marrow transplant patient. In Buchsel PC, Yarbro CH (eds): *Oncology Nursing in the Ambulatory Setting.* Boston: Jones and Bartlett, 1993, pp 185-216.
3. Franco T, Gould DA: Allogeneic bone marrow transplantation. *Semin Oncol Nurs* 10:3-11, 1994.
4. Whedon MB, Wujcik D (eds): *Stem Cell and Marrow Transplantation Principles, Practice, and Nursing Insights* (2nd ed). Boston: Jones and Bartlett, 1997.

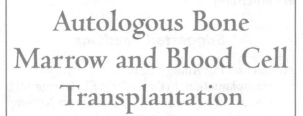

CHAPTER 12

Autologous Bone Marrow and Blood Cell Transplantation

Overview

Autologous bone marrow transplantation (ABMT)

1. Patient receives his or her own bone marrow
2. Diseases treated with ABMT include
   * Acute and chronic leukemia
   * Lymphomas
   * Some solid tumors
3. Advantages
   * Absence of graft-versus-host disease (GVHD)

∗ Fewer toxicities compared with allogeneic BMT

Blood cell transplantation (BCT)

1. Stem cells are collected from patient's peripheral blood by apheresis
2. Diseases treated with BCT

   ∗ Acute and chronic leukemia

   ∗ Lymphoma

   ∗ Multiple myeloma

   ∗ Some solid tumors

3. Advantages

   ∗ More rapid recovery of neutrophils and platelets when progenitor cells are used

   ∗ No anesthesia required

   ∗ Fewer complications

   ∗ Candidates are patients ineligible for ABMT because their marrow is hypoplasitc or metastatic

4. Standards for transplantation have been established
5. Centers of excellence for ABMT and BCT are being developed and mandated by insurers

Process of ABMT and BCT

Evaluate patient for eligibility and type of transplant

Cells for transplant

1. With ABMT, cells are obtained through a bone marrow procedure in surgery and then cells are harvested
2. With BCT, mobilization takes place to

   * Release an increased number of peripheral stem cells (PSCs) and progenitor cells

   * Hematopoietic growth factors, chemotherapy, or both increase these cells 100-fold to 500-fold

   * After mobilization, blood cell separators collect the PSCs and progenitor cells by apheresis

Cell processing and storage

1. Cells from ABMT and BCT are cryopreserved in same way
2. Purging of cells from ABMT and BCT may be done to decrease the risk of tumor contamination
3. Purging is done after the harvest or apheresis and before cryopreservation

Conditioning therapy

1. Given to patients to remove any remaining malignant cells
2. Chemotherapy, total body irradiation, or both may be used to deplete the marrow
3. Protocols vary in length from 4 to 7 days before transplant or blood cell reinfusion

Reinfusion

1. Procedure usually takes less than 1 hour
2. IV hydration is recommended for 2 hours before reinfusion

3. Antiemetic prophylaxis is recommended
4. Cells are brought to bedside in liquid nitrogen, thawed, and given by IV push or rapid IV drip
5. Nausea, vomiting, chills, cramping and bad taste in mouth from DMSO (cell preservative) are complications that occur during or immediately after infusion

Post-Transplant Care

Requires a multidisciplinary team skilled in the management of severely myelosuppressed patients

Complications after ABMT and BCT include

1. Infection

   * Patients receiving BCT have a shorter period of neutropenia

   * Patients do not have extended immunosuppression, therefore less risk of late infections

   * Standard prophylaxis and empirical antibiotic therapy are used to manage infections

2. Bleeding

   * Nose and mouth most common sites of bleeding

   * Platelet transfusions may be required

3. Anemia

   * Fatigue is common

4. Gastrointestinal toxicity

  ∗ Nausea, vomiting, diarrhea, and stomatitis may be severe

5. Urinary system toxicity

  ∗ Hemorrhagic cystitis may be severe

Outpatient Care

1. More care is being done in the outpatient setting
2. Requires significant allocation of resources
3. Treatment and supportive care protocols must facilitate outpatient care
4. Care must be available 24 hours per day, 7 days per week
5. Housing for out of town patients must be convenient

Future applications

Allogeneic BCT may be used in the future

Treatment with a combination of ABMT and BCT is being investigated

Suggested Readings

1. Wujcik D: Autologous bone marrow and blood cell transplantation. In Groenwald SL, Frogge MH, Goodman M, Yarbro CH (eds): *Cancer Nursing: Principles and Practice* (4th ed). Boston: Jones and Bartlett, 1997, pp 507–525.

2. Whedon MB, Wujcik D (eds): *Stem Cell and Marrow Transplantation: Principles, Practice and Nursing Insights* (2nd ed). Boston: Jones and Bartlett, 1997.

PART III

Symptom Management

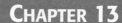
Bleeding Disorders

Overview

Bleeding is one of the most serious, potentially life-threatening problems for the person with cancer

Minor bleeding may be presenting symptom of cancer

Severe bleeding may indicate onset of progressive disease

Causes of bleeding in cancer

1. Tumor factors

* Blood vessel invasion, erosion, and subsequent rupture

* Ulcerative effects of local infections at vessel sites

* Invasion and replacement of bone marrow by tumor

2. Platelet abnormalities

  * Quantitative abnormalities

    Thrombocytosis

    Disorder involving increased number of circulating platelets (400,000 to 600,000 cells/mm^3)

    Associated with chronic granulocytic anemia and cancers of lung, ovary, pancreas, breast, kidney, and gastrointestinal (GI) tract

    Venous thrombosis can occur, especially in patients with platelet counts of more than 1 million cells/mm^3

    Thrombocytopenia

    Disorder involving reduction in number of circulating platelets

    May result from

      Decreased platelet production caused by tumor invasion of bone marrow or acute or delayed effect of chemotherapy or radiotherapy

      90% of platelet production can be sequestered in spleen in patients with hypersplenism; thus, platelets are unavailable in circulation

Idiopathic thrombocytopenic purpura can result in antibodies being formed against individual's own platelets

Rapid replacement of intravascular volume of stored platelet-poor blood dilutes thrombocytes already present

Platelet function decreases because of decreased adhesiveness and decreased aggregation (e.g., with aspirin and nonsteroidal anti-inflammatory drugs [NSAIDs])

* Qualitative abnormalities

Platelet malfunction

Bleeding occurs despite normal platelet counts and coagulation factors

May be caused by malignancy itself or by partial release of platelet contents after contact with malignant tissue

Many drugs also decrease platelet function (e.g., aspirin, NSAIDs, beta-lactam antibiotics, psychotropic drugs, some chemotherapeutic agents)

* Hypocoagulation

Risk factors

Tumor load

Liver disease

Vitamin K deficiency

Excessive frozen plasma transfusions

* Hypercoagulation

*Disseminated intravascular coagulopathy (DIC)
is most commonly caused by*

Infection

Tumor

Liver disease

Intravascular hemorrhage

*Coagulation mechanism is triggered
inappropriately by underlying disease process
with abnormal activation of thrombin, upsetting
balance of hemostasis*

Approaches to Care

Assessment

1. Comprehensive history for patient at risk for bleeding

   * Bleeding tendencies

   * Family history of any bleeding abnormalities

   * Drugs and chemicals that interfere with coagulation

   * General performance status

   * Current blood component therapy

   * Nutritional status; i.e., vitamin K or vitamin C deficiency

   * Anemia

2. Physical examination

   * Integumentary system

Bruising

Petechiae

Purpura

Ecchymosis

Acrocyanosis

Oozing from venipuncture, biopsy, or injection sites, or central lines, catheters, or nasogastric tubes

* Eyes and ears

  Visual disturbances

  Periorbital edema

  Subconjunctival hemorrhage

  Headache

  Ear pain

* Nose, mouth, and throat

  Petechiae on nasal or oral mucosa

  Epistaxis

  Tenderness or bleeding from gums or oral mucosa

* Cardiopulmonary system

  Crackles

  Wheezes

  Stridor

  Dyspnea

  Tachypnea

  Cyanosis

    Hemoptysis

    Changes in vital signs

    Color and temperature of all extremities

    Peripheral pulses

* Genitourinary system

  Bleeding

  Character and amount of menses

  Urinary output

* Musculoskeletal system

  Bleeding into joints

* Central nervous system (CNS)

  Mental status changes

  - Restlessness
  - Obtundation
  - Confusion
  - Seizures
  - Lethargy
  - Coma
  - Dizziness

3. Screening tests

   * Bleeding time
   * Platelet count
   * Whole-blood clot retraction test
   * Prothrombin time
   * Partial thromboplastin time

✴ Fibrin degradation products (FDP) test

4. Manifestations

✴ Internal bleeding may present as

Massive hemoptysis

Severe hematemesis

Vaginal hemorrhage

Loss of consciousness

Hypovolemic shock

✴ Loss of 6 to 8 cc of blood per day will precipitate iron-deficiency anemia

Diagnostic indications of iron-deficiency anemia

Absence of stainable iron levels

Diminished plasma iron levels

Increased level of unsaturated iron-binding capacity

Reduced serum ferritin level

Symptoms of anemia

Fatigue

Dyspnea

Weakness

Tachycardia

Irritability

✴ Clinical evidence of DIC

Easy and spontaneous bleeding

Minor coagulation disorders or overt bleeding

Prolonged prothrombin time

Prolonged partial thromboplastin time

Decreased platelet count

Increased results on FDP test

Interventions

1. General bleeding

   * Direct and steady pressure to site of bleeding

   * Mechanical pressure, if bleeding site is not directly accessible

   * Prophylactic arterial ligation

   * Blood transfusions to restore circulatory volume and oxygen-carrying capacity

   * Oral or parenteral iron supplements may be indicated

   * Human erythropoietin may stimulate erythropoiesis

2. Thrombocytosis

   * *Thrombocytapheresis:* Rapidly removes large numbers of platelets

   * *Marrow suppressive therapy:* Alkylating agents may be used to suppress hyperproliferative marrow

   * *Radiation therapy:* Radioactive phosphorous may suppress hyperproliferative marrow

3. Thrombocytopenia

   * Platelet transfusions

* Provide safe environment
* Minimal use of aspirin and NSAIDs
* Treat primary disease

4. Hypocoagulation

   * Effective tumor therapy
   * Plasma and plasma derivative therapy
   * Albumin transfusions
   * Plasma component therapy
   * Parenteral vitamin K

5. Hypercoagulation

   * Treatment of precipitating cause (i.e., sepsis or tumor)
   * Heparin therapy may be useful in chronic DIC for inhibiting formation of new clots
   * ϵ-aminocaproic acid (Amicar) is a fibrinolytic inhibitor and useful in management of DIC
   * Blood replacement therapy

6. Nursing interventions for persons at risk for or experiencing bleeding

   * Provide for person's physical safety
   * Maintain person's skin integrity
   * Apply pressure to injection sites
   * Consider pharmacologic suppression of menses
   * Instruct patient to avoid forceful coughing, sneezing, or nose blowing

* Provide for liberal use of stool softeners and laxatives

7. Blood component therapy

* Anemia

   Transfusions indicated when patient is short of breath

   One unit of packed red blood cells raises hematocrit by 3% and hemoglobin by 1 g/dl

   Patients who are prone to transfusion reactions require leukocyte-poor blood component therapy

   Plasma component therapy is administered for severe bleeding and shock

   All blood products given to a severely immunocompromised host should be irradiated to prevent lymphocyte engraftment

* Thrombocytopenia

   Platelet transfusions are required when patient is at risk for bleeding or when bleeding occurs in patient with low platelet count

   One unit of platelets increases peripheral blood platelet level by 10,000 to 12,000 cells/mm^3

   Goal is to maintain platelet count above 20,000 cells/mm^3 to prevent spontaneous bleeding

   Failure to maintain an adequate platelet count often results from infection, fever, DIC, or splenomegaly

   Fever caused by platelets may be prevented by premedicating with antipyretics, corticosteroids, and/or antihistamines; meperidine may be given if patient is having shaking chills

Repeated exposure to human lymphocyte antigens (HLAs) on donor platelets may result in ineffective platelet therapy, requiring HLA-matched or leukocyte-poor transfusions

* Transfusion complications include

Hemolytic and nonhemolytic transfusion reactions

Transmission of diseases

Graft-versus-host disease (in patients who had bone marrow transplantation)

* Home transfusion therapy: Basic criteria include

Physical limitations of patient that make travel difficult

Need for blood is not acute; patient does not need more than two units of blood

Stable cardiopulmonary status

Absence of reactions to most recent transfusion

Presence of responsible adult during and after transfusion

Telephone available for medical needs

Suggested Readings

1. Gobel BH: Bleeding disorders. In Groenwald S, Frogge M, Goodman M, and Yarbro CH (eds): *Cancer Nursing: Principles and Practice* (4th ed). Boston: Jones and Bartlett, 1997, pp 604-639.

2. Haeuber D, Spross JA: Alterations in protective mechanisms: Hematopoiesis and bone marrow depression. In Baird SB, McCorkle R, Grant M (eds): *Cancer Nursing: A Comprehensive Textbook.* Philadelphia: WB Saunders, 1991, pp 759-781.

3. Bagby GC, Segal GM: Growth factors and the control of hematopoiesis. In Hoffman R, Benz EJ, Shattil SJ, et al (eds): *Hematology: Basic Principles and Practice.* New York: Churchill-Livingstone, 1991, pp 97-121.

4. Feinstein DI: Treatment of disseminated intravascular coagulation. *Semin Thromb Hemost* 14:339-348, 1988.

5. Pisciotto PT (ed): *Blood Transfusion Therapy: A Physician's Handbook* (3rd ed). Arlington, VA: American Association of Blood Banks, 1989.

6. Rutman R, Kakaiya P, Miller WV: Home transfusion for the cancer patient. *Semin Oncol Nurs* 6:163-167, 1990.

CHAPTER 14

Cardiac Tamponade

Overview

Occurs when excessive fluid accumulates in pericardial space

Excess fluid severely compromises heart, resulting in

1. Disruption in pressure gradients
2. Decreased diastolic filling
3. Decreased stroke volume and cardiac output

Both cancer and cancer therapy can initiate cardiac tamponade

Neoplastic involvement of heart is rarely diagnosed before patient dies

About 16% of cancer patients symptomatic for pericardial effusion develop cardiac tamponade

Pericardial effusion and constrictive pericarditis can be caused by tumors that have metastasized to pericardium or have directly extended into pericardium

Radiation therapy to mediastinum can damage pericardium, causing constrictive pericarditis

Rate of fluid accumulation, compliance of pericardium, myocardial size, and intravascular volume affect rate of onset and severity of pericardial effusion

Tumors most commonly involved are

1. Breast
2. Lung
3. Leukemia
4. Lymphoma
5. Melanoma
6. Sarcoma

Approaches to Care

Assessment

1. Clinical manifestations

   * Increased heart rate

- ✷ Peripheral vasoconstriction
- ✷ Fluid retention
- ✷ Early symptoms and signs

  Weakness

  Retrosternal chest pain

  Shortness of breath (dyspnea)

  Venous distention

  Distant heart sounds

  Pulsus paradoxus

- ✷ Late symptoms and signs

  Hypotension

  Tachycardia

  Diminished arterial pulse

  Cough

  Peripheral edema

  Profuse diaphoresis

  Abdominal distention, nausea, vomiting (vague complaints)

  Confusion, anxiety

  Cyanosis, ashen color

2. Diagnostic measures

   - ✷ Echocardiogram is fastest and most precise
   - ✷ Computed tomographic scan to estimate volume of effusion and thickness of pericardium
   - ✷ Chest x-ray film reveals enlarged, globular, bottle-shaped heart

* Pericardial fluid examination

Treatment

1. Supportive therapy, initiated immediately, includes

   * Volume expanders
   * Fresh-frozen plasma
   * Vasoactive agents
   * Oxygen

2. Pericardiocentesis

   * Performed under echocardiographic guidance
   * Fluid is sent for cytologic study to determine most appropriate cancer therapy

3. Permanent resolution occurs through systemic therapy or local treatment of cancer

4. Further palliation of effusion may be obtained through surgical interventions

   * Subxiphoid pericardiotomy, or pericardial window
   * Balloon pericardiotomy
   * Pericardioperitoneal shunt
   * Pleurocardial window
   * Pericardioscentesis with sclerosing agent instillation

5. Potential surgical complications

   * Infection
   * Pleural effusion

* Arrhythmias
* Pneumothorax
* Bleeding
* Costochondritis
* Atelectasis

6. Sclerosing therapy is effective in about 50% of attempts

   * Agents used are tetracycline, quinacrine, thiotepa, radioactive gold or phosphorus, and 5-fluorouracil

7. Radiation therapy has been used to treat extremely radiosensitive tumors
8. Unsuccessful resolution can severely debilitate person or result in death
9. If effusion is chronic condition, limited outlook for survival exists
10. Supportive terminal care is usually needed

Suggested Readings

1. Maxwell MB: Malignant Effusions and Edemas. In Groenwald SL, Frogge MH, Goodman M, Yarbro CY (eds): *Cancer Nursing: Principles and Practice* (4th ed). Jones and Bartlett, 1997, pp 729-733.
2. Wilkes JD, Fideas P, Vaikius L, et al: Malignancy-related pericardial effusion. *Cancer* 76:1377-1387, 1995.
3. Wang N, Feikes JR, Morenson T, et al: Pericardioperitoneal shunt: An alternative treatment for malignant pericardial effusion. *Ann Thorac Surg* 57: 289-292, 1994.

4. Okamoto H, Shinkai T, Yamakido M, et al: Cardiac tamponade caused by primary lung cancer and the management of pericardial effusion. *Cancer* 73: 93-98, 1993.
5. Joiner GA: Neoplastic cardiac tamponade. Crit Care Nurs 11(2):50-58, 1991.

CHAPTER 15

Disseminated Intravascular Coagulation

Overview

DIC represents an inappropriate and exaggerated overstimulation of normal coagulation, in which both thrombosis and hemorrhage may occur simultaneously.

Occurs in approximately 10% of persons with cancer

This syndrome is always secondary to an underlying disease process.

Associated conditions include

1. Infection is the most common cause of DIC
2. Intravascular hemolysis

179

3. Viremia (cytomegalovirus, hepatitis, varicella)
4. Mucin-producing adenocarcinomas (e.g., gastric, lung, pancreatic, prostate)
5. Hematologic malignancy (i.e., leukemia, lymphoma)
6. Implanted devices
7. Liver disease

Microvascular thrombosis and bleeding from multiple sites occur simultaneously with disseminated intravascular coagulation (DIC)

1. Fibrinogen is consumed by thrombin-induced clotting and plasmin-induced fibrinolysis
2. Decreased macrophage-clearing function limits removal of activated clotting factors
3. Rapid coagulation exceeds ability of liver to clear fibrin split products (FSPs)
4. Excess FSPs inhibit clotting
5. Consumable factors I, II, V, and VIII are depleted by microvascular clotting

Approaches to Care

Assessment

1. Clinical manifestations

   * Early symptoms and signs

     Anxiety, restlessness

     Tachycardia, tachypnea

     Headache

     Conjunctival hemorrhage

     Periorbital petechiae

Oozing blood

Bleeding gums

* Late symptoms and signs

Change in mentation

Frank hematuria

Joint pain

Hemoptysis

Tarry stool, melena

2. Diagnostic measures

* DIC is defined by the presence of two or more of the following abnormalities

Prothrombin time increased by 3 or more seconds over control time

Activated partial thromboplastin time increased by 5 or more seconds over control time

Thrombin time prolonged by 3 or more seconds over control time

Fibrinogen less than 150 mg/dl

Fibrin split products equal to or greater than 40 µg/ml

Decreased platelet count

Treatment

1. Treatment of the underlying malignancy is vital because the tumor is the underlying stimulus; all other measures are only supportive
2. Give platelets and fresh-frozen plasma to replace consumed blood components

3. Give fresh-frozen plasma and antithrombin III concentrate to neutralize excess thrombin and slow DIC process

4. Administer heparin (7.5 U/kg/hr) as continuous infusion to avoid peaks in effect

   * Inhibits factors IX and X to halt clotting cascade

   * Contraindicated if there is any sign of intracranial bleeding (e.g. headache), open wounds, or recent surgery

   * Stopped immediately if person complains of headache or displays signs of frank bleeding

   * Considered controversial therapy

5. Give e-aminocaproic acid in conjunction with heparin to maintain platelet and fibrinogen levels

   * Controversial

   * Not used in most cases because inhibition of fibrinolytic system can lead to widespread fibrin deposition in microcirculation

6. Monitor vital signs, urine output, and blood loss

7. Maintain quiet environment

8. Give medications to suppress symptoms (e.g., cough, vomiting) that increase intracranial pressure

9. Initiate bleeding precautions

10. Monitor for signs of cardiogenic shock: hypovolemia, hypoxia, hypotension, oliguria
11. Effective control of DIC is measured by normal coagulation screen and platelet count
12. Nursing measures

   * Reduce potential for injury

   * Enhance tissue perfusion

   * Educate patient regarding early signs

Suggested Readings

1. Gobel BH, Bleeding Disorders. In Groenwald SL, Frogge MH, Goodman M, Yarbro CH, (4th ed.) *Cancer Nursing: Principles and Practice*, Boston: Jones and Bartlett, 1997, pp. 604-639.
2. Bick RL: Disseminated intravascular coagulation: Objective criteria for diagnosis and management. *Med Clin North Am* 78:511-543, 1994.
3. Bell TN: Disseminated intravascular coagulation and shock. *Crit Care Nurs Clin North Am* 2:255-268, 1990.
4. Rutherford CJ, Frenkel EP: Thrombocytopenia: Issues in diagnosis and therapy. *Med Clin North Am* 78:555-575, 1994.

CHAPTER 16

Fatigue

Overview

Definition

1. Fatigue is a complex concept associated with

   * Tiredness
   * Weakness
   * Exhaustion
   * Asthenia
   * Weariness
   * Somnolence
   * Drowsiness

* Lack of energy
* Malaise

2. Objective indicator of fatigue relates to person's ability to maintain specific activities
3. Subjective experience of fatigue relates to feeling state; it has voluntary component

Pathophysiology

1. Acute fatigue is an expected outcome of strenuous physical and mental activity and has same protective effect as acute pain
2. Fatigue in individuals with cancer

   * Does not respond to rest
   * Persists over time
   * Often interferes with performance of usual daily activities

3. Cause of chronic fatigue in cancer has not been established but is a combination of physical factors such as

   * Tumor burden
   * Physical stress of treatment
   * Environmental changes during hospitalization
   * Psychologic factors, such as fear of death
   * Changes in social relationships and roles
   * Nutritional changes
   * Side effects of treatment
   * Symptoms of disease

* Loss of sleep from side effects or symptoms
  of disease and psychologic factors
  such as

  Anxiety

  Depression

Approaches to Care

Assessment

1. Patient describes problems associated with
   fatigue
2. Nurse observes individual's

   Appearance

   Level of consciousness

   Activity level

3. Patient describes his or her current activities
   in comparison to usual daily activities
4. Nurse assesses patient's acceptance of
   limitations imposed by fatigue

Treatment interventions

1. Prepare patient in advance of treatment for
   what to expect in relation to fatigue
2. Plan for rest periods
3. Prioritize and rearrange patient's activities
4. Exercise helps relieve fatigue in some
   individuals
5. Manipulate patient's environment to allow
   undisturbed time for sleep and rest

Suggested Readings

1. Nail LM: Fatigue. In Groenwald SL, Frogge MH, Goodman M, Yarbro CH (eds): *Cancer Nursing: Principles and Practice* (4th ed). Boston: Jones and Bartlett, 1997, pp 640-654.
2. Winninghan ML, Nail LM, Burke MB, et al: Fatigue and the cancer experience: The state of the knowledge. *Oncol Nurs Forum* 21:23-34, 1994.
3. Richardson A: Fatigue in cancer patients: A review of the literature. *Eur J Cancer Care* 4:20-32, 1995.
4. Smets E, Garssen B, Schuster-Vitterhoeve A, et al: Fatigue in cancer patients. *Br J Cancer* 68:220-224, 1993.

CHAPTER 17

Hypercalcemia

Overview

Occurs most frequently in patients with lung cancer, breast cancer, multiple myeloma or head and neck cancer

Uncorrected hypercalcemia leads to dehydration, renal failure, coma, and death

Most common life-threatening metabolic abnormality in cancer patients

Occurs in 10% to 20% of persons with cancer

Occurs as result of increased bone resorption caused by

1. Bone destruction by tumor invasion
2. Increased levels of parathyroid hormone, osteoclast-activating factor, or prostaglandin produced by tumor

Risk factors

1. Primary tumors of breast, lung, kidney
2. Osteolytic bone lesions
3. Hematologic malignancies
4. Squamous cell lung cancer
5. Head and neck cancers
6. Hyperparathyroidism
7. Immobilization
8. Anorexia, nausea, vomiting
9. Renal failure

Humoral mediator factors involved include

1. Transforming growth factor (TGF)
2. Interleukin-1 (IL-1)
3. Tumor necrosis factor (TNF)
4. Prostaglandins given after hormone therapy

Approaches to Care

Assessment

1. Clinical manifestations relate to effects of excess calcium on smooth, skeletal, and cardiac muscle

   * Gastrointestinal

Etiology: Elevated extracellular calcium levels depress smooth muscle contractility leading to delayed gastric emptying and decreased GI motility.

Symptoms: Anorexia, nausea, vomiting, constipation, pain, dehydration

* Neuromuscular

Etiology: Elevated extracellular calcium affect both central nervous system and neuromuscular function

Symptoms: Lethargy, confusion, stupor, convulsions, hyporeflexia, profound muscle weakness and hypotonia

* Cardiac

Etiology: Calcium ions affect smooth, skeletal and cardiac muscle contractility, cell membrane permeability and conduction of electrical impulses within the heart

Symptoms: Bradycardia, tachycardia, EKG changes (increased PR interval, prolonged QT intervals in moderate hypercalcemia)

Atrioventricular block and asystole may occur when the serum calcium level reaches 18mg/dl

* Renal

Etiology: Elevated calcium interferes with the action of ADH on the kidney's collecting tubules, causing an inability to concentrate urine and polyuria

Symptoms: Polyuria, polydypsia, decreased renal concentrating ability, renal insufficiency

2. Diagnostic measures

   * Laboratory studies provide definitive diagnosis

   * Three categories of hypercalcemia have been defined

     Serum calcium level of 10.5 to 12.0 mg/dl and asymptomatic

     Serum calcium level of 12 to 13 mg/dl and asymptomatic

     Serum calcium level of 13 mg/dl or more and symptomatic

   * Serum calcium level must be "corrected" to be accurate; it can be calculated as:

     Corrected serum calcium = Measured serum calcium + $(4.0 - \text{serum albumin}) \times 0.8$

Treatment

1. Tumor control is only long-term effective measure
2. Emergency intervention is needed if serum calcium level is greater than 13 mg/dl
3. Major focus of therapy

   * Vigorous hydration with 4 to 6 liters of normal saline per day to

     Restore normal fluid volume

     Increase glomerular filtration

     Promote urinary calcium excretion

   * Parenteral furosemide, 40 to 80 mg every 6 hours

* Monitor fluid and electrolyte balance closely

  Vigorous hydration can lead to hypokalemia, hypocalcemia, and hypomagnesemia

  Blood urea nitrogen and creatinine levels are monitors of renal function

* Calcitonin 4-12 units/kg of body weight subcutaneously every 8-12 hours or as rectal suppositories at a dose of 300mg three times daily for seven days. It acts by inhibiting bone resorption.

  Rapid effect, duration of response is limited

  Response limited to 24 to 72 hours

  Glucocorticoids are given to improve effect

  Risk of anaphylaxis (skin testing prior to starting)

  Side-effects include mild nausea and vomiting, flushing, skin rashes and occasional allergic reactions

* Bisphosphonates are potent inhibitors of osteoclastic bone resorption

  Well tolerated, minimal side effects

  Two agents available in U.S.

    Etidronate (7.5 mg/kg/d intravenously)

    Pamidronate (60-90 mg intravenously)

  Produce normocalcemia in 5 to 9 days

  Duration of response is 2 to 4 weeks

* Pamidronate 60-90mg over 2-4 hours every 3-4 weeks is associated with a decrease in bone pain in women with breast cancer

Clinical trials are under way to evaluate the role of pamidronate in preventing the development of osteolytic metastases

* Gallium nitrate inhibits bone resorption

  Give 200 mg/m² in continuous intravenous infusion for 5 days

  Produces normocalcemia in more than 80% of cases

  Nephrotoxic

  Inconvenient administration schedule

* Oral phosphate 1 to 3 mg three times a day can control chronic, mild hypercalcemia

  Diarrhea may be limiting side effect

  Perianal care is important to prevent skin breakdown

  Encourage patient to take sitz baths

Suggested Readings

1. Lang-Kummer J, Hypercalcemia. In Groenwald SL, Frogge MH, Goodman M, Yarbro CH (eds): *Cancer Nursing: Principles and Practice* (4th ed). Boston: Jones and Bartlett, 1997, pp 684-701.
2. Ling PJ, A'Hern RP, Hardy JR: Analysis of survival following treatment of tumor-induced hypercalcemia with intravenous pamidronate. *Br J Cancer* 72;206-209, 1995
3. Houston SJ, Rubers RD: The systemic treatment of bone metastasis. *Clin Orthop* 312:95-104, 1995.

4. Mundy GR: Pathophysiology of cancer-associated hypercalcemia. *Semin Oncol* 17(suppl. 5):10-15, 1990.
5. Bajorunas DR: Clinical manifestations of cancer-related hypercalcemia. *Semin Oncol* 17(suppl. 5):16-25, 1990.
6. Heath D: The treatment of hypercalcemia of malignancy. *Clin Endocrinol* 34:155-157, 1991.

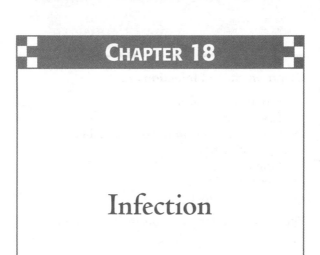

CHAPTER 18

Infection

Overview

Major cause of morbidity and mortality

Risk factors

1. Immunosuppression
2. Prolonged hospitalization
3. Acquired immunodeficiency syndrome (AIDS)
4. Malnutrition
5. Intensive cancer therapies
6. Disruption of natural physical barriers

Common sites of infection are

1. Mouth and pharynx
2. Respiratory tract
3. Skin, soft tissue, intravascular catheters
4. Perineal region
5. Urinary tract
6. Nose and sinuses
7. Gastrointestinal (GI) tract

Types of infection and specific treatments

1. Bacterial

   * Gram-negative bacteria; e.g., *Escherichia coli, Klebsiella pneumoniae, Pseudomonas aeruginosa*

     Primary cause of infection in granulocytopenic patients

   * Gram-positive bacteria; e.g., *Staphylococcus aureus, Staphylococcus epidermidis, Streptococcus*

   * Treatment begins immediately

     Immediate empiric antibiotic therapy

     Highly specific therapy initiated once an organism is identified

     Combination antibiotic therapy usually includes a beta-lactam antibiotic and an aminoglycoside

2. Mycobacterial

   * Less common

   * Usually associated with defects in cellular immunity

   * Latent mycobacterial tuberculosis may be reactivated

* *Mycobacterium avium-intracellulare* (MAI) is common with AIDS

* Treatment for tuberculosis is isoniazid

* Treatment for MAI is combination antibiotic therapy

3. Fungi

   * Increasingly important cause of infections for cancer patients

   * Contributing factors include

     Prolonged granulocytopenia

     Implanted vascular access devices

     Administration of parenteral nutrition

     Corticosteroids

     Prolonged antibiotic therapy

   * *Candida* species are most common causative agents

   * *Aspergillus, Cryptococcus, Histoplasma, Phycomycetes,* and *Coccidioides* species are common fungi

   * Treatment is confounded by

     Difficulty culturing organisms

     Limited number of effective agents

   * Amphotericin B is drug of choice

     Side effects, including fever, chills, rigors, nausea, vomiting, hypotension, bronchospasm, and seizures, require intensive support

     Nephrotoxicity is the major toxicity

* Flucytosine (5-FC), fluconazole, ketoconazole, and miconazole are also used

4. Viral

   * Usually herpes simplex virus (HSV), varicella zoster virus (VZV), cytomegalovirus (CMV), and hepatitis A or B virus

   * Acyclovir is drug of choice for HSV and VZV

   * Vidarabine is effective if used early

   * Ganciclovir and foscarnet are used for CMV

5. Protozoal and parasitic

   * Infections associated with defects in cell-mediated immunity

   * Can be difficult to treat

   * Can quickly become life-threatening

   * *Pneumocystis carinii, Toxoplasma gondii, Cryptosporidium* species are common

   * Treatment of *P carinii* infection

      Fatal if untreated

      Trimethoprim-sulfamethoxazole, dapsone, or pentamidine

      High-risk patients (e.g., AIDS patients) are sometimes treated prophylactically

   * Treatment of *T gondii* infection

      Pyrimethamine plus sulfamethoxazoleo

   * No treatment is known for *Cryptosporidium* species infection

Approaches to Care

Prevention

1. Meticulous handwashing by caregivers
2. Avoidance of crowds and infected individuals
3. If granulocytopenia is present, invasive procedures should be avoided
4. Adequate nutrition
5. Meticulous personal hygiene
6. Avoidance of skin trauma

Assessment

1. If number of circulating polymorphonuclear neutrophils (PMNs) is decreased, defenses are reduced

   * Absolute granulocyte count (AGC) is measure of risk

     AGC = Total white blood cell count ×
     (% PMNs + % bands)

   * Individuals whose AGC is less than $1000/mm^3$ are granulocytopenic

   * If AGC is less than $500/mm^3$, patient is severely granulocytopenic

2. Culture from all potential sites of infection before giving antibiotics
3. Closely observe patient's response to therapy
4. Monitor efficacy of treatment, vital signs, chest x-ray films, and laboratory data
5. Assess for signs of septic shock

   * Early shock

     Low-grade fever, possible shaking chills

Flushed, warm skin

Tachycardia, normal to slightly low blood pressure

Transient decrease in urine output

Hyperventilation

Alert, possible mild confusion, apprehension

Nausea, vomiting, diarrhea

* Late shock

Fever

Cold, clammy, acrocyanosis

Hypotension, decreased cardiac output, peripheral edema

Oliguria, anuria

Pulmonary edema

Restlessness, anxiety, confusion, lethargy, coma

Possible blood in stool or emesis

Treatment of patient with granulocytopenia and fever

1. Empiric broad-spectrum antibiotic therapy
2. Isolation precautions and protected environment
3. Administration of colony-stimulating factors (CSFs) (granulocyte and granulocyte-macrophage)
4. Supportive care to maintain fluid and electrolyte levels; oxygen when needed; nutritional support

Treatment of patient with gram-negative sepsis

1. Septic shock develops in 27% to 46% of cases
2. Mortality can reach 80% unless aggressive therapy is initiated
3. Treatment measures to reverse shock and sepsis include

   * Adequate oxygenation

   * Effective circulation with fluid replacement and vasoactive agents

   * Immediate broad-spectrum antibiotic therapy

   * Observation for complications of sepsis: disseminated intravascular coagulation, renal failure, heart failure, GI ulcers, hepatic abnormalities

Nursing interventions

1. Practice meticulous handwashing and hygiene
2. Take appropriate protective measures and wear protective clothing
3. Ensure that patient has adequate fluid and dietary intake
4. Ensure that patient receives adequate rest
5. Use aseptic technique for invasive procedures
6. Avoid trauma, especially to skin
7. Culture suspicious areas
8. Avoid potential sources of infection

Suggested Readings

1. Ellerhorst-Ryan J: Infection. In Groenwald SL, Frogge MH, Goodman M, Yarbro CH (eds): Cancer Nursing: Principles and Practice (4th ed). Boston: Jones and Bartlett, 1997, pp 585-603.
2. Workman ML: Inflammatory responses. In Workman ML, Ellerhorst-Ryan JM, Koertge VH (eds): *Nursing Care of the Immunocompromised Patient*. Philadelphia: WB Saunders, 1993, pp 14-31.
3. Shimpff SC: Infections in the cancer patient: Diagnosis, prevention and treatment. In Mandell GL, Bennett JE, Dolin R (eds): *Principles and Practice of Infectious Diseases* (4th ed). New York: Churchill-Livingstone, 1995, pp 2666-2675.

CHAPTER 19

Integumentary Alterations

Overview

Alterations to skin

1. Radiotherapy

   * Major effect of radiation on dividing cells is cell death

   * Radiosensitivity of cells varies

     Cells with rapid turnover (e.g., skin cells, mucous membrane cells, hematopoietic stem cells) are radiosensitive

     Cells that do not divide regularly or at all (e.g., muscle cells, nerve cells) are radioresistant

203

* Factors that determine degree, onset, and duration of radiation-induced skin reactions

  Equipment: Energy or particular beam quality of machine influences surface or skin dose

  Bolus material on skin reduces skin-sparing effect of radiation therapy, allowing for maximum dose at level of skin

  Tangential field increases skin dose

  Concomitant chemotherapy enhances radiation effect

  Treatment of areas of skin apposition are prone to increased reactions secondary to warmth, moisture, and lack of aeration

  Epidermis thins with age, has diminished elasticity, and decreased dermal turgor resulting in delayed healing

2. Chemotherapy effects

   * Hyperpigmentation

     Occurs in dark-skinned individuals

     Drugs

     Cyclophosphamide

     Methotrexate

     Doxorubicin

     5-Fluorouracil

   * Hypersensitivity

     l-asparaginase: *Acute urticaria*

     Taxol: *Hypotension, rash, bradycardia, dyspnea*

Cisplatin: *Pruritis, cough, dyspnea, angioedema, bronchospasm, rash, urticaria*

Teniposide and etoposide: *Dyspnea, wheezing, hypotension, urticaria, pruritis, angioedema, facial flushing, and rash*

Dactinomycin: *Folliculitis*

* Acral erythema: Intensely painful erythema, scaling, and epidermal sloughing from palms and soles followed by desquamation; occurs with

   Continuous infusions of 5-fluorouracil

   Doxorubicin

   High-dose cytarabine

   Floxuridine

* Pruritis; occurs in

   Hodgkin's disease

   Multiple myeloma

   Aminoglutethimide

   Antibiotic reaction

   Radiation skin changes

* Photosensitivity (enhanced skin response to ultraviolet [UV] radiation)

   May present as sunburn-like with erythema, edema, blisters, hyperpigmentation, and desquamation or peeling

   Occurs after skin exposure to UV light with

   5-Fluorouracil

Dacarbazine

Vinblastine

High-dose methotrexate

* Vesicant chemotherapy extravasation

  Infiltration of chemotherapeutic agent (vesicant) that, if infiltrated, can cause blistering, pain, ulceration, necrosis, and sloughing of damaged tissue

  Occurs in 0.5% to 5.0% of patients receiving peripheral intravenous chemotherapy

3. Malignant wounds

   * Most often seen in patients with cancers of breast, stomach, lung, uterus, kidney, ovary, colon, and bladder, and melanoma, sarcoma, lymphoma, and AIDS-K5

   * Poor vascular perfusion and altered collagen synthesis result in tissue ischemia and necrosis

   * Mycosis fungoides is a T-cell lymphoma that can develop into fungating skin lesions

Alterations to hair

1. Radiation effects

   * Extent and duration of radiation-induced alopecia depend on

     Individual's normal hair growth rate

     Area being treated

     Dose per fraction

     Total dose delivered to area

* Complete scalp hair loss is seen after whole-brain radiation
* Significant hair loss occurs after dose of 45 to 55 Gy
* Hair loss may be permanent if higher doses of radiation are given
* If hair regrows, it usually begins 8 to 9 weeks after completion of treatment

2. Chemotherapy effects

   * Extent of hair loss depends on

     Type of chemotherapy

     Schedule

     Dose of drug

   * Drugs most commonly associated with alopecia

     Bleomycin

     Doxorubicin

     Cyclophosphamide

     Vinblastine

     Dactinomycin

     Taxol

     Daunorubicin

     Docetaxel

   * Hair loss occurs by

     Atrophy of hair root; hair falls out over 2 to 3 weeks

     Partial atrophy of hair bulb and narrowing of hairshaft that causes breakage

* Hair loss is temporary

   Regrowth is evident in 4 to 6 weeks after chemotherapy

   Hair returns to its normal color and texture in about 1 year

Alterations of nails

1. Radiation to nails can result in decreased growth rates and development of ridges when nail attempts to grow
2. Chemotherapy causes

   * Pigmentation, with doxorubicin, 5-fluorouracil

   * *Beau's lines:* Transverse white lines or grooves

   * *Onycholysis:* Partial nail separation seen with 5-fluorouracil, bleomycin, doxorubicin, taxol, and taxotere

Alterations of glands

1. Radiation to skin

   * Destruction of sebaceous glands

   * Subsequent pruritis and inelasticity

2. Complete and permanent destruction of sweat gland function occurs with skin doses of more than 30 Gy delivered in 3 weeks or less

Approaches to Care

Skin

1. Radiation therapy

★ Assessment

Assess condition of skin before treatment, weekly during treatment, 1 to 2 weeks after completion of treatment, and at each follow-up appointment thereafter

Consistency of assessment and documentation is imperative

Grading scales provide an objective system of categorizing impaired skin integrity

★ Clinical manifestations

Acute skin reactions

Occur weeks to months after first exposure

Usually temporary

Include erythema, dry desquamation, pruritis, hyperpigmentation, and moist desquamation

Higher doses given over shorter periods of time to larger volumes of tissue result in more severe acute reactions

Late skin reactions

Usually manifest months to years after exposure

Usually permanent and often become more severe as time goes on

Include photosensitivity, pigmentation changes, atrophy, fibrosis, telangiectasia, and, rarely, ulceration and necrosis

★ Interventions

Patient education before therapy to promote self-care behavior

Anticipated skin reactions

Onset and duration of reactions

Skin care guidelines to follow before and after radiation

During treatment patient should

Shower or bathe using lukewarm water

Avoid harsh soap

Avoid ointments, creams, lotions, deodorant, perfume, cologne, powder, and cosmetics on skin

If instructed, apply recommended mild, water-soluble lubricant to reduce itching and discomfort

Avoid shaving treated areas if possible

Avoid extremes of temperature

Avoid tight-fitting clothing made of irritating fabric

Avoid exposing skin to sun

Avoid applying tape or adhesive bandages to skin in radiation treatment field

Drink at least 3 quarts of fluid each day

2 to 3 weeks after treatment, patient should

Apply unscented hydrophilic emollient (lotion or cream) two to three times daily for 1 to 2 months after treatment and then daily

Always avoid exposing previously irradiated skin to sun, or use sunscreen with sun protection factor (SPF) 15 or greater

Severe acute radiation skin reactions

Dry desquamation with pruritis

Increase frequency of lubricants, but avoid application for 3 hours before treatment

Apply cloths soaked in mild astringent to irritated area for 15 minutes three to four times daily

Use mild topical corticosteroids, avoiding application 3 hours before treatment

Moist desquamation

Use mild astringent soaks as described above

Apply hydrogel primary wound dressings, cover with nonadherent dressing, and secure with paper tape

Apply occlusive hydrocolloid dressings

2. Chemotherapy

 ∗ Cutaneous hypersensitivity

Manifestations

Early manifestations are urticaria and angioedema

Hypotension, rash, dyspnea, and bronchospasm may occur within 10 minutes of initiating the drug

May progress to severe anaphylaxis

Treatment

Decrease infusion rate

Premedicate with antihistamines and steroids

* Acral edema

  Manifestations

    Intensely painful erythema, scaling, and epidermal sloughing from the palms and soles

    Followed by desquamation and re-epithelialization of skin

  Treatment

    Suspension of chemotherapy until symptoms have subsided

    If symptoms recur, therapy may be discontinued

* Pruritis

  Assessment

    For possible cause of itching and aggravating factors

    Localization, onset, duration, and intensity of itching

    Prior history of pruritis

    Past or present cancer, cancer treatment, noncancer systemic disease, or use of analgesics or antibiotics

    For presence of infection

  Treatment

    Encourage adequate water intake

    Suggest medicated baths to soothe

    Apply local anesthetic creams

    Encourage patient to employ alternate cutaneous stimulation methods (e.g., massage, pressure, or rubbing with soft cloth) to relieve the urge to scratch

Keep room humidity at 30% to 40% and room temperature cool

Cotton clothing and sheets should be washed in hypoallergenic soaps

Distractions, such as music, imagery, or relaxation, may ease the itch sensation

Medications may help relieve itch, depending on cause (antihistamines and corticosteroid for drug reaction; cholestyramine for biliary obstruction)

* Photosensitivity

Manifestations

Exposed area becomes erythematous within a few hours; erythema gradually subsides

Rarely, photoallergy similar to contact dermatitis with immediate wheal-and-flare reactions or delayed reactions

With dacarbazine, pruritis and erythematous edematous eruptions of face, neck, and dorsal surfaces of both hands occur with sun exposure within 1 to 2 hours after drug administration

Treatment

Obtain complete list of all medications patient has recently taken or is currently taking

Educate patients about dangers of exposure to UV radiation after treatment with radiation or certain chemotherapeutic agents

Provide verbal and written instructions
regarding ways to reduce risk

Avoid tanning booths

Limit exposure to sun

Wear protective clothing and hats

Use sunscreens properly

* Vesicant chemotherapy extravasation

Prevented by

Professional training in chemotherapy drug
administration

Having available guidelines for management

Following management guidelines in event of
true or suspected extravasation

Completing documentation tool and
establishing follow-up

Manifestations

Bleb formation

Pain

Stinging or burning

Lack of blood return

Persistent complaints of pain or discomfort at
site despite blood return

Treatment

Stop drug administration

Disconnect chemotherapy drug infusion,
connect syringe, and attempt to aspirate any
blood or residual drug in tubing and at site

If you are unable to aspirate any blood, remove needle

Apply sterile 2 × 2-inch gauze pad at site

If antidote exists, prepare antidote and inject into pre-existing syringe; if syringe has been removed, inject into site

Nitrogen mustard: antidote is sodium thiosulfate

Vinblastine: antidote is hyaluronidase

Vincristine: antidote is hyaluronidase

Remove needle

Avoid application of direct manual pressure to site

Photograph site

Apply warm pack for 15 minutes four times daily for 24 hours, if hyaluronidase has been used

Apply cold pack for 15 minutes or more every 3 to 4 hours for 24 to 48 hours as tolerated for all other extravasations

Notify physician that true or suspected extravasation has occurred

Elevate extremity for 48 hours

After 48 hours, instruct patient to use extremity to prevent contracture formation

Arrange for return appointment once or twice weekly to monitor site

Consult surgeon if pain persists beyond 7 to 10 days

If extravasation has occurred from central line, stop infusion and notify physician

3. Malignant wounds

   * Manifestions

     Excessive purulent drainage

     Odor

     Infection

     May progress to tissue ischemia and necrosis

   * Management

     Surgery, radiation, chemotherapy, and hyperthermia

     Debridement: *Necrotic tissue and eschar are removed to reduce infection and odor*

     Topical or systemic antibiotics to control infection

     Hemostasis: *Bleeding is most often result of trauma and can usually be prevented by proper wound care*

     Odor management

       Frequent cleaning

       Topical chlorophyll-containing ointment and solutions

       Charcoal-impregnated dressings

       Room deodorizers

     Cleansing with solutions designed to minimize infection and odor

     Wound dressings

       Maintain moist environment to prevent trauma from drying

Stimulate epithelial-cell migration and resurfacing

Hair

1. Assessment

    * For patient's risk of hair loss related to therapy

    * For impact of hair loss on patient and significant others

2. Prevention

    * Scalp hypothermia and scalp tourniquet cause vasoconstriction; neither method has proved particularly useful and they are not widely employed

    * Hair preservation techniques are not recommended for patients with hematologic malignancies

3. Nursing interventions

    * Inform patient of approximate time of hair loss and how it will occur, if possible

    * Explain rationale for alopecia specific to therapy

      Why hair falls out with specific therapy

      Variability of hair loss depending on therapy

      Possibility of hair regrowth—stress regrowth when appropriate

      Potential change in color and texture of new hair when regrowth occurs

    * Provide written literature

* Encourage patient to speak with others who have experienced and adjusted to hair loss

* Offer tips to minimize degree of alopecia

  Shampoo gently one to two times weekly with mild protein-based shampoo; check with radiation therapist before washing hair if marks have been placed on scalp

  Rinse well with lukewarm water and gently pat dry with soft towel

  Use soft-bristled hairbrush or wide-toothed comb to reduce stress on hairshaft

  Use satin pillowcase to minimize rubbing friction on scalp hair while lying down

  Avoid use of hot rollers, hair dryers, curling irons, permanent waves, and hair dyes

  Avoid rollers in hair while sleeping, braids, ponytails, and cornrows

  Consider short haircut

  Use hair-preserving measures when appropriate

* Provide information regarding wigs or hairpieces before hair loss

  Types of wigs

  Cost, fit, and style

  Area retailers or available wig banks

  Reimbursement

* Identify wig alternatives

  Scarves, turbans, bandannas, sports caps, hats

  Use of wardrobe, makeup, and jewelry to highlight other features

* Encourage use of eyebrow pencil, false eyelashes, and wide-brimmed eyeglasses to minimize loss of eyebrows and eyelashes

* Inform patient of American Cancer Society's "Look Good...Feel Better Program"

* Instruct patient on ways to reduce trauma to remaining hair and skin of exposed scalp

    Wash scalp gently with mild shampoo one to two times weekly

    Use head covering to protect scalp from wind, cold, and sun

    Always apply sunscreen with SPF of 15 or more when sun exposure is expected

    While receiving radiation therapy, apply water-soluble, mild lubricant, such as Natural Care Gel (Catalin Corporation), or Skin Balm (Carrington Laboratories), two to three times daily (do not apply for 3 hours before receiving treatment)

    With chemotherapy cycles or after radiation treatments are completed, apply hydrophilic lubricant containing no perfume two to three times daily; continue applying until hair regrowth begins

    Ensure wig lining is comfortable and nonirritating

* Instruct patient on measures to protect eyes from injury (e.g., use of sunglasses, wide-brimmed hats, false eyelashes)

* Although controversial and limited in success, hair transplantation by punch or graft technique is only reported treatment for permanent radiation-induced alopecia

Nails

1. Inform patient of potential changes

   * Decreased growth rates
   * Development of ridges

Glands

1. Protect dry, irradiated skin, because it is more susceptible to fissuring, infection, and necrosis from lack of lubrication by sweat and sebaceous glands

Suggested Readings

1. Goodman M, Ladd LA, Purl S: Integumentary and mucous membrane alterations. In Groenwald SL, Frogge MH, Goodman M, Yarbro CH (eds): *Cancer Nursing: Principles and Practice* (4th ed). Boston: Jones and Bartlett, 1997, pp 768-822.

2. McDonald AE: Skin ulceration. In Groenweld S, Frogge M, Goodman M, Yarbro CH (eds): *Cancer Symptom Management*. Boston: Jones and Bartlett,1996, pp 364-376.

3. Perez CA, Brady LW: *Principles and Practice of Radiation Oncology* (2nd ed). Philadelphia: JB Lippincott, 1992.

4. Dow KH, Hilderley LJ: *Nursing Care in Radiation Oncology*. Philadelphia: WB Saunders, 1992.

5. Dorr RT: Antidotes to vesicant chemotherapy extravasation. *Blood Rev* 4:41-60, 1990.

CHAPTER 20

Malignant Cerebral Edema

Overview

Results from increase in fluid content of brain

Metastasis to brain is prime source of cerebral edema

Usually accompanies primary or metastatic brain tumors or carcinomatous meningitis

Primary tumors that metastasize to brain most often are

1. Lung
2. Breast

221

3. Melanoma
4. Renal carcinoma

Cerebral edema can result from

1. Direct injury to vascular endothelium
2. Dysplastic vascular structures within tumor
3. Biochemical alteration of capillary permeability
4. Less stable blood-brain barrier

Tumors can continuously produce fluid which causes edema

When cerebral edema exceeds compensatory limits of brain, herniation can occur

Approaches to Care

Assessment

1. Clinical manifestations

   * Headache
   * Weakness, focal
   * Mental disturbance
   * Seizures
   * Gait disorder
   * Visual disturbance
   * Language disturbance
   * Hemiparesis
   * Impaired cognition
   * Sensory loss (unilateral)
   * Papilledema

* Ataxia
* Aphasia

2. Diagnostic measures

   * Neurologic examination
   * Computed tomographic (CT) scan
   * Magnetic resonance imaging (MRI) (best for visualizing edema)
   * Stereotactic needle biopsy may be required for tissue diagnosis

Interventions

1. Aggressive therapy to sustain or restore optimal neurologic function
2. Radiation therapy is principal treatment

   * Whole brain usually included in radiation field
   * Treatment typically lasts 2 to 3 weeks
   * Interstitial brachytherapy with seeds (^{120}iodine or ^{192}iridium) to boost field occasionally used

3. Corticosteroids and osmotherapy to reduce edema

   * Corticosteroids

     Rapidly reduce rate of fluid formation

     Reduce intracranial pressure

     Increase cerebral blood flow

     Are tapered once neurologic symptoms are controlled and reduced

 * Mannitol osmotherapy produces profound
   reduction of edema

4. Surgical decompression may be used for
   refractory or recurrent situations

   * Significant risks: infection, hemorrhage,
     operative mortality

5. Nursing management

   * Assessment

   * Side-effect management

   * Safety and seizure precautions

   * Prevention of complications of immobility

   * Changes in vital signs are warning signs of
     intercranial hypertension

   * Early detection of brain herniation

     Decreased level of consciousness

     Change in pupil size

     Altered motor response

Suggested Readings

1. Maxwell MB: Malignant effusions and edema.
   In Groenwald SL, Frogge MH, Goodman M,
   Yarbro CH (eds): *Cancer Nursing: Principles and
   Practice* (4th ed). Boston: Jones and Bartlett,
   1997, pp 736-738.
2. Wright DC, Delaney TF, Buckner JC:
   Treatment of metastatic cancers to the brain. In
   DeVita VT, Hellman S, Rosenberg SA (eds):
   Cancer: Principles and Practice of Oncology

(4th ed). Philadelphia: JB Lippincott, 1993, pp 2170-2183.

3. Reulen HJ, Huber P, Ito U, et al: Peritumoral brain edema. In Long D, et al (eds): *Advances in Neurology* (vol 52.). New York: Raven Press, 1990.

4. Saba MT, Magolan JM: Understanding cerebral edema: Implications for oncology nurses. *Oncol Nurs Forum* 18:499-505, 1991.

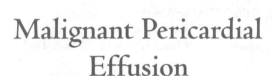

CHAPTER 21

Malignant Pericardial Effusion

Overview

Fluid accumulation in pericardial sac

Only 8% to 20% develop metastasis to pericardium

Only 33% develop symptoms of pericardial effusion

Most patients are asymptomatic or have nonspecific symptoms

Not often detected before death

Types of tumors associated with pericardial effusion

1. Lung
2. Breast
3. Leukemia and lymphoma
4. Sarcoma
5. Melanoma

Causes include

1. Pericardial metastasis
2. Tumor implants or direct invasion
3. Radiation-induced fibrosis
4. Obstruction of lymphatic and venous drainage of heart

Effects of effusion are related to

1. Rate of fluid exudation
2. Physical compliance capacity of pericardial cavity
3. Cardiac efficacy
4. Interference with cardiac function by reducing volume of heart in diastole

Approaches to Care

Assessment

1. Clinical manifestations

   * Tachycardia to offset decreased stroke volume

   * Systemic and pulmonary venous pressure increase to improve ventricular filling

   * Increased blood pressure

* Dyspnea
* Cough
* Chest pain
* Orthopnea
* Weakness
* Dysphagia
* Syncope
* Palpitations
* Pleural effusion
* Jugular venous distention
* Hepatomegaly
* Peripheral edema
* Pulsus paradoxus

2. Diagnostic measures

* Echocardiogram, electrocardiogram
* Pericardiocentesis for pericardial fluid; fluid usually has a bloody appearance
* Cytologic examination of fluid

Treatment

1. Dictated by specific physiologic impairment and degree of tamponade
2. If patient is asymptomatic, most clinicians wait and watch
3. If patient is symptomatic, treat to remove fluid and prevent fluid reaccumulation
4. To remove pericardial fluid, approaches are

* Pericardiocentesis alone

Guided by echocardiography

Needle is inserted into pericardial sac

Fluid is aspirated

Fluid can reaccumulate in short time

Procedure is critical if tamponade is occurring

* Subxiphoid pericardiotomy

  Allows for longer period of drainage and examination of pericardial space

  Direct pericardial biopsy possible

* Balloon pericardiotomy

  Balloon catheter is inserted to create window

  Fluid then drains into pleural space

* Pericardioperitoneal shunt

  Shunt drains pericardial fluid into peritoneal cavity

5. To obliterate pericardial space, therapies are

* Pericardiocentesis with sclerosing agent instillation

  Associated with significant toxicity

  Agents are tetracycline, 5-fluorouracil, radioactive gold or phosphorous, quinacrine, and thiotepa

  Fluid reaccumulates in 50% of cases

* Surgery

  Pleuropericardial window for effusions unresponsive to other treatments

Partial Pericardiectomy can be used for recurrences

* Radiation

    Lymphomas are extremely radiosensitive

    Effective in 50% of cases

    Breast and lung cancers may also respond

6. Nursing measures

   * Support patient and family through anxious period

   * Maintain optimal cardiac output and function

   * Prevent infection from invasive procedures

   * Reduce patient's pain

Suggested Readings

1. Maxwell MB: Malignant effusions and edema. In Groenwald SL, Frogge MH, Goodman M, Yarbro CH (eds): *Cancer Nursing: Principles and Practice* (4th ed). Boston: Jones and Bartlett, 1997, pp 729-733.
2. Wilkes JD, Fideas P, Vaikus L, et al: Malignancy-related pericardial effusion. *Cancer* 76: 1377-1387, 1995.
3. Joiner GA, Kolodychuk GR: Neoplastic cardiac tamponade. *Crit Care Nurs* 11:50-58, 1991.
4. Vaikus PT, Hermann HC, Winter MM: Treatment of malignant pericardial effusion. *JAMA* 272:59-64, 1994.

CHAPTER 22

Malignant Peritoneal Effusion

Overview

Commonly referred to as *ascites*

Occurs when volume of fluid that accumulates in peritoneal space exceeds capacity of lymphatic channels to drain

Most common with ovarian cancer; develops in over 60% of patients

Usually sign of advanced disease

Tumors associated with peritoneal effusion are

231

1. Ovarian
2. Breast
3. Gastric
4. Lymphoma
5. Endometrial
6. Colon
7. Pancreatic
8. Mesothelioma

Causes include

1. Tumor seeding peritoneum
2. Excess intraperitoneal fluid production
3. Humoral factors produced by tumor cause increased capillary leakage of proteins and fluids into peritoneum
4. Hypoalbuminemia and low serum protein

Approaches to Care

Assessment

1. Clinical manifestations

    * Several liters of fluid can accumulate in peritoneal space
    * Pressure and restrictiveness are hallmark symptoms
    * Fullness
    * Early satiety
    * Indigestion
    * Swollen ankles
    * Fatigue
    * Shortness of breath

* Constipation
* Reduced bladder capacity
* Weight gain
* Distended abdomen
* Fluid wave
* Shifting dullness
* Bulging flanks
* Everted umbilicus

2. Diagnostic measures

   * Physical examination
   * Paracentesis
   * Fluid cytology

Treatment

1. Only effective therapy is control of primary disease
2. If patient is asymptomatic, wait and see
3. If patient is symptomatic, initiate definitive therapy
4. Ascites fluid can be removed by

   * Paracentesis

     Fluid can reaccumulate rapidly

     Risk of protein depletion and electrolyte abnormality

     Risk of infection

   * Obliteration of intraperitoneal space

     Instillation of chemotherapeutic agents; e.g., cisplatin

Administered by intraperitoneal route

* Peritoneovenous shunting

  Used to recirculate ascitic fluid to intravascular space

  Reserved for patients for whom other treatment options failed

  Complications

    Clotting

    Disseminated intravascular coagulation

    Pulmonary embolism

    Infection

    Shunt malfunction

Suggested Readings

1. Maxwell MB: Malignant effusions and edema. In Groenwald SL, Frogge MH, Goodman M, Yarbro CH (eds): *Cancer Nursing: Principles and Practice* (4th ed). Boston: Jones and Bartlett, 1997, pp 733-736.
2. Baker AR, Weber JS: Treatment of malignant ascites. In DeVita VT, Hellamn S, Rosenberg SA (eds): *Cancer: Principles and Practice* (4th ed). Philadelphia: JB Lippincott, 1993, pp 2255-2261.
3. Ratliff CR, Hutchinson M, Conner C: Rapid paracentesis of large volumes of ascitic fluid. *Oncol Nurs Forum* 18:1461, 1991.
4. Hrozencik SP, Ness EA: Intraperitoneal chemotherapy via the Groshong catheter in

the patient with gynecologic cancer. *Oncol Nurs Forum* 18:1245, 1991.

5. Kehoe C: Malignant ascites: Etiology, diagnosis, and treatment. *Oncol Nurs Forum* 18:523-530, 1991.

CHAPTER 23

Malignant Pleural Effusion

Overview

Malignant pleural effusion occurs when malignant process prevents reabsorption and fluid accumulates in intrapleural space

May be initial symptom of cancer or may signal advanced disease

Typically recurs, unless underlying disease is controlled or cured

50% of all cancer patients develop pleural effusion

Occurs most often with following tumors (in order of incidence):

1. Lung
2. Breast
3. Adenocarcinoma
4. Leukemia, lymphoma
5. Reproductive tract
6. Gastrointestinal tract
7. Primary unknown

Causes of malignant pleural effusion

1. Implantation of cancer cells on pleural surface
2. Tumor obstruction of lymphatic channels
3. Tumor obstruction of pulmonary veins leads to increased capillary hydrostatic pressure
4. Necrotic tumor cells shed into pleural space and increase osmotic pressure
5. Thoracic duct perforation, producing chylous pleural effusion

Approaches to Care

Assessment

1. Clinical manifestations

   * Dyspnea
   * Orthopnea
   * Dry, nonproductive cough
   * Chest pain, heaviness
   * Labored breathing
   * Tachypnea
   * Dullness to percussion

* Restricted chest wall expansion
* Impaired transmission of breath sounds

2. Diagnostic measures

  * Chest x-rays
  * Pleural fluid examination
  * Thoracoscopy with direct pleural biopsy
  * Bloody effusion is strongest indicator of malignancy

Interventions

1. Definite treatment is based on tumor type and previous therapy

   * If tumor causing effusion is responsive, systemic chemotherapy is initiated
   * If tumor is questionably responsive, trial of systemic chemotherapy is initiated and thoracostomy tube is inserted to relieve symptoms
   * If tumor is refractory to treatment, thoracostomy tube is inserted and pleurodesis is performed

2. Short-term relief of symptoms is accomplished by

   * Thoracentesis

     Pleural fluid is removed by needle aspiration or via implanted port through chest wall

     Complications include pneumothorax, pain, hypotension, or pulmonary edema

Effective for diagnosis, palliation, or relief of acute distress

* Thoracostomy tube

  Inserted to remove fluid

  Can be left in place to assess degree of fluid accumulation

  Can be used to instill sclerosing agents

3. Sclerosing the pleural space

   * Is aggressive measure to prevent fluid reaccumulation

   * Instillation of chemical agent causes visceral and parietal pleura to become permanently adhered together

   * Sclerosing agent most commonly used is bleomycin

   * Other investigational methods for treatment include

     Antibody-guided radiation using monoclonal antibodies radiolabelled with iodine 131

     Biologic agents: interferons, interleukins

     Indwelling small-bore drainage catheter

4. Surgical methods

   * Used when above measures are unsuccessful

   * Pleurectomy is effective in some cases

   * Pleuroperitoneal shunt can also be inserted to divert pleural fluid into subcutaneous tissue via valved pump

5. Radiation

   * Used if underlying tumor is responsive to radiotherapy

   * Pulmonary fibrosis is potential complication

Suggested Readings

1. Maxwell MB: Malignant effusions and edema. In Groenwald SL, Frogge MH, Goodman M, Yarbro CH (eds): *Cancer Nursing: Principles and Practice* (4th ed). Boston: Jones and Bartlett, 1997, pp 724-729.
2. Petrou M, Kaplan D, Goldstraw P: Management of malignant pleural effusions. *Cancer* 75: 801-805, 1995.
3. Bealani CP, Aisner J, Patz E, et al: Ambulatory sclerotherapy for malignant pleural effusion. *Proc Am Soc Clin Oncol* 14: 524, 1995.
4. Moores DW: Malignant pleural effusion. *Semin Oncol* 18(suppl):59-61, 1991.

CHAPTER 24

Mucous Membrane Alterations

Overview

Stomatitis

1. Risk factors

   * Dose-intensive chemotherapy

   * Radiation therapy to head and neck region

   * Higher doses of stomatotoxic drugs: 5-fluorouracil, methotrexate, bleomycin, doxorubicin, vinblastine, cytosine arabinoside, taxol, taxotere

   * Concomitant administration of radiation and chemotherapy

- ∗ Liver or kidney dysfunction that may alter metabolism or elimination of stomatotoxic drug
- ∗ Higher doses of radiation given over shorter periods
- ∗ Poor nutritional status
- ∗ Tobacco and alcohol use

2. Risk of oral cavity infections after radiation or chemotherapy, or both, is directly related to degree and duration of granulocytopenia
3. Immunosuppression from treatment further increases susceptibility to oral infection

Xerostomia

1. Salivary glands highly sensitive to radiation
2. Decrease in quantity and quality of saliva

Taste changes

1. Chemotherapy and radiation cause direct injury to taste cells that results in taste changes
2. Radiation taste changes can be long-term, even permanent

Esophagitis

1. Both chemotherapy and radiation damage sensitive epithelial cells lining esophagus
2. Risk factors

- ∗ Stomatotoxic drugs: Dactinomycin, doxorubicin, 5-fluorouracil, methotrexate, hydroxyurea, procarbazine, vinblastine, taxol, and taxotere
- ∗ Concomitant chemotherapy and radiation to esophagus

* Alcohol consumption, tobacco use
* Ulcer disease

Enteritis

1. Three to five bowel movements daily or bowel movements of loose or watery consistency
2. Risk factors

   * High-dose radiation to gastrointestinal (GI) tract
   * Large volume field
   * Concomitant chemotherapy and radiation therapy
   * Chemotherapeutic agents most likely to cause diarrhea include 5-fluorouracil, dactinomycin, methotrexate, doxorubicin, irinotecan floxuridine
   * Poor nutrition, preexisting bowel disorders, diabetes, and hypertension may enhance enteritis

3. Other causes of diarrhea in cancer patient include

   * Acute graft-versus-host disease
   * Radiation
   * Antibiotics
   * Fecal impaction
   * GI mucosal changes

Genitourinary mucositis

1. Cystitis and urethritis can occur in patients who have had radiation to prostate, cervix, and bladder

2. Vaginitis can occur in women who have radiation for gynecologic and colorectal malignancies

Approaches to Care

Stomatitis

1. Assessment

   * Conduct dental evaluation and prophylactic care before treatment
   * Care for periodontal disease before treatment with radiation or chemotherapy
   * Daily fluoride treatments and good oral hygiene can reduce incidence of oral complications
   * During treatment, assess oral cavity daily

2. Clinical manifestations

   * Histologic changes within 5 to 7 days of exposure
   * Inflammation and oral ulceration at 7 to 10 days
   * Resolution within 2 to 3 weeks
   * If healing does not proceed, secondary infection leading to sepsis can occur
   * Oral pain is major clinical problem

3. Management

   * Treatment is palliative
   * Depends on severity or grade of toxicity

Grade 0: potential stomatitis

Encourage routine oral hygiene regimen after meals and at bedtime

Brush with soft toothbrush

Floss with unwaxed dental floss

Rinse with mouthwash of patient preference—avoid mouthwashes with high alcohol content

Remove, cleanse, and replace dental prostheses after oral care; store nightly in denture antiseptic solution

Apply lip lubricant

Use oxidizing agent as needed

3% hydrogen peroxide solution and water (1: 4 mixture)—swish, gargle, and expectorate

Sodium bicarbonate solution (e.g., 1 tsp in 8 oz water)—swish, gargle, and expectorate

Rinse with warm water or saline

Remove thick, tenacious mucus with swab as needed

Use prophylactic chlorhexidine mouth rinse, 15 ml—high-risk patients should swish, gargle, and expectorate every 8 hours

Consult dentist

Grade 1: erythema of oral mucosa, and Grade 2: isolated small ulcerations

Assess oral cavity twice daily

Follow oral hygiene regimen (see above) every 2 hours while awake and every 6 hours during night

> Use normal saline mouthwash if no crusts are present

> Alternate oxidizing agent with warm saline mouthwash if crusts are present

> Omit flossing if pain results or bleeding occurs in patients with a low platelet count

> Remove, cleanse, and do not replace dental prostheses, except for meals; store nightly in denture antiseptic solution

Culture suspicious oral lesions

Apply topical anesthetics before meals and as needed for local pain control

Use oral analgesics for systemic pain control

Adapt diet to ensure maximum nutrition and fluid intake

> Encourage frequent small feedings

> Soft, bland foods

> Increase fluids to 3 liters/day

> Diet should be high in protein and calories

> Avoid irritants

> Consult dietitian as needed

Grade 3: confluent ulcerations covering more than 25% of oral cavity, or Grade 4: hemorrhagic ulceration

> Assess oral cavity every 8 hours

Assess for evidence of infection; culture any suspicious lesion(s)

Institute aggressive and timely antimicrobial therapy as ordered by physician

Cleanse mouth every 2 hours while awake and every 4 hours at night

> Alternate warm saline mouthwash with antifungal or antibacterial oral suspension

> Use oxidizing agent for mucolytic area every 4 hours followed by saline rinse

Gently brush teeth every 4 hours, avoiding trauma to gums; substitute soft foam toothettes if bleeding occurs or brushing is too painful

Apply lip lubricant every 2 hours; if lips are bleeding or ulcerated, apply warm saline soaks every 4 hours for 20 minutes

Remove and cleanse dental prostheses—do not replace; store in denture antiseptic solution

Institute local pain control measures

Use systemic analgesics as needed, especially after meals

Provide adequate nutritional and fluid intake

> Liquid or pureed diet

> Intravenous fluids to prevent dehydration

> Enteral or total parenteral nutrition may be needed until healing occurs

Frequency of oral care increases as severity of stomatitis increases

Solutions commonly used to rinse oral cavity

Normal saline

Sodium bicarbonate

Hydrogen peroxide

Pain management includes local anesthetics (lidocaine, Cetacaine, or Hurricaine spray) and systemic analgesics, depending on severity of oral discomfort

Lip care includes moisture and lubrication

Xerostomia

1. Manifestations

 * Mouth is dry, saliva becomes thick and ropey

 * Nutrition, taste, and speech may be impaired

 * Patient at risk for oral caries and candidal infections

2. Management

 * Assess oral cavity daily

 * Instruct patient to

 Increase fluids and eat soft foods or food moistened with milk or gravy

 Humidify air

 Avoid irritants, such as tobacco, alcohol, carbonated beverages, and caffeine

 Take frequent sips of water to decrease oral irritation

 Use saliva substitutes

 Use sialagogues to stimulate secretion of saliva

Taste changes

1. Manifestations

   * Patients complain of lowered threshold for bitter taste and increased threshold for sweet taste

   * Metallic taste is commonly associated with cyclophosphamide

2. Management: Instruct patient to

   * Engage in frequent and consistent oral hygiene

   * Increase seasoning of food

   * Use hard candy to mask taste associated with chemotherapy

Esophagitis

1. Manifestations

   * Dysphagia

   * Odynophagia

   * Epigastric pain may progress to ulceration, hemorrhage, and secondary infection

   * Pain and difficulty swallowing can lead to dehydration and weight loss

2. Management: Instruct patient to

   * Avoid hot, spicy, rough foods

   * Eat foods that are soft and moist, like gravies

   * Drink at least 8 glasses of fluid per day

   * Humidify environment

* Avoid smoking or chewing any form of tobacco
* Take medicine prescribed for pain and discomfort
* Increase frequency of oral hygiene
* Tell physician about any dysphagia or pain, fever, or inability to drink fluids

Enteritis

1. Manifestations

   * Chemotherapy-induced enteritis is manifested by diarrhea accompanied by abdominal cramping and rectal urgency
   * Infection or antibiotic-associated colitis should be investigated and treated before antidiarrheal therapy that inhibits gut motility

2. Management: Instruct patient to

   * Begin low-fat, low-fiber diet when symptoms occur
   * Reduce or eliminate lactose from diet
   * Use lactase enzyme caplets or lactose-free milk if helpful
   * Avoid

     Raw fruits and vegetables

     Cooked broccoli

     Butter

     Margarine

     Sauces

    Whole-grain breads

    Fatty foods

    Nuts

    Caffeine

    Alcohol

    Milk

    Milk products

  * Pharmacologic measures

    Mild antidiarrheals, such as Pepto-Bismol, Kaopectate, Lomotil, and Imodium

    Opiates, such as opium tincture, paregoric elixir, and codeine, may decrease peristalsis

    Octreotide acetate (Sandostatin), given subcutaneously, may control diarrhea by suppressing secretion of serotonin and gastroenteropancreatic peptides

Genitourinary mucositis

1. Urinary tract

  * Manifestations

    Bladder irritation

    Dysuria

    Frequency and urgency

    Hemorrhagic cystitis from decreased capillary permeability and increased pressure of bloodflow

  * Treatment

    Instruct patient to

      Increase fluid intake

Use urinary anesthetics as needed

Use antispasmodics

2. Vaginitis

   ✳ Manifestations

   Erythema

   Inflammation

   Atrophy

   Fibrosis

   Hypopigmentation

   Telangiectasia

   Inelasticity

   Ulceration

   Tissue necrosis, fistula formation, and hemorrhage can occur in patients who receive higher doses or radiation

   ✳ Management: Instruct patient to

   Dilate vagina with vaginal dilator or sexual intercourse

   Use good personal hygiene to minimize risk of secondary infection

   Report symptoms of vaginitis, such as vaginal discharge, itching, odor, pain, soreness, bleeding, or dyspareunia

   Use analgesics if needed to relieve severe discomfort or pain

   Use topical and systemic medications (miconazole nitrate or clotrimazole cream or suppositories)

Suggested Readings

1. Goodman M, Ladd LA, Purl S: Integumentary and mucous membrane alterations. In Groenwald SL, Frogge MH, Goodman M, Yarbro CH (eds): *Cancer Nursing: Principles and Practice* (4th ed). Boston: Jones and Bartlett, 1997, pp 769-822.

2. Perez CA, Brady LW: *Principles and Practice of Radiation Oncology* (2nd ed). Philadelphia: JB Lippincott, 1992.

3. Dow KH, Hilderley LJ: *Nursing Care in Radiation Oncology.* Philadelphia: WB Saunders, 1992.

4. Beck SL: Mucositis. In Groenwald SL, Frogge M, Goodman M, Yarbro CH (eds): *Cancer Symptom Management.* Boston: Jones and Bartlett, 1996, pp 308-321.

5. Berger AM, Kilroy TJ: Oral complications. In DeVita VT, Hellman S, Rosenberg SA (eds): *Cancer Principles and Practice of Oncology* (5th ed). Philadelphia: Lippincott-Raven, 1997, pp 2714-2720.

CHAPTER 25

Nutritional
Disturbances

Overview

Nutritional disturbances

1. Are a common consequence of cancer or its treatment
2. Predispose individuals to infection
3. Diminish patient's tolerance to therapy
4. Are important prognosticators of morbidity and survival
5. Are important issues in quality of life

Pathophysiology of malnutrition in cancer

1. Metabolic effects of tumor

* Tumors produce peptides that cause cancer cachexia

* Carbohydrate, protein, and lipid metabolisms are altered

* Fluid and electrolyte abnormalities result from action of ectopic hormones

* Excessive energy requirements of tumors cause greater energy expenditures for individual

* Taste is altered

* Anorexia occurs in almost all cancer patients at some time during illness; this condition compounds weight loss and cachexia

* Immunosuppression occurs

2. Mechanical effects of tumor

* Expanding tumors cause local tissue damage with potential nutritional consequences such as

   Infection

   Loss of appetite

   Nausea and vomiting

   Edema

3. Nutritional consequences of cancer treatment

* Anorexia

* Constipation

* Diarrhea

* Fistulae

* Fluid and electrolyte imbalances
* Infection
* Malabsorption

  Interruption of bowel structure

  Damage to absorptive surface of bowel

  Lack of substance necessary for absorption of nutrients

* Mucositis
* Nausea and vomiting
* Taste changes

Approaches to Care

Nutritional assessment

1. Medical history

   * Duration and type of malignancy
   * Frequency, type, and severity of complications (e.g., infections, draining lesions)
   * Type and duration of therapy
   * Specific chemotherapeutic agents used
   * Radiation sites
   * Antibiotics used
   * Other drugs used
   * Surgical procedures performed (site, type, and date)

  ∗ Side effects of therapy (diarrhea, anorexia, nausea, and vomiting)

  ∗ Concomitant medical conditions (diabetes, heart disease, liver failure, kidney failure, infection)

2. Physical examination

  ∗ General appearance

  ∗ Condition of hair

  ∗ Condition of skin

  ∗ Condition of teeth

  ∗ Condition of mouth, gums, and throat

  ∗ Edema

  ∗ Performance status

  ∗ Identification of nutritionally-related problems (fistula, pain, stomatitis, xerostomia, infection, constipation, diarrhea, nausea and vomiting, obstruction)

3. Dietary history

  ∗ 24-hour recall of foods eaten, including snacks

  ∗ Composition of food taken in 24 hours

  ∗ Time of day meals and snacks eaten

  ∗ Past or current diet modifications

  ∗ Self-feeding ability

  ∗ Special cancer diet

  ∗ Vitamins, minerals, or other supplements

* Modifications of diet or eating habits as result of treatment or illness
* Foods withheld or given on basis of personal or religious grounds
* Food preferences
* Food allergies or intolerances

4. Socioeconomic history

   * Number of persons living in home
   * Presence of kitchen facilities
   * Income
   * Food purchased by
   * Food prepared by
   * Amount spent on food per month
   * Outside provision of meals

5. Anthropometric data

   * Height
   * Weight
   * Weight as percentage of ideal
   * Weight change as percentage of usual
   * Triceps skinfold measurement (as indicator of subcutaneous body fat)
   * Triceps skinfold as percentage of standard
   * Midarm circumference (as index of protein status)
   * Midarm muscle circumference
   * Midarm muscle circumference as percentage of standard

6. Biochemical data

* Hematocrit
* Hemoglobin level
* Serum albumin level
* Serum transferrin level
* Creatinine clearance
* Creatinine height index
* Total lymphocyte count
* Delayed hypersensitivity response (skin testing)
* Nitrogen balance
* Blood urea nitrogen level
* Sodium, potassium, carbon dioxide, chloride levels
* Glucose level

Planning

1. Identify goal of nutritional therapy
2. Establish individual's caloric requirements
3. Compose diet

Approaches to problems that interfere with normal nutrition

1. Dysphagia: Encourage patient to

* Eat soft or liquid foods
* Blenderize solid foods
* Moisten foods with cream, gravies, or oils
* Eat bland foods that are smooth in texture and tepid to minimize pain

2. Nausea and vomiting: Encourage patient to

  * Avoid acidic foods, such as citrus juice and tomatoes
  * Eat salty foods, or add salt to foods
  * Avoid overly sweet, greasy, or high-fat foods
  * Drink clear, cool beverages
  * Eat dry foods, such as toast or crackers, especially after getting up in morning
  * Eat slowly and chew food thoroughly
  * Eat small, frequent meals
  * Eat frozen juice sticks or gelatin for fluid
  * Rest with head elevated after eating
  * Avoid rich, sweet foods
  * Wear loose clothing
  * Avoid favorite foods during chemotherapy to avoid developing aversion to them
  * Take antinausea, antiemetic, and tranquilizing medications as prescribed

3. Early satiety: Encourage patient to

  * Eat five or six small meals per day
  * Keep nutritious snacks available between meals
  * Eat foods high in calories and low in fat
  * Avoid greasy foods
  * Chew foods slowly
  * Avoid liquids with meals; take them 30 minutes before or after meals

* Drink nutritious liquids, such as juice, milk, or milkshakes

4. Pancreatic insufficiency: Encourage patient to

   * Take digestive enzymes as prescribed
   * Follow a diet low in fat and high in calories and protein
   * Take commercial food supplements as prescribed

5. Anorexia: Encourage patient to

   * Eat small, frequent meals
   * Make changes in diet or surroundings
   * Try new recipes or foods, eat with friends, or go to favorite restaurant
   * Stimulate appetite with light exercise
   * Time meals to coincide with "best time" of day
   * Eat nutritious, high-protein snacks
   * Avoid "empty calorie" foods, such as coffee or diet soda
   * Take medications with high-calorie foods or nutritional supplements
   * Add powdered milk to foods during cooking to increase protein content
   * Drink small glass of wine or fruit juice before meals to stimulate appetite
   * Avoid fatty foods
   * Try foods served cold; they may be easier to tolerate

6. Dumping syndrome: Encourage patient to

   * Eat foods low in concentrated carbohydrate but high in protein

   * Eat several small, dry meals during day

   * Avoid liquids with meals; take them 30 minutes before or after meals

   * Avoid sugar, candy, jam, jelly, honey, and desserts

7. Constipation: Encourage patient to

   * Drink at least 2 liters of fluid daily

   * Eat high-fiber foods

   * Engage in light, regular exercise

   * Take previously successful bowel stimulants

8. Diarrhea: Encourage patient to

   * Drink plenty of fluids to avoid dehydration

   * Avoid milk or milk products, unless they are treated with lactase enzyme

   * Take electrolyte replacement fluids if diarrhea persists

   * Avoid foods high in fiber

   * Avoid high-fat, spicy, and gas-forming foods

   * Eat foods rich in potassium

9. Dyspepsia: Encourage patient to

   * Avoid fatty foods

   * Avoid spicy foods

* Elevate upper trunk after meals
* Use antacids

10. Stomatitis: Encourage patient to

   * Eat soft or liquid foods
   * Avoid irritating foods that are rough or acidic
   * Use warm saline irrigants to cleanse mouth
   * Eat cold or frozen foods to numb pain
   * Avoid extremely hot beverages

11. Taste changes: Encourage patient to

   * Marinate red meat with sweet marinades or soy sauce
   * Substitute poultry, fish, eggs, or cheese for red meat
   * Serve meats chilled rather than hot
   * Use high-protein liquid supplements if meat is not tolerated
   * Rinse mouth with carbonated water or a lemon wedge before meals to clear palate
   * Eat mildly acidic foods, such as lemonade, tea with lemon, pickled foods, and citrus fruits and juices to stimulate taste buds
   * Try extra spices, onion, or garlic to improve flavor of food
   * Keep experimenting; foods previously avoided may now be acceptable as a result of taste changes

12. Xerostomia: Encourage patient to

* Moisten foods with gravies or sauces
* Use artificial saliva as prescribed
* Blenderize or process foods to make them easier to eat
* Soak foods in coffee, tea, milk, cocoa, or warm beverages
* Avoid dry foods, such as crackers or toast
* Swallow liquid with each bite of food
* Use humidifier or steam kettle in room where food is eaten

13. General: Encourage patient to

* Drink plenty of fluids
* Make mealtime pleasant with different surroundings and pleasant company
* Serve food attractively; use garnishes
* Experiment with recipes, flavoring, spices
* Avoid empty-calorie foods, such as soda
* Eat high-calorie foods
* Take advantage of best time of day for eating
* Eat early in day if energy levels are higher then
* Keep nutritious snacks handy to increase nutrient intake

Administration of nutritional therapy

1. Oral feeding

* Regular diet is preferred if individual is able to consume adequate quantity of foods orally

* For those unable to eat adequate amounts, supplemental calories, protein, vitamins, and minerals may be indicated

* Liquid nutritional formulas may be used

2. Enteral (tube) feeding

* Indicated if oral intake cannot prevent weight loss or if person's physical condition prevents oral intake

* Requires functioning gastrointestinal (GI) tract

* For tumors of head and neck, lung, or upper GI tract, feeding directly into small intestine may be indicated

* May be administered by nasogastric or nasointestinal means

* For more permanent feeding, surgically placed esophagostomy, gastrostomy, or jejunostomy tube may be indicated

* Formulas may be prepared from regular food or may be commercially prepared

* Side effects tend to lessen over time, making enteral feeding appropriate for long-term use

Diarrhea

Attributed to formula-related factors including lactose content, bacterial contamination, and osmolality

If not resolved within 2 to 3 days, medical work-up may be indicated

Antidiarrheal medication may be prescribed

Fluid and electrolyte disturbances may occur

Monitor fluid status daily

Hyperglycemia may occur during initial stages of feeding and continue in individuals with diabetes

Monitor blood and urine glucose levels

3. Total parenteral nutrition (TPN)

  * Intravenous infusion of concentrated mixture of amino acids, glucose, fluid, vitamins, minerals, electrolytes, and trace elements into central vein, usually superior vena cava

  * Indicated when enteral feedings are impossible because of lack of GI function

  * Allows bowel of individual on cancer therapy to rest, thereby allowing individual to complete course of therapy

  * Complications

    Infection

    From contamination of TPN solution, insertion site, or equipment

    Offending organisms are usually skin microorganisms, such as the bacteria *Staphylococcus*, *Klebsiella*, and *Corynebacterium* species and the fungi *Candida* species

Early detection is an important nursing responsibility

First sign may be sudden glycosuria (or hyperglycemia) in previously stable individual

Clinical signs of sepsis include fever, hypotension, tachycardia, and tachypnea

If there is temperature spike, peripheral blood and blood drawn from catheter are cultured for bacteria and fungi

If culture results are positive, catheter is assumed to be source of infection and is removed

New catheter not inserted until all blood cultures show negative results

Bacterial sepsis treated with antibiotics

Fungal sepsis treated with fungicidal agent

Mechanical complications

Improper functioning of central line resulting from

Blockage of line from catheter crimping

Thrombosis

Malfunction of infusion pump

Failure of infusion set

Can be minimized if personnel are knowledgeable and skilled and if there is standardized protocol for care of TPN equipment

Thrombosis of central vein

Is a rare, but serious complication

Requires prompt removal of catheter and administration of heparin sodium

Signs include erythema, edema of catheter insertion site, pain along course of vein, fever, tachycardia, tachypnea, malaise, and ipsilateral swelling of arm, neck, or face

Air embolism

Is rare, but potentially fatal

Is prevented by clamping tubing securely to prevent air from entering system

Inspect infusion system regularly for leaks or cracks

Signs of sudden vascular collapse are

Chest pain

Apprehension

Tachycardia

Hypotension

Cyanosis, progressing to seizures

Loss of consciousness

Cardiac arrest

Immediate emergency nursing action is to position person on his or her left side with head down to allow air to dissipate gradually through pulmonary artery. Action may take several minutes, but eliminates vascular obstruction

Metabolic complications

Most common is hyperglycemia, which occurs in 15% of all individuals receiving TPN therapy; results when

Infusion is too rapid

Insulin response is inadequate

There are increased insulin demands on individual

Monitored with fractional urine tests or finger sticks for blood glucose every 6 hours

Symptoms include dry mouth, flushed skin, thirst, malaise, polyuria, nausea, or vomiting

Treated by addition of insulin to each TPN solution

Hypoglycemia occurs when too much insulin is administered or when TPN infusion is interrupted or discontinued shortly after insulin is given

Symptoms include headache, drowsiness, dizziness, tachycardia, and tremor

Corrected when TPN infusion is balanced against insulin administration

Essential fatty acid deficiency occurs as result of prolonged reduction of fat intake

Symptoms are

- Scaling of skin over lower calf and dorsum of foot

- Alopecia

- Delayed wound healing

- Increased capillary fragility

- Thrombocytopenia

Deficiency is treated by administering lipid emulsion to individuals who receive TPN for longer than 14 days without dietary fat intake

- Prevents essential fatty acid deficiency

- Provides concentrated energy source

- Is isotonic and therefore does not damage endothelium

- Does not require insulin

- Guidelines for lipid emulsion infusion

Do not use emulsion if color or texture is inconsistent

Do not shake container excessively

Nothing can be added to lipid infusion

Infuse in same line as TPN solution using Y-connector located near infusion site

Lipid infusion should be hung higher than TPN or it will run up TPN line

Do not use filter

Initial maximum rate of infusion is 1 cc/min for first 30 minutes If there are no untoward reactions, increase to 500 cc over 4 to 12 hours

Observe for allergic reactions, dyspnea, cyanosis, nausea, vomiting, headache, flushing, fever, chills, pain in chest or back, irritation at infusion site, and diaphoresis; if any reactions occur, discontinue infusion

Discard remaining solution—do not store for later use

Suggested Readings

1. Foltz AT: Nutritional disturbances. In Groenwald SL, Frogge MH, Goodman M, Yarbro CH (eds): *Cancer Nursing: Principles and Practice* (4th ed). Boston: Jones and Bartlett, 1997, pp 655-679.

2. Skipper A, Szeluga DJ, Groenwald SL: Nutritional disturbances. In Groenwald SL, Frogge MH, Goodman M, Yarbro CH (eds): *Cancer Nursing: Principles and Practice* (3rd ed). Boston: Jones and Bartlett, 1993, pp 620-643.

3. Ropka M: Nutrition. In Gross J, Johnson BL (eds): *Handbook of Oncology Nursing* (2nd ed). Boston: Jones and Bartlett, 1994, pp 329-372.

4. Shils M: Nutrition and diet in cancer management. In Olson J, Shike M (eds): *Modern Nutrition in Health and Disease* (8th ed). Philadelphia: Lea and Febiger, 1994, pp 1319-1342.

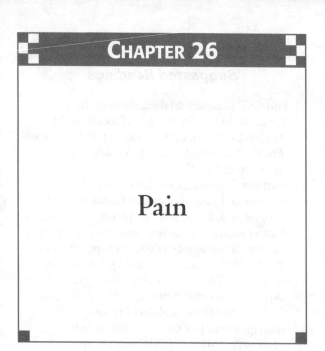

CHAPTER 26

Pain

Overview

Pain is an unpleasant sensory and emotional experience associated with tissue damage

Chronic pain and acute pain are different

There are three types of pain in patients with cancer, each with a different etiology

1. Tumor-related pain caused by

   * Infiltration of bone

   * Infiltration of nerves

   * Infiltration of intestinal tract and viscera

2. Treatment-related pain caused by

   * Diagnostic procedures
   * Surgery
   * Radiotherapy
   * Chemotherapy
   * Complications

3. Pain unrelated to either tumor or treatment

Pain is most prevalent in patients with

1. Advanced disease
2. Lung cancer
3. Breast cancer
4. Pancreatic cancer
5. Primary bone cancer

Cancer pain is poorly managed worldwide by health professionals

Obstacles to successful pain management include

1. Lack of understanding about pain
2. Expectation that pain should be present
3. Relief of pain not viewed as goal of treatment
4. Inadequate or nonexistent assessment
5. Undertreatment with analgesics
6. Inadequate knowledge of drugs or other interventions
7. Fears of addiction, sedation, respiratory depression
8. Perceptual differences between patients and health care providers

9. Legal impediments

Approaches to Care

Assessment

There are six dimensions to the cancer pain experience that need to be assessed

1. Physiologic dimension

    * Onset

    * Duration

        Acute pain: Self-limiting

        Chronic pain: Lasts 3 months or longer

    * Pattern

        Brief or transient

        Periodic or intermittent

        Continuous or constant

2. Sensory dimension

    * Location of pain

    * Intensity (e.g., mild, moderate, severe) of pain

    * Quality (e.g., burning, stabbing, throbbing) of pain

3. Affective dimension

    * Depression

    * Anxiety

    * Mental state

* Perception of suffering

4. Cognitive dimension

   * Meaning of pain
   * Coping strategies
   * Knowledge, attitudes, beliefs
   * Previous treatments
   * Influencing factors (positive and negative)

5. Behavioral dimension

   * Level of activity
   * Use of medications
   * Communication with others
   * Sleep and rest patterns
   * Behaviors to control pain
   * Interpersonal relationships
   * Fatigue

6. Sociocultural dimension

   * Ethnocultural background
   * Family and social life
   * Work and home responsibilities
   * Environment
   * Familial attitudes, beliefs, and behaviors
   * Personal attitudes, beliefs, and behaviors

7. The Oncology Nursing Society has stated nurse's role as

   * Describing pain

* Identifying aggravating and relieving
  factors
* Determining meaning of pain and its cause
* Determining individual's definition of pain
  relief
* Deriving nursing diagnoses
* Assisting in selection of interventions
* Evaluating efficacy of interventions

8. Standardized pain assessment tools and
   documentation procedures facilitate
   management of pain
9. Children, elderly patients, individuals with
   history of substance abuse, individuals from
   diverse cultural backgrounds, and terminally
   ill patients require special consideration in
   pain assessment and management

Interventions

1. Treat underlying pathology by

   * Chemotherapeutic agents to palliate
     symptoms
   * Hormonal therapy to provide relief of
     painful bone metastases from breast and
     prostate cancers
   * Radiotherapy to provide fast pain relief in
     patients with

     Bone, brain, and hepatic metastases

     Epidural cord compression

     Nerve root infiltration

   * Surgery (palliative) to

Resolve oncologic emergencies

Reduce tumor burden

Provide direct access to tumor (e.g., implants of infusion pumps or radiation seeds)

Prevent and repair fractures from metastatic disease

Interrupt pain pathway

2. Pharmacologic therapy

   ∗ Nonopioids

   Nonsteroidal anti-inflammatory drugs (NSAIDs) used alone or with an opioid for

   Mild to moderate pain

   Metastatic bone pain

   Pain from compression of tendons, muscles, pleura, and peritoneum

   Visceral pain

   Commonly used nonopioids are

   Acetaminophen

   Acetylsalicylic acid

   Choline magnesium trisalicylate

   Diclofenac

   Diflunisal

   Ibuprofen

   Indomethacin

   Ketorolac

   Naproxen

Major toxicities of NSAIDs are

    Gastrointestinal (GI) disorders: Nausea, vomiting, epigastric pain, ulcers, bleeding, diarrhea, constipation

    Renal dysfunction

    Sodium and water retention

    Skin rashes

    Headaches

* Opioids

Opioid agnonists are very useful for cancer pain and include

    Codeine

    Fentanyl

    Hydromorphone

    Methadone

    Morphine

Morphine is most frequently used opioid for moderate to severe pain; advantages include

    Long-acting form with scheduled doses once daily or every 8 to 12 hours

    Flexibility in dosing with tablet formulations of 15, 30, 60, and 100 mg

    Oral, parenteral, rectal, and intraspinal preparations

Addiction is highly unlikely

Most common side effects

    Sedation

Respiratory depression (treat with naloxone)

Nausea and vomiting

Constipation

* Adjuvant analgesics

Antidepressants are used for neuropathic pain (e.g., continuous burning) caused by tumor infiltration of nerves; agents include

Amitriptyline

Doxepin

Nortriptyline

Trazodone

Imipramine

Maprotiline

Desipramine

Anticonvulsants are used for lancinating and stabbing neuropathic pain

Phenytoin

Clonazepam

Carbamazepine

Valproic acid

Psychostimulants counteract sedation of opioid analgesics

Amphetamines

Methylphenidate

3. Routes of opioid administration

* Oral route

Convenient and safe

Inexpensive

Should be used as long as possible

* Parenteral (intramuscular, subcutaneous, intravenous) route

  Occasional intramuscular or subcutaneous injection for immediate pain relief if no peripheral or central venous access

  Consider continuous infusion if analgesic needed every 2 hours or less

  Continuous intravenous infusions provide steady blood levels of opioid

  Morphine and hydromorphone most common for continuous subcutaneous infusions

* Transdermal route

  Fentanyl only opioid available via this route

* Rectal route

* Intraspinal route

  Criteria for intraspinal opioids include

    Unacceptable toxicities from systemic opioids

    Neuroablative or anesthetic procedures unsuccessful or not indicated

    Good home and family support

    Life expectancy of more than 3 months

4. Patient-controlled analgesia (PCA)

   * Allows patient to self-administer analgesics from special infusion pump

* Used with intravenous, subcutaneous, and epidural routes

* Avoids highs and lows of (PRN) administration

* Methods are bolus dosing or bolus with continuous infusion

* Appropriate use for PCA

    When patient wants self-control

    When oral route not available

    For breakthrough pain

5. Anesthetic and nerve-block procedures

* Prevent generation and conduction of nerve impulses

* Used for intractable pain

* Nondestructive nerve blocks and destructive neurosurgical procedures based on

    Anatomy

    Extent of disease

    Type of pain

    Potential benefits

6. Nonpharmacologic interventions

* Do not affect pathology or alter sensation or perception of pain

* Practical components of nursing practice

* Selected interventions

    Counterirritant cutaneous stimulation

Mentholated ointments

Heat

Cold

Massage

Transcutaneous electrical nerve stimulation (TENS)

Immobilization and mobilization

Distraction

Conversation

Visualization and imagery

Breathing exercises

Counting, reading, watching television

Speaking to others

Relaxation and guided imagery

Music therapy

Laughter therapy

Biofeedback

Hypnosis

* These techniques are used in conjunction with pharmacologic interventions and require careful assessment and evaluation

7. Accurate and appropriate pain education for patients and families is essential for pain management

Suggested Readings

1. McGuire DB, Sheidler VR: Pain. In Groenwald SL, Frogge MH, Goodman M, Yarbro CH (eds): *Cancer Nursing: Principles and Practice.* (4th ed). Boston: Jones and Bartlett, 1997, pp 529-584.
2. Spross JA, McGuire DB, Schmidt R: Oncology Nursing Society position paper on cancer pain. *Oncol Nurs Forum* 17:595-614, 751-760, 825, 944-955, 1990.
3. McGuire DB, Yarbro CH, Ferrell BR (eds): *Cancer Pain Management*. Boston: Jones and Bartlett, 1996.

CHAPTER 27

Septic Shock

Overview

Develops in approximately 27% to 46% of patients with gram-negative bacteremia, resulting in inadequate tissue perfusion and cirulatory collapse

Results from septicemia, a systemic blood infection

Characterized by

1. Hemodynamic instability
2. Coagulopathy

3. Altered metabolism

Incidence is increasing as a result of numerous invasive procedures

Mortality rate is 75% for cancer patients who develop septic shock

Risk factors include

1. Local effects of tumor growth
2. Immunologic effects of cancer or treatment
3. Granulocyte count of less than $100/mm^3$
4. Iatrogenic factors
5. Nosocomial sources
6. Invasive procedures

Approaches to Care

Assessment

1. Clinical manifestations

    * Early signs (early stage lasts from 30 minutes to 16 hours)

        Tachycardia

        Fever or hypothermia

        Rigors

        Hypertension

    * Late signs

        Bilateral rales

        Oliguria

        Evidence of inadequate tissue perfusion

Cyanosis, hypotension, mental changes

Adult respiratory distress syndrome

2. Diagnostic measures

   ∗ Early identification is critical to prevent death

   ∗ Blood cultures to identify microorganisms

   ∗ Chest x-ray films

Treatment

Based on two main objectives

1. Reverse shock
2. Treat underlying sepsis
3. Initiate empiric broad-spectrum antibiotic therapy immediately
4. Initial treatment usually includes aminoglycoside, penicillin, and cephalosporin
5. If *Staphylococcus epidermidis* infection is suspected, add vancomycin
6. If shock develops during prolonged antibiotic therapy, suspect fungal source and treat with amphotericin B
7. In 30% of cancer patients, infecting organism cannot be identified
8. Monitor vital signs, central venous or pulmonary artery pressure, and urine output
9. Vigorous fluid replacement expands volume
10. Fresh-frozen plasma increases mean arterial pressure
11. Give vasopressors if patient is unresponsive to fluid therapy
12. Corticosteroid therapy produces anti-inflammatory response

13. Give oxygen and monitor blood gases
14. Metabolic acidosis is possible
15. Mechanical ventilation may be needed
16. Effective therapy is measured by stable vital signs, adequate pressures, and urine output
17. Educate patient regarding preventive measures

Suggested Readings

1. Ellerhorst-Ryan JM: Infection. In Groenwald SL, Frogge MH, Goodman M, Yarbro CH (eds): *Cancer Nursing: Principles and Practice* (4th ed). Boston: Jones and Bartlett, 1997, pp 585-603.

2. Dietz KA, Flaherty AM: Oncologic emergencies. In Groenwald SL, Frogge MH, Goodman M, Yarbro CH (eds): *Cancer Nursing: Principles and Practice* (3rd ed). Boston: Jones and Bartlett, 1993, pp 801-805.

3. Parrillo JE: Management of septic shock: Present and future. *Ann Intern Med* 115:491-493, 1991.

4. Truett L: The septic syndrome: An oncologic treatment challenge. *Cancer Nurs* 14:175-180, 1991.

5. Bone RC: A critical evaluation of new agents for the treatment of sepsis. *JAMA* 266:1686-1691, 1991.

CHAPTER 28

Spinal Cord Compression

Overview

Spinal cord compression (SCC) occurs by:

1. Direct extension of the tumor into the epidural space
2. Vertebral collapse and displacement of bone into the epidural space
3. Direct extension through the intervertebral foramina

Neurologic emergency requiring prompt diagnosis and treatment to preserve person's neurologic function

Can cause partial or complete paralysis if not recognized or treated early

Is classified according to location of tumor that is causing compression as intramedullary, intradural, extravertebral, or extradural

Site of compression is related to primary cancer

1. Cervical compression—breast
2. Thoracic compression—lung, breast, prostate
3. Lumbosacral—gastrointestinal (GI) cancers

About 5%-10% of cancer patients develop spinal cord compression (SCC)

Over 95% of SCC cases are caused by tumor that has metastasized to vertebral column

Risk factors

1. Tumors that metastasize to bone
2. Primary cancers are

   * Breast
   * Lung
   * Sarcoma
   * Prostate
   * Neuroblastoma
   * GI cancer
   * Thyroid
   * Unknown primary

Approaches to Care

Assessment

1. Clinical manifestations

   * Over 95% of SCC patients present with pain

   * Pain is either radicular or localized

   * Pain with or without neurologic symptoms can indicate degree of blockage of spinal cord

   * Thoracic SCC is described as constrictive band around waist

   * Pain is usually within one or two vertebrae of compression

   * Radicular pain can follow dermatome of involved nerve root

   * Motor weakness occurs in about 75% of patients and is rarely presenting symptom; usually described as heaviness or stiffness

   * Sensory loss begins with numbness and paresthesia, but can progress to loss of light touch, pain, then thermal sensation

   * Loss of proprioception, deep pressure, or position represents more severe cord compression

   * Autonomic dysfunction includes bladder and bowel disturbances; loss of sphincter control is most common

2. Diagnostic measures

   * Pain can be elicited by percussion of

vertebrae near SCC, or by either straight leg raising or neck flexion

* Pain is aggravated by coughing, sneezing, or Valsalva's maneuver

* Pain is not relieved by lying down

* Distinguishing cause of pain as SCC or metastases can be difficult

* Hallmark of SCC pain is that it changes location, intensity, or nature

* Single most important prognostic indicator with SCC is neurologic status before initiation of therapy; the less extensive the injury to cord, the greater the potential for recovery

* Imminent compression should be suspected in individuals who have known metastases, progressive back pain associated with weakness, parsthesias, bowel or bladder dysfunction, or gait disturbances

* Assessment parameters include pain, sensory changes, muscle weakness, hyperreflexia, urinary changes, and bowel changes

* Spine films

* MRI is most definitive tool

* Myelography and computed tomographic (CT) scan are also used

Treatment

1. Timely treatment is as important as rapid diagnosis

* If treated early, neurologic deficits are rare

* Effective treatment is directly related to prolonged survival and quality of life

2. Controversy exists regarding initial treatment of choice

   * Radiation therapy

   * Surgical decompression

   * Combined approach of surgery and radiation

3. Radiation therapy

   * Most often used

   * Total dose of 30 to 40 Gy is given to port that includes one or two vertebrae above and below compression

   * Side effects are minimal unless patient has less than optimal bone marrow function, which may be suppressed further

4. Surgical decompression with laminectomy or vertebral body resection

   * Used for prompt relief

   * Used as first line of therapy if patient is neurologically unstable, tumor is radioresistant or previously irradiated, or spine is unstable

   * Primary goal is decompression by providing alternate space for tumor and for spine stabilization

5. Surgery followed by radiation therapy

appears to offer no greater advantage than
radiotherapy alone

6. Steroids are included in any management
   approach

   ∗ Often given before definitive diagnosis is
     made

   ∗ Aid in reducing inflammation and edema

   ∗ Can have oncolytic effect

7. Pain management is achieved with
   pharmacologic and nonpharmacologic
   measures

8. Nursing measures

   ∗ Pain control

   ∗ Protection of patient from sensory, motor, or
     neurologic injury

   ∗ Rehabilitation

     *Depending on pretreatment status of patient,
     rehabilitation approaches vary*

     *If pretreatment neurologic status is poor, patient
     will not likely regain function*

     *Extensive rehabilitation can aid in maximizing
     recovery or providing adaptive measures*

Suggested Readings

1. Belford K: Central nervous system cancers. In
   Groenwald SL, Frogge MH, Goodman M,
   Yarbro CH (eds): *Cancer Nursing: Principles and
   Practice* (4th ed). Boston: Jones and Bartlett,
   1997, pp 980-1035.

2. Grant R, Papadopoulos SM, Sandler HM, et al: Metastatic Epidural Spinal Cord Compression: Current Concepts and Treatment. *J Neurooncol* 19:79-92, 1994.

3. Glover D, Glick JH: Oncologic emergencies: Spinal cord compression. In Holleb AI, Fink DJ, Murphy GP (eds): *American Cancer Society Textbook of Clinical Oncology.* Atlanta: American Cancer Society, 1991, pp 513-533.

4. Fuller BG, Heiss J, Oldfield EH: Spinal Cord Compression. In DeVita VT, Hellman S, Rosenberg SA (eds): Cancer Principles and Practice of Oncology (5th ed). Philadelphia: Lippincott-Raven, 1997, pp 2476-2484.

CHAPTER 29

Superior Vena Cava Syndrome

Overview

Obstruction of superior vena cava is usually caused by

1. External compression by tumor or lymph nodes
2. Direct invasion of vessel wall by tumor
3. Thrombosis of vessel

Development of superior vena cava syndrome (SVCS) depends on

1. Degree and location of obstruction
2. Aggressiveness of tumor
3. Competency of collateral circulation

295

If untreated, SVCS can lead to

1. Thrombosis
2. Cerebral edema
3. Pulmonary complications
4. Death

SVCS may be presenting sign of malignancy

Occurs in 3% to 4% of oncology patients, yet 97% of SVCS cases are caused by cancer

Risk factors

1. Lung cancer and lymphoma
2. Thrombus formation around central venous catheter
3. Radiation-induced fibrosis of vessel

Approaches to Care

Assessment

1. Clinical manifestations

    * Elevated venous pressure and congestion result in signs and symptoms that are hallmarks of this syndrome

    * Severity of symptoms is related to rapidity of onset and adequacy of collateral circulation to reduce congestion

    * Early signs and symptoms

      Facial, trunk, and upper extremity edema

      Pronounced venous pattern on trunk

      Neck vein distention

Dusky blue color of face

Lips deeply cyanotic

Cough

* Late signs

Hoarseness

Stridor

Engorged conjunctiva

Headache

Dizziness

Visual disturbances

Changes in mental status

Acute respiratory distress

2. Diagnostic measures

* Chest x-ray film may reveal mediastinal mass or adenopathy

* Histopathologic diagnosis via biopsy or cytology if condition is not threatening

Treatment

1. Immediate intervention to prevent respiratory arrest includes

* High doses of fractionated radiation to mediastinum (300 to 400 cGy/day)

* Doses may be tapered but achieve cumulative dose of 3000 to 3500 cGy

2. For nonthreatening SVCS

* Tissue diagnosis first

* Subsequent appropriate cancer therapy (e.g., small-cell lung cancer is chemosensitive and thus treated; if unresponsive, then radiation is given)

3. Steroids are sometimes given to further reduce edema
4. Anticoagulants can prevent thrombosis secondary to decreased blood flow through vessel
5. Antifibrinolytics are sometimes given to reduce intramural thrombi
6. Catheter-induced SVCS is treated with fibrinolytic agents (streptokinase, urokinase, tissue plasminogen activator)
7. Surgical procedures, bypass graft, and stent placement are reserved for person with good prognosis for whom other options have been exhausted
8. Maintain adequate cardiopulmonary status
9. Monitor progression of SVCS
10. Reduce patient's anxiety
11. Avoid invasive or constrictive procedures of upper extremities

    * Take blood pressure measurements on thigh

    * Perform venipuncture on lower extremities

12. Administration of vesicant or irritant chemotherapy agents is controversial because lower extremities are used; surgical cannulation of femoral vein is safest route if administration is necessary
13. Provide fluid therapy and diuresis therapy to avoid overload and further venous congestion

14. Position patient with head of bed elevated to help maximize breathing and allay anxiety
15. Provide calm environment with visible support, reinforcement of temporary nature of patient's physical appearance, and clear understanding of treatment plan
16. Resolution of syndrome usually occurs within 24 to 72 hours after therapy is initiated; if syndrome does not respond, thrombus formation is suspected and surgical intervention may be needed
17. Routine follow-up care is usually all that is needed once SVCS is resolved with effective therapy

Suggested Readings

1. Ingle RJ: Lung cancers: In Groenwald SL, Frogge MH, Goodman M, Yarbro CH (eds). *Cancer Nursing: Principles and Practice* (4th ed). Boston: Jones and Bartlett, 1997, pp 1260-1290.
2. Dietz KA, Flaherty AM: Oncologic emergencies. In Groenwald SL, Frogge MH, Goodman M, Yarbro CH (eds): *Cancer Nursing: Principles and Practice* (3rd ed). Boston: Jones and Bartlett, 1993, pp 810-813.
3. Schaefer SL: Oncologic complications: Superior vena cava syndrome. In Otto SE (ed): *Oncology Nursing*. St. Louis: Mosby Year Book, 1991, pp 468-526.
4. Greenberg S, Kosinski R, Daniels J: Treatment of SVC thrombosis with rTPA. *Chest* 99(5):1298-1301, 1991.

CHAPTER 30

Syndrome of Inappropriate Diuresis

Overview

Syndrome of inappropriate diuresis (SIAD) or secretion of inappropriate antidiuretic hormone (SIADH) is described as tumor production of ADH or arginine vasopressin (AVP) resulting in

1. A syndrome of hyponatremia
2. Urine inappropriately higher in osmolality than the plasma
3. High urinary sodium despite serum hyponatremia.

Normally the body maintains fluid volume and concentration within a very narrow range regulated by the effect of the neurohypophyseal peptide arginine vasopressin (AVP) on the kidney.

When AVP is present the collecting duct is permeable to water resulting in water reabsorption and concentrated urine.

Suppression of AVP leads to urine dilution

1. Excess AVP stimulation leads to water intoxication from an expanded extracellular volume, serum hypo-osmolality, hyponatremia, and hypertonic urine.

SIADH is more commonly referred to as SIAD or syndrome of inappropriate diuresis to reflect that vasopressin may not be the only agent to effect sodium excretion.

Excess ADH can result from

1. Ectopic production
2. Abnormal stimulation of hypothalamus-pituitary network
3. ADH effects on kidney that are mimicked or enhanced

Results of water intoxication

1. Drop in plasma osmolality
2. Dilutional hyponatremia
3. Increased urinary excretion of sodium
4. Further hyponatremia

About 1% to 2% of cancer patients develop syndrome of inappropriate diuresis

Risk factors

1. Often associated with small-cell lung cancer, which accounts for 80% of the cases
2. Only about 9-14% of patients with small-cell lung cancer have full-blown SIAD.
3. Often presenting symptom of lung cancer
4. Other cancers associated with SIAD:

   * Non-small cell lung cancer
   * Gastrointestinal cancers (esophagus, pancreas, colon)
   * Carcinoid
   * Squamous cell carcinoma of the head and neck
   * Thymoma
   * Lymphoma
   * Hodgkin's disease
   * Bladder cancer
   * Prostate cancer
   * Sarcoma

5. Other factors can induce SIAD by increasing AVP production

   * Cyclophosphamide directly affects the renal tubule
   * Vincristine
   * Morphine
   * Nicotine

* Ethanol
* Cisplatin is associated with SIADH, but mechanism is unknown

6. Other risk factors

* Pulmonary and central nervous system infection
* Neurologic trauma
* Anesthesia
* Prolonged intubation
* Brain tumors

Approaches to Care

Assessment

1. Clinical manifestations: The severity of SIAD usually correlates with the extent of malignant disease

* Early symptoms and signs

   Thirst

   Muscle cramps

   Headache

   Lethargy

   Anorexia

* Late symptoms and signs

   Nausea, vomiting

   Weight gain without edema

   Hyporeflexia

Confusion

Oliguria

Seizures

Coma

2. Diagnostic measures

  ∗ Blood and urine chemistries confirm
     diagnosis

     Serum sodium level, < 130 mEq/l

     Plasma osmolality, < 280 mOsm/kg

     Urine osmolality, > 330 mOsm/kg

     Urine sodium level, > 20 mEq/l

  ∗ Water load test can be done by
     administering specific amount of water and
     measuring urine output, osmolality, and
     specific gravity; this is not done if patient is
     symptomatic or serum sodium is less than
     125 mEq/l

Interventions

1. Measures are dependent on severity of
   syndrome and patient's general condition
2. If possible, initiate systemic chemotherapy
   immediately
3. Tumor control is only truly effective measure
   to reverse tumor-induced ectopic syndrome
4. Since most chemotherapy regimens require
   hydration, control fluid levels carefully
5. If hyponatremia is mild to moderate (serum
   sodium level of 120–134 mEq/l) and patient is

clinically stable, fluid restriction of 800 to 1000 ml every 24 hours is effective

6. If hyponatremia is severe (serum sodium level below 115 mEq/l) and/or patient is unstable, more aggressive intervention is needed

  * Restrict fluid to 500 ml every 24 hours

  * Administer hypertonic 3% saline solution intravenously

  * Give furosemide intravenously

  * Once fluid/electrolyte balance and neurologic status are stabilized, begin chemotherapy

7. SIADH that persists despite initial therapy may be treated with demeclocycline (900-1200 mg/day)

  * Inhibits action of ADH

  * Induces reversible diabetes insipidus

  * Absorption is affected by foods high in calcium

  * Should be taken on empty stomach

8. Lithium carbonate stimulates diuresis by impairing the effect of AVP on the renal tubule (Not often used due to side effects)

9. Nursing measures

  * Administer and manage chemotherapy

  * Educate patient's family

  * Provide support to patient and family

10. Self-care measures

    * Restrict fluid
    * Measure intake and output
    * Recognize signs of hyponatremia
    * Know when to contact physician

11. If untreated, SIADH can lead to seizure, coma, and death

12. Overall prognosis is related to underlying cause and effectiveness of therapy directed toward it

Suggested Readings

1. Haapoja IS, Paraneoplastic Syndromes. In Groenwald SL, Frogge MH, Goodman M, Yarbro CH (eds): *Cancer Nursing: Principles and Practice* (4th ed). Boston: Jones and Bartlett, 1997, pp 702-720.

2. Block JB: Paraneoplastic Syndromes. In Haskell CM, Berek JS (eds): Cancer Treatment (cd. 4) Philadelphia, Saunders, 1995, pp 245-264.

3. Becker KL, Silva OL; Paraneoplastic endocrine syndromes in Becker KL (ed): *Principles and Practice of Endocrinology and Metabolism* (2nd ed). Philadelphia: Lippincott, 1995, pp 1842-1852.

4. Poe CM, Taylor LM: Syndrome of inappropriate antidiuretic hormone: Assessment and nursing implications. *Oncol Nurs Forum* 16(3):373-382, 1989.

CHAPTER 31

Tumor Lysis Syndrome

Overview

Complication of cancer therapy that occurs most commonly in patients with tumors that have a high proliferation index and are highly sensitive to chemotherapy. When many rapidly proliferating cells are lysed they release intracellular contents (uric acid) into the circulation

When rapidly dividing cells are lysed, they release intracellular contents into the circulation

Degree of metabolic abnormality depends on renal function

Metabolic abnormalities can develop alone or in combination

1. Hyperuricemia can lead to renal tubular obstruction/acute renal failure
2. Hyperkalemia can lead to lethal cardiac arrhythmias
3. Hyperphosphatemia may result in acute renal failure
4. Hypocalcemia (caused by hyperphosphatemia) can cause muscle cramps, cardiac arrhythmias, and tetany

Risk factors

1. Most commonly occurs with high-grade lymphoma or lymphoblastic leukemia

   * These cells are highly chemosensitive
   * These cells rapidly lyse during induction therapy
   * Immature lymphoblasts contain abnormally high levels of phosphorous

2. Rapidly growing solid tumor that undergoes profound cell destruction
3. Acute or chronic myelogenous leukemia
4. Non–Hodgkin's lymphoma
5. Large tumor burden
6. High white blood cell count
7. Lymphadenopathy
8. Splenomegaly
9. Elevated lactate hydrogenase

Approaches to Care

Assessment

1. Clinical manifestations

   * Early symptoms and signs

     Weakness, paresthesia

     Muscle cramps

     Nausea, vomiting, diarrhea

     Lethargy

   * Late symptoms and signs

     Ascending flaccid paralysis

     Bradycardia, hypotension

     Oliguria, anuria, edema

     Hematuria, crystalluria

     Azotemia, flank pain

     Carpopedal spasm, laryngospasm

     Tetany, convulsion

2. Diagnostic measures

   * Close monitoring of metabolic parameters enables early identification; factors are levels of

     Potassium

     Uric acid

     Phosphorus

     Blood urea nitrogen

Calcium

Creatinine

* Assess baseline renal function

Interventions

1. Control of hyperuricemia

   * Begin allopurinol administration at 600 to
     900 mg/day and reduce to half that dose
     after 3 to 4 days

2. Urinary alkalinization

   * Maintain a urine pH of 7 by addition of 50
     to 100 mEq of $NaHCO_3$ to each liter of
     intravenous fluid

   * Acetazolamide, 250 to 500 mg intravenous
     daily, if above measure is ineffective or
     serum HCO_3 is more than 27 mEq/l

   * Discontinue urinary alkalinization once
     hyperuricemia is corrected (serum uric acid
     <10 mg/dl)

3. Forced diuresis

   * Maintain urine flow at more than 150 to 200
     ml/hour with infusion of 5% dextrose 0.5
     NS at 200 ml/hour

   * Initiate low-dose dopamine and diuretics in
     patients with pre-existing evidence of fluid
     retention (marked edema or ascites) or
     oliguria

   * Do not insert Foley catheter unless patient
     has altered mental status or evidence of
     urinary retention

4. Maintain fluid balance

    * Avoid fluid overload: administer
      intravenous furosemide (20 to 100 mg every
      4 to 8 hours) if urine output falls below
      fluid intake

    * Obtain daily weights

    * Maintain scrupulous records of intake and
      output

5. Monitoring of blood chemistries

    * Serum electrolyte, blood urea nitrogen,
      creatinine, uric acid, calcium, phosphorous,
      and magnesium levels should be
      determined every 6 to 8 hours during the
      first 72 hours after chemotherapy

6. Acute hyperkalemia

    * Initiate intravenous infusion of hypertonic
      glucose and insulin and sodium
      polystyrene sulfonate (Kayexalate) and
      furosemide

7. Hyperphosphatemia

    * Initiate hypertonic glucose and insulin
      infusion and oral antacids

8. Resolution occurs when metabolic parameters
    return to normal

Suggested Readings

1. Dietz KA, Flaherty AM: Oncologic
   emergencies. In Groenwald SL, Frogge MH,

    Goodman M, Yarbro CH (eds): *Cancer Nursing: Principles and Practice* (3rd ed). Boston: Jones and Bartlett, 1993, pp 821-824.

2. Camp-Sorrell D, Chemotherapy: Toxicity Management. In Groenwald SL, Frogge MH, Goodman M, Yarbro CH (eds): *Cancer Nursing: Principles and Practice* (4th ed). Boston: Jones and Bartlett, 1997, pp 385-425.

3. Simmons ED, Somberg KH: Acute tumor lysis syndrome after intrathecal methotrexate administration. *Cancer* 67:2062-2065, 1991.

4. Marcus SL, Einzig AI: Acute tumor lysis syndrome, prevention and management. In Dutcher JP, Wiernik PH (eds): *Handbook of Hematologic and Oncologic Emergencies*. New York: Plenum, 1987, pp 9-16.

5. Warrell RP, Metabolic Emergencies. In DeVita VT, Hellman S, and Rosenberg SA, (eds). *Cancer Principles and Practice of Oncology* (5th ed). Philadelphia: Lippincott-Raven, 1997, pp 2486-2496.

PART IV

The Care
of Individuals
with Cancer

CHAPTER 32

AIDS-Related Malignancies

Overview

30% to 70% of patients with acquired immunodeficiency syndrome (AIDS) develop a malignancy

Four most common malignancies in AIDS are

1. Kaposi's sarcoma (KS)

    * More predominant in homosexual and bisexual men

    * Mean survival duration is 72 weeks

    * Etiologic factors may include

Sexually transmitted agent

Virus (cytomegalovirus has been found in KS lesions)

2. Non–Hodgkin's lymphoma (NHL)

   * French Registry of human immunodeficiency virus–associated tumors reported that 33% of patients with AIDS had NHL

   * Risk factors include

   Epstein-Barr virus

   Therapeutic immunosuppression

3. Central nervous system (CNS) lymphoma

   * Most patients are immunocompromised

   * Rare malignancy, accounting for 0.3% to 2% of newly diagnosed lymphomas

   * Cell of origin is same as that causing NHL

4. Invasive squamous cell cancer (SCC) of the cervix

   * High prevalence of cervical intraepithelian neoplasia (CIN) and human papillomavirus (HPV) in women with HIV

   * Usual risk factors associated with SCC of cervix do not correlate with the HIV-infected population

   * In 1993, Centers for Disease Control added this diagnosis to the surveillance definition of AIDS

Approaches to Patient Care: Kaposi's Sarcoma

Assessment

1. Clinical manifestations

   * Multicentric skin lesions on any part of body

   * Pigmentation ranges from brown, brown-red, and purple to dark red and violet

   * Lesions may be raised nodules or flat and painless

   * Visceral and lymphatic involvement

   * Progressive disease can result in

     Enlarging lesions

     Severe edema resulting from compromised lymphatic drainage and blood circulation

     Protein-losing enteropathy caused by gastrointestinal involvement

     Respiratory distress because of lung involvement

2. Diagnostic measures

   * Self-observation of cutaneous lesions

   * Biopsy suspicious lesions

   * Histologic examination confirms diagnosis

Interventions

1. Treatment is complex

   * Need to control tumor without exacerbating immunodeficiency

* Radiation therapy for local control of lesions

* Chemotherapeutic agents, alone or in combination may be beneficial

* Responders to interferon include

  Patients with CD4 counts higher than 200/mm3

  No "B" symptoms (fever, night sweats, weight loss)

  No prior AIDS diagnosis

2. Nursing care

   * Determine patient's risk group and whether KS is first diagnosis

   * Consider psychosocial aspects

   * Aggressively assess potential complications

     Side effects from chemotherapy are more severe in AIDS patients

     If severe jaw pain occurs with first dose of vincristine, discontinue drug

   * Realistic goals are necessary because of manipulative and drug-seeking behavior of some patients

Approaches to Patient Care: Non–Hodgkin's Lymphoma

Assessment

1. Clinical manifestations

* Usually presents with advanced disease involving extranodal sites (CNS, bone marrow, bowel, and anorectum)

* Peripheral lymphadenopathy may be absent

* Majority of patients present with high-grade lymphoma

2. Diagnostic measures

* Biopsy specimen determines diagnosis and classification

* Staging work-up includes

  History, physical examination

  Laboratory tests

  Chest x-ray

  Bone marrow biopsy

  Lumbar puncture

  Computed tomographic (CT) scans of chest, abdomen, and pelvis

Interventions

1. Grade of tumor determines treatment options

* Low-grade tumors are uncommon

* Intermediate-grade tumors are treated with chemotherapy or radiation therapy

* High-grade tumors are treated with combination chemotherapy and CNS prophylaxis

2. Nursing care

* Care is same as for those with non–AIDS-related NHL
* Patients with bulky, high-grade disease are at risk for tumor lysis syndrome, which may occur 24 hours after chemotherapy
* Patients at risk for tumor lysis syndrome should receive

  Vigorous hydration (300 to 500 ml/hr)

  Allopurinol intravenously or by mouth

  Urine output monitored every hour

  Serum chemistry levels monitored every 6 hours

  Sodium bicarbonate if ordered

Approaches to Patient Care: Primary CNS Lymphoma

Assessment

1. Clinical manifestations

   * Confusion
   * Lethargy
   * Memory loss
   * Alterations in personality and behavior
   * Hemiparesis
   * Aphasia
   * Seizures and focal neurologic symptoms

2. Diagnostic measures

* CT and magnetic resonance imaging (MRI) reveal single or multiple discrete lesions

* Toxoplasmosis titers and VDRL tests rule out toxoplasmosis and syphilis

Interventions

1. Whether or not patient is treated, outcome remains same

   * Survival ranges from 1.7 to 5.5 months

2. Nursing care

   * Monitor focal findings, motor incoordination, and cognitive deficits

   * Establish safe environment in acute and home setting

   * Provide emotional support to patient and family

   * Plans may be needed for skilled nursing care facility

   * If patient is legally incompetent, legal guardian must be appointed

Approaches to Patient Care: Invasive Squamous Cell Cancer of the Cervix

Assessment

1. Clinical manifestations

   * HIV infected women are more likely to have advanced disease at presentation

2. Diagnostic measures

 * Cervical pap smear

Interventions

1. Surgery, radiotherapy and chemotherapy
2. More research is needed in this area

Suggested Readings

1. Moran T: AIDS-related malignancies. In Groenwald SL, Frogge MH, Goodman M, Yarbro CH (eds): *Cancer Nursing: Principles and Practice* (4th ed). Boston: Jones and Bartlett, 1997, pp 845-862.
2. Miles SA, Aboulafia DM, Mitsuyasu RT: AIDS-related malignancies. In DeVita VT, Hellman S, Rosenberg SA (eds): *Cancer: Principles and Practice of Oncology* (5th ed). Philadelphia: Lippincott-Raven, 1997, pp 2445-2467.
3. Stanley H, Fluetsch-Bloom M, Bunce-Clyma M: HIV-related non-Hodgkin's lymphoma. *Oncol Nurs Forum* 18:875-880, 1991.
4. Jacob JL, Baird BF, Haller S, et al: AIDS-related Kaposi's sarcoma: Concepts of care. *Semin Oncol Nurs* 5:263-275, 1989.

CHAPTER 33

Bladder
Cancer

Overview

Second most common urologic cancer after prostate cancer

Occurs in men more often than in women and incidence is higher in white men

Average age at diagnosis is 65

Risk factors include

1. Cigarette smoking
2. Occupational exposure to industrial chemicals

3. Exposure to schistosomiasis (rare in U.S.)
4. Exposure to other carcinogenic agents

Approximately 90% to 95% are transitional cell carcinoma

Grading of bladder tumors helps to predict recurrence (i.e., low-grade have slower growth rate and better prognosis)

5-year survival ranges from 87% for those with localized disease to 9% for those with distant metastasis

Approaches to Care

Assessment

1. Clinical manifestations

   * Gross hematuria

   * Dysuria

   * Urinary frequency, urgency, and burning

   * Decrease in urinary stream

   * Flank, rectal, back, or suprapubic pain

2. Diagnostic measures

   * Intravenous pyelogram (excretory urogram)

   * Cystoscopy provides view of tumor, biopsies, and bladder washings for cytology and flow cytometry

   * Computed tomographic (CT) scan, bone scan, and chest x-ray

✳ Serum chemistries

Interventions

1. Treatment selection depends on stage and grade of tumor

   ✳ Carcinoma in situ treatment options are

   Transurethral resection

   Intravesical therapy with thiotepa, Calmette-Guérin bacillus, mitomycin C, or doxorubicin

   Radical cystectomy with urinary diversion

   ✳ Superficial, low-grade tumors

   More than 70% of patients present with superficial tumors

   Treatment options are

      Transurethral surgery with resection and fulguration

      Intravesical therapy with thiotepa, Calmette-Guérin bacillus, mitomycin C, or doxorubicin

      Laser therapy

      Partial cystectomy, which preserves bladder and male erectile function

   ✳ Invasive tumors

   Treatment options are

      Radiation alone or in combination with chemotherapy for nonsurgical candidates

      Radical cystectomy with urinary diversion with or without pelvic lymph node dissection

      Combination chemotherapy for metastatic disease

✳ Types of urinary diversion

Ileal conduit

Loop stoma

Continent urinary diversion allows patient to control voiding and urinary reflux after cystectomy

  Kock pouch

  Indiana reservoir

2. Sexual dysfunctions caused by radical cystectomy

  ✳ Body image affected by stoma and appliance

  ✳ Penile prosthesis may help erectile impotence

  ✳ Intercourse is restricted in women and clitoral sensation may be altered

3. Nursing care involves

  ✳ Preoperative selection of stoma site and teaching self-catheterization

  ✳ Postoperative care depends on method of urinary diversion or bladder substitution

  ✳ Urinary diversion with ileal conduit

    Assess viability of stoma

    Appliance must be worn at all times

      Pouch should adhere for 3 days before changing

Good skin care is essential

✳ Continent urinary diversion

Produces much mucus and needs regular irrigation in early postoperative period; mucus decreases over time

No appliance necessary

Patient teaching focuses on self-catheterization of pouch; stoma care; and care of catheter

Suggested Readings

1. Lind J, Hagan L: Bladder and kidney cancer. In Groenwald SL, Frogge MH, Goodman M, Yarbro CH (eds): *Cancer Nursing: Principles and Practice* (4th ed). Boston: Jones and Bartlett, 1997, pp 889-915.
2. Hossan E, Striegel A: Carcinoma of the bladder. *Semin Oncol Nurs* 9:252-266, 1993.
3. Razor B: Continent urinary reservoirs. *Semin Oncol Nurs* 9:272-285, 1993.

CHAPTER 34

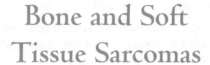

Bone and Soft Tissue Sarcomas

Overview

2000 new cases of bone cancer and 6000 new cases of soft tissue sarcoma are diagnosed annually

Risk factors

1. High dose radiation, such as that used in cancer therapy, has been linked to the development of bone and soft tissue sarcoma
2. Chemicals, such as vinyl chloride gas, arsenic, and dioxin (Agent Orange), have been associated with soft tissue sarcomas

3. Family history is implicated in both bone and soft tissue sarcomas
4. Paget's disease is a risk factor, primarily for bone tumors
5. Skeletal maldevelopment and abnormal skeletal growth patterns are associated with bone sarcomas
6. Genetic predisposition may be a risk factor for certain sarcomas

Common bone tumors:

1. Osteosarcoma (osteogenic sarcoma)

   * Most common osseous malignant bone tumor
   * Greatest incidence between 10 and 25 years of age
   * Incidence twice as high in men compared with women
   * Incidence increased in adults with Paget's disease
   * Most common sites are distal end of femur, proximal end of tibia, and proximal end of humerus
   * Metastasizes primarily to lungs
   * 5-year survival rates are low (10% to 20%)
   * Adjuvant chemotherapy after surgery demonstrates a significant increase in disease-free survival

2. Chondrosarcoma

   * Accounts for approximately 14% of malignant bone tumors

* Occurs between ages 30 and 60 in males only
* Associated with syndromes of skeletal maldevelopment
* Most frequent sites are pelvic bone, long bones, scapula, and ribs
* Most remain localized and slow growing
* If metastasis occurs, it is usually to lungs

3. Fibrosarcoma

* Accounts for fewer than 7% of primary malignant bone tumors
* Rare in children
* No gender predominance
* Paget's disease and therapeutic radiation may be predisposing factors
* The femur and the tibia are the most common sites of occurrence
* Metastasis occurs primarily to the lungs
* Surgery is the treatment of choice
* Fibrosarcomas are considered to be radioresistant

4. Ewing's sarcoma

* Accounts for 6% of all malignant bone tumors
* 80% are diagnosed in individuals between the ages of 5 and 15; 66% more males are affected than females
* Commonly located in pelvis and diaphyseal or metadiaphyseal regions of long bones

* Metastasis may be present in nearly 20% of individuals at diagnosis

Common soft tissue sarcomas

1. Include

    * Malignant fibrous histiocytoma
    * Liposarcoma
    * Fibrosarcoma
    * Synovial sarcoma
    * Rhabdomyosarcoma
    * Leiomosarcoma

2. Soft tissue sarcomas occur primarily in the extremities; some also occur in the head and neck or retroperitoneum
3. Nodal metastasis is common
4. Most metastases occur to the lungs within the first 2 years of treatment

Metastatic bone tumors

1. Primary tumors that metastasize to bone include

    * Lung
    * Gastric
    * Breast
    * Colon
    * Prostate
    * Pancreatic
    * Kidney
    * Testicular
    * Thyroid

2. More common sites of metastases include
   * Spine
   * Pelvis
   * Ribs

3. Tumors spread to bone from the primary tumor by three basic routes

   * Direct extension to adjacent bones
   * Arterial embolization
   * Direct venous spread through the pelvic and vertebral veins (Batson's plexus)

Approaches to Patient Care

Osteosarcoma

1. Assessment

   * Clinical manifestions

     Typically presents as pain and a mass

     Pain is more severe at night

     Limb becomes swollen with dilated superficial veins

     Weight loss and anemia may be seen

     Pathologic fractures may occur

   * Diagnostic measures

     Elevation in serum alkaline phosphatase level is common

     Bone scans

     Arteriography

Computed tomographic (CT) scan

Fluoroscopy

Magnetic resonance imaging (MRI)

Biopsy

CT scan of chest and regional nodes for metastatic disease

2. Treatment

* Chemotherapy

   Adjuvant chemotherapy after surgery significantly prolongs disease-free interval

   Chemotherapy protocols include doxorubicin, high-dose cyclophosphamide, ifosfamide, cisplatin, or high-dose methotrexate with leucovorin rescue; drugs are given intravenously or intra-arterially

   Preoperative chemotherapy effectiveness is assessed at time of tumor resection

   If there is high degree of tumor necrosis, chemotherapy is continued postoperatively

   The greater the necrosis, the greater the survival

   Improved response with chemotherapy has sparked interest in limb salvage surgery

* Surgery

   Amputations are indicated for patients with large, invasive tumors of extremities

   Types

      Immediate fitting prosthesis

- Rigid dressing and cast are applied to stump at time of surgery
- Socket on distal end of cast attaches to prosthetic unit

Delayed fitting

- Individual fitted with temporary or intermediate prosthesis at approximately 3 to 6 weeks
- Ambulation with weight-bearing is encouraged
- 3 months after surgery, individual is fitted with permanent prosthesis

Hemipelvectomy

Phantom limb pain

35% of patients experience phantom limb pain

Severe cramping, throbbing, or burning pain in various areas of amputated limb

Occurs for 1 to 4 weeks after surgery

May be triggered by fatigue, excitement, sickness, weather change, and stress

Incidence is greater when amputation site is more proximal

Pain worsens over time for 5% to 10% of amputees

Resection of pulmonary metastases with follow-up chemotherapy has resulted in increased survival

Reconstruction techniques after bone resection

Arthrodesis: fusion

Arthroplasty: bone allograft or metallic implant

Allograft: bone graft to provide scaffold in which new host bone to may grow

* Radiation is reserved for palliation of inoperable tumors

Chondrosarcoma

1. Assessment

   * Clinical manifestations

     *Medical advice is usually sought for slow-growing mass with intermittent dull, aching pain at
     tumor site*

     May be a firm enlargement over affected area

     Joints may be swollen and exhibit restricted motion

   * Diagnostic measures

     Bone scan

     Arteriography

     CT scan

     Fluoroscopy

     MRI

     Biopsy

     CT scan of chest and regional nodes for metastatic disease

2. **Treatment**

* If tumor is of central origin and has not extended through cortex, wide resection and reconstruction are considered

* Limb salvage surgery or amputation are options

* Chondrosarcomas are generally avascular; consequently, intravenous chemotherapy is not usually beneficial

* Radiation has limited effectiveness

Ewing's sarcoma

1. Assessment

   * Clinical manifestations

     Examination usually reveals palpable and tender mass

     Temperature may be increased over the mass and small superficial blood vessels may be visible

     Individual often has history of pain that has become increasingly severe

     Patients often present with fever and anemia

   * Diagnostic measures

     Patients may present with high erythrocyte sedimentation rates and leukocytosis, indicating aggressive disease

     Radiographic studies of the bone

2. Treatment

   * Radiation or surgery, or both, in combination with chemotherapy, is treatment of choice

* Ewing's sarcoma is radiosensitive and responds well to variety of antineoplastic agents

  Ifosfamide

  Vincristine

  Actinomycin

  Cyclophosphamide

  Doxorubicin

* Surgery combined with radiotherapy improves local control rate and can decrease need for extremely high radiation doses

* Limb salvage and amputation are both options

Soft Tissue Sarcomas

1. Assessment

   * Patients present with a painless mass, unless the tumor is impinging on nerves, blood vessels, or viscera

   * Pulmonary assessment includes history of hemoptysis, chest pain, or cough

   * Assess family history, exposure to toxic substances, and history of Paget's disease

2. Diagnostic Measures

   * MRI, CT scan, and ultrasonography are useful in determining size and density of a soft tissue mass

   * Open or incisional biopsy is the most common type of biopsy used for diagnosis

3. Treatment

  * Surgery and radiation are the treatment of choice for local control

  * Preoperative chemotherapy may be given intra-arterially to shrink the tumor

  * Combination chemotherapy (doxorubicin, cyclophosphamide, or ifosfamide) as adjuvant therapy may improve long-term survival

Metastatic bone tumors

1. Assessment

  * Clinical manifestations

    Initial presentation may include

      Complaints of dull, aching bone pain, which increases steadily as day progresses, and is worst at night

      Tumor weakens bone and can result in pathologic fracture

      Pain, both local and leg pain, is most often seen in spine metastases

      Neurologic dysfunction can precede pain in lesions of thoracic spine (e.g., heavy limb sensation, leg buckling)

  * Spinal compression may lead to paralysis; may present as pain, hyperreflexia, weakness of lower limbs, sensory loss, and loss of bowel and bladder control

  * Tenderness or warmth, or both, over lesion may be found on physical examination

* Diagnostic measures

  Conventional radiography

  Bone scan

  Biopsy is not necessary if appearance of lesion is consistent with known primary tumor

  Biopsy is indicated in absence of known or suspected primary tumor

  Hypercalcemia in presence of normal alkaline phosphatase level is associated with breast carcinoma

  Elevations of serum acid phosphatase occur with prostatic cancer

  Additional imaging with MRI, CT, or myelogram may be required

2. Treatment

   * Surgery

     Goals

       Augment material strength of bone, increasing resistance to fracture

       Improve functional use of the part

       Resume ambulatory status

       Even a bedridden patient with metastatic carcinoma and a femur fracture would benefit from surgery because of pain relief and increased mobility

       Prophylactic pinning of impending pathologic hip fracture reduces complications

     Indications for surgical intervention of metastatic spinal disease

Intractable pain unresponsive to nonoperative management

Progressive neurologic changes during or after radiotherapy

Presence of radioresistant tumor

Decompression of neural element, or spinal instability

* Radiation

Goals

Shrink tumor to facilitate surgical intervention

Palliate pain

Postoperatively, to kill tumor cells and allow surgical implant to maintain anatomic alignment

* Chemotherapy

May be used to reduce tumor cell mass

* Nursing care

Stump care

Elevate stump for 24 hours after surgery to prevent edema

Patient should lie in prone position 3 to 4 times per day to prevent joint contractures

Initiate exercises to maintain muscle tone and prevent edema, joint contractures, and muscle atrophy on first postoperative day

Wrap stump with elastic bandages or stump shrinkers

Patient should dangle at side of bed and transfer to chair as tolerated

Patient should begin crutch walking as soon as possible

Sutures or staples removed approximately 2 weeks after surgery

Wash stump and prosthesis with mild soap and water

Inspect stump daily for redness, blisters, or abrasions

Patient sees prosthetist every 4 to 6 weeks for first postoperative year

Phantom limb sensation

Apply heat to stump

Apply pressure with elastic bandages

Administer tranquilizers, muscle relaxants, or local anesthesia

Recommend psychotherapy and behavioral therapy

Suggest hypnosis, nerve blocks, sympathectomy cordotomy, acupuncture, biofeedback, and transcutaneous nerve stimulation

Posthemipelvectomy care

Mobilization usually begins on second or third postoperative day

Permanent prosthesis may be fitted within 12 weeks

Bucket prosthesis is fabricated to facilitate sitting in absence of ischium

Suggested Readings

1. Piasecki PA: Bone and soft tissue sarcoma. In Groenwald SL, Frogge MH, Goodman M, Yarbro CH (eds): *Cancer Nursing: Principles and Practice* (4th ed). Boston: Jones and Bartlett, 1997, pp 863-888.

2. Brennan MF, Casper ES, Harrison LB: Soft Tissue Sarcoma. In Devita VT, Hellman S, Rosenberg SA (eds): *Cancer Principles and Practice of Oncology* (5th ed). Philadelphia: Lippincott-Raven, 1997, pp 1738-1782.

3. Malawer MM, Link MP, Donaldson SS: Sarcomas of Bone. In Devita VT, Hellman S, Rosenberg SA (eds): *Cancer Principles and Practice of Oncology* (5th ed). Philadelphia: Lippincott-Raven, 1997, pp 1789-1816.

4. Mazanet R, Antman K: Sarcomas of soft tissue and bone. *Cancer* 68:463-473, 1991.

5. Piasecki P: The nursing role in limb salvage surgery. *Nurs Clin North Am* 26:33-41, 1991.

6. Williamson V: Amputation of the lower extremity: An overview. *Orthop Nurs* 11:55-65, 1992.

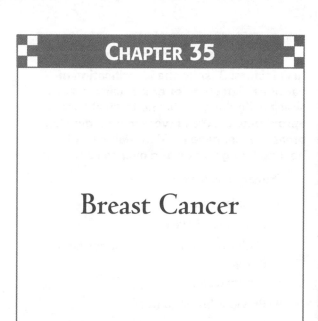

CHAPTER 35

Breast Cancer

Overview

Leading cause of death in women 40 to 44 years of age. Incidence in U.S. is 1 in 8 women; incidence varies across the country More than 70% of breast cancers occur in women 50 years of age and older Second leading cause of cancer deaths in women; lung cancer is first

Mortality rates have begun to decline; more decline in white women compared with African-American women

Risk factors: Despite the identification of various risk factors for breast cancer, specifically the genetic and familial factors, aproximatelly 50% of women who develop breast cancer have no identifiable risk factors beyond being female and over the age of 50

1. Primary risk factors

   * Female gender

   * Older than 50 years

   * Native of North America or northern Europe

   * Family history

   * Previous breast cancer

   * Breast cancer in two or more first-degree relatives

   * Bilateral or premenopausal breast cancer in first-degree relative

   * Breast cancer susceptibility genes, which appear to be transmitted in an autosomal dominant manner

   * Mutations of BRCA1, BRCA2, and the p53 tumor suppressor gene are associated with a markedly increased risk of breast cancer

2. Secondary risk factors

   * Postmenopausal obesity

   * Menarche before age 12 years; menopause after age 55

   * First full-term pregnancy after age 35

- ∗ Use of oral contraceptives before age 20 and persisting for 6 or more years
- ∗ Ionizing radiation exposure to chest before age 35
- ∗ Benign breast disease

3. Other risk factors

- ∗ Nulliparity
- ∗ Ingestion of more than two alcoholic drinks per day
- ∗ High-fat diet in adolescence may be a risk factor; no association between fat consumption and breast cancer risk in adults has been found

Prevention of breast cancer

1. Chemoprevention is the use of a chemical agent such as tamoxifen to prevent breast cancer in women with high-risk
2. Prophylactic mastectomy may be appropriate for some women who are at high genetic risk and psychologically distraught over the possibility of having breast cancer

Types of breast tumors

1. 48% of all breast cancers are adenocarcinomas located in upper outer quadrant of breast
2. Infiltrating ductal carcinoma

- ∗ Prominent lump; stony hardness on palpation
- ∗ Primarily affects women in early fifties
- ∗ 10-year survival rate is 50% to 60%

3. Invasive lobular carcinoma

   * Multicentric bilaterality in 30% of patients
   * Accounts for 5% to 10% of all breast cancers
   * Primarily affects women in their fifties
   * 10-year survival is 50% to 60%

4. Tubular carcinoma

   * Uncommon; 2% of all breast cancers
   * Well-differentiated adenocarcinoma
   * Primarily affects women over age 55
   * Microcalcification often present, facilitating early detection on mammography

5. Medullary carcinomas

   * Account for 5% to 7% of all breast cancers
   * Primarily affects women younger than 55 years
   * Lymph node involvement in 40% at diagnosis
   * Well circumscribed, rapid growth rate, bilaterality

6. Mucinous (colloid) carcinomas

   * Uncommon; 3% of all breast cancers
   * Primarily affects women 60 to 70 years old
   * Characterized by large pools of mucin with small islands of tumor cells
   * Slow growing, bulky

7. Other malignant breast tumors

* Sarcomas
* Invasive cribriform
* Papillary carcinoma
* Paget's disease
* Apocrine
* Inflammatory breast cancer

Classification and staging of breast cancer

1. Nodal involvement determined only by pathologic evaluation
2. Breast cancer staged clinically on basis of primary tumor characteristics, physical examination of axillary nodes, and presence of distant metastases

   * Stage I is localized disease only
   * Stage II has axillary nodal involvement on pathology or no nodes but a larger tumor
   * Stage III is more advanced locoregional disease with no distant metastasis
   * Stage IV involves presence of distant metastasis

Approaches to Patient Care

Assessment

1. Clinical manifestations of malignant disease

   * Boundaries of mass not distinct
   * Lack of mobility of mass, resulting from tumor infiltration into adjacent tissues

* Pain not common; may be present in advanced disease

* Pink or bloody, spontaneous, unilateral discharge from nipple

* Elevation or retraction of nipples, resulting from tumor fixation or infiltration into underlying tissues

* Skin dimpling or retraction, possibly caused by invasion of suspensory ligaments and fixation to chest wall

* Heat and erythema may signify inflammatory breast carcinoma

* Skin edema (peau d'orange) may be caused by tumor invasion and obstruction of dermal lymphatics

* Ulceration of skin with secondary infection

* Isolated skin nodules signify tumor invasion of blood vessels and lymphatics

* Ulceration or scaly skin at nipple may indicate Paget's disease

* May also include, or may be limited to, signs of local or distant metastatic disease

2. Diagnostic procedures

* Screening mammogram

   Used for routine observation of breast tissue in asymptomatic women

   Goal is to detect malignancy before it becomes clinically apparent

   Recommended every 1 to 2 years for women aged 40 to 49; yearly for women aged 50 and older

* Diagnostic mammogram

  Done when patient reports specific symptoms, when clinical findings are suspicious, or when screening mammogram reveals abnormality

  Information learned on diagnostic mammography may prevent need for open biopsy

* Sonogram or ultrasound

  Used to determine whether lesion is solid or cystic

  Not used for screening purposes because they are less sensitive and less specific compared to mammograms

  Useful for pregnant women and young women whose breasts are dense with fibroglandular tissue that may obscure a lesion on mammogram

* Magnetic resonance imaging (MRI)

  May allow earlier detection because it can determine smaller lesions and finer detail

  Complement to mammography and clinical examination in distinguishing benign from malignant lesions and avoiding benign biopsy

* Positron emission tomography (PET)

  PET employs metabolic activity to image the breast tissue; it may be able to differentiate benign and malignant disease

* Fine-needle aspiration

  Used when abnormality is known to be solid or to determine whether lump is cystic

Surgical biopsy may still be necessary for lesion that is not malignant on histologic study but remains clinically suspicious

* Stereotactic needle-guided biopsy

  Most often used to target and identify nonpalpable lesions detected on mammography

  Permits diagnosis of benign disease without trauma or scarring related to open biopsy

* Wire localization biopsy

  Primarily used to assist in location of nonpalpable lesions for excisional biopsy

* Open biopsy

  Objective to remove lump or identified area along with small amount of surrounding normal tissue

  Reasons for excisional biopsy

    Sonogram reveals solid lesion

    Insufficient findings on histologic or cytologic studies, or both

    Suspicious findings on mammogram or on clinical examination

    Patient with probable low-risk lesion requests biopsy to alleviate anxiety

Interventions

1. Most women with stage I and stage II breast cancer with positive or negative nodes can be treated by breast conservation procedures

- ✴ Lumpectomy
- ✴ Partial mastectomy
- ✴ Segmental resection
- ✴ Quadrantectomy and breast irradiation

2. Invasive breast cancer requires level I and II axillary node dissection for staging purposes; Sentinal node biopsy may be adequate to determine need for adjuvant chemotherapy

3. Women who require chemotherapy because of the characteristics of their tumor in the absence of palpable axillary nodes may not require an axillary node dissection, since information gained would not add to the decision making process

4. Modified radical mastectomy is indicated for

- ✴ Larger tumors
- ✴ Multicentric disease
- ✴ When cosmesis is otherwise not achievable
- ✴ Women who prefer not to undergo radiation therapy
- ✴ Involves removal of all breast tissue and nipple areola complex and level I and II axillary node dissection
- ✴ May also be used as definitive treatment after local recurrence in those who fail conservative surgery and radiation therapy

5. Carcinoma in situ is being detected more often by mammography

* Lobular carcinoma usually discovered during removal of benign tumor

  Tends to be bilateral and multicentric

  If not treated, there is 50% chance of invasive breast cancer developing in either breast

  Management includes

  Observation with annual mammography and frequent physical examination

  Ipsilateral mastectomy with contralateral biopsy

  Bilateral mastectomy with immediate or delayed reconstruction

* Intraductal carcinoma generally presents as clustered microcalcifications on mammography

  Rarely carries risk of axillary node involvement

  Treatment options

  Total mastectomy with low axillary dissection

  Wide excision followed by radiation

  Wide excision alone with tumor-free margins

  Invasive carcinoma develops in 30% to 50% of patients within 10 years when treated with excisional biopsy alone

  Total mastectomy and low axillary dissection are recommended as definitive treatment in presence of poor prognostic indicators, such as ploidy and high nuclear grade

6. Conservative surgery plus radiation now considered preferable to mastectomy in most women

Criteria for selecting patients are feasibility of resecting primary tumor without causing major cosmetic deformity and likelihood of tumor recurrence in breast

* Radiation more successful when all gross disease has been resected

* When chemotherapy is also used, radiation is usually given when chemotherapy is finished to avoid skin toxicity

7. Adjuvant systemic therapy for

* Early stage I and stage II breast cancer

Metastatic disease occurs in 30% to 50% of women with node-negative breast cancer

Systemic chemotherapy is indicated for women with large, poorly differentiated tumors

The rate of disease recurrence in node-negative disease can be reduced 20% to 50% by adjuvant therapy

Potential drug combinations

Methotrexate, followed in 1 hour by 5-fluorouracil (M-F); leucovorin calcium (L) is given beginning 24 hours after administration of methotrexate

Regimen given on days 1 and 8, every 28 days, for 6 cycles

Appears to be less toxic in terms of myelosuppression and hair loss; does not have the leukemogenic potential of alkylating agent–containing regimen

Cyclophosphamide, methotrexate, and 5-fluorouracil (CMF)

Methotrexate and 5-fluorouracil given on days 1 and 8; cyclophosphamide given orally for 14 days; CMF combination administered every 28 days for 6 cycles

Myelosuppression, hair loss, and gonadal dysfunction more pronounced with this regimen, because cyclophosphamide is alkylating agent

More effective than M-F+L regimen for treatment of premenopausal women; this may be because of alkylating agent

Doxorubicin and cyclophosphamide, given in standard doses every 3 weeks for 4 cycles

Treatment option for women with high-risk node-negative disease or with node-positive disease

Dose-intensive regimens may be employed, using colony-stimulating factors to boost marrow recovery

The taxanes (docetaxel and paclitaxel) are promising new agents in breast cancer and currently being combined with other standard therapies to determine efficacy in the adjuvant setting

Treatment with tamoxifen may be appropriate, based on patient age (over 50) and estrogen receptor status

May be given alone or in combination chemotherapy

Goserelin acetate (luteinizing hormone-releasing hormone antagonist), with or without tamoxifen and chemotherapy, may be used to

treat premenopausal women with estrogen
receptor-positive, node-positive disease

* Locally advanced (stage III) breast cancer

*More likely to metastasize to distant sites; larger
primary tumor and greater number of
histologically positive lymph nodes, greater risk
of metastasis*

Distant metastasis is presumed present at
diagnosis

*Treatment of choice is modified radical
mastectomy*

*Clinical characteristics include large or
unresectable primary tumors, fixed axillary
nodes, internal mammary node involvement,
and presence of classic inflammatory carcinoma*

Potential treatment options

Primary chemotherapy to evaluate tumor's in
vivo response to drug combination; if
significant tumor reduction occurs, surgery
may be indicated, followed by chemotherapy
and radiation therapy

High-dose chemotherapy with autologous
bone marrow rescue and support with
hematopoietic growth factor is currently
treatment option for women with high-risk
advanced disease

8. Chemotherapy

* Premenopausal women often experience
symptoms of menopause because of effects
of drugs on ovarian function

Less subjective sexual desire and arousability

Vaginal dryness

Vulvar or vaginal soreness

Light spotting after intercourse

Hot flashes or night sweats

Sleep disturbances

* Measures to minimize symptoms of ovarian failure

Lower thermostat in home, especially in sleeping area

Avoid highly seasoned foods

Avoid caffeine and alcohol

Dress in loose-fitting clothing and in layers

Take vitamin E, 800 international units per day, or Bellergal-S, 1 tablet twice daily, or use clonidine patch, 0.1 to 0.2 mg

* Some women experience weight gain and may require nutritional counseling

* Fatigue is common complaint; advise patient to rest and begin regular exercise program, such as walking, aerobics, or water aerobics

* Nausea and vomiting are predictable based on type of chemotherapy or hormone therapy; give prophylactic treatment with antiemetics, such as granisetron or ondansetron, dexamethasone, and lorazepam in combination

* High doses of doxorubicin and cyclophosphamide, with or without a

taxane, causes hair loss, with total hair loss occurring 17 to 21 days after first treatment; CMF treatment causes more gradual thinning over the six-course treatment and may not require patient to use wig

9. Radiation

* Generally begins 3 to 4 weeks after chemotherapy

* Side effects include fatigue and some nausea; primary side effects are skin changes and arm swelling

   Skin reactions occur in all patients and include itching, dryness, scaling, redness, and tenderness

      Dry desquamation can progress to moist desquamation with infection

* If chemotherapy is being given along with radiation, chemotherapy should be held until skin heals

10. Breast reconstruction

* Ideal candidate is woman with early-stage disease, no nodal involvement, and low-risk factors for recurrence

* Women who are pregnant or breastfeeding, or who have tissue abnormalities, infection, lupus, scleroderma, or uncontrolled diabetes are not candidates

* Those with radiation damage, vascularization problems, or who have inadequate tissue available are not eligible

* Procedures

Silicone implants are used when there is adequate skin for coverage after mastectomy

Ideal candidate is small-breasted and has minimum of ptosis on contralateral breast

Incision is made in previous scar and pocket is made beneath chest wall muscles, where silicone implant is placed

Complications

Contracture

Infection

Hematoma

Flap necrosis

Saline tissue expanders are used when there is inadequate supply of skin after mastectomy or when the breast is large and/or ptotic

Expander is placed behind muscles of chest wall using lines of mastectomy incision

Filling port is injected with saline over 6 to 8 weeks until device is overinflated by 50%; it is left overinflated for several months to allow for stretching and more natural contour

Expander is removed after several months and replaced with permanent prosthesis

Latissimus dorsi flap is used when adequate skin is not available at mastectomy site and/or if additional tissue is needed to fill supraclavicular hollow and create anterior axillary fold after mastectomy

Transverse rectus abdominis muscle flap, or "tummy tuck"

Incision is made over lower abdomen; abdominal muscle and fat are tunneled under abdominal skin to mastectomy site

Possible complications include hernia at donor site and flap necrosis

Obese patients, patients with circulatory problems, smokers, and patients over 65 are not candidates

Use of free flap entails removal of skin and fat from buttocks or lower abdomen and grafting them to mastectomy site

Main complication is failure to maintain sufficient perfusion during postoperative period; flap death occurs within 6 hours if flow is interrupted or cannot be sustained

Nipple areolar construction by using tissue from opposite breast or from like tissue on inner thigh or postauricular area

Tattooing may be necessary to darken skin

Raising and folding skin over itself creates more natural nipple projection, called skate flap

11. Breast cancer in men

* Similar to breast cancer in women in terms of epidemiology, natural history, treatment options, and response to treatment

* Occurs most commonly in men aged 50 to 70; most are estrogen receptor–positive

* Typically presents as infiltrating ductal carcinoma, fixed to underlying fascia and skin; nipple retraction and bloody discharge may be present

* Because it is usually first diagnosed at advanced stage, prognosis is generally poor

* Treatment is usually by modified radical mastectomy

* Hormonal manipulation is indicated, using tamoxifen, arimidex, or zoladex, unless disease is life-threatening or aggressive, indicating use of chemotherapy

12. Metastatic breast cancer

* Present at clinical diagnosis in approximately 10% of women diagnosed with breast cancer

* Disease metastasizes in 30% to 40% of women diagnosed and treated for potentially curable breast cancer; these women die of disease

* Relapse occurs within 2 years of diagnosis in most patients

* Median survival for patients with stage IV disease is 2 to 3 years

* Metastases most commonly occur to bone, specifically spine, ribs, and proximal long bones

   Pathologic fractures may occur, despite efforts to protect weakened bone

* Early symptoms of liver involvement include loss of appetite and abnormal liver function tests

* Pulmonary involvement may be manifested as nonproductive cough or shortness of breath

   Lymphangitic pulmonary spread is ominous sign of rapidly progressing disease

   Pleural effusions may progress slowly over time and may respond temporarily to drainage and sclerosing

* Metastasis to brain or meningeal carcinomatosis may present as seizures or cranial nerve palsies

* Management

   Judicious use of both local and systemic measures to palliate symptoms and improve patient's quality of life

   Initial choice of therapy is one that is least toxic with highest response rate

   Chemotherapy

      Candidates include women whose disease is hormone-receptor negative, who are refractory to hormone therapy, or who have aggressive disease in liver or pulmonary system

      Most chemotherapy regimens include some combination of methotrexate, 5-fluorouracil, cyclophosphamide, doxorubicin, paclitaxel, docetaxel, navelbine or mitoxantrone every 3 to 4 weeks

After response to treatment is seen, interval between treatments can be lengthened; therapeutic benefit is not compromised, but cost and inconvenience to patient are decreased

Endocrine therapy

Hormone minipulation is the main treatment for metastatic disease that is estrogen-receptor-positive

Steroid hormones promote tumor growth in hormonally dependent breast cancer; therefore, surgical removal of hormone source or medical manipulation of hormone balance results in significant tumor regression, but not cure

Antiestrogen therapy

Tamoxifen is the most widely used antiestrogen; it acts by binding to the estrogen receptor, thereby blocking the effects of the endogenous estrogens; if the woman has been on tamoxifen and experienced recurrence, the tamoxifen would be stopped and another form of hormone manipulation would be given

Side effects of tamoxifen are minimal, including hot flashes, mild nausea, fluid retention and ankle swelling, vaginal cornification, and postmenopausal bleeding

Androgen therapy

Most effective in women who are 5 or more years postmenopause

Indicated for treatment of soft-tissue or bone metastases

Therapeutic effect exerted through androgen's opposition of endogenous estrogens

Side effects of fluoxymesterone include fluid retention, erythrocytosis, and masculinization

Patient may experience increased libido, hair loss, amenorrhea, nausea, and anorexia

Progestin therapy

Megestrol acetate is progesterone agent that is tolerated as well as tamoxifen and has comparable efficacy

Side effects of megestrol acetate include weight gain, hot flashes, vaginal bleeding, hypercalcemia, tumor flare, and thrombophlebitis

Corticosteroid therapy

Corticosteroids are often used as adjunct to radiotherapy in cerebral metastasis, in chemotherapy for liver and lung metastasis, and in management of hypercalcemia

Side effects include bleeding peptic ulcer, muscle weakness, hypertension, infection, edema, glucose intolerance, moon faces, and osteoporosis

Oophorectomy

Generally reserved for women with recurrent or metastatic disease, if disease is not life-threatening at time of recurrence. Zoladex injections may be used instead of an oophorectomy, because they essentially create a medical oophorectomy. The effect of zoladex is not as immediate as oophorectomy

Surgical oophorectomy, tamoxifen, or ovarian radiation are equally effective in removing endogenous estrogen sources in premenopausal women and in some perimenopausal women

Secondary endocrine ablation

Aminoglutethimide effectively blocks adrenal corticosteroid synthesis and inhibits peripheral conversion of androgens to estrogens

Hydrocortisone replacement needed because of adrenal suppression

Side effects include lethargy and skin rash, which subside if hydrocortisone dose is increased temporarily

Arimidex is an aromatase inhibitor that is well-tolerated without need for cortisol replacement. Side effects include slight headache, hot flashes, tiredness, and fatigue

Symptom Management and Supportive Care

Bone metastasis

1. Bone pain may occur before skeletal changes are seen on radiography; bone scan is sensitive method to detect metastatic disease
2. CA 15-3, a human breast tumor associated antigen, is a sensitive marker in breast cancer

metastases and may be used as a screening
test for bone metastases

3. Metastasis to bone marrow is indicated by
anemia, thrombocytopenia, leukocytosis, and
immature forms of nucleated red blood cells;
serum alkaline phosphatase level and serum
calcium level may be increased

4. Patients who have back pain should undergo
thorough neurologic examination and
radiographic evaluation of spine; MRI may
determine whether spinal cord compression is
present or imminent

5. Radiation to symptomatic areas often results
in effective pain relief and bone recalcification

6. Surgery may stabilize bone by internal fixation
or replacement to avoid impending fracture

7. Bisphosphonates (etidronate, clodronate,
pamidronate) are used to inhibit bone
demineralization and to reduce incidence of
bone pain, hypercalcemia, and even metastatic
disease progression in bone; treatment is
usually monthly

Spinal cord compression

1. Constitutes emergency because of potential for
paraplegia; pain is usually present for several
weeks before other neurologic symptoms
develop

2. May be secondary to epidural tumor or altered
bone alignment because of pathologic fracture

3. Imminent compression should be suspected in
those with known bone disease; progressive
back pain associated with weakness;
paresthesias; bowel or bladder dysfunction; or
gait disturbances

4. MRI should be done as soon as diagnosis is suspected to determine exact level of compression and to identify other occult extradural lesions

5. Optimal results and return to ambulation can be accomplished by combined therapy with radiotherapy and corticosteroids

6. When spinal cord compression develops and diagnosis of epidural metastasis is in doubt, or if patient's neurologic state worsens as radiotherapy progresses, decompression laminectomy may be performed

Brain metastasis and leptomeningeal carcinomatosis

1. Brain metastasis occurs in approximately 30% of patients

   * Signs include

     Headaches

     Motor weakness

     Seizures

     Mental changes

     Visual defects

   * Symptoms of brain metastasis can be managed by total-brain irradiation and corticosteroids

2. Leptomeningeal carcinomatosis

   * Most common signs are

     Headache

     Cranial nerve dysfunction

Changes in mental status

* Treatment is with total-brain irradiation followed by intraventricular-intrathecal chemotherapy, usually through Ommaya reservoir

Chronic lymphedema

1. Occurs most commonly in women who have undergone axillary dissection followed by radiation therapy
2. Most often caused by infection and tumor recurrence or tumor enlargement in axilla
3. Management techniques include

    * Elevation of arm

    * Use of elastic stockinette

    * Therapeutic massage

    * Intermittent compression with extremity pump

    * Weight loss and weight control may be advised

Suggested Readings

1. Chapman D, Goodman M: Breast cancer. In Groenwald SL, Frogge MH, Goodman M, and Yarbro CH (eds). *Cancer Nursing: Principles and Practice* (4th ed). Boston: Jones and Bartlett, 1997, pp 916-979.
2. Parker SL, Tong T, Bolden, J, et al: Cancer Statistics *CA: Cancer J Clin* 46: 5-28, 1996.
3. Henderson BE, Bernstein L: Endogenous and exogenous hormonal factors. In Harris JR,

Lippman ME, Morrow M, and Hellman S (eds): *Diseases of the Breast*. Philadelphia: Lippincott-Raven, 1996, pp 185-200.

4. Harris J, Morrow M, Norton L: Malignant tumors of the breast. In DeVita VT, Hellman S, and Rosenberg SA (eds). *Cancer Principles and Practice of Oncology* (5th ed). Philadelphia: Lippincott-Raven, 1997, pp 1557-1616.

5. Bonadonna G: Evolving concepts in the systemic adjuvant treatment of breast cancer. *Cancer Res* 52:2127-2137, 1992.

6. Weber B: Genetic testing for breast cancer. *Sci Am* 3:12-21, 1996.

7. Leitch AM, Dodd GD, Costanza M, et al: American Cancer Society Guidelines for the Early Detection of Breast Cancer: Update 1997. *CA Cancer J Clin* 47:3,150-154, 1997.

CHAPTER 36

Cancer of the Kidney

Overview

Accounts for only 3% of all cancers
Occurs most often between 50 to 60 years of age
Risk factors include

1. Smoking (cigarette, cigar, pipe)
2. Occupational exposure to hydrocarbon, cadmium, asbestos, and lead
3. Analgesic use
4. Genetic link to renal cell carcinoma

Common forms of kidney cancer are

1. Renal cell carcinoma, which accounts for 75% to 85% of kidney cancers
2. Cancer of renal pelvis

Approaches to Patient Care

Assessment

1. Clinical manifestations

   * Hematuria
   * Pain
   * Palpable abdominal mass
   * Fever
   * Weight loss
   * Anemia
   * High association with paraneoplastic syndromes
   * 30% to 50% of patients have metastasis at diagnosis

2. Diagnostic measures

   * Radiographs of kidney, ureter, and bladder
   * Nephrotomograms
   * Excretory urogram (intravenous pyelogram)
   * Ultrasound
   * Computed tomographic (CT) scan
   * Urinary cytology
   * DNA flow cytometry

Interventions

1. Treatment of renal cell carcinoma includes

   * Surgical removal of kidney and tumor thrombus if there is vena caval involvement

   * Regional lymphadenectomy is controversial

   * Interleukin-2 and interferon therapy are under investigation

   * Radiotherapy, surgery, chemotherapy, hormonal therapy, and immunotherapy have been used for advanced disease

2. Treatment of cancer of renal pelvis

   * Nephroureterectomy is standard treatment

   * Use of radiation therapy is controversial

3. Preoperative and postoperative nursing care of patient undergoing radical nephrectomy is similar to that of individual undergoing laparotomy

Suggested Readings

1. Lind J, Hagan L: Bladder and kidney cancers. In Groenwald SL, Frogge MH, Goodman M, Yarbro CH (eds): *Cancer Nursing: Principles and Practice* (4th ed). Boston: Jones and Bartlett, 1997, pp 889-915.
2. Davis M: Renal cell carcinoma. *Semin Oncol Nurs* 9:267-271, 1993.

CHAPTER 37

Central Nervous System Cancers

Overview

Involvement of tumor within central nervous system (CNS) as result of primary or metastatic disease is associated with high degree of morbidity and mortality

Increased survival of persons with cancer have resulted in relative increase in incidence of brain metastases from primary sites, such as lung, breast, and colon

More than 50% of primary brain tumors are malignant

Approximately 17,900 new primary brain and CNS tumors are diagnosed each year in U.S., and account for approximately 2.5% of cancer-related deaths

The incidence of spinal cord tumors is about 15% of CNS tumors with the majority being from metastatic cancers

Etiology

1. Genetic disorders
   * Neurofibromatosis type 1 is an autosomal dominant disorder associated with optic nerve gliomas, astrocytomas, ependymomas, and meningiomas
   * Li-Fraumeni syndrome and Turcot syndrome are both autosomal dominant disorders associated with an increased incidence of gliomas, medulloblastomas, and pituitary adenomas
2. Chemical and environmental factors
   * Chemicals in pesticides, herbicides, and fertilizers
   * Synthetic rubber, petrochemicals, industrial chemicals, and nuclear energy
3. Viral factors
   * Epstein-Barr virus
   * Acquired immunosuppression, e.g. primary central nervous system lymphoma
4. Radiation to brain for benign conditions or for acute lymphoblastic leukemia

Types of CNS tumors

1. Primary brain tumors arise from neuroepithelial cells (glial cells) and are called gliomas

   * Astrocytomas

     Incidence greatest in fifth and sixth decades of life

     60% of all primary brain tumors

     Generally arise in cerebral hemispheres

     Range from well differentiated to highly malignant

   * Oligodendrogliomas

     5% of primary brain tumors

     Usually located in frontal lobe

     Slow-growing

     Commonly present as seizure disorder

   * Glioblastomas

     These are high-grade astrocytomas with a necrotic component

     Arise in cerebral hemispheres; predilection for frontal lobe

     Occur in fifth and sixth decades of life

     Typically grade IV tumor

2. Primary central nervous system lymphomas (PCNSL)

   * Number of cases of PCNSL is increasing,

with the highest incidence occurring in patients with AIDS, in which PCNSL develops in up to 6% of cases

* Commonly disseminates within the CNS and eyes

* Generally presents with lethargy, confusion, apathy, headache, nausea, vomiting, hemiparesis, visual disturbances, and seizures

3. Metastatic brain tumors

   * 24% of patients with systemic cancer develop brain metastases

   * Brain metastases occur at three sites

     The brain parenchyma

     The skull and dura

     The leptomeninges

   * Most brain metastases occur to the cerebral hemispheres

   * Symptoms include: headache, nausea, vomiting, change in level of consciousness, diminished cognitive function, personality changes, hemiparesis, language problems, and seizures

4. Meningeal carcinomatosis from adenocarcinoma of breast, lung, gastrointestinal tract, melanoma, and childhood leukemia occurs in approximately 4% of cases

5. Spinal cord tumors
   * Metastatic spinal cord tumors most often

originate from cancers of the breast, lung, prostate, kidney, and multiple myeloma

* Spinal cord compression occurs either by direct extension into the epidural space, by vertebral collapse, or by direct extension through the vertebral foramina

* Thoracic spine is the most frequent site of epidural spinal cord compression.

Approaches to Patient Care

Assessment

1. Clinical manifestations

   * Caused by increased intracranial pressure (ICP)

     Brain tumors displace components of intracranial cavity because of

     Tumor size

     Cerebral edema

     Obstruction of cerebrospinal fluid (CSF) pathways

     Clinical manifestations produced by effects of increasing pressure on nerve cells, blood vessels, and dura include

     Mental changes

     Papilledema

     Headache

     Vomiting

     Changes in vital signs

Prolonged increase in ICP produces nerve cell damage and cell death

* Caused by secondary effects of displacement of brain structures

    Shifting brain tissue causes compression damage, cerebral edema, and ischemia, causing effects that may be irreversible

    Two classifications of herniations

    Supratentorial herniations cause changes in level of consciousness and in ocular, motor, and respiratory signs

    Infratentorial herniations cause loss of consciousness and changes in cardiac and respiratory signs

* Focal effects

    Caused by direct compression of nerve tissue or destruction and invasion of brain tissues; deficits directly related to affected area of brain

    Focal or generalized seizures are major symptoms of brain tumors; first clinical manifestation of disease in many adults

* Patients with metastatic brain tumors commonly have headache first, followed by focal weakness, mental disturbances, and seizures; aphasia and visual abnormalities may also occur

2. Diagnostic studies

    * Document both focal and generalized symptoms

Examine each symptom with regard to location, onset, and duration (if applicable)

* Take baseline measurement of neurologic function

* CT views one plane of cranium over a few seconds

Photographs give exact location and size of nodules

Demonstrates amount of edema surrounding tumor

Less costly than MRI

* MRI allows multiplane imaging

Provides information regarding histology and pathology of lesions and extent of tissue invasion

Detects deep lesions and cyst formation, amount of edema surrounding tumor, and calcium aggregates

* Positron-emission tomography (PET) combines properties of conventional nuclear scanning with physical characteristics of positron-emitting radionuclides

Provides information about tumor metabolism, bloodflow, and oxygen and glucose use

* Clinical staging based on neurologic signs and symptoms and on results of diagnostic tests

* Pathologic staging based on results of

histopathologic studies, tumor grade, and microscopic evidence of completeness of tumor resection

Treatment

1. Surgery

   * Primary treatment for resectable primary brain tumors and some isolated metastatic lesions

   * Factors in evaluating surgical option

     Tumor location

     Tumor size

     Method of tumor spread

     Patient's general condition

     Patient's neurologic status

   * Goals of surgery

     Primary treatment

     Facilitation of nonsurgical therapy

       Partial resection debulks the tumor and relieves symptoms

     Treatment of metastatic brain tumors

   * Complications

     Intracranial bleeding

     Cerebral edema

     Water intoxication

   * Signs and symptoms of neurosurgery complications

Decreasing level of consciousness

Increased ICP

Progressive hemiparesis

Signs of herniation

Seizures

2. Radiosurgery

* Stereotactic radiosurgery is noninvasive technique that delivers a single large fraction of ionizing radiation to small, well-defined intracranial target—this technique is performed using a modified linear accelerator (gamma knife)

* A laser is used to vaporize the tumor

* Especially effective in treatment of tumors in or near sensitive target structures

3. Radiotherapy

* Used for both primary and metastatic disease; response is based on cell type and tissue of origin

* Corticosteroid therapy may be needed to relieve cerebral swelling and promote improvement of symptoms

* Presence of hypoxic malignant cells limits effectiveness of radiation therapy

* Administration of intraoperative radiation may help to shield normal tissue from radiation effects while exposing tumor to maximum radiation effects

* Three-dimensional conformal radiation therapy is a new method of high-precision

RT using CT information—the radiation dose is delivered to conform to the anatomic boundaries of the tumor.

4. Chemotherapy and related drugs

* Most chemotherapeutic agents do not cross blood-brain barrier

* Nitrosoureas are drugs that are lipid-soluble and can penetrate blood-brain barrier

* Certain chemotherapeatic agents are used to enhance the effect of radiation, e.g., 5-fluorouracl, BCNU

* Chemotherapy is indicated for histologic grade III or grade IV tumors

* Intraarterial, intrathecal, and intratumoral drug delivery may circumvent blood-brain barrier

5. General supportive measures

* Prepare family and home environment for patient to be cared for at home

* Cerebral edema

  Corticosteroids are usually prescribed

  Reduction of edema may occur over period of hours or days

  Less helpful in treatment of acutely increased ICP

  Osmotherapy is used to reduce amount of fluid in brain tissue

  Hyperosmolar agent such as mannitol is administered intravenously

Fluid intake is restricted

* Increased ICP

    Avoid Valsalva's maneuver, isometric muscle contractions, emotional arousal

    Elevate head of bed, avoid head rotation, neck flexion, and extension

    Avoid sneezing, coughing, straining

    Avoid hip flexion, prone position

    Monitor ICP level

* Seizures

    Provide prophylactic anticonvulsants

    Provide safe environment

    Prevent harm during seizure activity

    Provide skin and oral hygiene after seizure activity

* Personality changes

    Maintain normal function

    Maintain orientation with clocks, calendars

    Encourage use of remaining cognitive function

    Encourage social activities

* Loss of sensation

    Monitor for visual disturbances

    Monitor for hearing loss

    Maintain orientation

    Provide safe environment and clothing

* Disturbances in coordination

  Provide safety devices (bed rails, walker)

  Close off stairways

  Prepare physical surroundings for safety

* Poor nutrition and hydration

  Prepare small, attractive, frequent meals

  Provide dietary supplements

  Encourage frequent oral fluids

  Use alternative feeding routes, if necessary

* Need for supportive care

  Assess roles and family functioning

  Provide resources

  Educate and support

  Prepare for impending death

Suggested Readings

1. Belford K: Central nervous system cancers. In Groenwald SL, Frogge MH, Goodman M, Yarbro CH (eds). *Cancer Nursing: Principles and Practice* (4th ed). Boston: Jones and Bartlett, 1997, pp 980-1032.
2. Gilman S: Advances in neurology. *N Engl J Med* 326:167-176, 1992.
3. Berleur MP, Cordier S: The role of chemical, physical, or viral exposures and health factors in neurocarcinogenesis: Implications for epidemiological studies of brain tumors. *Cancer Causes Control* 6:240-256, 1995.

4. Swartz RB: Neuroradiology of brain tumors. In Wen PY, Black PM (eds): *Neurologic Clinics: Brain Tumors in Adults.* Philadelphia: Saunders, 1995, pp 723-756.

5. Wegmann JA: CNS tumors: Supportive management of the patient and family. *Oncology* 5:109-112, 1991.

CHAPTER 38

Cervical Cancer

Overview

Approximately 15,700 new cases and 4900 deaths from cervical cancer occurred in 1996 in U.S.

Mortality has decreased in women over age 45 but has increased in women under age 35

Overall incidence of invasive cancer has decreased by 50%

Incidence of carcinoma in situ (CIS) has dramatically increased since 1945

1. Over 65,000 new cases of CIS were diagnosed in 1996
2. Women in their 20s are most often diagnosed with cervical dysplasia
3. Women aged 30 to 39 are most often diagnosed with CIS
4. Women over age 40 are most often diagnosed with invasive cancer

Risk factors

1. Predominantly personal or lifestyle factors
2. Low socioeconomic groups
3. Smoking
4. Early sexual activity (before age 17)
5. Sexually transmitted infections
6. Higher titers of herpes simplex virus type 2 than controls
7. Human papillomavirus (HPV 16 and 18)
8. Multiple sexual partners
9. Spouse whose previous wife had cervical cancer
10. Maternal use of diethylstilbestrol
11. Immunosuppression
12. Multiparous
13. Spouse with cancer of penis
14. African American or Hispanic origin

Certain behaviors may actually lower risk of cervical cancer

1. Barrier-type contraception
2. Vasectomy
3. Recommended daily allowances of Vitamin A & C, betacarotene
4. Limited number of sexual partners
5. Sexual activity initiated at later age

Pathophysiology

1. 80% to 90% of cervical tumors are squamous
2. Cervical cancer is progressive disease
3. Begins with neoplastic alteration of cells at squamocolumnar junction
4. Gradually progresses to involve full thickness of epithelium and invade stroma
5. There are two major divisions for progression of cervical cancer:

   * Preinvasive or premalignant disease: CIN, cervical intraepithelial neoplasia (I, II, III)

   * Invasive or malignant disease

6. The Bethesda System is typically used to report cervical cytologic diagnosis

   * Two terms are used: CIN and SIL

7. CIN I, II, and III describe progression of disease and whether disease is considered invasive or malignant
8. Low-grade or high-grade SIL (squamous intraepithelial lesion) describes cellular changes

   * CIN I or low-grade SIL indicates dysplasia or atypical changes involving less than one-third thickness of epithelium

   * CIN II or high-grade SIL indicates dysplasia involving two-thirds thickness of epithelium

   * CIN III or high-grade SIL indicates severe dysplasia or CIS, involves up to full-thickness of epithelium

* CIN III is more likely to progress than CIN I or II; there is no way to predict which will progress

9. Invasive disease is malignant disease that extends beyond basement membrane
10. Cervical cancer can regress, persist, or invade
11. Invasive cancer spreads by three routes

* Direct extension: Throughout entire cervix, into parametrium, uterus, bladder, and rectum

* Lymphatic: obturator, hypogastric, external iliac, and then parametrial, presacral, and inferior gluteal nodes

* Hematogenous: Venous plexus, paracervical veins

12. Distant sites: Lung, liver, bone, mediastinal and supraclavicular nodes

Approaches to Care

Assessment

1. Clinical manifestations

* In preinvasive and early stages, asymptomatic except for watery vaginal discharge

* Later disease symptoms include

    Postcoital bleeding

    Intermenstrual bleeding

    Heavy menstrual flow

    Symptoms related to anemia

Foul-smelling, serous vaginal discharge

Pain in pelvis, hypogastrium, flank, leg

Urinary or rectal symptoms

* End-stage disease

   Edema of lower extremities

   Massive vaginal hemorrhage

   Renal failure

2. Diagnostic measures

   * Pap smear

      Most effective tool for assessing and diagnosing preinvasive disease and cervical cancer

      Recommended annually for all sexually active women or those over 18 years of age; pelvic exam also to be done

      Frequency of exams may be altered by individual's physician

   * If smear shows CIN or SIL, then next steps are

      Colposcopy

      Biopsy

      Possibly treatment

   * Staging is based on clinical findings, with confirmation from examination completed under anesthesia

      Initial staging is one of best prognostic indicators

      5-year survival rates (approximate) are

Stage I: 80.5%

Stage II: 59%

Stage III: 33%

Stage IV: 7%

* Clinical work-up for cervical cancer includes:

  Cervical biopsies

  Endocervical curettage

  Cystoscopy

  Proctosigmoidoscopy

  Metastatic work-up: Chest x-ray, intravenous pyelogram, barium enema, hematologic profile, liver scan, CT or MRI, node biopsies, DNA subtyping

Interventions

1. Accurate evaluation of extent of disease before treatment is critical
2. Treatment for CIN or SIL varies greatly from that for invasive disease
3. CIN or SIL treatment selection

   * Is based on extent of disease
   * Is based on woman's desire to preserve reproductive function
   * treatment options include:

     Cervical biopsy

     Electrocautery

     Cryosurgery

       Most used method

Painless

Low morbidity

Outpatient procedure

Patients experience watery discharge for 2 to 4 weeks

Laser surgery

80% to 90% of CIN or SIL can be eradicated

Less disease-free tissue removed

Slight discomfort

Little vaginal discharge

Heals in 2 to 3 weeks

Electrosurgery: loop diathermy excision (LEEP)

Increasingly popular

One outpatient visit

Minimal tissue ablation

Slight discharge

Cone biopsy

Removes cone-shaped piece of tissue from endocervix and exocervix

General anesthesia

Outpatient procedure

Diagnostic or therapeutic

Potential hemorrhage or perforation

Delayed complications include

Bleeding

Cervical stenosis

Infertility

Increased chances of preterm delivery

Complications relate to amount of endocervix removed

Hysterectomy for high-grade SIL

May be used for treatment of women who are beyond childbearing years or who do not wish to have more children

4. Invasive disease treatment

* Based on woman's age, medical condition, and extent of disease

* Either surgery or radiation can be used equally effectively for patients with early stage disease

* In general, stages IIb to IV are initially treated with radiotherapy

* Treatment selection is related to stage of disease

Stage Ia (microinvasive)

Hysterectomy: Abdominal or vaginal, for women who do not desire childbearing

Conization for patients who are poor surgical risks or prefer to preserve fertility

Stages Ib and IIa

Treatment selection is controversial, related to preserving ovarian function

Radical abdominal hysterectomy and pelvic lymphadenectomy: Ovarian function preserved; vagina more pliable than with radiation; shorter treatment time

Definitive radiation with external beam radiotherapy and/or intracavitary insertions

Stages IIb, III, and IV

Pretreatment staging laparotomy is controversial

Can identify candidates for specific therapies, but is plagued by complications and minimal improvement in survival

Alternative is extraperitoneal exploration for staging

High doses of external beam radiation with parametrial boosts: 5500 to 6000 cGy over 5 to 6 weeks; interstitial implants to supplement

Intracavitary radiation

Pelvic exenteration

Used only in selected group of patients with recurrent centralized disease not adherent to pelvic side walls or involving lymph nodes

Complications include

- Vaginal stenosis
- Cystitis
- Fistula
- Hemorrhage
- Stricture
- Abscess

Recurrent or persistent disease

About 35% of women have recurrent or persistent disease

Follow-up is critical, though recurrence is difficult to detect

Most recur within 2 years

75% of recurrences are local

25% of recurrences are distant sites

Signs include

Unexplained weight loss

Leg edema

Pain in pelvis or thigh

Serosanguinous vaginal discharge

Cough, hemoptysis, chest pain

Triad of weight loss, leg edema, and pelvic pain leads to grim outlook

Aim of treatment is palliation

Survival averages 6 to 10 months

Treatment for recurrent disease is

Surgery

Pelvic exenteration for central recurrence

Psychosexual and social rehabilitation needed

Postoperative problems include

- Embolism

- Pulmonary edema

- Cerebrovascular accident

- Sepsis

- Bowel obstruction

- Myocardial infarction

Chemotherapy

> Complicated by decreased pelvic vascular perfusion, limited bone marrow reserve, and poor renal function
>
> Response rates range from none to 48%
>
> No long-term benefit
>
> Response rates higher in patients with no prior chemotherapy or radiation
>
> Cisplatin has greatest single-agent activity; carboplatin may be used as first-line therapy
>
> Other agents include doxorubicin, dibromoducitol, ifosfamide, carboplatin
>
> Combination agents are not more effective than single agents
>
> Pelvic intra-arterial infusions have been tried
>
> Can be used as radiosensitizer, particularly hydroxyurea or cisplatin
>
> Biologic response modifiers are being investigated

Radiotherapy

> May be used to treat metastatic disease outside initial radiation field
>
> Selectively used within previous fields

Nursing managements

1. Essentials include

   * Education of patient
   * Pretreatment knowledge and understanding

* Treatment-induced complications and side-effects

* Counseling on sexuality issues and concerns

* Assessment of response and anticipation of recurrence

Suggested Readings

1. Walczak JR, Klemm PR, Guarnieri C: Gynecologic cancers. In Groenwald SL, Frogge MH, Goodman M, Yarbro CH (eds): *Cancer Nursing: Principles and Practice* (4th ed). Boston: Jones and Bartlett, 1997, pp 1163-1181.

2. Shingleton HM, Orr JW: *Cancer of the Cervix*. Philadelphia: JB Lippincott, 1995.

3. Fowler J, Montz FJ: Malignancies of the uterine cervix. In Cameron RB (ed): *Practical Oncology*. Norwalk, CT: Appleton & Lange, 1994, pp 364-376.

4. Thigpen R, Vance RB, Khansur T: Carcinoma of the uterine cervix: current status and future directions. *Semin Oncol* 21(suppl):43-54, 1994.

CHAPTER 39

Colon, Rectal, and Anal Cancers

Overview

Improvements in survival attributable to earlier diagnosis and decreased treatment-related morbidity

Overall 5-year survival rate of 62%

Incidence rate

1. Third most commonly diagnosed cancer in US; third leading cause of death from cancer

   * There are an estimated 134,500 new cases each year

2. There are 54,900 deaths each year resulting from colorectal cancer

Occurrence rate

1. Increases after age 40; rises sharply at age 55 and doubles each decade thereafter
2. Incidence and mortality among males is constant
3. Incidence and mortality among females is decreasing slightly

Risk factors

1. Age
2. Dietary factors appear to have dominant role

   * Dietary fat increases risk of colon cancer

   * High-fiber diets may decrease effects of fatty acids, increase fecal bulk and stool transit time, and hence reduce potential carcinogenic action

3. Alcohol consumption, particularly beer and whiskey
4. Occupational risks are not significant
5. Genetics

   * Familial adenomatous polyposis

   * Gardner's, Turcot, Peutz-Jeghers syndromes

   * Family history of colorectal cancer

   * Familial adenocarcinomatosis

6. Inflammatory bowel conditions

   * Ulcerative colitis

   * Crohn's disease

7. Radiation therapy to pelvis
8. Ureterosigmoidostomy leads to increased risk 25 to 30 years after surgery
9. Chemoprotective agents include ascorbic acid, cruciferous foods, calcium, aspirin, nonsteroidal anti-inflammatory drugs (NSAIDs), exogenous estrogen

Adenocarcinoma is most common histologic type

Most common anatomic sites affected are descending and sigmoid colon

Progression of disease does not relate to symptoms

1. Develops first in mucosa
2. Will invade locally by direct extension
3. Submucosal involvement leads to lymph and vascular spread
4. Liver is major site of metastases
5. Can spread to lungs, bone, brain

5-year disease-free rates in Dukes' classification system are

1. Dukes' A, more than 90%
2. Dukes' B, 70% to 85%
3. Dukes' C, 30% to 60%
4. Duke's D, 5% or less

Approaches to Care

Assessment

1. Clinical manifestations

* Relate to location of tumor
* Asymptomatic early in disease
* Tumors in ascending colon can become large before symptoms develop

    Fatigue, palpitations, iron deficiency anemia

    Palpable mass when lesion is large

* Tumors of transverse colon

    Constipation alternating with diarrhea

    Melena

    May lead to bowel obstruction and pain

* Tumors of sigmoid colon tend to obstruct

    Pain

    Nausea and vomiting

    Changes in bowel habits

    Melena

* Tumors of rectum

    Bleeding with bright red blood

    Sense of incomplete evacuation

    Tenesmus, sense of fullness

    Stool caliber becomes pencil-like

    Pain as tumor invades regionally

* Many patients have lymph node involvement at time of presentation

2. Diagnostic measures

    * Physical examination is focused on

Specific gastrointestinal symptoms

Prior medical and family risk factors

Digital examination of rectal area

Vaginal examination for fistulas

* Diagnostic studies

Endoscopic examination; proctosigmoidoscopy

Barium enema

Fecal occult blood testing

Hematologic studies

Chest x-ray

Carcinoembryonic antigen (CEA) levels

CA 19-9 assay

DNA content analysis by flow cytometry

Metastatic work-up: abdominal films and scans, liver function studies

* Classification and staging by Dukes' or tumor-node-metastasis (TNM) system; both are widely accepted

Interventions

1. Surgery is treatment of choice

   * Adequate margins and complete excision provide best outcomes

   * Preoperative preparation includes bowel cleansing

   * Common surgical procedures

     Right hemicolectomy for tumors of cecum and ascending colon

Transverse colectomy for tumors in middle and left transverse colon

Left hemicolectomy or partial colectomy for tumors of descending and sigmoid colon

Rectal cancer procedures are more specific to region

Low anterior resection for tumors of proximal and mid-rectal area

No need for permanent colostomy

External anal sphincter control maintained

Internal sphincter may be damaged, and complete continence may not be possible

Abdominal perineal resection for poorly-differentiated lesions and more advanced disease

Permanent colostomy is usually needed

Site selection is best done before surgery

Requires extensive adaptation to permanent colostomy

Associated with high morbidity

Requires temporary perineal wound for drainage

Associated with sexual dysfunction from nerve severance

Radiolabelled monoclonal antibodies can be used intraoperatively to identify occult disease

Laser therapy can be used for small tumors

Postoperative complications can include:

Anastomotic leak

Intra-abdominal abscess

Staphylococcal enteritis

Obstruction

Genitourinary tract injury

2. Chemotherapy

* 5-Fluorouracil (5-FU) is most commonly used cytotoxic agent

* 5-FU is administered by several routes: oral, intravenous, intraperitoneal, and intra-arterial

* Major side effects are hematologic and gastrointestinal

* 5-FU is commonly administered with other cytotoxic drugs

* Levamisole is used to enhance the effects of 5-FU

* Irinotecan is being studied for disease refractory to 5-FU

* Advanced colorectal cancer is treated with 5-FU

3. Immunotherapy

* Levamisole is an immunomodulator that enhances effect of 5-FU as adjuvant therapy for stage III colon cancer

* Alpha-interferon and γ-interferon, interleukin-2, and bacillus Calmette-Guérin (BCG) are being studied extensively

4. Radiation therapy

* Used as adjuvant therapy to prevent local recurrence
* Radiation can be used in preoperative, intraoperative, and postoperative treatment
* Radiation is used primarily to treat rectal cancers
* Preoperative radiation is given to decrease existing tumor burden
* Intraoperative radiation aims to reduce local recurrence
* Postoperative radiation is used most often with rectal tumors
* Combinations of radiation and 5-FU have increased effectiveness
* Most common injury to large bowel from radiation is proctosigmoiditis with symptoms of bleeding and tenesmus

Symptom Management and Supportive Care

Hepatic metastases

1. 70% of persons with colon cancer develop liver metastases
2. Symptoms are right upper quadrant pain, weight loss, anorexia, bowel changes, mass
3. CEA levels and liver function test levels may rise
4. Ultrasound and CT aid in diagnosis
5. Treatment involves a myriad of approaches:

* Surgical resection
* Cryotherapy
* Chemotherapy
* Radiotherapy
* Immunotherapy

6. Ascites can be treated with intermittent paracentesis
7. Pain from pressure on liver capsule can be reduced with radiation and aggressive use of pain medications
8. Pruritis from bile salt accumulation can be treated with increased fluid intake, topical anesthetics, and antihistamines

Ureteral obstruction

1. Occurs in 38% of cases
2. Presents with oliguria and elevated serum creatinine level
3. Cystoscopy and retrograde pyelogram used to diagnose
4. Urinary stents can provide relief
5. Nephrostomy tubes may be needed

Pulmonary Metastases

1. May present as solitary mass or multiple nodules
2. 85% of pulmonary metastases are asymptomatic
3. Chest x-ray to diagnose
4. Resection of metastatic area is best option, if possible
5. Poor prognosis if resection is not possible

Suggested Readings

1. Hoebler L: Colon and Rectal Cancer. In Groenwald SL, Frogge MH, Goodman M, Yarbro CH (eds): *Cancer Nursing: Principles and Practice* (4th ed). Boston: Jones and Bartlett, 1997, pp 1036-1054.

2. Beart RW: Colon and Rectum. In Abeloff MD, Armitage JO, Lichter AS, Niederhuber JE: *Clin Oncol.* New York: Churchill Livingston, 1995, pp 1267-1286.

3. Haskell CM, Lavey RS, Ramming KP: Colon and rectum. In Haskell CM: *Cancer Treatment* (4th ed). Philadelphia: WB Saunders, 1995, pp 469-497.

4. Fong Y, Blumgart LH, Cohen AM: Surgical treatment of colorectal metastases to the liver. *CA Cancer J Clin* 45:50-62, 1995.

CHAPTER 40

Endocrine Cancers

Overview

Most common endocrine malignancies are

1. Thyroid cancer

   * Rare; accounts for approximately 1% of total cancers and 0.2% of cancer deaths

   * Women have more than twice the risk of developing thyroid cancer

   * Most cases occur between ages 25 and 65

   * Higher incidence in adults who received head and neck irradiation during childhood or adolescence

* Medullary thyroid cancer associated with genetically transmitted multiple endocrine neoplasia (MEN) syndrome

* Types

Papillary carcinoma

Indolent, well differentiated

Survival measured in decades, even in patients with metastases

Cervical lymph node involvement usually occurs early in disease

Metastasis occurs to lungs and, less often, to bone

Occurs at all ages

Biologic behavior and prognosis vary by age; tumors in patients older than 40 years are more aggressive and rapidly growing

Death usually caused by recurrent or uncontrolled local disease, even with distant metastases

Follicular carcinoma

Tends to be more locally invasive than papillary form

Average age at diagnosis is 45 to 50

Cervical lymph node involvement common

Bone metastases more frequent

May retain ability to produce T3 and T4 thyroid hormones, causing hyperthyroidism

Poorer prognosis with tumors that have capsular or vascular invasion

Death usually caused by growth of local recurrences

Medullary carcinoma

Approximately 20% of cases occur as part of genetically transmitted MEN syndrome

Especially virulent

Incidence equal in both genders

Diagnosis usually made at age 45 to 50

Lymph node involvement is present in approximately 50% of cases; metastasis occurs later in lung, bone, and liver

Anaplastic carcinoma

Generally rapidly growing and lethal; death occurs within months of diagnosis

Females affected more often than males

Average age at diagnosis is 65

Local invasion is common

Metastasizes to lung

2. Pituitary tumors

* Rare

* Occur primarily in middle-aged and older adults

* Many adenomas are well differentiated, slow-growing, and confined, retaining their hormone-producing capabilities; however, tumor cells do not respond to normal regulatory mechanisms of body, producing hormones regardless of feedback from target organs

* Others are more aggressive, invading adjacent tissue and compressing vital structures

3. Adrenal tumors

   * Rare

   * Incidence same for men and women

   * In 60% to 70% of patients, functional tumors produce excessive amounts of corticosteroids

   * Types

     Adrenocortical carcinomas

       Aggressive malignancies; most patients have locally advanced or metastatic disease on diagnosis

       Most common sites of metastases are lung, liver, and lymph nodes

       Local tumor extension involves kidneys, liver, vena cava, pancreas, and diaphragm

     Pheochromocytomas

       Rare, catecholamine-secreting, benign or malignant tumors

       Occasionally associated with other endocrine tumors as part of MEN syndrome

       Genetic predisposition exists

4. Parathyroid tumors

   * Rare; account for 1% to 4% of all cases of primary hyperparathyroidism

   * Increased risk for those with previous head

and neck irradiation, especially in childhood

* Most are biologically functional and cause clinical effects of hypercalcemia because of hypersecretion of parathyroid hormone

* Prolonged survival has been seen, even in patients with metastatic disease

Approaches to Patient Care

Thyroid cancers

1. Assessment

   * Clinical manifestations

     Most commonly present asymptomatically with thyroid mass and cervical adenopathy

     Patients may have sensation of tightness or fullness in neck, which may progress to dyspnea or stridor, if trachea is compressed or infiltrated

     Hoarseness or dysphagia may result from infiltration or destruction of recurrent laryngeal or vagus nerves by malignant cells

     Pain is uncommon and is usually sign of advanced disease

   * Diagnostic evaluation

     Patient history includes family history, prior irradiation, and rate of tumor growth

     Physical examination includes checking thyroid and adjacent neck structures and regional lymph nodes for symmetry and palpating for masses

Patients with thyroid nodule should undergo examination of head and neck by laryngoscopy

Evaluation of altered hormone secretion

Symptoms of hyperthyroidism

> Fine tremors
>
> Lid lag
>
> Brisk tendon reflexes
>
> Increased appetite and weight loss
>
> Tachycardia
>
> Heat intolerance
>
> Proptosis
>
> Irritability
>
> Muscle weakness

Symptoms of hypothyroidism

> Dry skin
>
> Slowed speech
>
> Hair loss
>
> Bradycardia
>
> Cold intolerance
>
> Decreased reflexes
>
> Weight gain
>
> Constipation

Fine-needle aspiration is most widely used technique to evaluate nodular thyroid disease

Radionuclide imaging of thyroid provides information about its functional status

Normal thyroid tissue concentrates iodine and is labeled "warm," nonfunctioning nodules are "cold," and hyperfunctioning nodules are "hot"

Test does not distinguish benign from malignant nodules

If thyroid dysfunction is suspected, laboratory tests are obtained, including radioactive iodine uptake, T3 uptake, total T4, free T4, and thyroid-stimulating hormone (TSH)

TSH is suppressed by administration of thyroxine to reduce size of nodules and prevent prolonged TSH stimulation of thyroid

2. Treatment

* Thyroid malignancies are managed aggressively

* Total thyroidectomy

Results in fewer local recurrences and increases effectiveness of ^{131}I therapy

Recommended for those with medullary thyroid cancer because of high incidence of bilateral involvement of thyroid gland

May require tracheostomy and gastrostomy, which can be performed at time of initial surgery

If nodes are involved, lymph node dissection is indicated

Thyroid suppressive treatment is given for several weeks before surgery to induce atrophy of thyroid and reduce vascularity and hemorrhage at time of surgery

Postoperative complications

Hemorrhage because of high vascularity of gland

Place patient in semi-Fowler's position

Assess hourly for bleeding

Assess for increased pressure at surgical site

Evaluate patency of suction catheters

Measure fluids

Hypoparathyroidism caused by reduced function of parathyroid glands

Hypocalcemia

Monitor serum calcium daily

Replace calcium as necessary

Watch for signs including

- Numbness

- Tingling

- Cramps in extremities

- Stiffening

- Twitching

- Positive Chvostek's or Trousseau's sign

Potential damage to recurrent laryngeal nerve, causing temporary or permanent vocal cord paralysis, leading to respiratory obstruction

Keep tracheostomy set at patient's bedside for first 24 hours after surgery

Emergency tracheostomy may be required

* Radiotherapy

    ^{131}I for ablation or treatment, or both, after surgical resection

    Isotope concentrates in functional tumor tissue, facilitating cancer cell death

    Patient admitted to hospital for 48 hours, after which patient is no longer radioactive

    Complications

    Nausea and vomiting

    Fatigue

    Headache

    Bone marrow suppression

    Sialadenitis

    Rarely, pulmonary radiation fibrosis and leukemia

    External beam radiation may be useful in palliation of painful bony metastases

* Chemotherapy

    Only doxorubicin has shown any significant antitumor activity

* Follow-up of patients

    Long-term follow-up important because of risk of late recurrence

    Serum thyroglobulin and serial isotope scanning are useful in locating recurrent disease

    Measurement of basal and stimulated calcitonin levels is useful in locating recurrent medullary thyroid cancer

Pituitary tumors

1. Assessment

   * Clinical manifestations

     Alterations in hormonal patterns

     Symptoms of compression

       Headache

       Visual disturbances

       Functional impairment of cranial nerves

   * Diagnostic measures

     Complete evaluation of endocrine system to help define functional status of tumor

     High-resolution MRI provides information about tumor margins and tumor's effect on adjacent structures

     Angiography to evaluate lumen of blood vessels; indicated if there is any concern about aneurysm

2. Treatment

   * Surgery

     Treatment of choice is complete or subtotal resection followed by postoperative radiation therapy; achieves normalization of hormone levels most rapidly

       For most adenomas, trans-sphenoidal route is adequate, permitting selective removal of tumor and preservation of normal pituitary tissue

Complications

Diabetes insipidus

Cerebrospinal fluid leak

Meningitis

During recovery period, sneezing and nose blowing are contraindicated to minimize pressure on operative site

Pituitary hormone levels are measured after surgery to assess effectiveness of removal of hypersecreting tumor tissue

* Radiotherapy

Indicated

When tumor is not resectable

To manage patients with incompletely resected or recurrent tumors

For treatment of some patients with persistent hyperfunctioning endocrinopathies

Major complication is hypopituitarism

Monitor endocrine function continuously

* Pharmacotherapy

Dopamine antagonists or somatostatin analogs may be used to treat hypersecreting pituitary adenomas to reduce hormone levels and shrink tumor

Adrenal cortical carcinomas

1. Assessment

* Clinical manifestations

Patients with nonfunctional tumors usually have palpable abdominal mass and may have abdominal or back pain

Fever, weight loss, weakness, and lethargy are seen primarily in patients with advanced disease

Patients with aldosterone hypersecreting tumors were present with hypertension, hypokalemia, and hypernatremia

Most functional tumors result in Cushing's disease, virilization and feminization syndromes

* Diagnostic measures

Functional tumors are detected by immunoassays of hormone precursors and mature hormones

CT is used most commonly to localize tumors; it provides information about hepatic, renal, and vena cava involvement

MRI can be used to differentiate benign adenomas from adrenocortical carcinomas and pheochromocytomas

2. Treatment

* Surgery is treatment of choice and may be curative for localized disease

* Glucocorticoid treatment may be needed either temporarily or permanently

* Drugs used in treatment act either by causing necrosis of adrenal cortex (e.g., mitotane) or by blocking corticosteroid secretion (e.g., aminoglutethimide); either may be used as adjuvant therapy or for treatment of inoperable disease

* Chemotherapy has limited activity
* Radiation therapy does not improve overall survival, but may palliate symptoms of invasive or metastatic cancer

Pheochromocytomas

1. Assessment

   * Clinical manifestations

     Excess production of catecholamines accounts for most of tumor's clinical manifestations

     Sustained or paroxysmal diastolic hypertension may be present

     Other symptoms

     Headache

     Palpitations

     Sweating

     Anxiety

     Nausea and vomiting

   * Diagnostic measures

     Urinary secretion tests for circulating catecholamines or their metabolites are the most sensitive in detecting pheochromocytoma.

     CT and MRI scans are used to localize tumor

     Meta-iodobenzylguanidine (MIBG) scan helps localize tumor

2. Treatment

* Surgery is treatment of choice
* Patients are monitored for signs of shock related to abrupt decrease in circulating catecholamines

Parathyroid tumors

1. Assessment

   * Clinical manifestions

     Hyperparathyroidism may be seen as elevated calcium level on routine laboratory evaluation or may be found incidentally during work-up for other unrelated symptoms

     Bone pain

     Urolithiasis

     Neuropsychiatric changes

     Gastrointestinal symptoms

     Palpable neck masses are seen rarely

   * Diagnostic measures

     Nuclear scanning, CT, and ultrasound are most useful methods to localize parathyroid mass

     Approximately half of patients with hyperparathyroidism have evidence of bony disease

2. Treatment

   * Surgery includes en bloc resection of abnormal parathyroid; if nodes are involved, radical neck dissection is done

   * Surgery may be used to resect recurrent disease; not curative, but helps control

hypercalcemia and disease symptoms

∗ Postoperative complications include

Hypoparathyroidism

Recurrent laryngeal nerve damage

Hemorrhage

∗ Neither radiation nor chemotherapy have been successful in treating either primary or metastatic disease

Multiple endocrine neoplasia (MEN)

1. Syndromes in which several endocrine malignancies occur
2. Often are familial and are inherited as an autosomal dominant gene
3. Screening is a major focus of management for families known to express MEN

Suggested Readings

1. Wickham R, Rohan K: Endocrine malignancies. In Groenwald SL, Frogge MH, Goodman M, Yarbro CH (eds): *Cancer Nursing: Principles and Practice* (4th ed). Boston: Jones and Bartlett, 1997, pp 1055-1081.
2. Fraker DL: Radiation exposure and other factors that predispose to human thyroid neoplasia. *Surg Clin North Am* 75:365-375 1995.
3. Molitch ME: Evaluation and treatment of the patient with a pituitary incidentaloma. J *Clin Endocrinal Metab* 80:8-11 1995.
4. Delellis RA: Multiple endocrine neoplasia syndromes revisited: Clinical, morphologic and molecular features. *Lab Invest* 72:494-505.

CHAPTER 41

Endometrial Cancers

Overview

Predominant cancer of female genital tract

Mortality rate is low

About 34,000 new cases diagnosed in 1996

Only approximately 6000 women died of the disease in 1996

In more than 79% of women, diagnosis is made when disease is localized

Overall good prognosis

Survival rates are

1. Stage I: 76%
2. Stage II: 50%
3. Stage III: 30%
4. Stage IV: 9%

Primarily disease of postmenopausal women

Most cases are diagnosed in women between ages 50 and 59

Risk factors

1. Obesity (more than 20 lb overweight)
2. Nulliparity
3. Late menopause (after age 52)
4. Diabetes
5. Hypertension
6. Infertility
7. Irregular menses
8. Failure of ovulation
9. History of breast or ovarian cancer
10. Adenomatous hyperplasia
11. Prolonged use of unopposed estrogen therapy

Protective factors include

1. Oral contraceptives
2. Smoking

90% of tumors are adenocarcinomas

Multiple factors affect prognosis

1. Uterine size

2. Histologic differentiation: less differentiated tumor, poorer prognosis
3. Stage of disease
4. Pattern or degree of invasion (especially myometrium)
5. Peritoneal cytology
6. Lymph node metastases
7. Adenexal metastasis

Metastatic spread is usually by direct extension and to

1. Endocervix
2. Cervix
3. Fallopian tubes
4. Ovaries
5. Pelvic and para-aortic nodes
6. Lung
7. Liver
8. Bone
9. Brain

Approaches to Care

Assessment

1. Clinical manifestations

   * Abnormal or new vaginal bleeding is hallmark signal

   * Postmenopausal bleeding

   * Less common symptoms are

     Premenopausal onset of heavy or irregular bleeding

     Pyometra

Hematuria

Lumbosacral, hypogastric, or pelvic pain

2. Diagnostic measures

- ✳ Thorough pelvic examination
- ✳ Endometrial biopsy (90% effective in detection)
- ✳ Chest x-ray
- ✳ Intravenous pyelogram
- ✳ Hematologic profiles
- ✳ Cystoscopy, barium enema, proctoscopy

Interventions

1. Initial treatment is surgical staging

- ✳ Surgical staging procedures involve

  Bimanual examination

  Peritoneal cytology

  Inspection and palpation of peritoneal surfaces

  Biopsies

  Selective pelvic and para-aortic lymphadenectomy

2. Definitive treatment is dependent upon stage
3. Stage I disease is usually treated with

- ✳ Total abdominal hysterectomy, bilateral salpingo-oophorectomy, and possible omentectomy
- ✳ Adjuvant radiation therapy for early cancer is sometimes used

If there is positive peritoneal cytology, intraperitoneal radioactive colloidal phosphorous can be helpful

External beam therapy is used for disease localized to pelvis

Whole-pelvis radiation allows treatment of all pelvic tissue

2. Advanced or recurrent disease is difficult to treat

* Vaginal recurrences are treated with surgery or radiotherapy

* Hormonal therapy or chemotherapy are used for recurrent and advanced disease

    Hormonal therapy

    Synthetic progestational agents produce 30% to 37% response rates

    Receptor status greatly affects response

    If both estrogen and progesterone receptors are positive, response rate is about 77%

    Megestrol acetate and medroxyprogesterone are most commonly used

    Side effects include fluid retention, phlebitis, and thrombosis

    Chemotherapy

    Few agents have demonstrated activity greater than progestin therapy

    Doxorubicin every 3 weeks is common

    High-dose cisplatin (100 mg/m^2) is used as

first-line therapy, with little effect on refractory disease

Information needs related to endometrial cancer

1. Estrogen replacement therapy (ERT)

   * Indications for use

     Vaginal atrophy with infection or sexual dysfunction

     Loss of pelvic support with incontinence

     Postmenopausal osteoporosis

     Perimenopausal emotional lability

     Early surgical or radiation castration

     Vasomotor instability

     Lowered morbidity and mortality for cardiovascular disease

   * Estrogen cycled with progesterone

   * Annual pelvic exam, histologic sampling of endometrium, and mammogram

   * Seek medical attention if any abnormal vaginal bleeding occurs, including postmenopausal bleeding

2. Breast self-examination (BSE)

   * Importance of BSE in conjunction with ERT

   * Technique for performing BSE and demonstration of skill

3. Diet and weight control

   * Low-fat, calcium-rich diet

* Maintain weight within normal range
* Weight-bearing exercises to decrease bone loss

4. Abnormal vaginal bleeding

   * Seek medical attention for new onset of abnormal bleeding
   * Evaluation includes pelvic examination and endometrial biopsy

5. Sexual role functioning

   * Dispel myths related to perceived loss of femininity due to surgery
   * Help redefine self in terms other than reproduction

6. Sexual functioning

   * Complete sexual assessment
   * Alteration in sexual response secondary to hysterectomy

     Cervix contributes to but is not essential for orgasm

     Uterus elevates during excitement phase and contracts rhythmically during orgasm

   * Alteration in sexual functioning secondary to radiation

     Vaginal dryness and stenosis may result in patient who is not sexually active, unless vaginal dilators and lubricants are employed

Use of water-soluble lubricants during intercourse; use of nonhormonal moisturizers three times per week

Suggested Readings

1. Walczak JR, Klemm PR, Guarnieri C: Gynecologic cancers. In Groenwald SL, Frogge MH, Goodman M, Yarbro CH (eds): *Cancer Nursing: Principles and Practice* (4th ed). Boston: Jones and Bartlett, 1997, pp 1146-1151.
2. DiSaia PJ, Creasman WT: *Clinical Gynecologic Oncology.* St. Louis: CV Mosby, 1993.
3. Feldman S, Cook EF, Harlow BL, et al: Predicting endometrial cancer among older women who present with abnormal vaginal bleeding. *Gynecol Oncol* 56:367-381, 1995.
4. Hoskins WJ, Perez C, Young RC: Gynecologic Tumors. In DeVita VT, Hellman S, Rosenberg SA (eds): *Cancer: Principles and Practice of Oncology* (4th ed). Philadelphia: JB Lippincott, 1993, pp 1152-1225.

CHAPTER 42

Esophageal Tumors

Overview

Grow rapidly, metastasize early, and are diagnosed late

Survival rates are poor

Uncommon in U.S.

Represent 1% of all cancer cases and 2% of cancer deaths

Only 7% to 11% of those affected are alive 5 years after diagnosis

More common among men than women

African-American males have highest incidence

Highest incidence among ages 50 to 70

Risk factors include

1. Heavy alcohol intake
2. Poor nutrition
3. Anemia
4. Nitrosamines in food
5. Plummer-Vinson syndrome
6. Heavy tobacco use
7. Cirrhosis
8. Poor oral hygiene
9. Chronic irritation: hiatal hernia, reflux, Barrett's esophagus
10. Tylosis palmaris

Histologic types

1. Squamous cell carcinoma: 85% of cases
2. Adenocarcinoma: 10 % of cases

Metastasis occurs by

1. Direct extension
2. Lymphatic system
3. Hematologic system

Approaches to Care

Assessment

1. Clinical manifestations

* Many people mistakenly attribute signs and symptoms to disorders of digestion that commonly affect older persons

* Early symptoms may be nonspecific and of little concern

* Definitive symptoms may be present for only weeks or months and disease may be well advanced

* Initial symptoms include pressure, fullness, indigestion, substernal distress

* Dysphagia is the classic symptom in 90% of cases

* Dysphagia is progressive and patient will attempt to modify food intake and mastication to accommodate progressive obstruction

* Pain on swallowing occurs in 50% of cases

* Weight loss is dramatic, sometimes 10% to 20% of body weight

* Characteristic cough-swallow sequence

2. Diagnostic measures

* Routine x-ray films and double-barium contrast studies

* CT scan for staging

* Endoscopy and biopsy

* Cytologic studies for tissue diagnosis

* Endoscopic ultrasound for staging

Treatment

1. Pretreatment preparation includes

* Intensive nutritional therapy
* Pulmonary hygiene
* Chest physiotherapy
* Control of secretions

2. Surgery, radiation, and chemotherapy are options; a combination of the three appears to offer best alternative

   * Radiotherapy

     Can result in rapid relief of obstruction

     Excellent modality for combination therapy

     Alternative for palliation of advanced disease

     Complications of radiotherapy

     Swallowing difficulties

     Skin reactions

     Esophageal fistula

     Stricture

     Radiation pneumonitis

   * Preoperative radiotherapy

     Reduces tumor bulk

     Improves surgical resectability

     Improves swallowing and nutritional status

   * Postoperative radiotherapy

     Eradicates residual tumor cells in surgical site

     Used for local control

   * Intracavitary radiation

Implants placed via endoscope

Provides therapeutic boost dose to local area

* Surgery

Employed selectively at all three levels of esophagus

Goal may be to cure or palliate

Curative intent

Eradicate tumor

Re-establish esophageal continuity

Stage I and II tumors without evidence of local or distant metastases are eligible

Palliative intent

Maintain esophageal patency

Improve quality of life

Surgical approaches

Left transthoracic approach for cancers of lower third of esophagus

Abdominal and right thoracotomy for cancers of upper and middle third of esophagus

Transhiatal esophagectomy for cancer at all three levels

Radical resection for curative intent involves removal of a tissue block that is completely surrounded by normal tissue and incorporates surrounding nodes

Reconstruction of esophageal continuity can be achieved by

Elevating stomach to create esophagogastrectomy

Interposing segment of colon

Elevating gastric tube created from stomach to reconstruct lumen

Special considerations necessary for cervical esophagus because of difficulties imposed by tumor location including

Radical neck dissection

Partial cervical esophagectomy

Reconstruction done with gastric pull-up as initial procedure or as second-stage procedure

* Postoperative care

Potential complications are

Fistula

Anastomotic leak

Atelectasis

Pneumonia

Pulmonary edema

Adult respiratory distress syndrome

* Important nursing measures are

Preoperative antibiotic regimen

Aggressive respiratory care

Tracheal intubation care

Chest physiotherapy

Chest tube care

Tracheobronchial hygiene

Prevent fluid overload

Prevent infection

Antibiotic therapy

Meticulous suture line care

Monitor drainage, output

Reduce anastomosis tension

Maintain patent gastrointestinal tubes

Help patient to maintain body alignment

Detect fistulas

Prevent reflux aspiration

Elevate head of bed

Encourage patient not to consume snacks or liquid after evening meal

Encourage patient to eat small amounts of food more often

Encourage patient to avoid bending from waist

Encourage patient to avoid heavy lifting

Control odor (with colon interposition)

   Help patient to maintain meticulous oral hygiene

   Encourage patient to avoid gas-producing foods

   Encourage use of mint candies

   Suggest use of charcoal carbonate tablets

* Chemotherapy

Integral part of managing locally confined disease

Agents currently used are

Cisplatin

5-Fluorouracil

Mitomycin-C

Mitoguazone

Doxorubicin

Bleomycin

Vindesine

Sequenced chemotherapy in multimodal approach offers promise

Preoperative chemoradiation therapy

Delivers local and systemic therapy simultaneously

Severe mucositis and myelosuppression are limiting toxicities

★ Palliative therapy

Objective is to relieve distressing symptoms

Progressive dysphagia is most debilitating symptom, occurring in 90% of patients

Radiotherapy of 3000 to 5000 cGy decreases tumor size and bleeding

Laser therapy alleviates esophageal obstruction and severe dysphagia

Resection or bypass relieves severe symptoms or reduces tumor bulk

Synthetic endoesophageal prosthetic tubes create open passage for swallowing

Care of person with endoprosthesis includes

Educating patient

Preventing reflux up tube

Elevating head of bed

Helping patient take all meals in upright position

Helping patient to eat smaller amounts of food more often

Helping patient to dislodge trapped food with nasogastric tube

Helping patient to drink half glass of water or carbonated beverage at end of meal to clear tube

Suggested Readings

1. Coleman JA: Gastrointestinal cancer: Esophagus, stomach, liver, and pancreatic cancers. In Groenwald SL, Frogge MH, Goodman M, Yarbro CH (eds): *Cancer Nursing: Principles and Practice* (4th ed). Boston: Jones and Bartlett, 1997, pp 1082-1095.
2. Heitmiller RF, Forastiere AA: Esophagus. In Abeloff MD, Armitage JO, Lichter AS, Neiderrhuber JE (eds): *Clinical Oncology.* New York: Churchill Livingstone, 1995, pp 1189-1208.
3. Roth JA, Lichner AS, Putnam JB, et al: Cancer of the esophagus. In DeVita VT, Hellman S, Rosenberg SA (eds): *Cancer: Principles and Practice of Oncology* (4th ed). Philadelphia: JB Lippincott, 1993, pp 776-817.
4. Davydov MI, Akhvlediani GG, Stilidi IS, et al: Surgical aspects in the treatment of esophageal cancer. *Semin Surg Oncol* 8:4-8, 1992.

CHAPTER 43

Head and Neck Malignancies

Overview

Represent 4% of total newly diagnosed cancers in U.S.

Incidence is 40% in cancer of oral cavity, 25% in laryngeal cancer, 15% in cancers of oropharynx and hypopharynx, 7% in cancers of major salivary glands, and 13% in remaining sites

Male to female incidence ratio is 3:1

439

Incidence of squamous carcinoma of all sites of the head and neck has increased in women due to increase in alcohol and tobacco usage

Incidence increases with age

Approximately 95% are squamous cell in origin

Most invade locally, deep into underlying structures, and along tissue planes; invasion into bone usually occurs late in disease

Important factor in determining prognosis is presence or absence of histologically proved lymph node metastasis

**Approximately 30% of individuals have second primary tumor; greatest risk of second primary tumor occurs within first 3-year period after treatment for primary cancer
Usually locally aggressive; spread first to sites within head and neck**

80-90% of oral cancers are 2 cm or more at initial presentation

Risk factors

1. Use of tobacco, including cigarettes, smokeless tobacco, pipes, and cigars
2. Use of alcohol; there may also be synergism between alcohol and tobacco
3. Exposure to dust from wood, metal, leather, or textiles
4. Poor oral hygiene; chronic irritation from loose-fitting dentures

5. Epstein-Barr virus (EBV) and nasopharyngeal cancer
6. Genetic predisposition
7. Nutritional deficiencies, such as Plummer-Vinson syndrome
8. Vitamin A deficiency

Types of head and neck cancers

1. Carcinoma of nasal cavity and paranasal sinuses

   * Maxillary sinus most commonly affected site

   * Affects individuals older than age 40; affects men twice as often as women

   * Risk factors: Exposure to

     Leather or nickel plating or work in furniture manufacturing

     Chromate compounds

     Hydrocarbons

     Nitrosamines

     Mustard gas

     Isopropyl alcohol

     Petroleum

     Dioxane

2. Carcinoma of nasopharynx

   * Incidence ratio of males to females is 3:1

   * Appears to be viral association with EBV

   * Genetic predisposition may exist in individuals from southern China; related

to size of nasal cavity and ingestion of salted fish

3. Carcinoma of oral cavity

   * Cure rates increase dramatically if disease is diagnosed early when tumor is small

   * Risk factors

     Smoking

     Alcohol abuse

     Systemic syphilis

     Poor oral hygiene

     Poorly fitting dentures or dental appliances

     Chewing betel nuts

   * Approximately 37% of individuals develop multiple primary cancers concurrently or subsequently

   * Not age-specific or sex-specific

4. Carcinoma of hypopharynx

   * Incidence ratio of males to females is 2:1

   * Most commonly affected sites are

     Pyriform sinus (70%)

     Postcricoid (15%)

     Posterolateral wall (15%)

   * Contributing causes include

     Excessive smoking

     Drinking alcohol

     Plummer-Vinson syndrome

5. Carcinoma of larynx

* Approximately 80% occur in persons older than 50 years

* Risk factors

  Use of tobacco and alcohol

  Previous exposure to ionizing radiation

* Multiple primary tumors occur in 5% to 10% of patients

* Divided into three types according to distinct anatomic areas

  Glottic carcinoma: *Located in space between true cords, including vocal folds and anterior and posterior glottis*

  Supraglottic carcinoma: *Located in area and structures above glottis, including epiglottis, aryepiglottic folds, arytenoids, and ventricular bands (false cords)*

  Subglottic carcinoma: *Located in area and structures below glottis*

Approaches to Patient Care

Carcinoma of nasal cavity and paranasal sinuses

1. Assessment

   * Clinical manifestations

     Symptoms of early disease mimic chronic sinusitis; later symptoms include

     Stuffy nose

    Epistaxis

    Sinus headache

    Cheek hypesthesia

    Dull facial pain

    Trismus

    Rhinorrhea

    Loose teeth

* Diagnostic measures

  Physical findings may include

      Diplopia

      Proptosis

      Submucosal palatal mass

      Maxillary fullness

      Cranial nerve deficit

  Cervical adenopathy is unfavorable finding that occurs in 10% of patients at diagnosis

2. Treatment

   * Early disease may be treated with either radiation or surgery; more advanced disease is usually treated with combination of radiation, surgery, and sometimes chemotherapy

   * Surgery

     Maxillectomy is treatment of choice for tumors in maxillary sinus; combination of radical maxillectomy and orbital exenteration may be performed if there is extensive disease with invasion into floor of orbit

Before surgery impression is made of hard and soft palate

Obturator is made and placed at time of surgery to restore nasal continuity, allow patient to eat and speak immediately after surgery, and protect wound from irritation and debris

Obturator remains in place for 5 days; it is then removed and replaced with more permanent obturator

Teach patient to remove obturator after each meal, irrigate it with alkaline-based fluid, and remove any crusting over defect

Do not remove obturator for long periods of time, as atrophy can occur

Monitor patients receiving chemotherapy or radiation therapy, or both, for mucositis

Cranial base surgery

Used to resect tumors that involve or have extended to skull base

Complications

Loss of vision if orbital exenteration is necessary

Temporary facial paralysis

Loss of feeling in middle or lower face

Loss of smell if olfactory nerves are transected

* Local disease recurs in 30% to 40% of patients with nasal and paranasal cavity cancer and in 60% of patients with maxillary sinus cancer

Carcinoma of nasopharynx

1. Assessment

   * Clinical manifestations

     First indicator may be presence of enlarged node in neck

     Nasal obstruction (with or without epistaxis)

     Hearing impairment and tinnitus secondary to eustachian tube obstruction

     Otitis media

     Late in disease, headache and facial pain may signify bony erosion and pressure on fifth cranial nerve

     Tumor invasion through base of skull results in cranial nerve involvement, causing cranial nerve abnormalities

   * Diagnostic measures

   * Physical examination with head mirror, tongue depressor, and laryngeal mirror

   * Palpate neck nodes thoroughly

   * CT scans and other radiographic tools, such as angiography, help to determine spread of disease and potential collateralization in cerebrovascular tree

2. Treatment

   * Radiotherapy is primary treatment

   * Chemotherapy may be given in conjunction with radiation to potentiate effects of radiation

Carcinoma of oral cavity

1. Assessment

   * Many people deny symptoms and do not seek medical help until lesion is large and painful

   * Referred pain to ear or jaw can indicate ulceration or pressure on adjacent nerves

   * Individual may have difficulty chewing and swallowing as lesion progresses

2. Treatment

   * Determined by tumor size

   * In early-stage lesions, surgery or radiation alone have comparable cure rates; choice of treatment depends on

     Functional and cosmetic results required

     Patient's general health

     Patient's preference

   * Chemotherapy used as adjuvant therapy; also plays role in palliation of symptoms in patients whose disease is not curable

   * In oral cavity, surgical resection often involves neck dissection in continuity with tumor and regional lymph nodes

   * Speaking and swallowing can be greatly affected depending on location of tumor

   * Laser therapy is very precise and helps decrease possibility of tumor spread by sealing lymphatics as tissue is removed

Carcinoma of hypopharynx

1. Assessment

   * Clinical manifestations

     Presenting symptoms include odynophagia, referred otalgia (usually unilateral), and dysphagia

     Weight loss as result of difficulty swallowing food

     Hoarseness or aspiration with more advanced disease

   * Diagnostic measures

     Physical examination of pharyngeal wall and pyriform sinus is with laryngeal mirror and tongue depressor

     Diagnostic studies include CT, direct laryngoscopy, and biopsy

     Cervical esophageal extension should be suspected if any of following are found

       Laryngeal tumor involvement

       Tumor invasion and mucosal involvement of posterior wall of pharynx

       Pooling of saliva in or around pyriform sinus and pharynx

2. Treatment

   * Most patients have advanced disease at first presentation

   * Surgery may be extensive and necessitate intricate reconstruction using skin and muscle flaps to facilitate closure

* Swallowing is often problem after surgery because resection of pharyngeal constrictors interferes with swallowing

* Risk of fistula formation is greatest in patients who have had both surgery and radiation therapy

   Pack with iodoform gauze

   Allow to heal gradually over few weeks

Glottic carcinoma

1. Assessment

   * Impairment of vocal cord motion may indicate extension of tumor into cricoarytenoid articulation and arytenoid region

2. Treatment
   * Early lesions treated with equal success by radiotherapy or conservation surgery

   When cord fixation is not needed, conservative laryngeal resection is usually treatment of choice

   Hemilaryngectomy indicated if tumor extends forward to anterior commissure or posteriorly to or beyond vocal process

   Radiotherapy is option for cure; if there is no response after reasonable dosage, therapy may be discontinued and surgery may be indicated

   * Advanced disease (T3 or T4) often requires total laryngectomy; any patient with obvious metastases to lateral neck nodes should undergo radical neck dissection

Permanent voice loss and alteration of airway occur when larynx is removed

Establish means of communication for postoperative period before surgery

Long-term options for communication include electrolarynx, esophageal speech, and voice restoration by esophageal prosthetic voice restoration

* Postoperative care

Laryngectomy stoma care, including instructions on how to remove and clean tube and care for stoma

Humidity is important to moisten, warm, and filter air

Teach patients importance of mobilizing secretions by coughing, drinking adequate fluids, and instilling saline into stoma to loosen secretions, if necessary

Hyposmia occurs in most laryngectomy patients; taste may also be affected

Swallowing may be affected by stricture; managed by periodic dilation

Radiation may contribute to fistula formation at suture line

Patients should not lift heavy objects, participate in water sports, or get dust or dirt into airway when gardening or doing housework

Supraglottic carcinoma

1. Assessment

* Generally few symptoms

* Pain may occur

* Poorly defined throat and neck discomfort during swallowing

* Referred otalgia may occur with throat pain

* Indirect laryngoscopy usually used to make diagnosis

2. Treatment

* Radiation is usually treatment of choice

* If radiation fails, total laryngectomy is usually needed as salvage procedure

   Standard supraglottic laryngectomy consists of resection of hyoid bone, epiglottis, pre-epiglottic space, thyrohyoid membrane, superior half of thyroid cartilage, and false vocal cords

   Temporary tracheostomy tube is placed at surgery and removed when patient can swallow without aspirating, usually 10 to 14 days after surgery

   Patient needs to learn new method of swallowing; liquids are most difficult

General treatment measures for head and neck cancers

1. Reconstruction: Goal is to restore function and maintain socially adequate cosmesis

* Myocutaneous flap

   Indicated in cases where large amount of tissue has been resected and bulk is needed to reconstruct defect

Flap consists of muscle, skin, and blood supply; in some cases bone or cartilage is included

Pectoralis major, sternocleidomastoid, trapezius, and latissimus dorsi are muscles most often used to reconstruct head and neck defects

* Free flap

  Microvascular anastomosis used to completely remove free flap from donor site and place into recipient site

  Advantage of free flap is immediate functional reconstructive replacement of removed tissue

* Deltopectoral flap

  Advantage is that well-vascularized tissue from area that has not been irradiated is brought to area that has been irradiated

  Disadvantages include several-step procedure and occurrence of strictures and fistulas

2. Chemotherapy

* Used as

  Primary chemotherapy (before surgery and radiation)

  Single-agent therapy

  Sequential therapy with radiation

* Attempted as means of preserving structure and function of tissues

* Chemotherapy, especially 5-FU and taxol, may be used as radiation sensitizers

* Cisplatin and 5-FU are effective in combination

3. Radiation therapy

* Often used as primary therapy; also used as adjuvant therapy with surgery or chemotherapy, or both

* Treatment methods include

    External beam radiation

    Implant therapy (brachytherapy)

    > Use of radioactive sources placed directly into tumor

    > Used to cure early-stage lesions in floor of mouth and anterior tongue

    > May be used to boost tumor that has already received external beam therapy

    > Radioactive seeds may be permanently implanted at surgery

    Intraoperative

    > Involves delivery of single, large dose of radiation to either gross disease or tumor bed after surgical resection and during operative procedure

* Hyperthermia may be combined with radiation therapy to enhance tumor response

* Increased numbers of tumor cells may be killed by combining radiation and chemotherapy

* Nursing managment

    Mucositis

May appear as early as first week of treatment; usually resolves within 3 weeks after end of treatment

Good oral care is essential to ease discomfort and prevent infection

Xerostomia and loss of taste occur because of high doses of radiation therapy; patients are encouraged to sip fluids frequently and to season their food as necessary

Loss of taste

4. Management of altered airway

   * Tracheostomy

     If tumor affects patient's breathing or if surgical procedure includes compromised airway, tracheostomy is necessary

     At time of surgery, cuffed tracheostomy tube is usually sutured in place

     Teach patients to suction tracheostomy tube, remove, and clean inner cannula, clean tracheostoma, and apply clean dressing, as necessary

     Tracheostomy tube is removed when it is no longer needed; slit incision is taped, and site heals over in 4 to 6 weeks

   * Laryngectomy

     No longer any communication between oral cavity and lungs

     Laryngectomy stoma leads directly into lungs; mouth leads directly to stomach, with no risk of aspiration

Adequate humidity is crucial; encourage
adequate fluid intake to maintain fluid
secretions that are easy to cough up

Suggested Readings

1. Bildstein CY: Head and neck malignancies. In Groenwald SL, Frogge MH, Goodman M, Yarbro CH (eds): *Cancer Nursing: Principles and Practice* (4th ed). Boston: Jones and Bartlett, 1997, pp 1199-1234.

2. Shah J, Lydiatt W: Treatment of cancer of the head and neck. *CA Cancer J Clin* 45:352-368, 1995.

3. Bol D, Lloyd J, Manley M. The role of the primary care physician in tobacco use, prevention, and cessation. *CA Cancer J Clin* 45:369-373, 1995.

4. Attanasiadis I, Vokes EE: Expanding the role of chemotherapy for head and neck squamous cell carcinoma. *Adv Oncol* 2:742-756, 1995.

5. Tayor SG, Marthy AK, et al.: Randomized comparison of neoadjuvant cesplatin and fluorouracil infusion followed by radiation versus concomitant treatment in advanced head and neck cancer. *J Clin Oncol* 12:385-395 1994.

CHAPTER 44

Hodgkin's Disease

Overview

Hodgkin's disease (HD) accounts for 15% of malignant lymphomas and less than 1% of all cancers

Incidence of HD has two peaks

1. Young adults aged 20 to 30
2. Adults over age 45

Cause remains unclear

1. Infectious source has been speculated
2. Familial patterns have been noted

Approaches to Patient Care

Assessment

1. Clinical manifestations

   * Enlarged lymph nodes > 1 cm

     Painless, firm, rubbery, and moveable

     Most located in cervical and supraclavicular areas

     Axillary and inguinal involvement in less than 10% of patients

   * Mediastinal adenopathy is common

   * Constitutional symptoms, or "B" symptoms, are more common in advanced disease and include

     Fever

     Malaise

     Night sweats

     Weight loss (more than 10% of normal body weight)

     Pruritus

2. Diagnostic measures

   * Biopsy of involved tissue

   * Histologic typing and staging are necessary to determine prognosis and therapy

   * HD is distinguished histologically by presence of Reed-Sternberg cell

   * There are four distinct subtypes of HD

Nodular sclerosis

   More common in women than men

   Incidence between ages 15 and 34 years

   Most asymptomatic at presentation

Lymphocyte-predominant

   Occurs in fourth or fifth decade of life

   Most asymptomatic at presentation

   Good prognosis

Mixed cellularity

   More common in men; wide age range

   More than 50% of patients have B symptoms and are stage III or IV

Lymphocyte-depleted

   More common in elderly men

   Most aggressive of four types

  * Staging determines extent of disease and treatment

Interventions

1. Majority of patients are curable with optimal therapy
2. Guidelines for treatment of HD are

   * Radiation therapy (RT) for limited disease

   * RT and combination chemotherapy for patients with mediastinal disease, B symptoms, and abdominal nodes

3. Combination therapy involves mechlorethamine, vincristine, procarbazine,

and prednisone (MOPP) regimen or doxorubicin, bleomycin, vinblastine, and dacarbazine (ABVD) regimen; they may also be alternated

4. Treatment success depends on dosage and timing of therapy

5. If patient relapses more than 12 months after initial therapy, patient may be treated with same agents

6. If relapse occurs less than 12 months after initial remission, patients are seldom cured; autologous bone marrow transplant may be an option

7. Long-term complications in cured patients

  * Gonadal dysfunction

    Consider reproductive counselling and sperm banking

  * Second malignancies

    Acute nonlymphocytic leukemia most common

  * Immunologic dysfunction resulting in infections

  * Herpes zoster

  * Progressive radiation myelopathy

  * Pneumonitis

  * Pericarditis and cardiomyopathy

8. Nurses play pivotal role in

  * Promoting compliance with treatment; clinical course is lengthy and toxic

  * Providing emotional support

MOPP Regimen

DRUG	DOSE	SCHEDULE
Nitrogen mustard	6 mg/m^2 IV	Days 1 and 8
Vincristine	1.4 mg/m^2 IV	Days 1 and 8
Procarbazine	100 mg/m^2 PO	Days 1-14
Prednisone*	40 mg/m^2 PO	Days 1-14

*Cycles 1 and 4 only

Repeat cycle every 28 days for minimum of six cycles; complete remission must be documented before discontinuing therapy.

ABVD Regimen

DRUG	DOSE	SCHEDULE
Doxorubicin	25 mg/m^2 IV	Days 1 and 15
Bleomycin	10 U/m^2 IV	Days 1 and 15
Vinblastine	6 mg/m^2 IV	Days 1 and 15
Dacarbazine (DTIC)	375 mg/m^2 IV	Days 1 and 15

Repeat cycle every 28 days for minimum of six cycles; complete remission must be documented before discontinuing therapy.

* Providing symptom management
* Rehabilitating individual to healthy lifestyle

Suggested Readings

1. Yarbro CH, McFadden ME: Malignant lymphomas. In Groenwald SL, Frogge MH, Goodman M, Yarbro CH (eds): Cancer Nursing: Principles and Practice (4th ed). Boston: Jones and Bartlett, 1997, pp 1291-1318.
2. Eyre HJ, Farver ML: Hodgkin's disease and non-Hodgkin's lymphoma. In Holleb AI, Fink DJ, Murphy GP (eds): Textbook of Clinical Oncology. Atlanta: American Cancer Society, 1991, pp 377-396.

CHAPTER 45

Leukemia

Overview

Represents group of hematologic malignancies that affect bone marrow and lymphatic tissue

Occurs more often in adults than in children

Approximately half of cases are acute and others are chronic

Common types of leukemia are

1. Acute myelogenous leukemia (AML)

* Median age at diagnosis is 50 to 60 years

2. Acute lymphocytic leukemia (ALL)

   * More common in children

3. Chronic myelogenous leukemia (CML)

   * Median age of occurrence is 49 years
   * Both sexes affected

4. Chronic lymphocytic leukemia (CLL)

   * Median age at diagnosis is 60 years
   * More common in males

Cause is not known but common etiologic factors considered are

1. Genetic factors

   * Family clustering
   * Chromosomal abnormalities

2. Radiation
3. Chemical exposure to

   * Benzene
   * Σ Paint
   * Σ Dye

4. Drugs

   * Alkylating agents
   * Chloramphenicol
   * Phenylbutazone

5. Viruses

Classified according to type of cell that is predominant and location where cell maturation stopped

1. Acute leukemia has more immature cells
2. Chronic leukemia has more mature cells that are ineffective

Regulatory mechanisms that control cell numbers and growth are missing or abnormal

Manifestations are related to three factors

1. Increase of immature white cells in bone marrow, spleen, liver, and lymph nodes
2. Infiltration of these leukemic cells into body tissues
3. Decrease in leukocytes, thrombocytes, and erythrocytes resulting from crowding of bone marrow with leukemic cells

Approaches to Patient Care

Assessment of acute leukemia

1. Clinical manifestations

   * Nonspecific complaints

     Fever

     Weight loss

     Fatigue

   * Recurrent infections

   * Unexplained bleeding

     Bruising

Petechiae

Nosebleeds

* Progressive anemia with shortness of breath, splenomegaly, weakness, and fatigue

* Joint pain

* Neurologic complaints

  Headache

  Vomiting

  Visual disturbances

2. Diagnostic measures

   * Must differentiate between AML and ALL, since treatment and prognosis are very different

   * Bone marrow biopsy and aspirate for definitive diagnosis

   * 90% of patients have blast cells in peripheral blood smear

   * Serum chemistries may reveal hyperuricemia

   * Chromosome analysis to determine classification

Interventions

1. Treatment of AML

   * Goal is to eradicate leukemic stem cell

   * Complete remission (CR) is restoration of normal blood counts and less than 5% blast cells

* Course of therapy is divided into two stages

  Induction therapy

    Cytosine arabinoside continuously for 7 days

    Anthracycline (e.g., daunorubicin, doxorubicin) for 3 days

    Bone marrow biopsy on day 14; if leukemic cells are present, begin a second course

    20% of AML patients remain in CR; the rest relapse in 1 to 2 years

  Postremission therapy

    Consolidation: Give high doses of induction therapy drugs for 1 to 2 courses

    Intensification: Give different drugs after CR

* Patients who relapse after induction or postremission therapy have 30% to 60% chance of second remission

* Bone marrow transplant (BMT) for AML is controversial

2. Treatment of ALL

  * Goal is to eradicate leukemic cells from marrow and lymph tissue and residual disease from central nervous system (CNS)

  * Treatment involves drugs that are more selective to lymphoblasts and less toxic to normal cells

  * Long-term survival more favorable with ALL than AML

  * Course of therapy is divided into three stages

Induction therapy

Vincristine, prednisone, and L-asparaginase

CR achieved in 93% of children; only 70% to 75% of adults achieve CR

CNS prophylaxis

Intracranial radiation and intrathecal methotrexate

Postremission therapy

Same drugs as with induction; methotrexate and 6-mercaptopurine may be added

Maintenance therapy often continues for 2 to 3 years

* Outlook is poor for patients who relapse during therapy

* There is better prognosis with BMT if it is performed during first remission

Assessment of CML

1. Clinical manifestations

* 20% of CML patients have no symptoms at diagnosis

* Left upper quadrant pain, abdominal fullness, early satiety are related to massive splenomegaly

* Malaise, fatigue

* Fever

* Weight loss

* Bone and joint pain

2. Diagnostic studies may reveal

   * White blood cell (WBC) count greater than 100,000/mm3

   * Anemia

   * Thrombocytosis

   * Philadelphia (Ph^1) chromosome in 90% of CML patients

Interventions

1. Treatment of CML

   * Only chance for cure is ablation of Ph^1 chromosome by high-dose chemotherapy and BMT; only 25% of patients have this option

   * Natural course of CML has two phases

     Chronic phase

       Treatment with oral busulfan or hydroxyurea

       Treatment does not prevent progression to terminal phase

     Terminal phase

       Blastic transformation can be detected 3 to 4 months before clinical signs are evident

       Blast crisis requires intensive chemotherapy, similar to agents used for AML

       Median survival after onset of terminal phase is less than 1 year

Assessment of CLL

1. Clinical manifestations

* Recurrent infections (skin and respiratory)
* Splenomegaly
* Lymphadenopathy in advanced disease

2. Diagnostic studies may reveal

* WBC count > 20,000/mm3 in early disease
* WBC count > 100,000/mm3 in advanced disease
* Hypogammaglobulinemia
* Bone marrow biopsy needed for definitive diagnosis

Interventions

1. Treatment of CLL

* Observe asymptomatic patients
* Treat symptomatic patients with oral chlorambucil or cyclophosphamide
* Give corticosteroids to control leukocytosis
* Perform splenectomy and radiation therapy when patients no longer respond to chemotherapy and corticosteroids
* Give combination therapy (cyclophosphamide, vincristine, doxorubicin, prednisone) for advanced disease
* Give fludarabine to patients who are refractory to alkylating agents

Supportive care interventions

1. Supportive therapies may improve quality of survival

2. Nurse plays key role in patient and family education, physical care, psychosocial support, and symptom management

3. Symptom management of common side effects

   * Neutropenia

     Absolute neutrophil count less than 1000/mm3 is common

     60% of leukemia patients develop infection

     Common sites of infection are

       Pharynx, esophagus

       Lungs

       Anorectal area

       Skin

       Sinuses

     Usual signs and symptoms of infection may be absent because of lack of inflammatory response

     Fever of more than 100°F requires cultures of blood, urine, sputum, and intravenous sites

     Empiric antibiotic therapy is used until organism is identified

     Give amphotericin B for life-threatening fungal infections and if fever continues 5 to 7 days after start of antibiotic therapy

     Give prophylactic fluconazole to prevent disseminated infections

     To prevent infection

       Maintain patient's skin integrity, sleep, and nutrition

Decrease invasive procedures

Provide private room, restrict visitors

Patient should avoid uncooked foods

Patient and caregivers should practice meticulous hand washing

Do not allow plants or fresh flowers

Adminster colony-stimulating factors to shorten period of neutropenia

* Erythrocytopenia

Give transfusions of red blood cells if there is sudden blood loss or symptomatic anemia

Thrombocytopenia

There is potential bleeding if platelet count is < 50,000/mm3

There is spontaneous bleeding if platelet count is < 20,000/mm3

First signs of bleeding may be

Petechiae or ecchymoses on mucous membranes or skin of dependent limbs

Oozing from gums, nose, or intravenous site

Give random donor platelets to keep platelet count > 20,000/mm3

Measures to prevent bleeding

Maintain patient's skin integrity

Prevent trauma

Patient should avoid medications with anticoagulant effects

Patient should take stool softeners to prevent straining

4. Nursing care plan should anticipate complications of disease or therapy

* Leukostasis

  Patients at risk have WBC count > 50,000/mm3

  Occurs more often in ALL

  Intracerebral hemorrhage most common manifestation

  Reduce burden of cells by

  High-dose chemotherapy

  Leukapheresis

  Cranial radiation

* Disseminated intravascular coagulation (DIC)

  May occur with any acute leukemia

  Correction of DIC depends on successful treatment of leukemia

  Nursing care focuses on

  Prevention of injury

  Administration of prescribed therapy

  Monitoring of lab results

* Oral complications

  Result of disease or therapy

  Gingival hypertrophy

Stomatitis

Provide routine oral care

* Cerebellar toxicity

Associated with high-dose cytosine arabinoside (HDCA) (doses of > 3 g/m2)

Increased risk in patients over age 50

Ataxia and nystagmus are early signs

Difficulty with speech and rapid movements are late signs

Toxicity is irreversible if not detected early

Complete neurologic assessment before each HDCA treatment

Suggested Readings

1. Wujcik D: Leukemia. In Groenwald SL, Frogge MH, Goodman M, Yarbro CH (eds): Cancer Nursing: Principles and Practice (4th ed). Boston: Jones and Bartlett, 1997, pp 1235-1259.
2. Wujcik D: Infection. In Groenwald SL, Frogge MH, Goodman M, Yarbro CH (eds): Cancer Symptom Management. Boston: Jones and Bartlett, 1996, pp 289-307.
3. Levinson JA, Lesko LM: Psychiatric aspects of adult leukemia. Semin Oncol Nurs 6:76-83, 1990.
4. McNally JL, Somerville ET, Miaskowski C, Rostad M (eds): Guidelines for Cancer Nursing Practice (2nd ed) Philadelphia: WB Saunders, 1991.

CHAPTER 46

Liver Cancer

Overview

Leading cause of death in Africa and Asia

In U.S., primary liver cancer is uncommon

More prevalent among men than women

Average age of onset is 60 to 70

Unusual clinical and pathologic features

Disseminates early and is diagnosed when advanced

No specific treatment effectively controls advanced disease

Risk factors

1. Hepatitis B or C virus
2. Exposure to aflatoxin
3. Cirrhosis

    * Alcoholic cirrhosis

    * Chronic hepatitis B infection

4. Hemochromatosis
5. Ingestion of estrogens and androgens
6. Thorotrast biliary contrast medium

Tumors may be primary, or secondary tumors metastasized from other sites

Differentiating whether tumor is primary or secondary is critical treatment issue

1. Primary liver cancers

    * 90% are hepatocellular

    * 7% are cholangiocarcinoma

    * Typically originate in right lobe

    * May be multicentric in origin or start with single focus

    * Usually soft and highly vascular

    * Often well differentiated with clearly defined margins

2. Secondary liver cancers

    * Twenty times more likely to occur than primary liver cancer

* Liver is repository for metastatic deposits from nearly all sites
* Metastases may occur as single mass or as multiple masses
* Metastases are often from

  Lung

  Kidney

  Breast

  Intestinal tract

Progression of disease occurs by direct extension within and around liver

Tumors typically alter bloodflow within the liver, resulting in rapid spread of tumor

Occlusion of liver vessels is common

In advanced disease

1. Pneumonia, hepatic failure, and hemorrhage are causes of death
2. Tamponade within liver can lead to necrosis and rupture or hemorrhage
3. Prognosis is poor, with overall 5-year survival of 5%
4. If untreated, death occurs in 6 to 8 weeks

Approaches to Care

Assessment

1. Clinical manifestations

* Can grow to huge proportions before detected

* Common signs are

   Right upper quadrant pain that is dull and aching

   Continuous pain that interrupts sleep and is aggravated by activity or lying on right side

   Profound, progressive weakness and fatigue

   Fullness in epigastrium

   Constipation or diarrhea

   Anorexia or weight loss

   Mild jaundice

   Ascites and signs of portal hypertension

   Hematemesis

2. Diagnostic measures

   * Definitive diagnostic tool is tissue diagnosis

   * Physical examination may reveal painful, enlarged liver

   * Other diagnostic studies

      Abdominal x-ray to show displacement or deformity of organs

      Ultrasound of abdomen

      CT of abdomen and lungs

      MRI is as effective as CT

      Radionuclide scanning outlines tumors in liver

      Selective hepatic arteriography shows vascular abnormalities in liver blood supply

Hematologic profiles

Liver function tests

Tumor marker alpha-fetoprotein (AFP)

Needle biopsy (only if tumor is unresectable)

Interventions

1. Choice of treatment depends on

   * Whether tumor is primary or secondary

   * Type and extent of tumor

   * Concomitant diseases

   * Liver function

   * Patient status

2. Pretreatment therapy

   * Anemia, clotting deficits, and fluid and electrolyte abnormalities should be corrected

   * Vitamins A, C, D, and B complex can reduce effect of jaundice

   * Pruritus can be relieved with good hygiene and by avoiding products that dry skin and by using oil-based lotions, antihistamines, and cholestyramine

   * Nutritional improvement is critical

3. Treatment

   * Cure is objective for

     Primary liver cancer that is localized

     Solitary mass without evidence of regional lymph node involvement

Secondary tumors that are solitary or well-defined

★ Control is objective if liver tumor is

Multicentric

Metastatic to other sites

Secondary deposit from other sites

★ Surgery

Is most definitive treatment for primary liver cancer

Selection of surgical technique depends on tumor size, location, and patient condition

Classic resections are: right or left lobectomy, trisegmentectomy

If cirrhosis is present, surgical risk is directly related to degree of cirrhosis

If opposite lobe is cancer-free or mildly cirrhotic, hepatic lobectomy can be undertaken

If tumor is localized and accessible, an en bloc excision is initial treatment of choice

Up to 85% of the noncirrhotic liver can be removed if the tumor is in posterior right lobe

Local resection, ultrasound-guided cryosurgery, or laser surgery may be possible

Hepatic artery occlusion or embolization can deprive tumor of its blood supply and cause necrosis

Postoperative care is concerned with

Hemorrhage

Infection

Subphrenic abscess

Atelectasis

Clotting defects

Biliary fistula

Transient metabolic changes

Pneumonia

Portal hypertension

* Chemotherapy

Administered by two aproaches: systemic or regional

May be treatment of choice if surgery is not option

Regional therapy

Alternative if disease is isolated to liver

Provides high concentration of drug directly to tumor, with minimal systemic exposure

Considered superior to systemic chemotherapy

Dose limitations are toxicity-related

Drugs include

Doxorubicin

Floxuradine

5-Fluorouracil

Cisplatin

Streptozocin

Etoposide

Folinic acid

Intraperitoneal chemotherapy

   Tolerated well

   Comparable results to regional chemotherapy

Biological and hormonal therapy

   Interferons in combination with chemotherapy

   Administered intramuscularly several times a week

   Hormones used alone or in combination with chemotherapy

* Radiation therapy

   Limited to palliation

   Poor tolerance of liver tissue

   Doses range from 1900 to 3100 cGy over 2 to 20 days

   Major side effects are nausea, vomiting, anorexia, fatigue

* Supportive therapy

   Most individuals die within 6 months of diagnosis

   Advanced disease manifests

      Hepatic failure

      Severe ascites

      Infection

      Bleeding

      Pain

      Weight loss

Weakness

Pneumonia

Pain is most difficult to manage

Worsens at night and is severe

Aggravated by movement

Suggested Readings

1. Coleman JA: Gastrointestinal cancer: Esophageal, stomach, liver, and pancreatic cancers. In Groenwald SL, Frogge MH, Goodman M, Yarbro CH (eds): *Cancer Nursing: Principles and Practice* (4th ed). Boston: Jones and Bartlett, 1997, pp 1082-1144.
2. Weimann A, Oldhafer KJ, Pichlmayr R: Primary liver cancers. *Curr Opin Oncol* 7:387-396, 1995.
3. Sherman M: Hepatocellular carcinoma. *Gastroenterologist* 3:55-66, 1995.
4. Scheele J, Stang R, Altendorf-Hofmann A, et al: Resection of colorectal metastases. *World J Surg* 19:59-71, 1995.

CHAPTER 47

Lung Cancer

Overview

Most common cancer killer

85% of cases are preventable if cigarette smoking is eliminated

Smoking cessation can reduce risk in a smoker

5-year survival is poor

Occurs after repeated exposures to substances that cause irritation and inflammation

Major risk factors are

1. Tobacco smoke
2. Passive smoke
3. Asbestos
4. Air pollution
5. Occupational exposure to toxic substances
6. Radon
7. Dietary factors

Two major histologic classes of lung cancer are

1. Small-cell lung cancer (SCLC)

   * Associated with smoking
   * Comprises 25% of all lung cancers
   * Aggressive tumors and metastasize early

2. Non–small-cell lung cancer (NSCLC)

   * Squamous cell carcinoma

     More common in males than females
     Associated with cigarette smoking
     Accounts for 30% of all lung cancers
     Slow growing and longer survival

   * Adenocarcinomas

     Most common of lung cancers
     Metastasis is common, especially to the brain

   * Large-cell carcinomas

     Accounts for 10% to 15% of lung cancers

Approaches to Patient Care

Assessment

1. Clinical manifestations

   * Cough
   * Chest pain
   * Dyspnea
   * Wheezing
   * Hemoptysis
   * Anorexia
   * Weight loss
   * Fatigue
   * Hoarseness
   * Dysphagia
   * Chest or shoulder pain
   * Paraneoplastic syndromes

2. Diagnostic measures

   * Rarely diagnosed in early stage
   * Sputum cytology
   * Chest x-ray
   * Bronchoscopy
   * Percutaneous needle biopsy
   * Mediastinoscopy
   * CT and MRI

Interventions

1. SCLC

   * Prognostic indicators are extent of disease, performance status, weight loss, and response to therapy

   * Combination chemotherapy with or without radiation therapy (RT) is standard treatment

   * Chemotherapy combinations have included

     Cyclophosphamide

     Etoposide

     Doxorubicin

     Cisplatin

     Vincristine

     Ifosfamide

   * High doses produce better response

   * RT to chest with chemotherapy has reduced intrathoracic relapse

   * Prophylactic brain irradiation has been used

2. NSCLC

   * Extent of disease determines treatment and prognosis

   * Surgery

     Complete surgical resection is only chance for cure in early stage disease

     Only 20% to 25% of NSCLC patients qualify for complete surgical resection

Lobectomy or pneumonectomy are surgical procedures for localized disease

* RT

  For patients who are not surgical candidates or have unresectable disease

* Chemotherapy

  NSCLCs less sensitive to chemotherapy

  Cisplatin and RT for inoperable patients has increased survival 4 to 6 months

  New agents are being investigated

3. Symptom management

   * Distressing physical symptoms include

     Cough

     Hemoptysis

     Pain

     Fatigue

     Dyspnea

     Gastrointestinal disturbances

   * Pulmonary fibrosis may occur as result of RT and chemotherapy

   * Psychosocial issues and dilemmas include

     Quality of life

     Fear of suffering

     Depression

     Limited survival

     Family disruptions

4. Because of poor survival, nurses coordinate and provide palliative interventions

Suggested Readings

1. Ingle RJ: Lung cancer. In Groenwald SL, Frogge MH, Goodman M, Yarbro CH (eds): *Cancer Nursing: Principles and Practice* (4th ed). Boston: Jones and Bartlett, 1997, pp 1260-1290.
2. Risser NL: Prevention of lung cancer: The key is to stop smoking. *Semin Oncol Nurs* 12:260-229, 1996.
3. Maxwell M: New developments in lung cancer. *Semin Oncol Nurs* 12: 249-324, 1997.
4. Klemm PR: Variables influencing psychosocial adjustment in lung cancer: A preliminary study. *Oncol Nurs Forum* 21: 1059-1062, 1994.

CHAPTER 48

Multiple Myeloma

Overview

Most common of malignant plasma cell disorders

Represents 1% of hematologic malignancies

Characterized by overproduction of one specific immunoglobulin, designated IgM, or M protein (myeloma or malignant protein)

About 80% to 90% of multiple myeloma patients have evidence of aberrant M protein in serum

Although excessive amount of immunoglobulin is produced, M protein is unable to produce antibody necessary for maintaining humoral immunity

Affects hematologic, skeletal, renal, and nervous systems

Onset is late

Peak incidence is between ages 50 and 70

More common among African-Americans than whites

Male predominance in incidence

Once symptoms present, median survival is 7 months; survival can extend to 3 years with standard therapy

Risk factors

1. Genetic linkage
2. Chronic low-level exposure to radiation
3. Chronic antigenic stimulation (recurrent infection, allergy)
4. Occupational exposure to wood, textiles, rubber, metal, petroleum, herbicides

Approaches to Care

Assessment

1. Clinical manifestations

* Multiple myeloma has a long prodromal, indolent, or asymptomatic period

* Once symptoms appear, systemic therapy begins

* Most frequent symptom at presentationis bone pain

* Skeletal involvement

    68% to 80% of patients present with destructive, painful osteolytic lesions

    Hypercalcemia (20% to 40% of patients)

    Pathologic fractures with acute and chronic pain

    Decreased mobility

    Diminished ability in activities of daily living

    Bony lesions can be of three types

        Solitary osteolytic lesion

        Diffuse osteoporosis

        Multiple discrete osteolytic lesions ("punched out" or "cannon ball" lesions)

    Eventually skeletal involvement can lead to

        Compression fractures of spine

        Refractory hypercalcemia

        Death from neurologic sequelae or severe hypercalcemia and renal failure

* Infection

    50% to 70% of patients die from bacterial infections

    Most common sites of infection are respiratory and urinary tract

Biphasic pattern is common

> *Streptococcus pneumoniae* and *Haemophilus influenzae* infections occur early in disease

> *Nonencapsulated gram-negative bacilli and S. auereus infections occur later*

> Mechanisms of infection

>> Deficiency in immunoglobulin response

>> Neutropenia associated with bone marrow suppression

>> Qualitative defects in neutrophil and complement system function

* Bone marrow involvement

> *Normocytic, normochromic anemia is found in more than 60% of patients at initial diagnosis*

> *Hemolysis caused by M protein coating on erythrocytes*

> *Bleeding caused by decreased platelets, M protein's effect on clotting factors, or by coating of platelets with immunoglobulins*

* Renal insufficiency

> *50% of patients develop insufficiency*

> *15% die from renal failure*

> *Intrinsic renal lesions associated with renal failure is called myeloma kidney*

> *Bence-Jones proteins develop and are toxic to renal epithelium*

> *Amyloid deposits can cause another type of renal lesion*

* Other sequelae leading to renal failure

  Untreated hypercalcemia

  Hyperuricemia occurs with large tumor burdens

  Dehydration

  Infection and sepsis

* Hyperviscosity syndrome

  Caused by high concentration of proteins that increases serum viscosity and results in vascular sludging

  Clinical signs

    Blurred vision

    Drowsiness

    Irritability

* Confusion

* Headache

2. Diagnostic measures

   * Bone marrow biopsy to check percentage of plasma cells

   * Serum protein electrophoresis to check for presence of M protein

   * Serum chemistry for hypercalcemia or renal function

   * Complete blood count for anemia, thrombocytopenia

   * Skeletal survey for bone lesions

   * Staging of multiple myeloma integrates clinical and laboratory findings

* Durie-Salmon system of stages I to III is commonly used

Interventions

1. Patients with indolent, asymptomatic multiple myeloma are usually not treated
2. Once symptoms occur, standard therapy is initiated
3. Chemotherapy is used with onset of symptoms (anemia, hypercalcemia, pain)

   * Melphalan and prednisone are standard first-line therapy

     Response rate is 50% and survival is 24 to 36 months

     Melphalan 8 mg/m^2/day for 4 days along with prednisone 75 mg/day for 4 days is cycle, repeated every 4 weeks

     Monitor patient closely for signs of renal impairment

     Bone marrow suppressive effects can be cumulative in older adults

     If myeloma is unresponsive, melphalan dose is increased

   * Other common protocol is vincristine, doxorubicin, and dexamethasone (VAD)

     May be used as initial therapy and for refractory disease

     Dosages vary by protocol followed

     Improved response rates (84%) and survival

     Clinicians must monitor

Total dose of doxorubicin and response

Signs of steroid toxicity

Severe dyspepsia

Fluid and sodium retention

Myopathy

Pancreatitis

Hyperglycemia

Psychosis

Signs of neurologic toxicity

Bone marrow suppression

Hepatic toxicity

* If drug resistance emerges, cyclophosphamide can be used as second-line therapy

* 30% to 40% of patients respond to first-line therapy; second-line therapies are commonly used with response rate of 70%

4. Interferon

* Stimulates host cells to inhibit plasma cell and myeloma stem cell growth

* Has been used for untreated patients and after standard first-line chemotherapy, to prolong response and survival

5. Radiation

* Used to palliate bone lesions and control pain

* Multiple myeloma is highly radioresponsive

* Hemibody irradiation has been used for refractory or advanced myeloma

6. Bone marrow transplantation has been attempted; technical difficulties in purging myeloma from marrow limits its use

    * Incorporate hematopoetic growth factors to reduce neutropenia after chemotherapy

7. Treatment-related acute leukemia

    * Develops after primary therapy

    * Cause is considered to be prolonged administration of alkylating agents

    * Can be refractory to treatment

    * Treated patients have dismal survival period of 4 to 8 months

8. Nursing management

    * Pain is usually caused by bony involvement; in addition to aggressive pain management approaches, positioning, braces, supports, and massages can help

    * Mental status changes can result from hypercalcemia, hyperviscosity, or drug toxicity; closely assess patient to prevent injury

    * Infection is leading cause of death; early recognition and prevention of infection and bleeding are needed

    * Provide respiratory care measures to prevent pooling of secretions and to increase gas exchange

* Because of decreased physical activity and medications, constipation is common; assess patient's activity changes and dietary intake

* Prevent or quickly reverse renal insufficiency by providing adequate hydration, administration of allopurinol, and close monitoring for signs of urinary tract infection

Suggested Readings

1. Sheridan CA: Multiple myeloma. In Groenwald SL, Frogge MH, Goodman M, Yarbro CH (eds): *Cancer Nursing: Principles and Practice* (4th ed). Boston: Jones and Bartlett, 1997, pp 1319-1333.
2. Sheridan CA: Multiple myeloma. *Semin Oncol Nurs* 12:1-12, 1996.
3. Alexanian R, Dimopoulos MA: Management of multiple myeloma. *Semin Hematol* 32:20-30, 1995.
4. Varterasian ML: Biologic and clinical advances in multiple myeloma. *Oncology* 9:417-424, 1995.

CHAPTER 49

Non–Hodgkin's Lymphoma

Overview

Incidence of non–Hodgkin's lymphoma (NHL) is escalating; in the U.S., it is now the fifth most common cancer in males and the sixth most common in females

Nearly six times more frequent than Hodgkin's disease, and death rate is 13 times greater

Incidence is higher in males and white population

Average age of occurrence is fifth decade

Variety of etiologic factors have been implicated

1. Viral infections
2. Genetic abnormalities
3. Exposure to pesticides, fertilizers, chemicals

Approaches to Patient Care

Assessment

1. Clinical manifestations

    * Can involve almost any organ or tissue
    * 80% of patients present with advanced disease (stage III or IV), reflected by

    Painless, generalized lymphadenopathy

    "B" symptoms

    Fever

    Night sweats

    Weight loss

    Gastrointestinal symptoms

    Pain

    Abdominal mass

    Anorexia

    Lung infiltration

    Cough

    Dyspnea

    Chest pain

    Pleural effusion

Superior vena cava syndrome

Bone, liver, brain manifestations

2. Diagnostic measures

   * Biopsy confirms histopathology
   * Staging work-up determines extent of disease, tumor mass, and potential complications
   * NHL occurs in many locations and requires numerous studies for staging

Interventions

1. Treatment depends on histology, extent of disease, and performance status

   * Low-grade lymphomas

     Occur in older individuals

     Occur equally in males and females

     Majority of patients are asymptomatic

     Usual presenting problem is painless lymphadenopathy

     Slow growing, with median survival of 7 to 9 years

     Treatment includes irradiation, single-agent chemotherapy, or combination chemotherapy

   * Intermediate-grade lymphomas

     Follicular NHL

       Aggressive clinical course

       Most patients have advanced disease

Diffuse patterns of NHL

Disease limited to one side of diaphragm

Occur mostly in adults

Nodal and extranodal involvement

If untreated, survival is less than 2 years

Treatment includes combination chemotherapy and irradiation

* High-grade lymphomas

Immunoblastic

Occurs in adults older than age 50

Anemia and "B" symptoms are common

High incidence of cutaneous disease

Poor response to chemotherapy and poor survival rate

Lymphoblastic

Occurs in adolescents and young adults

More predominant in men than in women

Majority of patients present with mediastinal mass

Lymph node involvement and bone lesions

Rapid, progressive disease

Non-Burkitt's lymphoma

Uncommon; median age is 34

Lymph node and extranodal presentation

Treatment is generally ineffective and survival is approximately 1 year

Aggressive combination chemotherapy is treatment for high-grade lymphomas

2. Nursing care related to radiation and chemotherapeutic side effects is covered in chapters 8 and 9
3. Delayed toxicities vary from minor to severe problems
4. Nurses play pivotal role in

    * Providing emotional support

    * Providing symptom management

    * Rehabilitating cured patient to return to healthy lifestyle

Suggested Readings

1. Yarbro CH, McFadden ME: Malignant lymphomas. In Groenwald SL, Frogge MH, Goodman M, Yarbro CH (eds): *Cancer Nursing: Principles and Practice* (4th ed). Boston: Jones and Bartlett, 1997, pp 1291-1318.
2. Rahr VA, Tucker R: Non-Hodgkin's lymphoma: Understanding the disease. *Cancer Nurs* 13:56-91, 1990.

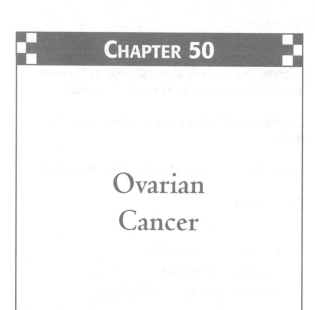

CHAPTER 50

Ovarian
Cancer

Overview

Most common cause of death from gynecologic cancers

Fifth leading cause of death overall in women in U.S.

Poor survival rate of 30% to 35% has been unchanged for 30 years because

1. Difficult to diagnosis early
2. Lack of curative treatments
3. Undefined high-risk group
4. Essentially unknown etiology

503

In 1996, there were about 26,700 new cases and 14,800 deaths from ovarian cancer

An estimated 1 in 71 women develops the disease

Occurs most often between ages 55 and 59

Risk factors

1. Environmental factors
   * Industrialized countries
   * Higher educational level
   * Higher socioeconomic level
   * Delayed childbearing pattern

2. Hormonal, menstrual, reproductive factors
   * Nulliparity
   * First pregnancy after age 35
   * Incessant ovulation (uninterrupted by pregnancy, lactation, contraceptives)
   * Early menarche
   * Late menopause
   * Hormonal therapy

3. Dietary factors (controversial)
   * High-fat diet

4. Hereditary factors
   * Family history of ovarian cancer
   * Family history of breast cancer
   * Family history of colon cancer

5. Protective factors

* Use of oral contraceptives
* Effect persists for 15 years after use

Ovarian cancers include several histologic types

1. Epithelial tumors constitute 80% to 90% of ovarian cancers
2. Tumors of low malignant potential, which represent 15% of epithelial tumors, are distinct entities between benign and invasive disease characterized by

   * Cellular proliferation
   * No invasive properties
   * Favorable prognosis

3. Histologic grade is important predictor of response and survival, especially stages I to II

75% of ovarian cancer patients have metastatic disease at diagnosis

Metastatic routes include

1. Invasion of stromal tissue
2. Penetration of capsule of ovary
3. Commonly spread by direct extension to adjacent organs, i.e., uterus, fallopian tubes, bladder, rectosigmoid colon, and pelvic peritoneum
4. Intraperitoneal seeding: Cells exfoliate and are carried to surfaces of organs within peritoneum
5. Lymphatic spread

Death is often secondary to intra-abdominal tumor dissemination that produces bowel and mesentery malfunction and alteration

Approaches to Care

Assessment

1. Clinical manifestations
   * No typical early manifestations
   * Abdominal fullness
   * Discomfort
   * Vague symptoms

2. Diagnostic measures
   * Routine pelvic examination
   * Barium enema
   * Proctosigmoidoscopy and gastrointestinal series
   * Chest x-ray
   * Ultrasound
   * CT scan
   * MRI for small lesions
   * Surgical staging and debulking

Interventions

1. Initial therapy involves surgical staging and cytoreduction
   * Surgical staging involves

   Evaluation of all peritoneal surfaces

Evaluation of subdiaphragmatic surfaces

Multiple biopsies

Palpation of all abdominal organs and surfaces

* Cytoreduction involves removing visible tumor to extent possible

* Stage I disease (15% to 20% of patients)

  90% survival rate with surgery alone

  If fertility is concern, conservative surgical treatment is used

  No standard adjuvant therapy is defined

* Stage II disease (tumor extends to peritoneal organs) is treated after cytoreduction with

  Intraperitoneal chromic phosphate (^{32}P)

  Whole-abdominal radiation

  Single-agent chemotherapy

  Platinum-based combination chemotherapy

* Stages III and IV disease (60% to 70% of patients)

  Requires more aggressive cytoreductive surgery and adjuvant therapy

  Platinum-based combination chemotherapy or whole-abdominal and pelvic radiation

  Survival rates are comparable for chemotherapy and radiation; morbidity is greater with radiation

2. Recurrent or persistent disease treatment approaches are of limited benefit and duration of response and include

* Second-look surgery is performed on those with complete clinical response after full-course chemotherapy

  To determine if therapy should stop

  To assess response and change therapy

  To perform secondary cytoreductive surgery

* Tumor-associated antigens can be monitored, but are not specific for ovarian cancer

  CA-125 is used to supplement standard disease monitoring

  CA-19-9 is used in combination with CA-125 to correlate response

* Chemotherapy is mainstay of adjuvant treatment for stages III and IV

  Single agents

    Cisplatin is most effective single agent; response rates as high as 55%

    A new drug, paclitaxel, has a 30% response rate in previously treated patients

    Topotecan is effective against refractory ovarian cancer

  Combination chemotherapy is extensively used; protocols of two to four agents typically include

    Hexamethylmelamine

    Cisplatin

    Cyclophosphamide

    Doxorubicin

    Methotrexate

Carboplatin

5-Fluorouracil

Taxol

Cisplatin, carboplatin, and taxol have generated much interest among researchers to determine effective recurrent disease protocol

Death can result from chemotherapy-refractory disease

Debulking surgeries reduce tumor burden and improve response to chemotherapy by reducing potentially refractory disease

Intraperitoneal chemotherapy

Benefits patients who have minimal residual disease after systemic therapy or who have high-grade tumors, or both

Is delivered via semipermanent dialysis catheter or port system implanted into abdominal cavity

Large volumes of fluid and chemotherapy can be administered

Hormone therapy

Has resulted in uneven responses

Tamoxifen has been investigated as second-line therapy for chemotherapy-refractory disease

* Radiotherapy

^{32}P can be administered by intraperitoneal infusion to produce even distribution of agent throughout abdomen

External-beam radiotherapy effectiveness is directly related to the volume of tumor to be treated

If tumor is less than 2 cm, equivalent results are achieved with radiation or chemotherapy

* Biologic therapy

  Includes monoclonal antibodies, adoptive cellular immunotherapy, and interferon

  Agents remain in abdominal cavity for prolonged periods

  Agents have manageable toxicities

* Management of side effects is reviewed in chapters 9 and 10

* General supportive measures

  Most women will develop abdominal ascites

  Self-care measures need to be learned

  Care of catheter

  Monitoring weight gain

  Measuring abdominal girth

  Diversional activities and guided imagery can help

Suggested Readings

1. Walczak JR, Klemm PR, Guarnieri C: Gynecologic cancers. In Groenwald SL, Frogge MH, Goodman M, Yarbro CH (eds): *Cancer Nursing: Principles and Practice* (4th ed). Boston: Jones and Bartlett, 1997, pp 1151-1163.

2. Young R, Perez CA, Hoskins WJ: Cancer of the ovary. In DeVita VT, Hellman S, Rosenberg SA (eds): *Cancer: Principles and Practice of Oncology* (4th ed) Philadelphia: JB Lippincott, 1993, pp 1226-1263.

3. Eriksson JH, Walczak JR: Ovarian cancer. *Semin Oncol Nurs* 6:214-227, 1990.

4. McGuire WP, Hoskins WJ, Brady MF, et al: Cyclophosphamide and cisplatin compared with paclitaxel and cisplatin in patients with Stage III and IV ovarian cancer. *N Engl J Med* 334:1-6, 1996.

CHAPTER 51

Pancreatic
Cancer

Overview

Fifth leading cause of cancer deaths in U.S.

5-year survival rate is only 3%

Fewer than 20% of persons are alive 1 year after diagnosis

Difficult to detect or diagnose before it is advanced

Accounts for 2% of all cancers

Peak incidence occurs between ages 60 and 70

Risk factors are few

1. Cigarette smoking
2. Diet high in animal fat

Protective effect from diet high in fresh fruits and vegetables

About 90% of tumors arise from endocrine pancreas

Adenocarcinoma is dominant morphologic type

Tumors occur in head of pancreas in 60 to 70% of cases

Pancreatic tumors grow slowly with late signs of pathology

Extension of tumor is usually into tissues behind pancreas or to vertebral column

At diagnosis, 90% of cases have perineural invasion, and 70% to 80% have lymphatic spread

Approaches to Care

Assessment

1. Clinical manifestations

   * Early signs are vague and contribute to delay in diagnosis

* Weight loss and abdominal pain are most prominent signs

  Weight loss is accelerated by pain, anorexia, nausea, vomiting

  Malabsorption can lead to diarrhea, constipation, steatorrhea, weakness

* Head of pancreas tumors manifest signs earlier than in other parts of pancreas

  Classic triad is seen: pain, jaundice, weight loss

  Pain

  In epigastric region

  Dull and intermittent

  Ameliorated by sitting in fetal position

  Profound weight loss

  Jaundice

  Presenting symptom in 80% of cases

  Jaundice with pain is more common than painless jaundice

  Patients complain of emotional disturbances and irritability

* Body of pancreas tumours manifest symptoms late in advanced stages

  Severe excruciating epigastric pain causes vomiting

  Splenomegaly

* Tail of pancreas tumours mimic other diseases

Generalized weakness

Upper abdominal pain

Indigestion, anorexia, weight loss

Diagnostic measures

1. Physical examination
2. Radiologic studies: Ultrasound, CT scan, endoscopic retrograde cholangiopancreatography (ERCP), arteriography, endoscopoic ultrasound, percutaneous fine needle aspiration
3. Laboratory profiles, tumor markers (CA 19-9, CA 242, CA 494)

Interventions

1. Radical therapy if cure is believed possible
2. Palliative therapy if disease is advanced
3. Multimodal therapy is being studied to determine if survival is extended
4. Surgery

   * Plagued by low resectability rates of less than 10% of cases

   * Surgical approaches for cure

   Pancreatoduodenectomy (Whipple procedure)

   Approach used most often when cure is objective

   Most commonly performed operation for pancreatic cancer

   Resect distal stomach, pancreas to superior mesenteric vein, duodenum, proximal jejunum, distal common duct, and gallbladder

   A modified approach, pylorus-preserving pancreaticoduodenectomy, is preferred by

some because stomach and cuff of duodenum
are preserved

Pancreatic fistula and delayed gastric emptying
are complications

Extended pancreatectomy

Resect entire pancreas, duodenum, gastric
antrum, bile duct, gallbladder, spleen, and
nodes

Lymph node involvement is important
prognostic indicator

Total pancreatectomy

En bloc resection including antrum, common
duct, gallbladder, pancreas, jejunum,
duodenum, and nodes

Distal pancreatectomy

Resect only involved pancreas and nodes

⁎ Surgical approaches for palliation

Used in over 85% of cases

*Obstructive jaundice, obstruction, and pain are
common symptoms needing palliation*

Decompression procedures

Cholecystojejunostomy

Choledochojejunostomy

Pancreatojejunostomy

Biliary bypass procedures

Percutaneous or endoscopic gastroenterostomy

Biliary stents

Chemical splanchnicectomy for pain

★ Postoperative care focuses on prevention of

Hemorrhage

Hypovolemia

Hypotension

Pulmonary complications

Exocrine and endocrine alterations

Endocrine function can be regulated with insulin

Exocrine function can result in malabsorption syndromes

Nutritional therapy, pancreatic enzyme supplements, and lipase administration may be needed

Diet therapy

Low-fat, high-carbohydrate foods

Small meals

Restrict caffeine

Restrict alcohol

5. Chemotherapy

★ Used as adjuvant therapy with limited results

★ Agents used

5-Fluorouracil

Ifosfamide

Mitomycin-c

Doxorubicin

Streptozocin

6. Radiotherapy

   * Used for both palliative and curative external therapy

   * Limitation to effectiveness is large volume of tissue to be irradiated

   * Combinations of radiotherapy and chemotherapy are used successfully to increase survival time

7. Supportive therapy: Most common measures

   * Continuous administration of pain relief measures

   * Nutritional support via oral feedings, supplemental mixtures, antiemetic therapy, feeding tube, pancreatic enzyme replacements

   * Relief of jaundice using cholestyramine, lotions, avoiding soaps

   * Relief of obstruction via percutaneous transhepatic biliary drainage

Suggested Readings

1. Coleman JA. Gastrointestinal cancer: Esophageal, stomach, liver, and pancreatic cancers. In Groenwald SL, Frogge MH, Goodman M, Yarbro CH (eds): *Cancer Nursing:*

Principles and Practice (4th ed). Boston: Jones and Bartlett, 1997, pp 1082-1144.

2. Coleman JA: Supportive management of the patient with pancreatic cancer: Role of the oncology nurse. *Oncology* 10(suppl):23-25, 1996.

3. Bell RH: Neoplasms of the exocrine pancreas. In Greenfield LJ, Mulholland M, Oldham KT, Zelenock GB, Lillemoe KD (eds): *Surgery: Scientific Principles and Practice* (2nd ed). Philadelphia: JB Lipppincott, 1997, pp 901-915.

4. Lillemoe KD: Current management of pancreatic carcinoma. Ann Surg 221:133-148, 1995.

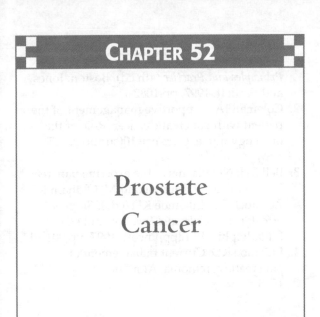

CHAPTER 52

Prostate Cancer

Overview

Most common cancer in American men and second leading cause of cancer death

Highest rate is among black Americans

Cause is unknown but risk factors include

1. Age: Risk increases on an yearly basis after age 50
2. Hormonal factors: Elevated testosterone levels
3. Family history
4. High-fat diet

Screening for prostate cancer involves digital rectal exmination (DRE), analysis of prostate specific antigen (PSA), and if necessary, transrectal ultrasound

National and international prospective randomized trials are evaluating issues related to screening

95% are adenocarcinomas and arise most often in posterior lobe of gland

Tumor growth varies from slow to moderately rapid

Survival related to extent of tumor and histologic grade

Approaches to Care

Assessment

1. Clinical manifestations

   * Usually asymptomatic in early stages
   * Routine rectal examination reveals nodule or mass
   * More than 50% of patients present with localized disease
   * Common symptoms include

     Prostatitis

     Urinary frequency

     Weak stream

Postvoid dribbling

Nocturia

Dysuria

Hematuria

Weight loss

Back pain

Erectile dysfunction

2. Diagnostic measures

    *   Digital rectal examination
    *   PSA levels reflect extent of disease
    *   Normal PSA results are

        | *Ages 40-49* | *0-2.5 ng/ml* |
        | *Ages 50-59* | *0-3.5 ng/ml* |
        | *Ages 60-69* | *0-4.5 ng/ml* |
        | *Ages 70-79* | *0-6.5 ng/ml* |

    *   All abnormal results require additional diagnostic studies
    *   Transrectal ultrasound and biopsy
    *   CT and bone scans, and MRI

Interventions

1. Treatment is controversial and varies
2. Treatment options depend on age, condition, grade and stage of tumor

    *   Watchful waiting or periodic observation

        Early stage (A & B) disease

        May be appropriate option for older men

* Radical prostatectomy

  Done in younger men in good health with localized tumors

  Complications include

  Impotence

  Urinary incontinence

* External beam radiotherapy

  Curative treatment for localized disease

  Palliation for advanced disease

  Common side effects

  Proctitis

  Urinary frequency

  Cystitis

  Diarrhea

  Incontinence and impotency

* Endocrine manipulation

  Used as palliation to reduce tumor size

  Most prostatic tumors are androgen-dependent; therapy attempts to block androgen formation or utilization

  Methods

  Bilateral orchiectomy

  Hormonal agents

    Diethylstilbestrol

    Flutamide

    Leuprolide

Aminoglutethimide

Goserelin acetate

Ketoconazole

Complications

Gynecomastia

Hot flashes

Nausea and vomiting

Edema

Decreased libido

Erectile impotence

79% of patients with advanced disease respond to hormonal manipulation

Duration of response is 1 to 3 years

* Chemotherapy

  Limited role for chemotherapy in advanced, hormonally unresponsive prostate cancer

  Both single-agent and combination regimens are being investigated

  No evidence that radiation or surgery is superior to the other in localized disease

3. Nursing interventions include

   * Encouraging men older than age 40 to have annual rectal examination

   * Provide suggestions for managing loss of libido, impotence, loss of fertility, or urinary incontinence

* Provide postoperative care: bladder
  irrigations, catheter care, prevention of
  infection, wound management, treatment
  for incontinence, pain management, and
  sexual assessment

* Teach patient about side effects of
  radiotherapy, hormonal therapy, and
  chemotherapy

* Patients with advanced disease may require

  Management of bone pain with analgesics

  *Mangement of leg and scrotal edema with
  scrotal elevation, diuretics, compression
  stockings*

  *Catheterization for bladder obstructive
  symptoms*

  *Monitoring for spinal cord compression,
  pulmonary embolism or disseminated
  intravascular coagulation*

Suggested Readings

1. Held-Warmkessel J: Prostate cancer. In
   Groenwald SL, Frogge MH, Goodman M,
   Yarbro CH (eds): *Cancer Nursing: Principles and
   Practice* (4th ed). Boston: Jones and Bartlett,
   1997, pp 1334-1354.
2. Maxwell MB: Cancer of the prostate. *Semin
   Oncol Nurs* 9:237-251, 1993.

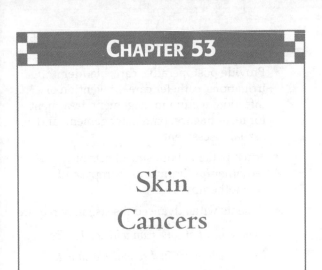

CHAPTER 53

Skin Cancers

Overview

Generally occur in adults and are rare in children

There are two groups

1. Nonmelanoma skin cancer (NMSC)

   * Basal cell carcinoma (BCC)

     Most common skin cancer in whites

     More frequent in men

     Least aggressive type

   * Squamous cell carcinoma (SCC)

      More frequent in men

      More aggressive than BCC

2. Malignant melanomas

   * Most are cutaneous melanomas (CM)

   * Primarily occur in whites

   * More frequent in men

NMSCs occur more often but have a lower mortality rate than malignant melanomas

Melanoma has a high mortality rate

Etiologic factors

1. Light skin, hair, and eyes; easily sunburned
2. Ultraviolet radiation
3. Chlorofluorocarbons
4. Precursor lesions
5. Atypical and changing moles
6. Ionizing radiation
7. Hereditary conditions

Approaches to Patient Care

NMSC

1. Assessment

   * Nodular BCC

      Small, firm, dome-shaped papule

      Pearly white, pink, or skin-colored

Ulcerates as it enlarges

Most common sites

  Face

  Head

  Neck

* Superficial BCC

Flat

Erythematous or pink scaling papules

Well-defined margins

Common sites

  Trunk

  Extremities

* SCC

Flesh-colored or erythematous

Raised, firm papule

May ulcerate and bleed

Common sites are areas exposed to sun

  Nose

  Back of hands

  Forehead

  Lower lip

  Ear

2. Interventions

  * Treatment selection depends on

    Tumor type

Location

Size

Growth pattern

Patient age and general health

* Primary goals of treatment are

  Cure

  Preservation of tissue and function

  Minimal risk

  Good cosmetic results

* There are five standard treatments for NMSCs

  Surgical excision

    Can be performed for any NMSC

    Allows for rapid healing

    Provides good specimen for histologic examination

    Provides good cosmetic results

  Chemosurgery (Mohs' micrographic surgery)

    Preserves maximum amount of tissue

    Complex and specialized technique

    Often used in high-risk areas (nose, ear)

  Curettage and electrodesiccation

    Used for small, superficial, or recurrent BCC because of poor margin control

  Radiotherapy for lesions that are

    Inoperable

Located in corner of nose, eyelid, lip, and canthus

Larger than 1 cm but smaller than 8 cm

Cryotherapy

Involves liquid nitrogen to freeze and thaw tissue; leads to tumor necrosis

Used for recurrent lesions, multiple superficial BCC, and lesions with well-defined margins

Melanoma

1. Assessment

    * There are three precursor lesions of CM

    Dysplastic nevi (DN)

    May occur in familial and nonfamilial settings

    Risk of CM is 100% in members of families with familial DN

    Normal nevi appear between ages of 5 and 8 years, with dysplastic changes after puberty

    Patient with "classic" DN has

    More than 100 moles

    One mole larger than 8 mm

    One mole with CM features

    DN appear on face, trunk, arms, buttocks, groin, scalp, and breast

    Pigmentation is irregular with mixtures of tan, brown and black, or red and pink

    Excisional biopsy is first line of treatment

Follow-up by

Periodic skin examinations

Total-body photographs every 3 to 6 months

Individuals with DN and family members
should be taught

To examine entire body every 1 to 2 months

Preventive behaviors

Melanoma risk factors

Congenital nevi

Present at birth or shortly thereafter

Range in size from large to small, covering
arms, hand, or trunk

Colors range from brown to black

Lesions may have irregular surface

Lifetime risk of malignant transformation is 6%
to 7%

Treatment consists of surgical excision

Lentigo maligna

Large

Tan with shades of brown

10 to 25 years before malignant transformation

∗ The "ABCDE" rule helps to identify CM

A = asymmetry

B = border irregularity

C = color variation or dark black color

    D = diameter more than 0.6 cm (pencil eraser size)

    E = elevation

* Four major types of CM are

    Lentigo maligna melanoma

      4% to 10% of CM

      Least serious type

      Common sites are areas exposed to sun

        Face

        Neck

        Back of hands

    Superficial spreading melanoma

      Accounts for 70% of CM

      Seen on trunk and back in men

      Seen on legs in women

      Aggressive

    Nodular

      Accounts for 15% to 30% of CM

      Common sites are head, neck, trunk

      Most aggressive

    Acral lentiginous

      Found in 35% to 60% of dark-skinned persons, primarily African-Americans, Asians, and Hispanics

      Occurs on palms, soles, nailbeds, mucous membranes

2. Treatment interventions

* Surgery

  Biopsy for suspected CM

  Wide excision for stage I CM

  Excision of primary lesions and surgical dissection of involved nodes for clinical stage II

  Elective lymph node dissection is controversial

* Chemotherapy

  Metastatic melanoma is resistant to chemotherapeutic agents

* Radiotherapy

  Most effective when tumor volume is low

  Often used for palliation

* Immunotherapy

  Several agents (interferons, interleukins, tumor necrosis factors, monoclonal antibodies) are under investigation

3. Preventive interventions

* Many skin cancers can be prevented by reducing exposure to risk factors

* Preventive behaviors

  Minimize sun exposure, especially between 10 am and 3 pm

  Wear protective clothing (hat, sunglasses)

  Use waterproof sunscreen with sun protective factor (SPF) of 15 or more

*Protect self when near surfaces that reflect
ultraviolet rays (water, sand, snow, concrete)*

*Be aware of photosensitivity caused by
medications*

Avoid tanning parlors

Keep infants well protected

* Early detection and diagnosis are essential
* High-risk individuals should receive
  periodic skin examinations

4. Nursing interventions

   * Interview that assesses patient's
     knowledge, medical history, and exposure
     to risk factors
   * Thorough skin assessment to identify
     suspicious lesions
   * Education about skin cancers
   * Posttreatment management and follow-up

Suggested Readings

1. Loescher LJ, Ketcham MA: Skin cancers. In
   Groenwald SL, Frogge MH, Goodman M,
   Yarbro CH (eds): *Cancer Nursing: Principles and
   Practice* (4th ed). Boston: Jones and Bartlett,
   1997, pp 1355-1373.
2. Berwick M, Bolognia JL, Heer C, et al: The role
   of the nurse in skin cancer prevention,
   screening, and early detection. *Semin Oncol
   Nurs* 7:64-71, 1991.

3. Loescher LJ: Skin cancer prevention and detection update. *Semin Oncol Nurs* 9:184-187, 1993.

4. Buller DBB, Callister MA, Reichert T: Skin cancer protection by parents of young children: Health information sources, skin cancer knowledge, and sun-protection practices. *Oncol Nurs Forum* 22: 1559-1566, 1995

CHAPTER 54

Stomach
Tumors

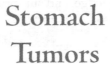

Overview

Gastric cancer is insidious in its onset and mimics other gastric maladies

If detected early and treated aggressively, it can be cured

Usually locally advanced or metastatic when first symptomatic

Overall survival rates are 5% to 15%

Incidence is increasing in some parts of the world, but decreasing in U.S.

In U.S., there are about 23,000 new cases and 14,000 deaths from gastric cancer each year

Higher incidence is seen among African Americans, Japanese immigrants, Chinese immigrants, and native Hawaiians

Risk factors

1. Environmental and genetic factors
2. Immigrants exhibit incidence rates similar to those of their country of origin
3. Those at greatest risk are over age 40 and possess one or more of the following

   * Low socioeconomic status

   * Poor nutritional habits

   * Vitamin A deficiency

   * Family history of gastric cancer

   * Previous gastric resection

   * Pernicious anemia

   * *Helicobacter pylori* infection

   * Gastric atrophy and chronic gastritis

   * Benign peptic ulcer disease

   * Occupation is rubber or coal worker

More than 95% of gastric cancers are adenocarcinoma

1. Most arise in gastric antrum
2. May be classified as polypoid, scirrhous, ulcerative, or superficial

Can progress and metastasize by several routes

1. By direct extension into adjacent structures
2. Local or distant nodal metastases
3. Bloodstream metastases
4. Intraperitoneal dissemination
5. Distant metastatic sites: lung, adrenals, bone, liver

Approaches to Care

Assessment

1. Clinical manifestations

   * Vague, nonspecific symptoms, which lead to delays in seeking medical help

   * Pain in back or epigastric or retrosternal area

   * Vague, uneasy sense of fullness, feeling heavy

   * Feeling moderate distention after meals

   * Progressive weight loss with advanced disease

   * Disturbance in appetite

   * Nausea, vomiting

   * Weakness, fatigue, anemia

   * Dysphagia

   * Hematemesis, melena

2. Diagnostic measures

   * Complete assessment of nutritional status and diet history

* Physical examination for abdominal mass, enlarged nodes, or hepatomegaly
* Rectal examination for metastatic deposits
* If obstruction exists, peristaltic activity moving left-to-right may be detected
* Anemia and jaundice
* Diagnostic studies include

    Upper endoscopic gastroduodenoscopy (EGD)

    Direct biopsy and brushings

    Endoscopic gastroscopy

    Endoscopic ultrasound

    Double-contrast upper gastrointestinal series

    CT scan for metastases and tumor extension

    Hematologic profiles

Interventions

1. Localized tumors are treated with curative intent

    * Aggressive surgery alone or in combination with chemotherapy or radiotherapy
    * About 50% of patients are candidates

2. Advanced tumors that are partially resectable, unresectable, or disseminated are treated with

    * Combination therapy using surgery and chemotherapy, with or without radiotherapy
    * Palliative surgery to

        Alleviate obstruction

        Restore intestinal continuity

3. Surgery

  * Surgery should always be considered, even
    with metastases

  * Surgical candidate has good performance
    status and no major medical problems

  * Types of surgical procedures

    *Total gastrectomy for resectable lesions located
    in midportion of stomach*

      Entire stomach, along with supporting
      mesentery and lymph nodes, is removed

      Esophagus is anastomosed to jejunum

    *Radical subtotal gastrectomy for lesions in
    middle and distal portions*

      Billroth I, or gastroduodenostomy, is choice for
      debilitated individuals, since it is not as
      extensive a resection as Billroth II

      Billroth II, or gastrojejunostomy, is used if
      person can tolerate more radical procedure and
      wider resection

    *Proximal subtotal gastrectomy for tumor located
    in proximal portion of stomach or cardia*

    *Surgical palliation for relief of symptoms, even
    if temporary*

  * Postoperative care

    Potential complications include

      Pneumonia

      Hemorrhage

      Infection

Reflux aspiration

Anastomotic leak

Gastric emptying is altered

Potential complications are typical postgastrectomy syndromes

Steatorrhea

Weight loss

Dumping syndrome

Diarrhea

Nausea

Vitamin deficiency

Vomiting

Anastomotic leak

Dumping syndrome is sequela that affects many but not all patients

Small, frequent feedings of low-carbohydrate, high-fat, high-protein foods recommended

Restrict fluid for 30 minutes before and after meal

Antispasmodics and antiperistaltics can reduce diarrhea

Vitamin B12 deficiency must be treated with replacement doses

4. Radiation therapy

* Gastric adenocarcinomas are generally radiosensitive

* Location and proximity to vital organs in abdomen restrict use

* May be administered in combination with chemotherapy or surgery for recurrent or advanced disease

* Used to augment locoregional control of residual or advanced disease

* Multimodal approaches can improve survival

* Intraoperative radiotherapy is used in Japan but not as much in U.S.

5. Chemotherapy

* No specific chemotherapy regimen alone effective

* Combination drug therapy superior to single agents

* Combinations used most often are

  FAM (5-fluorouracil [5-FU], doxorubicin, mitomycin-C)

  FAP (5-FU, doxorubicin, platinol)

  EAP (etoposide, doxorubicin, platinol)

  FAMTX (5-FU, doxorubicin, leucovorin)

* Intrahepatic and intraperitoneal administration being investigated

6. Supportive therapy

* Nutrition therapy is problematic, either because of obstruction or dysfunction; nutritional support is nursing priority

* Lack of gastric secretory function leads to enzyme and nutrient deficiencies
* Management of pain, pulmonary complications, and dehydration

Suggested Readings

1. Coleman JA. Gastrointestinal cancer: Esophageal, stomach, liver, and pancreatic cancers. In Groenwald SL, Frogge MH, Goodman M, Yarbro CH (eds): *Cancer Nursing: Principles and Practice* (4th ed). Boston: Jones and Bartlett, 1997, pp 1082-1144.
2. Vezeridis MP, Wanebo HJ: Gastric cancer: Surgical approach. In Ahlgren JD, Macdonald JS (eds): *Gastrointestinal Oncology.* Philadelphia: JB Lippincott, 1992, pp 159-170.
3. Alexander HR, Kelsen DP, Tepper JE: Cancer of the stomach. In DeVita VT, Hellman S, Rosenberg SA (eds): *Cancer: Principles and Practice of Oncology* (4th ed). Philadelphia: JB Lippincott, 1993, pp 818-848.
4. Rugge M, Cassaro M, Leandro G, et al: *Helicobacter pylori* in promotion of gastric carcinogenesis. *Dig Dsi Sci* 41:950-955, 1996.

CHAPTER 55

Testicular Cancer

Overview

Accounts for 1% to 2% of all cancers in men

Most common solid tumor in men between ages 20 and 30

Higher incidence in upper socioeconomic classes

Highly curable but has tremendous impact on economic, emotional, and social status

Etiologic factors

1. Cryptorchidism
2. Exogenous estrogens taken by mother
3. Cytogenetic abnormality on chromosome 12

Testicular tumors arise from germ tissue and are classified as

1. Nonseminomatous germ cell tumors
2. Seminoma

Metastasis occurs either by extension or via lymphatics

Young men should practice monthly testicular self-examination

Approaches to Patient Care

Assessment

1. Clinical manifestations

   * Painless enlarged testicle
   * Symptoms related to metastasis include

     Lumbar pain

     Abdominal or supraclavicular masses

     Cough

     Gynecomastia

2. Diagnostic measures

   * Inguinal orchiectomy for definitive pathologic diagnosis
   * Fine-needle biopsy and transcrotal approach to orchiectomy are contraindicated because they may increase recurrence and metastasis

* Radiographic studies

    Chest x-ray

    Intravenous pyelogram

    CT scans

    Ultrasound

* Laboratory studies

* Serum alpha-fetoprotein (AFP) level

* Lactic acid dehydrogenase level

* Human chorionic gonadotropin (HCG) level

* AFP and HCG tumor markers aid in diagnosis, response to treatment, and detection of residual tumor

* AFP and HCG levels are elevated in 85% of males with disseminated testicular cancer

Interventions

1. Treatment of nonseminomas

    * Retroperitoneal lymphadenectomy (RPLND) for stage I

    * Adjuvant cisplatin-based chemotherapy after RPLND in stage II disease prevents relapse in nearly 100% of men

    * Disseminated disease treated with cisplatin-based chemotherapy; 30% require surgery (RPLND) after chemotherapy

2. Treatment of seminomas

* Seminomas uniquely sensitive to
  radiotherapy

* Stage I and stage II (nonbulky) disease

  *Adjuvant radiotherapy following radical
  orchiectomy*

* Stage IIC and disseminated disease

  *Primary chemotherapy using cisplatin-based
  regimen*

3. Salvage therapy in recurrent disease

   * One of few cancers where second-line
     chemotherapy offers chance of cure

   * High-dose chemotherapy with stem cell
     rescue being investigated in patients
     refractory to cisplatin therapy

4. Nursing care includes

   * Fertility evaluation for man who wishes to
     father a child later

   * Anticipation of anxiety and threat to
     masculinity, sexual potency, and fertility

   * Assurance that loss of ejaculatory ability
     after RPLND is usually not permanent

   * Assurance of normal sexual functioning
     after unilateral orchiectomy

   * Monitoring and management of side effects
     related to radiotherapy and chemotherapy

   * Education, encouragement, and emotional
     support help men cope with testicular
     cancer and its treatment

Suggested Readings

1. Brock DL, Fox SM: Testicular germ cell cancer. In Groenwald SL, Frogge MH, Goodman M, Yarbro CH (eds): *Cancer Nursing: Principles and Practice* (4th ed). Boston: Jones and Bartlett, 1997, pp 1374-1389.
2. Brock D, Fox S, Gosling G, et al: Testicular cancer. *Semin Oncol Nurs* 9:224-236, 1993.

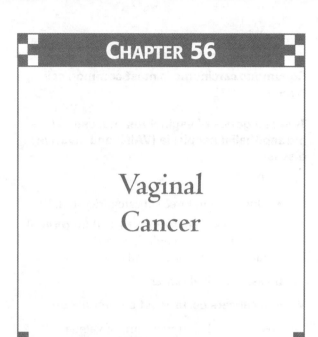

CHAPTER 56

Vaginal Cancer

Overview

One of rarest gynecologic tumors

Accounts for 1% to 2% of gynecologic tumors

Peak incidence is in women between ages 50 and 70

Rates are highest in

1. African-American populations
2. Low socioeconomic levels

Vaginal tumors are usually secondary sites of metastatic disease

549

Squamous carcinoma is most common cell type

Two categories of vaginal tumors, vaginal intraepithelial neoplasia (VAIN) and invasive disease:

1. VAIN

    * Divided into three subcategories: I, II, III
    * Usually seen in women treated for cervical intraepithelial neoplasia or after radiotherapy for cervical cancer

2. Invasive vaginal cancer

Vaginal cancers occur most commonly on

1. Posterior wall of upper third of vagina
2. Anterior wall of lower third of vagina

Tumor may spread along vaginal wall into cervix or vulva

Metastasis to lungs and supraclavicular nodes

Overall survival rate is 40% to 50%

There is little consensus on treatment

Risk factors include

1. History of human papillomavirus (HPV)
2. Vaginal trauma
3. Previous abdominal hysterectomy
4. Lack of regular Pap smears
5. Age (risk increases with age)
6. Young women exposed to diethylstilbestrol

Approaches to Care

Assessment

1. Clinical manifestations

   * Abnormal Pap smear
   * Abnormal vaginal bleeding
   * Foul-smelling discharge
   * Dysuria
   * Urinary symptoms

2. Diagnostic measures

   * Visual examination
   * Palpation of vagina
   * Pap smear (for squamous cell, not adenocarcinoma)
   * Colposcopy
   * Vaginal and cervical biopsies
   * Chest x-ray
   * Biochemical profile
   * Intravenous pyelogram, barium enema
   * Cystoscopy
   * Proctosigmoidoscopy

Interventions

1. Treatment of VAIN

   * Depends on location and whether lesion is single focus or multifocal
   * Depends on size of lesion

* Local excision is used for single-focus lesions

* Total vaginectomy for women who fail conservative therapy

* Local application of 5-fluorouracil cream can eradicate preinvasive lesions

* Laser therapy for single-focus or multifocal lesions

* For poor surgical candidates, irradiation is used

2. Treatment of invasive disease

* Treatment of choice is radiotherapy, especially for women with stage I and stage II disease

* Small lesions may be treated with local radiation

* Larger lesions may require both local and regional radiation

* Lesions that do not respond to radiation can be treated with surgery

3. Nursing measures

* Education and support during aggressive therapies

* Vaginal fibrosis and scarring with loss of blood supply lead to the need for measures to preserve vaginal elasticity

* Frequent intercourse or use of a vaginal dilator can help maintain vaginal flexibility

* Open communication is essential

* Excellent clinical assessments and astute interventions facilitate therapeutic outcomes

Suggested Readings

1. Walczak JR, Klemm PR, Guarnieri C: Gynecologic cancers. In Groenwald SL, Frogge MH, Goodman M, Yarbro CH (eds): *Cancer Nursing: Principles and Practice* (4th ed). Boston: Jones and Bartlett, 1997, pp 1185-1187.

2. Chamorro T: Cancer of the vulva and vagina. *Semin Oncol Nurs* 6:198-205, 1990.

3. Aho M, Vesterinen E, Meyer B, et al: Natural history of vaginal intraepithelial neoplasia. *Cancer* 68(1):195-197, 1991.

4. Kucera H, Vavra N: Radiation management of primary carcinoma of the vagina: Clinical and histopathologic variables associated with survival. *Gynecol Oncol* 40:12-16, 1991.

Chapter 57

Vulvar Cancer

Overview

Disease of elderly that occurs rarely; accounts for 3% to 4% of all gynecologic cancers

Peak incidence occurs between ages 70 and 80

Usually remains localized

Has overall 5-year survival rate of between 70% and 75% for all stages; survival is even higher for women with disease-negative nodes

Treatment is predominantly surgical

554

Vulvar cancer is categorized as either:

1. Preinvasive vulvar lesions: Vulvar intraepithelial neoplasia (VIN I,II,III)
2. Invasive vulvar cancer

Etiology of VIN and invasive vulvar cancer is unknown

Risk factors

1. Advanced age (age 60 or older)
2. Chronic vulvar disease
3. Previous malignancy of lower genital tract
4. History of breast cancer
5. Human papillomavirus
6. Herpes simplex virus type 2 (HSV2)
7. Chronic irritation
8. Exposure to coal tar derivatives
9. Multiple sexual partners
10. Venereal warts
11. Cigarette smoking

Labia are sites of 70% of vulvar cancer

1. Labia majora involved three times more than labia minora
2. Can develop in clitoris

Vulvar cancer

1. Localized disease with well-defined margins
2. Squamous cell cancer (90% of cases)

Common routes of metastatic spread

1. Direct extension
2. Lymphatic dissemination to regional nodes (46% of cases)

Approaches to Care

Assessment

1. Clinical manifestations

   * VIN

     50% of patients are asymptomatic

     Vulvar pruritus

     Burning (vulvodynia)

     Woman may delay seeking treatment, sometimes for 2 to 16 months

   * Invasive vulvar cancer

     20% of patients are asymptomatic

     Lesions detected during routine examinations

     Presence of mass

     Growth in vulvar area

     Vulvar pain and bleeding

2. Diagnostic measures

   * Invasive vulvar cancer

     Local excisional biopsy

     Colposcopy

     Pap smear

     Complete examination of vulva, cervix, and vagina

   * VIN

     Inspection

Toluidine stain

Colposcopy

Biopsy

* Metastatic work-up

Chest x-ray

Proctosigmoidoscopy

Cystoscopy

Barium enema

Intravenous pyelogram

Biochsemical profile

* Staging is according to International Federation of Gynecology and Obstetrics (FIGO) system

Interventions

1. Local disease

   * VIN treatment is controversial

     Wide local excision with primary closure skin flaps or skin grafts

     Multicentric disease treatment

       Skinning vulvectomy: Vulvar skin is excised and split-thickness skin graft is applied; requires prolonged bed rest for healing to occur

       Simple vulvectomy can be used for elderly or those with chronic diseases

   * Alternative to vulvectomy is laser, cryosurgery, or cautery

May cause painful ulcerations that take 3 months to heal

* Topical 5% 5-fluorouracil in daily applications may cause painful, slow-healing ulcers

2. Invasive vulvar cancer is treated with surgery

   * En bloc dissection of tumor, regional inguinal and femoral nodes, vulva, and sometimes pelvic nodes

   * Nodal dissection can also be achieved through separate incisions in groin, rather than by en bloc approach

   * Early lesions: Stage I (less than 2 cm lesion with less than 5 mm of stromal invasion) are treated with modified radical vulvectomy without groin dissection

   * Stage II and III lesions require more extensive surgery

     Radical vulvectomy

     Bilateral inguinal-femoral lymphadenectomy

     If needed, resection of surrounding organs: urethra, vagina, anus, rectum

   * Stage IV disease

     Pelvic exenteration may be required in addition to

     Radical vulvectomy (if rectum or bladder is involved)

     Radiotherapy may be used if tumor is fixed or distant metastases

★ Possible complications after radical surgery

Wound breakdown, infection

Chronic leg edema

Recurrent cellulitis of leg

Deep venous thrombosis

Pulmonary embolism

Genital prolapse

Urinary stress incontinence

★ Radiotherapy can be used in combination with surgery

Useful for those considered at high risk for recurrence

Potential wound-healing problems with radiation

★ 80% of recurrences occur within first 2 years of treatment

Surgery is used to treat local recurrence

Recurrence may be treated with radiotherapy and surgery

3. Nursing measures concentrate on patient education

★ Explain disease and treatment

★ Instruct patient in self-care

Address concerns about sexual functioning

Discuss changes in libido, orgasm, coital frequency, fertility

★ Stress importance of follow-up

Discuss possibility of treatment failure

Assess patient for anxiety, depression, changes in self-image or body image

Suggested Readings

1. Walczak JR, Klemm PR, Guarnieri C: Gynecologic cancers. In Groenwald SL, Frogge MH, Goodman M, Yarbro CH (eds): *Cancer Nursing: Principles and Practice* (4th ed). Boston: Jones and Bartlett, 1997, pp 1181-1185.

2. Chammaro T: Cancer of the vulva and vagina. *Semin Oncol Nurs* 6:198-205, 1990.

3. di Paola GR, Belardi MG: Squamous vulvar intraepithelial neoplasia. In Knapstein PG, diRe F, Disaia P, et al (eds): *Malignancies of the Vulva*. New York: Thieme Medical Publishers, 1991, pp 57-72.

4. Hacker MF: Vulvar cancer. In Berek JS, Hacker MF (eds): *Practical Gynecologic Oncology*. Baltimore: Williams & Wilkins, 1994, pp 403-439.

PART V

Issues in Cancer Survivorship

CHAPTER 58

Psychosocial
Responses
to Cancer

Overview

**Psychosocial responses to cancer experience
are determined by**

1. Characteristics of cancer
2. Person with or at risk for cancer
3. Social system and environment of significance
   to individual

Cancer poses a universal threat

1. Cancer is among the most feared of all
   diseases because

   * It occurs without warning

563

* It spreads without control
* It is incurable beyond a certain point
* It is associated with pain and discomfort
* It generates social and professional attitudes of hopelessness
* It is difficult to diagnose
* It sometimes requires mutilating surgery
* It has an unknown cause
* Cooperation with treatment does not necessarily lead to successful outcomes

2. Perceived absence of pathology is never certain; there is constant threat of cancer that can alter achievement of societal roles and self-actualization

The stigma of cancer persists

1. Individuals with cancer experience

   * Insurance cancellation
   * Job discrimination
   * Problems with reintegration into school and workplace

Disease and treatment are marked by uncertainty

1. Uncertainty is compounded by

   * Delays in diagnosis
   * Unpredictable prognoses
   * Early death

Cancer trajectory is manifested by chronicity

1. Simple crisis resolution models are not sufficient to address scope of problems encountered
2. People with cancer are confronted with continuing series of stressors, rather than a single, time-limited crisis
3. Lifelong fear of recurrence is one of the most disruptive aspects
4. Outcome goal is to maintain quality of life throughout all phases of illness
5. "Recovery model" of chronic disease of cancer focuses on survival versus dying and emphasizes self-care over professional intervention
6. Self-care and social and professional support strengthen recovery and influence quality of life throughout recovery process

Individual Responses to Cancer

Help-seeking responses

1. Patients search for psychosocial resources to deal with actual or potential threat of cancer
2. Patients do self-appraisal and then expand spheres to significant others and finally to members of health care professions
3. Return to health is manifested by professional returning responsibility for health care to family and ultimately to patient

Culturally determined responses

1. Specific culture of individual shapes his or her view of health

2. Health and illness responses and behaviors are acquired through lifelong socialization

3. Cancer can challenge lifelong values and beliefs and may result in changed cognitive, affective, and behavioral responses

Stress, emotions, and coping responses

1. Stress is

   * Relationship between person and environment in which demands tax or exceed person's resources

   * System of interdependent processes, including appraisal and coping, that mediate frequency, intensity, duration, and type of psychologic and somatic responses

   * Not an inherent characteristic of person or environment

2. Coping

   * Consists of cognitive and behavioral efforts to manage stress

   * Responses used initially by patients may be outmoded as disease and its treatment progress

   Past experience with stressful situations affects ability to adapt to current stress

   Unresolved past stresses may make current stressors difficult or impossible to cope with

Anxiety

1. Described, with depression, as most common psychosocial reaction experienced by people with cancer

2. Defined as

   * Individual perceives certain beliefs, values, and conditions essential to secure existence

   * Individual experiences nonspecific internal or external stimuli perceived as threats to secure existence

   * Individual responds to perceived threat affectively with increased level of arousal associated with vague, unpleasant, and uneasy feelings defined as anxiety

3. Individuals with cancer have higher levels of anxiety than individuals with nonmalignant condition
4. Anxiety increases at diagnosis and remains elevated in varying levels throughout course of treatment
5. Anxiety at minimal or moderate levels may be motivating for patient
6. Interventions

   * Help patient to recognize various manifestations

   * Determine if patient desires to do anything about response

   * Activate coping strategies to control anxiety levels

   Teach patient through formal and informal educational programs

   Assist in problem solving through counseling

   Role model with anxiety-reducing techniques, such as relaxation training or music therapy

    * Refer patient to support groups within care institution and community

Depression

1. When depressed, the

    * Individual perceives certain goals for future and attributes possibilities for success to self

    * Individual's attempts to attain goals are blocked

    * Individual attributes failure to attain goals to personal inadequacies

    * Individual's perceived loss of self-esteem results in cluster of affective, behavioral, and cognitive responses

2. Defining characteristics of depression must

    * Indicate a change from previous functioning

    * Be persistent

    * Occur for most of day

    * Occur more days than not

    * Be present for at least 2 weeks

    * Include

       Expressions of hopelessness, despair

       Inability to concentrate

       Change in physical activities, eating, sleeping, sexual activity

       Lowered self-esteem

Feelings of failure

Withdrawal from others

Threats or attempts to commit suicide

Suspicion and sensitivity to words and actions of others

Misdirected anger toward self

General irritability

Guilt feelings

Dependency on others

3. Treatment includes

* Identification of stimuli that have resulted in loss of self-esteem

* Referral to another member of health care team if patient presents with longstanding history of depression

* Assisting patient to acknowledge feelings of hopelessness and despair by giving permission to discuss feelings through

Attentive listening

Acknowledgment of feelings

Exploration of methods to deal positively with feelings

* Assisting patient to focus on immediate goals of care to reduce overwhelming feelings of powerlessness

* Focusing on positive abilities of patient, contracting short-term goals of care

Hopelessness

1. Defined as subjective state in which individual sees limited or no alternatives or personal choices available and is unable to mobilize energy on own behalf

2. Characterized by

   * Passivity
   * Decreased verbalization
   * Flat affect
   * Verbalization of despondent or hopeless content
   * Lack of initiative
   * Decreased response to stimuli
   * Lack of involvement in care
   * Turning away from speaker
   * Decreased appetite
   * Increased sleep

3. Interventions include

   * Assisting with reality surveillance

     Review changes in and current health status

     Seek perceptions of patient with respect to health

     Confirm accurate perception

     Correct misconceptions of reality

     Encourage patient to discuss reality with others in same situation

   * Reinforcing personal power and ability

Review perceived strengths of patient and family

Include patient in planning care, goals, schedule

Encourage review of past successes in stressful times

Reward approximations of goals

Encourage value of use of needed external resources

* Encouraging supportive relationships

Review number, types, and availability of supportive relationships

Assist in helping patient to ask for support

Encourage patient to continue contacts with supportive people

Respect relationship of patient to higher being

Encourage patient to express faith, if applicable

* Creating future perspective

Review past occasions for hope

Discuss meaning of hope from patient's perspective

Establish short-term goals with patient and family

Evaluate progress in achieving goals on routine basis

Encourage expressions of hope for future

Altered sexual health

1. Defined as inability to express one's sexuality consistent with personal needs and preferences

2. Sexual health of people with cancer threatened by the sequelae associated with radical surgery, radiation, chemotherapy, and biotherapy

3. Characterized by

   * Verbalizations of problems in sexuality

   * Alterations in achieving perceived sex role

   * Actual or perceived limitation imposed by disease or therapy

   * Conflicts involving values

   * Alteration in achieving sexual satisfaction

   * Inability to achieve desired sexual satisfaction

   * Frequent seeking of confirmation of desirability

   * Alteration in relationship with significant other

   * Change of interest in self and others

4. Interventions include

   * Legitimizing patient's sexual concerns

   * Encouraging patient to express sexual concerns with partner and health care team

   * Providing anticipatory guidance with respect to sexual concerns

   * Providing information needed for rehabilitation

   * Discussing coping skills for changes experienced in communication, roles, relationships

* Helping patient to modify behaviors to accommodate limitations imposed by cancer or treatment
* Referring patient to professional therapist

Social and Family Responses to Stress of Cancer

Overview

1. Supportive relationships at home and in community assist individual responses to stress
2. Family of origin or choice is most important social support for individual
3. Nurse's personal definitions of family or family values may vary from those of patients
4. Diagnosis of cancer precipitates significant changes for individual, members of family unit, and community
5. Responses vary among family members, across developmental stages of family, and with respect to economic and psychosocial resources

Psychosocial problems experienced by family members

1. Impaired relationships with family or significant others, or both
2. Impaired relationships with health care providers
3. Somatic side effects of disease and treatment
4. Difficulties in compliance with treatment
5. Mood disturbances

6. Difficulties in family roles
7. Difficulties in self-management
8. Financial difficulties
9. Transportation difficulties
10. Equipment difficulties
11. Significant concerns about body image
12. Denial
13. Cognitive impairment

Needs of family

1. Information

   * Family has assumed more responsibility in care of patient because of increased use of home health care services, outpatient care, and hospice services

   * Families need to be taught how to administer care and where to find appropriate resources

2. Communication

   * Communication becomes primary issue among family members as caregiving demands increase

   * As demands of care increase, mood disturbances among family members, particularly anxiety and depression, become more prominent

   * Communication patterns between patient and spouse, and between parents and children are strained

   * Nurse plays important role in facilitating communication among family members via

One-on-one counseling

Group sessions on communication

Role modeling of facilitative communication

Role-playing communications with individual family members

3. Coping skills

   * Modifying roles and relationship rules within family to meet demands imposed by illness

   * Seeking help from outside sources

   * Mobilizing action within household family

4. Support services

   * Type, amount, and usage of support systems and services needed by caregivers of differing age, sex, and socioeconomic status is concern for health care providers

   * Support services include

   Home management

   Financial counseling

   Anticipatory guidance

   Transportation

   Child care

   * Families have difficulty knowing where to go to get needed resources and often have difficulty asking for help

   * Nurses can help families identify and access support by

Role-playing how to ask for help

Making list of tasks to be done

Giving extended family and friends opportunity to help, being specific about type and amount of help needed

Communicating needs via

Church newsletter or bulletins

Community newsletters or papers

Handwritten, duplicated updates on how things are going to all supporters

Development of telephone tree

Professional Responses to Cancer

Distancing

1. Unconscious response of professionals, especially to people who are dying by

   * Delays in answering call lights
   * Infrequent visits
   * Failure to communicate
   * Maintaining "professionalism" in highly emotional situations

2. Especially prevalent when patient is not told truth
3. Enhances loneliness and fear of seriously ill
4. Showing genuine concern, being flexible, and being good listener lessen professional distancing

5. Through communication strategies, nurses with high levels of interpersonal competence effect behavioral changes, comfort, establish and maintain relationships, create positive self-image for patient, and relay information

6. Nurses can enhance interpersonal skills by

   * Audiotaping and videotaping for feedback

   * Studying the literature to learn communication strategies

   * Attending multidisciplinary conferences dealing with psychosocial needs of patients and families

Caring

1. Process that helps person attain or maintain health or peaceful death
2. Action-oriented and its intent is helpful
3. Moral commitment to protect human dignity
4. Begins with interest in another
5. Expands through knowledge and becomes commitment to help person to exist and to grow
6. Patients define caring behaviors among nurses as

   * Physical care that is humane (e.g., considerate, competent, gentle, timely, and accessible)

   * Emotional care that includes concern, involvement, sharing, touching (when culturally condoned), voluntary presence, and humor

7. Potentially negative outcomes of caring by nurses are overinvolvement and burnout

Suggested Readings

1. Barsevick AM, Much J, Sweeney C: Psychosocial responses to cancer. In Groenwald SG, Frogge MH, Goodman M, Yarbro CH (eds): *Cancer Nursing: Principles and Practice* (4th ed). Boston: Jones and Bartlett, 1997, pp 1393-1411.

2. Fawzy FI, Fawzy NW, Arndt LA, et al: Critical review of psychosocial interventions in cancer care. Arch Gen Psychiatry 52:100-133, 1995.

3. Clark J: Psychosocial responses of the patient. In Groenwald SL, Frogge MH, Goodman M, Yarbro CH (eds): *Cancer Nursing: Principles and Practice* (3rd ed). Boston: Jones and Bartlett, 1993, pp 449-467.

4. Clark J: Psychosocial responses of the family. In Groenwald SL, Frogge MH, Goodman M, Yarbro CH (eds): *Cancer Nursing: Principles and Practice* (3rd ed). Boston: Jones and Bartlett, 1993, pp 468-483.

CHAPTER 59

Physical, Economic, and Psychosocial Adaptation of the Cancer Survivor

Overview

Early literature regarding cancer survivorship focused on rehabilitation and functional adaptation to specific physical deficits caused by disease and its treatment

Growing cancer survivorship movement renewed interest in cancer rehabilitation concepts and began to emphasize psychosocial as well as physical functioning aspects of cancer rehabilitation

579

In 1989, Oncology Nursing Society defined cancer rehabilitation as "a process by which individuals, within their environments, are assisted to achieve optimal functioning within the limits imposed by cancer"; this definition

1. Allowed consideration of both the psychosocial and physical functioning aspects of cancer rehabilitation
2. Allowed cancer rehabilitation to be considered as a conceptual approach to cancer care as well as a specific program of services that addresses survivorship issues

Many cancer patients do not fit the classic picture of "a rehabilitation patient" as the functional status of individuals with cancer is more often limited by pain, fatigue, nausea, or other symptoms rather than by specific physical disabilities

Today cancer rehabilitation concerns any aspect of an individual's quality of life affected by the disease or its treatment, including

1. Psychological factors
2. Social factors
3. Sexual functioning
4. Nutrition
5. Fitness and exercise
6. Pain
7. Symptom management
8. Elimination
9. Skin care
10. Adaptation to physical and functional deficits

A diverse interdisciplinary cancer rehabilitation team is essential, including

1. Physicians (possibly from different specialties)
2. Nurses (from different specialties)
3. Clergy
4. Community volunteers
5. Family members
6. Friends
7. Physical, occupational, or speech therapists
8. Nutritionist
9. Teachers or tutors
10. Social worker
11. Vocational counselor
12. Recreation, art, or music therapists
13. Respiratory therapist
14. Enterostomal therapist
15. Psychologist and counselor
16. Homemaker
17. Home health aide

Nurses may serve in role of case manager to coordinate care provided by all disciplines

Development Considerations for Adult Cancer Survivors

Young adulthood (aged early 20s through 45)

1. Employment

    * In past, there was reluctance to share cancer history with employers for fear of discrimination

    * Shift of treatment from inpatient to ambulatory and home care settings has

enabled more patients undergoing active treatment to continue working successfully

* Americans with Disabilities Act prohibits discrimination against individuals with serious illnesses

2. Insurance coverage

   * In U.S., health coverage closely tied to employment

   * As of July 1997, insurance companies can no longer deny coverage for or impose restrictive waiting periods on individuals with preexisting illnesses such as cancer, allowing greater job mobility for cancer survivors

3. Parenting

   * Cancer patients who are parents of young children may need assistance

     Talking with their children about their disease

     Balancing demands of home, work and cancer treatment

     Enlisting children's help with tasks and chores

     Dealing with feelings of guilt and inadequacy regarding their abilities as parents

   * The nurse may refer the patient to another member of the cancer rehabilitation team, such as a child's teacher or social worker, for an identified problem or for further assessment

4. Fertility

* Many cancer patients experience infertility or premature menopause resulting from cancer treatment

* Sperm can be retrieved and stored indefinitely for assisted reproduction attempts, but there are no known methods of preserving eggs

5. Sexuality

* A number of factors affect a cancer patient's sexual rehabilitation

    Presence of a partner during diagnosis and treatment

    Disclosure of history to new partners

    Uncertainty about cancer survival or recurrence

    Prior sexual activity

    Religious and cultural beliefs and values

    Obvious physical changes in anatomy, functioning or appearance

    Presence of appliances or prostheses

    Changes or limitations in sexual and nonsexual functions

    Loss of reproductive organs

    Meaning of cancer diagnosis to patient and partner

    Meaning of sexual activity to patient and partner

* Because patients may be reluctant to discuss these issues, nurses should address early in treatment

Middle adulthood (aged 45 to 64)

1. Career advancement and stability

   * Concerns about job security may negatively affect patient's ability to optimize treatment

     Individuals may not be able to take essential time and energy away from work in order to devote it to cancer treatment

     Advances in telecommunications and use of home-based business equipment and services may allow some individuals to continue working productively while they receive treatment at home

     Americans with Disabilities Act protects individuals to certain extent, but may be difficult for some individuals to take advantage of

     Individual may suffer extraordinary expenses for treatment and face additional stresses if job is lost

2. Sexuality and body image

   * Marital and family relationships may be stressed

Older adulthood (aged 65 and older)

1. Co-morbid conditions

   * Success of cancer treatment may be affected by other pre-existing conditions

2. Social support

* Social network of older adults may be compromised because of death, disease, or disability

Disease Trajectory Considerations

Individual prognosis and limitations imposed by cancer must be considered in determining goals and interventions to achieve optimal functional status

1. Level 1: No disfigurement or disability; life expectancy good

   * Goal of rehabilitation

     Promote recovery from acute episode

     Prevent treatment complications

     Return to level of functioning before illness in all areas of life, including work, recreation, nutrition, sexuality, significant relationships

2. Level 2: Physical or psychological disability or disfigurement; life expectancy good

   * Goal of rehabilitation

     Same as for level 1, except that return to prior levels of functioning may not be possible in all life areas

     Adaptation to disabilities or disfigurements to promote optimal functioning within limitations

     Control of co-morbid conditions

3. Level 3: Shortened life expectancy, with or without disability or disfigurement

* Goal of rehabilitation

  Short-term return to normal functioning within limits imposed by disease if remission occurs

  Maintainance of adaptive functioning with relapse and terminal disease

  Focus on pain and symptom management, nutrition, elimination, skin care, and psychosocial needs

Suggested Readings

1. Blesch KS: Physical, economic, and social adaptation of the cancer survivor. In Groenwald SL, Frogge MH, Goodman M, Yarbro CH (eds). *Cancer Nursing: Principles and Practice* (4th ed). Boston: Jones and Bartlett, 1997, pp 1412-1420.
2. Blesch KS: Rehabilitation of the cancer patient at home. *Semin Oncol Nurs* 12:219-225, 1996.
3. Mellett SJ: Cancer rehabilitation. *J Natl Cancer Inst* 85:781-784, 1993.
4. Watson PG: Cancer rehabilitation: An overview. *Semin Oncol Nurs* 8:167-173, 1992.

CHAPTER 60

Spiritual and Ethical End-of-Life Concerns

Definitions

Spirituality refers to that dimension of being human and motivates meaning-making and self-transcendence—or intrapersonal, interpersonal, and transpersonal connectedness

1. Described as an integrating energy and innate human quality
2. Prompts individuals to make sense of their universe and to relate harmoniously with self, nature, and others—including any gods, as conceptualized by each person

587

Religion is viewed as a narrower concept

1. The representation and expression of spirituality
2. Offers an individual a specific world view and an explanation that seeks to provide answers to the questions of ultimate meaning
3. May recommend how to live harmoniously with self, others, nature, and god(s)
4. May or may not be of an institutional nature

Ethics involves reflecting systematically about "oughts," theorizing about right conduct and how to live as a good person

1. An ethical dilemma arises when a choice must be made between the lesser of evils or the best of goods
2. In addressing ethical conflicts, certain frameworks (utilitarianism, deontology) and principles (respect for autonomy, beneficence, nonmaleficence, justice, veracity) are considered during the decision-making process

Spirituality and the Cancer Experience

Research and clinical observations suggest that there is heightened spiritual awareness among individuals surviving cancer

1. May manifest as spiritual or existential distress or increased spiritual well-being

    * Cancer diagnosis creates the realization of personal mortality and vulnerability

* The closer to death an individual with cancer gets, the more she or he becomes aware and concerned with personal spirituality

2. Cancer survivors experience numerous losses and changes, such as loss of mobility and independence, changes in social roles, loss of the future

   * Significant losses and changes cause individuals to search for meaning as they try to make sense of such a negative experience

   * This process makes individuals reexamine their beliefs about their world, including religious beliefs

3. Those facing the reality of death:

   * Seek immortality through belief in an after-death life and by leaving legacies that benefit others

   * Experience anxiety

   * Confront existential questions

   * Feel powerless and vulnerable

   * Experience isolation and loneliness

Fundamental "End-of Life" Questions

How shall I die?

1. Where do I want to die?

   * At home, in a hospice, or somewhere else?

2. When do I want to die?

   * When "nature takes its course" or before
     conditions, such as pain or dementia, reach
     an unbearable threshold?

3. When should death be delayed, if at all?

   * If delayed, to what extent should "heroic"
     and resuscitation measures be used?

4. How do I want to die?

   * Alone or with loved ones present?

   * Naturally or with assistance?

5. What would constitute a good or dignified
   death?

**Some ask these questions openly, although
others avoid such discussion**

**Regardless of whether an active or passive
answer is given, a decision is inevitably made**

**Questions introduce ethical and spiritual
issues**

1. Is it right to hasten a death when suffering is
   unbearable?
2. Is it right to cause a death, or assist with a
   death, when life is present?
3. Suicide is the intentional taking of one's own
   life

   * Cancer survivors have a higher suicide rate
     than the general population because of

     Advanced illness, poor prognosis

Inadequately managed severe physical symptoms, such as pain, fatigue, exhaustion

Delirium, disinhibition

Hospitalization

Hopelessness, helplessness

Depression

Loss of self-esteem, loss of control

Fear of abandonment

Anxiety

Caregiver fatigue

4. Euthanasia refers to the act of assisting or enabling a sufferer's death, preferably without pain
5. Nurses are obligated to protect the moral and legal rights of care recipients

How Shall I Live Before I Die?

1. How to ascribe meaning to life, illness and death

   * What caused the cancer

     Personal lifestyles

     Environment causes

     Heredity

     Randomness

     Stressors

     Blaming themselves allows them to feel control, but may also cause a sense of shame, guilt, and spiritual distress

* Why the cancer happened to them in particular

  Because God knew I was strong and could handle it

  Because I deserve it

* What the significance or meaningfulness of the cancer is

  Teaching a lesson

  Reconsider personal values and priorities

  Develop appreciation and joy for life

  Increase spiritual sensitivity

  Improve self-knowledge

2. How to relate to themselves and others

   * Realize anew their intense appreciation for family and friends

   * Restructure lives to spend more time with loved ones

   * May be more selective about the people with whom they spend time

   * May intensify relationship with deity or spiritual beings

   * May feel they are a burden to loved ones and society

     Activities that help a person to return gifts of love include

       Praying for others

       Listening to others

Sharing personal wisdom gained from the cancer experience

Creating legacy gifts, such as poems, prose, crafts

Approaches to Making Spiritual and Ethical End-of-Life Decisions

The goal of nursing care is to facilitate and promote informed decision-making; the nurse

1. Encourages activities that increase the individual's sense of meaningfulness, self-awareness, and spiritual sensitivity
2. Offers a caring relationship and is open to dialogue
3. Provides information about decision-making and the issues confronted

Approaches that can assist one in resolving spiritual and ethical issues, regardless of the individual's beliefs about religion

1. Dedication to a mission or cause

    * May be sociopolitical, artistic, or scientific in nature

    * Provides a sense of purpose and "something to live for"

    * Offers the person perspective

    * Distracts from personal suffering

2. Leaving a legacy

    * Writing or taping personal histories or messages for descendants

* Leaving something special for descendants

3. Storytelling

   * Life stories and reminiscences answer questions about meaning of life

     Transmit beliefs and values, world views, and frameworks for meaning

     Promotes well-being by helping organize the person's thoughts and experiences and helps make sense of life

4. Prayer, meditation, and journal writing

   * Can develop inward awareness and spiritual sensitivity

5. Spiritual mentoring

   * Provides comfort, encouragement, companionship, and guidance

6. Cognitive strategies

   * When assumptions about the world are shattered, patients work to reconstruct their world view, so that it includes assumptions that are more mature and wiser

7. Confronting the reality of death
8. Advance directives

   * Patient Self-Determination Act

     Requires that all health care institutions receiving Medicare or Medicaid reimbursement ask the patients they admit if they have an advance directive; if not, the institution is obligated to provide written information about such directives

* An advance directive is a statement made by a competent person that directs their medical care in the event that they become incompetent

* A directive to physician, or living will, allows individuals to state their wishes regarding medical treatment in the event they become unable to do so

* A durable power of attorney for health care allows an individual to designate an agent who will make health care decisions on his or her behalf in the event he or she becomes incompetent

* Advance directives provide

    Clarification of individual's wishes and values

    Guidance for family members concerning choices

    Direction for the health care team

    Protection of assets from depletion caused by futile, high-cost care

* Nurses inform patients about advance directives and facilitate discussions between patients and families

Suggested Readings

1. Taylor EJ: Spiritual and ethical end-of-life concerns. In Groenwald SL, Frogge MH, Goodman M, Yarbro CH (eds): *Cancer Nursing: Principles and Practice (4th ed)*. Boston: Jones and Bartlett, 1997, pp 1421-1434

2. Brown-Saltzman KA: Tending the spirit. *Oncol Nurs Forum* 21:1001-1006, 1994.

3. Mansen TJ: The spiritual dimension of individuals: Conceptual development. *Nurs Diag* 4:140-147, 1993.

4. Highfield MF: Spiritual health of oncology patients: Nurse and patient perspectives. *Cancer Nurs* 15:1-8, 1992.

5. Reed PG: An emerging paradigm for the investigation of spirituality in nursing. *Res Nurs Health* 15:349-357, 1992.

PART VI

Delivery Systems
for Cancer Care

CHAPTER 61

Ambulatory Care

Overview

Has increasingly important role in cancer care

80% to 90% of cancer care is delivered in ambulatory setting

Settings include

1. Freestanding cancer centers
2. 24-hour clinics
3. Day surgery
4. Outpatient clinics and treatment centers
5. Outreach and satellite centers
6. Office practices

7. Other ambulatory centers (screening, rehabilitation, genetic)

Nurses have complex roles

1. Planning care and delivery
2. Direct nursing care process
3. Technical procedures
4. Teaching and advocacy
5. Telephone communications and care management
6. Coordination of care and services

Ambulatory Care Issues

Models of nursing care delivery

1. Primary nursing
2. Case management
3. Collaborative nurse-physician practice
4. Paired-partners approach

Patient classification and nurse productivity systems

1. Many systems have been proposed and examined, but few can capture many direct and indirect activities of nurse in these settings

Quality and outcomes improvement

1. Ensures that care is provided at or above established standards of care
2. Patient satisfaction with care has become an area of intense interest
3. Ambulatory patient needs and satisfactions may differ significantly from those factors nurse might identify as important

4. Conflicts can relate to cost-containment versus quality of care

Occupational hazards and safety

1. OSHA regulations revised in 1995, yet not as highly regulated as in acute setting
2. Safely handle antineoplastic agents, radioactive materials, and blood and body fluids
3. Applies to outpatient setting and the home
4. Adhere to current safety practices to avoid occupational hazards

Continuity of care

1. Enhanced in outpatient setting by electronic communications
2. Development of tools and documentation materials appropriate to any patient care setting
3. Critical elements for continuity

   * Uniform access to care

   * Comprehensive planning

   * Responsiveness to patient and family needs

   * Availability of resources and services

   * Coordination of care

   * Monitoring quality of care

Nurse's Role in Ambulatory Care

Major elements

1. Enabling operation of outpatient setting
2. Technical procedures and treatments

3. Nursing process and planning
4. Telephone communications and care management
5. Advocacy
6. Teaching patient self-care and family care-giving
7. Care coordination and referrals
8. Expert practice within setting
9. Quality improvement
10. Research
11. Continuing education

Nurses in ambulatory care are involved in fastest growing segment of cancer care

Challenges of growth, reimbursement, volumes, acuity, care standards, delivery systems, and coordination are but a few of the issues and opportunities ahead

Suggested Readings

1. Otte DM: Ambulatory Care. In Groenwald SL, Frogge MH, Goodman M, Yarbro CH (eds): *Cancer Nursing: Principles and Practice* (4th ed). Boston: Jones and Bartlett, 1997, pp 1465-1500.

2. Houston DA, Houston GR: Administrative issues and concepts in ambulatory care. In Buchsel PC, Yarbro CH (eds): *Oncology Nursing in the Ambulatory Setting: Issues and Models of Care*. Boston: Jones and Bartlett, 1993, pp 3-19.

3. Lamkin L: Outpatient oncology settings: A variety of services. *Semin Oncol Nurs* 10:229-236, 1994.

4. Hackbarth DP, Haas SA, Kavanagh JA, et al: Dimensions of the staff nurse role in ambulatory care: Part I. Methodology and analysis of data on current staff nurse practice. *Nurs Econ* 13:89-98, 1995.

CHAPTER 62

Home Care

Overview

One of most rapidly growing and changing fields in health care

Can be preventive, diagnostic, therapeutic, rehabilitative, or for long-term maintenance care

Services typically include

1. Nursing
2. Homemaker–home health aide
3. Physical therapy

4. Occupational therapy
5. Speech-language pathology
6. Social work
7. Nutrition services

Types of agencies

1. Official public health agencies
2. Medicare-certified agencies
3. Private-duty agencies
4. Specialized services agencies: infusion therapy, durable medical equipment

Unique Characteristics

Patient and family determine when and how care is implemented

Patient and family assume responsibility for care

Environmental barriers to safe care can exist

1. Lack of utilities or facilities for providing care
2. Potential presence of vermin or hazards
3. Inadequate insurance coverage and financial limitations are common

Home Care Issues

Situations that evoke stress for caregivers

1. Managing physical care and treatment
2. Managing own home and patient's home and finances

3. Need to be available 24 hours a day, 7 days a week
4. Fear of leaving patient alone
5. Change in relationship or communications between patient and caregiver
6. Disruption in household routines
7. Preparing different meals
8. Inability to spend time with own spouse and children
9. Often trying to balance need to work outside home with care of patient
10. Inability to meet expectations of health care system because of lack of time, knowledge, or skill or just being overwhelmed

Most helpful nursing interventions as identified by patients include

1. Giving excellent, knowledgeable, skilled, and personalized nursing care to patient
2. Providing patient with necessary emergency measures if need arises
3. Assuring patient that nursing services are available 24 hours a day, 7 days a week
4. Allowing patient to do as much for himself or herself as possible
5. Teaching family members how to keep patient physically comfortable
6. Answering questions honestly, openly, and willingly
7. Supporting cohesion of family by initiating and promoting interaction, communication, cooperation, and social and emotional involvement
8. Directing nursing intervention toward daily problem solving

Economic issues

1. Are significant struggle for home care providers
2. Nurses must be familiar with reimbursement guidelines

   * Eligibility criteria
   * Definitions of levels of service
   * Nuances of documenting for reimbursement

Ethical concerns

1. Certain possessions, routines, and family structures may not be conducive to provision of care in home
2. Nurses develop creative alternatives or intervene carefully in adjusting environment as much as possible
3. Withholding treatment for personal or financial reasons are among most common issues faced

Home Nursing Roles and Activities

Direct nursing care and treatments

1. Completes physical examination of patient during each home visit
2. Demonstrates all nursing care procedures being taught to caregivers in home
3. Performs all procedures requring skill of nurse (e.g., administration of intravenous fluid, insertion of feeding tube)

4. Administers chemotherapy prescribed by physician

5. Obtains laboratory specimens requested by physician to monitor effects of disease or disease treatment (e.g., specimens of blood, urine, sputum, or wound cultures)

Observation and reporting of disease, treatment response, and family response

1. Assesses and reports signs and symptoms of emergency medical problem resulting from side effects of medical treatment of disease (e.g., bone marrow depression after chemotherapy)

2. Assesses and reports potential signs and symptoms of emergency medical problem resulting from tumor (e.g., hypercalcemia)

3. Assesses and reports signs and symptoms of disease progression

4. Evaluates patient's response to prescribed medications and therapies

5. Assesses patient's and family's emotional response to course of disease or treatment

Supervision of self-care or caregivers

1. Identifies current and potential problems influencing patient's care, including ability of patient to obtain needed care in home

2. Plans nursing care to correct, improve, or manage identified patient problems

3. Provides written instructions of medication schedules or patient care procedures for caregivers in patient's home

4. Supervises care given to patient in home by

family, friends, volunteers, or home health aides

5. Coordinates admission to hospital if need arises

Health and disease management teaching

1. Teaches actual and potential effects of disease process based on patient's or caregiver's readiness and ability to learn
2. Teaches actual and potential effects of disease and treatment
3. Teaches signs and symptoms requiring immediate notification of nurse or physician
4. Teaches purpose, side effects, amount, frequency, and method of administering each medication and treatment prescribed (e.g., analgesics, colostomy care, decubitus ulcer care)
5. Teaches nutrition and hydration requirements, including methods appropriate for individual patient
6. Teaches rehabilitation and self-care techniques (e.g., ambulation with walker, range-of-motion exercises for lymphedema, energy saving and comfort measures)
7. Teaches prevention of complications and infections, including environmental safety and hygiene
8. Teaches health promotion and maintenance, with emphasis on prevention and early detection of disease

Counseling and support

1. Identifies emotional, spiritual, or social

problems experienced by patient and
family
2. Assists patient and family to identify and
   express their feelings about effects of disease
   or treatments
3. Facilitates referral to appropriate resources for
   extended counselling

Coordination and collaboration of home care community supports and medical care

1. Assists patient and family to use formal and
   informal support services within community
2. Assesses and prioritizes patient and family
   needs; integrates and coordinates appropriate
   home health services into the plan of care (e.g.,
   home health aide, medical social work,
   occupational therapy, physical therapy, speech
   therapy, nutrition consultation)

   * (Source: Michigan Cancer Foundation
     Services, Inc. Home Care Program,
     Detroit MI)

Home health agencies are integrating the role of Advanced Practice Nurse to meet complex care requirements of cancer patients

Specialized cancer care

1. Infusion therapy

   * Most rapidly growing segment within
     home health care
   * Venous access devices and pumps enable
     home infusions

* Home parenteral infusion and home antibiotic therapy are also becoming common

2. Chemotherapy administration

* Continuous infusion of chemotherapeutic agents through ambulatory infusion pumps most frequent delivery system

* Often cost-effective

* Other factors

  Criteria for patient selection must be met

  Patient has to be able to receive chemotherapy in home

  Insurance reimbursement varies and should be thoroughly checked to avoid unnecessary financial stresses

  Procedures for administration are well documented

  Staff are educated in processes, particularly

  Safety considerations of drug transport

  Preparation of drugs

  Spills

  Patient care

  Disposal of drugs and supplies

  Patient and family responsibility and education

3. Pain management

* Develop analgesic regimen that is simple to administer and provides sufficient pain relief to allow optimal functioning

* Ensure that pain medications are given around clock, not as needed

* Employ measures other than analgesics consistently and effectively (e.g., relaxation techniques)

* Initiate interventions to prevent potential side effects of narcotic analgesic regimen concurrently (e.g., anticonstipation medications)

* Provide ongoing comprehensive assessment of patient's pain (identify source of pain whenever possible and do not assume that patient's pain is caused by malignant process)

* Identify and dispel patient and family misconceptions about use and abuse of narcotic analgesics

Quality Assessment in Home Care Setting

Measure care with established standards for home care

A move is underway to shift emphasis from measuring structure or process to examining links between processes of care and desired patient outcomes

Suggested Readings

1. McNally JC: Home care. In Groenwald SL, Frogge MH, Goodman M, Yarbro CH (eds): *Cancer: Principles and Practice* (4th ed). Boston: Jones and Bartlett, 1997, pp 1501-1530.
2. McNally JC: Home care for the oncology patient. *Semin Oncol Nurs* 12:177-248, 1996

CHAPTER 63

Hospice Care

Overview

Objective is to facilitate comfortable and natural death

Palliative medical management is pivotal

Relief of suffering in dying goes beyond identifying and treating physical symptoms to also addressing emotional, spiritual, and existential components of suffering and pain

Principles of palliative care

1. Overall goal of treatment is to optimize quality of life; i.e., hopes and desires of patient are fulfilled
2. Death is regarded as natural process, to be neither hastened nor prolonged
3. Diagnostic tests and other invasive procedures are minimized, unless likely to result in alleviation of symptoms
4. Use of "heroic" treatment measures is discouraged
5. When using narcotic analgesics, correct dose is the dose that provides pain relief without unacceptable side effects
6. Patient is the expert on whether pain and symptoms have been adequately relieved
7. Patients eat if they are hungry and drink if thirsty; fluids and feedings are not forced
8. Care is individualized and based on goals of patient and family, as unit of care

Models of Hospice Care

Independent, community-based programs

Hospital-owned programs

Part of home-health agency

Coalition programs or nursing home programs

Acute care hospitals may have beds or units for inpatient care of hospice patients

Reimbursement and funding methods

1. 72% of hospices are Medicare-certified to receive funding
2. 89% of current hospices are operated as not-for-profit organizations

Patient Services

Reimbursemnt is on a per diem basis

Case management is used for hospice care

At least 80% of a patient's aggregate days of care must be provided in the patient's home

Each hospice program has its own criteria for selecting patients to receive hospice care

In most programs, the patient must

1. Have a primary caregiver
2. Reside in geographic area of providing hospice
3. Agree to palliative, not curative, treatment

Nursing and Hospice Care Services

Core services usually include

1. Medical director
2. Nurse coordinators
3. Social services
4. Pastoral care
5. Trained volunteers

Other services could include

1. Dietary counseling
2. Occupational therapy
3. Physical therapy
4. Speech therapy
5. Art therapy
6. Home health aide–homemaker
7. Psychologist
8. Volunteer and bereavement coordinator

Hospice nurse's role includes

1. Being experienced practitioner with specialized skill in terminal care
2. Working cooperatively and communicating effectively within multidisciplinary framework
3. Demonstrating self-direction and initiative
4. Coordinating care and services provided
5. Being leader within multidisciplinary hospice team
6. Individualizing plan of care to maximize patient's comfort
7. Ability to foster relaxed, warm, personal relationship with patient, family, and other team members

Death in Home

Unique to hospice is approach to death in home

Advantages of home death are predominantly sense of family's role in contributing to social being of family

Much unwanted medical intervention that would typically accompany hospitalization is avoided

Some caregivers may find physical and emotional tasks of providing care at home too difficult

Occasionally the patient's symptoms may be too difficult to manage at home (e.g., hemorrhage) and hospitalization may be better choice

Preparation of patient and family for death is emphasized by hospice team

Hospice team is available at all times, which is of utmost importance to family

Facilitating grief and providing for bereavement care are critical elements

1. Bereavement involves

   * Accepting reality of loss
   * Experiencing pain of grief
   * Adjusting to environment in which deceased is missing
   * Withdrawing emotional energy and replacing it into another relationship

2. Abnormal grief can be

   * Prolonged
   * Masked in behavioral or physical symptoms

* Manifested in exaggerated or excessive
  expressions of normal grief reactions

Legal and Ethical Issues Surrounding Hospice Care

Advance directives require informed decision and ongoing support

Hospice supports clear and informed decision

Euthanasia and suicide contain moral, ethical, and legal questions that have remained unanswered for centuries

Hospice does not support involvement in either, but promotes treatment for cause of despair and support during process of dying

Underserved populations (e.g., poor, minorities) are also underserved by hospice programs

Active hospice staff and volunteers are attempting to broaden coverage of hospice care to underserved populations

Integration of hospice into health care practices has been fostered by agencies such as JCAHO

Suggested Readings

1. Martinez J, Wagner S: Hospice care. In Groenwald SL, Frogge MH, Goodman M, Yarbro CH (eds): *Cancer Nursing: Principles and Practice* (4thd ed). Boston: Jones and Bartlett, 1997, pp 1531-1549.

2. Thal AE: *Proactive responses to the assisted suicide/euthanasia debate.* Publication No. 713438. Washington DC: National Hospice Organization, 1996.

3. Kristjonson LJ, et al: Research in palliative care populations: Ethical issues. *Palliat Care* 10(3):10-15, 1994.

4. Stuart B: *Medical Guidelines for Determining Prognosis in Selected Non-Cancer Diseases* (2nd ed). Arlington, VA: National Hospice Organization, 1996.

PART VII

Professional Issues
for the Cancer Nurse

CHAPTER 64

Ethical Issues in Cancer Nursing Practice

General Ethical Issues in Cancer Nursing Practice

Autonomy

1. Respect for individual's freedom to make choices about treatment and care
2. Individuals are responsible for their own moral acts and must make their own moral rules

Beneficence

1. Health care professionals must act in best interest of patient

623

Nonmaleficence

1. To help, or at least to do no harm to patient

Justice

1. Requires that each person is given his or her due

Compassion

1. Comprehension of suffering experienced by another

Termination of treatment

1. Withholding and withdrawing treatment

   * Is intent hastening death, or diminishing suffering?

   * Issues under debate are whether to

     Legalize active euthanasia

     Provide aid in dying

     Provide physician-assisted suicide

   * Planning for good death leads to restraint of technologic interventions at various stages in course of disease, depending on patient's values and willingness to trade possible severe side effects for chance for improved, albeit temporary, quality of life

   * Nurses can assist families to make decisions in advance so that some control can be exerted over dying

   * Patients have common law and constitutional right to refuse treatment, even if they are not dying

* Ethical considerations arise when individuals are not able to make decisions on their own and have not given prior instructions

* Many states require that advance directives be written

  Preferred instrument is durable power of attorney for health care

    Names in advance the individual who speaks for patient when patient is incompetent to make decisions about health care

    Limited in time to duration of incompetence

    Limited in scope to decisions about health care

  Without durable power of attorney, state may determine patient and family rights

  Obtain advance directives from all patients, especially seriously ill ones

Access to care

1. Some argue that health care options should be limited for elderly as means of allocating scarce resources
2. Ethics dictate that limits are set by whether treatment provides meaningful change in outcome for patients during last years, rather than by age
3. Statistics show that elderly choose highly technical interventions less often than younger cancer patients

Guidelines for Nursing Care

Duty to protect patient's life lies primarily in protecting his or her autonomy and value hierarchy

1. Pay close attention to discovering patient's value system through

   * Values assessment interview
   * Constant discussion with patient and family throughout course of treatment

Require patients to update advance directive on entering health care institution, nursing home, or hospice, in accordance with current Patient Self-Determination Act procedures

1. Supply patients with instructions as to their right to issue advance directives and sample forms with instructions for how to prepare them
2. Teaching guides should be developed to train health care professionals in process of implementing patient advance directives

Suggested Readings

1. Thomasma DC: Ethical issues in cancer nursing practice. In Groenwald SL, Frogge MH, Goodman M, Yarbro CH (eds): *Cancer Nursing: Principles and Practice* (3rd ed). Boston: Jones and Bartlett, 1997, pp 1608-1624.
2. Engelhardt HT Jr: *Foundations of Bioethics* (2nd ed) New York: Oxford Univ Press, 1996.

3. Veatch R: *A Theory of Medical Ethics* (2nd ed). New York: Basic Books, 1996
4. Beauchamp T, Childress J: *Principals of Biomedical Ethics* (3rd ed). New York: Oxford University Press, 1995.

CHAPTER 65

Alternative Methods of Cancer Therapy

Overview

Each year more than half of the million Americans diagnosed with cancer are cured with scientifically sound therapies

Each year thousands of cancer patients use alternative cancer remedies to prevent, diagnose, or treat cancer

Oncology nurses are involved with complementary therapies that are proven adjuncts in the care of cancer patients

Office of Alternative Medicine at National Institutes of Health and many other centers are conducting alternative medicine research

Alternative methods include diagnostic tests or therapeutic methods that

1. Have not shown activity in animal models or in scientific clinical trials
2. Do not protect consumer, because they do not meet requirements of U.S. Food, Drug, and Cosmetic Act

Popular Alternative Methods

Promoted as cure or prevention of cancer; methods include

1. Metabolic therapy (manipulation of diet and detoxification by enemas)
2. Macrobiotic diet

    * Cancer preventive effects under investigation

3. Megavitamins

    * Excessive vitamin intake is toxic

    * Studies underway with retinoids (vitamin A)

4. Laetrile

    * Although numerous studies have proven its ineffectiveness and potential harm, it is still being used alone or in combination with metabolic therapy

5. Herbal therapy
6. Live-cell therapy (injection of cells from animals)

   ∗ Serious side-effects have resulted from this therapy

7. Oxymedicine (hydrogen peroxide, ozone gas)

   ∗ Administered orally, rectally, intravenously, intramuscularly, and vaginally

8. Antineoplastins
9. Cancell (formula of chemicals that supposedly reacts with body electrically and lowers voltage of cancer cell)
10. Immunoaugmentative therapy
11. Shark cartilage

Tijuana, Mexico has become haven for alternative treatment facilities

Promoters rely on testimonials and anecdotes

Who Seeks Alternative Cancer Treatments, and Why?

Limited studies report that patients who seek such therapies are

1. White
2. Educated
3. Have relatively higher income
4. Want to relieve symptoms

Motivations and reasons for use include

1. Fear
2. Desire for self-control
3. Antiestablishment beliefs
4. Social pressures from family and friends

Control of Alternative Methods

Any new method of cancer treatment in U.S. must meet certain scientific standards before it receives government approval for interstate distribution

State governments also participate in regulation

Organizations provide information to health professionals and public about alternative methods

1. American Cancer Society, phone (800) ACS-2345
2. National Cancer Institute, phone (800) 4-CANCER
3. Food and Drug Administration, phone (301) 443-5006
4. Consumer Health Information and Research Institute, phone (816) 753-8850
5. National Council Against Health Fraud, phone (714) 824-4690

Nursing Interventions

Identification of unproven therapies

1. Is treatment based on unproven theory?
2. Is there purported need for special nutritional support?
3. Is there claim for painless, nontoxic therapy?
4. Have claims been published in peer-reviewed scientific journal?
5. Has treatment been compared to placebo?
6. Are proponents recognized cancer experts?
7. Do proponents claim benefit for treatment as well as prevention?
8. Is preparation a secret?
9. Is there an attack on medical establishment?
10. Do promoters demand "freedom of choice"?

Be knowledgeable of risks of such methods and toxicity if patient is using them in combination with standard therapy

Assess communication channels and patient motivations for potential use

Maintain positive communication channels with patient and family who may be interested in or participating in such methods

Maintain patient participation in health care

Patient education is most powerful approach towards controlling questionable remedies

Suggested Readings

1. Yarbro CH: Alternative methods of cancer therapy. In Groenwald SL, Frogge MH, Goodman M, Yarbro CH (eds). *Cancer Nursing: Principles and Practice* (4th ed). Boston: Jones and Bartlett, 1997, pp 1625-1641.
2. Lerner I, Kennedy BJ: *Questionable Methods of Cancer Treatment*. Atlanta, GA: American Cancer Society, 1993.

CHAPTER 66

Cultural Diversity Among Individuals with Cancer

Introduction

Culture is a fundamental element that uniquely shapes each individual

United States is becoming increasingly culturally diverse

1. Until recently largely limited to Caucasian immigrants from Europe
2. Immigration in the twentieth century included many people from southeast Asia, China, Japan, Korea, the Philippines, Mexico, and Caribbean

3. Ethnic minority populations growing at rates surpassing rest of population
4. Composition of health care professionals does not match this trend of increasing ethnic populations
5. Health care beliefs and practices of many ethnic groups may not be congruent with those of most health care professionals

Epidemiology

Factors contributing to these variations in cancer incidence and mortality in different ethnic groups include:

1. Environmental and/or socioeconomic factors
2. Access to health care
3. Cultural values, beliefs, and health practices
4. Genetic predisposition

Transcultural Nursing

Aim is to understand and assist diverse cultural groups and members of such groups with nursing and health care needs

1. Nursing interventions that are culturally relevant and sensitive to needs of patient decrease stress or conflict
2. Nurses must be sensitized to their own cultural biases and behaviors as well as to those of their patients
3. Nurses must avoid stereotyping or projecting onto patients their own cultural uniqueness in

order to do a thorough and relevant
assessment

Cultural Assessment

Nurses need to provide care that is free of gender, race, or religious bias

1. Based on accurate and systematic appraisal of individuals, groups and communities as to their cultural beliefs, values, and practices.
2. Patient needs and nursing interventions are identified within the cultural context of the people being evaluated

Six essential phenomena of Transcultural Assessment Model:

1. Communication

    * Language spoken
    * Voice quality
    * Pronunciation
    * Use of silence
    * Use of nonverbal

2. Space

    * Degree of comfort observed (conversation)
    * Proximity to others
    * Body movement
    * Perception of space

3. Social orientation

    * Culture

- * Race
- * Ethnicity
- * Family role function
- * Work
- * Leisure
- * Church
- * Friends

4. Time

- * Use of
- * Measures
- * Definition
- * Social time
- * Work time
- * Time orientation (future, present, past)

5. Environmental control

- * Cultural health practices (efficacious, neutral, dysfunctional, uncertain)
- * Values
- * Definition of health and illness

6. Biological variations

- * Body structure
- * Skin color
- * Hair color
- * Other physical dimensions
- * Enzymatic and genetic existence of diseases specific to populations

* Susceptibility to illness and disease
* Nutritional preferences and deficiencies
* Psychological characteristics (coping)

African-Americans

Represent about one-third of the population below poverty level; one-fourth are unemployed

Many worked or continue to work in occupations that place them at risk for certain cancers

Overall incidence rate for males is about 16% higher than that for Caucasian males

Highest incidence and mortality rates for cancers of the esophagus, larynx, pancreas, and prostate, and for multiple myeloma

Woman have the highest mortality rate for cervical cancer and men have the highest incidence and mortality rates for lung cancer

Women experience significantly more cervical cancer and early-age breast cancer than Caucasians

Five-year survival rate from all cancers is about 16% lower for African-Americans than that for Caucasians

Health beliefs and practices

1. Tendency to categorize events as either desirable or undesirable
2. Illness just another undesirable event along with bad luck, poverty and unemployment
3. Some believe illness results from their failure to live according to or to accept God's will
4. Strong relationship between faith and healing.
5. All blessings come from God and only God can heal the sick
6. Illness may be perceived as a natural occurrence resulting from disharmony and conflict in individual's life

   * Divine punishment

   * Impaired social relationships

   * Environmental hazards

7. Everything has an opposite
8. May respond to pain stoically out of desire to be perfect patient
9. Diet contains little fresh produce, is highly seasoned and includes frequent use of smoked and fatty meats as seasoning

   * Saturated fat intake may be high

   * African American women are more likely to be obese, while African American men are more likely to be underweight

   * 75% of African-Americans are lactose intolerant

   * Alcoholism is a major health problem and a risk factor for cancers of the

mouth, larynx, tongue, esophagus, lung, and liver

10. Less knowledgeable about cancer than Caucasians
11. Tend to underestimate prevalence of cancer and significance of common warning signs
12. More fatalistic and less likely to believe that early detection or treatment can make a difference in outcome

   * Diagnosis is often at a later stage of illness, resulting in a poorer prognosis and higher mortality rates

Healing practices

1. Folk healers are well respected and are often used

   * Understand the beliefs and needs of the people they serve

2. Religion incorporated as part of therapy; is means to a cure
3. Lay referral system services the health needs of the community and determines whether Western practitioners can be trusted and incorporated into treatment plan
4. Cure involves self-treatment, consultation with neighbor knowledgeable in home remedies, a physician, or someone regarded to have unusual powers

Social organization

1. Legalized segregation in U.S. caused African-

Americans to be isolated from mainstream society for many years

2. Many have not assimilated still, maintaining separate and often unequal lifestyles compared to other Americans

3. Under slavery, role of the African-American male as husband and father was obliterated.

4. Almost half of all African-American households are headed by the female who is charged with responsibility for protecting the health of family members

5. Most African-Americans have strong religious orientation and large social networks

Communication

1. Dialect spoken by many African-Americans is sufficiently different from standard English in pronunciation, grammar, and syntax as to be classified as "black English"

   * Use of black English varies and is sometimes related to educational level and socioeconomic status

   * Is a unifying factor for maintaining cultural and ethnic identity

2. Non-verbal communication may be very important to African-Americans

Space and time

1. Many have a "today" or "present" health orientation

   * Approach to the prevention of cancer may be to work out problems as they occur, rather than trying to prevent them

* Believe that planning for the future is hopeless and that the future will be the same as their present and past

Death and dying issues

1. Life is viewed as cyclical, beginning with birth and evolving to adulthood, old age and death
2. All events are given by God
3. Death is a natural part of the cycle of life and is unavoidable. It is familiar and near and evokes no great fear or awe
4. Care of terminally ill is public rather than private undertaking
5. Grief openly expressed and often loudly expressed

Biological variations

1. Major variation is skin color

   * Fairer skinned at greater risk for developing skin cancers
   * Darker skin makes more difficult the assessment of pallor, jaundice, ecchymosis or erythema

Asian/Pacific Islanders

Fastest growing ethnic minority group in the U.S.

Heterogeneous group composed of people from 28 Asian countries and 25 identified Pacific Island cultures; 95% are Asian Americans

Health belief and practices

1. Health is a state of harmony in body, mind, and spirit with nature and the universe
2. A balance between "hot"(yin) and "cold" (yang) elements is essential for good health

   * Yin is female, dark, negative energy
   * Yang is male, light, positive energy
   * Illness results from an imbalance of these two forces
   * The body, illness, foods possess yin or yang characteristics and treatment is aimed at reestablishing the balance

3. Belief that suffering is part of life

   * May result in postponement in seeking medical treatment
4. Many have a fatalistic view of life
5. Blood is a life force that cannot be replaced or, if taken, will disrupt the body's balance causing weakness and even death

   * Many fear venipuncture and blood transfusions

6. Chinese and Vietnamese may refuse surgery when organs or body parts are to be removed—believe human body must be intact at the time of death
7. High rate of smoking among southeast Asian men makes them at higher risk for lung cancer
8. Have lowest participation rate in Pap smears, mammography, breast examination or

smoking cessation counseling compared to all other ethnic groups

* Lack of health education programs targeted specifically for this group, fatalism belief, and decreased access to health care

Healing practices

1. Practice use of herbal medications, seek traditional healers, and perform healing ceremonies

   * Nurse must ascertain if, and what, herbal preparations are being used to anticipate drug interactions

2. Depending on perceived cause of illness, traditional healers may be consulted before Western medical practitioners

Social organization

1. Strong, family-centered systems

   * Health decisions often made by the family or social network rather than by the individual

   * Patrilineal authority

   * Filial piety

   * Respect for elders

     Eldest son or male head of the clan is the spokesperson for the patient

2. Family members are likely to actively participate in the patient's daily care

Communication

1. Value politeness, respect for authority, and avoidance of shame

   * May prevent from asking questions or challenging proposed treatment plan

   * May result in poor communication with health care professional

2. Some interpret direct eye contact as rude, challenging, and culturally unacceptable
3. Many prefer limited or no physical contact
4. May be language barriers, requiring the use of interpreters

Space and time

1. Many value privacy and are very modest

   * Limit exposure of patient's body as much as possible

2. Japanese are present and future oriented so are prompt and adhere to fixed schedules
3. Chinese are more present oriented and may be late for appointments
4. Filipinos are past and present oriented and may disregard health-related matters

Death and dying issues

1. Patient autonomy and self-determination may not be culturally acceptable or valued. The family or family spokesperson frequently makes decisions about the patient's care rather than the patient
2. Filipinos are Catholic and may view discontinuing life support as morally wrong

3. Koreans consider stopping life support as interfering with God's will; however, the initiation of life support is not

4. Conflict may arise between Western medicine value of open disclosure of terminal illness and API belief that telling someone he or she is dying is rude and may make the person die sooner

5. Many prefer to die at home rather than the hospital due to value placed on family and belief that those who die among strangers and away from home are orphan souls

Biological variations

1. Incidence rate for liver cancer is exceptionally high, particularly the southeast Asian groups

   * Linked to high incidence of hepatitis B infection

2. Japanese, Koreans, and Vietnamese have high rates of stomach cancer

   * Attributed in part to genetic factors as well as the frequent ingestion of sodium, hot and spicy foods, and nitrates

3. Lactose intolerance is common
4. The physical characteristics may necessitate adjusting the dosage of certain medications

   * In Chinese men, propranolol dose may need to be decreased due to greater sensitivity on heart rate and blood pressure

5. Many have distinguishing yellow cast to their skin, making recognition of jaundice more challenging

Hispanics

Umbrella term for people of Mexican, Puerto Rican, Cuban, Caribbean, and Central and South American origin

Population growing five times faster than rest of U.S. population

1. Expected to be largest U.S. minority by year 2050

Cancer incidence ranks in middle compared to other ethnic groups

Many delay seeking treatment for symptoms and continue to use folk remedies as first choice in health care

Largest concentration in the U.S. is in Los Angeles

1. High risk of gallbladder, cervical and stomach cancers
2. Intermediate risk of pancreatic and prostate cancers
3. Low risk of melanoma and colorectal, lung, and reproductive cancers

Appears to be genetic predisposition and higher incidence of gallbladder cancer among Hispanic men and women in New Mexico

Liver cancer rates increase dramatically after the age of 50

Compared to Caucasian women, Hispanic women with cervical cancer were younger, less educated, and had fewer sexual partners but were younger when they first had sex and had more children

Incidence of breast cancer is low, but mortality rate is high

1. Possibly due to cultural factors responsible for delays in seeking health care and larger, more advanced tumors at diagnosis

Health beliefs and practices

1. Health is believed to be the result of good luck or a reward from God for good behavior
2. Disease is God's will
3. Terminal illnesses are seen as the result of an indiscretion against God
4. Often a fatalistic belief that one is at the mercy of the environment and has little control over what happens

   * Hispanics often do not believe that they are personally responsible for present or future successes or failures

5. An equilibrium exists between "hot" and "cold" elements in a healthy body

   * To ensure good health, individuals must ingest both hot and cold foods
   * Internal factors such as a change in body temperature can affect the hot/cold balance

6. Evil eye occurs when someone with a powerful glance looks improperly at a child

* Believed to be manifestation of "witchcraft"

* Treatment is ceremonial ritual

7. Mental illness is seen as inevitable and affected person is viewed as a victim of consequence

8. Moral illness such as alcoholism is caused by the individual and the treatment is the responsibility of family members

9. Cancer is seen as God's will, and it goes against principle to aggressively treat the disease

10. Cancer viewed as contagious and hard to prevent because it is caused by many things

11. One in four lives at or below the poverty level

* Fear because of economic status, may receive inferior care in U.S.

* If cannot afford care, may not seek care

12. Believe it is not appropriate to question those giving care because of fear of retaliation

13. Believe that touch can promote healing

14. May perceive treatment without prayer as ineffective

Healing practices

1. Home remedies are first line of treatment

* To cure hot or cold imbalance, the opposite quality of the causative agent is applied

2. Usually a family folk healer who has knowledge of folk medicine

* Healing practices are passed from mother to daughter

3. If home remedies do not work, Mexican Americans send for the traditional folk medicine healer

   * Receives his or her skills through an apprenticeship or as a gift from God

   * Knowledgeable in the use of herbs, diet, massage, prayer, and ritual

4. Puerto Ricans seek a folk healer with the gift of contacting the spirit world and healing through powers of spirits

5. Diet is high in fiber and carbohydrates from staples such as rice, beans and corn but contains few leafy green vegetables

   * Use of lard and common practice of frying foods contribute to high fat content of Hispanic diet

   * High-risk behaviors include obesity, alcohol consumption and sexual promiscuity and infrequent use of condoms by males

6. Low socioeconomic status and low levels of education often result in infrequent Pap smears, infrequent use of barrier contraceptives, and lack of reporting of genital warts

Social organization

1. Nuclear family

   * Men are breadwinners, assume the dominant role and are considered big and strong

* Hesitancy of a woman or child to make a decision may be due to need to inform and obtain approval of the husband and father

* Women are primary caretakers

2. Extended family is valued and family's needs supersede those of the individual members

* Extended family frequently involved in patient's care

3. Roman Catholicism is predominant religion and important in health beliefs

Communication

1. Spanish is primary language with many dialectal differences
2. Politeness and courtesy are highly regarded
3. Manner of expression is often elaborate and indirect to avoid disagreement
4. Body language may be dramatic when expressing pain or emotion

Space and time

1. Adults are tactile in their relationships, but with a high degree of modesty

* Do not like being touched by others or having to touch themselves

* Uncomfortable being examined by health care professionals of the opposite sex

2. Generally have present orientation causing them to be late for appointments

Death and dying issues

1. Believe in the afterlife of heaven and hell
2. Religious practices like baptism of the dying and administration of the sacrament of he sick are important
3. Family serves as protective network for helping the dying
4. Patient often not told directly by family of his or her condition but demonstrates awareness of death's likelihood
5. Although preference is to die at home, dying in a hospital is acceptable alternative
6. Public expression of grief is expected, especially among women

Biological variations

1. Skin color can vary from a natural tan to dark brown

Natives of Continental United States

Diverse group consisting of over 400 federally recognized nations each with own traditions and cultural heritage

Smallest of defined U.S. minority groups

33 states have Indian reservations

1. High percentage of very young members and of people over 55
2. Poverty and welfare dependence are common

Two-thirds live away from reservations where they are separated from family and familiar culture

Cancer ranked as third leading cause of death after accidents and heart disease

Have lowest cancer incidence and rank mid to low in mortality rates of all U.S. minority populations

1. Incidence rates among both males and females are significantly lower than among the white population
2. May be due to high population of young people and shorter life expectancy as result of obesity and diseases associated with alcohol and tobacco use

Many do not have insurance or money to pay for health care

Many live long distances from health care facilities and are resistant to hospital treatment

Health beliefs and practices

1. Most tribes link health beliefs and religion

   * Religion is something that surrounds an individual at all times and has a profound influence on the entire being

2. Health is both a physical and a spiritual state

* It is the person's response or attitude toward circumstances that creates harmony or lack of it

3. Health reflects living in harmony with nature and humans have an intimate relationship with nature

4. The earth is considered a living being, the body of a higher individual with a will and desire to be well

   * The earth is periodically healthy or ill just as humans are

5. Individual is expected to treat both his or her body and the earth with respect

   * If individual harms the earth, he or she harms him or herself and vice versa

6. Illness is caused by the disharmony of mind, body, and spirit

   * Natural illness is caused by the violation of a sacred or tribal taboo

   * Treatment focused on external causative factors and not on the illness or injury itself

7. Illness may also be caused by witchcraft

   * Treatment is exorcism of the bad spirits

8. Alternatively use traditional medicine and Western medicine, either independent of each other, or simultaneously

   * One treats the physical disease; the other helps the individual heal himself by restoring harmony

9. Preventive measures are practiced to ward off effects of witchcraft, to reestablish harmony, or to prevent possession by an evil spirit

10. Some tribes are not receptive to invasive bodily procedures and may only reluctantly agree to surgery

   ∗ May wish a body part back after surgery for burial

11. Offering food shows concern, caring, friendship and neighborliness

12. Stoicism is valued

13. May expect medication as part of treatment and be disappointed if none is prescribed

14. High incidence of obesity and alcohol abuse

   ∗ Disruption and subsequent loss caused by European settlement of North America left many native Americans feeling powerless and hopeless

   May contribute to many social problems

Healing practices

1. Traditional healer is medicine person who is wise in ways of land and nature

   ∗ Determines first the cause of illness, the proper treatment, and performs special ceremonies that may take several days

   ∗ Medicine person is "chosen" and divinely inspired

   ∗ They are gifted with extrasensory perception that allows them to make mythological associations

* Spend many years learning their skills and servicing as apprentices

2. Healing may require involvement of several medicine people
3. Goal of treatment is to enhance total healing
4. Western physician seen as type of herbalist who can cure symptoms but cannot restore the individual's harmonious relationship with nature because they do not know important rituals

Social organization

1. Families are very involved in making decisions about patient's health care and may make decision for the patient
2. Matrilineal society

* Patient may not give consent for anything until permission is obtained from mother, grandmother, or aunt

* Sometimes permission may not be granted until ceremony is performed

3. Rely on family, tribe, and land to cope with stress
4. Extended family is very important especially during periods of crisis
5. Interpersonal relationships are carefully spelled out among Indian tribes

* Who one speaks to, when the speaking occurs, how one speaks, and the sequence of speaking are very important

Communication

1. Older individuals may speak only traditional language; often there are not comparable medical terms in the tribal language
2. Some tribes believe that discussion with one person about another is a sign of disrespect and could violate a cultural taboo
3. Person may be silent rather than admitting to not understanding
4. Direct eye contact may be viewed as looking into one's soul and could result in loss
5. Spoken word considered an integral part of sacred nature of humans

   * Language promotes values of generosity, bravery, compassion, respect for elders and concern for tribal entity

   * Periods of silence are important to observe

6. Sensitive to body language

   * Do not close or cross arms

7. Private people who do not readily volunteer information

   * Heavy questioning is resisted and information may be withheld

8. Many speak in a very soft voice
9. Note taking considered taboo for some Native Americans
10. Firm handshake may be considered sign of aggression

Space and time

1. Busy atmosphere of hospital or clinic may be uncomfortable
2. Hospital may be viewed as place to die
3. Modesty very significant; limited exposure of body parts is suggested

   * Permission should be asked to perform physical exam
   * Women may prefer a female practitioner

4. Time runs from one hour to a few days later than standard time

   * Often have no clocks in their home
   * Often do not eat on regular schedule

Death and dying issues

1. Existence is circular and continuous

   * Before birth, exist as spirit being with the supreme creator
   * At death, spirit joins creator and eventually returns to the physical world in another form
   * Death consists of joining one's ancestors and good or bad deeds have nothing to do with this reunion

2. Attitudes and approaches to death and dying vary considerably among tribes

Biological variations

1. Many are lactose intolerant

2. Dark skinned; conditions such as jaundice or cyanosis present differently than fairer-skinned Americans

Nursing Issues

Cancer, Poverty, and Ethnicity

1. The high rate of poverty among minorities contributes to a higher incidence and mortality rate for cancer, especially cancer of the breast, cervix, esophagus, male lung, pancreas and stomach
2. Poverty does not eliminate the ethnic differences in incidence rates for cancers of the bladder, prostate, uterus, and multiple myeloma
3. Recommendations for improving access to health care include:

   * Establishing programs where the economically disadvantaged or ethnic minorities can gather in emergency rooms, neighborhood clinics or churches

   * Developing culturally relevant educational materials that may be translated into different languages

   * Recruiting and training health care providers and volunteers from the targeted groups in the special needs of the poor or of a particular ethnic group

Clinical Trials and Cancer Research

1. Under-representation of minorities in clinical trials due to:

* Ethnic minorities' distrust of outsiders doing research in their communities
* Lack of culturally sensitive and specific educational materials
* Transportation difficulties
* Inconvenient clinic hours
* Lack of day care
* Differences in language
* Lack of understanding
* Fear of being denied care because of inadequate financial support
* Fear that researchers will take advantage
* Not understanding the value of the research to the participant

2. Factors that facilitate participation in clinical trials among ethnic minorities who are socioeconomically disadvantaged include:

* Adequate information and education about the risks, benefits, costs, and time commitment required
* Peer group norms that are supportive of the goals of the trial
* Endorsement of the goals of clinical trials by church, the cultural or social groups, and the employer
* Improved access to the health care system and the specific location where the trial is being conducted

* A perceived benefit to the individual from participation
* Minimal actual cost to the individual in terms of time lost from work, transportation, and child care

Resources

1. Specific resources have been created to meet the needs of our culturally diverse populations including educational materials and professional organizations

   * Office of Minority Health Resource Center
   * National Cancer Institute's Cancer Information Service
   * American Cancer Society
   * Oncology Nursing Society's Multicultural Advisory Council and Transcultural Nursing Issues Special Interest Group
   * Asian American/Pacific Islander Nurses' Association
   * Association of Chicana/Latina Nurses
   * Council of Black Nurses
   * National Association of Hispanic Nurses
   * National Black Nurses' Association
   * National Center for the Advancement of Blacks in the Health Professions
   * Philippine Nurses' Association of American
   * American Indian Health Care Association

Suggested Readings

1. Taoka KN, Itano JK: Cultural diversity among individuals with cancer concerns. In Groenwald SL, Frogge MH, Goodman M, Yarbro CH (eds): *Cancer Nursing: Principles and Practice,* (4th ed). Boston: Jones and Bartlett, 1997, pp 1691-1735.
2. Spector RE: Cultural factors in health, in Potter PA, Perry AG (eds): *Fundamentals of Nursing: Concepts, Process, and Practice* (3rd ed). St. Louis, Mosby-Year Book, 1993, pp 94-119.
3. Leininger MM: The theory of culture care diversity and universality, in Leininger MM (ed): *Cultural Care Diversity and Universality: A Theory of Nursing.* New York: National League for Nursing Press, 1991, pp 5-68.
4. Galanti G: Basic concepts, in Galanti G: *Caring for Patients From Different Cultures.* Philadelphia, University of Pennsylvania Press, 1991, pp 1-14.